W9-AUD-238

Fodor's

NORTHERN
CALIFORNIA

1ST EDITION

Where to Stay and Eat
for All Budgets

Must-See Sights
and Local Secrets

Ratings You Can Trust

Excerpted from *Fodor's California*

Fodor's Travel Publications   New York, Toronto, London, Sydney, Auckland
www.fodors.com

FODOR'S NORTHERN CALIFORNIA
Editor: Constance Jones

Editorial Production: David Downing
Editorial Contributors: Lisa Hamilton, Daniel Hindin, Satu Hummasti, Deborah Kaufman, Alison Lucian, Jane Onstott, Reed Parsell, Amanda Theunissen, John Vlahides, Christine Vovakes
Maps: David Lindroth, *cartographer;* Bob Blake and Rebecca Baer, *map editors*
Design: Fabrizio La Rocca, *creative director;* Guido Caroti, *art director;* Melanie Marin, *senior picture editor*
Production/Manufacturing: Robert B. Shields
Cover Photo (Yosemite National Park): Darrell Gulin/Corbis

COPYRIGHT
Copyright © 2004 by Fodors LLC

Fodor's is a registered trademark of Random House, Inc.

All rights reserved under International and Pan-American Copyright Conventions. Published in the United States by Fodor's Travel Publications, a unit of Fodors LLC, a subsidiary of Random House, Inc., and simultaneously in Canada by Random House of Canada Limited, Toronto. Distributed by Random House, Inc., New York.

No maps, illustrations, or other portions of this book may be reproduced in any form without written permission from the publisher.

ISBN 1–4000–1300–3

ISSN 1543–1045

First Edition

SPECIAL SALES
Fodor's Travel Publications are available at special discounts for bulk purchases for sales promotions or premiums. Special editions, including personalized covers, excerpts of existing guides, and corporate imprints, can be created in large quantities for special needs. For more information, contact your local bookseller or write to Special Markets, Fodor's Travel Publications, 1745 Broadway, New York, New York 10019. Inquiries from Canada should be directed to your local Canadian bookseller or sent to Random House of Canada, Ltd., Marketing Department, 2775 Matheson Boulevard East, Mississauga, Ontario L4W 4P7. Inquiries from the United Kingdom should be sent to Fodor's Travel Publications, 20 Vauxhall Bridge Road, London SW1V 2SA, England.

AN IMPORTANT TIP & AN INVITATION
Although all prices, opening times, and other details in this book are based on information supplied to us at press time, changes occur all the time in the travel world, and Fodor's cannot accept responsibility for facts that become outdated or for inadvertent errors or omissions. So **always confirm information when it matters,** especially if you're making a detour to visit a specific place. Your experiences—positive and negative—matter to us. If we have missed or misstated something, **please write to us.** We follow up on all suggestions. Contact the Northern California editor at editors@fodors.com or c/o Fodor's at 1745 Broadway, New York, New York 10019.

PRINTED IN THE UNITED STATES OF AMERICA

10 9 8 7 6 5 4 3 2

DESTINATION NORTHERN CALIFORNIA

Northern California is a source of endless wonder, natural and man-made. "Wow!" is a word you hear often here—at Half Dome in Yosemite, when a whale breaches off the coast, or driving through the redwood forest. If Texas is big and New York is stylish, Northern California is dramatic. Here, the sun shines, and all is beautiful; then the earth shakes, and all is shattered. But the region always bounces back, and its restless people continue to build their nirvana. The drama of constant change and the diversity of its landscape make Northern California seem vast, and fill it with charming surprises. If you are looking for natural beauty, the Shasta-Cascade region isn't a bad place to start, but it's only one gem on a long, long list. If you favor worldly pleasures, San Francisco and the Wine Country beckon. Fans of Wild West history will want to head to the Gold Country for a dose of excitement. Wherever you go in the Golden State, there's plenty to fall in love with: very few visitors go home unsmitten. Have a fabulous trip!

Karen Cure, Editorial Director

CONTENTS

ABOUT THIS BOOK

There's no doubt that the best source for travel advice is a like-minded friend who's just been where you're headed. But with or without that friend, you'll have a better trip with a Fodor's guide in hand. Once you've learned to find your way around its pages, you'll be in great shape to find your way around your destination.

SELECTION
Our goal is to cover the best properties, sights, and activities in their category, as well as the most interesting communities to visit. We make a point of including local food-lovers' hot spots as well as neighborhood options, and we avoid all that's touristy unless it's really worth your time. You can go on the assumption that everything you read about in this book is recommended wholeheartedly by our writers and editors. Flip to On the Road with Fodor's to learn more about who they are. It goes without saying that no property mentioned in the book has paid to be included.

RATINGS
Orange stars ★ denote sights and properties that our editors and writers consider the very best in the area covered by the entire book. These, the best of the best, are listed in the Fodor's Choice section in the front of the book. Black stars ★ highlight the sights and properties we deem Highly Recommended, the don't-miss sights within any region. Fodor's Choice and Highly Recommended options in each region are usually listed on the title page of the chapter covering that region. Use the index to find complete descriptions. In cities, sights pinpointed with numbered map bullets ❶ in the margins tend to be more important than those without bullets.

SPECIAL SPOTS
Pleasures & Pastimes focuses on types of experiences that reveal the spirit of the destination. Watch for Off the Beaten Path sights. Some are out of the way, some are quirky, and all are worth your while. If the munchies hit while you're exploring, look for Need a Break? suggestions.

TIME IT RIGHT
Wondering when to go? Check On the Calendar up front and chapters' Timing sections for weather and crowd overviews and best days and times to visit.

SEE IT ALL
Use Fodor's exclusive Great Itineraries as a model for your trip. (For a good overview of the entire destination, follow those that begin the book, or mix regional itineraries from several chapters.) In cities, Good Walks guide you to important sights in each neighborhood; ► indicates the starting points of walks and itineraries in the text and on the map.

BUDGET WELL
Hotel and restaurant price categories from ¢ to $$$$ are defined in the opening pages of each chapter—expect to find a balancedselection for every budget. For attractions, we always give standard adult admission fees; reductions are usually available for children, students, and senior citizens. Look in Discounts & Deals in Smart Travel Tips for information on destination-wide ticket schemes. Want to pay with plastic? AE, D, DC, MC, V following restaurant and hotel listings indicate whether American Express, Discover, Diner's Club, MasterCard, or Visa are accepted.

BASIC INFO	Smart Travel Tips lists travel essentials for the entire area covered by the book; city- and region-specific basics end each chapter. To find the best way to get around, see the transportation section; see individual modes of travel ("By Car," "By Train") for details. We assume you'll check Web sites or call for particulars.
ON THE MAPS	Maps throughout the book show you what's where and help you find your way around. Black and orange numbered bullets ❶ ❶ in the text correlate to bullets on maps.
FIND IT FAST	Within the book, Chapters are divided into small regions, within which towns are covered in logical geographical order; attractive routes and interesting places between towns are flagged as En Route. Heads at the top of each page help you find what you need within a chapter.
DON'T FORGET	Restaurants are open for lunch and dinner daily unless we state otherwise; we mention dress only when there's a specific requirement and reservations only when they're essential or not accepted—it's always best to book ahead. Unless we state otherwise, hotels have private baths, phone, TVs, and air-conditioning and operate on the European Plan (a.k.a. EP, meaning without meals). We always list facilities but not whether you'll be charged extra to use them, so when pricing accommodations, find out what's included.

SYMBOLS

Many Listings

★ Fodor's Choice
★ Highly recommended
⊠ Physical address
✛ Directions
⌖ Mailing address
☎ Telephone
🖷 Fax
⊕ On the Web
✍ E-mail
🎫 Admission fee
☉ Open/closed times
► Start of walk/itinerary
Ⓜ Metro stations
⊟ Credit cards

Outdoors

⚡ Golf
⚠ Camping

Hotels & Restaurants

🏨 Hotel
🛏 Number of rooms
⚴ Facilities
🍽 Meal plans
✕ Restaurant
✍ Reservations
👗 Dress code
🚭 Smoking
🍷 BYOB
✕🏨 Hotel with restaurant that warrants a visit

Other

🅒 Family-friendly
🛈 Contact information
⇨ See also
⊠ Branch address
☞ Take note

Northern
California

Crescent
City
Redwood
National   Klamath
Park

KLAMATH
NATIONAL
FOREST

Yreka

96

Mt. Shasta
FAR
NORTH

Mt.
Shasta ▲

97

89

3

Arcata
Eureka

299

Weaverville

ShastaLake

29°

Redding

44

Ferndale   36

TRINITY
NATIONAL
FOREST

36

Red Bluff

101

Eel R.

Garberville

Leggett

MENDOCINO
NATIONAL
FOREST

Sacramento Valley

5

99

45

1

101

Fort Bragg   Willits

20

Willows

Mendocino

128   Ukiah

Boonville   253

Clear
Lake

20

Yubo

Point Arena

Gualala

16

505

WINE
COUNTRY
Santa Rosa

1

Healdsburg
Jenner

29   Napa

Sonoma

Petaluma   Fairfield

Novato
Point Reyes
National
Seashore   Berkeley

80   680

Cor

SAN FRANCISCO   Oakland

San Mateo

Palo Alto

1   9

17

Santa Cruz

PACIFIC   OCEAN

0   50 miles
0   75 km

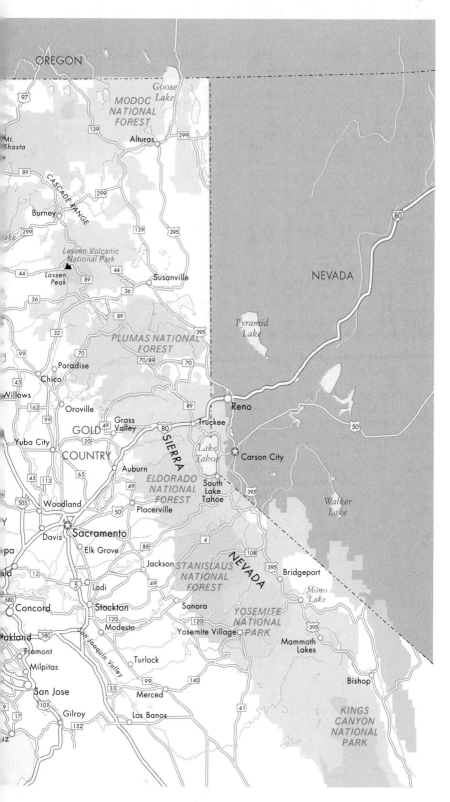

ON THE ROAD WITH FODOR'S

A trip takes you out of yourself. Concerns of life at home completely disappear, driven away by more immediate thoughts—about, say, what marvels will beguile the next day, or where you'll have dinner. That's where Fodor's comes in. We make sure that you know all your options, so that you don't miss something that's around the next bend just because you didn't know it was there. Because the best memories of your trip might well have nothing to do with what you came to Northern California to see, we guide you to sights large and small all over the region. You might set out to see where the Gold Rush of 1849 started, but back at home you find yourself unable to forget the taste of the wine at that Alexander Valley vineyard or the otherworldly thrill of a hike in Lassen Volcanic National Park. With Fodor's at your side, serendipitous discoveries are never far away.

Our success in showing you every corner of Northern California is a credit to our extraordinary writers. Although there's no substitute for travel advice from a good friend who knows your style, our contributors are the next best thing—the kind of people you would poll for travel advice if you knew them.

When not writing about California travel and outdoors, North Coast and Peninsula/South Bay updater Lisa M. Hamilton can be found at the beach. Accounts of the Marin County writer/photographer's food-related journeys have appeared in *National Geographic Traveler, Gastronomica,* and *Z Magazine.*

Daniel Hindin, features editor and weekly columnist at the *Watsonville Register-Pajaronian,* has found paradise in his adopted home of Santa Cruz. He poured his passion for the region into updating the Monterey Bay chapter.

Reed Parsell, who updated the Gold Country chapter, has been in the newspaper business for 20 years. He is currently a copy editor for the *Sacramento Bee* and a part-time travel writer.

Southern Sierra, Lake Tahoe, and Smart Travel Tips updater John Andrew Vlahides lives in San Francisco, spending his free time skiing the Sierra, touring California by motorcycle, and sunning on the beach beneath the Golden Gate Bridge. A columnist, essayist, and former *Clefs d'Or* concierge, he is a regular contributor to Fodor's guides.

A freelance correspondent for the *Sacramento Bee,* Far North updater Christine Vovakes regularly covers area news and writes newspaper features about the region. She considers her home turf of 23 years the undiscovered gem of California.

A frequent contributor to Fodor's, Sharron Wood has been happy to call the San Francisco Bay Area home for more than 12 years. She updated the Wine Country chapter for us.

WHAT'S WHERE

Northern California can be visualized as three long strips of land: coastal, central, and eastern. From Fresno in the Central Valley to Susanville in the far north, the region is divided south to north by the mighty Sierra Nevada. Likewise, along many stretches closer to the Pacific Ocean, the Coast ranges separate the shore towns and cities from the interior of the region. Few roads cross the mountains, and those that do can be narrow and twisting, so getting from points west to points east or vice versa in Northern California often involves long, circuitous drives. Along the coast or through the central zone that parallels the coast, the south–north drive is long but direct.

Northern California's biggest city—San Francisco—is on the coast. I–5 is the quickest route to the north or south, but many tourists travel the coastal route—a combination of U.S. 101 and Highway 1 (the Pacific Coast Highway)—from the Monterey Peninsula to the Oregon state line, making stops at Santa Cruz, Point Reyes National Seashore, Mendocino, and other points along the way.

① San Francisco

This is, arguably, the most beautiful city in the United States and one of the most beautiful in the world. Here you can rub elbows with those lucky enough to live here in the city's cable cars and stroll along thoroughfares like Lombard Street—the most crooked street in the United States—or lively Market Street. But sightseeing is only part of the San Francisco experience. The essence of the city is the diversity of its people. When you cross between neighborhoods—bohemian yet ethnic North Beach, busy and crowded Chinatown, prosperous Pacific Heights, transporting Japantown, the Castro with its gay denizens, the Haight with its countercultural legacy—you know it.

② The Wine Country

America's answer to Tuscany, the wine country looks and feels like its Italian counterpart, complete with gentle green hills and a soft coastal climate. The wine-centered life in Napa and Sonoma counties makes them a vibrant destination for food and wine lovers. If you're lucky, you might arrive in time to see the grape harvest, but whenever you visit, you will be greeted by row upon row of vines and wonderful food in scores of superb restaurants. But between wine tastings remember to do some sightseeing—the towns and countryside are gorgeous.

③ The North Coast

Migrating whales and other sea mammals swim past the dramatic bluffs of the 400 mi of shoreline between San Francisco and the Oregon state line. California's north coast is a place for retreat, for restoring the soul. Its pleasures are low-key, but they are hardly unrefined. Elegant country inns, and cozy Victorian B&Bs, await in Mendocino and other towns whose architecture reflects the New England origins of their founders. And then there is the beauty of the land. The north coast's majestic redwoods inspire awe, even reverence. If no gold rush had built San Francisco, if Los Angeles were still a bunch of orange groves in search of a freeway, this glory would still be worth the trip.

④ The Peninsula and South Bay

San Francisco lies at the tip of an approximately 35-mi peninsula bounded by San Francisco Bay on the east and the Pacific Ocean on the west. Highway 1 runs up the rugged coast past Año Nuevo State Reserve and Half Moon Bay, while I–280 or U.S. 101 runs down the interior Peninsula through congested Silicon Valley to San Jose and the

South Bay. In the prosperous interior Peninsula and South Bay cultural institutions glitter—from Stanford University's Iris and B. Gerald Cantor Center for Visual Arts to San Jose's Tech Museum of Innovation—and fine dining is abundant in cities such as Palo Alto.

5) Monterey Bay

Monterey Bay forms a crescent that begins near Carmel to the south and ends near Santa Cruz to the north. For many the coast here is Northern California at its best. The things that make the region so wonderful to visit converge here—from history, on view at the Carmel Mission, to natural splendor, unforgettable on 17-Mile Drive, to Pebble Beach, where golfing pilgrims come to perform their devotions. The coastal towns will charm you with pretty streets, great food, and occasional quirkiness.

6) The Central Valley

The Central Valley, one of the world's most fertile agricultural zones, is California's heartland. This sunbaked region—whose anchors are Bakersfield in the south and Lodi 260 mi to the north—contains a wealth of rivers, lakes, and waterways. The sun and the water nurture vineyards, dairy farms, orchards, fields, and pastures that stretch to the horizon. The vast agricultural tracts of the valley can be beautiful, and markets and festivals celebrating their bounty are numerous. Munch on fresh strawberries and other fruit sold up and down the valley at roadside stands, and when you're fortified, take in attractions ranging from Victorian houses to the whitewater of the Kern River.

7) The Southern Sierra

The highlight for many Northern California travelers is a visit to one of the national parks in the southern portion of the Sierra Nevada. At Sequoia, Kings Canyon, and Yosemite national parks, nature has outdone itself, carving magnificent glacial valleys out of a landscape sized for titans. In summer and early fall (or whenever snows aren't blocking the Tioga Pass), you can drive east from Yosemite National Park to see Mono Lake's tufa towers, resembling a giant's fingers. The Mammoth Lakes area, with skiing in winter and many outdoor sports in summer, is south of Mono Lake.

8) The Gold Country

This is where modern-day California began, along the American River on a winter's day in 1848, when James Marshall first glimpsed something shiny in the bottom of a ditch. Besides making California, gold made Sacramento, paying for the construction of the state capitol. Many a museum and historic site commemorate the gold rush—reenactors make it come alive at Coloma's Marshall Gold Discovery State Historic Park, and mining towns have been gussied up. Sacramento's California State Railroad Museum is a must for train buffs.

9) Lake Tahoe

Deep, clear, intensely blue-green, the largest alpine lake in North America straddles the California–Nevada border. That strict environmental controls have kept it and the surrounding forests pristine is no small feat, considering the area's popularity. If you're staying on the California side, you can golf, fish, hike, or ski at Squaw Valley USA. Pop in to see Vikingsholm, an authentic replica of a 1,200-year-old Viking castle, built in 1929 on the shore of jewel-like Emerald Bay. On the Nevada side gambling is king and casinos abound, but once you leave the bright lights of the gaming tables, natural wonders surround you again.

(10) The Far North

One of Northern California's best-kept secrets is its far northeast corner. This is a region of soaring mountain peaks, wild rivers brimming with fish, and almost infinite recreational possibilities. Mt. Shasta, a dormant volcano that tops 14,000 ft, is the subject of eerie folklore, but its size and beauty are fantastical enough. Tramping up it in summer and schussing down it in winter are two of the joys of being here. Anglers and boaters flock to Lake Shasta for its many watery diversions, including houseboating. At Lassen Volcanic National Park hot springs, steam vents, and mud pots await discovery by hikers with a sense of wonder.

GREAT ITINERARIES

Any tour of Northern California inevitably involves driving long distances—even 200 mi or more on some days. But the time in the car will be balanced by the sometimes spectacular scenery and places to stop along the way.

Highlights of Northern California
13 to 15 days

In contrast to the wide beaches and year-round sunshine that most people associate with California, Northern California is a place of remote and woodsy towns and lush agricultural areas where colors are deep and intense rather than sun-washed. Residents of the north have never disputed the image of California as a set of sunny beaches. They're happy to keep their emerald trees and sapphire seas a secret. San Francisco is the best city in which to begin and end this tour.

INVERNESS
2 days. Throughout Marin County, the California coast shows one of its most dramatic incarnations. Cliffs drop into secret coves. Waves spill over the horizon. Pelicans migrate from one volcanic sea stack to another. Stinson Beach is a placid stretch of white sand amid the geological chaos. Inland, the shade of Muir Woods National Monument offers ample room for contemplation. Point Reyes National Seashore is a dazzling jewel in the crown that is the Pacific Coast. Don't miss the black, white, and red sand beaches and sentinel lighthouse. ⇨ *Chapter 3*

MENDOCINO
1 or 2 days. North into Mendocino County, the coast is tamer but no less striking. Year-round blooms and Victorian buildings filled with shops, restaurants, and bed-and-breakfasts make Mendocino feel uniquely refined. If the weather is divine (which it can be at any time of year), take advantage of the local state parks' rugged and uncrowded shorelines. ⇨ *Chapter 3*

NAPA
2 days. The hills of Napa and Sonoma counties offer wineries as varied and colorful as the vintages they produce. French castles and farmhouses mingle with long rows of grapevines. Vineyards offer distinctive wines in beautiful and sometimes bustling settings. Fine dining is a way of life. ⇨ *Chapter 2*

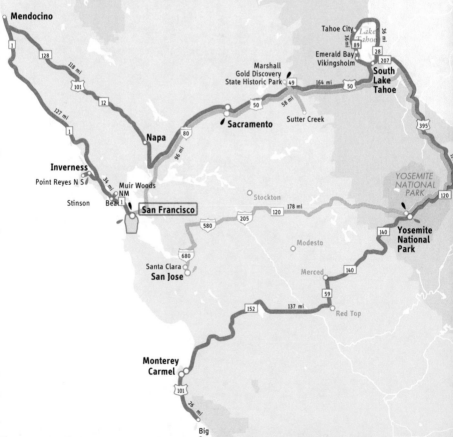

SACRAMENTO

2 days. Filled with gold-rush history, California's state capitol is the gateway to the Gold Country. Small towns scattered along Highway 49 are all that remain from that frenzied time when hundreds of thousands of fortune-seekers descended on the Mother Lode. But many of them have worked hard to preserve their heritage, and you can still stroll boardwalks past Old West storefronts.
⇨ Chapter 8

SOUTH LAKE TAHOE

2 or 3 days. Although deep powdery snow is rightly the Lake Tahoe area's most famous commodity, outdoor adventure abounds year-round. From Tahoe City you can bicycle, rock climb, and water-ski—or spend the day golfing. On the lake's southern shore, hike the steep trail down to Vikingsholm for a tour of this elaborately decorated neo-Nordic mansion, then cool off in tropical-looking Emerald Bay. In South Lake Tahoe, be sure to ride the Heavenly Gondola for a panoramic view of the area, which is, well, heavenly. ⇨ Chapter 9

YOSEMITE

2 days. The incomparable majesty of marvels like Half Dome and the sublime smell of sweet meadow air make Yosemite a world unto itself. Yosemite Valley is home to the park's most picturesque creations: gushing Yosemite Falls, proud and mighty El Capitan, and untamed Bridalveil Falls. The Mariposa Grove of Big Trees is both humbling and inspiring. Sunrise and starlight from atop Glacier Point are sensational. Be prepared for the long drive to the coast. ⇨ Chapter 7

MONTEREY & CARMEL

3 days. As you drive the Pacific Coast Highway through Big Sur, delight in delicate waterfalls, dense redwood groves, and breathtaking coastal cliffs. This earthly beauty is a way of life in Carmel and Monterey, where the crashing ocean and twisted splendor of cypresses provide a backdrop for shops and restaurants. The 17-Mile Drive gives you a glimpse of the mansions and golf courses of Pebble Beach.
⇨ Chapter 5

Northern California with Kids
12 to 15 days

As a real-world land of make-believe, California seems to have been created just for children. Fantasy comes to life in ghost towns, museums, and giant forests. Check local newspapers for seasonal children's events.

SAN FRANCISCO

2 or 3 days. Seeing the city from a cable car is sure to thrill, and you can take in another panorama from Coit Tower. But high above the bay, the Golden Gate Bridge wins for best photo opportunity. Along the water, sample the chocolates that gave Ghirardelli Square its name and bark back at the sea lions lounging at Pier 39. Ride a ferry to Alcatraz to see the island prison. Golden Gate Park's green pastures, woods, and water can offer a whole day of entertainment. If the weather doesn't cooperate, head inside to the Exploratorium or California Academy of Sciences for awesome hands-on exhibits.
⇨ Chapter 1

SACRAMENTO

2 days. You won't strike it rich in the Gold Country, but you can catch the spirit of the Mother Lode at Marshall Gold Discovery State Historic Park. Along historic Highway 49, towns such as Sutter Creek maintain the charm of the area's colorful past. Save an afternoon to wander the streets of Old Sacramento. Ride a tugboat taxi and marvel at old locomotives in the California State Railroad Museum. ⇨ Chapter 8

YOSEMITE

2 or 3 days. Supersized geological formations such as Half Dome and El Capitan and the rushing waters of Bridalveil and Yosemite Falls make Yosemite Valley a truly awesome place. Take a hike among the giant sequoias, wander through a re-created Indian village, and stop by a homesteader's cabin. Along the way, earn a Junior Ranger badge, and don't miss the opportunity to camp out under the stars of the inky Sierra Nevada sky. ⇨ Chapter 7

SAN JOSE

2 days. There's a whole lot more to San Jose than high-tech firms in corporate parks. Climb aboard a real fire truck at the Children's Discovery Museum, take a spin on the carousel in Guadalupe River Park, and meet a robot at the Tech Museum of Innovation. At the Winchester Mystery House you can climb some stairs to nowhere, then head to Paramount's Great America, a huge theme park in Santa Clara. ⇨ Chapter 4

MAP KEY
Highlights of Northern California
Northern California with Kids

114 mi

120

WHEN TO GO

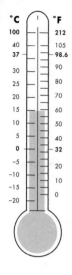

Any time of the year is the right time to go to Northern California. It's likely to be rainy along the coast in the fall and winter months. But San Francisco is pleasant year-round.

Climate

The climate varies amazingly in Northern California, sometimes within an hour's drive. A foggy, cool August day in San Francisco makes you grateful for a sweater, but head north 50 mi to the Napa Valley, and you'll probably need no more than short sleeves. Similarly, nighttime temperatures may differ greatly from daytime temperatures. For instance, in the Central Valley city of Sacramento, summer afternoons can be very warm, in the 90s and occasionally more than 100°F. But the nights cool down, the temperature often dropping by 30 degrees.

Because the weather is so varied throughout the region, it's hard to generalize much about it. Rain comes in the winter, with snow at higher elevations. Summers are dry everywhere. As a rule, compared to the coastal areas, which are cool year-round, inland regions are warmer in summer and cooler in winter. As you climb into the mountains, the climate changes more distinctly with the seasons: winter brings snow, autumn is crisp, spring is variable, and summer is clear and warm, with only an occasional thundershower.

🔂 Forecasts **Weather Channel Connection** ☎ 900/932–8437, 95¢ per minute from a Touch-Tone phone ⊕ www.weather.com.

SAN FRANCISCO

Jan.	55F	13C	May	66F	19C	Sept.	73F	23C
	41	5		48	9		51	11
Feb.	59F	15C	June	69F	21C	Oct.	69F	21C
	42	6		51	11		50	10
Mar.	60F	16C	July	69F	21C	Nov.	64F	18C
	44	7		51	11		44	7
Apr.	62F	17C	Aug.	69F	21C	Dec.	57F	14C
	46	8		53	12		42	6

ON THE CALENDAR

Hundreds of festivals and events are held annually in Northern California. Here are a few of the favorites. If you plan to visit during a big festival, book your accommodations and event tickets well in advance.

WINTER

Dec.

Over the first two weekends in December the Miners' Christmas Celebration (☎ 209/536–1672) in Columbia is an extravaganza of costumed carolers and children's piñatas. Related events include a Victorian Christmas feast at the City Hotel, lamplight tours, an equestrian parade, and Las Posadas Nativity Procession.

The internationally acclaimed El Teatro Campesino (☎ 831/623–2444) annually stages one of two nativity plays, *La Virgen del Tepeyac* or *La Pastorela,* in the Mission San Juan Bautista.

Feb.

The legendary AT&T Pebble Beach National Pro-Am golf tournament (formerly the Bing Crosby Pro-Am; ☎ 831/649–1533) begins in late January and ends in early February.

San Francisco's Chinatown is the scene of parades and noisy fireworks, all part of a several-day Chinese New Year celebration (☎ 415/391–9680).

SPRING

Mar.

The Mendocino/Fort Bragg Whale Festival (☎ 800/726–2780) includes whale-watching excursions, marine art exhibits, wine and beer tastings, crafts displays, and a chowder contest.

Apr.

The Cherry Blossom Festival (☎ 415/974–6900), an elaborate presentation of Japanese culture and customs, winds up with a colorful parade through San Francisco's Japantown.

May

Inspired by Mark Twain's story "The Notorious Jumping Frog of Calaveras County," the Jumping Frog Jubilee (☎ 209/736–2561), in Angels Camp, is for frogs and trainers who take their competition seriously.

Sacramento hosts the four-day Sacramento Jazz Jubilee (☎ 916/372–5277); the late-May event is the world's largest Dixieland festival, with 125 bands from around the world.

Thousands sign up to run the San Francisco Bay to Breakers Race (☎ 415/826–1100), a 7½-mi route from the Bay side to the ocean side that's a hallowed San Francisco tradition.

SUMMER

June

The last week in June, the San Francisco Lesbian, Gay, Bisexual, and Transgender Pride Celebration (☎ 415/864–3733 or 415/677–7959 ⊕ www.sfpride.com) culminates on Sunday, with a giant parade and festival, one of the largest of its kind in the world.

	The Napa Valley Wine Auction (☎ 707/963–3388 or 800/982–1371 📠 707/963–3488), in St. Helena, is accompanied by open houses and a wine tasting. Preregistration by fax, phone, or e-mail in early March is required.
July	During the three weeks of the Carmel Bach Festival (☎ 831/624–2046), the works of Johann Sebastian Bach and 18th-century contemporaries are performed; events include concerts, recitals, and seminars.
	During the last full weekend in July, Gilroy, self-styled "garlic capital of the world," celebrates its smelly but delicious product with the Gilroy Garlic Festival (☎ 408/842–1625), featuring such unusual concoctions as garlic ice cream.
Aug.	The Cabrillo Festival of Contemporary Music (☎ 831/426–6966), in Santa Cruz, one of the longest-running contemporary orchestral festivals, brings in American and other composers for two weeks in early August.
	The California State Fair (☎ 916/263–3247) showcases the state's agricultural side, with a rodeo, horse racing, a carnival, and big-name entertainment. It runs 18 days from August to Labor Day in Sacramento.
FALL	
Sept.	The San Francisco Blues Festival (☎ 415/979–5588) is held at Fort Mason in late September.
Oct.	The Grand National Rodeo, Horse, and Stock Show (☎ 415/404–4100), at San Francisco's Cow Palace, is a 10-day world-class competition straddling the end of October and the beginning of November.
	The Tor House Fall Festival (☎ 831/624–1813) honors the late poet Robinson Jeffers, a Carmel area resident for many years.

PLEASURES & PASTIMES

California Cuisine

California's name has come to signify a certain type of healthful, sophisticated cuisine made from local ingredients, creatively combined and served in often stunning presentations. The state also lies along the North American edge of the Pacific Rim, so Asian flavors and preparations are part of the scene. San Francisco and the Wine Country contain top-notch restaurants—an expensive meal at one of these culinary shrines is often the high point of a trip to Northern California. In coastal areas most menus include some seafood fresh off the boat. Don't neglect the region's many ethnic eateries—among them Mexican, Chinese, Japanese, Scandinavian, Italian, French, Belgian, Vietnamese, English, Thai, and German.

Downhill Skiing

Snow skiing in Northern California is generally limited to the period between Thanksgiving and late April, though in years of heavy snowfall skiers can hit some trails as late as July. The region's best skiing is to be had in the Sierra Nevada. Six major ski resorts and several minor ones surround Lake Tahoe, most notable among them Squaw Valley USA, site of the 1960 winter Olympics. Farther south in the Sierra, Mammoth Mountain is one of the biggest and best ski resorts in the West. Other Northern California ski options include Lassen Volcanic National Park and Mt. Shasta, in the far north; and Badger Pass, in Yosemite National Park.

Golf Heaven

Temperate weather throughout most of the region makes golf a year-round sport in Northern California. Many courses have spectacular settings alongside the ocean, in mountain forests, or in wide-open valleys. The most famous course in California, and one of the most famous in the world, is Pebble Beach Golf Links, set on the stunning coastline along 17-Mile Drive.

National and State Parks

Northern California's national parks are among the country's most awe-inspiring: Kings Canyon, Lassen Volcanic, Redwood, Sequoia, and Yosemite. National monuments include Muir Woods, north of San Francisco. Northern California also has three national recreation areas: Golden Gate, with 87,000 acres both north and south of the Golden Gate Bridge in San Francisco; and Whiskeytown-Shasta-Trinity, with 240,000 acres, including four major lakes, in the far north. The Point Reyes National Seashore is on a peninsula north of San Francisco.

California's state park system includes more than 200 sites; many are recreational and scenic, others historic or scientific. Among the most popular are Angel Island, in San Francisco Bay, reached by ferry from San Francisco or Tiburon; Humboldt Redwoods, with its tall trees; and Empire Mine, one of the richest mines in the Mother Lode, in Grass Valley. Most state parks are open year-round.

On the Beach

Though the beaches of Northern California don't generally fit the stereotype inspired by Southern California's broad, powdery strands, the region is well supplied with beaches. You can walk, sun, and snooze on them, watch seabirds and hunt for shells, dig clams, or spot seals and sea otters at play. From December through March you can witness the migrations of gray whales. Access to beaches in Northern California is generally excellent. The state park system includes many fine beaches, and ocean-side communities maintain public beaches. Through the work of the California Coastal Commission, many stretches of private property that would otherwise seal off a beach from outsiders have public-access paths. But you can't always swim at these beaches. From San Francisco northward the water is too cold for all but the hardiest souls, and some beaches are too dangerous for swimming because of the undertow. Look for signs and postings and take them seriously.

Take a Hike

Redwood groves, lava beds, or mountains, Northern California's landscape begs to be explored on foot. Whatever your level of ability, there are ample opportunities for you to get up-close and personal with nature. Especially rewarding are hikes along the Pacific Coast bluffs in Point Reyes National Seashore, amid the granite peaks and glacial valleys of Desolation Wilderness near Lake Tahoe, and in the shadow of Mount Shasta in Castle Crags State Park. For the serious backpacker, the Pacific Crest Trail and the John Muir Trail await.

Wine Tasting

You can visit wineries in many parts of Northern California, and not only in the Sonoma and Napa valleys. Mendocino County and the Monterey Bay area have become major players in the world of high-quality wine. Respected appellations now include the Anderson Valley and the Santa Cruz Mountains—even the Gold Country is producing wine. Most winegrowing areas publish brochures with lists of local wineries that have tours or tastings. Wineries and good wine stores throughout the region will package your purchases for safe travel or shipping.

FODOR'S CHOICE

The sights, restaurants, hotels, and other travel experiences on these pages are our editors' top picks—our Fodor's Choices. They're the best of their type in Northern California—not to be missed and always worth your time. In the regional chapters that follow, you will find all the details.

LODGING

$$$$	**Ahwahnee Hotel & Dining Room**, Yosemite National Park. Dating back to the 1920s, this mountain lodge constructed of rocks and sugar-pine logs is a National Historical Landmark. Rooms have luxury amenities.
$$$$	**Auberge du Soleil**, Rutherford. One of the Wine Country's best-known inns stands amid olive orchards that you can gaze upon from your terrace. The style is simple, but make no mistake—you will be cosseted here.
$$$$	**Château du Sureau**, Oakhurst. Like a storybook castle transported to the forest, this inn prides itself on European style and service. Fireplaces and down comforters are but two of the indulgences here.
$$$$	**Four Seasons Hotel San Francisco**. Elegant decor, cityscape views, and free access to the magnificent Sports Club/LA facilities.
$$$$	**Gaige House Inn**, Glen Ellen. At this oh-so-civilized country house, classic American architecture and landscaping are accented with Asian details. You might stay in a poolside cottage or in a room with a fireplace or whirlpool tub.
$$$$	**Hotel Monaco**, San Francisco. Decor is a riot of color and pattern; staff is devoted to pampering.
$$$$	**Mandarin Oriental**, San Francisco. The posh hotel occupies the top floors of one of the city's tallest buildings. The views are great even if you don't use the binoculars in your room.
$$$$	**Palace Hotel**, San Francisco. A landmark building graced with a stunning entryway, high ceilings, and marble bathrooms.
$$$$	**Ritz-Carlton, San Francisco**. The opulent lobby and elegant rooms result in the Ritz's ranking among the world's best hotels.
$$$$	**Sherman House**, San Francisco. A historic mansion in Pacific Heights is San Francisco's most luxurious small hotel.
$$$$	**Stonepine Estate Resort**, Carmel Valley. Hike, bike, or ride on the resort's expansive grounds before retiring to your suite or cottage for a massage or afternoon tea.
$$$–$$$$	**Black Bear Inn B&B**, South Lake Tahoe. A log lodge removed from the bustle of the main drag provides the kind of quiet luxury seldom seen on the south shore of Lake Tahoe. Every detail has been attended to, from the hand-knotted Persian rugs to the knotty-pine cathedral ceilings.
$$$–$$$$	**Hotel Rex**, San Francisco. Richly decorated rooms and literary soirées evoke the spirit of salon society in the 1920s.

$$$–$$$$	**Old Monterey Inn,** Monterey. In a Tudor-style inn surrounded by grand old trees, indulge yourself with featherbeds, down comforters, a sumptuous breakfast, and legendary bathroom amenities.
$$$–$$$$	**PlumpJack Squaw Valley Inn,** Olympic Valley. Bringing urban style to the mountains, this small hotel eschews the generic ski-and-golf resort aesthetic. Imagine, hipness in the heart of Olympic Village.
$$–$$$$	**Thistle Dew Inn,** Sonoma. Only half a block from Sonoma Plaza, this inn offers a sense of privacy that's more than welcome in the Wine Country. Borrow the inn's bicycles, then soak away your sore spots in the hot tub.
$$–$$$$	**Union Street Inn,** San Francisco. This romantic getaway has an old-fashioned English garden, elaborate complimentary breakfast, and personable owners.
$$–$$$	**MacCallum House,** Mendocino. Whether in the main mansion, the cottages, or the converted barn and water tower, the rooms here are lavishly appointed. Rose bushes flourish on the grounds and the excellent restaurant makes everything from scratch.
$–$$$$	**Tamarack Lodge Resort,** Mammoth Lakes. A log lodge surrounded by 25 cabins places you smack in the middle of the wilderness. You hardly have to leave the grounds to hike, bike, fish, or canoe.
$–$$	**Alamo Square Inn,** San Francisco. Two houses—a Queen Anne Victorian and a Tudor Revival—and a small apartment building form this lovely B&B.

RESTAURANTS

$$$$	**Erna's Elderberry House,** Oakhurst. The cute name belies the formal elegance of the setting and service here. All is refinement and grace as the staff serves the six-course prix-fixe dinner with perfect choreography.
$$$$	**Fifth Floor,** San Francisco. The fare is sophisticated and the presentation stunning at this intimate space in Hotel Palomar.
$$$$	**French Laundry,** Yountville. If you manage to get a reservation for a table at this contemporary American restaurant, you can expect to spend lots of time and money on your meal. But from the first bit to the last, the experience is worth it.
$$$$	**Gary Danko,** San Francisco. Usually solidly booked six weeks in advance, Gary Danko gets rave reviews for its contemporary cuisine, making it a must for visiting foodies.
$$$$	**Masa's,** San Francisco. Chef Ron Siegel, famous for besting Japan's Iron Chef, is at the helm of this celebrated temple to food. The prix-fixe dinner menus include a vegetarian option.
$$$–$$$$	**Farallon,** San Francisco. Lamps take the shape of jellyfish and columns are covered in kelp at this stylish and fun seafood restaurant.
$$$–$$$$	**Jardinière,** San Francisco. One of the city's most talked-about restaurants is a serious pre-theater event, thanks in large part to the incredible cooking of chef-owner Traci Des Jardins.

$$-$$$$	**Wild Goose,** Tahoe Vista. Tucked beneath towering pines overlooking Lake Tahoe is a French-California restaurant worthy of any big city. The menu is inventive and the clientele semi-chic.
$$-$$$	**Cafe Beaujolais,** Mendocino. Peaceful, backwoods Mendocino charm pervades this cottage, and the cooking is great, to boot. The cross-cultural menu highlights the freshest of organic, local, and hormone-free ingredients.
$$-$$$	**Montrio Bistro,** Monterey. If you like hearty cooking and clean, strong flavors, this European-inspired American bistro, a montage of brick, rawhide, and wrought iron, is the place for dinner.
$$-$$$	**PlumpJack,** Olympic Valley. After a day of skiing or hiking you can sink into your seat here and enjoy expertly prepared contemporary food. The kitchen strives to maximize the natural flavors of ingredients in the deceptively simple dishes.
$$-$$$	**Zuni Café,** San Francisco. Chef Judy Rodgers' Italian-Mediterranean fare is refined, not fussy, and attracts an eclectic crowd late into the night.
$-$$	**Delfina,** San Francisco. The simple but exquisite Italian fare at this casual, lively spot is what makes diners return again and again.

BUDGET RESTAURANTS

$	**L'Osteria del Forno,** San Francisco. As you enter this modest North Beach storefront, you're likely to feel as if you've been transported to Italy.
¢-$	**Chow,** San Francisco. The highest-quality local ingredients at low prices. Be prepared to wait along with the other folks hoping to snag a table.
¢-$	**Swan Oyster Depot,** San Francisco. Grab a stool at the counter of this fish market–diner lunchtime favorite and order some chowder, if you want hot food, or perhaps oysters or shrimp salad.

DRIVES

17-Mile Drive, Pebble Beach. The wonders are both man-made and natural along this detour from Highway 1 between Pacific Grove and Carmel. Robert Louis Stevenson described the gnarled and twisted Monterey cypresses en route as "ghosts fleeing before the wind."

HISTORY

Bodie Ghost Town, Bodie State Historic Park. Preserved in a state of "arrested decay," this once wild mining town is now a great place to come for a glimpse of prospecting life. A museum tells all about the buildings outside.

California State Railroad Museum, Sacramento. Even if you're not a railroad buff, this museum is bound to captivate you with its inside look at rail travel in the 19th century, not to mention the 21 locomotives and railroad cars on display.

Columbia State Historic Park, Columbia. Ride a stagecoach and pan for gold, then visit this restored Gold-Rush town and its blast-from-the-past merchants, blacksmiths, barkeeps, and newspapermen.

MUSEUMS

San Francisco Museum of Modern Art, San Francisco. Crossing the sky bridge in the atrium, you'll appreciate the cutting-edge designs of architect Mario Botta.

Tech Museum of Innovation, San Jose. The capital of Silicon Valley is home to a hands-on museum of technology. A visit here is a fun way to learn about everything from virtual reality to robotics to criminal forensics.

NATURE

Lassen Volcanic National Park, Mineral. Thermal features like boiling springs, steam vents, and mud pots, and volcanic domes and flows provide an eerie glimpse of California's origins.

Point Reyes National Seashore, Marin County. Elephant seals, 225 bird species, starfish, sea anemones and purple urchins thrive in the waters and grasslands along this raggedly magnificent stretch of coastline.

SIGHTS

Lombard Street, San Francisco. The "crookedest street in the world," with its winding brick paths and its well-tended flowerbeds, is worth the queue.

Palace of Fine Arts, San Francisco. This rosy rococo palace, a San Francisco landmark, was built for the 1915 Panama-Pacific International Exposition.

TASTES OF NORTHERN CALIFORNIA

Clos Pegase, Calistoga. Even the tunnels of the wine cave are bedecked with artworks at this winery in a radically post-modern building. The quirkiness of the architecture reflects the eccentricity of the winery, which produces chardonnay, and sauvignon blanc, pinot noir, merlot and cabernet sauvignon.

Copia: The American Center for Wine, Food & the Arts, Napa. When you visit this temple of American food and wine you can have a look at the exhibits, take a tour, participate in a tasting, or listen to a lecture. Your taste buds will never be the same again.

Niebaum-Coppola Estate, Rutherford. At Francis Ford Coppola's winery you can combine your wine tasting with a glimpse of Hollywood history, in the form of some of Coppola's memorabilia. But the wines—especially the reds—are as serious as any in the region.

VIEWS

Emerald Bay State Park, Lake Tahoe. Massive glaciers carved this fjordlike bay millions of years ago. Famed for its jewel-like shape and colors, it surrounds Fannette, Tahoe's only island. Survey the glorious scene from the lookout above.

Glacier Point, Yosemite National Park. For incredible vistas of Yosemite Valley and the High Sierra, especially at sunset drive or hike to this scenic overlook. From here you can see Nevada as well as Yosemite's landmarks.

Heavenly Gondola, South Lake Tahoe. From the middle of town, you can reach the trails of Heavenly Ski Resort in only 11 minutes. Getting there is at least half the fun, as your car affords magnificent views over the Lake Tahoe basin.

SMART TRAVEL TIPS

Finding out about your destination before you leave home means you won't squander time organizing everyday minutiae once you've arrived. The organizations in this section can provide information to supplement this guide; contact them for up-to-the-minute details, and consult the A to Z sections that end each chapter for facts on the various topics as they relate to Northern California's many regions. Happy landings!

AIR TRAVEL

BOOKING

When you book look for nonstop flights and remember that "direct" flights stop at least once. Try to avoid connecting flights, which require a change of plane. Because of frequent fog and weather delays there, avoid booking tight connections in San Francisco. For more booking tips and to check prices and make on-line flight reservations, log on to ⊕ www.fodors.com

CARRIERS

United, with a hub in San Francisco, has the greatest number of flights into and within Northern California. But most national and many international airlines fly here.

🔓 Major Airlines **Air Canada** ☎ 888/247-2262 ⊕ www.aircanada.com. **Alaska** ☎ 800/426-0333 ⊕ www.alaskaair.com. **America West** ☎ 800/235-9292 ⊕ www.americawest.com. **American** ☎ 800/433-7300 ⊕ www.aa.com. **British Airways** ☎ 800/247-9297 ⊕ www.britishairways.com. **Cathay Pacific** ☎ 800/233-2742 ⊕ www.cathaypacific.com. **Continental** ☎ 800/525-0280 ⊕ www.continental.com. **Delta** ☎ 800/221-1212 ⊕ www.delta.com. **Japan Air Lines** ☎ 800/525-3663 ⊕ www.japanair.com. **Northwest/KLM** ☎ 800/225-2525 ⊕ www.northwest.com. **Qantas** ☎ 800/227-4500 ⊕ www.qantas.com. **Southwest** ☎ 800/435-9792 ⊕ www.southwest.com. **United** ☎ 800/241-6522 ⊕ www.united.com. **US Airways** ☎ 800/428-4322 ⊕ www.usairways.com.

🔓 Smaller Airlines **American Trans Air** ☎ 800/435-9282 ⊕ www.ata.com. **Horizon** ☎ 800/547-9308 ⊕ www.horizonair.com. **Midwest Express** ☎ 800/452-2022 ⊕ www.midwestexpress.com.

🔓 From the U.K. **American** ☎ 0345/789-789. **British Airways** ☎ 0345/222-111. **Delta** ☎ 0800/414-767. **United** ☎ 0800/888-555. **Virgin Atlantic** ☎ 01293/747-747.

CHECK-IN AND BOARDING

Always ask your carrier about its check-in policy. Plan to arrive at the airport about two hours before your scheduled departure time for domestic flights and 2½ to 3 hours before international flights. You may need to arrive earlier if you're flying from one of the busier airports or during peak air-traffic times. To avoid delays at airport-security checkpoints, try not to wear any metal. Jewelry, belt and other buckles, steel-toe shoes, barrettes, and underwire bras are among the items that can set off detectors.

Assuming that not everyone with a ticket will show up, airlines routinely overbook planes. When everyone does, airlines ask for volunteers to give up their seats. In return, these volunteers usually get a several-hundred-dollar flight voucher, which can be used toward the purchase of another ticket, and are rebooked on the next flight out. If there are not enough volunteers, the airline must choose who will be denied boarding. The first to get bumped are passengers who checked in late and those flying on discounted tickets, so get to the gate and check in as early as possible, especially during peak periods.

Always **bring a government-issued photo I.D. to the airport;** even when it's not required, a passport is best.

CUTTING COSTS

The least expensive airfares to Northern California are priced for round-trip travel and must usually be purchased in advance. Airlines generally allow you to change your return date for a fee; most low-fare tickets, however, are nonrefundable. It's smart to call a number of airlines and check the Internet; when you are quoted a good price, book it on the spot—the same fare may not be available the next day, or even the next hour. Always check different routings and look into using alternate airports. Also, price off-peak flights, which may be significantly less expensive than others. Travel agents, especially low-fare specialists (⇨ Discounts and Deals), are helpful.

Consolidators are another good source. They buy tickets for scheduled flights at reduced rates from the airlines, then sell them at prices that beat the best fare available directly from the airlines. Sometimes you can even get your money back if you need to return the ticket. Carefully read the fine print detailing penalties for changes and cancellations, purchase the ticket with a credit card, and confirm your consolidator reservation with the airline.

When you fly as a courier, you trade your checked-luggage space for a ticket deeply subsidized by a courier service. There are restrictions on when you can book and how long you can stay. Some courier companies list with membership organizations, such as the Air Courier Association and the International Association of Air Travel Couriers; these require you to become a member before you can book a flight.

Many airlines, singly or in collaboration, offer discount air passes that allow foreigners to travel economically in a particular country or region. These visitor passes usually must be reserved and purchased before you leave home. Information about passes can be found on most airlines' international Web pages, which tend to be aimed at travelers from outside the carrier's home country. Also, try typing the name of the pass into a search engine, or search for "pass" within the carrier's Web site.

⚑ Consolidators **AirlineConsolidator.com** ☎ 888/468-5385 ⊕ www.airlineconsolidator.com; for international tickets. **Best Fares** ☎ 800/576-8255 or 800/576-1600 ⊕ www.bestfares.com; $59.90 annual membership. **Cheap Tickets** ☎ 800/377-1000 or 888/922-8849 ⊕ www.cheaptickets.com. **Expedia** ☎ 404/728-8787 or 800/397-3342 ⊕ www.expedia.com. **Hotwire** ☎ 920/330-9418 or 866/468-9473 ⊕ www.hotwire.com. **Now Voyager Travel** ⊠ 45 W. 21st St., New York, NY 10010 ☎ 212/459-1616 ₤ 212/243-2711 ⊕ www.nowvoyagertravel.com. **Onetravel.com** ⊕ www.onetravel.com. **Orbitz** ☎ 888/656-4546 ⊕ www.orbitz.com. **Priceline.com** ⊕ www.priceline.com. **Travelocity** ☎ 888/709-5983, 877/282-2925 in Canada, 0870/876-3876 in the U.K. ⊕ www.travelocity.com.
⚑ Courier Resources **Air Courier Association/Cheaptrips.com** ☎ 800/282-1202 ⊕ www.aircourier.org or www.cheaptrips.com. **International Association of Air Travel Couriers** ☎ 308/632-3273 ⊕ www.courier.org. **Now Voyager Travel** ⊠ 315 W. 49th St. Plaza Arcade, New York, NY 10019 ☎ 212/459-1616 ₤ 212/262-7407 ⊕ www.nowvoyagertravel.com.
⚑ Discount Passes **All Asia Pass**, Cathay Pacific, ☎ 800/233-2742 ⊕ www.cathay-usa.com. **Boomerang Pass**, Qantas, ☎ 800/227-4500, 0845/774-7767 in the U.K., 131-313 in Australia, 0800/

808-767 in New Zealand ⊕ www.qantas.com. **FlightPass, EuropebyAir,** ☎ 888/387-2479 ⊕ www.europebyair.com. **Pacific Explorer Airpass,** Hideaway Holidays, ☎ 61-2/9743-0253 in Australia 🖷 61-2/9743-3568 in Australia, 530/325-4069 in the U.S. ⊕ www.hideawayholidays.com.au. **Polypass,** Polynesian Airlines, ☎ 800/264-0823 or 808/842-7659, 020/8846-0519 in the U.K., 1300/653737 in Australia, 0800/800-993 in New Zealand ⊕ www.polynesianairlines.co.nz. **SAS Air Passes,** Scandinavian Airlines, ☎ 800/221-2350, 0845/6072-7727 in the U.K., 1300/727707 in Australia ⊕ www.scandinavian.net.

ENJOYING THE FLIGHT

State your seat preference when purchasing your ticket, and then repeat it when you confirm and when you check in. For more legroom, you can request one of the few emergency-aisle seats at check-in, if you are capable of lifting at least 50 pounds—a Federal Aviation Administration requirement of passengers in these seats. Seats behind a bulkhead also offer more legroom, but they don't have underseat storage. Don't sit in the row in front of the emergency aisle or in front of a bulkhead, where seats may not recline.

Ask the airline whether a snack or meal is served on the flight. If you have dietary concerns, request special meals when booking. These can be vegetarian, low-cholesterol, or kosher, for example. It's a good idea to pack some healthful snacks and a small (plastic) bottle of water in your carry-on bag. On long flights, try to maintain a normal routine, to help fight jet lag. At night, get some sleep. By day, eat light meals, drink water (not alcohol), and move around the cabin to stretch your legs. For additional jet-lag tips consult *Fodor's FYI: Travel Fit & Healthy* (available at bookstores everywhere).

Smoking policies vary from carrier to carrier. Many airlines prohibit smoking on all of their flights; others allow smoking only on certain routes or certain departures. Ask your carrier about its policy.

FLYING TIMES

Flying time to Northern California is roughly six hours from New York and four hours from Chicago. Travel from London to San Francisco takes about 10 hours and from Sydney approximately 14. Flying between San Francisco and Los Angeles takes one hour.

HOW TO COMPLAIN

If your baggage goes astray or your flight goes awry, complain right away. Most carriers require that you file a claim immediately. The Aviation Consumer Protection Division of the Department of Transportation publishes *Fly-Rights*, which discusses airlines and consumer issues and is available on-line. You can also find articles and information on mytravelrights.com, the Web site of the nonprofit Consumer Travel Rights Center.

🛃 Airline Complaints **Aviation Consumer Protection Division** ⊠ U.S. Department of Transportation, C-75, Room 4107, 400 7th St. NW, Washington, DC 20590 ☎ 202/366-2220 ⊕ www.dot.gov/airconsumer. **Federal Aviation Administration Consumer Hotline** ⊠ for inquiries: FAA, 800 Independence Ave. SW, Room 810, Washington, DC 20591 ☎ 800/322-7873 ⊕ www.faa.gov.

RECONFIRMING

Check the status of your flight before you leave for the airport. You can do this on your carrier's Web site, by linking to a flight-status checker (many Web booking services offer these), or by calling your carrier or travel agent.

AIRPORTS

The major gateway to Northern California is San Francisco International Airport (SFO).

🛃 Airport Information **San Francisco International Airport** ☎ 650/761-0800 ⊕ www.flysfo.com.

BIKE TRAVEL

There are beautiful places to bike throughout Northern California. For each part of the region, please see the specific chapter on that area for biking ideas.

BIKES IN FLIGHT

Most airlines accommodate bikes as luggage, provided they are dismantled and boxed; check with individual airlines about packing requirements. Some airlines sell bike boxes, which are often free at bike shops, for about $15 (bike bags can be considerably more expensive). International travelers often can substitute a bike for a piece of checked luggage at no charge; otherwise, the cost is about $100. U.S. and Canadian airlines charge $40–$80 each way.

BUSINESS HOURS

Banks in Northern California are typically open from 9 to 4 and are closed most holidays (⇨ Holidays). Smaller shops usually operate from 10 to 6, with larger stores remaining open until 8 or later. Hours vary for museums and historical sites, and many are closed one or more days a week. It's a good idea to **check before you visit a tourist site.** Many gas stations are open 24 hours, especially on interstate highways. In rural areas many close early, so fill up before nightfall.

BUS TRAVEL

Because of the region's size, traveling by bus in Northern California can be slow. But if you don't want to rent a car and wish to go where the train does not, a bus may be your only option. Greyhound is the major carrier for intermediate and long distances, though smaller, regional bus service is available in metropolitan areas. Check the specific chapters for the regions you plan to visit. Smoking is prohibited on all buses in California.

🚹 Bus Information **Greyhound** ☎ 800/231-2222 ⊕ www.greyhound.com.

CAMERAS AND PHOTOGRAPHY

The pounding surf, majestic mountains, towering trees, and rugged beaches—not to mention the cities and towns in between—make Northern California a photographer's dream destination. Bring lots of film (or plenty of digital memory) to capture the special moments of your trip.

The *Kodak Guide to Shooting Great Travel Pictures* (available at bookstores everywhere) is loaded with tips.

🚹 Photo Help **Kodak Information Center** ☎ 800/242-2424 ⊕ www.kodak.com.

EQUIPMENT PRECAUTIONS

Don't pack film and equipment in checked luggage, where it is much more susceptible to damage. X-ray machines used to view checked luggage are extremely powerful and therefore are likely to ruin your film. Try to ask for hand inspection of film, which becomes clouded after repeated exposure to airport X-ray machines, and keep videotapes and computer disks away from metal detectors. Always keep film, tape, and computer disks out of the sun.

Carry an extra supply of batteries, and be prepared to turn on your camera, camcorder, or laptop to prove to airport security personnel that the device is real.

CAR RENTAL

A car is essential in most parts of Northern California, though in compact San Francisco it's better to use public transportation to avoid parking headaches.

Rates at San Francisco airports begin around $30 a day and $140–$200 a week. The tax is 8½%. If you pick up at an airport, there may also be a facility charge of as much as $12 per rental. Vehicle license fees are no longer legal in California.

🚹 Major Agencies **Alamo** ☎ 800/327-9633 ⊕ www.alamo.com. **Avis** ☎ 800/331-1212, 800/879-2847 or 800/272-5871 in Canada, 0870/606-0100 in the U.K., 02/9353-9000 in Australia, 09/526-2847 in New Zealand ⊕ www.avis.com. **Budget** ☎ 800/527-0700, 0870/156-5656 in the U.K. ⊕ www.budget.com. **Dollar** ☎ 800/800-4000, 0124/622-0111 in the U.K., where it's affiliated with Sixt, 02/9223-1444 in Australia ⊕ www.dollar.com. **Hertz** ☎ 800/654-3131, 800/263-0600 in Canada, 0870/844-8844 in the U.K., 02/9669-2444 in Australia, 09/256-8690 in New Zealand ⊕ www.hertz.com. **National Car Rental** ☎ 800/227-7368, 0870/600-6666 in the U.K. ⊕ www.nationalcar.com.

CONVERTIBLES AND SUVS

If you dream of driving along the coast with the top down, or you want to explore a mountain landscape not visible from the road, consider renting a specialty vehicle. Agencies that specialize in convertibles and sport-utility vehicles will often arrange airport delivery in larger cities.

🚹 Specialty Car Agencies In San Francisco, **SpecialtyRentals.com** ☎ 800/400-8412

CUTTING COSTS

For a good deal, book through a travel agent who will shop around. Also, price local car-rental companies—whose prices may be lower still, although their service and maintenance may not be as good as those of major rental agencies—and research rates on the Internet. Remember to ask about required deposits, cancellation penalties, and drop-off charges if you're planning to pick up the car in one city and leave it in another. If you're traveling during a holiday period, also make sure that a confirmed reservation guarantees you a car.

INSURANCE

When driving a rented car you are generally responsible for any damage to or loss of the vehicle. You also may be liable for any property damage or personal injury that you may cause while driving. Before you rent, see what coverage you already have under the terms of your personal auto-insurance policy and credit cards.

For about $10 to $25 a day, rental companies sell protection, known as a collision- or loss-damage waiver (CDW or LDW), that eliminates your liability for damage to the car; it's always optional and should never be automatically added to your bill. In most states you don't need a CDW if you have personal auto insurance or other liability insurance. Some states, including California, have capped the price of the CDW and LDW. However, **make sure you have enough coverage to pay for the car.** If you do not have auto insurance or an umbrella policy that covers damage to third parties, purchasing liability insurance and a CDW or LDW is highly recommended.

REQUIREMENTS AND RESTRICTIONS

In California you must be 21 to rent a car, and rates may be higher if you're under 25. Some agencies will not rent to those under 25; check when you book. You'll pay extra for child seats (about $5 per day), which are compulsory for children under five. Children up to age six or 60 pounds must be placed in booster seats. There is no extra charge for an additional driver. Non–U.S. residents must have a license whose text is in the Roman alphabet, though it need not be in English. An international license is recommended but not required.

SURCHARGES

Before you pick up a car in one city and leave it in another, ask about drop-off charges or one-way service fees, which can be substantial. Note, too, that some rental agencies charge extra if you return the car before the time specified in your contract. To avoid a hefty refueling fee, fill the tank just before you turn in the car, but be aware that gas stations near the rental outlet may overcharge. It's almost never a deal to buy the tank of gas that's in the car when you rent it; the understanding is that you'll return it empty, but some fuel usually remains. Surcharges may apply if

you're under 25 or if you take the car outside the area approved by the rental agency. You'll pay extra for child seats (about $6 a day), which are compulsory for children under five, and usually for additional drivers (about $10 per day).

CAR TRAVEL

Three major highways—Interstate 5 (I–5), U.S. 101, and Highway 1—run north–south through Northern California. The main route into the region from the east is I–80.

EMERGENCIES

Dial 911 to report accidents on the road and to reach police, the California Highway Patrol, or the fire department. On some rural highways and on most interstates, look for emergency phones on the side of the road.

GASOLINE

Gasoline prices in Northern California vary widely depending on location (more expensive in small towns and other areas away from major highways), oil company, and whether you buy it at a full-serve or self-serve pump. At press time regular unleaded gasoline costs about $1.70 a gallon. If you are planning to travel near Nevada, you can save a lot by purchasing gas over the border.

Gas stations are plentiful throughout the region. Most stay open late (24 hours along major highways and in big cities), except in rural areas, where Sunday hours are limited and where you may drive long stretches without a chance to refuel.

ROAD CONDITIONS

Rainy weather can make driving along the coast or in the mountains treacherous. Some of the smaller routes over the mountain ranges are prone to flash flooding. When the rains are severe, coastal Highway 1 can quickly become a slippery nightmare, buffeted by strong winds and obstructed by falling debris from the cliffs above. When the weather is particularly bad, Highway 1 may be closed. Drivers should **check road and weather conditions before heading out.**

Many smaller roads over the Sierra Nevada are closed in winter, and if it is snowing, tire chains may be required on routes that are open, most notably those to Yosemite and Lake Tahoe. If it is raining along the coast, it is usually snowing at higher elevations. Do not wait until the highway patrol's chain-control checkpoint to look for chains; you'll be unable to turn around, and you will get stuck and have to wait out the storm. Rent a four-wheel-drive vehicle or purchase chains before you get to the mountains. If you delay and purchase them in the vicinity of the chain-control area, the cost may double. Be aware that most rental-car companies prohibit chain installation on their vehicles. If you choose to risk it and do not tighten them properly, they may snap; insurance will not cover the damage that could result. Uniformed chain installers on I–80 and U.S. 50 will apply them at the checkpoint for $20 or take them off for $10. On smaller roads you are on your own. Always carry extra clothing, blankets, and food when driving to the mountains in the winter, and keep your gas tank full to prevent the fuel line from freezing.

In larger cities the biggest driving hazards are traffic jams. Avoid major urban highways, especially at rush hour.
7 Road Conditions **Statewide hot line** ☎ 800/427-7623 from a touch-tone telephone, 916/445-1534 from a rotary-dial telephone ⊕ www.dot.ca. gov/hq/roadinfo.
7 Weather Conditions **National Weather Service** ☎ 707/443-6484 (northernmost California), 831/656-1725 (San Francisco Bay area and Central California), 775/673-8100 (Lake Tahoe and the northern Sierra) ⊕ weather.gov.

ROAD MAPS

You can buy detailed maps in bookstores and gas stations and at some grocery stores and drugstores.

RULES OF THE ROAD

Always strap children under age six or weighing 60 pounds or less into approved child-safety seats; also children up to age six and weighing up to 60 pounds must be placed in booster seats designed to reduce seat belt injuries. Seat belts are required at all times; tickets can be given for failing to comply. Children must wear seat belts regardless of where they're seated (studies show that children are safest in the rear seats).

Unless otherwise indicated, right turns are allowed at red lights after you've come to a full stop. Left turns between two one-way streets are allowed at red lights after you've come to a full stop. Drivers with a blood-alcohol level higher than 0.08 who are stopped by police are subject to arrest, and police officers can detain those with a level of 0.05 if they appear impaired. California's drunk-driving laws are extremely tough. The licenses of violators may immediately be suspended, and offenders may have to spend the night in jail and pay hefty fines.

The speed limit on many rural highways is 70 mph. In the cities, freeway speed limits are between 50 mph and 65 mph. Many city routes have commuter lanes, but the rules vary from city to city: in San Francisco you need three people in a car to use these lanes.

CHILDREN IN NORTHERN CALIFORNIA

Northern California is made to order for traveling with children: youngsters love the Monterey Aquarium; San Francisco cable cars; the gold mine in Placerville; Forestiere Underground Gardens, in Fresno; and the caverns near Lake Shasta. *Fodor's Around San Francisco with Kids* (available in bookstores everywhere) can help you plan your days together.

If you are renting a car, don't forget to arrange for a car seat when you reserve. For general advice about traveling with children, consult *Fodor's FYI: Travel with Your Baby* (available in bookstores everywhere).

FLYING

If your children are two or older, ask about children's airfares. As a general rule, infants under two not occupying a seat fly at greatly reduced fares or even for free. But if you want to guarantee a seat for an infant, you have to pay full fare. Consider flying during off-peak days and times; most airlines will grant an infant a seat without a ticket if there are available seats.

Experts agree that it's a good idea to use safety seats aloft for children weighing less than 40 pounds. Airlines set their own policies: if you use a safety seat, U.S. carriers usually require that the child be ticketed, even if he or she is young enough to ride free, because the seats must be strapped into regular seats. And even if you pay the full adult fare for the seat, it may be worth it, especially on longer trips. Do check your airline's policy about using safety seats during takeoff and landing. Safety seats are not allowed everywhere in the plane, so get your seat assignments as early as possible.

When reserving, request children's meals or a freestanding bassinet (not available at all airlines) if you need them. But note that bulkhead seats, where you must sit to use the bassinet, may lack an overhead bin or storage space on the floor.

LODGING

Most hotels in Northern California allow children under a certain age to stay in their parents' room at no extra charge, but others charge for them as extra adults; be sure to **find out the cutoff age for children's discounts.**

SIGHTS AND ATTRACTIONS

Places that are especially appealing to children are indicated by a rubber-duckie icon (🐤) in the margin.

CONSUMER PROTECTION

Whether you're shopping for gifts or purchasing travel services, **pay with a major credit card** whenever possible, so you can cancel payment or get reimbursed if there's a problem (and you can provide documentation). If you're doing business with a particular company for the first time, contact your local Better Business Bureau and the attorney general's offices in your state and (for U.S. businesses) the company's home state as well. Have any complaints been filed? Finally, if you're buying a package or tour, always consider travel insurance that includes default coverage (⇨ Insurance).

🔢 BBBs **Council of Better Business Bureaus** ✉ **4200 Wilson Blvd., Suite 800, Arlington, VA 22203** ☎ 703/276-0100 🖷 703/525-8277 ⊕ www. bbb.org.

CUSTOMS AND DUTIES

When shopping abroad, keep receipts for all purchases. Upon reentering the country, be ready to show customs officials what you've bought. Pack purchases together in an easily accessible place. If you think a duty is incorrect, appeal the assessment. If you object to the way your clearance was handled, note the inspec-

tor's badge number. In either case, first ask to see a supervisor. If the problem isn't resolved, write to the appropriate authorities, beginning with the port director at your point of entry.

IN AUSTRALIA

Australian residents who are 18 or older may bring home A$400 worth of souvenirs and gifts (including jewelry), 250 cigarettes or 250 grams of cigars or other tobacco products, and 1,125 ml of alcohol (including wine, beer, and spirits). Residents under 18 may bring back A$200 worth of goods. Members of the same family traveling together may pool their allowances. Prohibited items include meat products. Seeds, plants, and fruits need to be declared upon arrival.

🔢 **Australian Customs Service** ⓓ Regional Director, Box 8, Sydney, NSW 2001 ☎ 02/9213-2000 or 1300/363263, 02/9364-7222 or 1800/803-006 quarantine-inquiry line 🖷 02/9213-4043 ⊕ www. customs.gov.au.

IN CANADA

Canadian residents who have been out of Canada for at least seven days may bring in C$750 worth of goods duty-free. If you've been away fewer than seven days but more than 48 hours, the duty-free allowance drops to C$200. If your trip lasts 24 to 48 hours, the allowance is C$50. You may not pool allowances with family members. Goods claimed under the C$750 exemption may follow you by mail; those claimed under the lesser exemptions must accompany you. Alcohol and tobacco products may be included in the seven-day and 48-hour exemptions but not in the 24-hour exemption. If you meet the age requirements of the province or territory through which you reenter Canada, you may bring in, duty-free, 1.5 liters of wine *or* 1.14 liters (40 imperial ounces) of liquor *or* 24 12-ounce cans or bottles of beer or ale. Also, if you meet the local age requirement for tobacco products, you may bring in, duty-free, 200 cigarettes and 50 cigars. Check ahead of time with the Canada Customs and Revenue Agency or the Department of Agriculture for policies regarding meat products, seeds, plants, and fruits.

You may send an unlimited number of gifts (only one gift per recipient, however) worth up to C$60 each duty-free to Canada. Label the package UNSOLICITED

GIFT—VALUE UNDER $60. Alcohol and to-bacco are excluded.

🚹 Canada Customs and Revenue Agency ✉ 2265 St. Laurent Blvd., Ottawa, Ontario K1G 4K3 ☎ 800/461-9999, 204/983-3500, 506/636-5064 ⊕ www.ccra.gc.ca.

IN NEW ZEALAND

All homeward-bound residents may bring back NZ$700 worth of souvenirs and gifts; passengers may not pool their al-lowances, and children can claim only the concession on goods intended for their own use. For those 17 or older, the duty-free allowance also includes 4.5 liters of wine or beer; one 1,125-ml bottle of spir-its; and either 200 cigarettes, 250 grams of tobacco, 50 cigars, *or* a combination of the three up to 250 grams. Meat products, seeds, plants, and fruits must be declared upon arrival to the Agricultural Services Department.

🚹 New Zealand Customs ✉ Head office: The Cus-tomhouse, 17–21 Whitmore St., Box 2218, Wellington ☎ 09/300–5399 or 0800/428–786 ⊕ www.customs.govt.nz.

IN THE U.K.

From countries outside the European Union, including the United States, you may bring home, duty-free, 200 cigarettes or 50 cigars; 1 liter of spirits or 2 liters of fortified or sparkling wine or liqueurs; 2 liters of still table wine; 60 ml of perfume; 250 ml of toilet water; plus £145 worth of other goods, including gifts and souvenirs. Prohibited items include meat products, seeds, plants, and fruits.

🚹 HM Customs and Excise ✉ Portcullis House, 21 Cowbridge Rd. E, Cardiff CF11 9SS ☎ 0845/010–9000 or 0208/929–0152, 0208/929–6731 or 0208/910–3602 complaints ⊕ www.hmce.gov.uk.

DISABILITIES AND ACCESSIBILITY

California is a national leader in making attractions and facilities accessible to peo-ple with disabilities.

LODGING

Despite the Americans with Disabilities Act, the definition of accessibility seems to differ from hotel to hotel. Some properties may be accessible by ADA standards for people with mobility problems but not for people with hearing or vision impairments, for example.

If you have mobility problems, ask for the lowest floor on which accessible services are offered. If you have a hearing impair-ment, check whether the hotel has devices to alert you visually to the ring of the tele-phone, a knock at the door, and a fire/emergency alarm. Some hotels provide these devices without charge. Discuss your needs with hotel personnel if this equip-ment isn't available, so that a staff mem-ber can personally alert you in the event of an emergency.

If you're bringing a guide dog, get autho-rization ahead of time and write down the name of the person with whom you spoke.

PARKS

The National Park Service provides a Golden Access Passport for all national parks free of charge to those who are med-ically blind or have a permanent disability; the passport covers the entry fee for the holder and anyone accompanying the holder in the same private vehicle as well as a 50% discount on camping and vari-ous other user fees. Apply for the passport in person at a national recreation facility that charges an entrance fee; proof of dis-ability is required.

RESERVATIONS

When discussing accessibility with an op-erator or reservations agent, ask hard questions. Are there any stairs, inside *or* out? Are there grab bars next to the toilet *and* in the shower/tub? How wide is the doorway to the room? To the bathroom? For the most extensive facilities meeting the latest legal specifications, **opt for newer accommodations.** If you reserve through a toll-free number, consider also calling the hotel's local number to confirm the information from the central reserva-tions office. Get confirmation in writing when you can.

TRANSPORTATION

Hertz and Avis (⇨ Car Rental) are able to supply cars modified for those with dis-abilities, but they require one to two days' advance notice. Discounts are available for travelers with disabilities on Amtrak (⇨ Train Travel). On Greyhound (⇨ Bus Travel), your companion can ride free.

🚹 Complaints Aviation Consumer Protection Di-vision (⇨ Air Travel) for airline-related problems. **Departmental Office of Civil Rights** ✉ for general inquiries, U.S. Department of Transportation, S-30,

400 7th St. SW, Room 10215, Washington, DC 20590 ☎ 202/366-4648 🖷 202/366-9371 ⊕ www.dot. gov/ost/docr/index.htm. **Disability Rights Section** ⊠ NYAV, U.S. Department of Justice, Civil Rights Division, 950 Pennsylvania Ave. NW, Washington, DC 20530 ☎ ADA information line 202/514-0301, 800/ 514-0301, 202/514-0383 TTY, 800/514-0383 TTY ⊕ www.ada.gov. **U.S. Department of Transportation Hotline** ☎ for disability-related air-travel problems, 800/778-4838 or 800/455-9880 TTY.

TRAVEL AGENCIES

In the United States, the Americans with Disabilities Act requires that travel firms serve the needs of all travelers. Some agencies specialize in working with people with disabilities.

⏩ Travelers with Mobility Problems Access Adventures ⊠ 206 Chestnut Ridge Rd., Scottsville, NY 14624 ☎ 585/889-9096 ✍ dltravel@prodigy. net, run by a former physical-rehabilitation counselor. **Accessible Vans of America** ⊠ 9 Spielman Rd., Fairfield, NJ 07004 ☎ 877/282-8267, 973/ 808-9709 reservations 🖷 973/808-9713 ⊕ www. accessiblevans.com. **CareVacations** ⊠ No. 5, 5110-50 Ave., Leduc, Alberta, Canada, T9E 6V4 ☎ 780/986-6404 or 877/478-7827 🖷 780/986-8332 ⊕ www.carevacations.com, for group tours and cruise vacations. **Flying Wheels Travel** ⊠ 143 W. Bridge St., Box 382, Owatonna, MN 55060 ☎ 507/451-5005 🖷 507/451-1685 ⊕ www. flyingwheelstravel.com.

⏩ Travelers with Developmental Disabilities New Directions ⊠ 5276 Hollister Ave., Suite 207, Santa Barbara, CA 93111 ☎ 805/967-2841 or 888/967-2841 🖷 805/964-7344 ⊕ www.newdirectionstravel.com. **Sprout** ⊠ 893 Amsterdam Ave., New York, NY 10025 ☎ 212/222-9575 or 888/222-9575 🖷 212/222-9768 ⊕ www.gosprout.org.

DISCOUNTS AND DEALS

Be a smart shopper and compare all your options before making decisions. A plane ticket bought with a promotional coupon from travel clubs, coupon books, and direct-mail offers or purchased on the Internet may not be cheaper than the least expensive fare from a discount ticket agency. And always keep in mind that what you get is just as important as what you save.

DISCOUNT RESERVATIONS

To save money, look into discount reservations services with Web sites and toll-free numbers, which use their buying power to get a better price on hotels, airline tickets

(⇨ Air Travel), even car rentals. When booking a room, always **call the hotel's local toll-free number** (if one is available) rather than the central reservations number—you'll often get a better price. Always ask about special packages or corporate rates.

⏩ Airline Tickets Air 4 Less ☎ 800/AIR4LESS; low-fare specialist.

⏩ Hotel Rooms Accommodations Express ☎ 800/444-7666 or 800/277-1064 ⊕ www. accommodationsexpress.com. **Central Reservation Service (CRS)** ☎ 800/555-7555 or 800/548-3311 ⊕ www.roomconnection.net. **Hotels.com** ☎ 214/ 369-1246 or 800/246-8357 ⊕ www.hotels.com. **Quikbook** ☎ 800/789-9887 ⊕ www.quikbook. com. **RMC Travel** ☎ 800/245-5738 ⊕ www. rmcwebtravel.com. **Steigenberger Reservation Service** ☎ 800/223-5652 ⊕ www.srs-worldhotels. com. **Turbotrip.com** ☎ 800/473-7829 ⊕ www. turbotrip.com.

PACKAGE DEALS

Don't confuse packages and guided tours. When you buy a package, you travel on your own, just as though you had planned the trip yourself. Fly/drive packages, which combine airfare and car rental, are often a good deal. In cities, ask the local visitor's bureau about hotel packages that include tickets to major museum exhibits or other special events.

DIVERS' ALERT

Do not fly within 24 hours of scuba diving.

EATING & DRINKING

California has led the pack in bringing natural and organic foods to the forefront of American cooking. Though rooted in European cuisine, California cooking has absorbed strong Asian and Latin influences. Wherever you go, you're likely to find that dishes are made with fresh produce and other local ingredients.

The restaurants we list are the cream of the crop in each price category. Properties indicated by an ✕🏠 are lodging establishments whose restaurant warrants a special trip. Lunch is typically served 11:30–2:30, and dinner service in most restaurants begins at 5:30 and ends at 10. Some restaurants in larger cities stay open until midnight or later.

In general, when you order a regular coffee, you get coffee with milk and sugar.

PRICES

CATEGORY	COST
$$$$	over $30
$$$	$23–$30
$$	$16–$22
$	$10–$15
¢	under $10

Prices are for a main course at dinner, excluding tip and tax.

MEALTIMES

Unless otherwise noted, the restaurants listed in this guide are open daily for lunch and dinner.

RESERVATIONS AND DRESS

Reservations are always a good idea; we mention them only when they're essential or not accepted. Book as far ahead as you can, and reconfirm as soon as you arrive. (Large parties should always call ahead to check the reservations policy.) We mention dress only when men are required to wear a jacket or a jacket and tie.

WINE, BEER, AND SPIRITS

If you like wine, your trip to Northern California won't be complete unless you try a few of the local vintages. Throughout the region, most famously in the Napa and Sonoma valleys, you can visit wineries, most of which have tasting rooms and many of which offer tours. The legal drinking age is 21.

ECOTOURISM

When traveling in wilderness areas and parks, remember to tread lightly. Do not drive an SUV through sensitive habitats, and **pack out what you pack in.** Many remote camping areas do not provide waste disposal. It's a good idea to bring plastic bags to store refuse until you can dispose of it properly. Recycling programs are abundant in California, and trash at many state and national parks is sorted. Look for appropriately labeled garbage containers. Numerous ecotours are available in Northern California (⇨ Tours and Packages).

GAY AND LESBIAN TRAVEL

San Francisco is among the American cities with the most visible lesbian and gay communities. Though it is usually safe to be visibly "out" in many areas, you should always use common sense when in unfamiliar places. Gay bashings still occur in both urban and rural areas. For details about the gay and lesbian scene, consult *Fodor's Gay Guide to the USA* (available in bookstores everywhere).

LOCAL INFORMATION

Many Northern California cities large and small have lesbian and gay publications available in sidewalk racks and at bars, bookstores, and other social spaces; most have extensive events and information listings.

▶ Community Centers **Billy DeFrank Lesbian & Gay Community Center** ✉ 938 The Alameda, San Jose 95126 ☎ 408/293-2429 ⊕ www.defrank.org. **Lambda Community Center** ✉ 1927 L St., Sacramento 95814 ☎ 916/442-0185 ⊕ www.lambda-sacramento.com. **Lavender Youth Recreation & Information Center** ✉ 127 Collingwood St., San Francisco 94114 ☎ 415/703-6150, 415/863-3636 for hot line. **Pacific Center Lesbian, Gay and Bisexual Switchboard** ✉ 2712 Telegraph Ave., Berkeley 94705 ☎ 510/548-8283 ⊕ www.pacificcenter.org.

The Center (San Francisco Lesbian, Gay, Bisexual, Transgender Community Center) ✉ 1800 Market St. ☎ 415/865-5555 ⊕ www.sfgaycenter.org. ▶ Local Publications **Bay Area Reporter** ✉ 395 9th St., San Francisco 94103 ☎ 415/861-5019. *Mom Guess What* ✉ 1725 L St., Sacramento 95814 ☎ 916/441-6397.

▶ Gay- and Lesbian-Friendly Travel Agencies **Different Roads Travel** ✉ 8383 Wilshire Blvd., Suite 520, Beverly Hills, CA 90211 ☎ 323/651-5557 or 800/429-8747 (Ext. 14 for both) 🖶 323/651-3678 ✉ lgernert@tzell.com. **Kennedy Travel** ✉ 130 W. 42nd St., Suite 401, New York, NY 10036 ☎ 212/840-8659 or 800/237-7433 🖶 212/730-2269 ⊕ www.kennedytravel.com. **Now, Voyager** ✉ 4406 18th St., San Francisco, CA 94114 ☎ 415/626-1169 or 800/255-6951 🖶 415/626-8626 ⊕ www.nowvoyager.com. **Skylink Travel and Tour** ✉ 1455 N. Dutton Ave., Suite A, Santa Rosa, CA 95401 ☎ 707/546-9888 or 800/225-5759 🖶 707/636-0951; serving lesbian travelers.

HOLIDAYS

Most traditional businesses are closed the following days, but tourist attractions and some restaurants are usually open except on Thanksgiving, Christmas, and New Year's Day.

Major national holidays are New Year's Day (Jan. 1); Martin Luther King Day (3rd Mon. in Jan.); Presidents' Day (3rd Mon. in Feb.); Memorial Day (last Mon. in May); Independence Day (July 4); Labor Day (1st Mon. in Sept.); Columbus Day

(2nd Mon. in Oct.); Thanksgiving Day (4th Thurs. in Nov.); Christmas Eve and Christmas Day (Dec. 24 and 25); and New Year's Eve (Dec. 31).

INSURANCE

The most useful travel-insurance plan is a comprehensive policy that includes coverage for trip cancellation and interruption, default, trip delay, and medical expenses (with a waiver for preexisting conditions).

Without insurance you'll lose all or most of your money if you cancel your trip, regardless of the reason. Default insurance covers you if your tour operator, airline, or cruise line goes out of business. Trip-delay covers expenses that arise because of bad weather or mechanical delays. Study the fine print when comparing policies.

U.K. residents can buy a travel-insurance policy valid for most vacations taken during the year in which it's purchased (but check preexisting-condition coverage).

Always **buy travel policies directly from the insurance company**; if you buy them from a cruise line, airline, or tour operator that goes out of business you probably won't be covered for the agency or operator's default, a major risk. Before making any purchase, review your existing health and home-owner's policies to find what they cover away from home.

▓ Travel Insurers In the U.S.: **Access America** ✉ 6600 W. Broad St., Richmond, VA 23230 ☎ 800/284-8300 🖷 804/673-1491 or 800/346-9265 ⊕ www.accessamerica.com. **Travel Guard International** ✉ 1145 Clark St., Stevens Point, WI 54481 ☎ 715/345-0505 or 800/826-1300 🖷 800/955-8785 ⊕ www.travelguard.com.

FOR INTERNATIONAL TRAVELERS

For information on customs restrictions, *see* Customs and Duties, *above.*

CAR RENTAL

When picking up a rental car, non-U.S. residents need a reservation voucher for any prepaid reservations that were made in the traveler's home country, a passport, a driver's license, and a travel policy that covers each driver.

CAR TRAVEL

Highways are well paved. Interstate highways—limited-access, multilane highways whose numbers are prefixed by "I–"—are the fastest routes. Interstates with three-digit numbers encircle urban areas, which may have other limited-access expressways, freeways, and parkways as well. Tolls may be levied on some limited-access highways. So-called U.S. highways and state highways are not necessarily limited-access but may have several lanes.

Along larger highways, roadside stops with rest rooms, fast-food restaurants, and sundries stores are well spaced. State police and tow trucks patrol major highways and lend assistance. If your car breaks down on an interstate, pull onto the shoulder and wait for help, or have your passengers wait while you walk to an emergency phone. If you carry a cell phone, dial *55, noting your location on the small green roadside mileage markers.

Driving in the United States is on the right. Do obey speed limits posted along roads and highways. Watch for lower limits in small towns and on back roads. California requires front-seat passengers to wear seat belts. On weekdays between 6 and 10 AM and again between 3 and 7 PM expect heavy traffic. To encourage carpooling, some freeways have special lanes for so-called high-occupancy vehicles (HOV)—cars carrying more than one or two passengers, depending on where you are. If you do not meet the criteria for travel in these lanes and you get stopped by the police, you'll get fined $200–$300 and receive a point on your license.

In California you may turn right at a red light after stopping if there is no oncoming traffic unless a sign forbids you to do so. You may also turn left on red between two one-way streets. But when in doubt, wait for the green. Be alert for one-way streets, "no left turn" intersections, and blocks closed to car traffic. Bookstores, gas stations, convenience stores, and rest stops sell maps (about $3) and multiregion road atlases (about $10). For more information on driving in California, *see* Car Travel, *above.*

CONSULATES AND EMBASSIES

▓ Australia **Australia** ✉ 625 Market St., Suite 200, San Francisco 94105 ☎ 415/536-1970. ▓ Canada **Canada** ✉ 555 Montgomery St., Suite 1288, San Francisco 94111 ☎ 415/834-3180. ▓ New Zealand **New Zealand** ✉ One Maritime Plaza, Suite 400 San Francisco 94111.

⁊ United Kingdom **United Kingdom** ⊠ 1 Sansome St., Suite 850, San Francisco 94104 ☎ 415/617-1300.

CURRENCY

The dollar is the basic unit of U.S. currency. It has 100 cents. Coins are the copper penny (1¢); the silvery nickel (5¢), dime (10¢), quarter (25¢), and half-dollar (50¢); and the golden $1 coin, replacing the Susan B. Anthony dollar coin (which too closely resembled a quarter) and the now-rare silver dollar. Bills are denominated $1, $5, $10, $20, $50, and $100, all green and identical in size; designs vary. In addition, you may come across a $2 bill, but the chances are slim. The exchange rate at this writing is US$1.59 per British pound, $.69 per Canadian dollar, $.62 per Australian dollar, and $.55 per New Zealand dollar.

ELECTRICITY

The U.S. standard is AC, 110 volts/60 cycles. Plugs have two flat pins set parallel to each other.

EMERGENCIES

For police, fire, or ambulance, **dial 911** (0 in rural areas).

INSURANCE

Britons and Australians need extra medical coverage when traveling overseas.

⁊ Insurance Information In the U.K.: **Association of British Insurers** ⊠ 51 Gresham St., London EC2V 7HQ ☎ 020/7600-3333 🖷 020/7696-8999 ⊕ www.abi.org.uk. In Australia: **Insurance Council of Australia** ⊠ Insurance Enquiries and Complaints, Level 3, 56 Pitt St., Sydney, NSW 2000 ☎ 1300/363683 or 02/9251-4456 🖷 02/9251-4453 ⊕ www.iecltd.com.au. In Canada: **RBC Insurance** ⊠ 6880 Financial Dr., Mississauga, Ontario L5N 7Y5 ☎ 800/565-3129 🖷 905/813-4704 ⊕ www.rbcinsurance.com. In New Zealand: **Insurance Council of New Zealand** ⊠ Level 7, 111-115 Customhouse Quay, Box 474, Wellington ☎ 04/472-5230 🖷 04/473-3011 ⊕ www.icnz.org.nz.

MAIL AND SHIPPING

You can buy stamps and aerograms and send letters and parcels in post offices. Stamp-dispensing machines can occasionally be found in airports, bus and train stations, office buildings, drugstores, and the like. You can also deposit mail in the stout, dark blue, steel bins at strategic locations everywhere and in the mail chutes of large buildings; pickup schedules are posted.

For mail sent within the United States, you need a 37¢ stamp for first-class letters weighing up to 1 ounce (23¢ for each additional ounce) and 23¢ for postcards. You pay 80¢ for 1-ounce airmail letters and 70¢ for airmail postcards to most other countries; to Canada and Mexico, you need a 60¢ stamp for a 1-ounce letter and 50¢ for a postcard. An aerogram—a single sheet of lightweight blue paper that folds into its own envelope, stamped for overseas airmail—costs 70¢.

To receive mail on the road, have it sent c/o General Delivery at your destination's main post office (use the correct five-digit ZIP code). You must pick up mail in person within 30 days and show a driver's license or passport.

PASSPORTS AND VISAS

When traveling internationally, carry your passport even if you don't need one (it's always the best form of I.D.) and **make two photocopies of the data page** (one for someone at home and another for you, carried separately from your passport). If you lose your passport, promptly call the nearest embassy or consulate and the local police.

Visitor visas aren't necessary for Canadian or European Union citizens, or for citizens of Australia who are staying fewer than 90 days.

⁊ Australian Citizens **Passports Australia** ☎ 131-232 ⊕ www.passports.gov.au. **United States Consulate General** ⊠ MLC Centre, Level 59, 19-29 Martin Pl., Sydney, NSW 2000 ☎ 02/9373-9200, 1902/941-641 fee-based visa-inquiry line ⊕ usembassy-australia.state.gov/sydney.

⁊ Canadian Citizens **Passport Office** ⊠ to mail in applications: 200 Promenade du Portage, Hull, Québec J8X 4B7 ☎ 819/994-3500 or 800/567-6868 ⊕ www.ppt.gc.ca.

⁊ New Zealand Citizens **New Zealand Passports Office** ⊠ For applications and information, Level 3, Boulcott House, 47 Boulcott St., Wellington ☎ 0800/22-5050 or 04/474-8100 ⊕ www.passports.govt.nz. **Embassy of the United States** ⊠ 29 Fitzherbert Terr., Thorndon, Wellington ☎ 04/462-6000 ⊕ usembassy.org.nz. **U.S. Consulate General** ⊠ Citibank Bldg., 3rd floor, 23 Customs St. E, Auckland ☎ 09/303-2724 ⊕ usembassy.org.nz.

U.K. Citizens U.K. Passport Service ☎ 0870/521-0410 ⊕ www.passport.gov.uk. **American Consulate General** ✉ Queen's House, 14 Queen St., Belfast, Northern Ireland BT1 6EQ ☎ 028/9032-8239 ⛁ 028/9024-8482 ⊕ www.usembassy.org.uk. **American Embassy** ✉ for visa and immigration information (enclose an SASE), Consular Information Unit, 24 Grosvenor Sq., London W1 1AE ✉ to submit an application via mail, Visa Branch, 5 Upper Grosvenor St., London W1A 2JB ☎ 09068/200-290 recorded visa information or 09055/444-546 operator service, both with per-minute charges, 0207/499-9000 main switchboard ⊕ www.usembassy.org.uk.

TELEPHONES

All U.S. telephone numbers consist of a three-digit area code and a seven-digit local number. Within many local calling areas, you dial only the seven-digit number. Within some area codes, you must dial "1" first for calls outside the local area. To call between area-code regions, dial "1" then all 10 digits; the same goes for calls to numbers prefixed by "800," "888," "866," and "877"—all toll free. For calls to numbers preceded by "900" you must pay—usually dearly.

For international calls, dial "011" followed by the country code and the local number. For help, dial "0" and ask for an overseas operator. The country code is 61 for Australia, 64 for New Zealand, 44 for the United Kingdom. Calling Canada is the same as calling within the United States. Most local phone books list country codes and U.S. area codes. The country code for the United States is 1.

For operator assistance, dial "0." To obtain someone's phone number, call directory assistance at 555–1212 or occasionally 411 (free at some public phones). To have the person you're calling foot the bill, phone collect; dial "0" instead of "1" before the 10-digit number.

At pay phones, instructions often are posted. Usually you insert coins in a slot (usually 35¢–50¢ for local calls) and wait for a steady tone before dialing. When you call long-distance, the operator tells you how much to insert; prepaid phone cards, widely available in various denominations, are easier. Call the number on the back, punch in the card's personal identification number when prompted, then dial your number.

Long-Distance Carriers AT&T ☎ 800/225-5288. **MCI** ☎ 800/888-8000. **Sprint** ☎ 800/366-2255.

LODGING

The lodgings we list are the cream of the crop in each price category. We always list the facilities that are available, but we don't specify whether they cost extra; when pricing accommodations, always ask what's included and what costs extra.

Properties are assigned price categories based on the range between their least and most expensive standard double room at high season (excluding holidays) to the most expensive.

Properties marked ✕⌂ are lodging establishments whose restaurants warrant a special trip.

Assume that hotels operate on the **European Plan** (EP, with no meals) unless we specify that they use the **Continental Plan** (CP, with a Continental breakfast), **Breakfast Plan** (BP, with a full breakfast), **Modified American Plan** (MAP, with breakfast and dinner), or the **Full American Plan** (FAP, with all meals).

PRICES

Properties are assigned price categories based on the range from their least-expensive standard double room at high season (excluding holidays) to the most expensive.

CATEGORY	COST
$$$$	over $250
$$$	$176–$250
$$	$121–$175
$	$90–$120
¢	under $90

Prices are for a standard double room in high season, excluding service charges and tax. Hotel taxes vary from city to city, but the average is around 10%, with higher rates in major urban areas.

APARTMENT, VILLA, AND HOUSE RENTALS

If you want a home base that's roomy enough for a family and comes with cooking facilities, consider a furnished rental. These can save you money, especially if you're traveling with a group. Home-exchange directories sometimes list rentals as well as exchanges.

International Agents Hideaways International ✉ 767 Islington St., Portsmouth, NH 03802 ☎ 603/430-4433 or 800/843-4433 ⛁ 603/430-4444 ⊕ www.hideaways.com, membership $129. Vacation Home Rentals Worldwide ✉ 235 Kensington

Ave., Norwood, NJ 07648 ☎ 201/767-9393 or 800/633-3284 🖷 201/767-5510 ⊕ www.vhrww.com.

CAMPING

Northern California offers numerous camping options, from family campgrounds with all the amenities to secluded hike-in campsites with no facilities. Some are operated by the state, others are on federal land, and still others are private. Rules vary for each. You can camp anywhere in a National Forest, but in a National Park, you must use only specific sites. Whenever possible, **book well in advance,** especially if your trip will be in summer or on a weekend. Contact the National Parks Reservation Service to reserve a campsite in a national park. ReserveAmerica handles reservations for campgrounds administered by the U.S. Forest Service and the Army Corps of Engineers; ReserveUSA handles reservations for many of the campgrounds in California state parks. On their Web sites you can search for locations, view campground maps, check availability, learn rules and regulations, and find driving directions.

🚩 Reservations **National Parks Reservation Service** ☎ 800/436-7275 or 800/365-2267 ⊕ reservations.nps.gov. **ReserveAmerica** ☎ 877/444-6777 ⊕ www.reserveamerica.com. **ReserveUSA** ☎ 800/444-7275 ⊕ www.reserveusa.com.

HOME EXCHANGES

If you would like to exchange your home for someone else's, join a home-exchange organization, which will send you its updated listings of available exchanges for a year and will include your own listing in at least one of them. It's up to you to make specific arrangements.

🚩 Exchange Clubs **HomeLink International** ⌂ Box 47747, Tampa, FL 33647 ☎ 813/975-9825 or 800/638-3841 🖷 813/910-8144 ⊕ www.homelink.org; $110 yearly for a listing, on-line access, and catalog; $40 without catalog. **Intervac U.S.** ⊠ 30 Corte San Fernando, Tiburon, CA 94920 ☎ 800/756-4663 🖷 415/435-7440 ⊕ www.intervacus.com; $105 yearly for a listing, on-line access, and a catalog; $50 without catalog.

HOSTELS

No matter what your age, you can save on lodging costs by staying at hostels. In some 4,500 locations in more than 70 countries around the world, Hostelling International (HI), the umbrella group for a number of national youth-hostel associations, offers single-sex, dorm-style beds and, at many hostels, rooms for couples and family accommodations. Membership in any HI national hostel association, open to travelers of all ages, allows you to stay in HI-affiliated hostels at member rates; one-year membership is about $28 for adults (C$35 for a two-year minimum membership in Canada, £13.50 in the U.K., A$52 in Australia, and NZ$40 in New Zealand); hostels charge about $10–$30 per night. Members have priority if the hostel is full; they're also eligible for discounts around the world, even on rail and bus travel in some countries.

🚩 Organizations **Hostelling International–USA** ⊠ 8401 Colesville Rd., Suite 600, Silver Spring, MD 20910 ☎ 301/495-1240 🖷 301/495-6697 ⊕ www.hiayh.org. **Hostelling International–Canada** ⊠ 400-205 Catherine St., Ottawa, Ontario K2P 1C3 ☎ 613/237-7884 or 800/663-5777 🖷 613/237-7868 ⊕ www.hihostels.ca. **YHA England and Wales** ⊠ Trevelyan House, Dimple Rd., Matlock, Derbyshire DE4 3YH, U.K. ☎ 0870/870-8808 🖷 0870/770-6127 ⊕ www.yha.org.uk. **YHA Australia** ⊠ 422 Kent St., Sydney, NSW 2001 ☎ 02/9261-1111 🖷 02/9261-1969 ⊕ www.yha.com.au. **YHA New Zealand** ⊠ Level 3, 193 Cashel St., Box 436, Christchurch ☎ 03/379-9970 or 0800/278-299 🖷 03/365-4476 ⊕ www.yha.org.nz.

HOTELS

All hotels listed have private bath unless otherwise noted.

Most major hotel chains are represented in Northern California. All hotels listed have private bath unless otherwise noted. Make any special needs known when you book your reservation. Guarantee your room with a credit card, or many hotels will automatically cancel your reservations if you don't show up by 4 PM. Many hotels, like airlines, overbook. It is best to **reconfirm your reservation directly with the hotel on the morning of your arrival date.**

🚩 Toll-Free Numbers **Best Western** ☎ 800/528-1234 ⊕ www.bestwestern.com. **Choice** ☎ 800/424-6423 ⊕ www.choicehotels.com. **Clarion** ☎ 800/424-6423 ⊕ www.choicehotels.com. **Comfort Inn** ☎ 800/424-6423 ⊕ www.choicehotels.com. **Days Inn** ☎ 800/325-2525 ⊕ www.daysinn.com. **Doubletree Hotels** ☎ 800/222-8733 ⊕ www.doubletree.com. **Embassy Suites** ☎ 800/362-2779 ⊕ www.embassysuites.com. **Fairfield Inn** ☎ 800/228-2800 ⊕ www.marriott.com. **Four Seasons** ☎ 800/332-3442 ⊕ www.fourseasons.com. **Hilton** ☎ 800/445-8667 ⊕ www.hilton.com. **Holiday**

Inn ☎ 800/465-4329 ⊕ www.sixcontinentshotels. com. **Howard Johnson** ☎ 800/446-4656 ⊕ www. hojo.com. **Hyatt Hotels & Resorts** ☎ 800/233-1234 ⊕ www.hyatt.com. **Inter-Continental** ☎ 800/327-0200 ⊕ www.intercontinental.com. **La Quinta** ☎ 800/531-5900 ⊕ www.laquinta.com. **Marriott** ☎ 800/228-9290 ⊕ www.marriott.com. **Nikko Hotels International** ☎ 800/645-5687 ⊕ www. nikkohotels.com. **Omni** ☎ 800/843-6664 ⊕ www. omnihotels.com. **Quality Inn** ☎ 800/424-6423 ⊕ www.choicehotels.com. **Radisson** ☎ 800/333-3333 ⊕ www.radisson.com. **Ramada** ☎ 800/228-2828, 800/854-7854 international reservations ⊕ www.ramada.com. **Red Lion and WestCoast Hotels and Inns** ☎ 800/733-5466 ⊕ www.redlion. com. **Renaissance Hotels & Resorts** ☎ 800/468-3571 ⊕ www.renaissancehotels.com. **Ritz-Carlton** ☎ 800/241-3333 ⊕ www.ritzcarlton.com. **Sheraton** ☎ 800/325-3535 ⊕ www.starwood.com/sheraton. **Sleep Inn** ☎ 800/424-6423 ⊕ www.choicehotels. com. **Westin Hotels & Resorts** ☎ 800/228-3000 ⊕ www.starwood.com/westin. **Wyndham Hotels & Resorts** ☎ 800/822-4200 ⊕ www.wyndham.com.

MEDIA

NEWSPAPERS AND MAGAZINES

Northern California's major daily newspaper, the *San Francisco Chronicle,* maintains an up-to-the-minute Web site. The region's weekly newspapers are usually the best source of arts and entertainment information, from what shows are on the boards to who's playing the clubs. Visit the Web sites of the *San Francisco Bay Guardian,* the *San Jose Metro* (MetroActive), and *SF Weekly* for the latest information on events in your destination.
🔎 **Web Sites MetroActive** ⊕ www.metroactive.com. *San Francisco Bay Guardian* ⊕ www.sfbayguardian. com. *San Francisco Chronicle* ⊕ www.sfchron.com. *SF Weekly* ⊕ www.sfweekly.com.

MONEY MATTERS

San Francisco tends to be an expensive city to visit, and rates at coastal resorts are almost as high. Hotel rates average $150–$250 a night (though you can find cheaper places), and dinners at even moderately priced restaurants often cost $20–$40 per person. Costs in the Gold Country and the Far North are considerably less—many fine Gold Country B&Bs charge around $100 a night, and some motels in the Far North charge $50–$70.

Prices throughout this guide are given for adults. Substantially reduced fees are al-most always available for children, students, and senior citizens. For information on taxes, *see* Taxes.

ATMS

ATMs are readily available throughout Northern California. If you withdraw cash from a bank other than your own, expect to pay a fee of up to $2.50. If you're going to very remote areas of the mountains, take some extra cash with you or find out ahead of time if you can pay with credit cards.

CREDIT CARDS

Throughout this guide, the following abbreviations are used: **AE,** American Express; **D,** Discover; **DC,** Diners Club; **MC,** MasterCard; and **V,** Visa.
🔎 **Reporting Lost Cards American Express** ☎ 800/441-0519. **Diners Club** ☎ 800/234-6377. **Discover** ☎ 800/347-2683. **MasterCard** ☎ 800/622-7747. **Visa** ☎ 800/ 847-2911.

NATIONAL PARKS

Look into discount passes to save money on park entrance fees. For $50, the National Parks Pass admits you (and any passengers in your private vehicle) to all national parks, monuments, and recreation areas, as well as other sites run by the National Park Service, for a year. (In parks that charge per person, the pass admits you, your spouse and children, and your parents, when you arrive together.) Camping and parking are extra. The $15 Golden Eagle Pass, a hologram you affix to your National Parks Pass, functions as an upgrade, granting entry to all sites run by the NPS, the U.S. Fish and Wildlife Service, the U.S. Forest Service, and the Bureau of Land Management. The upgrade, which expires with the parks pass, is sold by most national-park, Fish-and-Wildlife, and BLM fee stations. A percentage of the proceeds from pass sales funds National Parks projects.

Both the Golden Age Passport ($10), for U.S. citizens or permanent residents who are 62 and older, and the Golden Access Passport (free), for those with disabilities, entitle holders (and any passengers in their private vehicles) to lifetime free entry to all national parks, plus 50% off fees for the use of many park facilities and services. (The discount doesn't always apply to companions.) To obtain them, you must show proof of age and of U.S. citizenship or permanent residency—such as a U.S. passport, driver's license, or birth certificate—and, if requesting Golden Access, proof of disability. The Golden Age and Golden Access passes are available only at NPS-run sites that charge an entrance fee. The National Parks Pass is also available by mail and via the Internet.

🔳 **National Park Foundation** ✉ 11 Dupont Circle NW, 6th floor, Washington, DC 20036 ☎ 202/238-4200 ⊕ www.nationalparks.org. **National Park Service** ✉ National Park Service/Department of Interior, 1849 C St. NW, Washington, DC 20240 ☎ 202/208-6843 ⊕ www.nps.gov. **National Parks Conservation Association** ✉ 1300 19th St. NW, Suite 300, Washington, DC 20036 ☎ 202/223-6722 ⊕ www.npca.org.

🔳 **Passes by Mail and On-Line National Park Foundation** ⊕ www.nationalparks.org. **National Parks Pass** 🖃 Box 34108, Washington, DC 20043 ☎ 888/467-2757 ⊕ www.nationalparks.org; include a check or money order payable to the National Park Service, plus $3.95 for shipping and handling, or call for passes by phone.

OUTDOORS AND SPORTS

In Northern California you can scale high peaks, hike through sequoia groves, fish, bike, sail, dive, ski, or golf. Whatever sport you love, you can do it in Northern California.

FISHING

You'll need a license to fish in California. State residents pay $30.70, but nonresidents are charged $82.45 for a one-year license or $30.70 for a 10-day license. Both residents and nonresidents can purchase a two-day license for $11.05. You can order licenses over the phone with a credit card; allow two weeks for delivery. The Web site of the California Department of Fish and Game provides information on fishing zones, licenses, and schedules.

🔳 **Department of Fish and Game; Licensing Dept.** ✉ 3211 S St., Sacramento 95816 ☎ 916/227-2245 ⊕ www.dfg.ca.gov/licensing/fishing/sportfishing.html.

STATE PARKS

🔳 **California State Park System** 🖃 Dept. of Parks and Recreation, Box 942896, Sacramento 94296 ☎ 916/653-6995 or 800/777-0369 ✍ info@parks.ca.gov ⊕ www.parks.ca.gov.

PACKING

When packing for a Northern California vacation, **prepare for changes in temperature.** Take along sweaters, jackets, and clothes for layering as your best insurance for coping with variations in temperature. Know that San Francisco and other coastal towns can be chilly at any time of the year, especially in summer, when the fog descends in the afternoon. Always tuck in a bathing suit; many lodgings have pools, spas, and saunas. Casual dressing is a hallmark of the California lifestyle, but in the evening men will need a jacket and tie at more formal restaurants, and women will be most comfortable in something dressier than sightseeing garb. Check *Fodor's How to Pack* (available in bookstores everywhere) for more tips.

In your carry-on luggage, pack an extra pair of eyeglasses or contact lenses and enough of any medication you take to last a few days longer than the entire trip. You may also ask your doctor to write a spare prescription using the drug's generic name, as brand names may vary from country to country. In luggage to be checked, **never pack prescription drugs, valuables, or undeveloped film.** And don't forget to carry with you the addresses of offices that handle refunds of lost traveler's checks. Check *Fodor's How to Pack* (available at on-line retailers and bookstores everywhere) for more tips.

To avoid customs and security delays, carry medications in their original packaging. Don't pack any sharp objects in your carry-on luggage, including knives of any size or material, scissors, and corkscrews, or anything else that might arouse suspicion.

To avoid having your checked luggage chosen for hand inspection, don't cram bags full. The U.S. Transportation Security Administration suggests packing shoes on top and placing personal items you don't want touched in clear plastic bags.

CHECKING LUGGAGE

You're allowed to carry aboard one bag and one personal article, such as a purse or a laptop computer. Make sure what you carry on fits under your seat or in the overhead bin. Get to the gate early, so you can board as soon as possible, before the overhead bins fill up.

Baggage allowances vary by carrier, destination, and ticket class. On international flights, you're usually allowed to check two bags weighing up to 70 pounds (32 kilograms) each, although a few airlines allow checked bags of up to 88 pounds (40 kilograms) in first class. Some international carriers don't allow more than 66 pounds (30 kilograms) per bag in business class and 44 pounds (20 kilograms) in economy. On domestic flights, the limit may be 50 pounds (23 kilograms) per bag. Most airlines won't accept bags that weigh more than 100 pounds (45 kilograms) on domestic or international flights. Check baggage restrictions with your carrier before you pack.

Airline liability for baggage is limited to $2,500 per person on flights within the United States. On international flights it amounts to $9.07 per pound or $20 per kilogram for checked baggage (roughly $640 per 70-pound bag) and $400 per passenger for unchecked baggage. You can buy additional coverage at check-in for about $10 per $1,000 of coverage, but it often excludes a rather extensive list of items, shown on your airline ticket.

Before departure, **itemize your bags' contents** and their worth, and label the bags with your name, address, and phone number. (If you use your home address, cover it so potential thieves can't see it readily.) Include a label inside each bag and pack a copy of your itinerary. At check-in, **make sure each bag is correctly tagged** with the destination airport's three-letter code. Because some checked bags will be opened for hand inspection, the U.S. Transportation Security Administration recommends that you leave luggage unlocked or use the plastic locks offered at check-in. TSA screeners place an inspection notice inside searched bags, which are re-sealed with a special lock.

If your bag has been searched and contents are missing or damaged, file a claim with the TSA Consumer Response Center as soon as possible. If your bags arrive damaged or fail to arrive at all, file a written report with the airline before leaving the airport.
🛂 Complaints **U.S. Transportation Security Administration Consumer Response Center** ☎ 866/289-9673 ⊕ www.tsa.gov.

SENIOR-CITIZEN TRAVEL

To qualify for age-related discounts, mention your senior-citizen status up front when booking hotel reservations (not when checking out) and before you're seated in restaurants (not when paying the bill). Be sure to have identification on hand. When renting a car, ask about promotional car-rental discounts, which can be cheaper than senior-citizen rates.
🛂 Educational Programs **Elderhostel** ⊠ 11 Ave. de Lafayette, Boston, MA 02111-1746 ☎ 978/323-4141 or 877/426-8056 🖷 617/426-0701 or 877/426-2166 ⊕ www.elderhostel.org. **Interhostel** ⊠ University of New Hampshire, 6 Garrison Ave., Durham, NH 03824 ☎ 603/862-1147 or 800/733-9753 🖷 603/862-1113 ⊕ www.learn.unh.edu/interhostel.

SMOKING

Smoking is illegal in all California bars and restaurants, except on outdoor patios or in smoking rooms. This law is typically not well enforced and some restaurants and bars do not comply, so take your cues from the locals. Hotels and motels are also decreasing their inventory of smoking rooms; inquire at the time you book your reservation if any are available. In addition, there is a selective tax on cigarettes sold in California, and prices can be as high as $6 per pack. You might want to bring a carton from home.

STUDENTS IN NORTHERN CALIFORNIA
🛂 I.D.s and Services **STA Travel** ⊠ 10 Downing St., New York, NY 10014 ☎ 212/627-3111 or 800/777-0112 🖷 212/627-3387 ⊕ www.sta.com. **Travel Cuts** ⊠ 187 College St., Toronto, Ontario M5T 1P7, Canada ☎ 416/979-2406, 800/592-2887, 866/246-9762 in Canada 🖷 416/979-8167 ⊕ www.travelcuts.com.

TAXES

Sales tax in Northern California varies from about 7¼% to 8½% and applies to all purchases except for prepackaged food; restaurant food is taxed. Airlines include departure taxes and surcharges in the price of the ticket.

TELEPHONES

Pay phones cost 35–50¢ in Northern California.

TIME

California is in the Pacific time zone. Pacific daylight time (PDT) is in effect from early April through late October; the rest of the year the clock is set to Pacific standard time (PST). Clocks are set ahead one hour when daylight saving time begins, back one hour when it ends.

TIPPING

At restaurants, a 15% tip is standard for waiters; up to 20% may be expected at more expensive establishments. The same goes for taxi drivers, bartenders, and hairdressers. Coat-check operators usually expect $1; bellhops and porters should get $1–$2 per bag; hotel maids in upscale hotels should get about $2 per day of your stay. A concierge typically receives a tip of $5–$10, with an additional gratuity for special services or favors.

On package tours, conductors and drivers usually get $1 per person from the group as a whole; check whether this has already been figured into your cost. For local sightseeing tours, you may individually tip the driver-guide 10%–15% if he or she has been helpful or informative. Ushers in theaters do not expect tips.

TOURS AND PACKAGES

Because everything is prearranged on a prepackaged tour or independent vacation, you spend less time planning—and often get it all at a good price.

BOOKING WITH AN AGENT

Travel agents are excellent resources. But it's a good idea to collect brochures from several agencies, as some agents' suggestions may be influenced by relationships with tour and package firms that reward them for volume sales. If you have a special interest, find an agent with expertise in that area; the American Society of Travel Agents (ASTA; ⇨ Travel Agencies) has a database of specialists worldwide.

Make sure your travel agent knows the accommodations and other services of the place being recommended. Ask about the hotel's location, room size, beds, and whether it has a pool, room service, or programs for children, if you care about these. Has your agent been there in person or sent others whom you can contact?

Do some homework on your own, too: local tourism boards can provide information about lesser-known and small-niche operators, some of which may sell only direct.

BUYER BEWARE

Each year consumers are stranded or lose their money when tour operators—even large ones with excellent reputations—go out of business. So check out the operator. Ask several travel agents about its reputation, and try to **book with a company that has a consumer-protection program.** (Look for information in the company's brochure.) In the United States, members of the National Tour Association and the United States Tour Operators Association are required to set aside funds to cover payments and travel arrangements in the event that the company defaults. It's also a good idea to choose a company that participates in the American Society of Travel Agents' Tour Operator Program; ASTA will act as mediator in any disputes between you and your tour operator.

Remember that the more your package or tour includes, the better you can predict the ultimate cost of your vacation. Make sure you know exactly what is covered, and **beware of hidden costs.** Are taxes, tips, and transfers included? Entertainment and excursions? These can add up.

🚩 Tour-Operator Recommendations **American Society of Travel Agents** (⇨ Travel Agencies). **National Tour Association** (NTA) ✉ 546 E. Main St., Lexington, KY 40508 ☎ 859/226-4444 or 800/682-8886 ⊕ www.ntaonline.com. **United States Tour Operators Association** (USTOA) ✉ 275 Madison Ave., Suite 2014, New York, NY 10016 ☎ 212/599-6599 or 800/468-7862 🖷 212/599-6744 ⊕ www.ustoa.com.

TRAIN TRAVEL

Amtrak's *California Zephyr* train from Chicago via Denver terminates in Oakland. The *Coast Starlight* train travels between southern California and the state of Washington.

🚩 Train Information **Amtrak** ☎ 800/872-7245 ⊕ www.amtrak.com.

TRAVEL AGENCIES

A good travel agent puts your needs first. Look for an agency that has been in business at least five years, emphasizes customer service, and has someone on staff who specializes in your destination. In addition, **make sure the agency belongs to a professional trade organization.** The American Society of Travel Agents (ASTA)—the largest and most influential in the field with more than 20,000 members in some 140 countries—maintains and enforces a strict code of ethics and will step in to help mediate any agent-client disputes involving ASTA members if necessary. ASTA (whose motto is "Without a travel agent, you're on your own") also maintains a Web site that includes a directory of agents. (If a travel agency is also acting as your tour operator, *see* Buyer Beware *in* Tours and Packages.)

Local Agent Referrals **American Society of Travel Agents (ASTA)** ✉ 1101 King St., Suite 200, Alexandria, VA 22314 ☎ 703/739-2782 or 800/965-2782 24-hr hot line 🖷 703/739-3268 ⊕ www.astanet.com. **Association of British Travel Agents** ✉ 68-71 Newman St., London W1T 3AH ☎ 020/7637-2444 🖷 020/7637-0713 ⊕ www.abtanet.com. **Association of Canadian Travel Agents** ✉ 130 Albert St., Suite 1705, Ottawa, Ontario K1P 5G4 ☎ 613/237-3657 🖷 613/237-7052 ⊕ www.acta.ca. **Australian Federation of Travel Agents** ✉ Level 3, 309 Pitt St., Sydney, NSW 2000 ☎ 02/9264-3299 🖷 02/9264-1085 ⊕ www.afta.com.au. **Travel Agents' Association of New Zealand** ✉ Level 5, Tourism and Travel House, 79 Boulcott St., Box 1888, Wellington 6001 ☎ 04/499-0104 🖷 04/499-0786 ⊕ www.taanz.org.nz.

VISITOR INFORMATION

For general information about Northern California, contact the California Division of Tourism. The California Division of Tourism Web site has travel tips, events calendars, and other resources, and the site will link you—via the Regions icon—to the Web sites of city and regional tourism offices and attractions. For the numbers of regional and city visitors bureaus and chambers of commerce *see* the A to Z section at the end of each chapter.

If you are coming to Northern California from overseas, you can check with your home government for official travel advisories and destination information. For a broader picture, consider information from more than one country.

Tourist Information **California Division of Tourism** ✉ 1102 Q St., Sacramento, CA 95814 ☎ 916/322-2881 or 800/862-2543 🖷 916/322-3402 ⊕ www.gocalif.ca.gov. **In the U.K.** **California Tourist Office** ✆ ABC California, Box 35, Abingdon, Oxfordshire OX14 4TB ☎ 0891/200-278 🖷 020/7242-2838. **Government Advisories** **Consular Affairs Bureau of Canada** ☎ 613/944-6788 or 800/267-6788 ⊕ www.voyage.gc.ca. **U.K. Foreign and Commonwealth Office** ✉ Travel Advice Unit, Consular Division, Old Admiralty Building, London SW1A 2PA ☎ 020/7008-0232 or 020/7008-0233 ⊕ www.fco.gov.uk/travel. **Australian Department of Foreign Affairs and Trade** ☎ 02/6261-1299 Consular Travel Advice Faxback Service ⊕ www.dfat.gov.au. **New Zealand Ministry of Foreign Affairs and Trade** ☎ 04/439-8000 ⊕ www.mft.govt.nz.

WEB SITES

Do check out the World Wide Web when planning your trip. You'll find everything from weather forecasts to virtual tours of famous cities. Be sure to **visit Fodors.com** (⊕ www.fodors.com), a complete travel-planning site. You can research prices and book plane tickets, hotel rooms, rental cars, vacation packages, and more. In addition, you can post your pressing questions in the Travel Talk section. Other planning tools include a currency converter and weather reports, and there are loads of links to travel resources.

The California Parks Department site has the lowdown on state-run parks and other recreational areas. A must-visit for outdoors and adventure travel enthusiasts, the Great Outdoor Recreation Page is arranged into easily navigated categories. The site of the Wine Institute, which is based in San Francisco, provides events listings and detailed information about the California wine industry and has links to the home pages of regional wine associations.

Web Sites **California Parks Department** ⊕ www. parks.ca.gov. **Great Outdoor Recreation Page** ⊕ www.gorp.com. **Wine Institute** ⊕ www.wineinstitute.org.

SAN FRANCISCO
WITH SAUSALITO & BERKELEY

1

FODOR'S CHOICE

Alamo Square Inn, *Western Addition*

Chez Panisse Café & Restaurant, *Berkeley*

Chow, *a casual American eatery in the Castro*

Claremont Resort and Spa, *Berkeley*

Delfina, *a sophisticated Italian restaurant in the Mission*

Farallon, *the spot for seafood in Union Sq.*

Fifth Floor, *Chef Laurent Gras's outpost in SoMa*

Four Seasons Hotel San Francisco, *SoMa*

Gary Danko, *a French eatery in Fisherman's Wharf*

Hotel Monaco, *Union Square*

Hotel Rex, *Union Square*

Jardinière, *contemporary food in Hayes Valley*

L'Osteria del Forno, *simple Italian fare in North Beach*

Lombard Street, *the crooked thoroughfare, in Russian Hill*

Mandarin Oriental, *a hotel with city views in the Financial District*

Masa's, *a nationally renowned French eatery in Nob Hill*

Palace Hotel, *SoMa*

Palace of Fine Arts, *Marina*

Ritz-Carlton, San Francisco, *Nob Hill*

San Francisco Museum of Modern Art, *SoMa*

Sherman House, *a luxurious hotel in Pacific Heights*

Swan Oyster Depot, *a fish market & diner in Van Ness/Polk*

Union Street Inn, *Cow Hollow*

Zuni Café, *Hayes Valley*

Many other great hotels, restaurants, and sights enliven San Francisco. To find them, look for the black stars as you read this chapter.

IN ITS FIRST LIFE, SAN FRANCISCO was little more than a small, well-situated settlement. Founded by Spaniards in 1776, it was prized for its natural harbor, so commodious that "all the navies of the world might fit inside it," as one visitor wrote. Around 1849 the discovery of gold at John Sutter's sawmill in the nearby Sierra foothills transformed the sleepy little settlement into a city of 30,000. Millions of dollars' worth of gold was panned and blasted out of the hills, the impetus for the development of a western Wall Street. Fueled by the 1859 discovery of a fabulously rich vein of silver in Virginia City, Nevada, San Francisco became the West Coast's cultural fulcrum and major transportation hub, and its population soared to 342,000. In 1869 the transcontinental railway was completed, linking the once-isolated western capital to the East. San Francisco had become a major city of the United States.

"Loose," "tolerant," and even "licentious" are words used to describe San Francisco. Bohemian communities thrive here. As early as the 1860s the Barbary Coast—a collection of taverns, whorehouses, and gambling joints along Pacific Avenue close to the waterfront—was famous, or infamous. North Beach, the city's Little Italy, became the home of the Beat movement in the 1950s. Lawrence Ferlinghetti's City Lights, a bookstore and publishing house that still stands on Columbus Avenue, brought out, among other titles, Allen Ginsberg's *Howl* and *Kaddish*. In the 1960s the Free Speech movement began at the University of California at Berkeley, and Stanford's David Harris, who went to prison for defying the draft, numbered among the nation's most famous student leaders. The Haight-Ashbury district became synonymous with hippiedom, giving rise to such legendary bands as Jefferson Airplane and the Grateful Dead. Southwest of the Haight is the onetime Irish neighborhood known as the Castro, which during the 1970s became identified with gay and lesbian liberation.

Technically speaking, San Francisco is only California's fourth-largest city, behind Los Angeles, San Diego, and nearby San Jose. But that statistic is misleading: the Bay Area, extending from the bedroom communities north of Oakland and Berkeley south through the peninsula and the San Jose area, is really one continuous megacity, with San Francisco as its heart.

EXPLORING SAN FRANCISCO

Updated by
Denise M. Leto

You could live in San Francisco a month and ask no greater entertainment than walking through it," wrote Inez Hayes Irwin, author of *The Californiacs,* an effusive 1921 homage to the state of California and the City by the Bay. Her claim remains true today: as in the 1920s, touring on foot is the best way to experience this diverse metropolis.

San Francisco is a relatively small city. About 800,000 residents live on a 46½-square-mi tip of land between the Pacific Ocean and San Francisco Bay. Yet this compact space is packed with sites of historical and architectural interest. San Franciscans cherish the city's colorful past—many older buildings have been nostalgically converted into modern offices and shops, and longtime locals still rue those that fell victim to acts of nature and the indifference of developers. In addition, the neighborhoods of San Francisco retain strong cultural, political, and ethnic identities. Locals know this pluralism is the real life of the city. Experiencing San Francisco means visiting the neighborhoods: the hip Mission District, the gay Castro, countercultural Haight Street, swank Pacific Heights, lively Chinatown, ever bohemian North Beach, and arts- and news media–oriented SoMa, among others.

Spend your first morning day checking out Fisherman's Wharf and Pier 39. Jump a cable car (the Powell-Hyde line is the most dramatic) at the wharf and take in sweeping views of the bay as you rattle your way to Union Square. Maiden Lane's charming galleries and boutiques are worth a look. On the second day, begin with a walk on the Golden Gate Bridge, then explore North Beach, the Italian quarter, filled with tempting food, Beat-era landmarks, and reminders of the city's bawdy past. Move on to labyrinthine Chinatown, where tea and herb shops, fish markets, and produce stalls spill onto the street. Begin your third day by taking a ferry from Pier 41 to the infamous Alcatraz prison. Spend the rest of the day in the whichever neighborhood most appeals to you: the Haight, the epicenter of 1960s counterculture, whose streets are lined with excellent music and book shops and cool vintage-clothing stores; colorful, gay-friendly Castro, brimming with shops and cafés; or the mural-filled Mission District, a neighborhood of twentysomething hipsters and working-class Latino families. Simple Mission Dolores, built in 1776, is San Francisco's oldest standing structure.

Follow the three-day itinerary above, and on the morning of your fourth day walk up Telegraph Hill to Coit Tower; you'll be rewarded with breathtaking views of the bay and the city's tightly stacked homes. Head for the Marina neighborhood, and if you love chocolate stop at Ghirardelli Square, which includes a shopping center and the tempting Ghirardelli Chocolate Factory. Make a beeline for the end of the Marina and the stunning Palace of Fine Arts. Don't miss the Palace's wacky and wonderful hands-on science museum, the Exploratorium. In the afternoon join in-line skaters, joggers, and walking enthusiasts in picnic-perfect Golden Gate Park—more than 1,000 acres of greenery stretching from the Haight to the Pacific. On day five, explore one of the neighborhoods you missed on day three, and in the afternoon take the ferry to Sausalito or head to the East Bay to explore formerly radical, still-offbeat Berkeley.

Numbers in the text correspond to numbers in the margin and on the neighborhood maps.

Union Square

Much of San Francisco may feel like a collection of small towns strung together, but the Union Square area bristles with big-city bravado. The city's finest department stores do business here, along with exclusive emporiums such as Tiffany & Co. and Prada and big-name franchises such as Niketown and the Virgin Megastore. Several dozen hotels within a three-block walk of the square cater to visitors. The downtown theater district and many fine arts galleries are nearby.

a good
walk

Begin three blocks south of Union Square at the **San Francisco Visitor Information Center** ❶ ⌐, on the lower level of Hallidie Plaza at Powell and Market streets. Up the escalators on the east side of the plaza, where Powell dead-ends into Market, lies the **cable-car terminus** ❷ for two of the city's three lines. Head north on Powell from the terminus to Geary Street, where the sturdy and stately **Westin St. Francis Hotel** ❸ dominates

Powell between Geary and Post streets. **Union Square ❹** is across Powell from the hotel's main entrance.

From the square head south on Stockton Street and make a right on **Maiden Lane ❺**, a two-block alley directly across Stockton from Union Square that runs east parallel to Geary. When the lane ends at Kearny Street, turn left, walk 1½ blocks to Sutter Street, make a right, and walk a half block to the **Hallidie Building ❻**. After viewing this historic building, reverse direction and head west 1½ blocks up Sutter to the fanciful beaux-arts–style **Hammersmith Building ❼**, on the southwest corner of Sutter Street and Grant Avenue. In the middle of the next block, at 450 Sutter, stands a glorious 1928 art deco skyscraper, a masterpiece of terra-cotta and other detailing; handsome Maya-inspired designs adorn its exterior and interior surfaces. From here, backtrack a half block east to Stockton Street and take a right. In front of the Grand Hyatt hotel sits **Ruth Asawa's Fantasy Fountain ❽**. Union Square is a half block south on Stockton.

TIMING Allow two hours to see everything around Union Square. If you're a shopper, give yourself extra time.

What to See

❷ **Cable-car terminus.** San Francisco's signature red cable cars were declared National Landmarks—the only ones that move—in 1964. Two of the three operating lines begin and end their runs in Union Square. The more dramatic Powell–Mason line climbs up Nob Hill, then winds through North Beach to Fisherman's Wharf. The Powell–Hyde line also crosses Nob Hill but then continues up Russian Hill and down Hyde Street to Victorian Park, across from the Buena Vista Café and near Ghirardelli Square. Buy your ticket ($2 one-way) on board, at nearby hotels, or at the police/information booth near the turnaround. If it's just the experience of riding a cable car you're after, board the less-busy California line at Van Ness Avenue and ride it down to the Hyatt Regency Hotel. ⊠ *Powell and Market Sts., Union Sq.*

❻ **Hallidie Building.** Named for cable-car inventor Andrew S. Hallidie, this 1918 structure is best viewed from across the street. Willis Polk's revolutionary glass-curtain wall—believed to be the world's first such facade—hangs a foot beyond the reinforced concrete of the frame. The reflecting glass, decorative exterior fire escapes that appear to be metal balconies, and Venetian Gothic cornice are worth noting. ⊠ *130 Sutter St., between Kearny and Montgomery Sts., Union Sq.*

❼ **Hammersmith Building.** Glass walls and a colorful design distinguish this four-story beaux-arts–style structure, built in 1907. The Foundation for Architectural Heritage once described the building as a "commercial jewel box." Appropriately, it was originally designed for use as a jewelry store. ⊠ *301 Sutter St., at Grant Ave., Union Sq.*

❺ **Maiden Lane.** Known as Morton Street in the raffish Barbary Coast era, this former red-light district reported at least one murder a week during the late 19th century. After the 1906 fire destroyed the brothels, the street emerged as Maiden Lane, and it has since become a chic pedestrian mall stretching two blocks, between Stockton and Kearny streets.

With its circular interior ramp and skylights, the handsome brick 1948 structure at **140 Maiden Lane,** the only Frank Lloyd Wright building in San Francisco, is said to have been his model for the Guggenheim Museum in New York. ⊠ *Between Stockton and Kearny Sts., Union Sq.*

❽ **Ruth Asawa's Fantasy Fountain.** Local artist Ruth Asawa's sculpture, a wonderland of real and mythical creatures, honors the city's hills,

The Bay & Its Bridges

The sight of a suit-clad stockbroker unloading a Windsurfer from his Land Rover is not uncommon in San Francisco, where the bay perpetually beckons to pleasure seekers of every stripe. On sunny weekends the bay teems with sailboats, and when the surf's up, daredevils in wet suits line the beaches. For those not inclined to get wet, various ferries, tour boats, and dinner cruises give those aboard a view of all three bridges—the Golden Gate Bridge, the Richmond, and the Bay—as well as Angel Island, Treasure Island, and the legendary Alcatraz.

The Fog

Every summer morning a white shroud of mist rolls down from the Marin Headlands, often obliterating all but the tops of the towers of the Golden Gate Bridge from view, and then it evaporates by noon. To native San Franciscans, summer fog is a part of life, as dependable as the sunrise. It's part of what makes San Francisco feel so exposed to the whims of nature.

Hidden Lanes & Stairways

Although it has its share of major boulevards, San Francisco is a city of small side streets—many one-way-only lanes and out-of-the-way stairways. Whether you're in Chinatown, Nob Hill, North Beach, Pacific Heights, Potrero Hill, or Russian Hill, there's always a quiet lane or stairway nearby. A few of the most scenic hidden corners are in Nob Hill, Russian Hill, and North Beach—but if you look carefully, you'll find them where they're least expected.

The Hills

Anyone who's afraid of heights would do well to stay away from San Francisco, where almost everything worth getting to lies at the top of or just beyond a steep hill. Driving the city feels like riding a roller coaster, but don't worry: your stomach catches up to the rest of you at the base of each extreme dip. But for all the challenges they present to drivers and walkers, the hills are what give San Francisco its distinctly European look and its dazzling bay views. It's a city of hills—Nob Hill, Russian Hill, Telegraph Hill, Potrero Hill, the smaller hills within neighborhoods—that looks out at larger hills across the bay.

Patches of Green

With its hills and fresh air, its myriad parks and waterfront promenades, San Francisco is an outdoors lover's dream. Golden Gate Park, with more than 1,000 acres of trails and fields, is deservedly popular, but there are other choices. The Presidio, a former military base, encompasses almost 1,500 acres of hilly, wooded trails interspersed with old army barracks. The Marina, which stretches from the Presidio to the northern waterfront, is the turf of choice for a stylishly outfitted crowd of runners and skaters. Along the western shore you find the 275-acre Lincoln Park and the Great Highway, a 3-mi ocean-side stretch with a paved jogging path.

Wining & Dining

Europhiles who bemoan the lack of a sophisticated food and wine culture in America have nothing to complain about in San Francisco. As the birthplace of California cuisine—cooking that combines fresh, locally grown ingredients in visually stunning ways—and as the neighbor of Napa Valley, the metro area has long been attracting notable chefs.

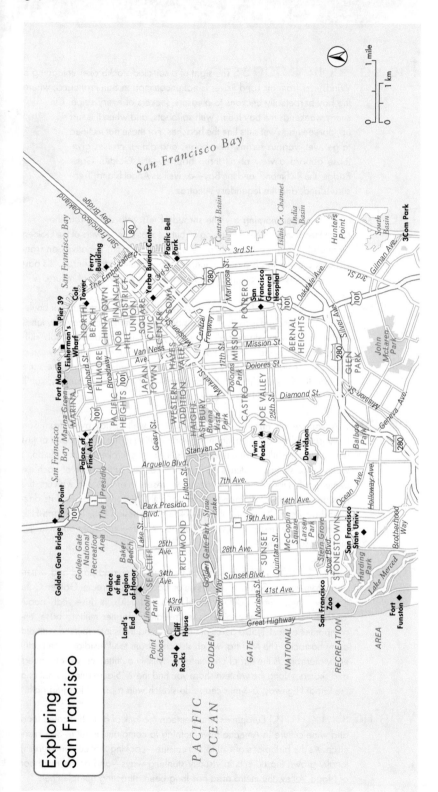

Exploring
San Francisco

bridges, and architecture. Children and friends helped Asawa shape the hundreds of tiny figures from baker's clay; these were assembled on 41 large panels from which molds were made for the bronze casting. ⊠ *In front of Grand Hyatt at 345 Stockton St., Union Sq.*

► ❶ **San Francisco Visitor Information Center.** A multilingual staff operates this facility below the cable-car terminus. Staffers answer questions and provide maps and pamphlets. You can also pick up discount coupons and hotel brochures here. ⊠ *Hallidie Plaza, lower level, Powell and Market Sts., Union Sq.* ☎ *415/391–2000 or 415/283–0177* ⊕ *www.sfvisitor. org* ⊙ *Weekdays 9–5, weekends 9–3.*

❹ **Union Square.** The heart of San Francisco's downtown since 1850, the 2½-acre square takes its name from the violent pro-union demonstrations staged here before the Civil War. At center stage, the *Victory Monument,* by Robert Ingersoll Aitken, commemorates Commodore George Dewey's victory over the Spanish fleet at Manila in 1898. The 97-foot Corinthian column, topped by a bronze figure symbolizing naval conquest, was dedicated by Theodore Roosevelt in 1903 and withstood the 1906 earthquake. An open-air stage and central plaza, an outdoor café, gardens, four sculptures by the artist R. M. Fischer, and a visitor information booth draw strollers to the square. ⊠ *Bordered by Powell, Stockton, Post, and Geary Sts., Union Sq.*

❸ **Westin St. Francis Hotel.** The second-oldest hotel in the city, established in 1904, was conceived by railroad baron and financier Charles Crocker and his associates as a hostelry for their millionaire friends. After the hotel was ravaged by the 1906 fire, a larger, more luxurious Italian Renaissance–style residence was opened in 1907. The hotel's checkered past includes the ill-fated 1921 bash in the suite of the silent-film comedian Fatty Arbuckle, at which a woman became ill and later died. Arbuckle endured three sensational trials for rape and murder before being acquitted, by which time his career was kaput. In 1975 Sara Jane Moore, standing among a crowd outside the hotel, attempted to shoot then-president Gerald R. Ford. ⊠ *335 Powell St., at Geary St., Union Sq.* ☎ *415/ 397–7000* ⊕ *www.westin.com.*

SoMa & the Embarcadero

SoMa was once known as South of the Slot, in reference to the cable-car slot that ran up Market Street. Industry took over most of the area after the 1906 earthquake collapsed most homes into their quicksand bases. When huge sections of the neighborhood were razed to make way for an ambitious multiuse redevelopment project in the 1960s and '70s, SoMa emerged as a focal point of San Francisco's cultural life. Alternative artists set up shop, and key players in San Francisco's arts scene then migrated to the area in the 1990s. Now glitzy projects such as the Four Seasons Hotel and residential complex are juxtaposed with still-gritty stretches of Mission and Market streets, creating a friction that keeps the neighborhood interesting.

a good walk

The **San Francisco Museum of Modern Art** ❾ ► dominates a half block of 3rd Street between Howard and Mission streets. Use the crosswalk near SFMOMA's entrance to head across 3rd Street into Yerba Buena Gardens, the centerpiece of the SoMa redevelopment area. To your right after you've walked a few steps, a sidewalk leads to the main entrance of the **Yerba Buena Center for the Arts** ❿. Straight ahead is the East Garden of Yerba Buena Gardens, surrounded by a circular walkway lined with benches and sculptures, and beyond that, on the 4th Street side of the block, is the **Metreon** ⓫ entertainment, retail, and restaurant com-

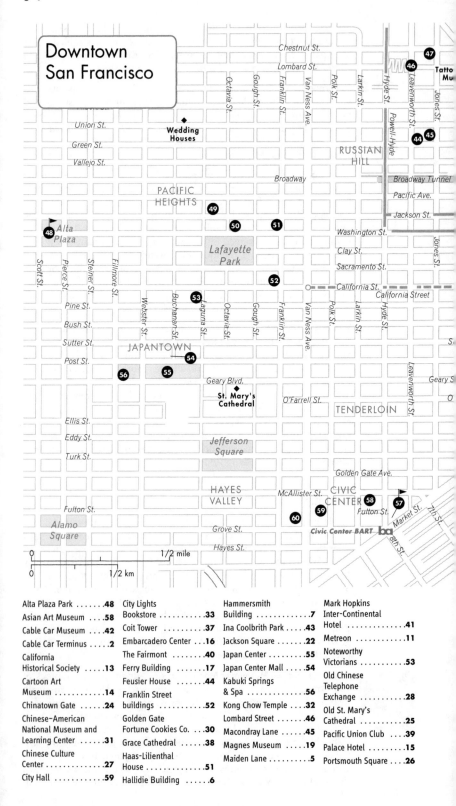

Downtown San Francisco

plex. A second-level walkway in the southern portion of the East Garden, above the Martin Luther King Jr. waterfall, arches over Howard Street, leading to the main (south) entrance to Moscone Convention Center and the **Rooftop@Yerba Buena Gardens** ⑫ facilities.

Exit the rooftop, head north up 4th Street to Mission Street and walk east on Mission (toward SFMOMA) past the monolithic San Francisco Marriott, also known as the "jukebox" Marriott because of its exterior design. Just before St. Patrick's Catholic Church, turn left onto the pedestrian walkway Yerba Buena Lane, due to open in fall 2004, past a water course, shops, and restaurants to the plaza on Market Street at the foot of Grant Avenue. (Also scheduled to open on this block of Mission Street in 2005 are the new Mexican Museum and a new home for the Magnes Museum.) A half block past 3rd Street on Mission is the headquarters of the **California Historical Society** ⑬. Across the street and a few steps farther east is the **Cartoon Art Museum** ⑭.

Continue east on Mission Street, turn left onto New Montgomery Street, and continue to Market Street and the **Palace Hotel** ⑮. Enter via the Market Street entrance, checking out the Pied Piper Bar, Garden Court restaurant, and main lobby. Exit via the lobby onto New Montgomery Street and make a left, which will bring you back to Market Street. Turn right and head toward the waterfront. Toward the end of Market a three-tier pedestrian mall connects the five buildings of the **Embarcadero Center** ⑯ office-retail complex. Across the busy Embarcadero roadway from the plaza stands the port's trademark, the **Ferry Building** ⑰.

The ground floor of the ornate 1889 Audiffred Building, on the southwest corner of the Embarcadero and Mission Street, houses Boulevard restaurant. Head west on Mission Street along the side of Boulevard and cross Steuart Street. In the middle of the block is the entrance to the historic sections of **Rincon Center** ⑱, worth seeing for the famous murals and the old Rincon Annex Post Office. Continue south within the center to its newer portions and make a left as you exit through the doors near Chalkers Billiards. Across Steuart Street is the Jewish Community Federation Building, which for now houses the **Magnes Museum** ⑲.

TIMING   The walk above takes a good two hours, more if you visit the museums and galleries. SFMOMA merits about two hours; the Center for the Arts and the Cartoon Art Museum, 45 minutes each.

What to See

⑬ **California Historical Society.** The society, founded in 1871, administers a vast repository of Californiana—500,000 photographs, 150,000 manuscripts, thousands of books, periodicals, and paintings as well as gold-rush paraphernalia. ⊠ *678 Mission St., SoMa* ☎ *415/357–1848* ⊕ *www.californiahistoricalsociety.org* ✉ *$3, free 1st Tues. of month* ☉ *Tues.–Sat. 11–5 (galleries close between exhibitions).*

⑭ **Cartoon Art Museum.** Krazy Kat, Zippy the Pinhead, Batman, and other colorful cartoon icons greet you at the Cartoon Art Museum. In addition to a 12,000-piece permanent collection, a 3,000-volume library, and a CD-ROM gallery, changing exhibits examine everything from the influence of underground comics to the output of women and African-American cartoonists. ⊠ *655 Mission St., SoMa* ☎ *415/227–8666* ⊕ *www.cartoonart.org* ✉ *$6, pay what you wish 1st Tues. of month* ☉ *Tues.–Sun. 11–5.*

⑯ **Embarcadero Center.** John Portman designed this five-block complex built during the 1970s and early 1980s. Shops and restaurants abound on the first three levels; there's ample office space on the floors above.

Louise Nevelson's 54-foot-tall black-steel sculpture, *Sky Tree,* stands guard over Building 3 and is among 20-plus artworks throughout the center. ⊠ *Clay St. between Battery St. (Embarcadero 1) and the Embarcadero (Embarcadero 5)* ☎ *415/772–0734* ⊕ *www.embarcaderocenter.com.*

★ **⑰ Ferry Building.** The beacon of the port area, erected in 1896, has a 230-foot clock tower modeled after the campanile of the cathedral in Seville, Spain. On April 18, 1906, the four great clock faces on the tower, powered by the swinging of a 14-foot pendulum, stopped at 5:17—the moment the great earthquake struck—and stayed still for 12 months. After a $70 million renovation, the Ferry Building has reopened with a skylit market hall on street level that bustles with restaurants, cafés, and local-food purveyors. A waterfront promenade extends from the piers on the north side of the building south to the Bay Bridge, and ferries behind the building sail to Sausalito, Larkspur, Tiburon, and the East Bay. ⊠ *The Embarcadero at foot of Market St., Embarcadero.*

⑲ Magnes Museum. The exhibits at this small museum survey Jewish art, history, and culture. Call ahead before visiting; the museum sometimes closes between exhibits. In 2005 the museum plans to move into state-of-the-art, Daniel Libeskind–designed quarters south of Market, on Mission Street between 3rd and 4th streets. ⊠ *121 Steuart St., Embarcadero* ☎ *415/788–9990* ⊕ *www.magnesmuseum.org* ⌦ *$5, free 1st Mon. of month* ☉ *Sun.–Thurs. noon–5.*

Ⓒ **⑪ Metreon.** Child's play meets the 21st century at this Sony entertainment center. An interactive play area is based on Maurice Sendak's *Where the Wild Things Are.* Portal 1, a high-tech interactive arcade, includes an Extreme Sports Adventure Room. In the Digital Solutions shop you can access the Internet for free. A 15-screen multiplex, an IMAX theater, retail shops, and outposts of some of the city's favorite restaurants are all part of the complex. ⊠ *101 4th St., between Mission and Howard Sts., SoMa* ☎ *800/638–7366* ⊕ *www.metreon.com.*

⑮ Palace Hotel. The city's oldest hotel, a Sheraton property, opened in 1875. Fire destroyed the original Palace after the 1906 earthquake, despite the hotel's 28,000-gallon reservoir fed by four artesian wells; the current building dates from 1909. President Warren Harding died at the Palace while still in office in 1923, and the body of King Kalakaua of Hawaii spent a night chilling here after he died in San Francisco in 1891. The managers play up this ghoulish past with talk of a haunted guest room. ⊠ *2 New Montgomery St., SoMa* ☎ *415/512–1111* ⊕ *www.sfpalace.com.*

⑱ Rincon Center. A sheer five-story column of water resembling a mini-rainstorm is the centerpiece of the indoor arcade at this mostly modern office-retail complex. The lobby of the streamline moderne–style former post office on the Mission Street side contains a Works Project Administration mural by Anton Refregier. The 27 panels depict California life from the days when Native Americans were the state's sole inhabitants through World War I. A permanent exhibit below the murals contains photographs and artifacts of life in the Rincon area in the 1800s. ⊠ *Between Steuart, Spear, Mission, and Howard Sts., SoMa.*

★ Ⓒ **⑫ Rooftop@Yerba Buena Gardens.** Fun is the order of the day among these brightly colored concrete and corrugated-metal buildings atop Moscone Convention Center South. The historic **Looff carousel** ($2 for two rides) twirls daily 11–6. South of the carousel is **Zeum** (☎ 415/777–2800 ⊕ www.zeum.org), a high-tech, interactive arts-and-technology center ($7) geared to children ages eight and over. Kids can make Claymation videos, work in a computer lab, and view exhibits and performances. Zeum is open 11–5 Tuesday through Sunday in summer and Wednesday through Sunday in winter. Also part of the rooftop complex are gardens, an ice-skating rink, and a bowling alley. ⊠ *4th St. between Howard and Folsom Sts., SoMa.*

▶ **❾** **San Francisco Museum of Modern Art.** Mario Botta designed the striking
FodorśChoice SFMOMA facility, completed in early 1995, which consists of a sienna
★ brick facade and a central tower of alternating bands of black and white stone. A black-and-gray stone staircase leads from the atrium to four floors of galleries. Works by Henri Matisse, Pablo Picasso, Georgia O'Keeffe, Frida Kahlo, Jackson Pollock, and Andy Warhol form the heart of the diverse permanent collection. The photography holdings are also strong. ⊠ *151 3rd St., SoMa* ☎ *415/357–4000* ⊕ *www.sfmoma. org* ⊠ *$10, free 1st Tues. of month, ½-price Thurs. 6–9* ☉ *Late May–early Sept., Fri.–Tues. 10–6, Thurs. 10–9; early Sept.–late May, Fri.–Tues. 11–6, Thurs. 11–9; call for hrs for special exhibits.*

❿ **Yerba Buena Center for the Arts.** The dance, music, theater, visual arts, films, and videos presented at this facility in Yerba Buena Gardens range from the community-based to the international and lean toward the cutting edge. ⊠ *701 Mission St., SoMa* ☎ *415/978–2787* ⊕ *www.yerbabuenaarts. org* ⊠ *Galleries $6, free 1st Tues. of month* ☉ *Galleries Tues.–Sun. 11–5, 1st Thurs. of month 11–8; box office Tues.–Sun. 11–6.*

Heart of the Barbary Coast

It was on Montgomery Street, in the Financial District, that Sam Brannan proclaimed the historic gold discovery that took place at Sutter's Mill on January 24, 1848. The gold rush brought streams of people from across America and Europe, and the population of San Francisco jumped from a mere 800 in 1848 to more than 25,000 in 1850 and to about 135,000 in 1870. Other fortune seekers, including saloon keepers, gamblers, and prostitutes, all flocked to the so-called Barbary Coast (now Jackson Square and the Financial District). Along with the quick money came a wave of violence. In 1852 the city suffered an average of two murders and one major fire each day. Since then the red-light establishments have edged upward to the Broadway strip of North Beach, and Jackson Square evolved into a sedate district of refurbished brick buildings decades ago.

a good walk

Bronze sidewalk plaques mark the street corners along the 50-sight, approximately 3¾-mi Barbary Coast Trail. The trail begins at the Old Mint, at 5th and Mission streets, and runs north through downtown, Chinatown, Jackson Square, North Beach, and Fisherman's Wharf, ending at Aquatic Park. For information about the sites on the trail, pick up a brochure at the San Francisco Visitor Information Center.

To catch the highlights of the Barbary Coast Trail and a glimpse of a few important Financial District structures, start on Montgomery Street, between California and Sacramento streets, at the **Wells Fargo Bank History Museum** ⓴.

Two blocks north on Montgomery from the Wells Fargo museum stands the **Transamerica Pyramid** ㉑, between Clay and Washington streets. Walk through the tranquil redwood grove on the pyramid's east side, and you'll exit on Washington Street, across which you can see Hotaling Place to your left. Walk west (left) to the corner, cross Washington Street, and walk back to Hotaling. This historic alley is your entrance to **Jackson Square** ㉒, the heart of the Barbary Coast. Of particular note here are the former A. P. Hotaling whiskey distillery, on the corner of Hotaling Place, and the 1850s structures around the corner in the 700 block of Montgomery Street. To see these buildings, walk west on Jackson from the distillery and make a left on Montgomery. Then head south on Montgomery to Washington Street, make a right, and cross Columbus Avenue. Head north (to the right) up Columbus to the **San Francisco Brewing Company** ㉓, the last standing saloon of the Barbary Coast era.

TIMING   Two hours should be enough time to see everything on this tour. The Wells Fargo museum (open only on weekdays) deserves a half hour.

What to See

㉒ **Jackson Square.** Here was the heart of the Barbary Coast of the Gay '90s. Although most of the red-light district was destroyed in the 1906 fire, old redbrick buildings and narrow alleys recall the romance and rowdiness of the early days. Some of the city's earliest business buildings, survivors of the 1906 quake, still stand in Jackson Square, between Montgomery and Sansome streets. Restored 19th-century brick buildings line Hotaling Place, which connects Washington and Jackson streets. The lane is named for the head of the **A. P. Hotaling Company whiskey distillery** (⊠ 451 Jackson St., at Hotaling Pl.), which was the largest liquor repository on the West Coast in its day. The Italianate Hotaling building reveals little of its infamous past, but a plaque on the side of the structure repeats a famous query about its surviving the quake: IF, AS THEY SAY, GOD SPANKED THE TOWN FOR BEING OVER FRISKY, WHY DID HE BURN THE CHURCHES DOWN AND SAVE HOTALING'S WHISKEY?

In the 700 block of **Montgomery Street,** Bret Harte wrote his novel *The Luck of Roaring Camp* at No. 730. He toiled as a typesetter for the spunky *golden-era* newspaper, which occupied No. 732 (now part of the building at No. 744). ⊠ *Jackson Square district bordered by Broadway and Washington, Montgomery, and Sansome Sts., Financial District.*

㉓ **San Francisco Brewing Company.** Built in 1907, this pub looks like a museum piece from the Barbary Coast days. An old upright piano sits in the corner under the original stained-glass windows. Take a seat at the mahogany bar, from where you can look down at the white-tile spittoon. An adjacent room holds the handmade copper brewing kettle used to produce a dozen beers—with names such as Pony Express—by means of old-fashioned gravity-flow methods. ⊠ *155 Columbus Ave., North Beach* ☎ *415/434–3344* ⊕ *www.sfbrewing.com* ☉ *Mon.–Sat. 11:30–2 AM, Sun. noon–2 AM.*

㉑ **Transamerica Pyramid.** The city's most photographed high-rise is this 853-foot structure. Designed by William Pereira and Associates in 1972, the initially controversial icon has become more acceptable to most locals over time. A fragrant redwood grove along the east side of the building, replete with benches and a cheerful fountain, is a placid patch in which to unwind. ⊠ *600 Montgomery St., Financial District* ⊕ *www.tapyramid.com.*

㉔ **Wells Fargo Bank History Museum.** There were no formal banks in San Francisco during the early years of the gold rush, and miners often entrusted their gold dust to saloon keepers. In 1852 Wells Fargo opened its first bank in the city, and the company established banking offices in the mother-lode camps, using stagecoaches and pony-express riders to service the burgeoning state. The museum displays samples of nuggets and gold dust from mines, a mural-size map of the Mother Lode, original art by western artists Charles M. Russell and Maynard Dixon, mementos of the poet bandit Black Bart, and an old telegraph machine on which you can practice sending codes. The showpiece is the red Concord stagecoach. ⊠ *420 Montgomery St., Financial District* ☎ *415/396–2619* 🖃 *Free* ☉ *Weekdays 9–5.*

Chinatown

Prepare to have your senses assaulted in Chinatown, bordered roughly by Bush, Kearny, and Powell streets, and Broadway. Pungent smells waft out of restaurants, fish markets, and produce stands. Good-luck banners of crimson and gold hang beside dragon-entwined lampposts, pagoda roofs, and street signs with Chinese calligraphy. Honking cars chime in with shoppers bargaining loudly in Cantonese or Mandarin. Add to this the sight of millions of Chinese-theme goods spilling out of the kitschy shops along Grant Avenue, and you get an idea of what Chinatown is all about.

a good
walk

While wandering through Chinatown's streets and alleys, don't forget to look up. Above street level, many older structures—mostly brick buildings that replaced rickety wooden ones destroyed during the 1906 earthquake—have ornate balconies and cornices. The architecture on the 900 block of Grant Avenue (at Washington Street) and Waverly Place (west of and parallel to Grant Avenue between Sacramento and Washington streets) is particularly noteworthy.

Enter Chinatown through the green-tile **Chinatown Gate** ㉔ ▶, on Grant Avenue at Bush Street. Shops selling souvenirs, jewelry, and home furnishings line Grant north past the gate. Dragon House, at No. 455, sells centuries-old antiques rather than six-month-old goods made in Taiwan. **Old St. Mary's Cathedral** ㉕ towers over the corner of Grant Avenue and California Street. Continue on Grant to Clay Street and turn right. A half block down on your left is **Portsmouth Square** ㉖. A walkway on the eastern edge of the park leads over Kearny Street to the third floor of the Holiday Inn, where you find the **Chinese Culture Center** ㉗.

Backtrack on the walkway to Portsmouth Square and head west up Washington Street a half block to the **Old Chinese Telephone Exchange** ㉘ (now the Bank of Canton), and then continue west on Washington Street. Cross Grant Avenue and look for Waverly Place a half block up on the left. One of the best examples of this alley's traditional architecture is the **Tin How Temple** ㉙. After visiting Waverly Place and Tin How, walk back to Washington Street. Several herb shops do business in this area. Two worth checking out are Superior Trading Company, at No. 839, and the Great China Herb Co., at No. 857.

Across Washington Street from Superior is Ross Alley. Head north on Ross toward Jackson Street, stopping along the way to watch the bakers at the **Golden Gate Fortune Cookies Co.** ㉚. Turn right on Jackson. When you get to Grant Avenue, don't cross it. For some of Chinatown's best pastries, turn left and stop by No. 1029, the Golden Gate Bakery. The markets in the 1100 block of Grant Avenue carry intriguing delicacies, such as braised pig noses and ears, eels, and all manner of live game birds and fish.

Head west on Pacific Avenue to Stockton Street, turn left, and walk south past Stockton Street's markets, where the locals do business. At Clay Street make a right and head halfway up the hill to the **Chinese-American National Museum and Learning Center** ㉛. Return to Stockton Street and make a right; a few doors down is the **Kong Chow Temple** ㉜, and next door is the elaborate Chinese Six Companies building, with its curved roof tiles and elaborate cornices.

TIMING Allow at least two hours to see Chinatown. Brief stops will suffice at the cultural center and temples.

What to See

► **㉔ Chinatown Gate.** Stone lions flank the base of the pagoda-topped gate, the official entrance to Chinatown. The lions and the glazed clay dragons atop the largest of the gate's three pagodas symbolize, among other things, wealth and prosperity. The fish whose mouths wrap tightly around the crest of this pagoda also symbolize prosperity. The four Chinese characters immediately beneath the pagoda represent the philosophy of Sun Yat-sen (1866–1925), the leader who unified China in the early 20th century. Sun Yat-sen promoted the notion of friendship and peace among all nations based on equality, justice, and goodwill. ⊠ *Grant Ave. at Bush St., Chinatown.*

㉛ Chinese-American National Museum and Learning Center. This airy, light-filled gallery has displays about the Chinese-American experience from 19th-century agriculture to 21st-century food and fashion trends. A separate room hosts rotating exhibits by contemporary Chinese-American artists; another describes the building's time as the Chinatown YWCA, which served as a meeting place and residence for Chinese women in need of social services. ⊠ *965 Clay St., Chinatown* ☎ *415/391–1188* ⊕ *www.chsa.org* ▨ *$3* ☉ *Tues.–Fri. 11–4, weekends noon–4.*

㉗ Chinese Culture Center. The San Francisco Redevelopment Commission agreed to let **Holiday Inn** build in Chinatown if the chain provided room for a Chinese culture center. Inside the center are the works of Chinese and Chinese-American artists as well as traveling exhibits relating to Chinese culture. Walking tours ($12; make reservations a week ahead) of historic points in Chinatown take place on most days at 10 AM. ⊠ *Holiday Inn, 750 Kearny St., 3rd floor, Chinatown* ☎ *415/986–1822* ⊕ *www.c-c-c.org* ▨ *Free* ☉ *Tues.–Sun. 10–4.*

☾ **㉚ Golden Gate Fortune Cookies Co.** Walk down Ross Alley and you'll likely be invited into this small cookie factory. The workers sit at circular motorized griddles and wait for dollops of batter to drop onto a tiny metal plate, which rotates into an oven. A few moments later out comes a cookie that's pliable and ready for folding. A bagful of cookies costs $2 or $3; personalized fortunes are also available. ⊠ *56 Ross Alley (west of and parallel to Grant Ave. between Washington and Jackson Sts.), Chinatown* ☎ *415/781–3956* ▨ *Free* ☉ *Daily 10–7.*

㉜ Kong Chow Temple. The god to whom the members of this temple pray represents honesty and trust. Take the elevator up to the fourth floor, where incense fills the air. You can show your respect by placing a dollar or two in the donation box. Amid the statuary, flowers, and richly colored altars, a couple of plaques announce that MRS. HARRY S. TRUMAN CAME TO THIS TEMPLE IN JUNE 1948 FOR A PREDICTION ON THE OUTCOME OF THE ELECTION . . . THIS FORTUNE CAME TRUE. The temple's balcony has a good view of Chinatown. ⊠ *855 Stockton St., Chinatown* ☎ *No phone* ▨ *Free* ☉ *Mon.–Sat. 9–4.*

㉘ Old Chinese Telephone Exchange. Most of Chinatown burned down after the 1906 earthquake, and this building—today the Bank of Canton—set the style for the new Chinatown. The intricate three-tier pagoda was built in 1909. The exchange's operators were renowned for their prodigious memories, about which the San Francisco Chamber of Commerce boasted in 1914: "These girls respond all day with hardly a mistake to calls that are given (in English or one of five Chinese dialects) by the name of the subscriber instead of by his number—a mental feat that would be practically impossible to most high-schooled American misses." ⊠ *Bank of Canton, 743 Washington St., Chinatown.*

㉕ **Old St. Mary's Cathedral.** The building served as the city's Catholic cathedral until 1891. The church needs to undergo seismic retrofitting and is in the process of raising funds for the procedure. Across California Street in **St. Mary's Park,** the late local sculptor Beniamino Bufano's 12-foot-tall statue of Sun Yat-sen towers over the site of the Chinese leader's favorite reading spot during his years in San Francisco. ⊠ *Grant Ave. and California St., Chinatown.*

㉖ **Portsmouth Square.** Captain John B. Montgomery raised the American flag here in 1846, claiming the area from Mexico. The square—a former potato patch—was the plaza for Yerba Buena, the Mexican settlement that was renamed San Francisco. Robert Louis Stevenson, the author of *Treasure Island,* lived on the edge of Chinatown in the late 19th century and often visited the square. Bruce Porter designed the bronze galleon that sits atop a 9-foot granite shaft in the square's northwestern corner in honor of the writer. With its pagoda-shape structures, Portsmouth Square is a favorite spot for morning tai chi and afternoon Chinese chess. ⊠ *Bordered by Walter Lum Pl. and Kearny, Washington, and Clay Sts., Chinatown.*

★ ㉙ **Tin How Temple.** Day Ju, one of the first three Chinese to arrive in San Francisco, dedicated this temple to the Queen of the Heavens and the Goddess of the Seven Seas in 1852. In the third-floor temple's entryway, elderly ladies can often be seen preparing "money" to be burned as offerings to various Buddhist gods or as funds for ancestors to use in the afterlife. A statue of Tin How sits in the middle back of the temple, flanked by a red lesser god and by a green one. Photography isn't permitted, and visitors are asked not to step onto the balcony. ⊠ *125 Waverly Pl., Chinatown* ☎ *No phone* ✉ *Free (donations accepted)* ◷ *Daily 9–4.*

North Beach

Novelist and resident Herbert Gold calls North Beach "the longest-running, most glorious American bohemian operetta outside Greenwich Village." Indeed, to anyone who's spent some time in its eccentric old bars and cafés or wandered the neighborhood, North Beach evokes everything from the Barbary Coast days to the no-less-rowdy beatnik era. Italian bakeries appear frozen in time, homages to Jack Kerouac and Allen Ginsberg pop up everywhere, and the modern equivalent of the Barbary Coast's "houses of ill repute," strip joints, do business on Broadway.

a good walk

The **City Lights Bookstore** ㉝ ☞, on Columbus Avenue, is a must-see city landmark in North Beach. To the south, the triangular Sentinel Building, where Kearny Street and Columbus Avenue meet at an angle, grabs the eye with its unusual shape and mellow green patina. To the north of Broadway and Columbus is the heart of Italian North Beach.

Walk southeast across Columbus to City Lights Bookstore. Three of the most atmospheric bars in San Francisco are near here: Vesuvio, Specs, and Tosca, where opera tunes stock the jukebox. For joltingly caffeinated espresso drinks, also to the tune of opera, head north on Columbus a block and a half on the same side of the avenue as City Lights to Caffè Puccini, at No. 411.

Head up the east side of Columbus Avenue past Grant Avenue. On the northeast corner of Columbus and Vallejo Street is the Victorian-era **St. Francis of Assisi Church** ㉞. Go east on Vallejo Street to Grant Avenue and make another left. Check out the eclectic shops and old-time bars and cafés between Vallejo and Union streets.

Turn left at Union Street and head west to Washington Square, an oasis of green amid the tightly packed streets of North Beach. On the north side of the park, on Filbert, stands the double-turreted **Saints Peter and Paul Catholic Church ㉟**.

After you've had your fill of North Beach, head up **Telegraph Hill ㊱** from Washington Square. Atop the hill is **Coit Tower ㊲**. Head east up Filbert Street at the park; turn left at Grant Avenue and go one block north, then right at Greenwich Street and ascend the steps on your right. Cross the street at the top of the first set of stairs and continue up the curving stone steps to Coit Tower. Coit Tower can also be reached by car (though parking is very tight) or public transportation.

TIMING   It takes a little more than an hour to walk the tour, but the point in both North Beach and Telegraph Hill is to linger—set aside at least a few hours.

What to See

▶ ★ ㉝ **City Lights Bookstore.** Designated a city landmark, the hangout of Beat-era writers—Allen Ginsberg and Lawrence Ferlinghetti among them—remains a vital part of San Francisco's literary scene. Still leftist at heart, the store has a replica of a revolutionary mural destroyed in Chiapas, Mexico, by military forces. ☒ *261 Columbus Ave., North Beach* ☏ *415/362–8193* ⊕ *www.citylights.com* ⊙ *Daily 10 AM–11:30 PM.*

★ ㊲ **Coit Tower.** Among San Francisco's most distinctive skyline sights, the 210-ft-tall Coit Tower stands as a monument to the city's volunteer firefighters. During the early days of the gold rush, Lillie Hitchcock Coit was said to have deserted a wedding party and chased down the street after her favorite engine, Knickerbocker No. 5, while clad in her bridesmaid finery. She was soon made an honorary member of the Knickerbocker Company. Lillie died in 1929 at the age of 86, leaving the city $125,000 to "expend in an appropriate manner . . . to the beauty of San Francisco." Inside the tower, 19 depression-era murals depict economic and political life in California. ☒ *Telegraph Hill Blvd. at Greenwich St. or Lombard St., North Beach* ☏ *415/362–0808* ▱ *$3.75* ⊙ *Daily 10–6.*

㉞ **St. Francis of Assisi Church.** The 1860 building stands on the site of the frame parish church that served the Catholic community during the gold rush. Its solid terra-cotta facade complements the many brightly colored restaurants and cafés nearby. ☒ *610 Vallejo St., North Beach* ☏ *415/983–0405* ⊕ *www.shrinesf.org* ⊙ *Daily 11–5.*

㉟ **Saints Peter and Paul Catholic Church.** Camera-toting visitors focus their lenses on the Romanesque splendor of what's often called the Italian Cathedral. Completed in 1924, the cathedral has Disneyesque stone-white towers that are local landmarks. ☒ *666 Filbert St., at Washington Square, North Beach* ☏ *415/421–0809* ⊕ *www.stspeterpaul.san-francisco.ca.us/church.*

㊱ **Telegraph Hill.** The name came from one of the hill's earliest functions—in 1853 it became the location of the first Morse Code Signal Station. Hill residents have some of the best views in the city, as well as the most difficult ascents to their aeries. The hill rises from the east end of Lombard Street to a height of 284 feet and is capped by Coit Tower. ☒ *Between Lombard, Filbert, Kearny, and Sansome Sts., North Beach.*

Nob Hill & Russian Hill

Once called the Hill of Golden Promise, Nob Hill was officially dubbed during the 1870s when "the Big Four"—Charles Crocker, Leland Stanford, Mark Hopkins, and Collis Huntington, who were involved in the construction of the transcontinental railroad—built their hilltop estates. The hill itself was called Snob Hill, a nickname that survives to this day. The 1906 earthquake and fire destroyed all the palatial mansions, except for portions of the Flood brownstone. The old San Francisco families of Russian Hill, a few blocks north of Nob Hill, were joined during the 1890s by bohemian artists and writers that included Charles Norris, George Sterling, and Maynard Dixon. Today, simple studios, spiffy pieds-à-terre, Victorian flats, Edwardian cottages, and boxlike condos rub elbows on the hill. The bay views here are some of the city's best.

a good walk

Begin on California and Taylor streets at the majestic **Grace Cathedral** 38 ☞. From the cathedral walk east (toward Mason Street and downtown) on California Street to the **Pacific Union Club** 39. Across Mason Street from the club is the lush hotel **The Fairmont** 40, with its quirky Tonga Room tiki bar. Directly across California Street is the **Mark Hopkins Inter-Continental Hotel** 41, famed for panoramic views from its Top of the Mark lounge. Head north on Mason Street to the **Cable Car Museum** 42, at Washington Street.

From the Cable Car Museum continue four blocks north on Mason Street to Vallejo Street, turn west, and start climbing the steps that lead to the multilevel **Ina Coolbrith Park** 43. The Flag House, one of several brown-shingle prequake buildings in this area, is to your left at Taylor Street. Cross Taylor Street and ascend the Vallejo steps; the view east takes in downtown and the Bay Bridge. Continue west from the top of the Vallejo steps to two secluded Russian Hill alleys. Down and to your left is Florence Place, an enclave of 1920s stucco homes, and down a bit farther on your right is Russian Hill Place, with a row of 1915 Mediterranean town houses designed by Willis Polk. After reemerging on Vallejo Street from the alleys, walk north (right) on Jones Street one short block to Green Street. Head west (left) halfway down the block to the octagonal **Feusier House** 44. Backtrack to Jones Street, and head north to **Macondray Lane** 45. Walk west (to the left) on Macondray and follow it to Leavenworth Street. Head north (to the right) on Leavenworth to the bottom of **Lombard Street** 46, the "Crookedest Street in the World." Continue north one block on Leavenworth and then east one block on Chestnut Street to the **San Francisco Art Institute** 47.

TIMING The tour covers a lot of ground, much of it steep. If you're in reasonably good shape, you can complete this walk in 3½ to 4 hours, including 30-minute stops at Grace Cathedral and the Cable Car Museum. Add time for gazing at the bay from Ina Coolbrith Park or enjoying tea or a cocktail at one of Nob Hill's grand hotels.

What to See

★ ☺ 42 **Cable Car Museum.** San Francisco once had more than a dozen cable-car barns and powerhouses. The only survivor, this 1907 redbrick structure, is an engaging stopover between Russian Hill and Nob Hill. Photographs, old cable cars, signposts, ticketing machines, and other memorabilia dating from 1873 document the history of these moving landmarks. The massive powerhouse wheels that move the entire cable-car system steal the show; the design is so simple it seems almost unreal. You can also go downstairs to the sheave room and check out the innards of the system. A 15-minute video describes how it all works—cables must be replaced every three to six months—or you can opt to read the detailed placards. The gift shop sells cable-car paraphernalia. ✉ *1201 Mason St., at Washington St., Nob Hill* ☎ *415/474–1887* ⊕ *www.cablecarmuseum.com* ✆ *Free* ☉ *Oct.–Mar., daily 10–5; Apr.–Sept., daily 10–6.*

CABLE CARS TO THE RESCUE

GAZE UP FROM THE BASE OF NOB HILL OR RUSSIAN HILL, *and you won't have trouble figuring out why the ASPCA became an early supporter of Andrew Smith Hallidie's proposal to add cable cars to San Francisco's mass-transit mix. Conductors of horse-drawn streetcars heading up these and other peaks in the 1850s and 1860s screamed at and fiercely whipped the animals, vainly encouraging them to muster the strength to halt their slides back down to the base.*

The "sorrowful plight" of the horses may have been one of Hallidie's inspirations, but he was also in the business of selling wire cable. He was the first person to manufacture it in California, beginning during the gold rush. Hallidie, a Scotsman, had come to California seeking gold. He didn't find much, but he did strike it rich selling his cable and building suspension bridges and mine conveyances. The technology for cable cars had been used for decades in mines, but it was Hallidie who successfully applied it to an urban environment.

Drop by the Cable Car Museum on Nob Hill to see how simple Hallidie's system, eventually employed by more than a dozen cities around the world, is. Four sets of cables—one for each of the streets (Powell, Hyde, Mason, and California) on which the cars now travel—spin on huge powerhouse wheels, making a continuous circuit beneath city streets. To put a car in motion, the conductor operates a handgrip, the end of which grabs the cable, allowing the car to move along with the cable. When the conductor releases the grip, the car comes to a halt. Brakes are also involved when the vehicle is on an incline.

San Francisco's system dates from 1873, when Hallidie demonstrated his first car on Clay Street. It's said that no one was brave enough to operate the car back down Nob Hill, so the inventor took the helm himself, guiding the car safely to the base of what's now Portsmouth Square at Kearny Street. Historians have pointed out that without cable cars the city's hills might well have been leveled, or at least reduced in height, as happened in Manhattan and other urban areas that expanded before the cars were invented. As it turned out, the cars made previously uninhabited or sparsely populated crests a magnet for the wealthy. The rich folk on Nob Hill built their own line, the California Street leg, in operation to this day, to bring them to and from the Financial District.

The heyday of cable cars was the two decades after their introduction. At the dawn of the 20th century, 500 cable cars zipped along a network of more than 100 mi. Today a few dozen cars travel on three lines, and the network covers 9½ mi. Most of the cars date from the 1800s, though the cars and lines had a complete overhaul during the early 1980s and the cables are replaced every three to six months.

— Daniel Mangin

40 The Fairmont. The hotel's dazzling opening was delayed a year by the 1906 quake, but since then the marble palace has hosted presidents, royalty, and movie stars. Things have changed since its early days, however: on the eve of World War I you could get a room for as low as $2.50 per night, meals included. Nowadays, prices go as high as $8,000, which buys a night in the eight-room, Persian art–filled penthouse suite that was showcased regularly in the 1980s TV series *Hotel.* ⊠ *950 Mason St., Nob Hill* ☎ *415/772–5000* ⊕ *www.fairmont.com.*

44 Feusier House. Octagonal houses were once thought to make the best use of space and enhance the physical and mental well-being of their occupants. A brief mid-19th-century craze inspired the construction of several in San Francisco. Only the Feusier House, built in 1857 and now a private residence amid lush gardens, and the Octagon House remain standing. ⊠ *1067 Green St., Russian Hill.*

➤ ③⑧ **Grace Cathedral.** The seat of the Episcopal Church in San Francisco, this soaring Gothic structure, erected on the site of Charles Crocker's mansion, took 53 years to build. The gilded bronze doors at the east entrance were taken from casts of Lorenzo Ghiberti's Gates of Paradise, which are on the baptistery in Florence, Italy. A black-and-bronze stone sculpture of St. Francis by Beniamino Bufano greets you as you enter. ⊠ *1100 California St., at Taylor St., Nob Hill* ☎ *415/749–6300* ⊕ *www.gracecathedral.org* ⊙ *Weekdays 7–5:45, weekends 7–5.*

④③ **Ina Coolbrith Park.** Beloved for its spectacular bay views and manicured gardens, this spot is unusual because it's vertical—that is, rather than being one open space, it's composed of a series of terraces up a very steep hill. A poet, Oakland librarian, and niece of Mormon prophet Joseph Smith, Ina Coolbrith (1842–1928) introduced Jack London and Isadora Duncan to the world of books. For years she entertained literary greats in her Macondray Lane home near the park. In 1915 she was named poet laureate of California. ⊠ *Vallejo St. between Mason and Taylor Sts., Russian Hill.*

④⑥ **Lombard Street.** The block-long "Crookedest Street in the World" makes
Fodor'sChoice eight switchbacks down the east face of Russian Hill between Hyde and
★   Leavenworth streets. Residents bemoan the traffic jam outside their front doors, and occasionally the city attempts to discourage drivers by posting a traffic cop near the top of the hill. If no one is standing guard, join the line of cars waiting to drive down the steep hill, or avoid the whole morass and walk down the steps on either side of Lombard. ⊠ *Lombard St. between Hyde and Leavenworth Sts., Russian Hill.*

④⑤ **Macondray Lane.** Enter this "secret garden" under a lovely wooden trellis and proceed down a quiet cobbled pedestrian street lined with Edwardian cottages and flowering plants and trees. A flight of steep wooden stairs at the end of the lane leads to Taylor Street—on the way down you can't miss the bay views. If you've read any of Armistead Maupin's *Tales of the City* or sequels, you may find the lane vaguely familiar. It's the thinly disguised setting for part of the series' action. ⊠ *Jones St. between Union and Green Sts., Russian Hill.*

④① **Mark Hopkins Inter-Continental Hotel.** Built on the ashes of railroad tycoon Mark Hopkins's grand estate, this 19-story hotel went up in 1926. A combination of French château and Spanish Renaissance architecture, with noteworthy terra-cotta detailing, it has hosted statesmen, royalty, and Hollywood celebrities. The 11-room penthouse was turned into a glass-walled cocktail lounge in 1939: the **Top of the Mark** is remembered fondly by thousands of World War II veterans who jammed the lounge before leaving for overseas duty. Wives and sweethearts watching the ships depart gave the room's northwest nook its name—Weepers' Corner. With its 360° views, the lounge is a wonderful spot for a nighttime drink. ⊠ *999 California St., at Mason St., Nob Hill* ☎ *415/392–3434* ⊕ *www.markhopkins.net.*

③⑨ **Pacific Union Club.** The former home of silver baron James Flood cost a whopping $1.5 million in 1886, when even a stylish Victorian like the Haas-Lilienthal House cost less than $20,000. All that cash did buy some structural stability. The Flood residence (to be precise, its shell) was the only Nob Hill mansion to survive the 1906 earthquake and fire. The Pacific Union Club, a bastion of the wealthy and powerful, purchased the house in 1907 and commissioned Willis Polk to redesign it; the architect added the semicircular wings and third floor. ⊠ *1000 California St., Nob Hill.*

47 **San Francisco Art Institute.** A Moorish-tile fountain in a tree-shaded courtyard draws the eye as soon as you enter the institute. The highlight of a visit is Mexican master Diego Rivera's *Making of a Fresco Showing the Building of a City* (1931), in the student gallery to your immediate left inside the entrance. Rivera himself is in the fresco—his back is to the viewer—and he's surrounded by his assistants. The older portions of the Art Institute were erected in 1926. Ansel Adams created the school's fine-arts photography department in 1946, and school directors established the country's first fine-arts film program. Notable faculty and alumni have included painter Richard Diebenkorn and photographers Dorothea Lange, Edward Weston, and Annie Leibovitz. The **Walter & McBean Galleries** (☎ 415/749–4563 ☉ Mon.–Sat. 11–6) exhibit the often provocative works of established artists. ⊠ *800 Chestnut St., North Beach* ☎ *415/771–7020* ⊕ *www.sanfranciscoart.edu* ⊠ *Galleries free* ☉ *Student gallery daily 9–9.*

Pacific Heights & Japantown

Some of the city's most expensive and dramatic real estate—including mansions and town houses priced in the millions—is in Pacific Heights. Grand Victorians line the streets, and from almost any point in this neighborhood you get a magnificent view. Japantown, or Nihonmachi, is centered on the southern slope of Pacific Heights, north of Geary Boulevard between Fillmore and Laguna streets. Around 1860 a wave of Japanese immigrants arrived in San Francisco, which they called Soko. By the 1930s they had opened shops, markets, meeting halls, and restaurants and established Shinto and Buddhist temples. Japantown is a relatively safe area, but the Western Addition, which lies to the south of Geary Boulevard, can be dangerous at night; after dark also avoid straying too far west of Fillmore Street just north of Geary.

a good walk

Pacific Heights lies on an east–west ridge along the city's northern flank from Van Ness Avenue to the Presidio and from California Street to the Marina. Begin your tour by taking in the views from **Alta Plaza Park** **48** ➤, at the intersection of Steiner and Jackson streets.

Walk east on Jackson Street several blocks to the **Whittier Mansion** **49**, on the corner of Jackson and Laguna streets. Make a right on Laguna and a left at the next block, Washington Street. The patch of green that spreads southeast from here is Lafayette Park, a four-block-square oasis for sunbathers and dog-and-Frisbee teams. Walk on Washington along the edge of Lafayette Park past the formal French **Spreckels Mansion** **50**, at the corner of Octavia Street, and continue east two more blocks to Franklin Street. Turn left (north); halfway down the block stands the handsome **Haas-Lilienthal House** **51**. Head back south on Franklin Street, stopping to view several **Franklin Street buildings** **52**. At California Street, turn right (west) to see more **noteworthy Victorians** **53** on that street and Laguna Street.

Continue west on California Street to begin the Japantown segment of your tour. When you reach Buchanan Street, turn left (south). The open-air **Japan Center Mall** **54** is a short block of shoji-screened buildings on Buchanan Street between Post and Sutter streets.

Cross Post Street and enter the three-block **Japan Center** **55** in the Kintetsu Building. There are usually several fine ikebana arrangements in the windows of the headquarters of the Ikenobo Ikebana Society of America. A few doors farther along at May's Coffee Stand you can pick up a lemonade and a tasty fish-shape waffle filled with red-bean paste. A second-level bridge spans Webster Street, connecting the Kinokuniya and

Kintetsu buildings. Among the shops of note are the Kinokuniya Bookstore and Ma-Shi'-Ko Folk Craft, both on the second floor. Exit the Kinokuniya Building onto Post Street. Take a left on Fillmore Street and head south toward Geary Boulevard. **Kabuki Springs & Spa ⑤⑥** is on the northeast corner of Geary and Fillmore.

TIMING   Set aside about two hours for the Pacific Heights portion of the tour, not including the tour of the Haas-Lilienthal House. Although most of the attractions are walk-bys, you are covering a good bit of pavement. The Japantown tour, on the other hand, is very compact. Not including a visit to the Kabuki Springs, an hour will probably suffice.

What to See

▶ ㊽ **Alta Plaza Park.** Landscape architect John McLaren, who also created Golden Gate Park, designed Alta Plaza in 1910, modeling its terracing on the Grand Casino in Monte Carlo, Monaco. From the top you can see Marin to the north, downtown to the east, Twin Peaks to the south, and Golden Gate Park to the west. ⊠ *Bordered by Clay, Steiner, Jackson, and Scott Sts., Pacific Heights.*

㊾ **Franklin Street buildings.** What at first looks like a stone facade on the **Golden Gate Church** (⊠ 1901 Franklin St., Pacific Heights) is actually redwood painted white. A Georgian-style residence built in the early 1900s for a coffee merchant sits at 1735 Franklin. On the northeast corner of Franklin and California streets is a **Christian Science church**; built in the Tuscan Revival style, it's noteworthy for its terra-cotta detailing. The **Coleman House** (⊠ 1701 Franklin St., Pacific Heights) is an impressive twin-turreted Queen Anne mansion that was built for a gold-rush mining and lumber baron. Don't miss the large, brilliant-purple stained-glass window on the house's north side. ⊠ *Franklin St. between Washington and California Sts., Pacific Heights.*

㊿ **Haas-Lilienthal House.** A small display of photographs on the bottom floor of this elaborate 1886 Queen Anne house, which cost a mere $18,500 to build, makes clear that it was modest compared with some of the giants that fell victim to the 1906 earthquake and fire. The Foundation for San Francisco's Architectural Heritage operates the home, whose carefully kept rooms provide an intriguing glimpse into late 19th-century life. Volunteers conduct one-hour house tours three days a week and an informative two-hour tour ($5) of the eastern portion of Pacific Heights on Sunday afternoon. ⊠ *2007 Franklin St., between Washington and Jackson Sts., Pacific Heights* ☎ *415/441–3004* ⊕ *www.sfheritage.org/ house.html* ⊠ *$5* ⊗ *Wed. and Sat. noon–4 (last tour at 3), Sun. 11–5 (last tour at 4). Pacific Heights tours leave the house Sun. at 12:30.*

⑤⑤ **Japan Center.** The noted American architect Minoru Yamasaki created this 5-acre complex, which opened in 1968. The development includes a hotel; a public garage with discounted validated parking; shops selling Japanese furnishings, clothing, cameras, tapes and records, porcelain, pearls, and paintings; an excellent spa; and a multiplex cinema. Between the Miyako Mall and Kintetsu Building are the five-tier, 100-foot-tall **Peace Pagoda** and the Peace Plaza. ⊠ *Bordered by Geary Blvd. and Fillmore, Post, and Laguna Sts., Japantown* ☎ *415/922–6776.*

㊼ **Japan Center Mall.** The buildings lining this open-air mall are of the shoji school of architecture. Seating in this area can be found on local artist Ruth Asawa's twin origami-style fountains, which sit in the middle of the mall; they're squat circular structures made of fieldstone, with three levels for sitting and a brick floor. ⊠ *Buchanan St. between Post and Sutter Sts., Japantown* ☎ *No phone.*

★ **56** **Kabuki Springs & Spa.** Japantown's house of tranquillity offers a treatment regimen that includes facials, salt scrubs, and mud and seaweed wraps. You can take your massage in a private room with a bath or in a curtained-off area. The communal baths ($15 before 5 PM, $18 after 5 and all weekend) contain hot and cold tubs, a large Japanese-style bath, a sauna, a steam room, and showers. ⊠ *1750 Geary Blvd., Japantown* ☎ *415/922–6000* ⊕ *www.kabukisprings.com* ⊘ *Daily 10–10.*

53 **Noteworthy Victorians.** Two **Italianate** Victorians (⊠ 1818 and 1834 California St., Pacific Heights) stand out on the 1800 block of California. A block farther is the Victorian-era **Atherton House** (⊠ 1990 California St., Pacific Heights), whose mildly daffy design incorporates Queen Anne, Stick-Eastlake, and other architectural elements. The oft-photographed **Laguna Street Victorians**, on the west side of the 1800 block of Laguna Street, cost between $2,000 and $2,600 when they were built in the 1870s. ⊠ *California St. between Franklin and Octavia Sts., and Laguna St. between Pine and Bush Sts., Pacific Heights.*

50 **Spreckels Mansion.** The estate was built for sugar heir Adolph Spreckels and his wife, Alma. Mrs. Spreckels was so pleased with her house that she commissioned George Applegarth to design another building in a similar vein: the California Palace of the Legion of Honor. One of the city's great iconoclasts, Alma Spreckels was the model for the bronze figure atop the Victory Monument in Union Square. ⊠ *2080 Washington St., at Octavia St., Pacific Heights.*

49 **Whittier Mansion.** With a Spanish-tile roof and scrolled bay windows on all four sides, this was one of the most elegant 19th-century houses in the state. An anomaly in a town that lost most of its grand mansions to the 1906 quake, the Whittier Mansion was built so solidly that only a chimney toppled over during the disaster. ⊠ *2090 Jackson St., Pacific Heights.*

Civic Center

The Civic Center—the beaux-arts complex between McAllister and Grove streets and Franklin and Hyde streets that includes City Hall, the War Memorial Opera House, the Veterans Building, and the old public library, now home of the Asian Art Museum and Cultural Center—is a product of the "City Beautiful" movement of the early 20th century. City Hall, completed in 1915 and renovated in 1999, is the centerpiece.

a good walk

Start at **United Nations Plaza** **57** ▶, set on an angle between Hyde and Market streets. BART and Muni trains stop here, and the Bus 5–Fulton, Bus 21–Hayes, and other lines serve the area. Walk west across the plaza toward Fulton Street, which dead-ends at Hyde Street, and cross Hyde. Towering over the block of Fulton between Hyde and Larkin streets is the Pioneers Monument. The new main branch of the San Francisco Public Library is south of the monument. North of it is the **Asian Art Museum** **58**, in the old library building. The patch of green west of the museum is Civic Center Plaza, and beyond that is **City Hall** **59**. If City Hall is open, walk through it, exiting on Van Ness Avenue and turning left. If the building's closed, walk around it to the south—to the left as you're facing it—and make a right at Grove. Either way you end up at Grove Street and Van Ness Avenue. Looking west (to the right) across the street on Van Ness, you see the **War Memorial Opera House** **60**. In the next block of Van Ness Avenue, across Grove Street from the opera house, is Louise M. Davies Symphony Hall, the fascinating and futuristic looking home of the San Francisco Symphony. From Davies, head west (to the right) on Grove Street to Franklin Street, turn left (south), walk one block to Hayes Street, and turn right (west). This takes you to Hayes Valley and the hip strip of galleries, shops, and restaurants between Franklin and Laguna streets. Like Japantown, the Civic Center borders the Western Addition; it's best not to stray west of Laguna at night.

TIMING   Walking around the Civic Center shouldn't take more than about 45 minutes. The Asian Art Museum merits an hour; another half hour or more can be spent browsing in the shops along Hayes Street. On Wednesday or Sunday allot some extra time to take in the farmers' market in United Nations Plaza.

What to See

★ **58** **Asian Art Museum.** One of the largest collections of Asian art in the world opened in this new location in early 2003. Holdings include more than 12,000 sculptures, paintings, and ceramics from 40 countries, illustrating major periods of Asian art. Although the bulk of the art and artifacts come from China, treasures from Korea, Iran, Turkey, Syria, India, Tibet, Nepal, Pakistan, India, Japan, Afghanistan, and Southeast Asia are also on view. ⊠ *200 Larkin St., between McAllister and Fulton Sts., Civic Center* ☎ *415/668–8921 or 415/379–8801* ⊕ *www.asianart.org* ⊠ *$10* ☉ *Tues., Wed., and Fri.–Sun. 10–5; Thurs. 10–9.*

59 **City Hall.** This masterpiece of granite and marble was modeled after St. Peter's cathedral in Rome. City Hall's bronze and gold-leaf dome, which is even higher than the U.S. Capitol's version, dominates the area. The classical influences of Paris-trained architect Arthur Brown Jr., who also designed Coit Tower and the War Memorial Opera House, can be seen throughout the structure. Some noteworthy events that have taken place here include the hosing—down the central staircase—of civil-rights and freedom-of-speech protesters in 1960 and the murders of Mayor George Moscone and openly gay supervisor Harvey Milk in 1978. Free tours are available Tuesday through Friday at 10, noon, and 2 and weekends at 12:30. Inside City Hall, the **Museum of the City of San Francisco** (☎ 415/928–0289 ⊕ www.sfmuseum.org ☉ weekdays 8–8, Sat. noon–4) displays historical items, maps, and photographs, as well as the 500-pound head of the Goddess of Progress statue, which crowned the City Hall building that crumbled during the 1906 earthquake. Museum admission is free. ⊠ *Between Van Ness Ave. and Polk, Grove, and McAllister Sts., Civic Center* ☎ *415/554–6023* ⊕ *www.ci.sf.ca.us/cityhall* ☉ *Weekdays 8–8, weekends noon–4.*

▶ **57** **United Nations Plaza.** Brick pillars listing various nations and the dates of their admittance into the United Nations line the plaza, and its floor is inscribed with the goals and philosophy of the United Nations charter, which was signed at the War Memorial Opera House in 1945. On Wednesday and Sunday a farmers' market fills the space with home-grown produce and plants. ⊠ *Fulton St. between Hyde and Market Sts., Civic Center.*

60 **War Memorial Opera House.** All the old opera houses were destroyed in the 1906 quake, but lusty support for opera continued. The opera didn't have a permanent home until the War Memorial Opera House was inaugurated in 1932 with a performance of *Tosca.* Modeled after its European counterparts, the building has a vaulted and coffered ceiling, marble foyer, two balconies, and a huge silver art deco chandelier that resembles a sunburst. ⊠ *301 Van Ness Ave., Civic Center* ☎ *415/621–6600.*

The Northern Waterfront

For the sights, sounds, and smells of the sea, hop the Powell–Hyde cable car from Union Square and take it to the end of the line. The views as

SWEET PAINTED LADIES

BRIGHT, CHEERFUL, AND STURDILY PROUD, San Francisco's Painted Ladies are wooden (mostly redwood) Victorian homes built in the 19th and early 20th centuries. They provide the perfect grace notes of exuberance for a metropolis that burst onto the scene as capriciously as did the City by the Bay. Though viewed as picturesque antiques these days, the homes, about 15,000 of which survive today, represented the height of modernity in their time.

Made possible by the newly created streetcar and cable-car lines—not to mention money from the gold and silver rushes of the 1800s—the Painted Ladies had indoor plumbing (the later ones electricity, too) and other modern touches. The older Victorians downtown perished in the 1906 earthquake and fire. But west of Van Ness Avenue, where grand mansions were dynamited to halt the fire's spread, and in the Haight, the outer Mission District, and Noe Valley, sterling examples remain.

Apparently the Painted Ladies were always as brilliantly hued as they are today. Accounts from the late 1800s mention bright, even "garish" colors. Some writers attributed this to the city's carefree attitudes, others to the desire of San Franciscans to create a visual reality as different as possible from that of the East Coast cities.

Three main Victorian styles emerged in San Francisco. The architecture of Renaissance Italy's palaces informed the Italianate style, characterized by Corinthian porch columns, tall and narrow doorways, and slanted bay windows. (The bay window was invented in San Francisco, where the standard lot is only 25 feet wide, to take advantage of water views.) The Stick style employs wood strips as ornamentation—as opposed to floral and other patterns—and squared-off bay windows. It evolved into what came to be known as the Stick-Eastlake style, with faux gables, mini-mansards, and other embellishments adding a playful quality to the basic Stick look. If you see a home with a rounded turret or other curvy elements, it's probably a Queen Anne, the third major San Francisco style. Angled roofs, lacy detailing, and jolly bits of froufrou—arching portals, wedding-cake trim, rounded shingling—enliven Queen Anne homes. There's plenty of overlapping of styles. Many Italianate houses built in the 1870s but remodeled in the 1890s, for example, acquired Queen Anne touches. The Atherton House daffily combines the Stick-Eastlake and Queen Anne styles. And you'll find Gothic, Tudor, and Greek Revival Victorians in much smaller numbers.

To view the quintessential strip of Victorians, head to Alamo Square and look east toward downtown. The Queen Anne homes—710–720 Steiner Street—in the foreground, which have been painted and photographed numerous times, are known as Postcard Row.

— Daniel Mangin

---

you descend Hyde Street toward the bay are breathtaking—tiny sail-boats bob in the whitecaps, Alcatraz hovers ominously in the distance, and the Marin Headlands form a rugged backdrop to the Golden Gate Bridge. Once you reach sea level at the cable-car turnaround, Aquatic Park and the National Maritime Museum are immediately to the west, and the commercial attractions of the Fisherman's Wharf area are to the east. Bring good walking shoes and a jacket or sweater for mid-afternoon breezes or foggy mists.

a good walk

Begin at Polk and Beach streets at the **National Maritime Museum** ❶ ➤. (Walk west from the cable-car turnaround; Bus 19 stops at Polk and Beach streets, and Bus 47–Van Ness stops a block west at Van Ness Avenue and Beach Street.) Across Beach from the museum is Ghirardelli Square, a complex of shops, cafés, and galleries in an old chocolate factory. Continue east on Beach to Hyde Street and make a left. At the end of Hyde is the **Hyde Street Pier** ❷. South on Hyde a block and a half is the former Del Monte **Cannery** ❸, which holds more shops, cafés, and restaurants. Walk east from the Cannery on Jefferson Street to **Fisherman's Wharf** ❹. A few blocks farther east is **Pier 39** ❺.

TIMING For the entire Northern Waterfront circuit, set aside a couple of hours, not including boat tours, which take from one to three hours or more. All attractions here are open daily.

What to See

★ **Alcatraz Island.** The boat ride to the island is brief (15 minutes) but affords beautiful views of the city, Marin County, and the East Bay. The audio tour, highly recommended, includes observations of guards and prisoners about life in one of America's most notorious penal colonies. A separate ranger-led tour surveys the island's ecology. Plan your schedule to allow at least three hours for the visit and boat rides combined. Reservations are recommended. ⊠ *Pier 41, Fisherman's Wharf* ☎ *415/ 773–1188 boat schedules and information, 415/705–5555 or 800/426– 8687 credit-card ticket orders, 415/705–1042 park information* 🖾 *$13.25 with audio, $9.25 without audio ($20.75 evening tours, including audio); add $2.25 per ticket to charge by phone* ☉ *Ferry departures Sept.–late May, daily 9:30–2:15 (4:20 for evening tour Thurs.–Sun. only); late May–Aug., daily 9:30–4:15 (6:30 and 7:30 for evening tour)* ⊕ *www.nps.gov/alcatraz.*

❸ **Cannery.** The three-story structure was built in 1894 to house what became the Del Monte Fruit and Vegetable Cannery. Today the Cannery contains shops, art galleries, a comedy club (Cobb's), and some unusual restaurants. ⊠ *2801 Leavenworth St., Fisherman's Wharf* ☎ *415/771– 3112* ⊕ *www.thecannery.com.*

🐾 ❹ **Fisherman's Wharf.** Ships creak at their moorings; seagulls cry out for a handout. By mid-afternoon the fishing fleet is back to port. The chaotic streets of the wharf have numerous seafood restaurants, among them sidewalk stands where shrimp and crab cocktails are sold in disposable containers. T-shirts and sweats, gold chains galore, redwood furniture, acres of artwork, and generally amusing street artists also beckon visitors.

Most of the entertainment at the wharf is schlocky and overpriced, with one notable exception: the splendid **Musée Mécanique** (☎ 415/346– 2000 ☉ Memorial Day–Labor Day, daily 10–8; rest of yr, weekdays 11–7, weekends 10–8), a time-warped arcade with antique mechanical contrivances, including peep shows and nickelodeons. Some favorites are the giant and rather creepy "Laughing Sal," an arm-wrestling machine, and mechanical fortune-telling figures who speak from their curtained boxes. Admission is free, but you may want to bring change to play the games.

The USS *Pampanito* (⊠ Pier 45, Fisherman's Wharf ☎ 415/775–1943 ☉ Oct.–Memorial Day, Sun.–Thurs. 9–6, Fri. and Sat. 9–8; Memorial Day–Sept., Thurs.–Tues. 9–8, Wed. 9–6) provides an intriguing if mildly claustrophobic glimpse into life on a submarine during World War II. Admission is $8. ⊠ *Jefferson St. between Leavenworth St. and Pier 39, Fisherman's Wharf.*

❷ **Hyde Street Pier.** The pier, one of the wharf area's best bargains, always crackles with activity. Depending on the time of day, you might see boatbuilders at work or children manning a ship as though it were still the early 1900s. The highlight of the pier is its collection of historic vessels, all of which can be boarded. ⊠ *Hyde and Jefferson Sts., Fisherman's Wharf* ☎ *415/561–7100* ⊕ *www.maritime.org* 🖾 *$5* ☉ *Mid-May–mid-Sept., daily 9:30–5:30; mid-Sept.–mid-May, daily 9:30–5.*

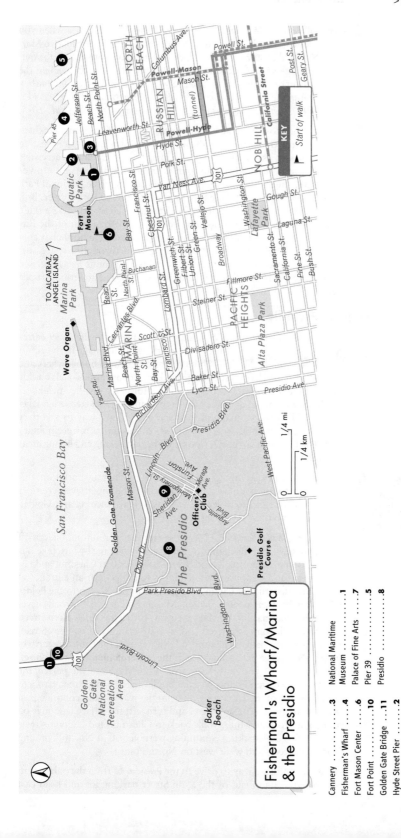

Fisherman's Wharf/Marina & the Presidio

NORTH BEACH

RUSSIAN HILL

NOB HILL

PACIFIC HEIGHTS

MARINA

The Presidio

San Francisco Bay

TO ALCATRAZ, ANGEL ISLAND

Golden Gate National Recreation Area

Baker Beach

Presidio Golf Course

Lafayette Park

Alta Plaza Park

Aquatic Park

Fort Mason

Marina Park

Wave Organ

Officers' Club

Golden Gate Promenade

KEY
▲ Start of walk

Powell-Mason

Powell-Hyde

Powell St.
Mason St. (tunnel)
Columbus Ave.
Jefferson St.
Beach St.
North Point St.
Leavenworth St.
Hyde St.
Polk St.
Van Ness Ave.
Francisco St.
Chestnut St.
Bay St.
Greenwich St.
Filbert St.
Union St.
Green St.
Vallejo St.
Broadway
Lombard St.
Steiner St.
Fillmore St.
Divisadero St.
Baker St.
Lyon St.
Scott St.
Buchanan
Cervantes Blvd.
Beach St.
North Point St.
Bay St.
Francisco St.
Marina Blvd.
Richardson Ave.
Presidio Ave.
Washington St.
Laguna St.
Gough St.
California Street
Post St.
Geary St.
Pine St.
Bush St.
Sacramento St.
California St.
Presidio Blvd.
West Pacific Ave.
Lincoln Blvd.
Funston Ave.
Montgomery St.
Moraga Ave.
Arguello Blvd.
Sheridan Ave.
Washington Blvd.
Park Presidio Blvd.
Lincoln Blvd.
Doyle Dr.
Mason St.
Yacht Rd.
Pier 45

1/4 mi
1/4 km

► ❶ **National Maritime Museum.** You'll feel as if you're out to sea when you step inside this sturdy, rounded structure. Part of the **San Francisco Maritime National Historical Park,** which includes Hyde Street Pier, the museum exhibits ship models, maps, and other artifacts chronicling the development of San Francisco and the West Coast through maritime history. ⊠ *Aquatic Park at the foot of Polk St., Fisherman's Wharf* ☎ *415/ 561–7100* ⊕ *www.nps.gov/safr* ⊠ *Donation suggested* ⊙ *Daily 10–5.*

🖐 ❺ **Pier 39.** The most popular—and commercial—of San Francisco's waterfront attractions, the pier draws millions of visitors each year to browse through its dozens of shops. Ongoing free entertainment, accessible validated parking, and nearby public transportation ensure crowds most days. Sales of books, maps, and collectibles at the **National Park Store** (☎ 415/433–7221) help to support the National Park Service. Brilliant colors enliven the double-decker **Venetian Carousel** (⊠ $2 a ride), often awhirl with happily howling children. At **Aquarium of the Bay** (☎ 415/623–5300 or 888/732–3483 ⊕ www.aquariumofthebay.com ⊠ $12.95), moving walkways transport you through a space surrounded on three sides by water filled with indigenous San Francisco Bay marine life, from fish and plankton to sharks. The aquarium is open weekdays 10–6, weekends 10–7.

The Marina & Presidio

The Marina district was a coveted place to live until the 1989 earthquake, when the area's homes suffered the worst damage in the city—largely because the Marina is built on landfill. Many homeowners and renters fled in search of more-solid ground, but young professionals quickly replaced them, changing the tenor of this formerly low-key neighborhood. The number of upscale coffee emporiums skyrocketed, a bank became a Williams-Sonoma, and the local grocer gave way to a Pottery Barn. West of the Marina is the sprawling Presidio, a former military base. The Presidio has superb views and the best hiking and biking areas in San Francisco.

a good drive

Though you can visit the sights below using public transportation, this is the place to use your car if you have one. You might even consider renting one for a day to cover the area, as well as Lincoln Park, Golden Gate Park, and the western shoreline.

Start at **Fort Mason Center** ❻ ►, whose entrance for automobiles is off Marina Boulevard at Buchanan Street. If you're coming by bus, take Bus 30–Stockton heading north (and later west); get off at Chestnut and Laguna streets and walk north three blocks to the pedestrian entrance at Marina Boulevard and Laguna. To get from Fort Mason to the **Palace of Fine Arts** ❼ by car, make a right on Marina Boulevard. The road curves past a small marina and the Marina Green. Turn left at Divisadero Street, right on North Point Street, left on Baker Street, and right on Bay Street, which passes the palace's lagoon and dead-ends at the Lyon Street parking lot. Part of the palace complex is the **Exploratorium,** a hands-on science museum. (If you're walking from Fort Mason to the palace, the directions are easier: Follow Marina Boulevard to Scott Street. Cross to the south side of the street—away from the water—and continue past Divisadero Street to Baker Street, and turn left; the palace lagoon is on your right. To take Muni, walk back to Chestnut and Laguna streets and take Bus 30–Stockton continuing west; get off at North Point and Broderick streets and walk west on North Point.)

The least confusing way to drive to the **Presidio** ❽ from the palace is to exit from the south end of the Lyon Street parking lot and head east (left) on Bay Street. Turn right (south) onto Baker Street, and right (west) on Francisco Street, taking it across Richardson Avenue to Lyon Street. Turn south (left) on Lyon and right (west) on Lombard Street, and go through the main gate to Presidio Boulevard. Turn right on Lincoln Boulevard and left on Funston Avenue to Moraga Avenue and the Presidio's **Mott Visitor Center** ❾ at the Officers' Club. (To take the bus to the Presidio, walk north from the palace to Lombard Street and catch Bus 28 heading west; it stops on Lincoln near the visitor center.)

From the visitor center head back up Funston Avenue and turn left on Lincoln Boulevard. Lincoln winds through the Presidio past a large cemetery and some vista points. After a couple of miles is a parking lot marked FORT POINT on the right. Park and follow the signs leading to **Fort Point** ❿, walking downhill through a lightly wooded area. To walk the short distance to the **Golden Gate Bridge** ⓫, follow the signs from the Fort Point parking lot; to drive across the bridge, continue on Lincoln Boulevard a bit and watch for the turnoff on the right. Bus 28 serves stops fairly near these last two attractions; ask the driver to call them out.

TIMING   The time it takes to see this area varies greatly, depending on whether you take public transportation or drive. If you drive, plan to spend at least three hours, not including a walk across the Golden Gate Bridge or hikes along the shoreline—each of which takes a few hours. A great way to see the area is on bicycle; the folks at the Mott Visitor Center can help you find the closest rental outfit. With or without kids, you could easily pass two hours at the Exploratorium.

What to See

★ ☾ **Exploratorium.** The curious of all ages flock to this fascinating "museum of science, art, and human perception" within the **Palace of Fine Arts.** The more than 650 exhibits focus on sea and insect life, computers, electricity, patterns and light, language, the weather, and much more. Reservations are required to crawl through the pitch-black, touchy-feely **Tactile Dome,** an adventure of 15 minutes. ✉ *3601 Lyon St., at Marina Blvd., Marina* ☎ *415/561–0360 general information, 415/561–0362 Tactile Dome reservations* ⊕ *www.exploratorium.edu* 🔊 *$10, free 1st Wed. of month; Tactile Dome $4 extra* ☉ *Tues.–Sun. 10–5.*

▶ ➏ **Fort Mason Center.** Originally a depot for the shipment of supplies to the Pacific during World War II, the fort was converted into a cultural center in 1977. In business here are the popular vegetarian restaurant Greens and shops, galleries, and performance spaces, most of which are closed Monday.

Two interesting small museums in Building C are the The **Museo Italo-Americano** (☎ 415/673–2200) and the **San Francisco African-American Historical and Cultural Society** (☎ 415/441–0640).

The **San Francisco Craft and Folk Art Museum** (☎ 415/775–0990) in Building A exhibits American folk art, tribal art, and contemporary crafts. Most of the museums and shops at Fort Mason close by 6 or 7. Museum admission fees range from pay-what-you-wish to $4. ✉ *Buchanan St. and Marina Blvd., Marina* ☎ *415/979–3010 event information* ⊕ *www.fortmason.org.*

☾ ❿ **Fort Point.** Designed to mount 126 cannons with a range of up to 2 mi, Fort Point was constructed between 1853 and 1861 to protect San Francisco from sea attack during the Civil War—but it was never used for that purpose. It was, however, used as a coastal defense–fortification post during World War II, when soldiers stood watch here. This National Historic Site is a museum filled with military memorabilia. On days when Fort Point is staffed, guided group tours and cannon drills take place. ⊠ *Marine Dr. off Lincoln Blvd., Presidio* ☎ *415/556–1693* ⊕ *www.nps.gov/fopo* 🚃 *Free* ☉ *Fri.–Sun. 10–5.*

★ ⑪ **Golden Gate Bridge.** The suspension bridge that connects San Francisco with Marin County has long wowed sightseers with its rust-color beauty, 750-foot towers, and simple but powerful art deco design. At nearly 2 mi, the Golden Gate, completed in 1937 after four years of construction, was built to withstand winds of more than 100 mph. The east walkway yields a glimpse of the San Francisco skyline as well as the islands of the bay. The view west takes in the wild hills of the Marin Headlands, the curving coast south to Land's End, and the majestic Pacific Ocean. Muni Buses 28 and 29 make stops at the Golden Gate Bridge toll plaza, on the San Francisco side. ⊠ *Lincoln Blvd. near Doyle Dr. and Fort Point, Presidio* ☎ *415/921–5858* ⊕ *www.goldengatebridge.org* ☉ *Pedestrians: daily sunrise–sunset.*

⑨ **Mott Visitor Center.** Tucked away in the Presidio's mission-style Officers' Club, the William P. Mott Jr. Visitor Center dispenses maps, brochures, and schedules for guided walking and bicycle tours, along with information about the Presidio's past, present, and future. History boards tell the story of the Presidio, from military outpost to self-sustaining park. ⊠ *50 Moraga Ave., Presidio* ☎ *415/561–4323* 🚃 *Free* ☉ *Daily 9–5.*

⑦ **Palace of Fine Arts.** The rosy rococo palace is the sole survivor of the many tinted-plaster structures built for the 1915 Panama-Pacific International Exposition, the world's fair that celebrated San Francisco's recovery from the 1906 earthquake and fire. Bernard Maybeck designed this faux Roman Classic beauty, which was reconstructed in concrete and reopened in 1967. The massive columns, great rotunda, and swan-filled lagoon have been used in countless fashion layouts and films. ⊠ *Baker and Beach Sts., Marina* ☎ *415/561–0364 palace tours* ⊕ *www.exploratorium.edu/palace.*

Fodor's Choice ★

⑧ **Presidio.** Part of the **Golden Gate National Recreation Area,** the Presidio was a military post for more than 200 years. Don Juan Bautista de Anza and a band of Spanish settlers first claimed the area in 1776. It became a Mexican garrison in 1822 when Mexico gained its independence from Spain; U.S. troops forcibly occupied the Presidio in 1846. The U.S. Sixth Army was stationed here until October 1994, when the coveted space was transferred into civilian hands. Today the area is being transformed into a self-sustaining national park with a combination of public, commercial, and residential projects. The more than 1,400 acres of hills, majestic woods, and redbrick army barracks include two beaches, a golf course, a visitor center, and picnic sites. ⊠ *Between the Marina and Lincoln Park, Presidio* ⊕ *www.nps.gov/prsf.*

Golden Gate Park

William Hammond Hall conceived one of the nation's great city parks and began in 1870 to put into action his plan for a natural reserve with no reminders of urban life. John McLaren finished Hall's work during his tenure as park superintendent, from 1890 to 1943, transforming 1,000 desolate brush- and sand-covered acres into a rolling, landscaped oasis. Urban reality now encroaches on all sides, but the park remains a great getaway. The fog can sweep into the park with amazing speed; always bring a sweatshirt or jacket.

Because the park is so large, a car comes in handy if you're going to tour it from one end to the other—though you'll still do a fair amount of walking. Muni serves the park. Buses 5–Fulton and 21–Hayes stop along its northern edge, and the N–Judah light-rail car stops a block south of the park between Stanyan Street and 9th Avenue, then two blocks south and the rest of the way west.

The **Conservatory of Flowers** ❶ ▶ is the first stop on this walk. To get here from the park's north side, head for the intersection of Fulton Street and 6th Avenue, where the Bus 5–Fulton and Bus 21–Hayes from downtown stop. Walk south into the park at 6th Avenue. The road you come to is John F. Kennedy Drive. Turn left on the blacktop sidewalk and head east. Across the drive on your right is the Rhododendron Dell. Past the first stop sign you see the exterior gardens of the conservatory on your left. Explore the gardens; then walk south (back toward Kennedy Drive) from the conservatory entrance. Continue east on Kennedy Drive a short way to the three-way intersection and turn right (south) at Middle Drive East.

Less than a block away at the intersection of Middle and Bowling Green drives is a sign for the National AIDS Memorial Grove. Before you enter the grove, follow the curve of Bowling Green Drive to the left, past the Bowling Green to the **Children's Playground** ❷. If you have kids in tow, you'll probably be spending time here. If not, still take a peek at the vintage Herschell-Spillman Carousel.

Reverse direction on Bowling Green Drive and enter the **National AIDS Memorial Grove** ❸, a sunken meadow that stretches west along Middle Drive East. At the end of the wheelchair-access ramp make a left to view the Circle of Friends; then continue west along the graded paths (ignore the staircase on the right halfway through the grove) to another circle with a poem by Thom Gunn. Exit north from this circle. As you're standing in the circle looking at the poem, the staircase to take is on your left. At the top of the staircase make a left and continue west on Middle Drive East. This brings you to the back entrance of the California Academy of Sciences, which closed at the end of 2003 for renovations.

A hundred feet shy of the 9th Avenue and Lincoln Way entrance to Golden Gate Park is the main entrance to **Strybing Arboretum & Botanical Gardens** ❹. Take the first right after the bookstore. Follow the path as it winds north and west. Take the second right and look for signs for the Fragrance and Biblical gardens.

Backtrack from the gardens to the path you started on and make a right. As the path continues to wind north and west, you see a large fountain off to the left. Just before you get to the fountain, make a right and head toward the duck pond. A wooden footbridge on the pond's left side crosses the water. Signs on the other side identify the fowl in the pond. Stay to the right on the path, heading toward the exit gate. Just before the gate, continue to the right to the Primitive Garden. Take the looped boardwalk past ferns, gingko, cycads, conifers, moss, and other plants. At the end of the loop, make a left and then a right, exiting via the Eugene L. Friend gate. Go straight ahead on the crosswalk to the blacktop path on the other side. Make a right, walk about 100 feet, and make a left on Tea Garden Drive. A few hundred feet east of here is the entrance to the **Japanese Tea Garden** ❺.

Tour the Japanese Tea Garden, exiting near the gate you entered. Make a left and continue past the former Asian Art Museum and the M. H. de Young Memorial Museum; both buildings are closed for construction. A crosswalk leads south to the Music Concourse, with its gnarled trees, century-old fountains and sculptures, and the Golden Gate Bandshell. Turn left at the closest of the fountains and head east toward the bronze sculpture of Francis Scott Key.

Turn left at the statue and proceed north through two underpasses. At the end of the second underpass, you'll have traveled about 2 mi. If you're ready to leave the park, take the short staircase to the left of the blue-and-green playground equipment. At the top of the staircase is the 10th Avenue and Fulton Street stop for Bus 5–Fulton heading back downtown. If you're game for walking ½ mi more, make an immediate left as you exit the second underpass, cross 10th Avenue, and make a right on John F. Kennedy Drive. After approximately ¼ mi the Rose Garden is on your right. Continue west to the first stop sign. To the left is a sign for **Stow Lake** ❻. Follow the road past the log cabin to the boathouse.

From Stow Lake it's the equivalent of 30 long blocks on John F. Kennedy Drive to the western end of the park and the ocean. If you walk, you pass meadows, the Portals of the Past, the buffalo paddock, and a 9-hole golf course. You can skip most of this walk by proceeding west on John F. Kennedy Drive from the stop sign mentioned above, making the first right after you walk underneath Cross-Over Drive, and following the road as it winds left toward 25th Avenue and Fulton. On the northwest corner of Fulton Street and 25th Avenue, catch Bus 5–Fulton heading west, get off at 46th Avenue, walk one block west to 47th Avenue, and make a left. Make a right on John F. Kennedy Drive.

By foot or vehicle, your goal is the **Dutch Windmill** ❼ and adjoining garden. A block to the south, wind up with a microbrew at the Beach Chalet.

TIMING   You can easily spend a whole day in Golden Gate Park, especially if you walk the whole distance. Set aside at least an hour for the Academy of Sciences. Even if you plan to explore just the eastern end of the park (up to Stow Lake), allot at least two hours.

What to See

❷ **Children's Playground.** Kids have been coming here to cut loose since the 1880s. The equipment has changed over the years, but the squeals and howls remain the same. A menagerie of handcrafted horses and other animals—among them cats, frogs, roosters, and a tiger—twirl on the 1912 Herschell-Spillman Carousel, inside a many-windowed circular structure. The Romanesque-style Sharon Building looms over the playground; the 1887 structure has been rebuilt twice, after the earthquake of 1906 and a 1980 fire. ⊠ *Bowling Green Dr., off Martin Luther King Jr. Dr., Golden Gate Park* ☎ *415/753–5210 or 415/831–2700* ✉ *Playground free, carousel $1* ☉ *Playground daily dawn–midnight; carousel June–Sept., daily 10–5, Oct.–May, Fri.–Sun. 9–4.*

❶ **Conservatory of Flowers.** Built in the late 1870s, this is the oldest building in the park, the last remaining wood-frame Victorian conservatory in the country, and a copy of the conservatory in the Royal Botanical Gardens in Kew, England. Heavily damaged during a 1995 storm, the whitewashed facility underwent extensive renovations. With its crown jewel—the 14-ton glass dome—back atop its perch, the conservatory and its garden are a worthy a stop. ⊠ *John F. Kennedy Dr. at Conservatory Dr., Golden Gate Park* ⊕ *www.conservatoryofflowers.org.*

❼ **Dutch Windmill.** Two windmills anchor the western end of Golden Gate Park. The restored 1902 Dutch Windmill once pumped 20,000 gallons of well water per hour to the reservoir on Strawberry Hill. With its heavy concrete bottom and wood-shingled arms and upper section, the windmill cuts quite the sturdy figure. The Murphy Windmill, on Martin Luther King Jr. Drive near the Great Highway, was the world's largest windmill when it was built in 1905 and also pumped water to the Strawberry Hill reservoir; today fund-raising efforts are under way to restore

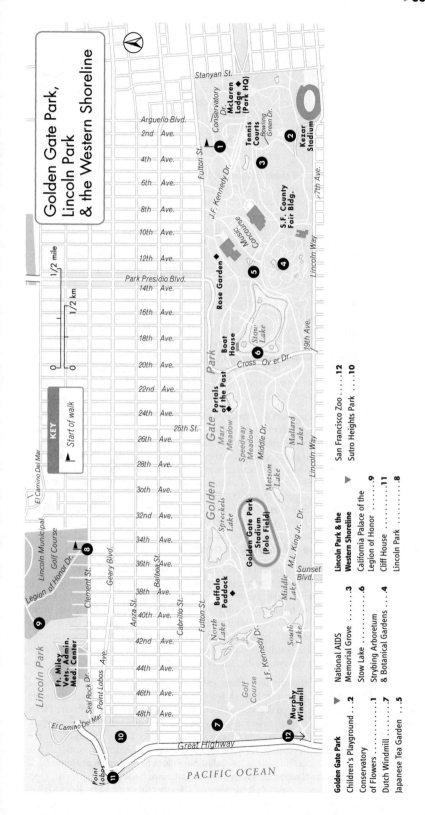

Golden Gate Park, Lincoln Park & the Western Shoreline

KEY

▲ Start of walk

1/2 mile

1/2 km

Stanyan St.
Arguello Blvd.
2nd Ave.
4th Ave.
6th Ave.
8th Ave.
10th Ave.
12th Ave.
Park Presidio Blvd.
14th Ave.
16th Ave.
18th Ave.
20th Ave.
22nd Ave.
24th Ave.
25th St.
26th Ave.
28th Ave.
30th Ave.
32nd Ave.
34th Ave.
36th Ave.
38th Ave.
40th Ave.
42nd Ave.
44th Ave.
46th Ave.
48th Ave.

El Camino Del Mar

Conservatory Dr.
McLaren Lodge ◆ (Park HQ)
Tennis Courts
Bowling Green Dr.
Kezar Stadium
S.F. County Fair Bldg.
Music Concourse
Rose Garden ◆
Stow Lake
Boat House
Cross Over Dr.
Portals of the Past ◆
Marx Meadow
Speedway Meadow
Middle Dr.
Mallard Lake
Metson Lake
Golden Gate Park Stadium (Polo Field)
Spreckels Lake
Buffalo Paddock ◆
Sunset Blvd.
Middle Lake
North Lake
South Lake
Golf Course
Murphy Windmill ◆

Fulton St.
J.F. Kennedy Dr.
Lincoln Way
19th Ave.
7th Ave.
Lincoln Way
M.L. King Jr. Dr.
Golden Gate Park

Geary Blvd.
Anza St.
Balboa St.
Cabrillo St.
Fulton St.
Clement St.
Lincoln Municipal Golf Course
Legion of Honor Dr.
Lincoln Park
Ft. Miley Vets. Admin. Med. Center
Seal Rock Dr.
Point Lobos Ave.
Point Lobos
El Camino Del Mar

Great Highway

PACIFIC OCEAN

Golden Gate Park

▶ Children's Playground . . . **2**
Conservatory of Flowers **1**
Dutch Windmill **7**
Japanese Tea Garden . . . **5**

▶ National AIDS Memorial Grove **3**
Stow Lake **6**
Strybing Arboretum & Botanical Gardens **4**

Lincoln Park & the Western Shoreline
▶ California Palace of the Legion of Honor **9**
Cliff House **11**
Lincoln Park **8**

San Francisco Zoo **12**
Sutro Heights Park **10**

the windmill, currently in disrepair. ⊠ *Between 47th Ave. and the Great Hwy., Golden Gate Park.*

★ ❺ **Japanese Tea Garden.** A serene 4-acre landscape of small ponds, streams, waterfalls, stone bridges, Japanese sculptures, *mumsai* (planted bonsai) trees, perfect miniature pagodas, and some nearly vertical wooden "humpback" bridges, the tea garden was created for the 1894 Mid-Winter Exposition. Go in the spring if you can, when the cherry blossoms are in bloom. ⊠ *Tea Garden Dr. off John F. Kennedy Dr., Golden Gate Park* 🕾 *415/752–4227 or 415/752–1171* 🖾 *$3.50* ☉ *Mar.–Sept., daily 9–6; Oct.–Feb., daily 9–5.*

❸ **National AIDS Memorial Grove.** San Francisco has lost many residents, gay and straight, to AIDS. This 15-acre grove, started in the early 1990s by people with AIDS and their families and friends, was conceived as a living memorial to those the disease has claimed. In 1996 the U.S. Congress passed a bill granting the grove status as a national memorial. Coast live oaks, Monterey pines, coast redwoods, and other trees flank the grove, which is anchored at its east end by the stone Circle of Friends. ⊠ *Middle Dr. E, west of tennis courts, Golden Gate Park* ⊕ *www.aidsmemorial.org.*

☿ ❻ **Stow Lake.** One of the most picturesque spots in Golden Gate Park, this placid body of water surrounds Strawberry Hill. A couple of bridges allow you to cross over and ascend the hill. A waterfall cascades from the top of the hill, and panoramic views make it worth the short hike up here. Just to the left of the waterfall sits the elaborate Chinese Pavilion, a gift from the city of Taipei. It was shipped in 6,000 pieces and assembled on the shore of Strawberry Hill Island in 1981. ⊠ *Off John F. Kennedy Dr., ½ mi west of 10th Ave., Golden Gate Park* 🕾 *415/752–0347.*

❹ **Strybing Arboretum & Botanical Gardens.** The 55-acre arboretum specializes in plants from areas with climates similar to that of the Bay Area, such as the west coast of Australia, South Africa, and the Mediterranean; more than 8,000 plant and tree varieties bloom in gardens throughout the grounds. Maps are available at the main and Eugene L. Friend entrances. ⊠ *9th Ave. at Lincoln Way, Golden Gate Park* 🕾 *415/661–1316* ⊕ *www.strybing.org* 🖾 *Free* ☉ *Weekdays 8–4:30, weekends 10–5* ☞ *Tours from bookstore weekdays at 1:30, weekends at 10:20 and 1:30; tours from Friend Gate Wed., Fri., and Sun. at 2.*

Lincoln Park & the Western Shoreline

From Land's End in Lincoln Park you have some of the best views of the Golden Gate (the name was originally given to the opening of San Francisco Bay, long before the bridge was built) and the Marin Headlands. From the historic Cliff House south to the sprawling San Francisco Zoo, the Great Highway and Ocean Beach run along the western edge of the city. The wind is often strong along the shoreline, summer fog can blanket the ocean beaches, and the water is cold and usually too rough for swimming. Carry a jacket and bring binoculars.

a good drive

A car is useful out here. There are plenty of hiking trails, and buses travel to all the sights mentioned, but the sights are far apart. Start at **Lincoln Park** ❽ ▶. The park entrance is at 34th Avenue and Clement Street. Those without a car can take Bus 38–Geary—get off at 33rd Avenue and walk north (to the right) one block on 34th Avenue to the entrance. At the end of 34th Avenue (labeled on some maps as Legion of Honor Drive within Lincoln Park) is the **California Palace of the Legion of Honor** ❾, a splendid art museum. From the museum, head back out to Clement Street and follow it west. At 45th Avenue, Clement turns into Seal Rock Drive.

When Seal Rock dead-ends at 48th Avenue, turn left on El Camino del Mar and right on Point Lobos Avenue. After a few hundred yards, you see parking lots for **Sutro Heights Park** ⑩ and the **Cliff House** ⑪. (To get from the Legion of Honor to Point Lobos Avenue by public transit, take Bus 18 from the Legion of Honor parking lot west to the corner of 48th and Point Lobos avenues.) Two large concrete lions near the southeast corner of 48th and Point Lobos guard the entrance to Sutro Heights Park. After taking a quick spin through the park, exit past the lions, cross Point Lobos, make a left, and walk down to the Cliff House. From the Cliff House it's a short walk farther downhill to Ocean Beach. The 3-mi beach has a beachside path that winds through landscaped sand dunes and a paved path that is good for biking and in-line skating.

The **San Francisco Zoo** ⑫ is a couple of miles south, at the intersection of the Great Highway and Sloat Boulevard. If you're driving, follow the Great Highway (heading south from the Cliff House, Point Lobos Avenue becomes the Great Highway), turn left on Sloat Boulevard, and park in the zoo's lot on Sloat. The hike along Ocean Beach from the Cliff House to the zoo is a flat but scenic 3 mi. To take public transportation from the Cliff House, reboard Bus 18, which continues south to the zoo.

TIMING Set aside at least three hours for this tour—more if you don't have a car. You can easily spend an hour in the Palace of the Legion of Honor and 1½ hours at the zoo.

What to See

★ ⑨ **California Palace of the Legion of Honor.** Spectacularly situated on cliffs overlooking the ocean, the Golden Gate Bridge, and the Marin Headlands, this landmark building is a fine repository of European art. A pyramidal glass skylight in the entrance court illuminates the lower-level galleries, which exhibit prints and drawings, English and European porcelain, and ancient Assyrian, Greek, Roman, and Egyptian art. The 20-plus galleries on the upper level display the permanent collection of European art from the 14th century to the present day. The noteworthy Auguste Rodin collection includes two galleries devoted to the master and a third with works by Rodin and other 19th-century sculptors. ⊠ *34th Ave. at Clement St., Lincoln Park* ☎ *415/863–3330* ⊕ *www.thinker.org* ⊠ *$8 ($2 off with Muni transfer), free Tues.* ☉ *Tues.–Sun. 9:30–5.*

⑪ **Cliff House.** The third incarnation of the Cliff House dates from 1909. The complex, which includes restaurants, a pub, and a gift shop, remains open while undergoing a gradual renovation to restore its early 20th-century look. Below the Cliff House is a fine observation deck and the **Golden Gate National Recreation Area Visitors' Center** (☎ 415/556–8642 ⊕ www.nps.gov/goga ☉ closed during the Cliff House renovation). To the north are the ruins of the glass-roof Sutro Baths. You can explore the ruins on your own or take ranger-led walks on weekends. The visitor center has information about these and other trails. ⊠ *1090 Point Lobos Ave., Lincoln Park* ☎ *415/386–3330* ⊕ *www.cliffhouse. com* ☉ *Weekdays 9 AM–10:30 PM, weekends 8:30 AM–11 PM.*

▶ ⑧ **Lincoln Park.** Large Monterey cypresses line the fairways at Lincoln Park's 18-hole golf course. There are scenic walks throughout the 275-acre park, with postcard-perfect views from many spots. The trail out to **Land's End** starts outside the Palace of the Legion of Honor, at the end of El Camino del Mar. Be careful if you hike here; landslides are frequent. ⊠ *Entrance at 34th Ave. at Clement St.*

ᘓ ⑫ **San Francisco Zoo.** More than 1,000 birds and animals—220 species altogether—reside here. Among the more than 130 endangered species are the snow leopard, Sumatran tiger, jaguar, and Asian elephant. African Kikuyu grass carpets the circular outer area of **Gorilla World,** one of the largest and most natural gorilla habitats of any zoo in the world. Trees and shrubs create communal play areas. Fifteen species of rare monkeys—including colobus monkeys, white ruffed lemurs, and macaques—live and play at the two-tier **Primate Discovery Center,** which contains 23 interactive learning exhibits on the ground level. The **Feline Conservation Center,** a natural setting for rare cats, plays a key role in the zoo's efforts to encourage breeding among endangered felines. ⊠ *Sloat Blvd. and 45th Ave., Sunset (Muni L–Taraval streetcar from downtown)* ☎ *415/753–7080* ⊕ *www.sfzoo.org* ☜ *$10 ($1 off with Muni transfer), free 1st Wed. of month* ☉ *Daily 10–5.*

❿ **Sutro Heights Park.** Monterey cypresses and Canary Island palms dot this cliff-top park on what were the grounds of the home of eccentric mining engineer and former San Francisco mayor Adolph Sutro. Photos on placards depict what you would have seen before the house burned down in 1896. All that remains of the main house is its foundation. Climb up for a sweeping view of the Pacific Ocean and the Cliff House below. ⊠ *Point Lobos and 48th Aves., Lincoln Park.*

The Mission

The sunny Mission district wins out in San Francisco's system of microclimates—it's always the last to succumb to fog. Italian and Irish in the early 20th century, the Mission became heavily Latino in the late 1960s, when immigrants from Mexico and Central America began arriving. Gentrification in the late 1990s led to skyrocketing rents, causing clashes between the longtime residents forced out and the wealthy yuppies moving in. Still a bit scruffy in patches, the Mission lacks some of the glamour of other neighborhoods, but a walk through it provides the opportunity to mix with a heady cross section of San Franciscans.

a good walk

The spiritual heart of the old Mission lies within the thick, white adobe walls of **Mission Dolores** ❶ ▶, where Dolores Street intersects with 16th Street. From the Mission, cross Dolores Street and head east on 16th Street. Tattooed and pierced hipsters abound a block from Mission Dolores, but the eclectic area still has room for a place like Creativity Explored, where people with developmental disabilities work on art and other projects. At the intersection of 16th and Valencia streets, head south (to the right). At 18th Street walk a half block west (right) to view the mural adorning the Women's Building.

Head south on Valencia Street and make a left on 24th Street. The atmosphere becomes distinctly Latin American. About a block east of Folsom Street is the **Precita Eyes Mural Arts and Visitors Center** ❷. From the center continue east past St. Peter's Church, where Isías Mata's mural *500 Years of Resistance,* on the exterior of the rectory, reflects on the struggles and survival of Latin-American cultures. At 24th and Bryant streets is the **Galería de la Raza/Studio 24** ❸ art space.

Diagonally across from the Galería, on Bryant at the northeast corner near 24th Street, you can catch Bus 27–Bryant to downtown.

TIMING The above walk takes about two hours, including brief stops at the various sights listed. If you plan to go on a mural walk with Precita Eyes or if you're a browser who tends to linger, add at least another hour.

What to See

❸ **Galería de la Raza/Studio 24.** San Francisco's premier showcase for Latino art, the gallery exhibits the works of local and international artists.

The Mission

Next door is the nonprofit Studio 24, which sells prints and paintings by Chicano artists, as well as folk art, mainly from Mexico. In early November the studio brims with art objects paying tribute to *Día de los Muertos* (Day of the Dead). ⊠ *2857 24th St., at Bryant St., Mission* ☎ *415/826–8009* ⊕ *www.galeriadelaraza.org* ☉ *Gallery Tues.–Sun. noon–6, Studio 24 Wed.–Sun. noon–6.*

★ ▶ ❶ **Mission Dolores.** Mission Dolores encompasses two churches standing side by side. Completed in 1791, the small adobe building known as **Mission San Francisco de Asís** is the oldest standing structure in San Francisco and the sixth of the 21 California missions founded by Father Junípero Serra in the 18th and early 19th centuries. Its ceiling depicts original Ohlone Indian basket designs, executed in vegetable dyes. The tiny chapel includes frescoes and a hand-painted wooden altar; some artifacts were brought from Mexico by mule in the late 18th century. There is a small museum, and the pretty little mission cemetery maintains the graves of mid-19th-century European immigrants. ⊠ *Dolores and 16th Sts., Mission* ☎ *415/621–8203* ⊕ *www.sfmuseum.org/hist5/ misdolor.html* ⊠ *Free (donations welcome), audio tour $7* ☉ *Daily 9–4.*

❷ **Precita Eyes Mural Arts and Visitors Center.** The nonprofit arts organization sponsors guided walks of the Mission District's murals. Most tours start with a 45-minute slide presentation. The bike and walking trips, which take between one and three hours, pass several dozen murals. You can pick up a map of 24th Street's murals at the center. ⊠ *2981 24th St., Mission* ☎ *415/285–2287* ⊕ *www.precitaeyes.org* ⊠ *Center free, tours $8–$12* ☉ *Center weekdays 10–5, Sat. 10–4, Sun. noon–4; walks weekends at 11 and 1:30 or by appointment.*

The Castro & the Haight

The Castro district—the social, cultural, and political center of the gay and lesbian community in San Francisco—is one of the liveliest and most welcoming neighborhoods in the city, especially on weekends. Come Saturday and Sunday, the streets teem with folks out shopping, pushing political causes, heading to art films, and lingering in bars and cafés.

Young people looking for an affordable spot in which they could live according to new precepts began to move into the big old Victorians in the Haight in the late 1950s and early 1960s. By 1966 the Haight had become a hot spot for rock bands including the Grateful Dead and Jefferson Airplane.

a good walk

Begin in the Castro at **Harvey Milk Plaza** ❶ ⚑ on the southwest corner of 17th and Market streets; it's outside the south entrance to the Castro Street Muni station (K, L, and M streetcars stop here). Across Castro Street from the plaza is the neighborhood's landmark, the **Castro Theatre** ❷. Many shops line Castro Street between 17th and 19th streets, 18th between Sanchez and Eureka streets, and Market Street heading east toward downtown. After exploring the shops on 18th and Castro streets, get ready for a strenuous walk. For an unforgettable vista, continue north on Castro Street two blocks to 16th Street, turn left, and head up the steep hill to Flint Street. Turn right on Flint and follow the trail on the left (just past the tennis courts) up the hill. The beige buildings on the left contain the **Randall Museum** ❸ for children. Turn right up the dirt path, which soon loops back up Corona Heights. At the top you're treated to an all-encompassing view of the city.

Now continue north to walk the Haight Street tour. Follow the trail down the other side of Corona Heights to a grassy field. The gate to the field is at the intersection of Roosevelt Way and Museum Way. Turn right on Roosevelt (head down the hill) and cross Roosevelt at Park Hill Terrace. Walk up Park Hill to Buena Vista Avenue, turn left, and follow the road as it loops west and south around Buena Vista Park to Central Avenue. Head down Central two blocks to Haight Street, and make a left.

Continue west to the fabled **Haight-Ashbury intersection** ❹. A motley contingent of folks attired in retro fashions and often sporting hippie-long hair hangs here. One block south of Haight and Ashbury (at 710 Ashbury) is the Grateful Dead house, the pad that Jerry Garcia and band inhabited in the 1960s. The stores along Haight Street up to Shrader Street are worth checking out. (You encounter many panhandlers along this walk.)

TIMING   Allot 60 to 90 minutes to visit the Castro district. Set aside an extra hour to hike Corona Heights and visit the Randall Museum. The distance covered in the Haight is only several blocks, and although there are shops aplenty and other amusements, an hour or so should be enough.

What to See

★ ❷ **Castro Theatre.** The neon marquee is the neighborhood's great landmark, and the 1,500-seat theater, which opened in 1922, is the grandest of San Francisco's few remaining movie palaces. The Castro's elaborate Spanish baroque interior is fairly well preserved. The crowd can be enthusiastic and vocal, talking back to the screen as loudly as it talks to them. ✉ *429 Castro St., Castro* ☎ *415/621–6120.*

❹ **Haight-Ashbury intersection.** On October 6, 1967, hippies took over the intersection of Haight and Ashbury streets to proclaim the "Death of Hip." If they thought hip was dead then, they'd find absolute confir-

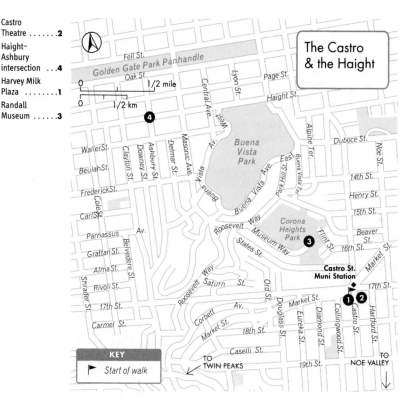

mation of it today, what with the Gap holding court on one quadrant of the famed corner. Among the folks who hung out in or near the Haight during the late 1960s were writers Richard Brautigan, Allen Ginsberg, Ken Kesey, and Gary Snyder; anarchist Abbie Hoffman; rock performers Marty Balin, Jerry Garcia, Janis Joplin, and Grace Slick; LSD champion Timothy Leary; and filmmaker Kenneth Anger.

❶ Harvey Milk Plaza. An 18-foot-long rainbow flag, a gay icon, flies above this plaza named for the man who electrified the city in 1977 by being elected to its Board of Supervisors as an openly gay candidate. The liberal Milk hadn't served a full year of his term before he and Mayor George Moscone, also a liberal, were shot in November 1978 at City Hall. Milk's assassination shocked the gay community, which became infuriated when the infamous "Twinkie defense"—that junk food had led to diminished mental capacity—resulted in a manslaughter verdict for White. During the so-called White Night Riot of May 21, 1979, gays and their sympathizers stormed City Hall, torching its lobby and several police cars. ⊠ *Southwest corner of Castro and Market Sts., Castro.*

☙ ❸ Randall Museum. The highlight of this facility is the educational animal room, popular with children, where you can observe birds, lizards, snakes, spiders, and other creatures that cannot be released to the wild because of injury or other problems. Also here are a greenhouse, woodworking and ceramics studios, and a theater. The Randall sits on 16 acres of public land; the hill that overlooks the museum is variously known as Red Rock, Museum Hill, and, correctly, Corona Heights. ⊠ *199 Museum Way, off Roosevelt Way, Castro* ☎ *415/554–9600* ⊕ *www.randallmuseum.org* ⊠ *Free* ⊗ *Tues.–Sat. 10–5.*

WHERE TO EAT

Reviewed by
Sharon Silva

Since its earliest days, San Francisco has been a destination for food lovers, a place where diversity rules and trends are set. Nearly every ethnic cuisine is represented—from Afghan to Indian to Vietnamese. And although locals have long headed to the Mission District for Latin food, to Chinatown and the Richmond District for Asian food, and to North Beach for Italian food, they also know that every part of the city offers dining experiences beyond the neighborhood tradition.

Prices

WHAT IT COSTS				
$$$$	$$$	$$	$	¢
AT DINNER	over $30	$23–$30	$16–$22	$10–$15	under $10

Prices are per person for a main course, excluding tax of 8.25%.

Union Square

Contemporary

★ **$$$–$$$$** ✕ **Postrio.** There's always a chance to catch a glimpse of some celebrity here, including the owner of this legendary eatery, superchef Wolfgang Puck, who periodically commutes here from Los Angeles. A stunning three-level bar and dining area is connected by copper handrails and accented with museum-quality contemporary paintings. The seasonal lunch and dinner menus are Californian with Mediterranean and Asian overtones. ⊠ *545 Post St., Union Sq.* ☎ *415/776–7825* ⚏ *Reservations essential* ⊟ *AE, D, DC, MC, V* ⊗ *No lunch Sun.*

French

$$$$ ✕ **Fleur de Lys.** The creative cooking of French chef–part owner Hubert Keller has brought every conceivable culinary award to this romantic spot. The interior's distinctive feature is its tented ceiling, 900 yards of draped and swathed fabric. The three-, four-, and five-course prix-fixe menus include dishes such as monkfish rolled in serrano ham, squab breast filled with foie gras and truffles, and filet mignon with braised endives. ⊠ *777 Sutter St., Union Sq.* ☎ *415/673–7779* ⚏ *Reservations essential* 🎩 *Jacket required* ⊟ *AE, DC, MC, V* ⊗ *Closed Sun. No lunch.*

Seafood

$$$–$$$$ ✕ **Farallon.** Outfitted with sculpted jellyfish lamps, kelp-covered columns,
Fodor'sChoice and sea-urchin chandeliers, this swanky Pat Kuleto–designed restaurant
★ is loaded with style *and* customers. Chef Mark Franz changes his menu regularly, but lobster bisque with truffle chantilly, Dungeness crab risotto, and cognac-roasted monkfish are sometimes among the exquisite dishes that draw serious diners from coast to coast. ⊠ *450 Post St., Union Sq.* ☎ *415/956–6969* ⊟ *AE, D, DC, MC, V* ⊗ *No lunch Sun. or Mon.*

Vietnamese

$$–$$$ ✕ **Le Colonial.** The stamped tin ceiling, period photographs, slow-moving fans, and tropical plants re-create a 1920s French colonial setting for the upscale Vietnamese food. Local blue bloods come for the banana blossom–and–prawn salad, hot-and-sour fish soup, wok-seared beef tenderloin, bass steamed in banana leaves with glass noodles, and other Southeast Asian flavors. ⊠ *20 Cosmo Pl., Union Sq.* ☎ *415/931–3600* ⚏ *Reservations essential* ⊟ *AE, MC, V* ⊗ *Closed Sun. No lunch.*

TAQUERIAS AROUND TOWN

SAN FRANCISCO'S TAQUERIAS *are ideal places to quell your hunger pangs quickly and cheaply— usually for no more than five bucks. Although the Mission District is loaded with these taco and burrito outposts, they turn up in other neighborhoods, too.*

In the Lower Haight, a neighborhood loaded with quick bites—shawarma, sushi, sausages, noodles—the modest **Botana** *(✉ 422 Haight St., near Webster St., Lower Haight ☎ 415/863–9113) has held its own. Regulars appreciate the fish tacos and bountiful burritos. In the Castro, across from the giant Safeway on Market Street and within steps of the Church Street MUNI Metro station,* **El Castillo** *(✉ 126 Church St., near Market St., Castro ☎ 415/621–3428), the always busy burrito purveyor, is known for its good food in hefty portions and fast service.* **La Corneta Taqueria** *(✉ 2731 Mission St., between 23rd and 24th Sts., Mission ☎ 415/643–7001) serves everything from tacos and burritos to flautas and quesadillas, in meat, seafood, and vegetarian versions. The particularly pleasant setting—blond-wood tables and plenty of light—is a plus in the neighborhood, where most taquerias are short on frills.* **La Taqueria** *(✉ 2889 Mission St., near 25th St., Mission ☎ 415/285–7117), with its attractive arched facade, opened in 1975. It has a wide variety of fillings for tacos and burritos, including an excellent version of*

carnitas (chunks of long-simmered pork). The line almost always snakes out the door at **Pancho Villa Taqueria** *(✉ 3071 16th St., between Mission and Valencia Sts., Mission ☎ 415/864–8840), a Mission institution. Most customers are waiting to order one of the big burritos heavy with rice, beans (black or pinto), meat, and salsa; guacamole and cheese are just pennies more. At art-filled* **Taqueria El Balazo** *(✉ 1654 Haight St., between Cole and Clayton Sts., Upper Haight ☎ 415/864–8608), plump burritos filled with meat or seafood, beans, rice, and guacamole and simpler tacos are the draw. A favorite of homesick Mexicans, the plain-Jane* **Taqueria San Jose** *(✉ 2830 Mission St., near 24th St., Mission ☎ 415/282–0203) stays open until the wee hours. Choices include a full array of meats for tacos, burritos, and tortas (sandwiches), all served in paper-lined baskets. Although* **Tlaloc** *(✉ 525 Commercial St., near Sansome St., Financial District ☎ 415/981–7800) charges more than places deep in the Mission, the salsa bar is a plus. So, too, are the seafood burritos. In the Mission, two silver* **Toyanese Taco Trucks** *are home to the most authentic tacos in the city: two small, soft, fresh tortillas, one atop the other, crowned with meat—pork, beef, brains, head, or tongue—and a spoonful of salsa. Pickled jalapeños sit alongside. One truck sits at 19th and Harrison streets, the other at 22nd and Harrison.*

SoMa & the Embarcadero

American

$–$$$ ✕ **Momo's.** Many of the baseball fans spilling out of the San Francisco Giants' ballpark like to stop at this former printing plant, now a serious drinking and dining hangout. A shiny stainless-steel exhibition kitchen delivers french fries with chipotle ketchup, thick steaks, and thin pizzas to crowds in the Craftsman-appointed dining room with its big banquettes and high ceilings. The large patio and long bar are gathering places for everyone from sports enthusiasts to businesspeople shaking hands on a deal. ✉ 760 2nd St., SoMa ☎ 415/227–8660 ⊟ AE, MC, V.

Where to Eat in
San Francisco

Contemporary

$$$$ ✕ **Fifth Floor.** Chef Laurent Gras puts together elegant, sophisticated, vi-
Fodor'sChoice sually stunning plates that keep interested—and well-heeled—diners
★ coming to this top-drawer restaurant. The 75-seat room, in dark wood,
and zebra-stripe carpeting, is where exquisite dishes such as venison saddle with coconut and lime, and slow-cooked pork belly with truffles are
served from a menu that changes with the seasons. ⊠ *Palomar Hotel,
12 4th St., SoMa* ☎ *415/348–1555* ⏣ *Reservations essential* ▭ *AE,
DC, MC, V* ⊘ *Closed Sun. No lunch.*

$$$–$$$$ ✕ **Bacar.** An understated brick-and-glass exterior hides one of the city's
most wine-savvy restaurants. The by-the-glass list runs pages; wines by
the bottle require a hefty book. In other words, serious wine drinkers
feel at home in this stylish place. The food menu is far smaller—and nicely
unfussy—with a half dozen or so choices in each category. Salt
cod–and–crab brandade, pizza with serrano ham and manchego cheese,
and rabbit rillettes (cooked pulverized meat) are among the starters. ⊠ *448
Brannan St., SoMa* ☎ *415/904–4100* ▭ *MC, V* ⊘ *No lunch.*

★ **$$$–$$$$** ✕ **Boulevard.** Two of San Francisco's top restaurant talents—chef Nancy
Oakes and designer Pat Kuleto—are responsible for this high-profile eatery
in the magnificent 1889 Audiffred Building. Oakes's menu is season-
ally in flux, but you can always count on her signature juxtaposition of
delicacies such as caviar with comfort foods like wood oven–roasted rack
of lamb. ⊠ *1 Mission St., Embarcadero* ☎ *415/543–6084* ⏣ *Reservations
essential* ▭ *AE, D, DC, MC, V* ⊘ *No lunch weekends.*

$$–$$$$ ✕ **One Market.** This huge, bustling brasserie across from the Ferry
Building is chef Bradley Ogden's popular San Francisco outpost. The
two-tier dining room, done in mustard tones, seats 170 and serves fine—
and homey—preparations that include cider-brined pork with sage
milk sauce, sea bream in a salt crust, and bittersweet chocolate tart with
caramel sauce and vanilla ice cream. ⊠ *1 Market St., Embarcadero*
☎ *415/777–5577* ⏣ *Reservations essential* ▭ *AE, DC, MC, V*
⊘ *Closed Sun. No lunch Sat.*

★ **$$–$$$** ✕ **Hawthorne Lane.** The stylish restaurant draws a crowd to a quiet alley
not far from the Yerba Buena Center. At the tables in the large, high-
ceiling bar, you can order a selection of irresistible small plates—tuna
tartare with nori chips, tempura green beans with mustard sauce—plus
anything on the full menu. Patrons in the formal, light-flooded dining
room engage in more-serious eating. ⊠ *22 Hawthorne St., SoMa* ☎ *415/
777–9779* ▭ *D, DC, MC, V* ⊘ *No lunch weekends.*

French

$$ ✕ **Piperade.** In a previous incarnation, this handsome restaurant, with
its wood-beam ceiling and sleek wooden banquettes, was called Pastis
and the kitchen turned out French-California food to a regular clien-
tele. These days chef-owner Gerald Hirogoyen is keeping those same loyal
customers happy with a French Basque menu full of the rustic dishes of
his childhood. Among them are *piperade* (peppers and tomatoes served
with serrano ham and a poached egg) and halibut in sherry sauce.
⊠ *1015 Battery St., Embarcadero* ☎ *415/391–2555* ▭ *AE, MC, V*
⊘ *Closed Sun. No lunch Sat.*

Mediterranean

★ **$–$$** ✕ **LuLu.** The food is satisfyingly uncomplicated and delectable. Beneath
a high barrel-vaulted ceiling, you can feast on a fritto misto of artichokes,
fennel, and lemon slices; mussels roasted in an iron skillet; wood-roasted
poultry, meats, and shellfish; plus pizzas and pastas. Specials include a
rotisserie-prepared main course that changes daily; Friday it's truly suc-
culent suckling pig. ⊠ *816 Folsom St., SoMa* ☎ *415/495–5775* ▭ *AE,
D, DC, MC, V.*

Vietnamese

★ **$–$$$** ✕ **Slanted Door.** Chef-owner Charles Phan first opened this location as "temporary" quarters after the original Slanted Door in the Mission District closed in 2002 for a major expansion. Phan's signature dishes—clay-pot chicken with chilies and ginger, shaking beef (tender beef cubes with garlic and onion), green papaya salad—made the move, too, to the cheers of his faithful customers. Indeed, this space has been so successful that Phan is keeping it going. ⊠ *100 Brannan St., Embarcadero* ☎*415/861–8032* ⊟ *MC, V.*

Financial District

Chinese

¢–$ ✕ **Yank Sing.** The city's oldest teahouse prepares 100 varieties of dim sum on a rotating basis, serving some 60 varieties daily. The Spear Street location, near one end of the Rincon Center atrium, is big and comfortable; the older, Stevenson Street site is smaller, a cozier refuge for neighborhood office workers who fuel up on steamed buns and parchment chicken at lunchtime. ⊠ *49 Stevenson St., Financial District* ☎ *415/541–4949* ♧ *Reservations essential* ⊟ *AE, DC, MC, V* ☾ *No dinner* ⊠ *One Rincon Center, 101 Spear St., Financial District* ☎ *415/957–9300* ♧ *Reservations essential* ⊟ *AE, DC, MC, V* ☾ *No dinner.*

French

★ **$–$$$** ✕ **Jeanty at Jack's.** Chef Philippe Jeanty, who made a name for himself in the wine country (first at Domaine Chandon and then at his own Bistro Jeanty), opened this brass-and-wood, three-story brasserie in the former Jack's restaurant, a San Francisco institution since 1864. The food is as French as the chef, with cassoulet, steak au poivre, bouillabaisse, and coq au vin among the traditional offerings. The second floor houses a series of private rooms, just as it did in the days of the original Jack's. ⊠ *615 Sacramento St., Financial District* ☎ *415/693–0941* ⊟ *AE, D, MC, V* ☾ *Closed Sun.*

Japanese

$$–$$$ ✕ **Kyo-ya.** With extraordinary authenticity, this showplace in the Palace Hotel replicates the refined experience—rarely found outside Japan—of dining in a first-class Japanese restaurant. In Japan a *kyo-ya* is a nonspecialized restaurant that serves a wide range of food. Here, the range is spectacular, encompassing tempuras, one-pot dishes, deep-fried and grilled meats, and two dozen sushi selections. ⊠ *Palace Hotel, 2 New Montgomery St., at Market St., Financial District* ☎*415/546–5000* ⊟*AE, D, DC, MC, V* ☾ *Closed Sun. and Mon. No lunch Sat.*

Seafood

★ **$$$$** ✕ **Aqua.** Quietly elegant, ultrafashionable, heavily mirrored, and populated by a society crowd, this spot is among the city's most lauded seafood restaurants—and among the most expensive. The kitchen is known for using exquisite ingredients, from which it assembles beautiful preparations that are elegant without being overly fussy. The signature mussel soufflé with chardonnay sauce, white-anchovy terrine, and seared tuna with foie gras are all especially good. ⊠ *252 California St., Financial District* ☎ *415/956–9662* ♧ *Reservations essential* 🏛 *Jacket and tie* ⊟ *AE, DC, MC, V* ☾ *No lunch weekends.*

$–$$ ✕ **Tadich Grill.** Owners and locations have changed many times since this old-timer opened during the gold-rush era, but the 19th-century atmosphere remains. Simple sautés are the best choices, or cioppino during crab season (October to May) and Pacific halibut in season (January to May). Seating is at the counter as well as in private booths, but expect long lines for a table at lunchtime on weekdays. ⊠ *240 California St.,*

Financial District ☎ *415/391–2373* ⚘ *Reservations not accepted* ☰ *MC, V* ⊘ *Closed Sun.*

Spanish

★ **$$** ✕ **B44.** The cluster of wonderful European eateries on Belden Place includes this spare, modern Spanish restaurant that draws locals with its menu of Catalan tapas and paellas. The open kitchen sends out small plates such as white anchovies with pears and Idiazábal cheese, warm octopus with tiny potatoes, and blood sausage with white beans. The paellas bring together inviting combinations such as chicken, rabbit, and mushrooms. ⊠ *44 Belden Pl., Financial District* ☎ *415/986–6287* ☰ *AE, MC, V* ⊘ *Closed Sun. No lunch Sat.*

Chinatown

Chinese

★ **$–$$$** ✕ **R&G Lounge.** The name conjures up an image of a dark bar with a cigarette-smoking piano player, but the restaurant is actually as bright as a new penny. Downstairs (entrance on Kearny Street) is a brightly lighted no-tablecloth dining room that's packed at lunch and dinner. The classier upstairs space (entrance on Commercial Street) is a favorite stop for Chinese businessmen on expense accounts and anyone else seeking Cantonese banquet fare. Decide among the many wonderful, sometimes pricey, always authentic dishes, such as salt-and-pepper Dungeness crab and steamed bean curd stuffed with shrimp. ⊠ *631 Kearny St., Chinatown* ☎ *415/982–7877 or 415/982–3811* ☰ *AE, D, DC, MC, V.*

¢–**$$$** ✕ **Great Eastern.** Cantonese chefs are known for their expertise with seafood, and the kitchen here continues that venerable tradition. Tanks filled with Dungeness crabs, black bass, abalone, catfish, shrimp, and other creatures of fresh- and saltwater occupy a corner of the main dining room, a handsome space with jade-green wainscoting and dark-wood accents. A wall-hung menu in both Chinese and English lists the cost of selecting what can be pricey indulgences. ⊠ *649 Jackson St., Chinatown* ☎ *415/986–2550* ☰ *AE, MC, V.*

North Beach

Contemporary

$$–$$$$ ✕ **Moose's.** Ed Moose and his wife, Mary Etta, are well known in San Francisco and beyond, so local and national politicians and media types typically turn up at their restaurant. The menu is a sophisticated take on familiar preparations, such as spinach salad with grapes, blue cheese, and champagne vinaigrette; double-cut pork chops with Mission figs, cabbage, and Yukon Gold potatoes; and key lime pie with coconut-rum sauce. ⊠ *1652 Stockton St., North Beach* ☎ *415/989–7800* ⚘ *Reservations essential* ☰ *AE, D, DC, MC, V* ⊘ *No lunch Mon.–Wed.*

Italian

★ **$–$$$** ✕ **Rose Pistola.** Chef-owner Reed Hearon's busy 130-seat spot draws huge crowds. The name honors one of North Beach's most revered barkeeps, and the food celebrates the neighborhood's Ligurian roots. An assortment of antipasti—roasted peppers, house-cured fish, fava beans dusted with pecorino shards—and wood-fired pizzas are favorites, as are the cioppino and fresh fish of the day served in various ways. A big bar area opens onto the sidewalk, and an exhibition kitchen lets you keep an eye on your order. ⊠ *532 Columbus Ave., North Beach* ☎ *415/399–0499* ☰ *AE, DC, MC, V.*

$$ ✕ **Capp's Corner.** At this pleasantly down-home spot, one of North Beach's last family-style trattorias, the men at the bar still roll dice for drinks and diners sit elbow to elbow at long oilcloth-covered tables. The fare consists of bountiful, well-prepared five-course dinners—not award-winning, but a meal here doesn't break the bank. Osso buco and roast lamb are good main-dish choices. ⊠ *1600 Powell St., North Beach* ☎ *415/ 989–2589* ☰ *AE, D, DC, MC, V.*

¢–$ ✕ **L'Osteria del Forno.** An Italian-speaking staff, a small and unpreten-
Fodor'sChoice   tious dining area, and irresistible aromas drifting from the open kitchen
★   make customers who pass through the door of this modest storefront operation feel as if they've stumbled into Italy. The kitchen produces small plates of simply cooked vegetables, a few baked pastas, a roast of the day, creamy polenta, and thin-crust pizzas—including a memorable "white" pie topped with porcini mushrooms and mozzarella. At lunch try one of the delectable focaccia sandwiches. ⊠ *519 Columbus Ave., North Beach* ☎ *415/982–1124* ⊜ *Reservations not accepted* ☰ *No credit cards* ☻ *Closed Tues.*

Nob Hill & Russian Hill

French

$$$$ ✕ **Masa's.** The restaurant, with its chocolate-brown walls, white fabric
Fodor'sChoice   ceiling, and red silk–shaded lanterns, is one of the country's most cele-
★   brated food temples. Chef Ron Siegel, famous for besting Japan's Iron Chef, is at the helm, and his efforts have pleased the fussiest restaurant critics. Dinners are prix fixe: a three-course tasting menu, two six-course tasting menus (one vegetarian), and one nine-course tasting menu. All are laced with plenty of fancy ingredients and priced accordingly. ⊠ *Hotel Vintage Court, 648 Bush St., Nob Hill* ☎ *415/989–7154* ⊜ *Reservations essential* 🏛 *Jacket required* ☰ *AE, D, DC, MC, V* ☻ *Closed Sun. and Mon. No lunch.*

Italian

★ $–$$ ✕ **Antica Trattoria.** The dining room, spare and classic, has off-white walls, dark wood, a partial view of the kitchen, and a strong sense of re-straint. The food is characterized by the same no-nonsense quality. A small menu delivers classic plates such as farro pasta with Bolognese sauce, monk-fish wrapped in pancetta, and venison medallions matched with wilted greens. The Italian wine list is fairly priced, and the genial service is pol-ished but not overly formal. ⊠ *2400 Polk St., Russian Hill* ☎ *415/928–5797* ⊜ *Reservations essential* ☰ *DC, MC, V* ☻ *Closed Mon. No lunch.*

Van Ness/Polk

Italian

$$$$ ✕ **Acquerello.** White linens, fresh flowers, and exquisite china set an el-egant scene at one of the most romantic spots in town. Pumpkin ravioli tossed with chestnuts, sage, and brown butter; red wine–and–truffle risotto; and green-onion fettuccine with crab and wine are all memorable, as are the fish dishes. Chef-owner Suzette Gresham is responsible for the kitchen's high standards, and co-owner Giancarlo Paterlini oversees the superb list of Italian wines. ⊠ *1722 Sacramento St., Van Ness/Polk* ☎ *415/567–5432* ☰ *AE, D, MC, V* ☻ *Closed Sun. and Mon. No lunch.*

Seafood

¢–$ ✕ **Swan Oyster Depot.** Half fish market and half diner, this small, slim
Fodor'sChoice   seafood operation, open since 1912, has no tables, only a narrow mar-
★   ble counter with about a dozen and a half stools. Most people come in to buy perfectly fresh salmon, halibut, crabs, and the like to take home. Everyone else hops onto one of the rickety stools to enjoy a bowl of clam chowder—the only hot food served—a dozen oysters, or half a cracked crab. ⊠ *1517 Polk St., Van Ness/Polk* ☎ *415/673–1101* ☰ *No credit cards* ☻ *Closed Sun. No dinner.*

Pacific Heights & Japantown

Contemporary

★ ¢–$$$ ✕ **Chez Nous.** The concept here is Spanish tapas, although the small dishes—duck-leg confit, baked goat cheese with oven-roasted tomatoes, french fries and aioli spiked with *harissa* (Moroccan chili sauce)—cross borders into other cuisines. Lamb rib chops seasoned with herbes de Provence and sautéed spinach tossed with raisins and pine nuts are among the other choices. The stylish yet casual and noisy dining room has wood floors, zinc-topped tables, and blue walls. It's usually packed with neighborhood residents and moviegoers from the nearby Clay Theater. ✉ *1911 Fillmore St., Lower Pacific Heights* ☎ *415/441–8044* ⌨ *Reservations not accepted* ▤ *MC, V* ☺ *Closed Mon. No lunch Tues.*

Italian

$–$$ ✕ **Vivande Porta Via.** Tucked in among the boutiques on upper Fillmore Street, this longtime Italian delicatessen-restaurant, operated by well-known chef and cookbook author Carlo Middione, draws a crowd at lunch and dinner for both its take-out and sit-down fare. Shelves are laden with wines, olives, and other gourmet goods. The regularly changing menu includes a half dozen pastas and risottos, as well as meat and fish main dishes. ✉ *2125 Fillmore St., Lower Pacific Heights* ☎ *415/346–4430* ▤ *AE, MC, V.*

Japanese

$–$$ ✕ **Mifune.** Thin, brown soba and thick, white udon are the specialties at this North American outpost of an Osaka-based noodle empire. A line often snakes out the door, but the house-made noodles are worth the wait. Seating is at wooden tables, where diners can be heard slurping down big bowls of such traditional Japanese combinations as fish cake–crowned udon and *tenzaru* (cold noodles and hot tempura with a gingery dipping sauce). ✉ *Japan Center, Kinetsu Bldg., 1737 Post St., Japantown* ☎ *415/922–0337* ⌨ *Reservations not accepted* ▤ *AE, D, DC, MC, V.*

¢–$ ✕ **Sanppo.** This venerable, modestly priced, casual spot has an enormous selection of Japanese food: *yaki* (charcoal-grilled fare) of every type, *nabemono* dishes (one-pot meals), *donburi* (meat- or chicken-topped rice bowls), udon, and soba, not to mention featherlight tempura and sushi. Tempting small dishes for snacking make Sanppo a favorite. If you drive here, ask for validated parking at the Japan Center garage. ✉ *1702 Post St., Japantown* ☎ *415/346–3486* ⌨ *Reservations not accepted* ▤ *MC, V.*

Civic Center

Contemporary

$$$–$$$$ ✕ **Jardinière.** One of the city's most talked-about restaurants since its opening in the late 1990s, Jardinière continues to be *the* place to dine before a performance at the nearby Opera House or any time you have something to celebrate. The chef-owner is Traci Des Jardins, and the sophisticated interior, with its eye-catching oval atrium and curving staircase, is the work of designer Pat Kuleto. From a foie gras first course to a perfectly roasted squab main to a berry-rich shortcake for dessert, the menu is a match for the decor. ✉ *300 Grove St., Hayes Valley* ☎ *415/861–5555* ⌨ *Reservations essential* ▤ *AE, DC, MC, V* ☺ *No lunch.*

FodorsChoice
★

German

$–$$ ✕ **Suppenkuche.** Bratwurst and braised red cabbage and a long list of German beers rule at this lively, hip outpost in the trendy Hayes Valley corridor. Strangers sit down together at unfinished pine tables. The food—potato pancakes with homemade applesauce, sauerbraten, cheese spaetzle, schnitzel, apple strudel—is tasty and easy on the pocketbook, and the brews are first-rate. ⊠ *601 Hayes St., Hayes Valley* ☎ *415/252–9289* ⊟ *AE, MC, V* ☺ *No lunch.*

Mediterranean

$$–$$$ ✕ **Zuni Café.** The Italian-Mediterranean menu, created by nationally
Fodor'sChoice known chef Judy Rodgers, packs in an eclectic crowd until late in the
★ evening. A balcony dining area overlooks the large zinc bar, where a first-rate oyster selection and drinks are dispensed. The menu changes daily, but the superb whole roast chicken and Tuscan bread salad for two are always on it. ⊠ *1658 Market St., Hayes Valley* ☎ *415/552–2522* ⚖ *Reservations essential* ⊟ *AE, MC, V* ☺ *Closed Mon.*

Fisherman's Wharf

French

$$$$ ✕ **Gary Danko.** Chef Gary Danko's daily-changing menu of highly so-
Fodor'sChoice phisticated plates has kept anyone able to finance a visit returning again
★ and again. The cost of a meal is pegged to the number of courses, from three to five, and the plates run the gamut from lobster paired with chanterelles to lemon-herb duck breast with cranberry compote. The wine list is the size of a small-town phone book. ⊠ *800 N. Point St., Fisherman's Wharf* ☎ *415/749–2060* ⚖ *Reservations essential* ⊟ *AE, D, DC, MC, V* ☺ *No lunch.*

Seafood

$–$$$ ✕ **McCormick & Kuleto's.** This seafood emporium in Ghirardelli Square is a visitor's dream come true: a fabulous view of the bay from every seat in the house, an Old San Francisco atmosphere, and dozens of varieties of fish and shellfish prepared in scores of international ways. The food has its ups and downs—stick with the simplest preparations, such as oysters on the half shell and grilled fish. ⊠ *Ghirardelli Sq. at Beach and Larkin Sts., Fisherman's Wharf* ☎ *415/929–1730* ⊟ *AE, D, DC, MC, V.*

Cow Hollow/Marina

Italian

★ **$$$$** ✕ **Merenda.** This cozy, friendly combination trattoria, *enoteca* (wine bar), and take-out counter is the domain of chef Keith Luce and his wife, Raney, who oversees the front of the house. The menu is prix fixe (two, three, or four courses) and the food is sophisticated Italian with some French touches—chicken-liver crostini, rabbit with tomato-porcini sauce, walnut torta. The wines are some of Italy's most intriguing bottlings. ⊠ *1809 Union St., Cow Hollow* ☎ *415/346–7373* ⚖ *Reservations essential* ⊟ *MC, V* ☺ *Closed Mon.–Tues. No lunch.*

Mediterranean

$$–$$$ ✕ **PlumpJack Café.** The clubby dining room, with its smartly attired clientele of bankers and brokers, socialites and society scions, takes its name from an opera composed by oil tycoon and music lover Gordon Getty, whose sons are two of the partners here. The regularly changing menu, the creation of chef James Ormsby, spans the Mediterranean. Dishes might include butternut risotto, grilled tuna with pistachio-laced couscous, or duck served three ways on one plate—roasted breast, crispy leg, and confit-filled spring roll. ⊠ *3127 Fillmore St., Cow Hollow* ☎ *415/463–4755* ⊟ *AE, MC, V* ☺ *No lunch weekends.*

The Mission

Contemporary

¢–$$$ ✕ **Andalu.** The menu includes some 30 globe-circling small plates, from duck-confit spring rolls and miniature tacos filled with tuna tartare to a fritto misto of artichokes and potatoes and a crock of *brandade* (puree of salt cod). The wine list is equally global, and many offerings come by the glass, tempting curious palates. The hip, bilevel dining room has tables outfitted in aquamarine and black. ⊠ *3198 16th St., Mission* ☏ *415/621–2211* ⊟ *MC, V* ☉ *No lunch.*

$–$$ ✕ **Foreign Cinema.** The Bay Area is home to many of the country's most respected independent filmmakers, so it's no surprise that this innovative spot is a hit. In the hip, loftlike space not only can you sit down to carpaccio with fried onions and horseradish sauce and pork chops with celery-root puree, but you also can watch varied film classics such as Terry Gilliam's *Brazil* and Martin Scorsese's *The Last Waltz* projected on the wall in the large inner courtyard. ⊠ *2534 Mission St., Mission* ☏ *415/648–7600* ⊟ *MC, V* ☉ *Closed Mon. No lunch.*

French

$$–$$$ ✕ **Chez Papa.** The small, simply outfitted restaurant has brought France to Potrero Hill. The menu has both small plates, such as mussels in wine, lamb chops on ratatouille, and deep-fried smelt with lemon, and big plates, such as lamb daube, roast chicken, and shellfish stew. ⊠ *1401 18th St., Potrero Hill* ☏ *415/824–8210* ⚘ *Reservations essential* ⊟ *AE, MC, V* ☉ *No lunch Sun.*

Italian

$–$$ ✕ **Delfina.** Regardless of the state of the economy, the loyal clientele keeps
Fodor'sChoice coming for Craig Stoll's simple yet exquisite Italian fare at this hopping
★ spot. The interior is simple, with hardwood floors, aluminum-top tables, a tiled bar, and a casual but sophisticated ambience. The menu changes daily, but among the usual offerings are house-made mozzarella with tomatoes; grilled squid on a bed of tiny white beans; and orecchiette with broccoli rabe and chickpeas. ⊠ *3621 18th St., Mission* ☏ *415/552–4055* ⚘ *Reservations essential* ⊟ *MC, V* ☉ *No lunch.*

Mexican

¢–$ ✕ **Los Jarritos.** The name of this cheery, sun-filled corner spot refers to the collection of hundreds of tiny earthenware cups that hang from the ceiling and decorate the walls—cups used for drinking tequila in Mexico. The *carne asada* (grilled strips of marinated meat) is excellent here, and the delicious *chilaquiles,* day-old tortillas cut into strips and cooked with cheese, eggs, chilies, and sauce, satisfy the hardiest appetites. ⊠ *901 Van Ness Ave., Mission* ☏ *415/648–8383* ⊟ *MC, V.*

The Castro & the Haight

American-Casual

¢–$ ✕ **Chow.** Chef-owner Tony Gulisano left the world of upmarket Italian
Fodor'sChoice cooking in the late 1990s to open this wildly popular, unpretentious spot.
★ The honest fare—pizzas from the wood-fired oven, thick burgers of grass-fed beef, spaghetti with meatballs—is made with the best local ingredients and priced for diners watching their wallets. The savvy try to leave room for an order of the superb cannoli, made according to a Gulisano family recipe. Because reservations are restricted to large parties, folks hoping to snag seats usually surround the doorway. ⊠ *215 Church St., Castro* ☏ *415/552–2469* ⚘ *Reservations not accepted* ⊟ *MC, V.*

Contemporary

¢ ✕ **Zao Noodle Bar.** Good prices, fresh ingredients, and generous portions have made this minichain a success. The menu items span Asia, from Vietnamese rice noodles with seared pork to Thai green curry–coconut prawns with ramen. Among the beverages are top-flight sakes served in martini glasses and Zao ginger–orange cooler. The noodles in creamy peanut sauce on the kids' menu should keep nearly any grammar-school student smiling. ⊠ *3583 16th St., Castro* ☎ *415/864–2888* ⌒ *Reservations not accepted* ⊟ *MC, V* ⊠ *2031 Chestnut St., Marina* ☎ *415/928–3088* ⌒ *Reservations not accepted* ⊟ *MC, V.*

Indian

¢–$$ ✕ **Indian Oven.** The tandoori specialties—chicken, lamb, breads—make this cozy Victorian storefront one of the Lower Haight's most popular restaurants. *Sag paneer* (spinach with Indian cheese) and *aloo gobhi* (potatoes and cauliflower with black mustard seeds and other spices) are also excellent. On Friday and Saturday nights, the mostly twenty- and thirtysomething clientele waiting for tables overflows onto the sidewalk. ⊠ *233 Fillmore St., Lower Haight* ☎ *415/626–1628* ⊟ *AE, D, DC, MC, V* ⊗ *No lunch.*

Thai

★ ¢–$$ ✕ **Thep Phanom.** The fine fare and the lovely interior at this Lower Haight institution keep local food critics and restaurantgoers singing Thep Phanom's praises. Duck is deliciously prepared in several ways—in a fragrant curry, minced for salad, atop a bed of spinach. Seafood (in various guises) is another specialty. ⊠ *400 Waller St., Lower Haight* ☎ *415/431–2526* ⊟ *AE, D, DC, MC, V* ⊗ *No lunch.*

Richmond District

Chinese

★ $–$$$ ✕ **Ton Kiang.** The lightly seasoned Hakka cuisine of southern China, rarely found in this country, was introduced to San Francisco at this restaurant, with such regional specialties as salt-baked chicken, braised stuffed bean curd, delicate fish balls, and clay pots of meats and seafood. Don't overlook the other seafood offerings here or the pea sprouts stir-fried with garlic. The dim sum is arguably the finest in the city. ⊠ *5821 Geary Blvd., Richmond* ☎ *415/387–8273* ⊟ *MC, V.*

Japanese

★ $–$$ ✕ **Kabuto Sushi.** Master chef Sachio Kojima flashes his knives before an admiring crowd who can't get enough of his buttery yellowfin tuna or golden sea urchin on pads of pearly rice. In addition to fine sushi and sashimi, traditional Japanese dinners are served in the adjoining dining room. Be sure to consider the excellent selection of sakes, each one rated for dryness and labeled with its place of origin. ⊠ *5116 Geary Blvd., Richmond* ☎ *415/752–5652* ⊟ *MC, V* ⊗ *Closed Mon. and last Sun. of month. No lunch.*

Sunset District

American-Casual

$$ ✕ **Beach Chalet.** In a historic colonnaded building with handsome Works Project Administration–produced murals depicting San Francisco in the mid-1930s, the Beach Chalet is the place to watch the waves break on the shore and the sun set over the Pacific Ocean. The fine microbrewery beers range from a light pilsner to a pale ale, but the eclectic dinner menu seldom produces more-than-okay food. At midday, the prices are lower, the food simpler, and the view better. ⊠ *1000 Great Hwy., Sunset* ☎ *415/386–8439* ⊟ *MC, V.*

WHERE TO STAY

Reviewed by
Andy Moore

Few U.S. cities can rival San Francisco's variety in lodging. Its plush hotels rank among the world's finest; renovated buildings house hostelries with European flair; grand Victorian-era homes serve as bed-and-breakfasts; and private residences of all types rent rooms, apartments, or cottages. You can even find accommodations in boats bobbing on the bay, but the popular chain hotels and motels found in most American cities are here, too. The city's hilly topography and diversity of neighborhoods contribute to each property's unique sense of place, and you may feel like a kid in a candy store as you go about choosing which of the approximately 31,000 rooms here will be your home-away-from-home.

WHAT IT COSTS					
	$$$$	**$$$**	**$$**	**$**	**¢**
FOR 2 PEOPLE	over $250	$176–$250	$121–$175	$90–$120	under $90

Prices are for two people in a standard double room in high season, excluding 14% tax.

Union Square/Downtown

★ **$$$$** 🏨 **Campton Place.** Highly attentive service is the hallmark of this small, top-tier hotel behind a simple brownstone facade. Many rooms are smallish, but all are elegant in a contemporary Italian style, with light earth tones and handsome pearwood paneling and cabinetry. Bathrooms have deep soaking tubs, and double-paned windows keep city noises out. ⊠ *340 Stockton St., Union Sq., 94108* 🕾 *415/781–5555 or 800/235–4300* 🖷 *415/955–5536* ⊕ *www.camptonplace.com* 📲 *101 rooms, 9 suites* ♻ *Restaurant, room service, in-room data ports, in-room safes, minibars, some microwaves, cable TV with movies, gym, bar, lobby lounge, dry cleaning, laundry service, concierge, business services, meeting room, parking (fee), some pets allowed (fee), no-smoking floors* ▤ *AE, DC, MC, V.*

$$$$ 🏨 **Clift.** Behind a stately, beige brick facade lies this "hotel as art" showplace, as conceived by entrepreneur Ian Schrager and artist-designer Philippe Starck. The cavernous lobby contains groupings of whimsical art objects meant to encourage a surreal mood. Spacious rooms, in shades of ivory, gray, and lavender, are furnished sparely with blond wood and see-through orange acrylic furniture, plus two huge mirrors on otherwise-empty walls. ⊠ *495 Geary St., Union Sq., 94102* 🕾 *415/775–4700 or 800/652–5438* 🖷 *415/441–4621* ⊕ *www.clifthotel.com* 📲 *363 rooms, 26 suites* ♻ *2 restaurants, room service, in-room data ports, in-room safes, minibars, cable TV with movies, in-room VCRs, gym, bar, lobby lounge, dry cleaning, laundry service, concierge, Internet, business services, meeting room, parking (fee), no-smoking floors* ▤ *AE, D, DC, MC, V.*

$$$$ 🏨 **Hotel Monaco.** A cheery 1910 beaux-arts facade and snappily dressed
FodorsChoice doormen welcome you into the plush lobby, with its grand marble staircase, French inglenook fireplace, and a vaulted ceiling with murals of
★ WW I planes and hot-air balloons. The hotel hosts a free wine and appetizer hour in this delightful space. Guest rooms, with Chinese-inspired armoires, canopy beds, and high-back upholstered chairs, have vivid colors. There are special amenities for pets. If you didn't bring a pet, request one of the "companion goldfishes" available. ⊠ *501 Geary St., Union Sq., 94102* 🕾 *415/292–0100 or 800/214–4220* 🖷 *415/292–*

0111 ⊕ *www.monaco-sf.com* ⟿ *181 rooms, 20 suites* ♿ *Restaurant, room service, in-room data ports, in-room fax, in-room safes, some in-room hot tubs, minibars, cable TV with movies and video games, some in-room VCRs, gym, massage, sauna, spa, steam room, bar, dry cleaning, laundry service, Internet, business services, parking (fee), some pets allowed, no-smoking floors* ▭ *AE, D, DC, MC, V.*

★ **$$$$** 🏨 **Hotel Nikko.** The vast marble lobby of this Japan Airlines–owned hotel is airy and serene, and its rooms are some of the most handsome in the city. They have furniture with clean, elegant lines; gold drapes; wheat-color wall coverings; and ingenious window shades that screen the sun while allowing views of the city. The staff is multilingual. Don't miss the excellent fifth-floor fitness facility ($6 fee), which has traditional *ofuros* (Japanese soaking tubs), a *kamaburo* (Japanese sauna), and a glass-enclosed rooftop pool and whirlpool. ⊠ *222 Mason St., Union Sq., 94102* ☎ *415/394–1111 or 800/645–5687* 🖷 *415/421–0455* ⊕ *www. hotelnikkosf.com* ⟿ *510 rooms, 22 suites* ♿ *Restaurant, room service, in-room data ports, some in-room hot tubs, some kitchenettes, minibars, cable TV with movies, indoor pool, gym, hair salon, Japanese baths, massage, sauna, bar, dry cleaning, laundry service, concierge, concierge floor, business services, meeting rooms, car rental, parking (fee), some pets allowed, no-smoking floors* ▭ *AE, D, DC, MC, V.*

★ **$$$$** 🏨 **Prescott Hotel.** Although not as famous as many hotels in the area, the Prescott has several advantages: the relatively small size means personalized service, and its relationship with Postrio, the Wolfgang Puck restaurant attached to its lobby, means you get preferred reservations. Rooms are traditional, with a rich hunter-green theme. Bathrooms have marble-top sinks. Complimentary coffee service and evening wine receptions are held by a flickering fireplace in the handsomely furnished living room off the lobby. ⊠ *545 Post St., Union Sq., 94102* ☎ *415/563–0303 or 800/ 283–7322* 🖷 *415/563–6831* ⊕ *www.prescotthotel.com* ⟿ *164 rooms, 32 suites* ♿ *Restaurant, room service, in-room data ports, in-room fax, some in-room hot tubs, minibars, cable TV with in-room movies and video games, some in-room VCRs, gym, bar, lobby lounge, concierge, concierge floor, business services, meeting room, parking (fee), some pets allowed, no-smoking floors* ▭ *AE, D, DC, MC, V.*

$$$
Fodor'sChoice
★ 🏨 **Hotel Rex.** Literary and artistic creativity are celebrated at this stylish place (named after writer Kenneth Rexroth), where thousands of books line the 1920s-style lobby. The proprietors even host book readings and round-table discussions in the lobby and in the petite bistro. Muted check bedspreads, striped carpets, and restored period furnishings upholstered in deep, rich hues may evoke the spirit of 1920s salon society, but the rooms also have such modern amenities as voice mail and CD players. ⊠ *562 Sutter St., Union Sq., 94102* ☎ *415/433–4434 or 800/433– 4434* 🖷 *415/433–3695* ⊕ *www.thehotelrex.com* ⟿ *92 rooms, 2 suites* ♿ *Restaurant, room service, in-room data ports, minibars, cable TV with movies, bar, lobby lounge, dry cleaning, laundry service, concierge, Internet, business services, meeting room, parking (fee), no-smoking floors* ▭ *AE, D, DC, MC, V.*

$–$$ 🏨 **Hotel Beresford Arms.** Fancy molding, 10-foot-tall windows, and an English grandfather clock grace the lobby of this ornate brick Victorian, on the National Register of Historic Places. Afternoon tea and wine are served in the large space, and the staff is especially friendly. Junior suites include sitting areas and either a wet bar or kitchenette; full suites have two queen beds in the bedroom, a Murphy bed in the living room, and a kitchen. Dark-wood antique-reproduction furniture is used throughout. ⊠ *701 Post St., Union Sq., 94109* ☎ *415/673–2600 or 800/ 533–6533* 🖷 *415/929–1535 or 800/533–5349* ⊕ *www.beresford.com* ⟿ *90 rooms, 12 suites* ♿ *In-room data ports, some in-room hot tubs,*

Where to Stay
in Downtown
San Francisco

some kitchens, some kitchenettes, minibars, some microwaves, some refrigerators, cable TV, in-room VCRs, dry cleaning, laundry service, Internet, business services, parking (fee), some pets allowed (fee), no-smoking floors ▤ *AE, D, DC, MC, V* ⑩ *CP.*

★ ¢–$ ▦ **Grant Plaza Hotel.** Amazingly low room rates for this part of town make the Grant Plaza a find for budget travelers wanting to look out their window at the striking architecture and fascinating street life of Chinatown. Rooms are small, modern, and sparkling clean. Those on the top floor are newer, slightly brighter, and a bit more expensive; for a quieter stay ask for one in the back. ⊠ *465 Grant Ave., Chinatown, 94108* ☏ *415/434–3883 or 800/472–6899* 🖷 *415/434–3886* ⊕ *www. grantplaza.com* ⬫ *71 rooms, 1 suite* ♤ *Some in-room VCRs, concierge, business services, parking (fee); no a/c* ▤ *AE, DC, MC, V.*

Financial District

★ $$$$ ▦ **Harbor Court.** The exemplary service of the friendly staff earns high marks for this cozy hotel overlooking the Embarcadero and within shouting distance of the Bay Bridge. Guest rooms are smallish but have double sets of soundproof windows and include fancy touches such as partially canopied upholstered beds, tasteful faux-textured walls, and fine reproductions of late 19th-century nautical and nature prints. Complimentary wine is served evenings in the lounge. Once an Army/Navy YMCA, the hotel offers free access to adjacent YMCA facilities and limousine service to the Financial District. ⊠ *165 Steuart St., SoMa 94105* ☏ *415/882–1300 or 800/346–0555* 🖷 *415/882–1313* ⊕ *www. harborcourthotel.com* ⬫ *130 rooms, 1 suite* ♤ *Room service, in-room data ports, minibars, room TVs with movies and video games, dry cleaning, laundry service, Internet, business services, parking (fee), some pets allowed, no-smoking floors* ▤ *AE, D, DC, MC, V.*

$$$$ ▦ **Mandarin Oriental.** Occupying the top 11 floors of San Francisco's
Fodor'sChoice third-tallest building, the hotel has panoramic vistas of the metro area
★ from every room (each has binoculars). The structure actually comprises two towers; glass-enclosed sky bridges connect them. Unlike in many modern buildings, windows here open so you can hear the "ding ding" of the cable cars some 40 floors below. In the Mandarin Rooms, extra-deep tubs sit next to picture windows. ⊠ *222 Sansome St., Financial District 94104* ☏ *415/276–9888 or 800/622–0404* 🖷 *415/433–0289* ⊕ *www.mandarinoriental.com* ⬫ *154 rooms, 4 suites* ♤ *Restaurant, room service, in-room data ports, in-room safes, minibars, cable TV with movies, some in-room VCRs, gym, lobby lounge, dry cleaning, laundry service, concierge, Internet, business services, meeting room, parking (fee), some pets allowed (fee), no-smoking floors* ▤ *AE, D, DC, MC, V.*

★ $$–$$$$ ▦ **Hyatt Regency.** The 20-story gray concrete structure, at the foot of Market Street, is the focal point of the Embarcadero Center, where more than 100 shops and restaurants cater to the Financial District. The spectacular 17-story atrium lobby is a marvel with sprawling trees, a shimmering stream, and a huge fountain. Glass elevators whisk you up to Equinox, the city's only revolving rooftop restaurant. Rooms—all with city or bay views and some with bay-view balconies—have an attractive, contemporary look with blond-wood furniture. ⊠ *5 Embarcadero Center, Embarcadero 94111* ☏ *415/788–1234 or 800/233–1234* 🖷 *415/ 398–2567* ⊕ *www.sanfranciscoregency.hyatt.com* ⬫ *760 rooms, 45 suites* ♤ *2 restaurants, room service, in-room data ports, in-room safes, some in-room hot tubs, cable TV with movies, some in-room VCRs, gym, bar, lobby lounge, concierge, business services, meeting rooms, parking (fee), no-smoking floors* ▤ *AE, D, DC, MC, V.*

SoMa

$$$$ 🏨 **Four Seasons Hotel San Francisco.** On floors 5–17 o. .
Fodor'sChoice luxurious hotel is sandwiched between multimillion-dollar condo...
★ a sports-and-fitness complex. Rooms overlook either Yerba Buena Gardens or other parts of the local cityscape. Some have deep soaking tubs and floor-to-ceiling windows. You get free access to Sports Club/LA, which has a 25-yard lap pool, an aerobics room with a spring-cushioned floor, and spa services. Both the hotel and its restaurant, Seasons, draw visiting celebrities. ⊠ *757 Market St., SoMa 94103* ☎ *415/633–3000* 🖷 *415/633–3009* ⊕ *www.fourseasons.com* ➥ *231 rooms, 46 suites* ⅋ *Restaurant, room service, in-room data ports, in-room safes, minibars, cable TV with movies and video games, some in-room VCRs, indoor pool, health club, sauna, spa, steam room, basketball, volleyball, bar, dry cleaning, laundry service, concierge, Internet, business services, meeting rooms, parking (fee), some pets allowed, no-smoking floors* ⊟ *AE, D, DC, MC, V.*

$$$$ 🏨 **Hotel Palomar.** The top five floors of the green-tiled and turreted 1908 Pacific Place Building provide an urbane and luxurious oasis above the busiest part of town. Guest rooms have muted leopard-pattern carpeting and drapes with bold navy-and-cream stripes. The sleek furniture echoes a 1930s moderne sensibility. Bathrooms sparkle; a "tub menu" with various herbal and botanical infusions tempts adventurous bathers. In-room spa services are arranged through Spa Equilibrium. ⊠ *12 4th St., SoMa, 94103* ☎ *415/348–1111 or 877/294–9711* 🖷 *415/348–0302* ⊕ *www.hotelpalomar.com* ➥ *182 rooms, 16 suites* ⅋ *Restaurant, room service, in-room data ports, in-room fax, some in-room hot tubs, in-room safes, minibars, room TVs with movies and video games, some in-room VCRs, gym, massage, bar, lobby lounge, dry cleaning, laundry service, concierge, Internet, business services, meeting room, parking (fee), some pets allowed (fee), no-smoking floors* ⊟ *AE, D, DC, MC, V.*

$$$$ 🏨 **Palace Hotel.** This landmark hotel was the world's largest and most Fodor'sChoice luxurious when it opened in 1875. Completely rebuilt after the earth★ quake and fire of 1906, the splendid hotel has a stunning entryway and the fabulous belle epoque Garden Court restaurant, with its stained-glass domed ceiling. Rooms have high ceilings, reproduction antique furnishings, and marble bathrooms. ⊠ *2 New Montgomery St., SoMa 94105* ☎ *415/512–1111* 🖷 *415/543–0671* ⊕ *www.sfpalace.com* ➥ *518 rooms, 34 suites* ⅋ *3 restaurants, room service, in-room data ports, in-room safes, some in-room hot tubs, refrigerators, cable TV with movies, indoor pool, health club, hot tub, sauna, spa, bar, dry cleaning, laundry service, concierge, business services, meeting rooms, parking (fee), no-smoking floors* ⊟ *AE, D, DC, MC, V.*

Nob Hill

★ **$$$$** 🏨 **Fairmont San Francisco.** Commanding the top of Nob Hill like a European palace, the Fairmont has experienced plenty of drama, including its triumph over the 1906 earthquake and the creation of the United Nations Charter here in 1945. Architect Julia Morgan's 1907 lobby design includes alabaster walls and gilt-embellished ceilings supported by Corinthian columns. Guest rooms all have high ceilings, fine dark-wood furniture, colorful Chinese porcelain lamps, and marble bathrooms. Rooms in the Tower are generally larger and have better views. An array of amenities and services (including free chicken soup if you're under the weather) keeps loyal guests coming back. ⊠ *950 Mason St., Nob Hill, 94108* ☎ *415/772–5000 or 800/527–4727* 🖷 *415/837–0587*

⊕ *www.fairmont.com* ⏎ *531 rooms, 65 suites* ⚕ *2 restaurants, room service, in-room data ports, in-room fax, in-room safes, minibars, room TVs with movies, health club, hair salon, 2 bars, nightclub, baby-sitting, dry cleaning, laundry service, concierge, business services, meeting room, car rental, parking (fee), some pets allowed (fee), no-smoking floors* ▭ *AE, D, DC, MC, V.*

★ **$$$$** ▣ **The Huntington Hotel.** The redbrick, ivy-covered hotel has provided stately and gracious personal service to everyone from Humphrey Bogart and Lauren Bacall to Pablo Picasso and Luciano Pavarotti. Rooms and suites, many of which have great views of Grace Cathedral, the bay, or the city skyline, are large because they used to be apartments. Most rooms have wet bars; all have large antique desks. At the spa, a sunny indoor-outdoor area with panoramic city views has an indoor pool and 10 rooms for massages, facials, and body wraps, plus a poolside fireplace lounge. ⊠ *1075 California St., Nob Hill 94108* ☎ *415/474–5400 or 800/227–4683* 🖷 *415/474–6227* ⊕ *www.huntingtonhotel. com* ⏎ *100 rooms, 35 suites* ⚕ *Restaurant, room service, in-room data ports, in-room safes, some in-room hot tubs, some kitchenettes, room TVs with movies, indoor pool, massage, sauna, spa, steam room, bar, dry cleaning, laundry service, concierge, meeting room, parking (fee), no-smoking floors* ▭ *AE, D, DC, MC, V.*

$$$$ ▣ **Ritz-Carlton, San Francisco.** This world-class hotel is a stunning trib-
Fodor'sChoice ute to beauty, and warm, sincere service. Beyond the 17 Ionic columns
★ of the neoclassic facade, crystal chandeliers illuminate Georgian antiques and museum-quality 18th- and 19th-century paintings in the lobby. The fitness center is a destination in its own right, with an indoor pool, steam baths, saunas, and a whirlpool. All rooms have feather beds with down comforters. Afternoon tea in the Lobby Lounge—overlooking the beautifully landscaped garden courtyard—is a San Francisco institution. ⊠ *600 Stockton St., at California St., Nob Hill 94108* ☎ *415/296–7465 or 800/241–3333* 🖷 *415/986–1268* ⊕ *www.ritzcarlton.com* ⏎ *294 rooms, 42 suites* ⚕ *2 restaurants, in-room data ports, in-room safes, minibars, cable TV with movies and video games, some in-room VCRs, indoor pool, health club, hot tub, sauna, 3 bars, lobby lounge, dry cleaning, laundry service, concierge, concierge floor, Internet, business services, meeting room, parking (fee), no-smoking floors* ▭ *AE, D, DC, MC, V.*

¢–**$$** ▣ **San Francisco Residence Club.** In contrast to the neighboring showplace hotels, here's a modest guest house with million-dollar views, a money-saving meal plan, and a pleasant garden patio. The building has seen better days, and most of the modest rooms share baths. The international clientele ranges from leisure travelers and business professionals to longer-term residents who take advantage of the full American breakfast *and* dinner, which are included in the daily, weekly, and four-week rate. An advance deposit via check is required. ⊠ *851 California St., Nob Hill 94108* ☎ *415/421–2220* 🖷 *415/421–2335* ⊕ *www.sfresclub. com* ⏎ *84 rooms* ⚕ *Dining room, some refrigerators, laundry facilities; no TV in some rooms* ▭ *No credit cards* ⏐⊙⏐ *MAP.*

Fisherman's Wharf

$$$ ▣ **Tuscan Inn.** The major attraction here is the friendly, attentive staff. The condolike exterior of the hotel—reddish brick with white concrete—gives little indication of the charm of the relatively small, Italy-influenced guest rooms, which have white-pine furniture and floral bedspreads and curtains. Cafe Pescatore, the Italian seafood restaurant off the lobby, provides room service. Morning coffee, tea, and biscotti are complimentary. In the oak-panel lobby, two impressive wooden lions flank a large fireplace. Complimentary limousine service to the Financial District is available. ✉ *425 N. Point St., at Mason St., Fisherman's Wharf 94133* ☎*415/561–1100 or 800/648–4626* 🖷*415/561–1199* ⊕*www.tuscaninn. com* ✍*209 rooms, 12 suites* ⚶ *Restaurant, room service, minibars, room TVs with movies and video games, some in-room VCRs, dry cleaning, laundry service, Internet, meeting room, parking (fee), some pets allowed (fee), no-smoking floors* ☰ *AE, D, DC, MC, V.*

★ **$$** 🖾 **Radisson Hotel at Fisherman's Wharf.** Occupying an entire city block, and part of a complex including 25 shops and restaurants, this is the only bay-front hotel at Fisherman's Wharf and the nearest to Pier 39 and the bay cruise docks. Eighty percent of the rooms have views of the bay and overlook a landscaped courtyard and pool. Rooms are contemporary, cleanly designed, and bright, with black-and-tan striped drapes and cherrywood furniture. ✉ *250 Beach St., Fisherman's Wharf 94133* ☎*415/ 392–6700 or 800/333–3333* 🖷*415/986–7853* ⊕ *www.radisson.com* ✍*355 rooms* ⚶ *3 restaurants, in-room data ports, some refrigerators, cable TV with movies and video games, pool, gym, concierge, business services, parking (fee), no-smoking rooms* ☰ *AE, D, DC, MC, V.*

★ **¢** 🖾 **San Remo Hotel.** This three-story 1906 Italianate Victorian was once home to longshoremen and Beats. A narrow stairway from the street leads to the front desk and labyrinthine hallways. Rooms are small but charming, with antique furnishings. About a third of the rooms have sinks, but all rooms share scrupulously clean black-and-white-tile shower and toilet facilities with pull-chain toilets. ✉ *2237 Mason St., North Beach 94133* ☎ *415/776–8688 or 800/352–7366* 🖷 *415/776–2811* ⊕ *www.sanremohotel.com* ✍ *62 rooms with shared baths* ⚶ *Laundry facilities, Internet, parking (fee); no room phones, no room TVs, no smoking* ☰ *AE, DC, MC, V.*

Pacific Heights & Cow Hollow

$$$$ 🖾 **Sherman House.** A magnificent Italianate mansion at the foot of res-
Fodor'sChoice idential Pacific Heights houses San Francisco's most luxurious small hotel.
★ Rooms have Biedermeier, English Jacobean, or French Second Empire antiques. Tapestrylike canopies over four-poster feather beds, wood-burning fireplaces with marble mantels, and sumptuous bathrooms with whirlpool baths enhance the decadent mood. The six romantic suites attract honeymooners from around the world. Room rates include valet parking, a full breakfast, and evening wine and hors d'oeuvres in the Gallery, a sitting room. ✉ *2160 Green St., Pacific Heights 94123* ☎ *415/563–3600 or 800/424–5777* 🖷*415/563–1882* ⊕*www.theshermanhouse.com* ✍ *8 rooms, 6 suites* ⚶ *Dining room, room service, cable TV, in-room VCRs, piano, concierge, Internet, meeting room, free parking; no a/c, no smoking* ☰ *AE, D, DC, MC, V* ⧉ *BP.*

$$–$$$$ 🖾 **Union Street Inn.** With the help of precious family antiques and unique
Fodor'sChoice artwork, innkeepers Jane Bertorelli and David Coyle turned this green-
★ and-cream-colored 1902 Edwardian into a delightful B&B. Equipped with candles, fresh flowers, and wineglasses, rooms are popular with honeymooners and romantics. The Carriage House, with its own hot tub, is set off from the main house by an old-fashioned English garden with lemon trees. ✉ *2229 Union St., Cow Hollow 94123* ☎ *415/346–0424* 🖷 *415/922–8046* ⊕*www.unionstreetinn.com* ✍*6 rooms* ⚶ *Cable TV, parking (fee); no smoking* ☰ *AE, MC, V* ⧉ *BP.*

$$ 🖾 **Hotel Del Sol.** Once a typical 1950s-style motor court, the Del Sol is now an anything-but-typical artistic statement. The sunny yellow-and-blue, three-story building and courtyard are a riot of stripes. Rooms open onto the courtyard's heated pool and hammock under palm trees and have plantation shutters, tropical-stripe bedspreads, and rattan chairs; some have brick fireplaces. Bathrooms are small. Family suites have child-friendly furnishings and games. ⊠ *3100 Webster St., Cow Hollow 94123* ☎ *415/921–5520 or 877/433–5765* 🖶 *415/931–4137* ⊕ *www. thehoteldelsol.com* 🖵 *47 rooms, 10 suites* ♿ *In-room data ports, in-room safes, some kitchenettes, cable TV with movies, pool, sauna, laundry service, concierge, free parking; no smoking* ▭ *AE, D, DC, MC, V.*

Civic Center/Van Ness

★ **$$$** 🖼 **Inn at the Opera.** Within a block or so of Davies Symphony Hall and the War Memorial Opera House, this hotel has hosted the likes of Luciano Pavarotti and Mikhail Baryshnikov. Beyond the marble-floor lobby, rooms have dark-wood furnishings, bureau drawers lined with sheet music, and queen-sized beds. Standard rooms are quite compact. The sumptuous, dimly lighted Ovation restaurant, where stars congregate before and after performances, is a major attraction. ⊠ *333 Fulton St., Van Ness/Civic Center, 94102* ☎ *415/863–8400 or 800/325–2708* 🖶 *415/861–0821* ⊕ *www.innattheopera.com* 🖵 *30 rooms, 18 suites* ♿ *Restaurant, room service, kitchenettes, cable TV with movies, lobby lounge, concierge, Internet, business services, parking (fee); no a/c, no smoking* ▭ *AE, DC, MC, V* ⦿ *CP.*

★ **$$–$$$** 🖼 **The Archbishop's Mansion.** A chandelier used in the movie *Gone With the Wind* hangs above a 1904 Bechstein grand piano once owned by Noël Coward in this romantic B&B's cavernous common areas. The guest rooms are individually decorated with intricately carved antiques; many have whirlpool tubs or fireplaces. Although it isn't within easy walking distance of many restaurants or attractions, its perch on the corner of Alamo Square near the Painted Ladies—San Francisco's famous Victorian homes—makes for a scenic, relaxed stay. ⊠ *1000 Fulton St., Western Addition/Alamo Sq., 94117* ☎ *415/563–7872 or 800/543–5820* 🖶 *415/885–3193* ⊕ *www.thearchbishopsmansion.com* 🖵 *10 rooms, 5 suites* ♿ *Some fans, in-room data ports, some in-room hot tubs, cable TV, in-room VCRs, piano, meeting room, free parking, no-smoking rooms; no a/c* ▭ *AE, MC, V* ⦿ *CP.*

$–$$
Fodor'sChoice
★ 🖼 **Alamo Square Inn.** Two large houses—an 1895 Queen Anne Victorian and an 1896 Tudor Revival—and a small apartment building form this extravagantly romantic and beautifully cared-for B&B overlooking a terraced, grassy hilltop park for which it is named. The parlors, dining rooms, hallways, and guest rooms in the Queen Anne house have elaborate wainscoting and are filled with period antiques. One suite has peaked ceilings and a sunken whirlpool tub; another has bookcases with hundreds of old volumes and a fireplace. Complimentary wine and tea are served each afternoon in one of the parlors. ⊠ *719 Scott St., at Fulton St., Western Addition 94117* ☎ *415/922–2055 or 800/345–9888* 🖶 *415/931–1304* ⊕ *www.alamoinn.com* 🖵 *9 rooms, 3 suites, 2 apartments* ♿ *Breakfast room, room service (breakfast only), 1 in-room hot tub, some kitchens, cable TV, meeting room, free parking, no smoking* ▭ *AE, MC, V* ⦿ *BP.*

The Airport

$$$$ 🖼 **Hotel Sofitel–San Francisco Bay.** Parisian boulevard lampposts, a métro sign, and a poster-covered kiosk bring an unexpected bit of Paris to this bay-side hotel. The French-theme public spaces—the Gigi Brasserie and La Terrasse bar—have a light, open, airy feeling that extends to the rooms, each of which has pale earth-tone walls and a writing desk. ⊠ *223 Twin Dolphin Dr., Redwood City 94065* ☎ *650/598–9000 or 800/763–4835* 🖶 *650/598–0459* ⊕ *www.hotelsofitelsfbay.com* 🖵 *379 rooms, 42 suites* ♿ *Restaurant, in-room data ports, minibars, room TVs with movies, gym, bar, lobby lounge, laundry service, concierge, Internet, busi-*

ness services, meeting room, airport shuttle, free parking, some pets allowed (fee), no-smoking floors ▭ *AE, DC, MC, V.*

$$–$$$$ ▧ **Hyatt Regency San Francisco Airport.** A spectacular 10-story lobby atrium encompasses 29,000 square foot of this dramatic hotel 2 mi south of the airport. With nearly 800 rooms, this is one of the largest airport convention hotels in Northern California. Almost every service and amenity you can think of are here, including athletic facilities and several dining and entertainment options. Rooms are modern and well equipped. ✉ *1333 Bayshore Hwy., Burlingame 94010* ☎ *650/347–1234* 🖷 *650/696–2669* ⊕ *www.sanfrancisco.hyatt.com* ↩ *767 rooms, 26 suites* ⚑ *Restaurant, café, snack bar, room service, in-room data ports, some in-room fax, cable TV with movies, pool, gym, outdoor hot tub, lobby lounge, sports bar, dry cleaning, laundry service, concierge, Internet, business services, convention center, meeting room, airport shuttle, car rental, parking (fee), no-smoking floors* ▭ *AE, D, DC, MC, V.*

NIGHTLIFE & THE ARTS

Updated by
Sharron Wood

From ultrasophisticated piano bars to come-as-you-are dives that reflect the city's gold-rush past, San Francisco has a tremendous variety of evening entertainment. Enjoy a night out at the opera in the Civic Center area or hit the hip SoMa neighborhood for straight-up rock or retro jazz. Except at some hotel lounges, you're not expected to dress up. Nevertheless, jeans are the exception and stylish dress the norm at most nightspots.

The Arts

The best guide to arts and entertainment events in San Francisco is the "Datebook" section, printed on pink paper, in the *San Francisco Sunday Chronicle.* Also consult any of the free alternative weeklies.

Half-price, same-day tickets for many local and touring stage shows go on sale (cash only) at 11 AM Tuesday through Saturday at the **TIX Bay Area** booth on Union Square (✉ Powell St. between Geary and Post Sts., Union Sq. ☎ 415/433–7827 ⊕ www.theatrebayarea.org/tix/tix.shtml) You can charge tickets for everything from jazz concerts to Giants games by phone through **Tickets.com** (☎ 415/776–1999, 510/762–2277, 800/955–5566 ⊕ tickets.com). **City Box Office** (✉ 180 Redwood St., Suite 100, Civic Center ☎ 415/392–4400 ⊕ www.cityboxoffice.com) has a charge-by-phone service for many concerts and lectures.

Dance

The **San Francisco Ballet,** under artistic director Helgi Tomasson, has won admiring reviews for both classical and contemporary works. Tickets and information are available at the **War Memorial Opera House** (✉ 301 Van Ness Ave., Civic Center ☎ 415/865–2000).

Music

The world-renowned **San Francisco Opera** company, founded in 1923, resides in the Civic Center's War Memorial Opera House. Over its season—September through January and June through July—the opera presents about 70 performances of 10 to 12 operas. ✉ *War Memorial Opera House, 301 Van Ness Ave., Civic Center* ☎ *415/864–3330 tickets* ⊕ *www.sfopera.com.*

The **San Francisco Symphony** performs from September through May, with additional summer performances of light classical musical and show tunes. ✉ *Davies Symphony Hall, 201 Van Ness Ave., Civic Center* ☎ *415/864–6000* ⊕ *www.sfsymphony.org.*

Theater

The city's major nonprofit theater company is the **American Conservatory Theater** (ACT; ✉ 415 Geary St., Union Square ⊕ www.act-sfbay. org), which was founded in the mid-1960s and quickly became one of the nation's leading regional theaters. The ACT ticket office is at 405 Geary Street (☎ 415/749–2228). The leading producer of new plays is the **Magic Theatre** (✉ Fort Mason, Bldg. D, Laguna St. at Marina Blvd., Marina ☎ 415/441–8822 ⊕ www.magictheatre.org). The Magic presents works by rising American playwrights, such as Matthew Wells, Karen Hartman, and Claire Chafee.

Nightlife

For information on who is performing where, check out the *San Francisco Chronicle*'s "Datebook" insert—or consult the *San Francisco Bay Guardian,* free and available in racks around the city, listing neighborhood, avant-garde, and budget-priced events. The *SF Weekly* is also free and packed with information on arts events around town. Another handy reference is the weekly magazine *Where,* offered free in most major hotel lobbies and at Hallidie Plaza (Market and Powell streets).

Bars

The **Beach Chalet** (✉ 1000 Great Hwy., Golden Gate Park ☎ 415/386–8439), in a historic building filled with Works Project Administration murals from the 1930s, has a stunning view overlooking the Pacific Ocean. **Buena Vista Café** (✉ 2765 Hyde St., Fisherman's Wharf ☎ 415/474–5044), the wharf area's most popular bar introduced Irish coffee to the New World—or so it says.

Carnelian Room (✉ 555 California St., Financial District ☎ 415/433–7500), on the 52nd floor of the Bank of America Building, has what is perhaps the loftiest view of San Francisco's magnificent skyline. **Harry Denton's Starlight Room** (✉ Sir Francis Drake Hotel, 450 Powell St., Union Sq. ☎ 415/395–8595), on the 21st floor of the Sir Francis Drake Hotel, re-creates the 1950s high life with rose velvet booths and romantic lighting. Attached to the restaurant Foreign Cinema, **Laszlo** (✉ 2532 Mission St., Mission ☎ 415/401–0810), with a bilevel design, dim lighting, and candles on each table, is a great spot for a romantic tête-à-tête over a classy cocktail or single-malt whisky.

Redwood Room (✉ 495 Geary St., Union Sq. ☎ 415/929–2372), paneled with wood from a 2,000-year-old tree and updated by über-hip designer Philippe Starck, draws a stylish young crowd nightly. You usually have to be on the guest list to get in Thursday through Saturday. **Specs'** (✉ 12 Saroyan Pl., North Beach ☎ 415/421–4112), a hidden hangout for artists, poets, and other heavy drinkers, is worth looking for. The **Tonga Room** (✉ 950 Mason St., Nob Hill ☎ 415/772–5278), on the Fairmont hotel's terrace level, has given San Francisco a taste of high Polynesian kitsch for more than 50 years.

Top of the Mark (✉ 999 California St., Nob Hill ☎ 415/616–6916), in the Mark Hopkins Inter-Continental, was immortalized by a famous magazine photograph as a hot spot for World War II servicemen on leave or about to ship out. **Tosca Café** (✉ 242 Columbus Ave., North Beach ☎ 415/391–1244) has an Italian flavor, with opera, big-band, and Italian standards on the jukebox, plus an antique espresso machine that's nothing less than a work of art. **Vesuvio Café** (✉ 255 Columbus Ave., North Beach ☎ 415/362–3370), near the legendary City Lights Bookstore, has a second-floor balcony that is a fine vantage point for watching the colorful Broadway-Columbus intersection.

Cabaret

At **asiaSF** (⊠ 201 9th St., SoMa ☎ 415/255–2742), the entertainment, as well as gracious food service, is provided by "gender illusionists." These gorgeous men don daring dresses and strut in impossibly high heels on top of the bar, which serves as a catwalk. **Club Fugazi** (⊠ 678 Green St., North Beach ☎ 415/421–4222) is famous for *Beach Blanket Babylon,* a wacky musical send-up that pokes fun at San Francisco moods and mores. Order tickets as far ahead as possible.

Dance Clubs

El Rio (⊠ 3158 Mission St., Mission ☎ 415/282–3325) is a casual spot with a range of acts, from an open mike on Tuesday to Arab dance music on Thursday and a packed world-music dance party on Friday. Live bands play on Saturday. No matter what day you attend, expect to find a diverse crowd. **Roccapulco** (⊠ 3140 Mission St., Mission ☎ 415/648–6611), a cavernous dance hall and restaurant that knows how to bring 'em in, has live music and salsa dancing on Friday and Saturday. Look for salsa lessons on Wednesday. **330 Ritch Street** (⊠ 330 Ritch St., SoMa ☎ 415/541–9574), a popular nightclub with a stylish modern look, has an extensive tapas menu, a dance floor, and extremely varied music lineup; soul, R&B, and Brit pop music are only some of the styles you'll hear here. The club is closed on Monday and Tuesday nights.

Gay & Lesbian Nightlife

MEN **Café Flore** (⊠ 2298 Market St., Castro ☎ 415/621–8579), more of a daytime destination, attracts a mixed crowd, including poets, punks, and poseurs. The **Cinch** (⊠ 1723 Polk St., Van Ness/Polk ☎ 415/776–4162), a Wild West–theme neighborhood bar, has pinball machines, pool tables, and a smoking patio. **Divas** (⊠ 1081 Post St., Tenderloin ☎ 415/928–6006), around the corner from the Polk Street bars in the rough-and-tumble Tenderloin, is *the* place for transvestites, transsexuals, and their admirers, with frequent stage performances.

Eagle Tavern (⊠ 398 12th St., SoMa ☎ 415/626–0880) is one of the few SoMa bars remaining from the days before AIDS and gentrification. Bikers are courted with endless drink specials. **Martuni's** (⊠ 4 Valencia St., Mission ☎ 415/241–0205), an elegant, low-key bar, draws a mixed crowd that enjoys cocktails in a refined environment; variations on the martini are a specialty. **Midnight Sun** (⊠ 4067 18th St., Castro ☎ 415/861–4186), one of the Castro's longest-standing and most popular bars, has giant video screens playing a mix of old sitcoms, *Queer as Folk* episodes, and musicals and show tunes. **The Stud** (⊠ 399 9th St., SoMa ☎ 415/252–7883) is still going strong seven days a week nearly four decades after its opening. Each night's music is different—from funk, soul, and hip-hop to 1980s tunes and disco favorites.

WOMEN The **Lexington Club** (⊠ 3464 19th St., Mission ☎ 415/863–2052) is where, according to its slogan, "every night is ladies' night." This all-girl club is geared toward lesbians in their twenties and thirties.

Jazz

Cafe du Nord (⊠ 2170 Market St., Castro ☎ 415/861–5016) hosts some of the coolest local jazz, blues, rock, and alternative sounds in town. The basement poolroom bar is "speakeasy hip." **Enrico's** (⊠ 504 Broadway, North Beach ☎ 415/982–6223) was the city's hippest North Beach hangout after its 1958 opening. Today it's hip once again, with an indoor-outdoor café, a fine menu (tapas and Italian), and mellow nightly jazz combos.

Moose's (⊠ 1652 Stockton St., North Beach ☎ 415/989–7800), a popular restaurant, also has great music in its small but stylish bar area. Combos play classic jazz nightly from 8 PM, as well as during Sunday brunch.

Piano Bars

The **Big 4 Bar** (⊠ 1075 California St., Nob Hill ☎ 415/474–5400), on the ground floor of the Huntington Hotel, is a quietly opulent spot for piano music daily from about 5 PM to 11:30. The elegant, dimly lit spot has polished wood and brass, green leather chairs, and a carved ceiling. **Ovation** (⊠ 333 Fulton St., Hayes Valley ☎ 415/553–8100), in the Inn at the Opera hotel, is a popular spot for a romantic rendezvous, especially weekends, when the pianist is playing.

At the **Ritz-Carlton Lobby Lounge** (⊠ 600 Stockton St., Nob Hill ☎ 415/296–7465), a harpist plays during high tea (approximately 3–4:30) and a jazz trio plays Saturday nights (9 to 1). **Seasons Bar** (⊠ 757 Market St., SoMa ☎ 415/633–3000) echoes the muted tones and elegant furnishings of the coolly minimalist Four Season Hotel. Discreet staff members in dark suits serve cocktails and salty nibbles while a piano player entertains, usually Tuesday through Saturday evenings.

Rock, Pop, Folk & Blues

Bimbo's 365 Club (⊠ 1025 Columbus Ave., North Beach ☎ 415/474–0365), in the same location since 1951, has a plush main room and an adjacent lounge that retain a retro vibe perfect for the "Cocktail Nation" programming that keeps the crowds entertained. **Boom Boom Room** (⊠ 1601 Fillmore St., Japantown ☎ 415/673–8000) attracts old-timers and hipsters alike with top-notch blues acts. The **Fillmore** (⊠ 1805 Geary Blvd., Western Addition ☎ 415/346–6000), San Francisco's most famous rock music hall, serves up a varied menu of national and local acts: rock, reggae, grunge, jazz, folk, acid house, and more.

Great American Music Hall (⊠ 859 O'Farrell St., Tenderloin ☎ 415/885–0750) has top-drawer entertainment, with acts running the gamut from the best in blues, folk, and jazz to alternative rock.

The **Saloon** (⊠ 1232 Grant Ave., North Beach ☎ 415/989–7666) is a favorite blues and rock spot among North Beach locals in the know. **Slim's** (⊠ 333 11th St., SoMa ☎ 415/522–0333), one of SoMa's most popular nightclubs, specializes in national touring acts—mostly classic rock, blues, jazz, and world music.

SPORTS & THE OUTDOORS

Reviewed by
John Andrew
Vlahides

Temperatures rarely drop below 50°F in San Francisco, so it's no surprise that visitors and residents alike are drawn outdoors. The captivating views are a major part of the appeal, as are the city's 3,500 acres of parks and open spaces. On the best of days, when the fog burns off early, even longtime city dwellers marvel at the sun sparkling on the bay and the cool, crisp air.

Beaches

Nestled in a quiet cove between the lush hills adjoining Fort Mason, Ghirardelli Square, and Fisherman's Wharf, **Aquatic Park** has a tiny, ¼-mi-long sandy beach with gentle water. Facilities include rest rooms and showers. **Baker Beach** has gorgeous views of the Golden Gate Bridge and the Marin Headlands, but the pounding surf makes swimming a dangerous prospect. Picnic tables, grills, rest rooms, and drinking water are available. **China Beach,** one of the city's safest swimming beaches, is a 600-foot strip of sand south of the Presidio and Baker Beach. It

A SHORE THING

SAN FRANCISCO'S BEACHES *are perfect backdrops for romantic sunsets. As for swimming, icy temperatures and treacherous currents make most waters too dangerous. On the occasional summer days when the coastal fog blows out to sea and the mercury rises, locals do head for the shore. Always bring a sweater; even the sunniest of days can become cold and foggy without warning.*

Nestled in a quiet cove between the lush hills adjoining Fort Mason, Ghirardelli Square, and Fisherman's Wharf, **Aquatic Park** *has a tiny, ¼-mi-long sandy beach with gentle water. Its cove and manicured lawns are part of the* San Francisco Maritime National Historic Park *(www.nps.gov/safr). Facilities include rest rooms and showers. Members of the* **Dolphin Club** *(415/441–9329) come every morning for a dip in the ice-cold waters of Aquatic Park. An especially large and raucous crowd braves the cold on New Year's Day.*

Baker Beach *(Gibson Rd., off Bowley St., southwest corner of Presidio), with gorgeous views of the Golden Gate Bridge and the Marin Headlands, is a local favorite. The pounding surf makes swimming a dangerous prospect, but the mile-long shoreline is ideal for fishing, building sand castles, or watching sea lions at play. On warm days, the entire beach is packed with bodies—including nudists at the north end—tanning in the sun. Picnic tables, grills, rest rooms, and drinking water are available. The first weekend of every month, rangers give tours of the 95,000-pound cannon at Battery Chamberlin, overlooking the beach. The 1904 weapon can still spring into firing position.*

China Beach, *one of the city's safest swimming beaches, was named for the poor Chinese fishermen who once camped here. (You may also find it marked on maps as James D. Phelan Beach.) This 600-foot strip of sand, south of the Presidio and Baker Beach, has gentle waters as well as changing rooms, bathrooms, showers, grills, drinking water, and picnic tables. Despite its humble*

beginnings, China Beach today is bordered by the multimillion-dollar homes of the Seacliff neighborhood, including a massive pink structure owned by actor Robin Williams.

Although **Ocean Beach** *isn't the city's cleanest shore, this wide, sandy expanse stretches for more than 3 mi along the Great Highway, south of the Cliff House, making it ideal for long walks and runs. (Rest rooms are at the north end.) You may spot sea lions sunning themselves atop the stony nearby islands, or daredevil surfers riding the roiling waves. Because of extremely dangerous currents, swimming isn't recommended. After the sun sets, bonfires form a string of lights along the beach. You don't need a permit for a fire but are prohibited from building one north of Fulton Street. The* United States Park Police *(415/561–5505) can provide particulars about beach bonfires. You can buy firewood at most supermarkets year-round.*

Less than an hour's drive south of San Francisco on scenic Highway 1 brings you to the popular, 2-mi-long **Half Moon Bay State Beach,** *a great spot for picnics. The best time to explore the tide pools of* **Fitzgerald Marine Reserve** *(650/728–3584 www.fitzgeraldreserve.org), near Montara, a few miles north of Half Moon Bay State Beach, is before and after low tide. (Wear nonslip rubber soles and tread lightly.) For a faster trip back to the city during non–rush hour periods, take Highway 92 east over the mountains to I–280 northbound.*

has gentle waters as well as changing rooms, bathrooms, showers, grills, drinking water, and picnic tables. **Ocean Beach,** south of the Cliff House, isn't the city's cleanest shore, but its wide, sandy expanse stretches for more than 3 mi along the Great Highway, making it ideal for long walks and runs. Because of extremely dangerous currents, swimming isn't recommended. Rest rooms are at the north end.

Baseball

The **San Francisco Giants** play at the downtown bay-front stadium, **Pacific Bell Park,** (✉ 24 Willie Mays Plaza, China Basin ☎ 415/972–2000 or 800/734–4268 ⊕ www.sfgiants.com). **Tickets.com** (☎ 510/762–2255 Baseball Line ⊕ www.tickets.com) sells game tickets. Its Baseball Line charges a $2.50 per-call processing fee; ticket-handling fees may also apply.

Football

The Bay Area is home to two professional football teams. The **San Francisco 49ers** play at **3Com Park,** near the San Mateo County border. (✉ 3Com Park, Jamestown Ave. and Harney Way, Bayview Heights ☎ 415/656–4900 ⊕ www.sf49ers.com). Single-game tickets, available via **Ticketmaster** (☎ 415/421–8497 ⊕ www.ticketmaster.com), almost always sell out far in advance.

SHOPPING

Shopping Neighborhoods

Updated by
Sharron Wood

The Castro. Often called the gay capital of the world, it's also a major shopping destination for nongay travelers, filled with men's clothing boutiques, home-accessories stores, and various specialty shops.

Chinatown. The intersection of Grant Avenue and Bush Street marks the gateway to 24 blocks of shops, restaurants, and markets. Dominating the exotic cityscape are the sights and smells of food: crates of bok choy, tanks of live crabs, and hanging whole chickens. Racks of Chinese silks, toy trinkets, colorful pottery, baskets, and carved figurines are displayed chockablock on the sidewalks.

Fisherman's Wharf. Sightseers crowd this area and with good reason: Pier 39, the Anchorage, Ghirardelli Square, and the Cannery. Each has shops and restaurants, as well as outdoor entertainment—musicians, mimes, and magicians. Best of all are the wharf's view of the bay and its proximity to cable-car lines, which can shuttle shoppers directly to Union Square.

The Haight. Haight Street is a perennial attraction for visitors, if only to see the sign at Haight and Ashbury streets—the geographic center of the Flower Power movement during the 1960s. These days chain stores such as Gap and Ben & Jerry's have taken over large storefronts near the famous intersection, but it's still possible to find high-quality vintage clothing, funky shoes, and folk art from around the world in this always-busy neighborhood.

Jackson Square. A dozen or so of San Francisco's finest retail antiques dealers, many of which occupy Victorian-era buildings, are here on the northeastern edge of the Financial District.

North Beach. Although this area is sometimes compared to New York City's Greenwich Village, it's only a fraction of the size, clustered tightly around Washington Square and Columbus Avenue. Most of its businesses are small eateries, cafés, and shops selling clothing, antiques, and vintage wares.

Pacific Heights. Residents seeking fine items for their luxurious homes head straight for Fillmore Street between Post Street and Pacific Avenue, and Sacramento Street between Lyon and Maple streets, where private residences alternate with fine clothing and gift shops and housewares stores.
SoMa. High San Francisco rents mean there aren't many discount outlets in the city, but a few do exist in the semi-industrial zone south of Market Street. At the other end of the spectrum is the gift shop of the San Francisco Museum of Modern Art, which sells books, handmade ceramics, art-related games, and other great gift items.
Union Square. Serious shoppers head straight to San Francisco's main shopping area and the site of most department stores, as well as the Virgin Megastore, the Disney Store, Borders Books and Music, and Frette. Nearby are the pricey international boutiques of Alfred Dunhill, Cartier, Emporio Armani, Gucci, Hermès of Paris, Louis Vuitton, and Versace.

Malls & Department Stores

Crocker Galleria. Forty or so mostly upscale shops and restaurants a few blocks east of Union Square are housed in this complex beneath a glass dome. ⊠ *50 Post St., at Kearny St., Financial District* ☎ *415/393–1505.*
Embarcadero Center. Shops, restaurants, and a popular movie theater—plus the Hyatt Regency hotel—are in the center's five modern towers. Most of the stores are branches of upscale national chains, like Ann Taylor, Banana Republic, and housewares giant Pottery Barn. It's one of the few major shopping centers with an underground parking garage. ⊠ *Clay and Sacramento Sts. between Battery and Drumm Sts.,* ☎ *415/ 772–0734.*
Japan Center. The three-block complex includes an 800-car public garage and three shop-filled buildings. Especially worthwhile are the Kintetsu and Kinokuniya buildings, where shops and showrooms sell bonsai trees, antique kimonos, and *tansu* (Japanese chests). ⊠ *Between Laguna, Fillmore, and Post Sts. and Geary Blvd.* ☎ *No phone.*
Gump's. Stocked with large decorative vases, ornate Asian-inspired furniture, and extravagant jewelry, this airy store exudes a museumlike aura. Luxurious bed linens are tucked away upstairs. ⊠ *135 Post St., between Grant Ave. and Kearny St., Union Sq.* ☎ *415/982–1616.*
Macy's. Downtown has two behemoth branches of this retailer. One—with entrances on Geary, Stockton, and O'Farrell streets—houses the women's, children's, furniture, and housewares departments. The men's department occupies its own building, across Stockton Street. ⊠ *170 O'Farrell St., at Stockton St., Union Sq.* ☎ *415/397–3333* ⊠ *Men's branch:* ⊠ *50 O'-Farrell St. (entrance on Stockton St.), Union Sq.* ☎ *415/397–3333.*
Neiman Marcus. The surroundings, which include a Philip Johnson–designed checkerboard facade, gilded atrium, and stained-glass skylight, are as high class as the goods showcased in them. The mix includes designer men's and women's clothing and accessories as well as posh household wares. ⊠ *150 Stockton St., at Geary Blvd., Union Sq.* ☎ *415/ 362–3900.*
Nordstrom. This service-oriented store specializes in designer fashions, accessories, cosmetics, and, most notably, shoes. The space, with spiral escalators circling a four-story atrium, is stunning. ⊠ *San Francisco Shopping Centre, 865 Market St., between 4th and 5th Sts., Union Sq.* ☎ *415/243–8500.*
San Francisco Shopping Centre. The center, across from the cable-car turnaround at Powell and Market streets, has spiral escalators that wind up through the sunlit atrium. Inside are 65 retailers, including Nordstrom and Godiva. ⊠ *865 Market St., between 4th and 5th Sts., Union Sq.* ☎ *415/495–5656.*

Saks Fifth Avenue. A central escalator ascends past a series of designer boutiques, which give Saks the feel of an exclusive multilevel mall. ⊠ *384 Post St., at Powell St., Union Sq.* ☎ *415/986–4300.*

SIDE TRIPS FROM SAN FRANCISCO

Updated by
Lisa M.
Hamilton &
Denise M. Leto

One of San Francisco's best assets is its surroundings. To the north is Marin County, where the lively waterfront town of Sausalito has bougainvillea-covered hillsides, an expansive yacht harbor, and an artists' colony. To the east is Berkeley, a colorful university town. Explore a bit beyond the city limits and you're bound to discover what makes the Bay Area such a coveted place to live.

Sausalito

Like much of San Francisco, Sausalito had a raffish reputation before it went upscale. The town served as a port for whaling ships during the 19th century. By the mid-1800s wealthy San Franciscans were making Sausalito their getaway across the bay. They built lavish Victorian summer homes in the hills, many of which still stand. In 1875 the railroad from the north connected with ferryboats to San Francisco, bringing the merchant and working classes with it. This influx of hardworking, fun-loving folk polarized the town into "wharf rats" and "hill snobs," and the waterfront area grew thick with saloons, gambling dens, and bordellos.

Sausalito developed its bohemian flair in the 1950s and '60s, when a group of artists established a houseboat community here. Today more than 450 houseboats are docked in Sausalito, which has since also become a major yachting center. The ferry is the best way to get to Sausalito from San Francisco; you get more romance (and less traffic) and disembark in the heart of downtown.

The U.S. Army Corps of Engineers uses the **Bay Model,** a 400-square-foot replica of the entire San Francisco Bay and the San Joaquin–Sacramento River delta, to reproduce the rise and fall of tides, the flow of currents, and the other physical forces at work on the bay. ⊠ *2100 Bridgeway, at Marinship Way* ☎ *415/332–3870* ⊕ *www.spn.usace.army.mil/bmvc* ☎ *Free* ☉ *Memorial Day–Labor Day, Tues.–Fri. 9–4, weekends 10–5; rest of yr. Tues.–Sat. 9–4.*

The **Bay Area Discovery Museum** fills five former military buildings with entertaining and enlightening hands-on exhibits related to science and the arts. Kids and their families can fish from a boat at the indoor wharf, explore the skeleton of a house, and make multitrack recordings. From San Francisco take the Alexander Avenue exit from U.S. 101 and follow signs to East Fort Baker. ⊠ *557 McReynolds Rd., at East Fort Baker* ☎ *415/487–4398* ⊕ *www.badm.org* ☎ *$7* ☉ *Tues.–Fri. 9–4, weekends 10–5.*

Freight and Salvage Coffee House is one of the finest folk houses in the country. Some of the most talented practitioners of folk, blues, Cajun, and bluegrass perform in this alcohol-free space. ⊠ *1111 Addison St.* ☎ *510/548–1761.*

Where to Stay & Eat

$$–$$$ ✕ **Ondine.** Jutting into the bay with clear views of San Francisco and Angel Island, this second-story restaurant is romantic for dinner or Sunday brunch. The kitchen pays careful attention to its ingredients and comes up with unusual combinations, such as English pea-and–morel soup with crème fraîche and macadamia nuts. There are a few traditional meat entrées, but the best dishes are fashioned from the menu's cornerstones: handpicked seafood and seasonal produce. ☒ *558 Bridgeway Ave.* ☏ *415/331–1133* ⌕ *Reservations essential* ☰ *AE, DC, MC, V* ☺ *No lunch.*

¢ ✕ **Bayside Cafe.** Members of the nearby houseboat community regularly patronize this dependable coffee shop steps from the bay. The breakfast menu is long, filled with dozens of egg dishes, waffles, pancakes, and combos. All kinds of sandwiches, salads, pastas, and burgers constitute the lunch listings, available until 4 PM. ☒ *1 Gate 6 Rd.* ☏ *415/331–2313* ☰ *AE, D, DC, MC, V* ☺ *No dinner.*

$$$$ ⌂ **Casa Madrona.** What began as a small inn with a handful of historic accommodations in a 19th-century landmark house has expanded over the decades to incorporate a variety of accommodations and a top-notch spa, all tiered down the hill in the center of town. The design in the original rooms and suites ranges from the cutesiness of what's called the Artist's Loft to elegant Mediterranean and Asia-inspired motifs. ☒ *801 Bridgeway, 94965* ☏ *415/332–0502 or 800/567–9524* ⎙ *415/332–2537* ⊕ *www.casamadrona.com* ⋙ *63 rooms, 14 suites* ⌕ *Restaurant, in-room data ports, minibars, cable TV, hot tub, spa* ☰ *AE, D, DC, MC, V* ◉ *CP.*

$$–$$$ ⌂ **Hotel Sausalito.** Soft yellow, green, and orange tones create a warm Mediterranean feel at this well-run inn with handmade furniture and tasteful original art and reproductions. The rooms, some of which have harbor or park views, range from small ones that are good for budget-minded travelers to commodious suites. ☒ *16 El Portal, 94965* ☏ *415/332–0700 or 888/442–0700* ⎙ *415/332–8788* ⊕ *www.hotelsausalito. com* ⋙ *14 rooms, 2 suites* ⌕ *In-room data ports, cable TV, concierge, no-smoking rooms* ☰ *AE, DC, MC, V* ◉ *CP.*

Berkeley

Although Berkeley has grown alongside the University of California, which dominates its history and contemporary life, the university and the town are not synonymous. The city of 100,000 facing San Francisco across the bay has other interesting attributes. It's culturally diverse and politically adventurous, a breeding ground for social trends, a bastion of the counterculture, and an important center for Bay Area writers, artists, and musicians.

The **Berkeley Visitor Information Center** (☒ University Hall, Room 101, 2200 University Ave., at Oxford St. ☏ 510/642–5215) is the starting point for the free, student-guided tours of the campus, which last 1½ hours and start at 10 on weekdays.

The **University of California Berkeley Art Museum** has an interesting collection of works that spans five centuries, with an emphasis on contemporary art. Changing exhibits line the spiral ramps and balcony galleries. Don't miss the museum's series of vibrant paintings by abstract expressionist Hans Hofmann. ☒ *2626 Bancroft Way* ☏ *510/642–0808, 510/642–1124 film-program information* ⊕ *www.bampfa.berkeley.edu* ▦ *$6* ☺ *Wed.–Sun. 11–7.*

About 13,500 species of plants from all over the world flourish in the 34-acre **University of California Botanical Garden**—thanks to Berkeley's temperate climate. Informative tours of the garden are given weekends at 1:30. Free garden tours, given Thursday, Saturday, and Sunday at 1:30, are informative. Benches and shady picnic tables make this a relaxing alternative to the busy main campus. ☒ *200 Centennial Dr.* ☏ *510/643–2755* ⊕ *www.mip.berkeley.edu/garden* ▦ *$3, free Thurs.* ☺ *Memorial*

Day–Labor Day, Mon.–Tues. 9–5 and Wed.–Sun. 9–8; rest of yr. daily 9–5. Closed 1st Tues. of month.

☉ The fortresslike **Lawrence Hall of Science**, a dazzling hands-on science center, lets kids look at insects under microscopes, solve crimes using chemical forensics, and explore the physics of baseball. ✉ *Centennial Dr. near Grizzly Peak Blvd.* ☎ *510/642–5132* ⊕ *www.lawrencehallofscience.org* ▭ *$8* ☉ *Daily 10–5.*

Where to Stay & Eat

$$$$ ✗ **Chez Panisse Café & Restaurant.** The downstairs portion of Alice Wa-
Fodor'sChoice   ters's legendary eatery is noted for its formality and personal service.
★   Here, the daily-changing multi-course dinners are prix-fixe and pricey. Upstairs, in the informal café, the crowd is livelier, the prices are lower, and the ever-changing menu is à la carte. The food is simpler, too: penne with new potatoes, arugula, and sheep's-milk cheese or fresh figs with Parmigiano-Reggiano cheese and arugula. ✉ *1517 Shattuck Ave., north of University Ave.* ☎ *510/548–5525 restaurant, 510/548–5049 café* ⌕ *Reservations essential* ▭ *AE, D, DC, MC, V* ☉ *Closed Sun.*

$$–$$$ ✗ **Café Rouge.** You can recover from 4th Street shopping in this spacious two-story bistro, complete with zinc bar, skylights, and festive lanterns. The short, seasonal menu ranges from sophisticated rack of lamb and juniper berry–cured pork chops to homey spit-roasted chicken or pork loin. ✉ *1782 4th St.* ☎ *510/525–1440* ▭ *MC, V* ☉ *No dinner Mon.*

$$ ✗ **Rivoli.** Italian-inspired dishes using fresh, mostly organic California ingredients star on a menu that changes every three weeks. Typical meals include fresh line-caught fish, pastas, and inventive dishes such as its trademark Portobello mushroom fritters with aioli. ✉ *1539 Solano Ave.* ☎ *510/526–2542* ⌕ *Reservations essential* ▭ *AE, D, DC, MC, V* ☉ *No lunch.*

¢–$ ✗ **Bette's Oceanview Diner.** Buttermilk pancakes are just one of the specialties at this 1930s-inspired diner, complete with checkered floors and burgundy booths. The wait for a seat can be long. If you're starving, Bette's to Go, next door, offers takeout. ✉ *1807 4th St.* ☎ *510/644–3230* ⌕ *Reservations not accepted* ▭ *MC, V* ☉ *No dinner.*

$$$$ ▤ **Claremont Resort and Spa.** The hotel beckons like a gleaming white
Fodor'sChoice   castle in the hills. Traveling executives come for the business amenities,
★   including 40 rooms outfitted with computer terminals, T-1 Internet connections, and guest e-mail addresses. The Claremont also shines for leisure travelers, drawing in honeymooners and families alike with its luxurious suites, therapeutic massages, and personalized yoga workouts at the on-site spa. You can drop your kids at the kids' club. ✉ *41 Tunnel Rd., at Ashby and Domingo Aves., 94705* ☎ *510/843–3000 or 800/323–7500* ▦ *510/843–6629* ⊕ *www.claremontresort.com* ⇔ *282 rooms* ⌕ *3 restaurants, in-room data ports, some minibars, some refrigerators, cable TV with movies, 10 tennis courts, 2 pools, health club, spa, 2 bars, children's programs (ages 6 wks–10 yrs), dry cleaning, concierge, Internet, business services, meeting rooms, parking (fee), no-smoking floor* ▭ *AE, D, DC, MC, V.*

$$–$$$$ ▤ **Hotel Durant.** Long the mainstay of parents visiting their children at U.C. Berkeley, the hotel is a good option for those who want to be a short walk from campus and from the restaurants and shops of Telegraph Avenue. Rooms, accented with dark woods set against tame shades of green and mauve, are small without feeling cramped. The hotel bar, Henry's, is where U.C. Berkeley sports fans congregate after football games. ✉ *2600 Durant Ave., 94704* ☎ *510/845–8981* ▦ *510/486–8336* ⊕ *www.hoteldurant.com* ⇔ *135 rooms, 5 suites* ⌕ *Restaurant, room service, cable TV with movies, bar, dry cleaning, laundry service,* *concierge, business services, meeting room, parking (fee), no-smoking rooms* ▤ *AE, D, DC, MC, V.*

$–$$ ▦ **French Hotel.** The only hotel in north Berkeley, this three-story brick structure has a certain *pensione* feel. Its 18 rooms have pastel or brick walls and modern touches such as white wire baskets in lieu of dressers. Balconies make the rooms seem larger than their modest dimensions. A ground-floor café buzzes day and night with aging intellectuals and other denizens of the Gourmet Ghetto. ⊠ *1538 Shattuck Ave., 94709* ☎ *510/548–9930* 🖷 *510/548–9930* ⇩ *18 rooms* ⚫ *Room service, concierge; no a/c* ▤ *AE, D, DC, MC, V.*

SAN FRANCISCO A TO Z

To research prices, get advice from other travelers, and book travel arrangements, visit ⊕ *www.fodors.com*

AIR TRAVEL

Heavy fog is infamous for causing chronic delays into and out of San Francisco. If you're heading to the East Bay, make every effort to fly into the Oakland airport. The Oakland airport, which is easy to navigate and accessible by public transit, is a good alternative to San Francisco International Airport. Of the major carriers, Alaska, America West, American, Continental, Delta, Southwest, United, and US Airways fly into both Oakland and San Francisco. Northwest flies into San Francisco only. Midwest Express and Frontier Airlines, two smaller carriers, both fly into San Francisco. *See* Air Travel *in* Smart Travel Tips A to Z for airline phone numbers.

AIRPORTS & TRANSFERS

The major gateway to San Francisco is San Francisco International Airport (SFO), off U.S. 101 15 mi south of the city. Oakland Airport (OAK) is across the bay, not much farther away from downtown San Francisco (via I–880 and I–80), but rush-hour traffic on the Bay Bridge may lengthen travel times.

🎦 **San Francisco International Airport (SFO)** ☎ 650/761–0800 ⊕ www.flysfo.com. **Oakland International Airport (OAK)** ☎ 510/577–4000 ⊕ www.flyoakland.com.

TRANSFERS **From San Francisco International Airport:** A taxi ride to downtown costs about $35. Airport shuttles are inexpensive and generally efficient. The SFO Airporter ($12.50) picks up passengers at baggage claim (lower level) and serves selected downtown hotels. Lorrie's Airport Shuttle and SuperShuttle both stop at the upper-level traffic islands and take you anywhere within the city limits of San Francisco. They charge $12.50 to $17, depending on your destination. Inexpensive shuttles to the East Bay, such as Bayporter Express, also depart from the upper-level traffic islands; expect to pay around $30. The least expensive way to get to San Francisco is via SamTrans Bus 292 (55 minutes, $2.50) and KX (35 minutes, $3.50; only one small carry-on bag permitted), or by taking Bus BX to the Colma BART train station. Board the SamTrans buses at the north end of the lower level. A BART extension connects SFO to downtown San Francisco directly; the trip from the International Terminal takes 29 minutes.

From Oakland International Airport: A taxi to downtown San Francisco costs $35 to $40. Bayporter Express and other shuttles serve major hotels and provide door-to-door service to the East Bay and San Francisco. Marin Door to Door serves Marin County for a flat $50 fee. The best way to get to San Francisco via public transit is to take the AIR BART bus ($2) to the Coliseum/Oakland International Airport BART station

(BART fares vary depending on where you're going; the ride to downtown San Francisco costs $2.75).

🔢 Taxis & Shuttles **American Airporter** ☎ 415/202-0733. **Bayporter Express** ☎ 415/467-1800. **East Bay Express Airporter** ☎ 510/547-0404. **Lorrie's Airport Shuttle** ☎ 415/334-9000. **Marin Door to Door** ☎ 415/457-2717. **SamTrans** ☎ 800/660-4287. **SFO Airporter** ☎ 800/532-8405 or 650/624-0500. **South & East Bay Airport Shuttle** ☎ 408/559-9477. **SuperShuttle** ☎ 415/558-8500 or 800/258-3826. **VIP Airport Shuttle** ☎ 408/885-1800 or 800/235-8847.

BOAT & FERRY TRAVEL

Blue & Gold Fleet ferries depart daily for Sausalito from Pier 41 at Fisherman's Wharf. Golden Gate Ferry crosses the bay to Sausalito from the south wing of the San Francisco Ferry Building on the Embarcadero. The trip to Sausalito takes 30 minutes.

🔢 **Blue & Gold Fleet** ☎ 415/705-5555 ⊕ www.blueandgoldfleet.com. **Golden Gate Ferry** ☎ 415/923-2000 ⊕ www.transitinfo.org.

BUS TRAVEL TO & FROM SAN FRANCISCO

Greyhound, the only long-distance bus company serving San Francisco, operates buses to and from most major cities in the country. Outside the city, AC Transit serves the East Bay, and Golden Gate Transit serves Marin County.

🔢 **AC Transit** ☎ 510/839-2882 ⊕ www.actransit.org. **Golden Gate Transit** ☎ 415/923-2000 ⊕ www.goldengate.org. **Greyhound** ✉ 425 Mission St. ☎ 415/495-1569 or 800/231-2222 ⊕ www.greyhound.com.

BUS & TRAIN TRAVEL WITHIN SAN FRANCISCO

BART: Bay Area Rapid Transit (BART) trains reach Oakland, Berkeley, Concord, Richmond, Fremont, Martinez, and Dublin/Pleasanton. Trains also travel south from San Francisco as far as Daly City and Colma. The BART-SFO Extension Project, under construction at this writing and scheduled for completion in 2003, will connect downtown San Francisco to the San Francisco International Airport. Fares range from $1.10 to $4.70; trains run until midnight.

CalTrain: CalTrain connects San Francisco to Palo Alto, San Jose, Santa Clara, and many smaller cities en route. In San Francisco, trains leave from the main depot, at 4th and King streets, and a rail-side stop at 22nd and Pennsylvania streets. One-way fares run $1.50 to $7.25. Trips last 1–1½ hours.

Muni: The San Francisco Municipal Railway, or Muni, operates light-rail vehicles, the historic streetcar line along Fisherman's Wharf and Market Street, trolley buses, and the world-famous cable cars. On buses and streetcars, the fare is $1. Exact change is required, and dollar bills are accepted in the fare boxes. For all Muni vehicles other than cable cars, 90-minute transfers are issued free upon request at the time the fare is paid. Transfers are valid for two additional transfers in any direction. Cable cars cost $2 and include no transfers.

🔢 **Bay Area Rapid Transit** ☎ 650/992-2278 ⊕ www.bart.gov. **CalTrain** ☎ 800/660-4287 ⊕ www.caltrain.com. **San Francisco Municipal Railway System** (Muni) ☎ 415/673-6864 ⊕ www.sfmuni.com.

CAR RENTAL

All of the national car-rental companies have offices at the San Francisco and Oakland airports. *See* Car Rental *in* Smart Travel Tips A to Z for national rental agency phone numbers.

CAR TRAVEL

Driving in San Francisco can be a challenge because of the hills, one-way streets, and traffic. Although "rush hour" is 6 to 10 AM and 3 to 7 PM, you can hit gridlock on any day at any time, especially over the Bay Bridge and leaving and/or entering the city from the south. Sunday afternoon traffic can be heavy as well.

PARKING Remember to curb your wheels when parking on hills—turn wheels away from the curb when facing uphill, toward the curb when facing downhill. On certain streets, parking is forbidden during rush hours. Look for the warning signs; illegally parked cars are towed. Downtown parking lots are often full and most are expensive. Large hotels often have parking available, but it doesn't come cheap; many charge as much as $40 a day for the privilege.

EMERGENCIES

In an emergency dial 911.

▪ Doctors and Dentists **California Pacific Center Physician Referral Service** ☎ 415/600-5333. **San Francisco Dental Society Referral Service** ☎ 415/421-1435.

▪ 24-Hour Pharmacies **Walgreens Drug Store** ✉ 498 Castro ☎ 415/861-3136 ✉ 3201 Divisadero St. ☎ 415/931-6417.

LODGING

The San Francisco Convention and Visitors Bureau publishes a free lodging guide with a map and listings of San Francisco and Bay Area hotels. You can also reserve a room, by phone or via the Internet, at more than 60 bureau-recommended hotels. San Francisco Reservations can arrange reservations at more than 200 Bay Area hotels, often at special discounted rates.

▪ **San Francisco Convention and Visitors Bureau** ☎ 415/391-2000 general information, 415/283-0177 or 888/782-9673 lodging service ⊕ www.sfvisitor.org. **San Francisco Reservations** ☎ 800/677-1500 ⊕ www.hotelres.com.

TAXIS

Taxi service is notoriously bad in San Francisco, and hailing a cab can be frustratingly difficult in some parts of the city, especially on weekends. In a pinch, hotel taxi stands are an option, as is calling ahead for a pickup. But be forewarned: taxi companies frequently don't answer the phone in peak periods. Taxis in San Francisco charge $2.85 for the first ⅕ of a mile, 45¢ for each additional ⅕ mile, and 45¢ per minute in stalled traffic. There is no charge for additional passengers; there is no surcharge for luggage.

▪ Taxi Companies **City Wide Cab** ☎ 415/920-0700. **DeSoto Cab** ☎ 415/970-1300. **Luxor Cab** ☎ 415/282-4141. **Veteran's Taxicab** ☎ 415/552-1300. **Yellow Cab** ☎ 415/626-2345.

TOURS

ORIENTATION TOURS In addition to bus and van tours of the city, most tour companies run excursions to various Bay Area and Northern California destinations such as Marin County. City tours generally last 3½ hours and cost $28–$37. Golden Gate Tours offers a combination bay cruise and city tour ($40) as well as standard city tours in vans or buses. San Francisco Sightseeing (Gray Line) offers bay cruises combined with city tours, using large motor coaches and motorized cable cars ($15–$37); Great Pacific Tours conducts city tours in passenger vans that seat fewer people (starting at $37).

▪ Tour Companies **Golden Gate Tours** ☎ 415/788-5775. **Great Pacific Tour** ☎ 415/626-4499 ⊕ www.greatpacifictour.com. **San Francisco Sightseeing** ☎ 415/558-9400 ⊕ www.graylinesanfrancisco.com.

WALKING TOURS The best way to see San Francisco is to hit the streets. Tours of various San Francisco neighborhoods generally cost $15–$40. Some tours explore culinary themes, such as Chinese food or coffeehouses: lunch and snacks are often included. Others focus on architecture or history.

🎇 Architecture Tours **"Victorian Home Walk"** 🖷 415/252-9485 ⊕ www.victorianwalk. com.

🎇 Culinary Tours **"Chinatown with the Wok Wiz"** 🖷 415/981-8989 ⊕ www.wokwiz. com. **"Javawalk"** 🖷 415/673-9255 ⊕ www.javawalk.com.

🎇 General Interest Tours **San Francisco Convention and Visitors Bureau** 🖷 415/391-2000 ⊕ www.sfcvb.org. **City Guides** 🖷 415/557-4266 ⊕ www.sfcityguides.org.

🎇 Historic Tours **Chinese Culture Center** 🖷 415/986-1822 ⊕ www.c-c-c.org. **Trevor Hailey** 🖷 415/550-8110 ⊕ www.webcastro.com/castrotour.

TRAIN TRAVEL TO & FROM SAN FRANCISCO

Amtrak trains travel to San Francisco and the Bay Area from different cities in California and the United States. The *Coast Starlight* travels north from Los Angeles to Seattle, passing the Bay Area along the way. Amtrak also has several inland routes between San Jose, Oakland, and Sacramento. The *California Zephyr* route travels from Chicago to the Bay Area. San Francisco doesn't have an Amtrak station, but there is one in Emeryville, just over the Bay Bridge, as well as in Oakland. A free shuttle operates between these two stations and the Ferry Building, the Cal-Train station, and several other points in downtown San Francisco.

🎇 Amtrak 🖷 800/872-7245 ⊕ www.amtrak.com.

VISITOR INFORMATION

🎇 **Berkeley Convention and Visitors Bureau** ✉ 2015 Center St., 1st floor, Berkeley 94704 🖷 800/847-4823, 800/220-5747 fax-on-demand service, 510/549-7040 ⊕ www. berkeleycvb.com. **San Francisco Convention and Visitors Bureau** 🗁 Box 429097, San Francisco 94142-9097 ✉ lower level of Hallidie Plaza 🖷 415/391-2000 or 415/974-6900 ⊕ www.sfvisitor.org. **Sausalito Visitor Center** ✉ 780 Bridgeway, 94965 🖷 415/332-0505 ⊕ www.sausalito.org.

THE WINE COUNTRY

2

FODOR'S CHOICE

Auberge du Soleil, *hotel in Rutherford*

Clos Pegase, *Calistoga winery*

Copia: The American Center for Wine, Food & the Arts, *Napa*

French Laundry, *Yountville restaurant*

Gaige House Inn, *Glen Ellen*

Niebaum-Coppola Estate, *winery in Rutherford*

Thistle Dew Inn, *Sonoma*

HIGHLY RECOMMENDED

SIGHTS   Beringer Vineyards, *St. Helena*

Frog's Leap, *Rutherford*

Hess Collection Winery and Vineyards, *Napa*

Hop Kiln Winery, *Healdsburg*

Matanzas Creek Winery, *Santa Rosa*

Many other great hotels and restaurants enliven the Wine Country. For other favorites, look for the black stars as you read this chapter.

Updated by
Sharron Wood

IN 1862, AFTER AN EXTENSIVE TOUR of the wine-producing areas of Europe, Count Agoston Haraszthy de Mokcsa reported a promising prognosis about his adopted California: "Of all the countries through which I passed, not one possessed the same advantages that are to be found in California. . . . California can produce as noble and generous a wine as any in Europe; more in quantity to the acre, and without repeated failures through frosts, summer rains, hailstorms, or other causes."

The "dormant resources" that the father of California's viticulture saw in the balmy days and cool nights of the temperate Napa and Sonoma valleys have come to fruition today. The wines produced here are praised and savored by connoisseurs throughout the world. The area also continues to be a proving ground for the latest techniques of grape growing and wine making.

Ever more competitive, vintners constantly hone their skills, aided by the scientific expertise of graduates of the nearby University of California at Davis and by the practical knowledge of the grape growers. They experiment with high-density vineyard planting, canopy management (to control the amount of sunlight that reaches the grapes), and filtration of the wine.

For many, wine making is a second career. Any would-be wine maker can rent the cumbersome, costly machinery needed to stem and press the grapes. Many say making wine is a good way to turn a large fortune into a small one, but that hasn't deterred the doctors, former college professors, publishing tycoons, art dealers, and others who come here to try their hand at it.

In 1975 Napa Valley had no more than 20 wineries; today there are more than 240. In Sonoma County, where the web of vineyards is looser, there are well over 150 wineries, and development is now claiming the cool Carneros region, at the head of the San Francisco Bay, deemed ideal for growing the chardonnay grape. Nowadays many individual grape growers produce their own wines instead of selling their grapes to larger wineries. As a result, smaller "boutique" wineries harvest excellent, reasonably priced wines that have caught the attention of connoisseurs and critics, while the larger wineries consolidate land and expand their varietals.

This state-of-the-art viticulture has also given rise to a gastronomic renaissance. Inspired by the creative spirit that produces the region's great wines, esteemed chefs are opening restaurants in record numbers, making culinary history in the process.

In addition to great food and wine, you'll find a wealth of California history in the Wine Country. The town of Sonoma is filled with remnants of Mexican California and the solid, ivy-covered, brick wineries built by Haraszthy and his followers. Calistoga is a virtual museum of Steamboat Gothic architecture, replete with the fretwork and clapboard beloved of gold-rush prospectors and late 19th-century spagoers. A later architectural fantasy, the beautiful art-nouveau mansion of the Beringer brothers, is in St. Helena, and the postmodern extravaganza of Clos Pegase is in Calistoga.

The area's natural beauty draws a continuous flow of tourists—from the spring, when the vineyards bloom yellow with wild mustard, to the fall, when the grapes are ripe. Haraszthy was right: this is a chosen place.

Exploring the Wine Country

The Wine Country is composed of two main areas—the Napa Valley and the Sonoma Valley—but also includes the Carneros district, which strad-

Because the Wine Country is expansive, and traveling between the Napa and Sonoma valleys usually requires a winding drive through a small mountain range, it's best to plan shorter, separate trips over the course of several days. You can get a feel for the area's towns and vineyards by taking to the open road over a weekend. Along the way you can stop at a winery or two, have a picnic lunch, and watch the countryside glide past your windshield. Four or five days gives you enough time to explore more towns and wineries and also indulge in dining adventures. You might even bike the Silverado Trail or fish the Russian River. A full week allows time for all of the above, plus pampering at the region's hot springs and mud baths, a round of golf, and a hot-air balloon ride.

2

**If you have
2 days**

Start at the circa-1857 **Buena Vista Carneros Winery** ㉟ ► just outside Sonoma. From there, take Highway 12 north to the Trinity Road/Oakville Grade. Drive east over the Mayacamas Mountains, taking time to admire the views as you descend into the Napa Valley. Take Highway 29 north into historic ⊠ **St. Helena** for lunch. After lunch in St. Helena, take the 30-minute tour of **Beringer Vineyards** ㉔. The next day continue up 29 North to **Calistoga** for an early-morning balloon ride, an afternoon trip to the mud baths, and a visit to **Clos Pegase** ㉚ before heading back to St. Helena for dinner at Greystone—the Culinary Institute of America's beautiful West Coast campus and highly acclaimed restaurant.

**If you have
4 days**

Concentrate on the Napa Valley, starting at Yountville and traveling north to Calistoga. Make your first stop in **Oakville** ►, where the circa-1880s Oakville Grocery—once a Wells Fargo Pony Express stop—is indisputably the most popular place for picnic supplies and an espresso. Enjoy the picnic grounds at **Robert Mondavi** ⑭ before touring the winery and tasting the wine. If time permits, spend the night in the town of ⊠ **Rutherford** and visit either **Rutherford Hill Winery** ㉑ or the **Niebaum-Coppola Estate** ⑮, or continue north to ⊠ **St. Helena.** Take a look at the Silverado Museum and visit the shopping complex surrounding the **Freemark Abbey Winery** ㉕. On the third day drive to ⊠ **Calistoga** for a balloon ride before heading north to Old Faithful Geyser of California; then continue on to Robert Louis Stevenson State Park, which encompasses the summit of Mt St. Helena. On the fourth day take Highway 29 just north of Calistoga proper, head west on Petrified Forest Road, and then go south on Calistoga Road, which runs into Highway 12. Follow Highway 12 southeast to rustic **Glen Ellen** for a taste of the Sonoma Valley. Visit Jack London State Historic Park, and then loop back north on Bennett Valley Road to beautiful **Matanzas Creek Winery** ㊷ in Santa Rosa.

**If you have
7 days**

Begin in the town of **Sonoma** ►, whose colorful plaza and mission evoke early California's Spanish past. Afterward, head north to ⊠ **Glen Ellen** and the Valley of the Moon. Picnic and explore the grounds at Jack London State Historic Park. Next morning visit **Kenwood Vineyards** ㊵ before heading north to ⊠ **Healdsburg** in Dry Creek Valley via Santa Rosa and U.S. 101. In this less-trafficked haven of northern Sonoma County, a host of "hidden" wineries—including **Ferrari-Carano Winery** ㊾—lie nestled in the woods along the roads. Spend the night in ⊠ **Healdsburg,** where a stroll around the plaza offers many opportunities for shopping and fine dining. On the third day cross over into Napa Valley—take Mark Springs Road east off U.S. 101's River Road exit and follow the signs on Porter Creek Road to Petrified Forest Road to Highway 29. Spend the day (and the night) in the western-style town of ☒ **Calistoga,** noted for its mud baths and mineral springs. Wake up early on the fourth day for a balloon ride. If you're feeling energetic, take to the Silverado Trail for a bike ride with stops at **Cuvaison** ㉘, **Stag's Leap Wine Cellars** ⓫, and **Clos du Val** ❻. On day five, visit the galleries, shops, and eateries of **St. Helena** before heading to Oakville for the Oakville Grocery, a must-see (and must-taste) landmark. Spend the night and visit the wineries in ☒ **Rutherford.** On day six, explore nearby **Yountville,** stopping for lunch at one of its many acclaimed restaurants before heading up the hill to the **Hess Collection Winery and Vineyards** ❽, on Mt. Veeder, where a brilliant art collection and excellent wines may keep you occupied for hours. Splurge on dinner at Domaine Chandon. On your last day return to the town of Sonoma via the Carneros Highway, moving on to the landmark **Buena Vista Carneros Winery** ㉟ or **Gloria Ferrer Champagne Caves** ㉝.

---

dles southern Sonoma and Napa counties. Five major paths cut through both valleys: U.S. 101 and Highways 12 and 121 through Sonoma County, and Highway 29 north from Napa. The 25-mi Silverado Trail, which runs parallel to Highway 29 north from Napa to Calistoga, is a more scenic, less crowded route with a number of distinguished wineries.

One of the most important viticultural areas in the Wine Country spreads across southern Sonoma and Napa counties. The Carneros region has a long, cool growing season tempered by maritime breezes and lingering fogs off the San Pablo Bay—optimum slow-growing conditions for pinot noir and chardonnay grapes. So exotic-looking are the misty Carneros marshlands that Francis Ford Coppola chose them as the location for scenes of the Mekong Delta in his 1979 movie *Apocalypse Now.* When the sun is shining, however, Carneros looks like a sprawling and scenic expanse of quintessential Wine Country, where wildflower meadows and vineyards stretch toward the horizon.

About the Restaurants

Many star chefs from urban areas throughout the United States have migrated to the Wine Country, drawn by the area's renowned produce and world-class wines—the products of fertile soil and near-perpetual sun during the growing season. As a result of this marriage of imported talent and indigenous bounty, food now rivals wine as the principal attraction of the region. Although excellent cuisine is available throughout the region, the little town of Yountville has become something of an epicurean crossroads. If you don't succeed at getting a much-coveted reservation at Thomas Keller's French Laundry, often described as one of the best restaurants in the country, then the more casual Bistro Jeanty and Bouchon, as well as a host of other restaurants in and around Yountville, are excellent choices.

Such high quality often means high prices, but you can also find appealing inexpensive eateries. High-end delis offer superb picnic fare, and brunch is a cost-effective strategy at pricey restaurants.

With few exceptions (which are noted in individual restaurant listings), dress is informal. Where reservations are indicated as essential, you may need to reserve a week or more ahead. In summer and early fall you may need to book several months ahead.

About the Hotels

Ranging from quaint to utterly luxurious, the area's many inns and ho-tels are usually exquisitely appointed. Most of the bed-and-breakfasts have historic Victorian and Spanish architecture and serve a full break-fast highlighting local produce. The newer hotels have spas with state-of-the-art buildings offering such comforts as massage treatments or spring water–fed pools. Many house first-class restaurants or are a short car ride away from gastronomic bliss.

All of this comes with a hefty price tag. As the cost of vineyards and grapes has risen, so have lodging rates. Santa Rosa, the largest popula-tion center in the area, has the widest selection of moderately priced rooms. Try there if you've failed to reserve in advance or have a limited bud-get. In general, all accommodations in the area often offer considerably lower rates on weeknights; rates are about 20% lower in winter.

On weekends, two- or even three-night minimum stays are commonly required, especially at smaller inns and B&Bs. Many B&Bs book up long in advance of the summer and fall seasons, and they're often not suit-able for children.

WHAT IT COSTS				
$$$$	**$$$**	**$$**	**$**	**¢**
RESTAURANTS over $30	$23–$30	$16–$22	$10–$15	under $10
HOTELS over $250	$176–$250	$121–$175	$90–$120	under $90

Restaurant prices are per person for a main course at dinner, excluding sales tax. Hotel prices are for two people in a standard double room in high season, exclud-ing service charges and tax.

Timing

"Crush," the term used to indicate the season when grapes are picked and crushed, usually takes place in September or October, depending on the weather. From September until December the entire Wine Coun-try celebrates its bounty with street fairs and festivals. The Sonoma County Harvest Fair, with its famous grape stomp, is held the first weekend in October. Golf tournaments, wine auctions, and art and food fairs occur throughout the fall.

In season (April through October), Napa Valley draws crowds of tourists, and traffic along Highway 29 from St. Helena to Calistoga is often backed up on weekends. The Sonoma Valley, Santa Rosa, and Healdsburg are less crowded. In season and over holiday weekends it's best to book lodg-ing, restaurant, and winery reservations well in advance. Many winer-ies give tours at specified times and require appointments.

To avoid crowds, visit the Wine Country during the week and get an early start (most wineries open around 10). Summer is usually hot and dry and autumn can be even hotter, so pack a sun hat if you go during these times.

Numbers in the text correspond to numbers on the Napa Valley and Sonoma Valley maps.

NAPA VALLEY

With more than 240 wineries, the Napa Valley is the undisputed capi-tal of American wine production. Famed for its unrivaled climate and neat rows of vineyards, the area is made up of small, quirky towns whose Victorian Gothic architecture—narrow, gingerbread facades and pointed arches—is reminiscent of a distant world. Yountville, in the lower Napa Valley, is compact and redolent of American history, yet fast becoming an up-to-the-minute culinary hub. St. Helena, in the middle of the valley, is posh, with tony shops and elegant restaurants. Calistoga, near the north border of Napa County, feels like an Old West frontier town, with wooden-plank storefronts and people in cowboy hats.

Napa

46 mi from San Francisco via I–80 east and north, Hwy. 37 west, and Hwy. 29 north.

Established in 1848 and with a population of about 120,000, Napa is the oldest town as well as the largest city in the valley. It has been undergoing a cultural rebirth, especially since the 2001 opening of Copia: The American Center for Wine, Food & the Arts, which coincided with the opening of several new restaurants and inns. In 2002, the 1879 Napa Valley Opera House reopened for its first public performance in nearly 90 years.

The commercial hub for one of the richest wine-producing regions in the world, the city itself is urban and busy. But it's surrounded by some of California's prettiest agricultural lands. Most destinations in both the Napa and Sonoma valleys are easily accessible from here. For those seeking an affordable alternative to the hotels and B&Bs in the heart of the Wine Country, Napa is a good option. But choose lodgings right downtown or on the north side of town near Yountville, as parts of Napa are downright seedy.

❶ **Domaine Carneros** occupies a 138-acre estate dominated by a classic château inspired by Champagne Taittinger's historic Château de la Marquetterie in France. Carved into the hillside beneath the winery, Domaine Carneros's cellars produce sparkling wines reminiscent of the Taittinger style and using only Carneros grapes. (It's in the Carneros wine district.) At night the château is a glowing beacon rising above the dark vineyards. By day activity buzzes throughout the visitor center, the touring and tasting rooms, and the kitchen and dining room, where private luncheons and dinners emphasize food and wine pairings. Complimentary appetizers are served with wines. ✉ *1240 Duhig Rd.* ☎ *707/257–0101* 🖷 *707/257–3020* ⊕ *www.domainecarneros.com* ✉ *Tasting fees vary, tour free* ☉ *Daily 10–6; tours daily at 10:15, 11, noon, 1, 2, 3, and 4.*

❷ **Artesa Vineyards & Winery,** formerly called Codorniu Napa, is bunkered into a Carneros hilltop. The Spanish owners now produce primarily still wines under the talented wine maker Don Van Staaveren (previously of Chateau St. Jean). With a modern, minimalist look in the tasting room and contemporary sculptures on the property, this place is a far cry from the many faux French châteaux and rustic Italian-style villas in the region. ✉ *1345 Henry Rd., north off Old Sonoma Rd. and Dealy La.* ☎ *707/224–1668* 🖷 *707/224–1672* ⊕ *www.artesawinery.com* ✉ *Tasting $2 and up, tour free* ☉ *Daily 10–5; tours daily at 11 and 2.*

❸ Instead of tasting wine you have the opportunity to try five types of sake at **Hakusan.** One of the more appealing choices is a plum-flavored dessert sake. Outside, a few placards near a Japanese garden explain the sake-making process. ✉ *1 Executive Way* ☎ *707/258–6160* ⊕ *www.hakusan. com* ✉ *Tasting $3* ☉ *Daily 10–5.*

❹ **Copia: The American Center for Wine, Food & the Arts** is a shrine to American food and wine. An enormous variety of food-related art exhibits, video screenings, and food and wine tastings, and tours are scheduled

Fodor'sChoice
★

2

Galleries & Museums

More and more artists and art dealers are discovering the Napa Valley as a showplace for original works of art. Internationally famous artists and local artists exhibit their work side by side in galleries that showcase artistic styles to suit every taste. Shows at most galleries are scheduled throughout the year, and exhibitions change frequently.

Hot-Air Ballooning

Day after day, colorful balloons fill the morning sky high above the Wine Country's valleys. To aficionados, peering down at vineyards from the vantage point of the clouds is the ultimate California experience. Balloon flights usually take place soon after sunrise, when the calmest, coolest conditions offer maximum lift and soft landings. Prices depend on the duration of the flight, number of passengers, and services. Some companies provide such extras as pickup at your lodging or champagne brunch after the flight. Expect to spend at least $175 per person.

Spas & Mud Baths

Mineral-water soaks, mud baths, and massage are rejuvenating local traditions. Calistoga, known worldwide as the Hot Springs of the West, is famous for its warm, spring water–fed mineral tubs and mud baths full of volcanic ash. Sonoma, St. Helena, and other towns also have full-service spas.

Wonderful World of Wine

Wine tasting can be an educational, fascinating, and even mysterious ritual. The sight of polished glasses and uniquely labeled bottles lined up in a row, the tour guide's commentary on the character of each wine, the decadent mood of the vineyards with their full-to-bursting grapes—all combine to create an anticipation that's gratified with the first sip of wine. Learning about the origin of the grapes, the terraces on which they're grown, the weather that nurtured them, and the methods by which they're transformed into wine will give you a new appreciation of wine—and a great afternoon (or all-day) diversion. For those new to the wine-tasting game, Robert Mondavi and Korbel Champagne Cellars give general tours geared toward teaching novices the basics on how wine and champagne are made and what to look for when tasting.

There are more than 400 wineries in Sonoma and Napa, so it pays to be selective when planning your visit. Better to mix up the wineries with other sights and diversions—a picnic, trips to local museums, a ride in a hot-air balloon—than attempt to visit too many in one day. Unless otherwise noted, the wineries in this chapter are open daily year-round and charge no fee for admission, tours, or tastings. In general, fees tend to be low or nonexistent in the Sonoma and Russian River valleys and from $3 to $10 in the Napa Valley. Sometimes tasting fees are refundable with the purchase of a bottle of wine.

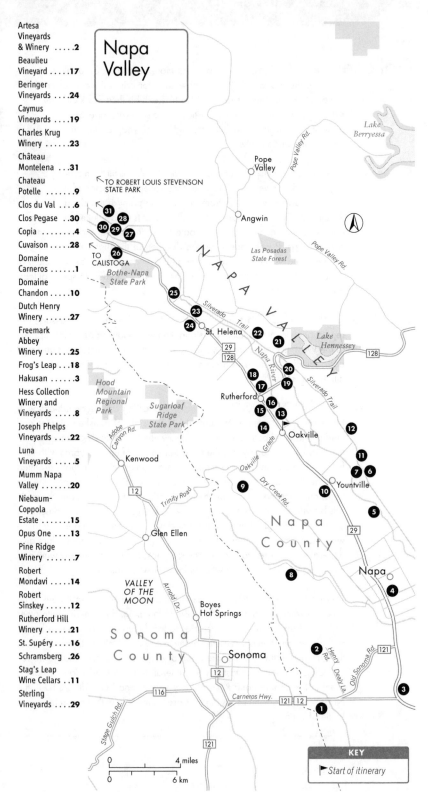

Napa
Valley

TO ROBERT LOUIS STEVENSON
STATE PARK

Pope
Valley

Angwin

Pope Valley Rd.

Lake
Berryessa

TO
CALISTOGA

Bothe-Napa
State Park

Las Posadas
State Forest

Pope Valley Rd.

N A P A

V A L L E Y

Silverado Trail

St. Helena

Napa River

Lake
Hennessey

128

Hood
Mountain
Regional
Park

Sugarloaf
Ridge
State Park

Adobe Canyon Rd.

Rutherford

Silverado Trail

Oakville Grade

Oakville

Kenwood

12

Trinity Road

Dry Creek Rd.

Yountville

Glen Ellen

Napa
County

29

VALLEY
OF THE
MOON

Arnold Dr.

Boyes
Hot Springs

Napa

Sonoma
County

Sonoma

12

Henry Rd.

Deely La.

Old Sonoma Rd.

121

116

Carneros Hwy.

121 12

Stage Gulch Rd.

121

0   4 miles

0   6 km

daily (pick up a schedule at the information desk on your way in). The entry fee allows you access to the exhibitions, informative tours, gift shop, and some introductory tastings and lectures. One-hour tours of the ever-changing gardens are very popular. Special programs, such as a luncheon exploration of wine and cheese pairings, are fantastic (additional fee required). ⊠ *500 1st St.* ☎ *707/259–1600* ⊕ *www.copia.org* ⊠ *$12.50* ⊘ *Mid-May–Sept., Mon., Wed., and Sun. 10–5, Thurs.–Sat. 10–7; Oct.–mid-May, Thurs.–Mon. 10–5.*

❺ Luna Vineyards, the southernmost winery on the Silverado Trail, was established in 1995 by veterans of the Napa wine industry intent on making less-conventional wines, particularly Italian varieties. They've planted pinot grigio on the historic property and also produce sangiovese and merlot. ⊠ *2921 Silverado Trail* ☎ *707/255–2474* ⊕ *www.lunavineyards. com* ⊠ *Tasting and tour $5* ⊘ *Daily 10–5; tours by appointment.*

❻ Clos du Val, founded by French owner Bernard Portet, produces a celebrated reserve cabernet. It also makes zinfandel, pinot noir, and chardonnay. Although the winery itself is austere, the French-style wines age beautifully. ⊠ *5330 Silverado Trail* ☎ *707/259–2200* ⊕ *www.closduval. com* ⊠ *Tasting and tour $5* ⊘ *Daily 10–5; tours by appointment.*

❼ Small **Pine Ridge Winery,** in the Stags Leap district, makes estate-bottled wines, including chardonnay, chenin blanc, and merlot, as well as a first-rate cabernet sauvignon. Tours include barrel tastings in the winery's caves. ⊠ *5901 Silverado Trail* ☎ *707/252–9777* ⊕ *www.pineridgewinery. com* ⊠ *Tasting fees vary; tour $20* ⊘ *Daily 10:30–4:30; tours (by appointment) at 10, noon, and 2.*

★ ❽ The **Hess Collection Winery and Vineyards** is a delightful discovery on a hilltop 9 mi northwest of the city of Napa. (Don't give up; the road leading to the winery is long and winding.) The simple, rustic limestone structure, circa 1903, contains Swiss owner Donald Hess's personal art collection, including works by contemporary European and American artists such as Robert Motherwell, Francis Bacon, and Frank Stella. Cabernet sauvignon is the real strength here, though Hess also produces some fine chardonnays. The winery and the art collection are open for self-guided tours (free). ⊠ *4411 Redwood Rd., west of Hwy. 29* ☎ *707/ 255–1144* 🖶 *707/253–1682* ⊕ *www.hesscollection.com* ⊠ *Tasting $3* ⊘ *Daily 10–4.*

❾ Chateau Potelle, on the slopes of Mt. Veeder, produces acclaimed estate zinfandel, chardonnay, and cabernet sauvignon, all of which thrive in the poor soil at nearly 2,000 feet above the valley floor. Jean-Noël and Marketta Fourmeaux were official tasters for the French government before establishing this winery in 1988. It's a quiet, out-of-the-way spot for a picnic. ⊠ *3875 Mt. Veeder Rd. (5 mi west of Hwy. 29 off the Oakville Grade)* ☎ *707/255–9440* ⊕ *www.chateaupotelle.com* ⊠ *Tasting free–$5* ⊘ *Nov.–mid-Apr., Thurs.–Mon. 11–5; rest of yr, daily 11–6.*

Where to Stay & Eat

$$–$$$$ ✕ **Silverado Country Club.** This large, famous resort includes two restaurants and a bar and grill. The elegant Vintner's Court, with California–Pacific Rim cuisine, serves dinner and Sunday brunch. The restaurant closes off-season and is open limited days in shoulder season, so inquire at the concierge desk. Royal Oak serves traditional American food—largely steak and seafood—nightly. The bar and grill is open for breakfast and lunch year-round. ⊠ *1600 Atlas Peak Rd. (follow signs to Lake Berryessa)* ☎ *707/257–0200 or 800/532–0500* ⚓ *Reservations essential for Vintner's Court* 🖃 *AE, D, DC, MC, V* ⊘ *Vintner's Court: Closed Nov.–Mar. and Mon. and Tues. No dinner Sun.*

$$–$$$ ✕ **Foothill Cafe.** On the less glamorous side of Highway 29, this low-key, whimsically decorated restaurant is a big favorite with locals, which is a high recommendation in such a food-savvy area. Typical dishes include oak-roasted prime rib with potato–Stilton gratin and salmon crusted with ginger and peppercorns. ✉ *2766 Old Sonoma Rd.* ☎ *707/252–6178* ▭ *MC, V* ⏲ *Closed Mon. and Tues. No lunch.*

$$–$$$ ✕ **Julia's Kitchen.** Named for Julia Child, the restaurant at Copia serves French-California cuisine that relies on the freshest regional ingredients. Salad greens and many other vegetables come from Copia's 3½ acres of organic gardens, just outside the door. The free-range chicken breast might come with braised endive and verjuice vinaigrette; calamari salad is sometimes garnished with freshly picked cucumbers. ✉ *500 1st St.* ☎ *707/265–5700* ▭ *AE, MC, V* ⏲ *No lunch Tues. No dinner Mon.–Wed.*

★ $–$$$ ✕ **Celadon.** Venture into downtown Napa for chef-owner Greg Cole's creative and enticing "global comfort food." Dishes such as flash-fried calamari with a chipotle chili–and–ginger glaze and small tasting plates such as a large crab cake laced with grainy mustard sauce make this an ideal place to sample contemporary cuisine accompanied by any of the dozen wines available by the glass. ✉ *500 Main St.* ☎ *707/254–9690* ▭ *AE, DC, MC, V.*

$–$$ ✕ **Bistro Don Giovanni.** Even in winter, the valley views from the covered patio are extraordinary. The wine list is as locally representative as the menu is eclectic. Don't miss the individual pizzas, the handmade pastas, or the focaccia sandwiches encasing grilled vegetables. Wood-roasted whole fish is a specialty and out of the ordinary. The terra-cotta tile floors and high ceilings create a casual Mediterranean feel. ✉ *4110 St. Helena Hwy. (Hwy. 29)* ☎ *707/224–3300* ▭ *AE, D, DC, MC, V.*

¢–$$$ ✕ **ZuZu.** Spanish glass lamps, a carved-wood Latin American goddess, and hammered-tin ceiling panels set the tone for a menu composed almost entirely of tapas. These little dishes so common in Spain are a rarity in the Wine Country, which may be why the in-crowd immediately adopted this lively place. White anchovies with endive, ratatouille, sea-scallop ceviche, and paella are typical fare. ✉ *829 Main St.* ☎ *707/224–8555* ▭ *AE, D, DC, MC, V* ⏲ *No lunch weekends.*

★ $$$$ 🏨 **Milliken Creek Inn.** Views of the property's lavish landscaping and the Napa River enhance the already beautiful rooms at this inn, which replicates the style of British-colonial Asia with khaki and cream walls, rattan furniture, and, in some rooms, gauzy canopy beds. In fair weather you can while away the day outdoors, where there's a fountain, Adirondack chairs, and a pavilion for outdoor massages. None of the rooms is particularly large, but all come with nice touches such as luscious bedding, DVD players, and finely adjustable spa tubs. ✉ *1815 Silverado Trail, 94558* ☎ *707/255–1197 or 888/622–5775* 🌐 *www.millikencreekinn.com* ⇨ *6 rooms, 6 suites* ♨ *In-room data ports, minibars, refrigerators, cable TV, in-room VCRs, hot tub, massage, wine bar, dry cleaning, concierge; no smoking* ▭ *AE, D, DC, MC, V.*

$$$$ 🏨 **Oak Knoll Inn.** Uncommonly spacious guest rooms with Napa fieldstone walls and high beamed ceilings give this small inn an expansive feel. Seating areas with plush chairs and couches are perfect for enjoying the fireplace in each room. The views take in the pool and the hundreds of acres of vineyard beyond. The bathrooms aren't as lavish as those at similarly priced B&Bs, but the food, beautifully presented at the wine hour every evening and at a decadent breakfast, is reason enough to visit, as is the service; the innkeepers are happy to arrange winery visits and other activities for you. ✉ *2200 E. Oak Knoll Ave. (4 mi south of Yountville)* ☎ *707/255–2200* 📠 *707/255–2296* 🌐 *www.oakknollinn.com* ⇨ *4 rooms* ♨ *In-room data ports, refrigerators, pool, hot tub; no room TVs, no smoking* ▭ *MC, V* 🍽 *BP.*

$$–$$$$ 🏨 **Napa River Inn.** A 2½-acre complex includes restaurants, shops, a spa, and this waterfront inn. Accommodations in the 1884 Hatt Building maintain some of the original architectural details, including maple hardwood floors; some rooms have canopy beds, fireplaces, and artwork depicting an 1880s river town. Brighter colors dominate in the adjacent Embarcadero building, where some rooms have small balconies and the decor has an understated nautical theme. ⊠ *500 Main St., 94559* ☎ *707/251–8500 or 877/251-8500* 📠 *707/251-8504* ⊕ *www.napariverinn.com* 🛏 *65 rooms, 1 suite* 🍴 *2 restaurants, café, patisserie, in-room data ports, in-room safes, refrigerators, cable TV, in-room VCRs, dry cleaning, laundry service, concierge, meeting rooms, some pets allowed (fee); no smoking* 🚬 *AE, D, DC, MC, V.*

$$ 🏨 **Chateau Hotel.** Despite the name, this is a pretty simple motel that makes only the barest nod to France. Clean rooms, its location at the entrance to the Napa Valley, the adjacent restaurant, and free stays for children under age 12 make up for its lack of charm. ⊠ *4195 Solano Ave. (west of Hwy. 29, exit at Trower Ave.), 94558* ☎ *707/253–9300, 800/253–6272 in CA* 📠 *707/253-0906* ⊕ *www.napavalleychateauhotel. com* 🛏 *109 rooms, 6 suites* 🍴 *Some refrigerators, cable TV, pool, hot tub* 🚬 *AE, D, DC, MC, V* ¹⊙¹ *CP.*

Nightlife & the Arts

In 1995, former telecommunications tycoon and vintner William Jarvis and his wife transformed a historic stone winery building in downtown Napa into the **Jarvis Conservatory,** an excellent venue for baroque French ballet and Spanish operetta known as zarzuela. Performances open to the public are held in conjunction with workshops and festivals centered on these two art forms. The conservatory presents opera nights featuring local talent the first Saturday of each month. ⊠ *1711 Main St.* ☎ *707/ 255–5445* ⊕ *www.jarvisconservatory.com.*

Sports & the Outdoors

BIKING   Thanks to the long country roads that wind through the region, bicycling is a popular pastime. The Silverado Trail, with its very gently rolling hills, is more scenic than Highway 29, which nevertheless tempts some bikers with its pancake-flat aspect. **Napa Valley Bike Tours and Rentals** (⊠ 4080 Byway E ☎ 707/255–3377) has bicycle rentals.

FISHING   You can fish from the banks of the Napa River at **John F. Kennedy Park** (⊠ 2291 Streblow Dr. ☎ 707/257–9529), which includes picnic facilities and barbecue pits. Call ahead for river conditions.

GOLF   The 18-hole **Chardonnay Golf Club** (⊠ 2555 Jameson Canyon Rd. ☎ 707/ 257–8950) course is a favorite among Bay Area golfers. The greens fee, $70 weekdays and $90 weekends in high season, includes a cart. Within the vicinity of the Silverado Trail, the **Silverado Country Club** (⊠ 1600 Atlas Peak Rd. ☎ 707/257–0200) has two challenging 18-hole courses with a beautiful view at every hole. The greens fee for guests at the resort is $140, including a cart; the reciprocal rate for members of other clubs is $155.

Yountville

13 mi north of the town of Napa on Hwy. 29.

Yountville has become the valley's boomtown. No other small town in the Wine Country has as many inns, restaurants, or shops. A popular Yountville attraction is **Vintage 1870** (⊠ 6525 Washington St. ☎ 707/ 944–2451), a 26-acre complex of boutiques, restaurants, and fancy-food stores. The vine-covered brick buildings were built in 1870 and housed a winery, livery stable, and distillery. The original mansion of the prop-

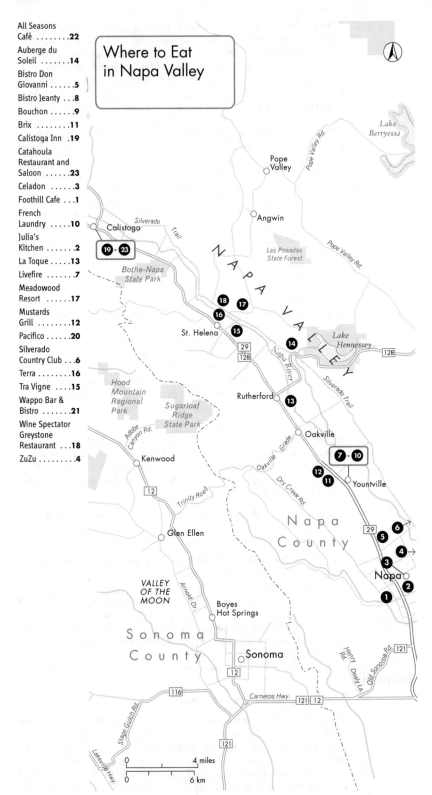

Where to Eat
in Napa Valley

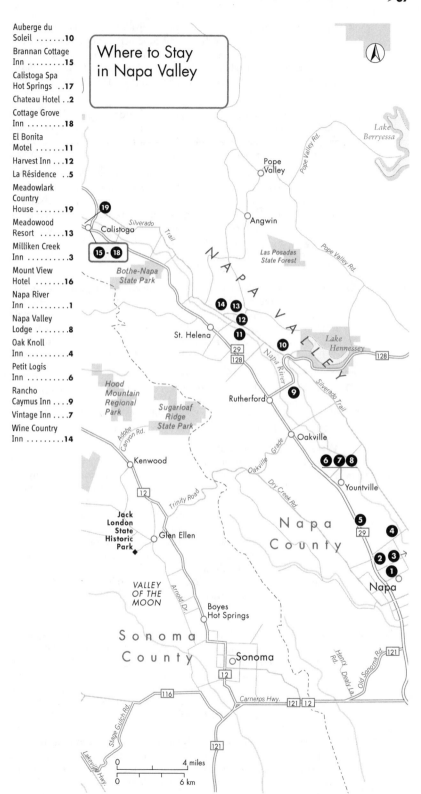

Where to Stay
in Napa Valley

erty is now the popular Mexican-style Compadres Bar and Grill. Nearby is the Pacific Blues Café. Although the food here is nothing special, the restaurant is housed in the train depot Samuel Brannan built in 1868 for his privately owned Napa Valley Railroad. At **Yountville Park** (⌧ Washington and Madison Sts.), there's a picnic area with tables, barbecue pits, and a view of grapevines.

At the intersection of Madison and Washington streets is Yountville's **Washington Square,** a complex of boutiques and restaurants. **Pioneer Cemetery,** the final resting place of the town's founder, George Yount, is nearby, on the far side of Washington Street.

⑩ French-owned **Domaine Chandon** claims one of Yountville's prime pieces of real estate, on a knoll west of downtown. Tours of the sleek, modern facilities on the beautifully maintained property include sample flutes of the méthode champenoise sparkling wine. Champagne is $4–$12 per glass, hors d'oeuvres are available, and an elegant restaurant beckons. ⌧ *1 California Dr., west of Hwy. 29* ☎ *707/944–2280* ⊕ *www.chandon.com* ☉ *Daily 10–6. Tours on the hr Mar.–Oct., daily 11–5; Nov.–Feb., Wed.–Sun. 11–5.*

⑪ It was the 1973 cabernet sauvignon produced by **Stag's Leap Wine Cellars** that put the winery—and the California wine industry—on the map by placing first in the famous Paris tasting of 1976. Today, Stag's Leap makes cabernet, as well as chardonnay, sauvignon blanc, white riesling, merlot, and a petite sirah. ⌧ *5766 Silverado Trail* ☎ *707/265–2441* ⊕ *www.cask23.com* ▤ *Tasting $10–$30; tour free* ☉ *Daily 10–4:30; tours by appointment.*

⑫ **Robert Sinskey** makes estate-bottled wines, including chardonnay, cabernet, and merlot, but is best known for its pinot noir. ⌧ *6320 Silverado Trail* ☎ *707/944–9090* 🖷 *707/994–9092* ⊕ *www.robertsinskey.com* ▤ *Tasting $10; tour free* ☉ *Daily 10–4:30; tours by appointment.*

Where to Stay & Eat

$$$$　✕ **French Laundry.** An old stone building houses the most acclaimed
Fodor'sChoice　restaurant in Napa Valley—and, indeed, one of the most highly re-
★　garded in the country. The prix-fixe menus ($110–$135), one of which is vegetarian, include five or nine courses and usually have two or three additional surprises, such as a tiny cone filled with salmon tartare. A full three hours will likely pass before you reach dessert. Chef Thomas Keller, with two James Beard awards, doesn't lack for admirers. Reservations are hard won and not accepted more than two months in advance (call two months ahead to the day). Didn't get a reservation? Try stopping by on the day you'd like to dine here to be considered if there's a cancellation. ⌧ *6640 Washington St.* ☎ *707/944–2380* ⚐ *Reservations essential* ▤ *AE, MC, V* ☉ *Closed 1st 2 wks in Jan. No lunch Mon.–Thurs.*

$$–$$$$　✕ **Brix.** The spacious dining room has artisan glass, fine woods, and an entire wall of west-facing windows that overlooks vineyards and the Mayacamas Mountains. Main dishes include tamari-glazed Atlantic salmon, spicy ahi on a futomaki sushi roll, and double-cut lamb chops with a goat cheese–potato gratin. A wood-burning oven is used for cooking pizzas. Desserts, such as a gingered pear-and-apple crisp, receive an Asian accent as well. ⌧ *7377 St. Helena Hwy. (Hwy. 29)* ☎ *707/944–2749* ▤ *AE, D, DC, MC, V.*

$$–$$$　✕ **Bistro Jeanty.** Philippe Jeanty's menu draws its inspiration from the cooking of his French childhood. His traditional cassoulet will warm those nostalgic for bistro cooking, and classic coq au vin rises above the ordinary with the infusion of a spicy red-wine sauce. The scene here is

Gallic through and through with a small bar and a handful of tables in two crowded rooms. The best tables are in the back room, near the fireplace. ⊠ *6510 Washington St.* ☎ *707/944–0103* ⌕ *Reservations essential* ⊟ *AE, MC, V.*

★ **$$–$$$** ✕ **Mustards Grill.** Owner-chef Cindy Pawlcyn's first restaurant (she's also responsible for San Francisco's Fog City Diner) attracts a capacity crowd almost every night. Grilled fish, steak, local fresh produce, and an impressive wine list are the trademarks of this boisterous bistro with a black-and-white marble floor and upbeat artwork. The thin, crisp, golden onion rings are addictive. ⊠ *7399 St. Helena Hwy. (Hwy. 29), 1 mi north of town* ☎ *707/944–2424* ⌕ *Reservations essential* ⊟ *D, DC, MC, V.*

★ **$–$$$** ✕ **Bouchon.** The team that brought the French Laundry to its current pinnacle is behind this place, where everything from the snazzy zinc bar to the black vests on the waiters to the traditional warm goat-cheese salad could have come straight from a Parisian bistro. *Boudin blanc* (white sausage) with potato puree and leg of lamb with white beans are among the hearty dishes served in the high-ceilinged room. Late-night diners are pleased it's open until at least 1 AM. ⊠ *6534 Washington St.* ☎ *707/ 944–8037* ⊟ *AE, MC, V.*

$–$$$ ✕ **Livefire.** Fred Halpert's rustic restaurant, on Yountville's expanding restaurant row, is a cozy spot warmed with earthy colors. The specialty is "wood cuisine," food cooked in a grill, rotisserie, or smoker with walnut or cherrywood chips—smoked pork chops or a platter of ribs, chicken sausage, and rotisserie chicken, for example. Service is top-notch. ⊠ *6518 Washington St., 1 mi north of town* ☎ *707/944–1500* ⊟ *AE, D, DC, MC, V.*

$$$$ ☶ **Napa Valley Lodge.** The balconies, covered walkways, and red-tile roof are reminiscent of a hacienda, and many of the rooms have fireplaces. Some second-floor rooms, which are spacious, have vineyard views. A large pool area is landscaped with lots of greenery. ⊠ *2230 Madison St., at Hwy. 29, 94599* ☎ *707/944–2468 or 800/368–2468* 🖷 *707/944– 9362* ⊕ *www.woodsidehotels.com/napa* ⇗ *50 rooms, 5 suites* ⌕ *In-room data ports, minibars, refrigerators, cable TV with movies, pool, gym, hot tub, sauna, dry cleaning, laundry service, concierge, meeting rooms; no smoking* ⊟ *AE, D, DC, MC, V* ⏆ *CP.*

★ **$$$–$$$$** ☶ **La Résidence.** These deluxe accommodations, romantic and secluded amid extensive landscaping, are in two buildings: the French Barn and the Mansion, a renovated 1870s Gothic Revival manor house built by a riverboat captain from New Orleans. Towering oaks bathe the entire property in shade. The spacious rooms have period antiques and fireplaces, and most have double French doors that open onto verandas or patios. ⊠ *4066 Howard La. (Hwy. 29 4 mi south of town), 94558* ☎ *707/ 253–0337* 🖷 *707/253–0382* ⊕ *www.laresidence.com* ⇗ *22 rooms, 1 suite* ⌕ *Some refrigerators, cable TV, pool, hot tub; no TV in some rooms, no smoking* ⊟ *AE, D, DC, MC, V* ⏆ *BP.*

$$$–$$$$ ☶ **Vintage Inn.** Rooms in this luxurious inn are housed in two-story villas scattered around the 3½-acre property. French fabrics and 19th-century antiques outfit guest rooms, all of which are airy and spacious and have a private patio or a balcony, and bathrooms include whirlpool tubs. Some private patios have vineyard views. You're treated to a bottle of wine, champagne at breakfast, and afternoon tea. ⊠ *6541 Washington St., 94599* ☎ *707/944–1112 or 800/351–1133* 🖷 *707/944–1617* ⊕ *www.vintageinn.com* ⇗ *72 rooms, 8 suites* ⌕ *Refrigerators, cable TV, tennis court, pool, hot tub, bicycles, concierge, business services, meeting rooms, no-smoking rooms* ⊟ *AE, DC, MC, V* ⏆ *CP.*

$$$ ☶ **Petit Logis Inn.** At this small, charming one-story inn—remodeled from what was a row of shops—murals and 11-foot ceilings infuse each room with a European elegance. Breakfast, included in the room rate, is offered at one of two nearby restaurants. The inn's proximity to many of Yountville's best restaurants (within walking distance) is another plus. ✉ *6527 Yount St., 94599* ☎ *707/944–2332 or 877/944–2332* 🖷 *707/944–2388* ⊕ *www.petitlogis.com* 🛏 *5 rooms* ♿ *In-room data ports, refrigerators, cable TV; no smoking* ⊟ *AE, MC, V* ⦿ *CP.*

Oakville

⚐ *2 mi west of Yountville on Hwy. 29.*

There are three reasons to visit the town of Oakville: its grocery store, its scenic mountain road, and its magnificent, highly exclusive winery. The **Oakville Grocery** (✉ 7856 St. Helena Hwy./Hwy. 29 ☎ 707/944–8802), built in 1881 as a general store, carries high-end fare and difficult-to-find wines; custom-packed picnic baskets are a specialty. It's a pleasant place to sit on a bench out front and sip an espresso. Along the mountain range that divides Napa and Sonoma, the **Oakville Grade** (✉ west off Hwy. 29) is a twisting half-hour route with breathtaking views of both valleys. Although the surface of the road is good, it can be difficult to negotiate at night, and trucks are advised not to attempt it at any time.

🔞 **Opus One,** the combined venture of California wine maker Robert Mondavi and the late French baron Philippe de Rothschild, is famed for its vast (1,000 barrels side by side on a single floor), semicircular cellar modeled on the Château Mouton Rothschild winery in France. The futuristic building is the work of the architects responsible for San Francisco's Transamerica Pyramid. The state-of-the-art facilities produce about 20,000 cases of ultrapremium Bordeaux-style red wine from grapes grown in the estate's vineyards and in the surrounding Oakville appellation. ✉ *7900 St. Helena Hwy. (Hwy. 29)* ☎ *707/963–1979* 🖷 *707/944–1753* ⊕ *www.opusonewines.com* 🍷 *Tasting $25; tour free* ⊙ *Daily 10–3:30; tasting and tours by appointment.*

🔞 At **Robert Mondavi,** perhaps the best-known winery in the United States, you're encouraged to take the 75- to 90-minute vineyard and winery tour ($10) followed by an appetizer and wine tasting. In-depth two- to four-hour tours and lunch tours are also popular. Afterward, visit the art gallery, or, in summer, stick around for a concert (from jazz to pop and world music). ✉ *7801 St. Helena Hwy. (Hwy. 29)* ☎ *707/259–9463* ⊕ *www.robertmondaviwinery.com* 🍷 *Tasting fees vary; tour $10* ⊙ *Daily 9–5; tours by appointment.*

Rutherford

1 mi northwest of Oakville on Hwy. 29.

From a fast-moving car, Rutherford is a quick blur of dark forest, a rustic barn or two, and maybe a country store. But don't speed by this tiny hamlet. With its singular microclimate and soil, this is an important viticultural center.

In the 1970s, filmmaker Francis Ford Coppola bought the old Niebaum property, a part of the world-famous Inglenook estate. He resurrected an early Inglenook-like quality red with his first bottle of Rubicon, released in 1985. Since then, the **Niebaum-Coppola Estate** has consistently **Fodor'sChoice** received high ratings, and in 1995 Coppola purchased the other half of ★ the Inglenook estate, the ancient, ivy-covered château, and an additional 95 acres. A small museum in the château houses displays documenting the history of the Inglenook estates as well as Coppola movie memorabilia, which includes Don Corleone's desk and chair from *The God-*

WINE TASTING 101

IF ONE OF YOUR REASONS for visiting the Wine Country is to learn about wine, your best friend should be the person who is pouring in a winery tasting room. The people who do this are only too happy to share their knowledge. Though wine bars and shops abound, many of them offering tastings at certain times, the best way to learn about wines is to visit the wineries themselves. True, you'll get to taste only one product line, but because most wineries make 5 or 10 or even more types, you can make a lot of headway after visiting one or two wineries.

Why do people make such a big deal about tasting wine? Because it's the only way to learn the differences among varieties of wines and styles of wine making. The more you know, the more you will get out of the experience. Certainly, you can pick up any decent bottle of chardonnay to have with tonight's chicken dinner without making a major production of it. But if you love wine, or think you might, you'll have a lot of fun doing some comparison tasting. You can learn why you like what you like and how to find similar wines anywhere in the world.

Contrary to the cartoon image, tasting wine is by no means an effete exercise. As long as you don't act pretentious—say, by tilting your glass with your pinkie finger in the air—you won't look silly.

So how do you go about tasting wine? You start by looking at it. Usually the pourer will give you between 1 and 1½ ounces of each wine you try. You can hold the glass by the stem or by the bowl; the former grip will keep the wine from heating up, but the latter is a good idea if the tasting room is so crowded you fear getting jostled. If you can hold the glass to the light, all the better. You're looking for clues to the grape variety as well as to the wine's age. Connecting the color with the wine grape is part of the sensory experience and is likely to help you remember the aromas and flavors better. As for how old the wine is, remember that red wines pale as they age, whereas white wines get darker.

Sniff once or twice to see if you smell anything recognizable. Next, swirl the wine gently in the glass. Aerating the wine this way releases more aromas. (This step works with just about every type of wine except the sparkling kind, which tends to go flat when the bubbles are crushed in the process.) Don't be afraid to stick your nose in the glass. The idea is get close enough to the liquid to pick up subtle scents. The receptor nerve cells in your nose can detect every scent and forward them to the brain's olfactory bulb. Those cells tire quickly, however, so be sure to assess the aromas as quickly as possible.

At this point, it is time to taste. Although smell plays an enormous role in taste memory, so can "mouth-feel," or the weight of the wine on your tongue. Is it light or watery? Is it rich like milk? Mentally record these impressions, along with any other tactile sensations such as smoothness or silkiness. Hold the wine in your mouth for a few seconds to give your taste buds a chance to pick up as many flavors as possible. Wines carry an almost infinite range of flavors, from butter to olives, mint to chocolate, pineapple to vanilla, or cherry, blackberry, or even violets.

Finally, if you can still perceive flavor well after you've swallowed the wine, you can say it has a long finish. And you can be assured that it's a wine you will remember.

— Marty Olmstead

father and costumes from *Bram Stoker's Dracula.* ✉ *1991 St. Helena Hwy. (Hwy. 29)* ☎ *707/963–9099* ⊕ *www.niebaum-coppola.com* 🍷 *Tasting $10, tour $20* ☉ *Daily 10–5; château tours daily at 10:30, 12:30, and 2:30; vineyard tours daily at 11.*

⑯ Fine sauvignon blancs, semillons, and cabernet sauvignons are among the wines at which **St. Supéry** excels. This winery's unique discovery center allows you to inhale distinct wine aromas and match them with actual black pepper, cherry, citrus, and the like. A restored century-old Victorian house is part of the excellent winery tour. ✉ *8440 St. Helena Hwy. S (Hwy. 29)* ☎ *707/963–4507* ⊕ *www.stsupery.com* 🍷 *Tasting $5 and up, tour $5* ☉ *May–Sept., daily 10–5:30; Oct.–Apr., daily 10–5; tours at 11, 1, and 3.*

⑰ **Beaulieu Vineyard** still uses the same wine-making process, from crush to bottle, as it did the day it opened in 1900. The winery's cabernet is a benchmark of the Napa Valley. The Georges de Latour Private Reserve consistently garners high marks from major wine publications. ✉ *1960 St. Helena Hwy. (Hwy. 29)* ☎ *707/967–5200* ⊕ *www.bvwines. com* 🍷 *Tasting $5 and up, tour free* ☉ *Daily 10–5. Tours daily at 11, 1, 2, 3, and 4.*

★ ⑱ **Frog's Leap** is the perfect place for wine novices to begin their education. Owners John and Julie Williams maintain a sense of humor and a humble attitude that translates into an informative and satisfying experience. They also happen to produce some of the finest zinfandel, cabernet sauvignon, and sauvignon blanc in the Wine Country. ✉ *8815 Conn Creek Rd.* ☎ *707/963–4704* ⊕ *www.frogsleap.com* 🍷 *Tasting and tour free* ☉ *Mon.–Sat. 10–4; tours and tastings by appointment.*

⑲ **Caymus Vineyards** is run by wine master Chuck Wagner, who started making wine on the property in 1972. His family, however, had been farming in the valley since 1906. Today a 100% cabernet sauvignon special selection is the winery's claim to fame. Caymus also turns out a superior white, the Conundrum, made of an unusual blend of grapes— sauvignon blanc, semillon, chardonnay, and viognier. Reserve to taste. ✉ *8700 Conn Creek Rd.* ☎ *707/963–4204* ⊕ *www.caymus.com* 🍷 *Tasting free* ☉ *Sales daily 10–4; tastings by appointment.*

⑳ A joint venture of Mumm—the French champagne house—and Seagram, **Mumm Napa Valley** is considered one of California's premier sparkling-wine producers. Its Napa Brut Prestige and ultrapremium Vintage Reserve are the best known. The excellent tour and comfortable tasting room are two more good reasons to visit. An art gallery contains a permanent exhibit of photographs by Ansel Adams that record the wine-making process. ✉ *8445 Silverado Trail* ☎ *707/942–3434* ⊕ *www. mummnapavalley.com* 🍷 *Tasting $5–$12, tour free* ☉ *Daily 10–5; tours daily on the hr 10–3.*

㉑ The wine at **Rutherford Hill Winery** is aged in French oak barrels stacked in more than 44,000 square feet of caves—one of the largest winery cave systems in the United States. Tours of the caves can be followed by a picnic in oak, olive, or madrone orchards. ✉ *200 Rutherford Hill Rd. (east of Silverado Trail)* ☎ *707/963–7194* ⊕ *www.rutherfordhill.com* 🍷 *Tasting $5–$10, tour $5* ☉ *Daily 10–5; tours daily at 11:30, 1:30, and 3:30.*

Where to Stay & Eat

$$$$ ✕🏨 **Auberge du Soleil.** Every room at this elegant hotel has at least a
Fodor'sChoice small terrace, from which you can take in the views of the stunning property and its steep, olive tree–studded slopes. Guest rooms are dressed
★

in cool tile and soothing earth tones, with a nod to the spare side of South-western style. Bathrooms are truly grand (as expected at this price level), many of them equipped with whirlpool tubs. The renowned Auberge du Soleil restaurant has a world-class wine list and serves dishes such as raw yellowfin tuna with baby beets and Florida red snapper with pureed cauliflower. The bar serves moderately priced fare—goat-cheese salads and mussels, for example—until 11 PM. ⊠ *180 Rutherford Hill Rd., off Silverado Trail north of Hwy. 128, 94573* ☎ *707/963–1211 or 800/348–5406* 🖷 *707/963–8764* ⊕ *www.aubergedusoleil.com* ➷ *18 rooms, 32 suites* ♿ *2 restaurants, in-room data ports, kitchenettes, refrigerators, cable TV, in-room VCRs, 3 tennis courts, pool, gym, hot tub, massage, sauna, spa, bar, concierge, business services, meeting rooms* ⊟ *AE, D, DC, MC, V* ⏝⃝ *EP.*

★ **$$$–$$$$** ✕⌖ **Rancho Caymus Inn and La Toque.** California-Spanish in style, this cozy inn has well-maintained gardens and large suites with kitchens and whirl-pool baths. Well-chosen details include wrought-iron lamps, tile murals, stoneware basins, and window seats. But even if you don't stay here, come for dinner at the understated La Toque, which gives Yountville's French Laundry its toughest competition for Wine Country diners' haute-cuisine dollars. Reservations are essential and jackets are preferred for men. Chef-owner Ken Frank's changing prix-fixe menu ($$$$) is loaded with intense flavors; dishes might include seared Sonoma foie gras and Maine lobster with Pernod and candied turnips. His cheese courses and desserts are worth saving room for. A special truffle menu is added from mid-January to mid-February. ⊠ *1140 Rutherford Rd., east of Hwy. 29, 94573* ☎ *707/963–1777 or 800/845–1777 inn, 707/963–9770 restaurant* 🖷 *707/963–5387* ⊕ *www.ranchocaymus.com* ➷ *27 suites* ♿ *Restaurant, dining room, in-room data ports, minibars, refrigerators, cable TV, wine bar; no smoking* ⊟ *AE, DC, MC, V* ⏝⃝ *Restaurant closed Mon., Tues., and 1st 2 wks in Jan. No lunch* ⏝⃝ *CP.*

St. Helena

2 mi northwest of Oakville on Hwy. 29.

By the time pioneer wine maker Charles Krug planted grapes in St. Helena around 1860, quite a few vineyards already existed in the area. Today the town greets you with its abundant selection of wineries—many of which lie along the route from Yountville to St. Helena—and restaurants, including Greystone on the West Coast campus of the Culinary Institute of America. Many Victorian and false-front buildings dating from the late 19th and early 20th centuries distinguish the downtown area. Arching sycamore trees bow across Main Street (Highway 29) to create a pleasant, shady drive.

For some nonalcoholic sightseeing, visit the **Robert Louis Stevenson Museum** (⊠ 1490 Library La. ☎ 707/963–3757 ⏝⃝ Tues.–Sun. noon–4), next door to the public library. Its Robert Louis Stevenson memorabilia consists of more than 8,000 artifacts, including first editions, manuscripts, and photographs. The museum is free (donation suggested). Grape-seed mud wraps and Ayurveda-inspired massages performed by two attendants are among the trademarks of the **Health Spa Napa Valley** (⊠ 1030 Main St. ☎ 707/967–8800), which has a pool, steam room, and fitness facilities. Don't worry if your treatments leave you too limp to operate your car: Tra Vigne and other St. Helena restaurants are within walking distance.

㉒ Bordeaux blends, Rhône varietals, and a cabernet sauvignon are the house specialties at **Joseph Phelps Vineyards.** One of Napa's top wineries, it first hit the mark with Johannisberg riesling. ⊠ *200 Taplin Rd.* ☎ 707/963–

*2745 ⊕ www.jpvwines.com ⊒ Tasting $5, tour $10–$15 ⊙ Mon.–Sat.
9–5, Sun. 10–4; tours and tastings by appointment.*

㉓ The first winery founded in the Napa Valley, **Charles Krug Winery** opened
in 1861 when Count Haraszthy lent Krug a small cider press. Today,
the Peter Mondavi family runs it. The gift shop stocks everything from
fancy food baskets with grape-shape pasta to books about the region
and its wines. At this writing, tours have been suspended indefinitely
because a major earthquake retrofit project is in the works, but you can
still come for tastings. ⊠ *2800 N. Main St.* ☎ *707/963–5057* ⊕ *www.
charleskrug.com* ⊒ *Tasting $5–$8* ⊙ *Daily 10:30–5.*

The West Coast headquarters of the **Culinary Institute of America,** the country's leading school for chefs, are in the **Greystone Winery,** the former site
of the Christian Brothers Winery and a national historic landmark. The
campus consists of 30 acres of herb and vegetable gardens, a 15-acre merlot vineyard, and a Mediterranean-inspired restaurant, which is open to
the public. Also on the property are a well-stocked culinary store, a quirky
corkscrew-and-winepress museum, and a culinary library. Daily cooking
demonstrations are scheduled for nonstudents. ⊠ *2555 Main St.* ☎ *707/
967–2600 or 800/333–9242* 🖶 *707/967–1113* ⊕ *www.ciachef.edu.*

★ **㉔** Arguably the most beautiful winery in Napa Valley, the 1876 **Beringer Vineyards** is also the oldest continuously operating one. In 1883 the Beringer
brothers, Frederick and Jacob, built the Rhine House Mansion, where tastings are held among Belgian art-nouveau hand-carved oak and walnut
furniture and stained-glass windows. Historical tours are offered frequently; tours focused on special topics such as food-and-wine pairings
aren't as frequent. ⊠ *2000 Main St. (Hwy. 29)* ☎ *707/963–4812* ⊕ *www.
beringer.com* ⊒ *Tasting $5 and up, tour $5 (includes tasting)* ⊙ *May–Oct.,
daily 10–6; Nov.–Apr., daily 10–5; tours daily every half hr 10:30–4.*

㉕ **Freemark Abbey Winery** was originally called the Tychson Winery, after
Josephine Tychson, the first woman to establish a winery in California.
It has long been known for its cabernets, whose grapes come from the
fertile Rutherford Bench. All other wines are estate grown, including a
much-touted late-harvest riesling. ⊠ *3022 St. Helena Hwy. N (Hwy. 29)*
☎ *707/963–9694* ⊕ *www.freemarkabbey.com* ⊒ *Tasting $5* ⊙ *Daily
10–5; tours by appointment.*

Where to Stay & Eat

★ **$$–$$$$** ✕ **Tra Vigne.** A fieldstone building has been transformed into a striking
trattoria with a huge wood bar, 30-foot ceilings, and plush banquettes.
Homemade mozzarella, dressed with olive oil and vinegar, and house-
cured pancetta and prosciutto are preludes to rustic Tuscan specialties
such as oak-grilled rabbit with fava beans. The outdoor courtyard in
summer and fall is a sun-splashed Mediterranean vision of striped um-
brellas and awnings, crowded café tables, and rustic pots overflowing
with flowers. ⊠ *1050 Charter Oak Ave., off Hwy. 29* ☎ *707/963–4444*
⌛ *Reservations essential* 🖭 *D, DC, MC, V.*

★ **$$–$$$** ✕ **Terra.** A romantic restaurant housed in an 1888 stone foundry, Terra
is especially known for its exquisite Mediterranean-inspired dishes,
many with Asian touches. The sweetbread ragout, grilled squab, and
sake-marinated Chilean sea bass are memorable. Desserts might in-
clude a huckleberry *crostata* (tart) with vanilla-bean ice cream. ⊠ *1345
Railroad Ave.* ☎ *707/963–8931* ⌛ *Reservations essential* 🖭 *DC, MC,
V* ⊙ *Closed Tues. No lunch.*

$$–$$$ ✕ **Wine Spectator Greystone Restaurant.** The Culinary Institute of Amer-
ica runs this place in the handsome old Christian Brothers Winery. Cen-
tury-old stone walls house a large and bustling restaurant, with cooking,

baking, and grilling stations in full view. The menu has a Mediterranean spirit and emphasizes such small plates as caramelized onion tart with black olives. Typical main courses include crispy striped bass with braised leeks and winter-vegetable potpie. ✉ *2555 Main St.* ☎ *707/967–1010* ▤ *AE, D, DC, MC, V.*

$$$$ ✕▥ **Meadowood Resort.** Secluded at the end of a semiprivate road, this 256-acre resort has accommodations in a rambling country lodge and several bungalows. You need never leave the luxurious confines of the resort, where you can indulge in golf, tennis, hiking, fitness classes, and other sporty activities as well as an array of spa treatments. The elegant dining room, open at dinner only, specializes in California Wine Country cooking. Seating is also available outdoors on a terrace overlooking the golf course. The Grill, a less formal, less expensive restaurant, serves a lighter menu of pizzas and spa food. ✉ *900 Meadowood La., 94574* ☎ *707/963–3646 or 800/458–8080* 🖷 *707/963–5863* ⊕ *www.meadowood.com* �’ *40 rooms, 45 suites* ᗌ *2 restaurants, room service, in-room data ports, refrigerators, cable TV, 9-hole golf course, 7 tennis courts, 2 pools, health club, hot tub, massage, sauna, steam room, croquet, bar, concierge, business services, meeting rooms; no smoking* ▤ *AE, D, DC, MC, V.*

$$$$ ▥ **Harvest Inn.** Most rooms in this Tudor-esque inn on lushly landscaped grounds have wet bars, antique furnishings, and fireplaces. Some of the rooms are housed in cottages scattered around 8 acres. Pets are allowed in two rooms for a $75 fee. Complimentary breakfast is served in the breakfast room and on the patio overlooking the vineyards. ✉ *1 Main St., 94574* ☎ *707/963–9463 or 800/950–8466* 🖷 *707/963–4402* ⊕ *www.harvestinn.com* �’ *51 rooms, 3 suites* ᗌ *Room service, in-room data ports, refrigerators, cable TV, in-room VCRs, 2 pools, 2 hot tubs, wine bar, concierge, meeting rooms, some pets allowed (fee)* ▤ *AE, D, DC, MC, V* ⦿ *CP.*

$$$–$$$$ ▥ **Wine Country Inn.** A pastoral landscape of hills surrounds this peaceful New England–style retreat. Comfortable country-style furniture fills the rooms, most of which overlook the vineyards with either a balcony, patio, or deck. Most guest rooms have fireplaces, and some have private hot tubs. A hearty country breakfast is served buffet-style in the sun-splashed common room, and wine tastings are scheduled in the afternoon. ✉ *1152 Lodi La. (off Hwy. 29), 94574* ☎ *707/963–7077* 🖷 *707/963–9018* ⊕ *www.winecountryinn.com* �’ *25 rooms, 4 suites* ᗌ *Refrigerators, pool, hot tub, business services; no room TVs, no smoking* ▤ *MC, V* ⦿ *BP.*

$$$ ▥ **El Bonita Motel.** Window boxes and landscaped grounds are some of the pleasant touches at this cute motel with relatively elegant furnishings. Walls are dressed in muted pastels and upholstery is floral. Family-friendly pluses include roll-away beds and cribs for a modest extra charge. ✉ *195 Main St. (Hwy. 29), 94574* ☎ *707/963–3216 or 800/541–3284* 🖷 *707/963–8838* ⊕ *www.elbonita.com* �’ *37 rooms, 4 suites* ᗌ *In-room data ports, kitchenettes, microwaves, refrigerators, cable TV, pool, hot tub, sauna, Internet, business services, some pets allowed (fee), no-smoking rooms* ▤ *AE, D, DC, MC, V.*

Shopping

Art on Main (✉ 1359 Main St. ☎ 707/963–3350), one of the oldest galleries in the region, sells oils, watercolors, ceramics, and etchings by Northern California artists. The **Campus Store** (✉ Culinary Institute of America, 2555 Main St. ☎ 888/424–2433) is the place to shop for all things related to preparing and cooking food, from chef's pants to fish stock to cutlery. **Dean & Deluca** (✉ 607 St. Helena Hwy. S/Hwy. 29 ☎ 707/967–9980), a branch of the famous Manhattan store, is crammed with everything you need in the kitchen—including terrific produce and deli items—as well as a huge wine selection. Many of the cheeses sold here are produced locally. Handcrafted candles made on the premises are for sale at the **Hurd Beeswax Candle Factory** (⊠ 3020 St. Helena Hwy. N/Hwy. 29 ☎ 707/963–7211). **I. Wolk Galleries** (⊠ 1354 Main St. ☎ 707/963–8800) has works by established and emerging American artists—everything from abstract and contemporary realist paintings to high-quality works on paper and sculpture. Call for an appointment. **On the Vine** (⊠ 1234 Main St. ☎ 707/963–2209) sells wearable art and unique jewelry with food and wine themes. Italian ceramics, tabletop decor, and other high-quality home accessories fill **Vanderbilt & Company** (⊠ 1429 Main St. ☎ 707/963–1010), the prettiest store in town. Bargain hunters delight in the many designer labels at the **Village Outlet Stores** complex on St. Helena Highway, across the street from Freemark Abbey Winery.

Calistoga

3 mi northwest of St. Helena on Hwy. 29.

In addition to its wineries, Calistoga is noted for its mineral water, hot mineral springs, mud baths, steam baths, and massages. The Calistoga Hot Springs Resort was founded in 1859 by maverick entrepreneur Sam Brannan, whose ambition was to found "the Saratoga of California." He reputedly tripped up the pronunciation of the phrase at a formal banquet—it came out "Calistoga"—and the name stuck.

㉖ **Schramsberg,** perched on a wooded knoll on the southeast side of Highway 29, is one of Napa's most historic wineries, with caves that were dug by Chinese laborers in 1880. The winery makes sparkling wines in several styles, in several price ranges. If you want to taste here, you must tour first. ⊠ *1400 Schramsberg Rd.* ☎ *707/942–4558* ⊕ *www.schramsberg. com* 🎟 *Tasting and tour $12* ☉ *Daily 10–4; tours by appointment.*

㉗ It's worth taking a slight detour off the main artery to find **Dutch Henry Winery,** a small winery whose wines are available only on-site or through mail order. Tastings are held in a working winery, where wine makers explain the process. This is a good place to try cabernet sauvignon and merlot. ⊠ *4310 Silverado Trail* ☎ *707/942–5771* ⊕ *www.dutchhenry. com* 🎟 *Tasting $5* ☉ *Daily 10–4:30.*

㉘ Of the wines produced by **Cuvaison,** 65% are chardonnays, with pinot noir, cabernet sauvignon, and merlot rounding out the offerings. Picnic grounds with a view of the valley are shaded by 350-year-old oak trees. ⊠ *4550 Silverado Trail* ☎ *707/942–6266* ⊕ *www.cuvaison.com* 🎟 *Tasting $8, tour free* ☉ *Daily 10–5; tours Mon.–Sat. at 10:30.*

㉙ **Sterling Vineyards** sits on a hilltop 1 mi south of Calistoga, its pristine white Mediterranean-style buildings reached by an aerial tramway from the valley floor. The view from the tasting room is superb, and the gift shop is one of the best in the valley. ⊠ *1111 Dunaweal La. (east off Hwy. 29)* ☎ *707/942–3300* ⊕ *www.sterlingvineyards.com* 🎟 *$10 (includes tramway, self-guided tour, and tasting)* ☉ *Daily 10:30–4:30.*

㉚ Designed by postmodern architect Michael Graves, the **Clos Pegase** winery is a one-of-a-kind structure packed with unusual art objects from the collection of art-book publisher and owner Jan Shrem. Works of art even appear in the underground wine tunnels. Cheese and other foods are for sale in the visitor center, so you can still enjoy the shady picnic area even if you forget to bring food. ⊠ *1060 Dunaweal La. (east off Hwy. 29)* ☎ *707/942–4981* ⊕ *www.clospegase.com* 🎟 *Tasting fees vary, tour free* ☉ *Daily 10:30–5; tours daily at 11 and 2.*

Fodor'sChoice ★

The **Sharpsteen Museum,** in the center of town, has a magnificent diorama of the Calistoga Hot Springs Resort in its heyday. Other exhibits document the history of the Wappo, the original inhabitants of the area, and the career of Ben Sharpsteen, an animator at the Walt Disney studio. ✉ *1311 Washington St.* ☎ *707/942–5911* ⊕ *www.sharpsteen-museum.org* 🎫 *$3 donation* ⊘ *Daily 11–4.*

Indian Springs, an old-time spa, has been pumping out 212°F water from its three geysers since the late 1800s. The place offers some of the best bargains on mud bathing and short massages and has an Olympic-size mineral-water pool. The 16 bungalows ($$$$) range from a studio duplex to a three-bedroom house. Reservations are recommended for spa treatments. ✉ *1712 Lincoln Ave./Hwy. 29* ☎ *707/942–4913* ⊕ *www.indianspringscalistoga.com* ⊘ *Daily 9–8.*

Ⓒ Many families bring children to Calistoga to see **Old Faithful Geyser of California** blast its 60-foot tower of steam and vapor about every 30 minutes. (The frequency is affected by the moon, barometric pressure, tectonic activity, and recent rainfall.) One of just three regularly erupting geysers in the world, it's fed by an underground river that heats to 350°F. The spout usually lasts three minutes. Picnic facilities are available. ✉ *1299 Tubbs La. (1 mi north of Calistoga)* ☎ *707/942–6463* ⊕ *www.oldfaithfulgeyser.com* 🎫 *$8* ⊘ *Apr.–Sept., daily 9–6; Oct.–Mar., daily 9–5.*

㉛ **Château Montelena** is a vine-covered stone French château constructed circa 1882 and set amid Chinese-inspired gardens, complete with a man-made lake with gliding swans and islands crowned by Chinese pavilions. Its wines include chardonnays, cabernet sauvignons, and a limited-production riesling. ✉ *1429 Tubbs La.* ☎ *707/942–5105* ⊕ *www.montelena.com* 🎫 *Tasting $10* ⊘ *Daily 10–4; tours at 9:30 and 1:30, by appointment.*

Ⓒ **Robert Louis Stevenson State Park** (✉ Hwy. 29 7 mi north of Calistoga ☎ 707/942–4575) encompasses the summit of **Mt. St. Helena.** It was here, in the summer of 1880, in an abandoned bunkhouse of the Silverado Mine, that Stevenson and his bride, Fanny Osbourne, spent their honeymoon. The stay inspired Stevenson's "The Silverado Squatters," and Spyglass Hill in *Treasure Island* is thought to be a portrait of Mt. St. Helena. The park's approximately 3,600 acres are mostly undeveloped except for a fire trail leading to the site of the bunkhouse—which is marked with a marble tablet—and to the summit beyond.

Ⓒ The **Petrified Forest** contains the remains of the volcanic eruptions of Mt. St. Helena 3.4 million years ago. The force of the explosion uprooted the gigantic redwoods, covered them with volcanic ash, and infiltrated the trees with silica and minerals, causing petrifaction. Explore the museum, and then picnic on the grounds. ✉ *4100 Petrified Forest Rd. (5 mi west of Calistoga)* ☎ *707/942–6667* ⊕ *www.petrifiedforest.org* 🎫 *$5* ⊘ *Late Apr.–early Sept., daily 10–6; early Sept.–late Apr., daily 10–5.*

Where to Stay & Eat

$$–$$$ ✕ **All Seasons Café.** Bistro cuisine takes a California spin in this sun-filled space with marble tables and a black-and-white checkerboard floor. The seasonal menu might include organic greens, seared day-boat scallops, local game birds, and house-smoked pork—plus there are homemade breads and dessert. The café shares space with a well-stocked wineshop. ✉ *1400 Lincoln Ave.* ☎ *707/942–9111* ▭ *D, DC, MC, V* ⊘ *No lunch Mon.–Wed.*

★ $–$$$ ✕ **Catahoula Restaurant and Saloon.** Chef Jan Birnbaum, whose credentials include stints at the Quilted Giraffe in New York and Campton Place in San Francisco, uses a large wood-burning oven to turn out dishes such

CloseUp
SPAS IN THE WINE COUNTRY

THE WINE COUNTRY *is in the forefront of America's love affair with hot springs, mud baths, and spa treatments. Blessed with natural mineral ash from nearby volcanoes and mineral springs, areas around Calistoga and Sonoma were popular with Native Americans long before the stressed-out white man arrived. Today you can find spas of every stripe throughout the Wine Country.*

Dr. Wilkinson's *is the oldest spa in Calistoga. Best known for its mud baths, it is perhaps the least chic of the bunch.* ✉ 1507 Lincoln Ave., Calistoga ☎ 707/942–4102 ⊕ www.drwilkinson.com.

Lincoln Avenue Spa *occupies a 19th-century bank building, a history suggested by elegant woodwork and a tiled steam room. House specialties include mint and green-tea wraps ($55).* ✉ 1339 Lincoln Ave., Calistoga ☎ 707/942–5296 ⊕ www.lincolnavenuespa.com.

The **Mount View Spa** *is the most elegant in town, though like most other Calistoga spas, it could be larger. You won't find mud baths at this retreat at the rear of the Mount View Hotel lobby, but it is one of the best places for facials.* ✉ 1457 Lincoln Ave., Calistoga ☎ 707/942–5789 ⊕ www.mountviewspa.com.

Nance's Hot Springs *has rows of cotlike beds that practically beg you to take a nap after a treatment. The spa offers mud baths, a mineral whirlpool bath, and mineral steam baths. You can find good bargains here if you arrive midweek; a hot mineral bath followed by a half-hour massage costs $50.* ✉ 1614 Lincoln Ave., Calistoga ☎ 707/942–6211.

Calistoga Spa Hot Springs *is the best choice if you have several hours to lounge around. A house special is "The Works" ($120), a two-hour marathon of mud bath, mineral whirlpool, steam bath, blanket wrap, and hour-long massage. If you're booking any treatment, you can pay $5 and get all-day pool access as well. You can try relaxing in four pools of varying size and temperature until you decide on a favorite. This spa dates to the 1920s, an era depicted in photographs lining the*

hallway. ✉ 1006 Washington St., Calistoga ☎ 707/942–6269 ⊕ www.calistogaspa.com.

Lavender Hill Spa *is in a country cottage on the edge of town. The nicest treatment rooms are in the rear, with views of the lavender garden. Freestanding bathhouses with two whirlpool tubs make this a particularly good spot for couples.* ✉ 1015 Foothill Blvd., Calistoga ☎ 707/942–4495 ⊕ www.lavenderhillspa.coms.

Health Spa Napa Valley *is in a complex shared with an inn and a restaurant. The house specialty is Ayurvedic treatments; for an unforgettable experience, you should book "The Abhyanga," which is performed by two practitioners ($180).* ✉ 1030 Main St., St. Helena ☎ 707/967–8800 ⊕ www.napavalleyspa.com.

The **Fairmont Sonoma Mission Inn & Spa** *is the most glamorous and best-known sybaritic hot spot in the Wine Country. You'll want to arrive at least 45 minutes in advance of your appointment to spend some time in the bathing ritual room.* ✉ 18140 Sonoma Hwy., Sonoma ☎ 707/938–9000 ⊕ www.sonomamissioninn.com.

Facilities at **Kenwood Inn & Spa** *claim the prettiest spa setting in the Wine Country, thanks to the vineyards across the road and the Mediterranean style of the inn.* ✉ 10400 Sonoma Hwy., Kenwood ☎ 707/833–1293 ⊕ www.kenwoodinn.com.

The **Garden Spa at MacArthur Place** *has larger-than-life floral murals and the nicest, most expensive gift shop of all the Wine Country spas. The treatments are based on herbs, flowers, or minerals, rather than a blend of two or three. The two-hour "Rose Garden" treatment ($194) includes a bath in rose petals, a rose-petal body polish, and an essential oil massage. This spa, part of an inn, also has a small pool and coed steam rooms.* ✉ 29 E. MacArthur St., Sonoma ☎ 707/933–3193 ⊕ www.macarthurplace.com.

as spicy gumbo with rooster and pork porterhouse at this sleek, innovative restaurant. The large barroom opposite the dining room has its own menu of small plates, which are ideal for sampling Birnbaum's kitchen wizardry. ⊠ *Mount View Hotel, 1457 Lincoln Ave.* ☎ *707/942–2275* ⚑ *Reservations essential* ▤ *MC, V* ⊘ *No lunch Mon.–Thurs. June–Dec., no lunch weekdays Jan.–May.*

$$ ✕ **Calistoga Inn.** Grilled meat and fish for dinner and soups, salads, and sandwiches for lunch are prepared with flair at this restaurant and microbrewery with a tree-shaded outdoor patio. Hearty main courses include filet mignon with cracked black peppercorns and Jamaican jerk chicken. ⊠ *1250 Lincoln Ave.* ☎ *707/942–4101* ▤ *AE, MC, V.*

$–$$ ✕ **Wappo Bar & Bistro.** With a menu ranging from tandoori chicken and Thai shrimp curry to chiles rellenos and Turkish meze, this colorful restaurant is an adventure in international dining. ⊠ *1226 S. Washington St.* ☎ *707/942–4712* ▤ *AE, MC, V* ⊘ *Closed Tues. and 1st 2 wks in Dec.*

¢–$ ✕ **Pacifico.** Technicolor ceramics and murals adorn this Mexican restaurant, which serves Oaxacan and other fare. Fajitas and moles are among the specialties. ⊠ *1237 Lincoln Ave.* ☎ *707/942–4400* ▤ *MC, V.*

$$$$ ▦ **Cottage Grove Inn.** Elm trees shade 16 elegant and contemporary cottages. Rooms have skylights and plush furnishings; fireplaces, CD players, two-person hot tubs, and porches with wicker rocking chairs add to the coziness. Spas and restaurants are within walking distance. Rates include afternoon wine and cheese. ⊠ *1711 Lincoln Ave., 94515* ☎ *707/ 942–8400 or 800/799–2284* 🖶 *707/942–2653* ⊕ *www.cottagegrove. com* ⚑ *16 rooms* ⚒ *In-room safes, minibars, refrigerators, cable TV, in-room VCRs; no smoking* ▤ *AE, D, DC, MC, V* ⎮○⎮ *CP.*

$$$–$$$$ ▦ **Meadowlark Country House.** Twenty hillside acres just north of downtown Calistoga surround this decidedly laid-back and sophisticated inn. Innkeeper Kurt Stevens prides himself on being helpful but not intrusive. The main house and a newer building hold unfussy but countrystylish rooms, and the pool house has a bar and kitchen. The pool and sauna area is clothing optional. ⊠ *601 Petrified Forest Rd., 94515* ☎ *707/942–5651 or 800/942–5651* 🖶 *707/942–5023* ⊕ *www. meadowlarkinn.com* ⚑ *8 rooms* ⚒ *Some refrigerators, cable TV, in-room VCRs, pool, hot tub, sauna, some pets allowed; no smoking* ▤ *AE, MC, V* ⎮○⎮ *BP.*

$$–$$$ ▦ **Mount View Hotel.** A National Historic Landmark, the Mount View is the largest Napa Valley hotel north of St. Helena. A full-service European spa provides state-of-the-art pampering, and three cottages are each equipped with a private redwood deck, whirlpool tub, and wet bar. The Catahoula restaurant-saloon adds to the allure. ⊠ *1457 Lincoln Ave., 94515* ☎ *707/942–6877* 🖶 *707/942–6904* ⊕ *www. mountviewhotel.com* ⚑ *20 rooms, 11 suites* ⚒ *Restaurant, some refrigerators, cable TV, pool, spa, bar, concierge, Internet; no smoking* ▤ *AE, D, MC, V* ⎮○⎮ *CP.*

$$ ▦ **Brannan Cottage Inn.** The pristine Victorian cottage with lacy white fretwork, large windows, and a shady porch is the only one of Sam Brannan's 1860 resort cottages still standing on its original site. Rooms have private entrances, and elegant stenciled friezes of stylized wildflowers cover the walls. ⊠ *109 Wapoo Ave., 94515* ☎ *707/942–4200* ⊕ *www. brannancottageinn.com* ⚑ *6 rooms* ⚒ *Refrigerators; no TV in some rooms, no smoking* ▤ *AE, MC, V* ⎮○⎮ *BP.*

$$ ▦ **Calistoga Spa Hot Springs.** No-nonsense motel-style rooms have kitchenettes stocked with utensils and coffeemakers, which makes them popular with families and travelers on a budget. (There's a supermarket a block away.) The on-premises spa includes mineral baths, mud baths, swimming pools, and a hot tub. ⊠ *1006 Washington St., 94515* ☎ *707/ 942–6269* 🖶 *707/942–4214* ⊕ *www.calistogaspa.com* ⚑ *51 rooms,*

1 suite ☼ Kitchenettes, cable TV, 2 pools, wading pool, gym, outdoor hot tub, spa, laundry facilities, meeting room; no smoking ⊟ MC, V.

Sports & the Outdoors
Getaway Adventures and Bike Shop (⊠ 1117 Lincoln Ave. ☎ 707/942–0332 or 800/499–2453) rents bikes, including tandem bikes, and conducts winery and other bike tours.

Shopping
For connoisseurs seeking hard-to-find wines, the **All Seasons Wine Shop** (⊠ 1400 Lincoln Ave. ☎ 707/942–6828) is the place to visit. The **Calistoga Wine Stop** (⊠ 1458 Lincoln Ave. ☎ 707/942–5556), inside California's second-oldest existing train depot, carries 500 wines.

SONOMA VALLEY

Although the Sonoma Valley may not have quite the cachet as neighboring Napa Valley, wineries here entice with their unpretentious attitude and smaller crowds. Its name is Miwok Indian for "many moons," but writer Jack London's nickname for the region—Valley of the Moon—is more fitting. The scenic valley, bounded by the Mayacamas Mountains on the east and Sonoma Mountain on the west, extends north from San Pablo Bay nearly 20 mi to the eastern outskirts of Santa Rosa. The varied terrain, soils, and climate (cooler in the south because of the bay influence and hotter toward the north) allow grape growers to raise cool-weather varietals such as chardonnay and pinot noir as well as merlot, cabernet sauvignon, and other heat-seeking vines. The valley is home to some three dozen wineries, most of them on or near Highway 12, a California Scenic Highway that runs the length of the valley, which is near the Sonoma–Napa county border. In addition to wineries, you can find a few tasting rooms on the historic plaza in the town of Sonoma.

Sonoma

▶ *14 mi west of Napa on Hwy. 12; 45 mi from San Francisco, north on U.S. 101, east on Hwy. 37, and north on Hwy. 121/12.*

Sonoma is the oldest town in the Wine Country. Its historic town plaza is the site of the last and the northernmost of the 21 missions established by the Franciscan order of Father Junípero Serra. It also includes the largest group of old adobes north of Monterey.

On your way into town from the south, you pass through the Carneros wine district, which straddles the southern sections of Sonoma and Napa counties. Sam Sebastiani, of the famous Sebastiani family, and his wife,
㉜ Vicki, have established their own hilltop winery, **Viansa,** in the Carneros district. Reminiscent of a Tuscan villa, the winery's ocher-color building is surrounded by olive trees and overlooks the valley. The varietals produced here depart from the traditionally Californian and include muscat canelli and nebbiolo. The Italian Marketplace on the premises sells delicious specialty sandwiches and salads to complement Viansa's Italian-style wines. The adjacent Wine Country Visitor Center has brochures and information. ⊠ *25200 Arnold Dr.* ☎ *707/935–4700* ⊕ *www.viansa. com* ⌑ *Tour free* ☉ *Daily 10–5; tours daily at 11 and 2.*

㉝ The sparkling and still wines at **Gloria Ferrer Champagne Caves** originated with a 700-year-old stock of Ferrer grapes. The method here is to age the wines in a "cava," or cellar, where several feet of earth maintain a constant temperature—an increasingly popular alternative to temperature-controlled warehouses. Call after 9:30 AM on the day of your visit for that day's tour schedule. ⊠ *23555 Carneros Hwy. (Hwy. 121)*

☎ 707/996–7256, 707/933–1917 *tour times* ⊕ *www.gloriaferrer.com* ✉ *Tasting fees vary, tour free* ☉ *Daily 10:30–5:30; tours daily 11–4.*

In town, the **Mission San Francisco Solano,** whose chapel and school were used to bring Christianity to the Native Americans, is now a museum with a fine collection of 19th-century watercolors. ⊠ *114 Spain St. E* ☎ *707/938–9560* ✉ *$1 (includes Sonoma Barracks on the central plaza and General Vallejo's home, Lachryma Montis)* ☉ *Daily 10–5.*

A tree-lined driveway leads to **Lachryma Montis,** which General Mariano G. Vallejo, the last Mexican governor of California, built for his large family in 1851; the state purchased the home in 1933. The Victorian Gothic house is secluded in the midst of beautiful gardens. Opulent furnishings, including a white-marble fireplace in every room, are particularly noteworthy. ⊠ *W. Spain St. near 3rd St. E* ☎ *707/938–9559* ✉ *$1* ☉ *Daily 10–5; tours by appointment.*

㉞ Originally planted by Franciscans of the Sonoma Mission in 1825, the **Sebastiani Vineyards** were bought by Samuele Sebastiani in 1904. Red wine is king here. To complement it, Sylvia Sebastiani has recorded her good Italian home cooking in a family recipe book, *Mangiamo.* On Sonoma's main plaza the Sebastiani winery operates **Sebastiani on the Square** (⊠ 40 W. Spain St. ☎ 707/933–3290), a wine bar with live music Thursday through Saturday evenings. ⊠ *389 4th St. E* ☎ *707/938–5532* ⊕ *www.sebastiani.com* ✉ *Tour $5* ☉ *Daily 10–5. Tours weekdays at 11 and 2; weekends at 10:45, noon, and 2.*

▶ ㉟ **Buena Vista Carneros Winery** is the oldest continually operating winery in California. It was here, in 1857, that Count Agoston Haraszthy de Mokcsa laid the basis for modern California wine making, bucking the conventional wisdom that vines should be planted on well-watered ground by instead planting on well-drained hillsides. Chinese laborers dug tunnels 100 feet into the hillside, and the limestone they extracted was used to build the main house. The winery, which is surrounded by redwood and eucalyptus trees, has a specialty-foods shop, an art gallery, and picnic areas. ⊠ *18000 Old Winery Rd., off Napa Rd. (follow signs from plaza)* ☎ *707/938–1266 or 800/678–8504* ⊕ *www.buenavistawinery.com* ✉ *Tasting fees vary, tour free* ☉ *Daily 10–5. Tours Jan.–June and Oct.–Dec., daily at 2; July–Sept., daily at 11 and 2.*

㊱ **Ravenswood,** literally dug into the mountains like a bunker, is famous for its zinfandel. The merlot should be tasted as well. Tours include barrel tastings of wines in progress in the cellar. ⊠ *18701 Gehricke Rd., off E. Spain St.* ☎ *707/938–1960* ⊕ *www.ravenswood-wine.com* ✉ *Tasting and tour $4* ☉ *Daily 10–4:30; tours at 10:30 by appointment.*

Where to Stay & Eat

$$–$$$ ✕ **The Girl & the Fig.** The popular restaurant was in Glen Ellen before migrating to the Sonoma Hotel, where it has revitalized the historic barroom with cozy banquettes and inventive French country cuisine. A seasonally changing menu may include something with figs, duck confit with green lentils, steak frites, or cassoulet. The wine list is notable for its inclusion of Rhône and other less-common varietals. ⊠ *Sonoma Hotel, Sonoma Plaza, 110 W. Spain St.* ☎ *707/938–3634* ▭ *AE, D, DC, MC, V.*

$$–$$$ ✕ **Santé.** The Fairmont Sonoma Mission Inn's formal restaurant focuses on using the freshest local ingredients rather than on elaborate preparations. The resulting meals are beautifully simple and healthful. An Asian influence shows up dishes such as the tuna tartare, but the California influence dominates in choices such as carrot–and–pumpkin seed ravioli and roasted beets with a soufflé of Sonoma goat cheese. ⊠ *Fairmont Sonoma Mission Inn & Spa, 18140 Sonoma Hwy. (2 mi north of*

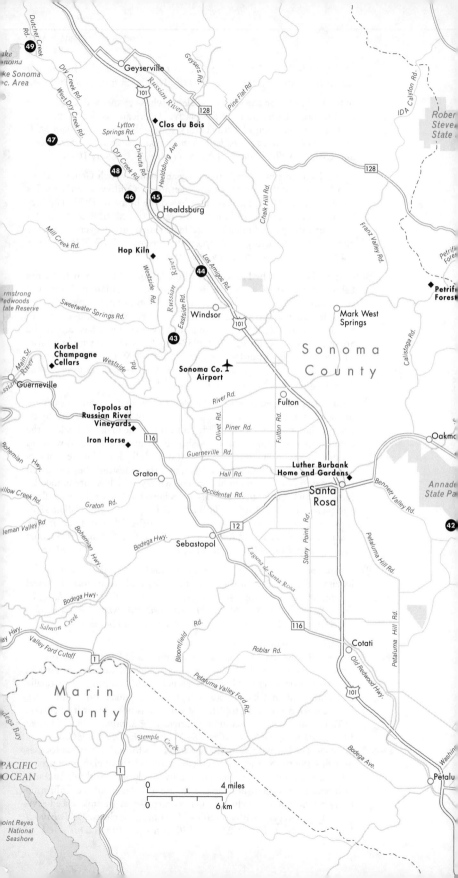

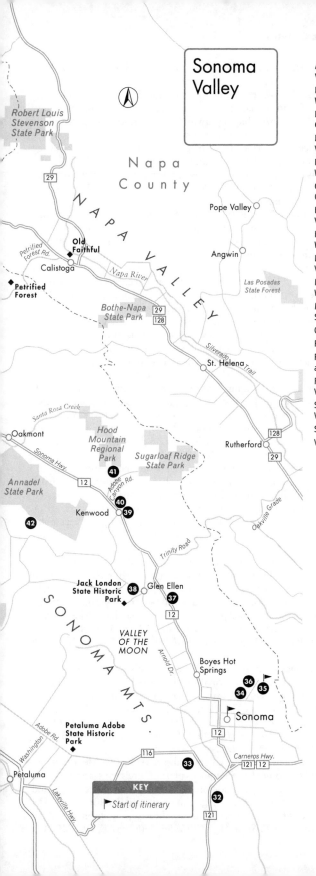

Sonoma Valley

Sonoma on Hwy. 12 at Boyes Blvd.), Boyes Hot Springs ☎ *707/939–2415* ▭ *AE, DC, MC, V* ⊘ *No lunch.*

$$ ✕ **La Salette.** Chef-owner Manny Azevedo, born in the Azores and raised in Sonoma, found culinary inspiration in his travels. The flavors of his dishes, such as Mozambique prawns with tomatoes and grilled plantains or salt cod baked with white onions, stand strong while complementing each other. The variety of ports on the wine list emphasizes Azevedo's Portuguese heritage. Paintings and sculpture enliven the off-white walls in this eatery, which has patio seating for balmy evenings. ✉ *18625 Hwy. 12, Boyes Hot Springs* ☎ *707/938–1927* ▭ *MC, V* ⊘ *Closed Mon. and Tues. No lunch.*

★ **$–$$$** ✕ **Cafe La Haye.** In a postage-stamp-size kitchen, skillful chefs turn out half a dozen main courses that star on a small but worthwhile menu emphasizing local ingredients. Chicken, beef, pasta, fish, and risotto get deluxe treatment without fuss or fanfare. This offbeat café turns out some of the best food for the price in the Wine Country. ✉ *140 E. Napa St.* ☎ *707/935–5994* ▭ *MC, V* ⊘ *Closed Mon. No dinner Sun., no lunch.*

$–$$$ ✕ **Meritage.** A fortuitous blend of southern French and northern Italian cuisine is the backbone of this restaurant, where chef Carlo Cavallo works wonders with house-made pastas, particularly *gemelli* (twists). An oyster bar augments extensive seafood choices, and breakfast is available Wednesday through Sunday. The wine list includes blends from the major players in both Napa and Sonoma. ✉ *522 Broadway* ☎ *707/938–9430* ▭ *AE, MC, V* ⊘ *Closed Tues.*

$–$$ ✕ **Della Santina's.** A longtime favorite with a charming, enclosed brick patio out back serves the most authentic Italian food in town. Daily fish and veal specials offer an alternative to other menu choices of classic northern Italian pastas and rotisserie meats. Of special note are the gnocchi and, when available, petrale sole and sand dabs. ✉ *133 E. Napa St.* ☎ *707/935–0576* ▭ *AE, D, MC, V.*

$–$$ ✕ **Piatti.** A beautiful room opens onto one of the finest patios in the valley at this restaurant, the first in a minichain of trattorias. Pizza from the wood-burning oven and northern Italian specials (spit-roasted chicken, ravioli with spinach-ricotta filling) are served on the terrace or in a rustic space with an open kitchen and pastel images of vegetables on the walls. ✉ *El Dorado Hotel, 405 1st St. W* ☎ *707/996–2351* ▭ *AE, MC, V.*

$–$$ ✕ **Saddles.** True to its name, this steak house is decorated with things horsey, from saddles to boots. Expect to find Midwestern corn-fed USDA prime beef, in addition to pork chops, chicken, fish, and a black-Angus burger. Side dishes include a sinful potato au gratin as well as green vegetable selections. Appetizers can be ordered in the bar, in case you want to sample from the martini list. ✉ *29 E. MacArthur St., at MacArthur Pl.* ☎ *707/938–2942* ▭ *AE, D, DC, MC, V* ⊘ *No lunch Mon.–Thurs.*

¢–$$ ✕ **The Big 3 Diner.** Overstuffed booths, ceiling fans, and an open kitchen give this corner bistro an informal feel. Country breakfasts, pizza from the wood-burning oven, and hearty American fare such as house-smoked meats are the specialties. The limited menu includes several spa-cuisine items. ✉ *Fairmont Sonoma Mission Inn & Spa, 18140 Sonoma Hwy. (2 mi north of Sonoma on Hwy. 12 at Boyes Blvd.), Boyes Hot Springs* ☎ *707/938–9000* ▭ *AE, DC, MC, V.*

¢–$$ ✕ **La Casa.** Whitewashed stucco and red tiles evoke Old Mexico at this spot around the corner from Sonoma's plaza. There's bar seating, a patio, and an extensive menu of traditional Mexican food: chimichangas and snapper Veracruz for entrées, sangria to drink, and flan for dessert. The food isn't really the draw here; locals love the casual atmosphere and the margaritas. ✉ *121 E. Spain St.* ☎ *707/996–3406* ▭ *AE, DC, MC, V.*

$$$$ 🏨 **MacArthur Place.** Chic country colors such as olive and lemon distinguish the accommodations at this sprawling complex. Rooms are in a remodeled historic mansion as well as in contemporary two-story structures tucked into the back of the property. Beyond the extensively landscaped grounds is a full-service spa, adjacent to the pool. ✉ *29 E. MacArthur St., at MacArthur Pl., 95476* ☎ *707/938–2929 or 800/722–1866* 🖷 *707/933–9833* ⊕ *www.macarthurplace.com* 🛏 *35 rooms, 29 suites* ♿ *Restaurant, room service, in-room data ports, some refrigerators, cable TV, in-room VCRs, pool, gym, hot tub, sauna, spa, croquet, bar, shop, dry cleaning, laundry service, concierge, Internet, business services; no smoking* ⊟ *AE, D, MC, V* ⍟ *CP.*

$$$–$$$$ 🏨 **The Fairmont Sonoma Mission Inn & Spa.** California Mission–style architecture combines with the elegance of a European luxury spa at this beautifully landscaped property. Everything here is on a grand scale, from the Olympic-size pool to the spa facilities, where warm mineral water is pumped up from wells beneath the property. Gourmet and classic spa food is served at the Santé restaurant. Thirty suites in a secluded, tree-shaded area have verandas or patios, whirlpools, and fireplaces. ✉ *18140 Hwy. 12 (2 mi north of Sonoma at Boyes Blvd.), Box 1447, Boyes Hot Springs 95476* ☎ *707/938–9000* 🖷 *707/938–4250* ⊕ *www.sonomamissioninn.com* 🛏 *168 rooms, 60 suites* ♿ *2 restaurants, room service, in-room data ports, in-room safes, minibars, refrigerators, cable TV, 2 pools, 18-hole golf course, pro shop, fitness classes, gym, hair salon, hot tub, spa, bicycles, hiking, 2 bars, shops, baby-sitting, dry cleaning, laundry service, concierge, business services, meeting rooms; no smoking* ⊟ *AE, DC, MC, V.*

$$$ 🏨 **El Dorado Hotel.** A modern hotel in a remodeled old building, this place has unusually spare and simple accommodations. Rooms reflect Sonoma's Mission era, with Mexican-tile floors and white walls. The best rooms are Nos. 3 and 4, which have larger balconies that overlook the Sonoma Plaza. ✉ *405 1st St. W, 95476* ☎ *707/996–3030 or 800/289–3031* 🖷 *707/996–3148* ⊕ *www.hoteleldorado.com* 🛏 *27 rooms* ♿ *Restaurant, in-room data ports, refrigerators, cable TV, in-room VCRs, pool, shops; no smoking* ⊟ *AE, MC, V* ⍟ *CP.*

$$–$$$$ 🏨 **Thistle Dew Inn.** The public rooms of this turn-of-the-20th-century Victorian home half a block from Sonoma Plaza are filled with collector's-quality Arts and Crafts furnishings. Four of the six rooms have private entrances and decks, and all have queen-size beds with antique quilts, private baths, and air-conditioning. Some rooms have fireplaces; some have whirlpools. Welcome bonuses include a hot tub and free use of the inn's bicycles. ✉ *171 W. Spain St., 95476* ☎ *707/938–2909, 800/382–7895 in CA* 🖷 *707/996–8413* ⊕ *www.thistledew.com* 🛏 *4 rooms, 2 suites* ♿ *In-room data ports, hot tub, bicycles; no TV in some rooms, no smoking* ⊟ *AE, D, DC, MC, V* ⍟ *BP.*

Fodor'sChoice ★

¢–$$$ 🏨 **Vineyard Inn.** Built as a roadside motor court in 1941, this B&B inn with red-tile roofs brings a touch of Mexican village charm to an otherwise lackluster and somewhat noisy location at the junction of two main highways. It's across from two vineyards and is the closest lodging to Sears Point Raceway. Rooms have queen-size beds, and Continental breakfast is included. ✉ *23000 Arnold Dr., at junction of Hwys. 116 and 121, 95476* ☎ *707/938–2350 or 800/359–4667* 🖷 *707/938–2353* ⊕ *www.sonomavineyardinn.com* 🛏 *17 rooms, 7 suites* ♿ *In-room data ports, cable TV, pool; no smoking* ⊟ *AE, MC, V* ⍟ *CP.*

Nightlife & the Arts

Small blues and jazz bands play Friday and Saturday nights at **Cucina Viansa** (✉ 400 1st St. E ☎ 707/935–5656) on the plaza, where the crowd is a mix of young to middle-age fans. The **Sebastiani Theatre**

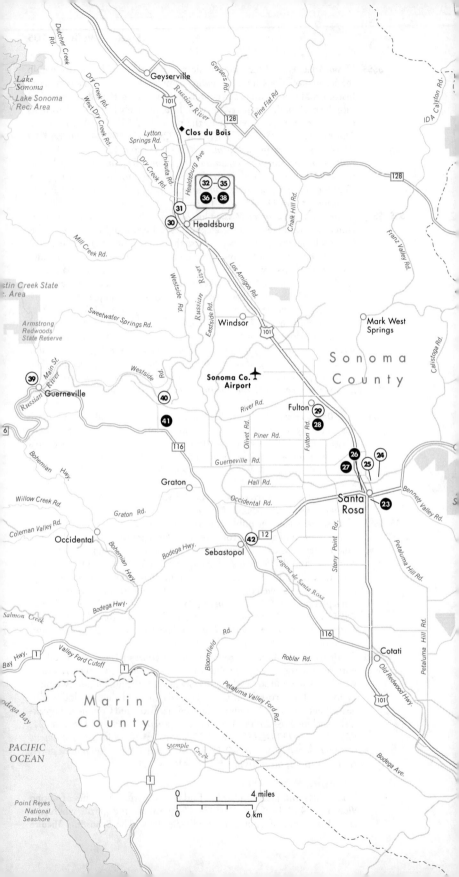

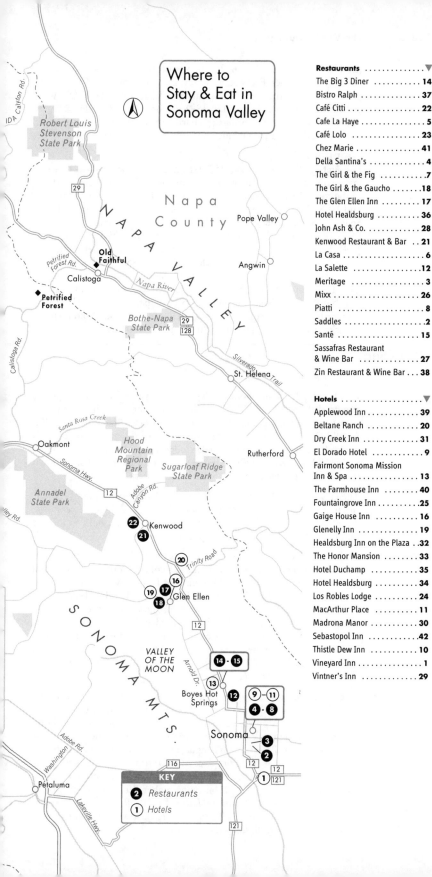

Where to Stay & Eat in Sonoma Valley

KEY

2 *Restaurants*

1 *Hotels*

(✉ 476 1st St. E ☎ 707/996–2020), on historic Sonoma Square, schedules first-run movies. Every Sunday in August and September **Shakespeare at Buena Vista,** at the Buena Vista Carneros Winery (✉ 18000 Old Winery Rd., off Napa Rd. ☎ 707/938–1266 or 800/678–8504 ⊕ www. buenavistawinery.com), brings the Bard to Sonoma. Performances are best enjoyed with a picnic lunch and a bottle of wine.

Shopping

Half-Pint (✉ Sonoma Plaza, 450 1st St. E ☎ 707/938–1722) carries fashionable clothing and accessories for infants and children. Several shops in the four-block **Sonoma Plaza** (✉ between E. Napa and E. Spain Sts. and 1st St. W and 1st St. E) attract food-lovers from miles around. The **Sonoma Cheese Factory and Deli** (✉ Sonoma Plaza, 2 Spain St. ☎ 707/ 996–1000), run by the same family for four generations, makes Sonoma Jack cheese and the tangy Sonoma Teleme. They have everything you could possibly need for a picnic. **Shushu Fufu** (✉ Sonoma Plaza, 452 1st St. E ☎ 707/938–3876) is a chic shoe boutique with labels including Cole-Haan and Arche, makers of fine French walking shoes. Glitzy it's not, but the **Total Living Company** (✉ 5 E. Napa St. ☎ 707/939–3900) is great for full-spectrum lightbulbs, well-designed household utensils, and clever items that make daily life easier.

Glen Ellen

7 mi north of Sonoma on Hwy. 12.

Jack London lived in Sonoma Valley for many years. The craggy, quirky, and creek-bisected town of Glen Ellen commemorates him with place-names and nostalgic establishments. The **Jack London Bookstore** (✉ 14300 Arnold Dr. ☎ 707/996–2888) carries many of the namesake author's books. Built in the early 1900s, **London Lodge** (✉ 13740 Arnold Dr. ☎ 707/ 996–3100 ⊕ www.jacklondonlodge.com) is tucked out of sight down the hill from the Jack London State Historic Park.

The **Olive Press** (✉ 14801 Arnold Dr. ☎ 707/939–8900) not only carries many local olive oils, serving bowls, books, and dining accessories, but also presses fruit for a number of local growers, usually in the late fall. It's in the Jack London Village complex.

In the hills above Glen Ellen—known as the Valley of the Moon—lies **Jack London State Historic Park.** London's collection of South Seas and other artifacts is on view at the House of Happy Walls, a museum of London's effects. The ruins of Wolf House, which London designed and which mysteriously burned down just before he was to move in, are close to the House of Happy Walls. Also restored and open to the public are a few farm outbuildings and the cottage where London lived and wrote. London is buried on the property. ✉ *2400 London Ranch Rd.* ☎ *707/ 938–5216* 🅿 *Parking $3* ☉ *Park Nov.–Mar., daily 9:30–5; Apr.–Oct., daily 9:30–7. Museum daily 10–5.*

③⑦ Arrowood Vineyards is neither as old nor as famous as some of its neighbors, but wine makers and critics are quite familiar with the excellent handcrafted wines produced here. The winery's harmonious architecture overlooking the Valley of the Moon earned it an award from the Sonoma Historic Preservation League, and the wine-making equipment is state-of-the-art. A stone fireplace in the tasting rooms makes this an especially enticing destination in winter. The winery has been owned by Robert Mondavi since 2000, but wine maker Richard Arrowood has stayed on. ✉ *14347 Sonoma Hwy.* ☎ *707/938–5170* ⊕ *www. arrowoodvineyards.com* 🍷 *Tasting fees vary, tour $10 (includes tasting)* ☉ *Daily 10–4:30; tours daily at noon.*

As you drive along Highway 12, you see orchards and rows of vineyards flanked by oak-covered mountain ranges. One of the best-known local **38** wineries is **Benziger Family Winery,** situated on a sprawling estate in a bowl with 360° sun exposure. Among the first wineries to identify certain vineyard blocks for particularly desirable flavors, Benziger is noted for its merlot, pinot blanc, chardonnay, and fumé blanc. Tram tours through the vineyards cover everything from regional microclimates and geography to a glimpse of the extensive cave system. Tours depart several times a day, weather permitting. ⊠ *1883 London Ranch Rd.* ☎ *707/935–3000, 888/490–2739 tram-tour schedule* ⊕ *www.benziger. com* ⊡ *Tasting and tour $5 and up* ☉ *Daily 10–4:30.*

Where to Stay & Eat

$$–$$$ ✕**The Glen Ellen Inn.** Recommended for romantic evenings, this restaurant adjusts its seafood and pasta offerings according to seasonal availability. Look for sesame-seared ahi tuna and filet mignon served with Parmesan potatoes. Desserts such as cinnamon-brandy bread pudding are large enough to share. ⊠ *13670 Arnold Dr.* ☎ *707/996–6409* ⊟ *AE, MC, V* ☉ *No lunch Wed.–Thurs.*

★ $$ ✕**The Girl & the Gaucho.** Rust-colored walls, the glow from myriad hanging lamps, and the smiling servers set a warm, intimate tone at this pan–Latin American restaurant. Large dishes, such as grilled rib eye or pan-roasted bass, can be served in the Spanish style, with a sherry-reduction sauce and pepper, olive, and caper relish, or in Cuban style, with tropical fruit salsa. Small plates, with paprika prawns and ceviche-and-avocado salad, for instance, are unusual and beautifully presented. ⊠ *13690 Arnold Dr.* ☎ *707/938–2130* ⊟ *AE, MC, V* ☉ *Closed Tues. and Wed. No lunch.*

$$$$ ▥**Gaige House Inn.** The comfort of a 19th-century residence blends with
Fodor'sChoice contemporary, uncluttered furnishings accented with Asian details at this ★ elegant country inn. Some of the largest accommodations—and the most private—are cottages behind the house, overlooking the pool or Calabazas Creek. Rooms in the main house have their own charms; some have fireplaces and one opens onto the pool. Another has one of the most glamorous bathrooms in the Wine Country—it's bigger than many hotel rooms and has a whirlpool tub and separate shower area more than large enough for two. The green lawn, striped awnings, white umbrellas, and magnolias around the large pool conjure up a manicured Hamptons-like glamour in the midst of rustic Glen Ellen. ⊠ *13540 Arnold Dr., 95442* ☎ *707/935–0237 or 800/935–0237* ☎ *707/935–6411* ⊕ *www.gaige.com* ↝ *12 rooms, 3 suites* ⚲ *In-room data ports, some in-room safes, refrigerators, cable TV, pool, hot tub; no smoking* ⊟ *AE, D, DC, MC, V* ⓧ *BP.*

$$–$$$ ▥**Beltane Ranch.** On a slope of the Mayacamas range on the eastern side of the Sonoma Valley lies this house, which is thought to have been built by Mary Ellen Pleasant, a shrewd San Francisco businesswoman who was the daughter of slaves. The Wood family, who have lived on the premises since 1936, have stocked the comfortable living room with dozens of books about the area. The rooms, furnished with antiques, open onto the building's wraparound porch. The cottage apartment, created out of the gardener's quarters, has a sitting room. ⊠ *11775 Sonoma Hwy. (Hwy. 12), 95442* ☎ *707/996–6501* ⊕ *www.beltaneranch.com* ↝ *3 rooms, 3 suites* ⚲ *Tennis court, hiking; no room TVs* ⊟ *No credit cards* ⓧ *BP.*

$$–$$$ ▥**Glenelly Inn.** On the outskirts of Glen Ellen, this sunny little establishment, built as an inn in 1916, offers all the comforts of home—plus a hot tub in the garden. Rooms, each individually decorated, tend toward a simple country style; many have four-poster beds and floral fabrics. Innkeeper

Kristi Hallamore Jeppesen serves breakfast in front of the common room's cobblestone fireplace and provides local delicacies in the afternoon. On sunny mornings you can eat outside under the shady oak trees. ⊠ *5131 Warm Springs Rd., 95442* ☎ *707/996–6720* 🖷 *707/996–5227* ⊕ *www.glenelly.com* ↪ *10 rooms* ♨ *Outdoor hot tub; no a/c in some rooms, no room TVs, no smoking* ▤ *AE, D, MC, V* ⧉| *BP.*

Kenwood

3 mi north of Glen Ellen on Hwy. 12.

Kenwood has a historic train depot and several restaurants and shops that specialize in locally produced goods. Its inns, restaurants, and winding roads nestle in soothing bucolic landscapes.

③⑨ **Kunde Estate Winery** lies on 2,000 acres and is managed by the fourth generation of Kunde-family grape growers and winemakers. The standard tour of the grounds includes its extensive caves. A tasting and dining room lies 175 feet below a chardonnay vineyard. Tastings usually include viognier, chardonnay, cabernet sauvignon, and zinfandel. ⊠ *10155 Hwy. 12,* ☎ *707/833–5501* ⊕ *www.kunde.com* 🖻 *Tasting $5, tour free* ⊘ *Daily 10:30–4:30. Tours Apr.–Oct., Fri.–Mon. 11–3; Nov.–Mar., Fri.–Sun. 11–3.*

④⓪ The beautifully rustic grounds at **Kenwood Vineyards** complement the tasting room and artistic bottle labels. Although Kenwood produces all premium varietals, the winery is best known for its Jack London Vineyard reds—pinot noir, zinfandel, merlot, and a unique Artist Series cabernet. Most weekends the winery offers a free food-and-wine pairing, but there are no tours. ⊠ *9592 Sonoma Hwy.* ☎ *707/833–5891* ⊕ *www.kenwoodvineyards.com* 🖻 *Free* ⊘ *Daily 10–4:30.*

④① The landscaping and design of **Landmark Vineyards,** established by the heirs of John Deere, are as classical as the winery's wine-making methods. Those methods include two fermentations in French oak barrels and the use of the yeasts present in the skins of the grapes rather than the addition of manufactured yeasts to create the wine. Landmark's chardonnays have been particularly well received, as has the winery's pinot noir. ⊠ *101 Adobe Canyon Rd. (off Sonoma Hwy.)* ☎ *707/833–1144 or 800/452–6365* ⊕ *www.landmarkwine.com* ⊘ *Daily 10–4:30; horse-drawn-wagon vineyard tours Apr.–Sept., Sat. 11:30–3:30.*

Where to Eat

$–$$$ ✕ **Kenwood Restaurant & Bar.** One of the enduring favorites in an area known for fine dining, this is where Napa and Sonoma chefs eat on their nights off. You can indulge in California country cuisine in the sunny, South of France–style dining room or head through the French doors to the patio for a memorable view of the vineyards. Dishes might include roast lamb, baked polenta with goat cheese, or house-made pastas. ⊠ *9900 Hwy. 12* ☎ *707/833–6326* ▤ *MC, V* ⊘ *Closed Mon.*

★ **¢–$$** ✕ **Café Citti.** The aroma of garlic envelops the neighborhood whenever the Italian chef-owner is roasting chickens at this homey roadside café. Deli items, hot pastas, and soups make this an excellent budget stop. ⊠ *9049 Hwy. 12* ☎ *707/833–2690* ▤ *MC, V.*

ELSEWHERE IN SONOMA COUNTY

At nearly 1,598 square mi, Sonoma is far too large a county to cover in one or two days. The landmass extends from San Pablo Bay south to Mendocino County and from the Mayacamas Mountains on the Napa side west to the Pacific Ocean. One of the fastest-growing counties in

Northern California, Sonoma is still rather sparsely populated; even the county seat, Santa Rosa, has fewer than 120,000 residents.

Within this varied terrain are hills and valleys, rivers, creeks, and lakes that beg to be explored. Wineries can be found from the cool flatlands of the south to the hot interior valleys to the foggy regions closer to the coast. Sonoma, though less famous than Napa, in fact has more award-winning wines. But to be sure, Sonoma offers much more than wine.

In addition to the Sonoma Valley, the major grape-growing appellations include the Alexander Valley and the Dry Creek Valley close to Healdsburg, and the Russian River Valley to the west of U.S. 101. The latter has been gaining an international reputation for its pinot noir, which thrives in the valley climate cooled by the presence of morning and evening fog. Guerneville, a popular summer destination for gays and lesbians, and neighboring Forestville are in the heart of the Russian River Valley. Dozens of small, winding roads and myriad wineries make this region a delight to explore, as do its small towns.

Santa Rosa

8 mi northwest of Kenwood on Hwy. 12.

Santa Rosa is the Wine Country's largest city and a good bet for moderately priced hotel rooms, especially for those who have not reserved in advance.

The **Luther Burbank Home and Gardens** commemorates the great botanist who lived and worked on these grounds for 50 years, single-handedly developing the modern techniques of hybridization. Arriving as a young man from New England, he wrote: "I firmly believe . . . that this is the chosen spot of all the earth, as far as nature is concerned." The Santa Rosa plum, Shasta daisy, and lily of the Nile agapanthus are among the 800 or so plants he developed or improved. In the music room of his house, a Webster's Dictionary of 1946 lies open to a page on which the verb "burbank" is defined as "to modify and improve plant life." ⊠ *Santa Rosa and Sonoma Aves.* ☎ *707/524–5445* ⊕ *www.lutherburbank.org* ⊠ *Gardens free, guided tour of house and greenhouse $3* ⊙ *Gardens daily 8–dusk; tours Apr.–Oct., Tues.–Sun. 10–4.*

★ ⓸ **Matanzas Creek Winery** specializes in three varietals—sauvignon blanc, merlot, and chardonnay—and makes a hard-to-find sparkling wine. All three varietals have won glowing reviews from various magazines. Huge windows in the visitor center overlook a field of 3,100 tiered and fragrant lavender plants. Acres and acres of gardens planted with unusual grasses and plants from all over the world have caught the attention of horticulturists. After you taste the wines, ask for the self-guided garden tour book before taking a stroll. ⊠ *6097 Bennett Valley Rd.* ☎ *707/528–6464 or 800/590–6464* ⊕ *www.matanzascreek.com* ⊠ *Tasting fees vary, tour free* ⊙ *Apr.–Dec., daily 10–4:30; Jan.–Mar., Thurs.–Sun. 10–4:30. Tours weekdays at 10:30 and 3, weekends at 10:30, by reservation.*

Where to Stay & Eat

$$–$$$ ✕ **John Ash & Co.** Patio seating, views out over vineyards, and a cozy indoor fireplace make this slightly formal restaurant a draw on both summer and winter evenings. The California cuisine incorporates a bit of France, Italy, and even Asia, but the ingredients are largely local: Hog Island oysters come from Tomales Bay, and the goat cheese in the ravioli comes from Laura Chenel, local cheese maker extraordinaire. Entrées may include Dungeness crab cakes or pan-seared ahi tuna. A café menu offers bites between meals. ⊠ *4330 Barnes Rd. (River Rd. exit*

west from U.S. 101) ☎ 707/527–7687 ♨ *Reservations essential* ▤ *AE, D, DC, MC, V* ◷ *No lunch Sat.*

$$–$$$ ✕ **Mixx.** Great service and an eclectic mix of dishes made with locally grown ingredients define this small restaurant with large windows, high ceilings, and Italian blown-glass chandeliers. House-made ravioli, grilled Cajun prawns, and grilled leg of lamb are among the favorites of the many regulars, and the kids' menu makes it a favorite with families. The frequently changing wine list includes more than a dozen choices by the glass. Occasional "Name That Wine" dinners feature local wine makers and artisanal cheese makers. ⊠ *135 4th St., at Davis St. (behind mall on Railroad Sq.)* ☎ 707/573–1344 ▤ *AE, D, MC, V* ◷ *Closed Sun.*

$–$$$ ✕ **Café Lolo.** This small, sophisticated spot is the territory of chef and co-owner Michael Quigley, who has single-handedly made downtown Santa Rosa a culinary destination. His dishes stress fresh ingredients and an eye for presentation. Don't pass up the foie gras terrine with caramelized apples. ⊠ *620 5th St.* ☎ 707/576–7822 ▤ *AE, MC, V* ◷ *Closed Sun. No lunch Sat.*

$–$$ ✕ **Sassafras Restaurant & Wine Bar.** Chef Scott Snyder changes the menu daily to reflect what's fresh at the market. The restaurant focuses on regional dishes from the United States, Cuba, and the Caribbean; the wine list is heavy on California vintages but also includes wines from Canada and the East Coast. Dishes that sound familiar get a contemporary twist: pizza with Creole-style ingredients, a meat loaf–with–ketchup that's really a venison-and-pork terrine with cranberry sauce, pecan pie with a lavender custard. ⊠ *1229 N. Dutton Ave.* ☎ 707/578–7600 ▤ *AE, D, DC, MC, V* ◷ *No lunch weekends.*

$$$–$$$$ ▦ **Vintner's Inn.** Set on 50 acres of vineyards, this French provincial inn has large rooms, many with wood-burning fireplaces, and a trellised sundeck. Breakfast is complimentary, and the close-by John Ash & Co. restaurant is tempting for other meals. Discount passes to an affiliated health club are available. ⊠ *4350 Barnes Rd. (River Rd. exit west from U.S. 101), 95403* ☎ 707/575–7350 *or* 800/421–2584 ☐ 707/575–1426 ⊕ *www.vintnersinn.com* ⇨ *38 rooms, 6 suites* ♨ *Restaurant, room service, in-room data ports, in-room safes, minibars, cable TV, hot tub, lounge, dry cleaning, laundry service, meeting room; no smoking* ▤ *AE, D, DC, MC, V* ¶◎¶ *CP.*

★ $$ ▦ **Fountaingrove Inn.** A redwood sculpture and a wall of cascading water distinguish the lobby at this elegant, comfortable hotel and conference center. A refined restaurant and bar has piano music and a stellar menu. For an additional fee you have access to a nearby 18-hole golf course, a tennis court, and a health club. ⊠ *101 Fountaingrove Pkwy. (near U.S. 101), 95403* ☎ 707/578–6101 *or* 800/222–6101 ☐ 707/544–3126 ⊕ *www.fountaingroveinn.com* ⇨ *88 rooms, 36 suites* ♨ *Restaurant, room service, in-room data ports, refrigerators, cable TV, golf privileges, pool, hot tub, bar, dry cleaning, laundry service, Internet, business services, meeting rooms, some pets allowed (fee), no-smoking rooms* ▤ *AE, D, DC, MC, V* ¶◎¶ *CP.*

$–$$ ▦ **Los Robles Lodge.** The pleasant, relaxed motel overlooks a pool that's set into a grassy landscape. Pets are allowed in some rooms. Some rooms have whirlpools. ⊠ *1985 Cleveland Ave. (Steele La. exit west from U.S. 101), 95401* ☎ 707/545–6330 *or* 800/255–6330 ☐ 707/575–5826 ⇨ *104 rooms* ♨ *Restaurant, coffee shop, in-room data ports, microwaves, refrigerators, cable TV, pool, hot tub, laundry facilities, business services, no-smoking rooms* ▤ *AE, DC, MC, V.*

Nightlife & the Arts

The **Luther Burbank Center for the Arts** (⊠ 50 Mark West Springs Rd. ☎ 707/546–3600) presents concerts, plays, and other performances by locally and internationally known artists. For symphony, ballet, and other live theater performances throughout the year, call the **Spreckels Performing Arts Center** (✉ 5409 Snyder La. ☎ 707/588–3434) in Rohnert Park.

Russian River Valley

5 mi northwest of Santa Rosa.

The Russian River flows all the way from Mendocino to the Pacific Ocean, but in terms of wine making, the Russian River Valley is centered on a triangle with points at Healdsburg, Guerneville, and Sebastopol. Tall redwoods shade many of the two-lane roads that access this scenic area, where, thanks to the cooling marine influence, pinot noir and chardonnay are the king and queen of grapes. For a free map of the area, contact **Russian River Wine Road** (✉ Box 46, Healdsburg 95448 ☎ 800/723–6336 ⊕ www.wineroad.com).

Rustic woods and a homey tasting room await you in a hop kiln–style building at the unusual **Topolos at Russian River Vineyards.** Michael Topolos is a leader in biodynamic farming, and he will gladly talk about environmentally friendly practices over a taste of port, alicante bouschet, or other unusual varieties. ✉ *5700 Gravenstein Hwy. N (Hwy. 116)* ☎ *707/887–1575* ⌕ *Tasting free* ☉ *Daily 11–5:30.*

Tucked into Green Valley, **Iron Horse,** a showplace estate, is equally successful at making still wine as it is the sparkling type. You should allow time to meander around the gardens, which are planted to bloom practically all year-round, thanks to the winery's proximity (12 mi) to the ocean. ✉ *9786 Ross Station Rd. (near Sebastopol)* ☎ *707/887–1507* ⊕ *www.ironhorsevineyards.com* ☉ *Daily 10:30–3:30.*

❹❸ **Rochioli Vineyards and Winery** claims one of the prettiest picnic sites in the area, with tables overlooking vineyards. The winery makes one of the county's best chardonnays but is especially known for its pinot noir and sauvignon blanc. ✉ *6192 Westside Rd.* ☎ *707/433–2305* ☉ *Feb.–Oct., daily 10–5; Nov.–Jan., daily 11–4.*

★ At **Hop Kiln Winery,** you can easily spot the triple towers of the old hop kiln, a California state historical landmark. One of the friendliest wineries in the Russian River area, Hop Kiln has a vast tasting room steps away from a duck pond where you can picnic. This is a good place to try light wines such as riesling or A Thousand Flowers (a fruity gewürztraminer blend), but be sure to try some of the big-bodied reds as well. ✉ *6050 Westside Rd., Healdsburg* ☎ *707/433–6491* ⊕ *www. hopkilnwinery.com* ⌕ *Tasting free* ☉ *Daily 10–5.*

Old Vine zinfandel, along with chardonnay and pinot noir, is top of the ❹❹ line at **Rodney Strong Vineyards.** Picnic areas overlook the vineyards. ✉ *11455 Old Redwood Hwy.* ☎ *707/433–6511* ⊕ *www.rodneystrong. com* ⌕ *Tasting free–$5, tour free* ☉ *Daily 10–5; tours daily at 11 and 3.*

off the beaten path

KORBEL CHAMPAGNE CELLARS – To be called champagne, a wine must be made in the French region of Champagne or it's just sparkling wine. But despite the objections of the French, champagne has entered the lexicon of California wine makers, and many refer to their sparkling wines as champagne. Whatever you call it, Korbel produces a tasty, reasonably priced wine as well as its own beer, which is available at a brew pub on the premises. The wine tour, one of the best in Sonoma County, clearly explains the process of making sparkling wine. The winery's 19th-century buildings and gorgeous rose gardens are a delight in their own right. ✉ *13250 River Rd.,*

Guerneville ☎ 707/824–7000 ⊕ www.korbel.com Tasting and tour free ⊙ Oct.–Apr., daily 9–4:30; May–Sept., daily 9–5; tours on the hr 10–3.

Where to Stay & Eat

$–$$ ✕ **Chez Marie.** It took a New Orleans chef to turn this tiny restaurant into a California auberge. Forestville is light on places to eat, so Chez Marie fills up with locals familiar with the rustic French specialties, such as cassoulet and chicken-liver pâté. Desserts tend to reflect the chef's New Orleans heritage; look for pecan pie in addition to crème brûlée. ✉ *6675 Front St., Forestville* ☎ *707/887–7503* ⊙ *Closed Mon.–Wed. No lunch.*

$$–$$$ ✕ **The Farmhouse Inn.** Deluxe accommodations in an 1873 farmhouse have feather beds, wood-burning fireplaces, and private saunas. The restaurant ($$–$$$), open for dinner Thursday through Sunday, relies largely on seasonal local products and fresh seafood. A meeting room and efficient staff make it a good place to mix business and pleasure. ✉ *7871 River Rd., Forestville 95436* ☎ *707/887–3300 or 800/464–6642* 🖷 *707/887–3311* ⊕ *www.farmhouseinn.com* *6 rooms, 2 suites* *Restaurant, refrigerators, pool, massage, sauna, boccie, croquet, concierge; no room TVs, no smoking* 💳 *AE, D, DC, MC, V* *BP.*

★ **$$$–$$$$** **Applewood Inn.** On a knoll in the shelter of towering redwoods, this hybrid inn has two distinct types of accommodations. Those in the original Belden House are comfortable but modest in scale. Most of the 10 accommodations in the newer buildings are larger and airier. The buildings cluster around a Mediterranean-style courtyard complete with gurgling fountains. Cooking classes are available at an on-site cooking school, La Buona Forchetta. ✉ *13555 Hwy. 116, Guerneville 95421* ☎ *707/869–9093 or 800/555–8509* 🖷 *707/869–9170* ⊕ *www.applewoodinn.com* *19 rooms* *Restaurant, cable TV, pool, outdoor hot tub; no smoking* 💳 *AE, MC, V* *BP.*

$$ **Sebastopol Inn.** Simple but stylish rooms in a California country style are tucked behind a historic train station; some have views over a wetlands preserve. The offbeat coffeehouse, Coffee Catz, on the property, is convenient for light meals. ✉ *6751 Sebastopol Ave., Sebastopol 95472* ☎ *707/829–2500* 🖷 *707/823–1535* ⊕ *www.sebastopolinn.com* *29 rooms, 2 suites* *Coffee shop, in-room data ports, microwaves, refrigerators, cable TV, pool, hot tub, spa, dry cleaning, laundry facilities, laundry service; no smoking* 💳 *AE, D, DC, MC, V.*

Healdsburg

17 mi north of Santa Rosa on U.S. 101.

The countryside around Dry Creek Valley and Healdsburg is a fantasy of pastoral bliss—beautifully overgrown and in constant repose. Alongside the relatively untrafficked roads, country stores offer just-plucked fruits and vine-ripened tomatoes. Wineries here are barely visible, tucked behind groves of eucalyptus or hidden high on fog-shrouded hills.

Healdsburg itself is centered on a fragrant plaza surrounded by shady trees, appealing antiques shops, spas, and restaurants. A whitewashed bandstand is the venue for free summer concerts, where the music ranges from jazz to bluegrass.

Where to Stay & Eat

$–$$$ ✕ **Bistro Ralph.** Ralph Tingle has discovered the formula for success with his California home-style cuisine, serving up a small menu that changes weekly. Typical dishes include peppered filet mignon with a brandy reduction and sautéed salmon with fava beans. The stark industrial space includes a stunning wine rack of graceful curves fashioned in metal and wood. Take a seat at the bar and chat with the locals, who love this place just as much as out-of-towners do. ✉ *109 Plaza St. (off Healdsburg Ave.)* ☎ *707/433–1380* ⌨ *Reservations essential* 🖃 *MC, V* ⊘ *No lunch weekends.*

$–$$ ✕ **Zin Restaurant and Wine Bar.** Concrete walls and floors, large canvases on the walls, and servers in jeans and white shirts give the restaurant a casual, industrial, and slightly artsy feel. The American cuisine—such as grilled hanger steak with Gruyère-potato gnocchi and wild mushrooms, or the wonderfully crisp saffron risotto cakes stuffed with goat cheese—is hearty and highly seasoned. True to the restaurant's name, the wine list includes dozens of zinfandels, including half a dozen by the glass. ✉ *344 Center St.* ☎ *707/473–0946* 🖃 *AE, MC, V* ⊘ *Closed Tues. No lunch weekends.*

$$$$ ✕▦ **Hotel Healdsburg.** The green facade of this three-story luxury hotel blends nicely with Healdburg's elegant town plaza, across the street. The attention to detail is striking, from the sleek modern decor to the wide, uncarpeted hallways and the Frette bathrobes. The attached restaurant, Dry Creek Kitchen, is one of the finest in Sonoma, serving celebrity chef Charlie Palmer's cuisine under a vaulted ceiling. ✉ *25 Matheson St., 95448* ☎ *707/431–2800 or 800/889–7188* 🖷 *707/431–0414* ⊕ *www.hotelhealdsburg.com* ⤵ *49 rooms, 6 suites* ⚅ *Restaurant, café, room service, in-room data ports, refrigerators, cable TV, in-room VCRs, pool, gym, hot tub, spa, bar, dry cleaning, laundry service, concierge, Internet, meeting rooms, no-smoking rooms* 🖃 *AE, D, DC, MC, V* ⑩ *CP.*

★ $$$$ ▦ **Hotel Duchamp.** Six identical, freestanding villas are archetypes of spare design, with concrete floors, white walls, and furniture composed strictly of right angles. Luxe lily-white bedding keeps the rooms from feeling spartan, as do CD players loaded with groovy global dance music. Bathrooms decked out in stainless steel and white tile have showers that could fit four and have just as many showerheads. The four cottages named after artists are larger and less minimalist, with mostly mid-century furniture and quirky, artsy touches. ✉ *421 Foss St.* ☎ *707/431–1300 or 800/431–9341* 🖷 *707/431–1333* ⊕ *www.duchamphotel.com* ⤵ *10 rooms* ⚅ *In-room data ports, in-room safes, minibars, cable TV, pool, hot tub, lawn bowling, wine bar, Internet, some pets allowed (fee); no smoking* 🖃 *AE, MC, V* ⑩ *CP.*

$$$–$$$$ ▦ **Healdsburg Inn on the Plaza.** This 1900 brick building on the town plaza has a bright solarium and a roof garden. The rooms, most with fireplaces, are spacious, with quilts and pillows piled high on antique beds. In the bathrooms claw-foot tubs are outfitted with rubber ducks; six rooms have whirlpool baths. Full champagne breakfast, afternoon coffee and cookies, and early-evening wine and hors d'oeuvres are included. ✉ *110 Matheson St., Box 1196, 95448* ☎ *707/433–6991 or 800/431–8663* 🖷 *707/433–9513* ⊕ *www.healdsburginn.com* ⤵ *11 rooms* ⚅ *In-room data ports, cable TV; no smoking* 🖃 *AE, D, MC, V* ⑩ *BP.*

$$$–$$$$ ▦ **The Honor Mansion.** Each room is unique at this photogenic 1883 Italianate Victorian. Rooms in the main house preserve a sense of the building's Victorian heritage, whereas the larger suites out back are comparatively understated. Luxurious touches such as lovely antiques and feather beds are found in every room, and suites have the added advantage of private outdoor hot tubs and a deck. ✉ *14891 Grove St., 95448* ☎ *707/433–4277 or 800/554–4667* 🖷 *707/431–7173* ⊕ *www.honormansion.com* ⤵ *5 rooms, 6 suites* ⚅ *In-room data ports, some refrigerators, some cable TV, some in-room VCRs, pool, hot tub* 🖃 *MC, V* ⑩ *BP.*

$$$–$$$$ ☒ **Madrona Manor.** The oldest continuously operating inn in the area, this 1881 Victorian mansion, surrounded by 8 acres of wooded and landscaped grounds, is straight out of a storybook. Sleep in the splendid three-story mansion, the carriage house, or one of two separate cottages. From May to November you can enjoy live jazz on the front porch Friday and Saturday evenings. ☒ *1001 Westside Rd. (take central Healdsburg exit from U.S. 101, turn left on Mill St.), Box 818, 95448* ☎ *707/433–4231 or 800/258–4003* ☒ *707/433–0703* ⊕ *www.madronamanor.com* ⇨ *17 rooms, 5 suites* ⚅ *Restaurant, in-room data ports, pool, bar, meeting rooms; no room TVs, no smoking* ☐ *MC, V* ⦿| *BP.*

Shopping

Oakville Grocery (☒ 124 Matheson St. ☎ 707/433–3200) has a bustling Healdsburg branch filled with wine, condiments, and deli items. A terrace with ample seating makes a good place for an impromptu picnic. For a good novel, children's literature, and books on interior design and gardening, head to **Levin & Company** (☒ 306 Center St. ☎ 707/433–1118), which also stocks a lot of CDs and tapes and has a small art gallery upstairs. **Tip Top Liquor Warehouse** (☒ 90 Dry Creek Rd. ☎ 707/431–0841) has a large selection of local wines, including some hard-to-find labels.

Every Saturday morning from early May through November, Healdsburg locals gather at the open-air **Farmers' Market** (☒ North Plaza parking lot, North and Vine Sts. ☎ 707/431–1956) to pick up supplies from local producers of vegetables, fruits, flowers, cheeses, and olive oils.

Dry Creek & Alexander Valleys

On the west side of U.S. 101, Dry Creek Valley remains one of the least-developed appellations in Sonoma. The valley made its name on the zinfandel grapes that flourish on the benchlands, whereas the gravelly, well-drained soil of the valley floor is better known for chardonnay and, in the north, sauvignon blanc. The wineries in this region tend to be smaller and clustered in bunches.

The Alexander Valley, which lies east of Healdsburg, has a number of family-owned wineries. Most can be found right on Hwy. 28, which runs through this scenic, diverse appellation where zinfandel and chardonnay grow particularly well.

㊺ Giuseppe and Pietro Simi, two brothers from Italy, began growing grapes in Sonoma in 1876. Though the operations at **Simi Winery,** in the Alexander Valley, are strictly high-tech these days, the winery's tree-studded entrance area and stone buildings recall a more genteel era. The tour highlights the winery's rich history. ☒ *16275 Healdsburg Ave. (take Dry Creek Rd. exit off U.S. 101)* ☎ *707/433–6981* ⊕ *www.simiwinery. com* ☒ *Tasting $5 and up, tour $3* ⊙ *Daily 10–5. Tours Mar.–Dec., daily at 11, 1, and 3; Jan. and Feb., daily at 11 and 2.*

㊻ **Dry Creek Vineyard,** whose fumé blanc is an industry benchmark, is also earning notice for its reds, especially zinfandels and cabernets. Picnic beneath the flowering magnolias and soaring redwoods. ☒ *3770 Lambert Bridge Rd.* ☎ *707/433–1000* ⊕ *www.drycreekvineyard.com* ☒ *Tasting free–$5* ⊙ *Daily 10:30–4:30; tours by appointment.*

㊼ Housed in a California Mission–style complex off the main drag, **Michel-Schlumberger** produces ultrapremium wines including chardonnay, merlot, and pinot blanc, but its reputation is based on the exquisite cabernet sauvignon. ☒ *4155 Wine Creek Rd.* ☎ *707/433–7427 or 800/447–3060* ⊕ *www.michelschlumberger.com* ☒ *Tasting and tour free* ⊙ *Tastings and tours at 11 and 2, by appointment.*

48 An unassuming winery in a wood–and–cinder block barn, **Quivira** produces some of the most interesting wines in Dry Creek Valley. Though it is known for its exquisitely balanced and fruity zinfandel, it also makes a superb blend of red varietals called Dry Creek Cuvée. Redwood and olive trees shade the picnic area. ⊠ *4900 W. Dry Creek Rd.* ☎ *707/431–8333* ⊕ *www.quivirawine.com* ⊡ *Tasting and tour free* ☉ *Daily 10–5; tours by appointment.*

Noted for its beautiful Italian villa–style winery and visitor center (the breezy courtyard is covered with just about every kind of flower imaginable), **Ferrari-Carano Winery** produces chardonnays, fumé blancs, and merlots. Tours take you between the rows of grapevines right into the vineyards themselves. ⊠ *8761 Dry Creek Rd., Dry Creek Valley* ☎ *707/433–6700* ⊕ *www.ferrari-carano.com* ⊡ *Tasting $3, tour free* ☉ *Daily 10–5; tours Mon.–Sat. at 10 AM, by appointment.*

49

off the
beaten
path

CLOS DU BOIS – Some of the best wines from Clos du Bois, 5 mi north of Healdsburg on Highway 116, are made from the relatively unusual purple-black Malbec grapes. Aged in oak barrels for 20 months, the wine goes well with rich meat dishes. Other standout wines include the reserve cabernet sauvignons and merlots. ⊠ *19410 Geyserville Ave., Geyserville* ☎ *707/857–3100 or 800/222–3189* ⊕ *www.closdubois.com* ⊡ *Tasting $5* ☉ *Daily 10–4:30. No tours.*

Where to Stay

$–$$$ ☒ **Dry Creek Inn.** Continental breakfast and a bottle of wine are complimentary at this three-story Spanish Mission–style motel. Midweek discounts are available. A casual family restaurant is next door. ⊠ *198 Dry Creek Rd., 95448* ☎ *707/433–0300 or 800/222–5784* ☐ *707/433–1129* ⊕ *www.drycreekinn.com* ⤴ *102 rooms, 1 suite* ☆ *In-room data ports, refrigerators, cable TV, pool, hot tub, laundry facilities, some pets allowed (fee), no-smoking rooms* ☰ *AE, D, DC, MC, V* ⊧ *CP.*

WINE COUNTRY A TO Z

To research prices, get advice from other travelers, and book travel arrangements, visit www.fodors.com.

BUS TRAVEL

Greyhound runs buses from the Transbay Terminal at 1st and Mission streets in San Francisco to Sonoma and Santa Rosa. Sonoma County Area Transit offers daily bus service to points all over the county. VINE (Valley Intracity Neighborhood Express) provides bus service within the city of Napa and between other Napa Valley towns.

🚌 Bus Lines **Greyhound** ☎ 800/231-2222. **Sonoma County Area Transit** ☎ 707/576-7433 or 800/345-7433. **VINE** (Valley Intracity Neighborhood Express) ☎ 707/255-7631.

CAR TRAVEL

Although traffic on the two-lane country roads can be heavy, the best way to get around the sprawling Wine Country is by private car.

From San Francisco, cross the Golden Gate Bridge, and then go north on U.S. 101, east on Highway 37, and north and east on Highway 121. For Sonoma wineries, head north at Highway 12; for Napa, turn left (to the northwest) when Highway 121 runs into Highway 29.

From Berkeley and other East Bay towns, take Interstate 80 north to Highway 37 west to Highway 29 north, which will take you directly up the middle of the Napa Valley. To reach Sonoma County, take Highway 121 west off Highway 29 south of the city of Napa. From points north of the Wine Country, take U.S. 101 south to Geyserville and take Highway 128 southeast to Calistoga and Highway 29. Most Sonoma County wine regions are clearly marked and accessible off U.S. 101; to reach the Sonoma Valley, take Highway 12 east from Santa Rosa.

LODGING

🏠 **Bed & Breakfast Association of Sonoma Valley** ✉ 3250 Trinity Rd., Glen Ellen 95442 ☎ 707/938-9513 or 800/969-4667 ⊕ www.sonomabb.com. **The Wine Country Inns of Sonoma County** ☎ 707/433-4667 or 800/946-3268 ⊕ www.winecountryinns.com. **Wine Country Reservations** ☎ 707/257-7757 ⊕ www.winecountryreservation.com.

TOURS

Full-day guided tours of the Wine Country usually include lunch and cost about $55–$72 per person. The guides, some of whom are winery owners themselves, know the area well and may show you some lesser-known cellars. Reservations are usually required.

Gray Line has buses that tour the Wine Country. Great Pacific Tour Co. operates full-day tours of Napa and Sonoma, including a restaurant lunch, in passenger vans that seat 14. HMS Travel Group offers customized tours of the Wine Country for six or more people, by appointment only. The Napa Valley Wine Train allows you to enjoy lunch, dinner, or weekend brunch on one of several restored 1915–17 Pullman railroad cars that run between Napa and St. Helena. Prices range from $59.50 for brunch to $70 for lunch to $79 for dinner. Special gourmet events and murder mystery packages are more expensive. In winter service is sometimes limited to Thursday through Sunday; call ahead.

🏠 Tour Companies **Gray Line** ✉ 350 8th St., San Francisco 94103 ☎ 415/558-9400. **Great Pacific Tour Co.** ✉ 518 Octavia St., Civic Center, San Francisco 94102 ☎ 415/626-4499 ⊕ www.greatpacifictour.com. **HMS Travel Group** ✉ 707-A 4th St., Santa Rosa 95404 ☎ 707/526-2922 or 800/367-5348. **Napa Valley Wine Train** ✉ 1275 McKinstry St., Napa 94559 ☎ 707/253-2111 or 800/427-4124 ⊕ www.winetrain.com.

HOT-AIR BALLOONING For views of the ocean coast, the Russian River, and San Francisco on a clear day, Above the Wine Country operates out of Santa Rosa, although many flights actually originate outside Healdsburg. The cost is $195 per person, including a champagne brunch. Balloons Above the Valley is a reliable organization; rides are $185 per person, including a champagne brunch after the flight. Bonaventura Balloon Company schedules early-morning flights (exact times vary) out of Calistoga or, depending on weather conditions, St. Helena, Oakville, or Rutherford. The company's deluxe balloon flight ($175–$215 per person, depending on optional activities) may include a picnic or a breakfast at the Meadowood Resort. Pilots are well versed in Napa Valley lore. Napa Valley Balloons charges $175 per person, including a catered brunch.

🏠 **Above the Wine Country** ☎ 707/829-9850 or 888/238-6359 ⊕ www.balloontours.com. **Balloons Above the Valley** ✍ Box 3838, Napa 94558 ☎ 707/253-2222, 800/464-6824 in CA. **Bonaventura Balloon Company** ☎ 707/944-2822 ⊕ www.bonaventuraballoons.com. **Napa Valley Balloons** ✉ Box 2860, Yountville 94599 ☎ 707/944-0228, 800/253-2224 in CA.

VISITOR INFORMATION

🏠 **Napa Valley Conference and Visitors Bureau** ✉ 1310 Napa Town Center, Napa 94559 ☎ 707/226-7459 ⊕ www.napavalley.com. **Sonoma County Tourism Program** ✉ 520 Mendocino Ave., Suite 210, Santa Rosa 95401 ☎ 707/565-5383 or 800/576-6662 ⊕ www.sonomacounty.com. **Sonoma Valley Visitors Bureau** ✉ 453 1st St. E, Sonoma 95476 ☎ 707/996-1090 ⊕ www.sonomavalley.com.

THE NORTH COAST

FROM MUIR BEACH TO CRESCENT CITY

FODOR'S CHOICE

Cafe Beaujolais, *Mendocino*

MacCallum House, *inn and restaurant in Mendocino*

Point Reyes National Seashore, *Marin County*

HIGHLY RECOMMENDED

RESTAURANTS   Larrupin' Cafe, *Trinidad*

Restaurant 301, *Eureka*

Samoa Cookhouse, *Eureka*

HOTELS   An Elegant Victorian Mansion, *Eureka*

Benbow Inn, *Garberville*

Brewery Gulch Inn, *Mendocino*

Glendeven Inn, *Little River*

The Inn at Occidental, *Occidental*

Manka's, *Inverness*

Pelican Inn, *Muir Beach*

Whitegate Inn, *Mendocino*

SIGHTS   MacKerricher State Park, *Fort Bragg*

Mendocino, *Victorian-era town*

Mendocino Coast Botanical Gardens, *Mendocino*

Muir Woods National Monument, *Marin County*

Patrick's Point State Park, *Trinidad*

Point Reyes Lighthouse Visitor Center, *Inverness*

Salt Point State Park, *Bodega Bay*

Updated by
Lisa M.
Hamilton

THE 386 MILES between San Francisco Bay and the Oregon state line is a land of spectacular scenery, secret beaches, and numerous national, state, and local parks, all without the crowds. Migrating whales and other sea mammals swim within sight of the dramatic bluffs that make the shoreline north of San Francisco one of the most photographed landscapes in the country. The area is also rich in human history, having been the successive domain of the Native American Miwok and Pomo, Russian fur traders, Hispanic settlers, and more contemporary fishing folk and loggers. All have left visible legacies.

After driving along lonely and lovely stretches of cypress- and redwood-studded highway, you'll be pleasantly surprised to come across iconoclastic small towns harboring art galleries, imaginative restaurants whose menus highlight locally grown produce, and small inns. Only a handful of towns in this sparsely populated region have more than 1,000 inhabitants.

About the Restaurants
Despite its small population, the North Coast lays claim to several well-regarded restaurants. Seafood is abundant, as are locally grown vegetables and herbs. In general, dining options are more varied near the coast than inland. Dress is usually informal, though dressy casual is the norm at some of the pricier establishments listed below.

About the Hotels
Restored Victorians, rustic lodges, country inns, and chic hotels are among the accommodations available along the North Coast. In several towns there are only one or two places to spend the night; some of these lodgings are destinations in themselves. Make summer and weekend B&B reservations as far ahead as possible—rooms at the best inns often sell out months in advance. During the winter you are likely to see reduced rates and nearly empty inns and bed-and-breakfasts. For some of the area's nicest lodging options, check out www.uniquenorthwestinns.com.

WHAT IT COSTS				
$$$$	**$$$**	**$$**	**$**	**¢**
RESTAURANTS over $30	$23–$30	$16–$22	$10–$15	under $10
HOTELS over $250	$176–$250	$121–$175	$90–$120	under $90

Restaurant prices are for a main course at dinner, excluding sales tax of 7¼% (depending on location). Hotel prices are for two people in a standard double room in high season, excluding service charges and 8%–10% tax.

Exploring the North Coast

Exploring the northern California coast is easiest by car. Highway 1 is a beautiful if sometimes slow and nerve-racking drive. You'll want to stop frequently to appreciate the views, and there are many portions of the highway along which you won't drive faster than 20–40 mph. You can still have a fine trip even if you don't have much time, but be realistic and don't plan to drive too far in one day. The itineraries below proceed north from Marin County, just north of San Francisco.

Timing
The North Coast is a year-round destination, though when you go determines what you will see. The migration of the Pacific gray whales is a wintertime phenomenon, roughly from mid-December to early April. In July and August views are often obstructed by fog. The coastal climate is quite similar to San Francisco's, although winter nights are colder than in the city.

3

If you have
3 days

Some of the finest redwoods in California are found less than 20 mi north of San Francisco in **Muir Woods National Monument** ❶ ▶. After walking through the woods, stop for an early lunch in **Inverness** ❻ (on Sir Francis Drake Boulevard, northwest from Highway 1) or continue on Highway 1 to **Fort Ross State Historic Park** ❿. Catch the sunset and stay the night in 🏨 **Gualala** ⓭. On day two drive to 🏨 **Mendocino** ⓱. Spend the next day and a half browsing in the many galleries and shops and visiting the historic sites, beaches, and parks of this cliff-side enclave. Return to San Francisco via Highway 1, or the quicker (3½ hours, versus up to five) and less winding route of Highway 128 east (off Highway 1 at the Navarro River, 10 mi south of Mendocino) to U.S. 101 south.

If you have
7 days

Early on your first day, walk through **Muir Woods National Monument** ❶ ▶. Then visit **Stinson Beach** ❷ for a walk on the shore and lunch. In springtime and early summer head north on Highway 1 to Bolinas Lagoon, where you can see birds nesting at **Audubon Canyon Ranch** ❸. At other times of the year (or after you've visited the ranch) continue north on Highway 1. One-third of a mile beyond **Olema,** look for a sign marking the turnoff for the **Bear Valley Visitor Center,** the gateway to the **Point Reyes National Seashore.** Tour the reconstructed Miwok village near the visitor center. Spend the night in nearby 🏨 **Inverness** ❻ or one of the other coastal Marin County towns. The next day stop at Goat Rock State Beach and **Fort Ross State Historic Park** ❿ on the way to 🏨 **Mendocino** ⓱. On your third morning head toward **Fort Bragg** ⓭ for a visit to the **Mendocino Coast Botanical Gardens.** If you're in the mood to splurge, drive inland on Highway 1 to U.S. 101 north and spend the night at the Benbow Inn in 🏨 **Garberville** ⓳. Otherwise, linger in the Mendocino area and drive inland the next morning. On day four continue north through parts of **Humboldt Redwoods State Park** ⓴, including the Avenue of the Giants. Stop for the night in the Victorian village of 🏨 **Ferndale** ㉑ and visit the cemetery and the Ferndale Museum. On day five drive to 🏨 **Eureka** ㉒. Have lunch in Old Town, visit the shops, and get a feel for local marine life on a Humboldt Bay cruise. Begin day six by driving to **Patrick's Point State Park** ㉕ to enjoy stunning views of the Pacific from a point high above the surf. Have a late lunch overlooking the harbor in **Trinidad** ㉔ before returning to Eureka for the night. Return to San Francisco on day seven. The drive back takes six hours on U.S. 101; it's nearly twice as long if you take Highway 1.

Numbers in the text correspond to numbers on the North Coast maps.

MARIN COUNTY

Much of the Marin County coastline is less than an hour from San Francisco, but the pace is slower. Most sights in the southern coastal Marin area can easily be done as day trips from the city.

Muir Woods National Monument

★ ▶ ❶ *17 mi from San Francisco, north on U.S. 101 and west on Hwy. 1 (take Mill Valley/Stinson Beach exit off U.S. 101 and follow signs).*

This grove of old-growth *Sequoia sempervirens* was one of the country's first national monuments. A number of easy hikes can be accomplished in an hour. There's even a short valley-floor trek, accessible to travelers with disabilities, that takes only 10 minutes to walk. The coast redwoods that grow here are mostly between 500 and 800 years old and as tall as 236 feet. Along Redwood Creek are other trees—live oak, madrone, and buckeye, as well as wildflowers (even in winter), ferns, and mushrooms. Parking is easier at Muir Woods before 10 and after 4. ⊠ *Panoramic Hwy. off Hwy. 1* ☎ *415/388–2595* ⊕ *www.nps.gov/ muwo* ⊡ *$3* ☉ *Daily 8 AM–sunset.*

> **off the beaten path**
>
> **MUIR BEACH –** Small but scenic, this rocky patch of shoreline 3 mi south of Muir Woods off Highway 1 is a good place to stretch your legs and gaze out at the Pacific. Locals often walk their dogs here, and anglers and boogie boarders share the gentle surf. At one end of the strand is a cluster of waterfront homes, and at the other are the bluffs of Golden Gate National Recreation Area.

Where to Stay & Eat

★ **$$$** ✕▥ **Pelican Inn.** With a fireplace nearly wherever you look, the Pelly is beloved by locals as the coziest place in southern Marin. It's surprising the building was erected in the 1980s, as it truly feels like a centuries-old farmhouse airlifted from the English countryside. Rooms are romantic and plush, many with canopy beds and pretty views. The downstairs lounge is lovely place to read or sip tea. The restaurant ($–$$; no lunch on Monday, November–April) is equally quaint, especially the dining room housed in a conservatory, although the food is heavy, hit-or-miss English fare. A better bet is chocolate cake, Guinness, and a game of darts in the small pub. ⊠ *10 Pacific Way (off Hwy. 1), Muir Beach 94965* ☎ *415/383–6000* ⊕ *www.pelicaninn.com* ⇨ *7 rooms* ⚬ *No room phones, no room TVs* ▭ *MC, V* ⧪ *BP.*

Stinson Beach

❷ *8 mi north of Muir Woods National Monument via Panoramic Hwy., 25 mi north of San Francisco, U.S. 101 to Hwy. 1.*

Stinson Beach has the most expansive sands in Marin County. It's as close (when the fog hasn't rolled in) as you'll get to the stereotypical feel of a southern California beach. On any hot summer weekend every road to Stinson Beach is jam-packed, so factor this into your plans.

Where to Stay & Eat

$–$$ ✕ **Parkside Cafe.** Most people only know of Parkside's beachfront snack bar, but inside you'll find the town's best restaurant. The food is classic California-style, favoring goat cheese, for example, and seasonal ingredients. Breakfast—a more traditional spread of pancakes and omelets—is a big hit with the locals. The sunny patio is less of a "scene" than those at other Stinson beach restaurants, and it's sheltered by vines to keep down the wind. If you can't stop for a full meal, consider one of the snack bar's superbly thick milkshakes. ⊠ *43 Arenal Ave.* ☎ *415/ 868–1272* ▭ *AE, D, MC, V.*

$–$$ ✕ **Sand Dollar.** The oldest restaurant in town has had a makeover since its longtime owner sold it in 2000. It still attracts all the old salts from Muir Beach to Bolinas, but now they sip whiskey over a new bar or on the spiffy deck. The menu is imaginative and the food is fine, but the real draw is the lively atmosphere. Live music happens sporadically, and sunny afternoons find the deck so full that people sip beer while sitting

3

Beaches The waters of the Pacific Ocean along the North Coast are fine for seals, but most humans find the temperatures downright arctic. When it comes to spectacular cliffs and seascapes, though, the North Coast beaches are second to none. Explore tidal pools, watch for sea life, or dive for abalone. Don't worry about crowds: on many of these beaches you will have the sands largely to yourself. South to north, Stinson Beach, Limantour Beach (at Point Reyes National Seashore), the beaches in Manchester and Van Damme state parks, and the 10-mi strand in MacKerricher State Park are among the most notable.

Fishing Depending on the season, you can fish for rockfish, salmon, and steelhead in rivers such as Gualala and Smith, and in lakes such as those in MacKerricher State Park. Deap-sea charters leave from Fort Bragg, Eureka, and elsewhere for ocean fishing. There's particularly good abalone diving around Jenner, Fort Ross, Point Arena, Westport, and Trinidad.

Whale-Watching From any number of excellent observation points along the coast, you can watch gray whales during their annual winter migration season (mid-December to early April) or, in the summer and fall, blue or humpback whales. Point Reyes Lighthouse, Gualala Point Regional Park, Point Arena Lighthouse, and Patrick's Point State Park are just a few of the places where you stand a good chance of spotting one of the giant sea creatures. Another option is a whale-watching cruise, perhaps from Bodega Bay or Fort Bragg.

---

on the railings. ⊠ *3458 Hwy. 1, Stinson Beach* ☎ *415/868–0434* ⊟ *AE, MC, V.*

$$$ 🖼 **The Beach Cottage.** Stinson Beach's best accommodation is rented out by Darrellyn Morris, a friendly longtime local who built a pleasant studio next to her seaside house. With its peaked cedar ceiling, the room was designed to emulate a provincial French church that Morris visited years ago. Breakfast is served on your private patio, which sits above the sand. ⊠ *28 Calle del Sierra, 94970* ☎ *415/868–0474* ⊕ *www. stinsonbeachfront.com* ⊶ *1 room* ⚐ *Minibar; no room TVs* ⌶⊙⌶ *CP* ⊟ *No credit cards.*

$–$$$ 🖼 **Stinson Beach Motel.** This will not likely be the place you return for a honeymoon, but it is among the least expensive places on the coast south of Fort Bragg. The building is older but everything is immaculate: freshly painted walls, new queen-sized beds, and lovingly tended gardens. This is right on the main street, which makes it convenient to everything but potentially loud on busy summer days. ⊠ *3416 Hwy. 1, 94970* ☎ *415/ 868–1712* 🖷 *415/868–1790* ⊕ *www.stinsonbeachmotel.com* ⊶ *7 rooms* ⚐ *Some kitchens and kitchenettes, cable TV* ⊟ *D, MC, V.*

Audubon Canyon Ranch

❸ *12 mi northwest of Stinson Beach.*

This 1,000-acre wildlife sanctuary along the Bolinas Lagoon gets the most traffic during late spring, when great blue herons and egrets nest in the trees covering the hillside. It is a spectacular sight, these large birds in white and gray dotting the tops of the evergreens; docent-led hikes offer the best access and viewing. Quiet trails through the rest of the

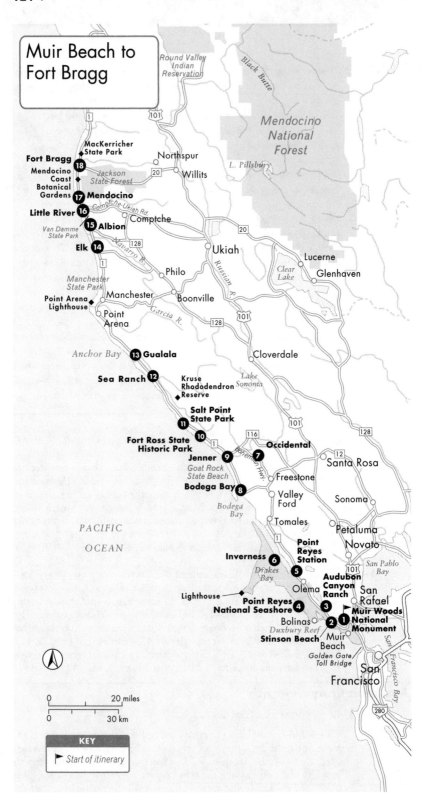

Muir Beach to Fort Bragg

Mendocino
National
Forest

*Round Valley
Indian
Reservation*

Black Butte

101

1

MacKerricher
State Park

Fort Bragg 18

Northspur

L. Pillsbury

Mendocino
Coast
Botanical
Gardens

*Jackson
State Forest*

20

Willits

17 **Mendocino**

Little River 16

Comptche-Ukiah Rd.

15 **Albion**

Comptche

*Van Damme
State Park*

20

Elk 14

Navarro R.

128

Ukiah

Lucerne

*Manchester
State Park*

Philo

Russian R.

*Clear
Lake*

Glenhaven

**Point Arena
Lighthouse**

Manchester

Point
Arena

Boonville

101

Garcia R.

128

Cloverdale

Anchor Bay

13 **Gualala**

Sea Ranch 12

Kruse
Rhododendron
Reserve

*Lake
Sonoma*

**Salt Point
State Park**

11

10

116

Occidental

**Fort Ross State
Historic Park**

Jenner 9

7

12 **Santa Rosa**

128

*Goat Rock
State Beach*

1

Bohemian Hwy.

Freestone

Bodega Bay 8

*Bodega
Bay*

Valley
Ford

Sonoma

**PACIFIC

OCEAN**

Tomales

1

Petaluma

Novato

**Point
Reyes
Station**

101

*San Pablo
Bay*

Inverness 6

5

*Drakes
Bay*

**Audubon
Canyon
Ranch**

San
Rafael

Lighthouse

**Point Reyes
National Seashore** 4

Olema

3

**Muir Woods
National
Monument**

Bolinas

2

1

Duxbury Reef

Muir
Beach

Stinson Beach

*Golden Gate
Toll Bridge*

San
Francisco

*San
Francisco Bay*

280

0 ___ 20 miles

0 ___ 30 km

KEY

▶ *Start of itinerary*

preserve offer tremendous vistas of the Bolinas Lagoon and Stinson Beach and fabulous birding. Access to these areas is available only on guided nature walks, well worth it if you can get a space. A small museum surveys the geology and natural history of the region. ☒ *4900 Hwy. 1, along Bolinas Lagoon* ☏ *415/868–9244* ⊕ *www.egret.org* ☒ *$10 donation requested* ☉ *Mid-Mar.–mid-July, weekends 10–4, year-round Tues.–Fri. 2–4 (midweek by appointment only).*

An unmarked road running west from Highway 1 about 2 mi beyond Audubon Canyon Ranch leads to the sleepy town of **Bolinas.** Don't expect a warm welcome or directions to this hidden town: residents have taken down the road signs that point to town so many times the state no longer bothers putting them up.

Point Reyes National Seashore

❹ *About 3 mi south of Audubon Canyon Ranch via Olema-Bolinas Rd.*
Fodor'sChoice *to Bolinas, then 4 mi northwest on Mesa Rd.*
★

Point Reyes National Seashore, which borders the northern reaches of the Golden Gate National Recreation Area in Marin County, is a great place for hiking to secluded beaches, viewing wildlife, and driving through rugged, rolling grasslands. Highlights include watching elephant seals from Chimney Rock during late winter and early spring and hiking the ½-mi Earthquake Trail, which passes by the epicenter of the 1906 quake that destroyed much of San Francisco. If you don't mind the steep stairs leading down, the late-19th–century Point Reyes Lighthouse is a good spot to watch for whales. Horses and mountain bikes are permitted on some trails. ☒ *Point Reyes 94956* ☏ *415/464–5100* 🖷 *415/663–8132* ⊕ *www.nps.gov/pore* ☒ *Free* ☉ *Daily sunrise–sunset.*

Those not interested in birds might find the **Point Reyes Bird Observatory** ho-hum, but birders adore it. The visitor center is small yet has excellent interpretive exhibits, including a comparative display of real birds' talons. What really warrants a visit, though, are the surrounding woods, which harbor nearly 225 bird species. As you hike the quiet trails through forest and along ocean cliffs, you're likely to see biologists banding birds to aid in studying their life cycles. The sanctuary is in the southernmost part of Point Reyes National Seashore, accessed through Bolinas. ☒ *Mesa Rd.* ☏ *415/868–0655* ⊕ *www.prbo.org* ☒ *Free* ☉ *Visitor center daily 9–5.*

Mile-long **Duxbury Reef** is the largest shale intertidal reef in North America. Look for starfish, barnacles, sea anemones, purple urchins, limpets, sea mussels, and the occasional abalone. But check a tide table if you plan to explore the reef—it's accessible only at low tide. ☒ *From Mesa Rd. turn left on Overlook Dr. and right on Elm Ave. to beach parking lot.*

Ⓒ Point Reyes National Seashore's **Bear Valley Visitor Center** has exhibits of park wildlife. The rangers here dispense advice about beaches, the Point Reyes Lighthouse, whale-watching, hiking trails, and camping. A reconstructed Miwok village, a short walk from the visitor center, provides insight into the daily lives of the region's first human inhabitants. ☒ *12 mi north of Bolinas to Olema via Hwy. 1, then west on Bear Valley Rd.* ☏ *415/464–5100* ⊕ *www.nps.gov/pore* ☒ *Free* ☉ *Weekdays 9–5, weekends 8–5.*

Sports & the Outdoors

Many of the beaches in Point Reyes National Seashore are accessible off Bear Valley Road. **Limantour Beach** (☒ end of Limantour Beach Rd.) is the most popular stretch of sand in the park, perhaps because it is generally the last to get foggy. The area closest to the parking lot can be busy with families, but the beach is long enough that walkers can find total tranquility. **Blue Waters Kayaking** (✉ 12938 Sir Francis Drake Blvd., Inverness ☎ 415/669–2600 ⊕ www.bwkayak.com) rents kayaks and offers tours and lessons. **Five Brooks Stables** (✉ 8001 Hwy. 1 ☎ 415/663–1570 ⊕ www.fivebrooks.com) rents horses and equipment. Trails from the stables wind through the Point Reyes woods and along the beaches.

Point Reyes Station

❺ *2 mi north of Olema on Hwy. 1.*

The best place to find out what's going on in Point Reyes Station, a stop on the North Pacific Coast narrow-gauge railroad until 1933, is Toby's Feed Barn. Toby's sells offbeat gifts (many of them "cow-themed") to tourists and locals, and feed and grain to local farmers. There's a market on Main Street for picking up picnic supplies.

Where to Stay & Eat

¢–$ ✕ **Tomales Bay Foods.** There are three separate businesses at this mecca for gourmands: a stand that showcases local, organic fruits, vegetables and breads; a shop that sells artisanal cheeses from around the world (including some made in the building, at the Cowgirl Creamery); and a kitchen that draws on both of its neighbors' products to create exquisite sandwiches, salads, and soups. You can eat here at a café table or on the lawn, but most customers take their gourmet picnics out to Point Reyes. ✉ 80 4th St. ☎ 415/663–9335 ▭ MC, V ☯ Closed Mon.–Tues.

¢ ▥ **Point Reyes Hostel.** These dorm-style lodgings in an old clapboard ranch house are a good deal for budget travelers. A family-size guest room is limited to those with children ages five and under and must be reserved well in advance. ✉ Off Limantour Rd., 94956 ☎ 415/663–8811 ⊕ www.norcalhostels.org ⇝ 44 beds. ☖ Kitchen ▭ MC, V.

Shopping

Gallery Route One (✉ 11101 Hwy. 1 ☎ 415/663–1347), a nonprofit co-operative, shows the works of area artists.

Inverness

❻ *4 mi from Point Reyes Station on Sir Francis Drake Blvd., northwest from Hwy. 1.*

Inverness boomed after the 1906 earthquake, when wealthy San Franciscans built summer homes in its hills. Today many structures serve as full-time residences or small inns. A deli, a grocery store, restaurants, and shops are along Sir Francis Drake Boulevard.

★ The **Point Reyes Lighthouse Visitor Center** is a 45-minute drive from Inverness, across rolling landscape that resembles Scottish heath. Parking near the lighthouse is difficult on weekends during summer. The view alone persuades most people to make the effort of walking down—and then back up—the hundreds of steps from the cliff tops to the lighthouse below. Because of a multi-stage restoration project, the lighthouse is periodically closed to the public; plus, rangers close the trail if the coastal winds are too strong, so call in advance. ✉ Western end of Sir Francis Drake Blvd. ☎ 415/669–1534 ⊕ www.nps.gov/pore ☯ Thurs.–Mon. 10–4:30.

Where to Stay & Eat

¢ ✕ **Grey Whale.** This casual place is a good stop for pizza, sandwiches, salad, pastries, and espresso. ✉ 12781 Sir Francis Drake Blvd. ☎ 415/669–1244 ▭ MC, V.

★ **$$$–$$$$** ×⊞ **Manka's.** Every detail of this 1917 hunting lodge is geared toward pleasing the senses. Rooms are rustic in nature but entirely indulgent, each with some combination of heavy leather and overstuffed armchairs, Tiffany lamps, and fireplaces. The 1902 fishing cabin has a private outdoor hot tub and shower. The restaurant ($$$$, reservations essential) is regarded as among the best in Northern California for the attention lavished on each hand-crafted culinary wonder—it feels like dinner at a chef friend's house. Nearly all the kitchen's ingredients come from within 15 mi of the lodge, so the dinner menu changes daily according to what local farmers, fishermen, and foragers offer chef-owner Margaret Grade. The dinner-only restaurant is closed Tuesday and Wednesday year-round and Sunday through Thursday January through March. ⊠ *30 Callender Way, 94937* ☎ *415/669–1034* ⊕ *www.mankas. com* ⤶ *14 rooms, 6 suites* ♨ *Restaurant, some in-room hot tubs, massage, concierge, meeting rooms, some pets allowed (fee); no room TVs, no smoking* ⊟ *MC, V* �|◯| *BP.*

$$$–$$$$ ⊞ **Blackthorne Inn.** There's no other inn quite like the Blackthorne, a combination of whimsy and sophistication in the woods. The giant tree house–looking structure has spiral staircases, a 3,500-square-foot deck, and a fireman's pole. The solarium was made with timbers from San Francisco wharves, and the outer walls are salvaged doors from a railway station. The best room is aptly named the Eagle's Nest, perched as it is in the glass-sheathed octagonal tower that crowns the inn. ⊠ *266 Vallejo Ave., 94937* ☎ *415/663–8621* ⊕ *www.blackthorneinn.com* ⤶ *5 rooms, 3 with bath* ♨ *Hot tub* ⊟ *MC, V* �|◯| *BP.*

$$–$$$ ⊞ **Ten Inverness Way.** This is the kind of place where you sit around after breakfast and share tips for hiking the nearby Point Reyes National Seashore. The living room of this low-key inn has a stone fireplace and library. The rooms contain dormer ceilings with skylights and such homespun touches as patchwork quilts and well-worn antiques. ⊠ *10 Inverness Way, 94937* ☎ *415/669–1648* 🖨 *415/669–7403* ⊕ *www. teninvernessway.com* ⤶ *5 rooms* ♨ *Hot tub* ⊟ *D, MC, V* �|◯| *BP.*

COASTAL SONOMA COUNTY

The gently rolling countryside of coastal Marin gives way to more dramatic scenery north of Bodega Bay. Cattle cling for their lives (or so it seems) to steep inclines alongside the increasingly curvy highway, now traveling right along the coast. The stunning vistas make this one of the most attractive stretches of coastline north of San Francisco.

Occidental

❼ *35 mi north of Inverness, via Hwy. 1 to Valley Ford, then east on Hwy. 12 (Bodega Hwy.) to Bohemian Hwy.*

A village in a clearing that's surrounded by the redwood forests, orchards, and vineyards of western Sonoma County, Occidental is so small that you might drive right through the town and barely take notice. A 19th-century logging hub with a present-day bohemian feel, Occidental has a top-notch B&B, good eats, and a handful of art galleries and crafts and clothing boutiques, all of which make the town an ideal base for day trips to Sonoma Coast beaches, Bodega Bay, Armstrong Redwoods Reserve, and Point Reyes National Seashore.

> **off the beaten path**
>
> **OSMOSIS ENZYME BATHS –** The tiny town of Freestone, 3 mi south of Occidental and 7½ mi east of Bodega Bay off Highway 12 (Bodega Highway), is famous regionally as the home of the unique Osmosis Enzyme Baths. This spa, in a two-story clapboard house on

extensive grounds, specializes in several treatments, including a detoxifying "dry" bath in a blend of enzymes and fragrant wood shavings. After 20 minutes in the tub, opt for a 75-minute massage in one of the freestanding Japanese-style pagodas near the creek that runs through the property. ⊠ *209 Bohemian Hwy., Freestone* ☎ *707/823–8231* ⊕ *www.osmosis.com.*

Where to Stay & Eat

$–$$ ✕ **Willow Wood Market Café.** About 5 mi east of Occidental in the village of Graton is one of the best-kept secrets of the north coast. Tucked among the market merchandise are a number of tables and a counter where casually dressed locals sit down to order freshly made soups and salads or heartier American fare such as a roasted half chicken served with mashed potatoes. ⊠ *9020 Graton Rd., Graton* ☎ *707/823–0233* ⌲ *Reservations not accepted* ⊟ *MC, V* ☾ *Closed Sun.*

★ **$$$–$$$$** ▥ **The Inn at Occidental.** Every room here showcases one of owner Jack Bullard's interesting collections. Antique English and Irish cut-glass jars decorate the Cut-Glass Suite, which has its own sunny garden and outdoor hot tub. A fireplace, fine Oriental rugs, and antique clocks create a cozy but dignified mood in the ground-floor living room. Antiques, quilts, and original artwork fill the guest rooms in the main house. This inn is a decidedly adult place. ⊠ *3657 Church St. 95465* ☎ *707/874–1047 or 800/522–6324* 🖷 *707/874–1078* ⊕ *www.innatoccidental.com* ⇲ *17 rooms* ☙ *In-room hot tubs, massage, concierge, meeting rooms, no-smoking rooms; no TV in some rooms, no kids under 12 except in cottage, shop* ⊟ *AE, D, MC, V* ▯◎▯ *BP.*

Bodega Bay

❽ *8 mi from Valley Ford on Hwy. 1, 65 mi north of San Francisco via U.S. 101 and Hwy. 1.*

The location of Alfred Hitchcock's film *The Birds* is also one of the busiest harbors on the Sonoma County coast. Commercial boats here haul in all kinds of fish and crustaceans, most famously the Dungeness crab. T-shirt shops and galleries line both sides of Highway 1; a short drive around the harbor leads to the Pacific. This is the last stop, townwise, before Gualala, and a good spot for stretching your legs and taking in the salt air. Visit the **Bodega Marine Laboratory** (☎ *707/875–2211* for directions ⊕ www-bml.ucdavis.edu ✉ $2 donation requested), on a 326-acre reserve on nearby Bodega Head. The lab gives one-hour tours and peeks at intertidal invertebrates, such as sea stars and sea anemones, on Friday from 2 to 3:45.

Where to Stay & Eat

$$–$$$ ✕▥ **Inn at the Tides.** The condominium-style buildings at this complex have spacious rooms with high ceilings and an uncluttered feel. All rooms have views of the harbor, and some have fireplaces. The inn's two restaurants ($$–$$$) serve both old-style and more adventurous seafood dishes. In season you can buy a slab of salmon or live crab at a seafood market across the highway and have the kitchen prepare it for you. ⊠ *800 Hwy. 1, 94923* ☎ *707/875–2751 or 800/541–7788* 🖷 *707/875–2669* ⊕ *www.innatthetides.com* ⇲ *86 rooms* ☙ *2 restaurants, room service, refrigerators, pool, hot tub, sauna, bar, laundry facilities* ⊟ *AE, D, MC, V* ▯◎▯ *CP.*

$$$$ ▥ **Sonoma Coast Villa.** In this secluded spot in the coastal hills between Valley Ford and Bodega Bay sits a most unusual inn. Founded as an Arabian horse ranch in 1976, the 60-acre property has two single-story rows of accommodations beside a swimming pool. Red-tile roofs, a stucco exterior, Mediterranean-style landscaping, and two courtyards create a southern European mood. Rooms have slate floors, French doors, beam ceilings, and wood-burning fireplaces. ✉ *16702 Hwy. 1, Bodega 94922* ☎ *707/876–9818 or 888/404–2255* 🖶 *707/876–9856* ⊕ *www.scvilla. com* ⟳ *16 rooms* ⚓ *Cable TV, in-room VCRs, pool, hot tub, spa, library, meeting rooms; no room phones, no smoking* ☰*AE, MC, V* ℹ*BP.*

Sports & the Outdoors

Bodega Bay Sportfishing (✉Bay Flat Rd. ☎707/875–3344) charters ocean-fishing boats and rents equipment. On weekends in March and April, **Oceanic Society Expeditions** (☎ 415/474–3385 ⊕ www.oceanic-society. org) conducts whale-watching cruises from Bodega Bay. The *New Sea Angler* and *Jaws* (☎ 707/875–3495) are charter fishing boats.

On the 700-acre **Chanslor Guest Ranch** (✉ 2660 Hwy. 1 ☎707/875-3333 ⊕ www.chanslorranch.com) you can take guided horseback rides.

Shopping

The **Ren Brown Gallery** (✉ 1781 Hwy. 1 ☎ 707/875–2922), in the north end of town, is renowned for its selection of Asian arts, crafts, and furnishings. This two-floor gallery also represents a number of local artists worth checking out.

Jenner

❾ *10 mi north of Bodega Bay on Hwy. 1.*

After meandering westward for miles, the Russian River arrives at its destination—the Pacific Ocean—at Jenner. Here, a number of state beaches offer tide-pooling and fishing. The town has a couple of good restaurants and some shops. South of the Russian River is windy **Goat Rock State Beach** (☎ 707/875–3483), where a colony of sea lions (walk north from the parking lot) resides most of the year. The beach, just west of Highway 1 about 1 mi south of Jenner, is open daily from 8 AM to sunset; there's no day-use fee.

Where to Eat

★ **$–$$$** ✗ **River's End.** The feeling is rustic rather than refined at this romantic restaurant where, at the right time of year, you can view sea lions lazing on the beach below. The creative and sometimes elaborately presented fare, however, belies the cabinlike ambience. Eclectic dishes run the gamut from Continental to Indonesian, with seafood dishes a specialty. Open hours sometimes vary, so call to confirm. ✉ *Hwy. 1, north end of Jenner* ☎ *707/865–2484* ☰ *MC, V* ⊘ *Closed Tues. and Wed. Apr.–Oct. and Mon.–Thurs. Nov.–Mar.*

Fort Ross State Historic Park

⚓ **❿** *12 mi north of Jenner on Hwy. 1.*

Fort Ross, completed in 1821, became Russia's major fur-trading outpost in California. The Russians brought Aleut hunters down from Alaska. By 1841 the area was depleted of seals and otters, and the Russians sold their post to John Sutter, later of gold-rush fame. After a local Anglo rebellion against the Mexicans, the land fell under U.S. domain, becoming part of California in 1850. The state park service has reconstructed Fort Ross, including its Russian Orthodox chapel, a redwood stockade, the officers' barracks, and a blockhouse. The excellent museum here documents the history of the fort and some of the North Coast. ✉*Hwy. 1* ☎ *707/847–3286* ⊕ *www.parks.ca.gov* ✉ *$3 per vehicle (day use)* ⊘ *Daily 10–4:30* ☞ *No dogs allowed past the parking lot.*

Where to Stay

¢–$$$ ⊡ **Fort Ross Lodge.** This comfortable lodge is a celebration of its wild natural setting, with lots of outdoor areas and a wind-bitten look that reflects the rough coastline's weather. Some rooms have views of the shoreline; others have private hot tubs. Six hillside units have saunas, hot tubs, and fireplaces. Visiting fishermen can cook up their catches on patio grills. ⊠ 20705 Hwy. 1, 95450 ☎ 707/847–3333 ⎙ 707/847–3330 ⊕ www. fortrosslodge.com ↪ 22 rooms ᠔ In-room VCRs, microwaves, refrigerators, some in-room hot tubs ⊟ AE, MC, V.

Salt Point State Park

★ ⓫ 2 mi north of Fort Ross on Hwy. 1.

Any noise made by other visitors to this 6,000-acre park is washed away by the sound of the surf pounding on the rocky shore. Seals sun themselves at Gerstle Cove, and the surrounding meadows of wild brush host more birds than humans. This is a good place to picnic or let off steam on a long drive. Don't miss the unusual *tafonis*—caverns in the sandstone caused by centuries of erosion by wind and rain—near the park's entrance at Fisk Mill Cove. A five-minute walk uphill from the parking lot leads to a dramatic view of Sentinel Rock, an excellent spot for sunsets. ⊠ Hwy. 1 ☎ 707/847–3221 ᠌ $2 per vehicle ⊙ Daily sunrise–sunset.

Kruse Rhododendron Reserve, a peaceful 317-acre forested park, has thousands of rhododendrons that bloom in light shade in the late spring. ⊠ Hwy. 1, north of Fisk Mill Cove ᠌ Free.

Where to Stay

¢ ⊡ **Stillwater Cove Ranch.** Six miles north of Jenner, this former boys' school overlooking Stillwater Cove has been transformed into a family-oriented lodge. Group accommodations are also available in a bunkhouse and a dairy barn. The grounds are pleasant, with 50 acres of forests and wide lawns traversed by resident peacocks. ⊠ 22555 Hwy. 1, 95450 ☎ 707/ 847–3227 ↪ 6 rooms ⊟ No credit cards.

⚠ **Salt Point State Park Campgrounds.** There are two excellent campsites in the park. Gerstle Cove campground, on the west side of Highway 1, is set on a wooded hill with some sites overlooking the ocean. Woodside campground offers more trees and protection from the wind; it is on the east side of Highway 1. Woodside is closed December–March 15. Reservations are accepted March–October. ᠔ Flush toilets, drinking water, fire grates, picnic tables ↪ Gerstle Cove, 29 sites; Woodside, 79 sites ⊠ 20705 Hwy. 1, 95450 ☎ 800/444–7275 ᠌ $12.

Sea Ranch

⓬ 18 mi northwest of Fort Ross on Hwy. 1.

Sea Ranch is a dramatically positioned development of stylish homes on 5,000 acres overlooking the Pacific. To appease critics, the developers provided public beach-access trails off Highway 1 south of Gualala. Even some militant environmentalists deem the structures designed by William Turnbull and Charles Moore to be reasonably congruent with the surroundings; some folks find the weathered wooden buildings beautiful.

Where to Stay & Eat

$$$–$$$$ ✕⊡ **Sea Ranch Lodge.** High on a bluff with ocean views, the lodge is close to beaches, trails, and golf. Some rooms have fireplaces, while others have hot tubs. Handcrafted wood furnishings and quilts create an earthy yet contemporary look. The restaurant ($$–$$$), which overlooks the

Pacific, serves good seafood and homemade desserts. Try the five-course chef's dinner for a special treat. ⊠ *60 Sea Walk Dr., 95497* ☎ *707/785–2371 or 800/732–7262* 🖷 *707/785–2917* ⊕ *www.searanchlodge.com* ᗐ *20 rooms, 2 suites* ♧ *Restaurant, massage, baby-sitting, shop, concierge, meeting rooms; no smoking* ⊟ *AE, MC, V* ¶O¶ *BP.*

$$–$$$$ 🖼 **Sea Ranch Escape.** The Sea Ranch houses, sparsely scattered on a grass meadow fronting a stretch of ocean, are a striking sight from Highway 1. Groups or families can rent fully furnished homes for two nights or more. You can dine at superb nearby restaurants or stock up on provisions from one of the markets in Gualala and make use of the full kitchens. ⊠ *60 Sea Walk Dr., Box 238, 95497* ☎ *707/785–2426 or 888/732–7262* 🖷 *707/785–1021* ⊕ *www.searanchvillage.com* ᗐ *71 houses* ♧ *In-room VCRs, some in-room hot tubs, pool, sauna, tennis courts, some pets allowed* ⊟ *MC, V.*

MENDOCINO COUNTY

The timber industry gave birth to most of the small towns strung along this stretch of the California coastline. Today tourism drives the economy, but the region's cities still retain much of their old-fashioned charm. And of course, the beauty of the coast has not changed.

Gualala

⑬ *11 mi north of Sea Ranch on Hwy. 1*

This former lumber port remains a sleepy drive-through except for the several ocean-view motels that serve as headquarters for exploring the coast. The town lies north of the Gualala River—a good place for fishing. On the Gualala River's Sonoma side, **Gualala Point Regional Park** (⊠ 1 mi south of Gualala on Hwy. 1 ☎ 707/785–2377), open daily from 8 AM until sunset, is an excellent whale-watching spot. The park has picnicking ($3 day-use fee) and camping.

Where to Stay & Eat

¢ ✕ **The Food Company.** This café serves "home-style gourmet" food, including breakfast, either to go or served on the sunny porch. The backbone is picnic-ready prepared foods (cucumber salad, barbecued pork, sesame noodles), as well as wine, cheese, and fresh bread. Nightly dinner specials are inventive—lamb pie with shallots, moussaka with Moroccan bread—and the gingersnaps are locally famous. ⊠ *Hwy. 1, ½ mile north of Gualala* ☎ *707/884–1400* ⊕ *www.thefoodcompanyonline. com* ⊟ *MC, V.*

¢ ✕ **Laura's Bakery.** This *panaderia*, or Mexican bakery, behind the Gualala Hotel is so small you can easily miss it; look for the sign on the parking lot's south side. Inside are authentic Mexican baked goods, including guava empanadas and sugar-dusted wedding cookies. ⊠ *Hwy. 1* ☎ *707/884–3175.*

¢–$$$ ✕🖼 **St. Orres.** Two onion-dome towers evoke the area's Russian heritage at one of the North Coast's most eye-catching inns. The main house is further accented by balconies, stained-glass windows, and wood-inlaid towers. Two rooms overlook the sea, and the other six have views of the garden or a stand of pines. In the tranquil woods behind the house are clusters of cottages somehow both rustic and opulent, all unique and appointed with romantic touches like in-rooms saunas and wood-burning stoves. The inn's restaurant (closed on Tuesday and Wednesday from October through June) serves dinner only, a fixed-price meal ($$$$). ⊠ *Hwy. 1, 2 mi north of Gualala, 95445* ☎ *707/884–3303* 🖷 *707/884–1840* ⊕ *www.saintorres.com* ᗐ *8 rooms without bath, 13 cottages* ♧ *Restau-*

rant, some in-room hot tubs, some in-room saunas, some kitchenettes, some fireplaces, hot tub, sauna, beach ▤ *MC, V* ⫴ *BP.*

$$$–$$$$ ⊡ **Whale Watch Inn.** The largest accommodations at this inn are in the main house, but all have their merits. Most rooms do indeed have views (through cypress trees) down the coast, where whales often come close to shore on their early spring migration. Year-round the scent of pine and salt-sea air fills the rooms, all of which have fireplaces and small decks. A 132-step stairway leads down to a small, virtually private beach. Breakfast is served in your room. There is a two-night minimum Friday and Saturday. ⊠ *35100 Hwy. 1, 95445* ☎ *707/884–3667 or 800/ 942–5342* ⊟ *707/884–4815* ⊕ *www.whalewatchinn.com* ⇔ *18 rooms* ⌂ *Some in-room hot tubs, some kitchenettes, beach* ▤ *AE, MC, V* ⫴ *BP.*

$$–$$$ ⊡ **Old Milano Hotel.** This not-so-old hotel—the 1905 mansion burned a few years back—is one of the most beautiful sunset spots on the coast. You can stay in one of five modern cottages or a train caboose. Some cottages have spa tubs; four have gas fireplaces. The caboose has a wood-burning stove and brakeman's seats. ⊠ *38300 Hwy. 1, 95445* ☎ *707/ 884–3256* ⊟ *707/884–4249* ⊕ *www.oldmilanohotel.com* ⇔ *5 cottages, 1 caboose* ⌂ *Hot tub* ▤ *MC, V* ⫴ *BP.*

¢ ⊡ **Gualala Hotel.** Gualala's oldest hotel, which once housed timber-mill workers, has small, no-nonsense rooms furnished with well-worn antiques. Most rooms share baths. Rooms in the front have ocean views (and some street noise). The rustic first-floor saloon was a haunt of Jack London's. ⊠ *39301 Hwy. 1, 95445* ☎ *707/884–3441* ⊟ *707/884– 3908* ⇔ *19 rooms, 5 with bath* ⌂ *Restaurant, bar* ▤ *AE, D, MC, V.*

⛺ **Gualala Point Regional Park Campground.** Right on the Gualala River, this campground offers riverfront campsites as well as more secluded sites that sit among the giants of a redwood forest. None of the sites has hook-ups. ⌂ *Flush toilets, drinking water, showers, fire pits* ⇔ *19 drive-in sites, 6 walk-in sites* ⊠ *Hwy. 1, one mi south of Gualala* ☎ *707/ 565–2267 reservations* ⊕ *www.sonoma-county.org/camping* ⊗ *Year-round* ▨ *$16.*

en route | For a dramatic view of the surf and, in winter, migrating whales, take the marked road off Highway 1 north of the fishing village of Point Arena to the **Point Arena Lighthouse** (☎ 707/882–2777). First constructed in 1870, the lighthouse was destroyed by the 1906 earthquake that devastated San Francisco. Rebuilt in 1907, it towers 115 feet above its base, which is 50 feet above the sea. The lighthouse is open for tours daily from 11 until 3:30, from 10 in summer; admission is $4. As you continue north on Highway 1 toward Mendocino, there are several beaches, most notably the one at **Manchester State Park,** 3 mi north of Point Arena. The area's best dinners are at **Pangaea** (⊠ 250 Main St., Point Arena ☎ 707/882– 3001), where the well-traveled chef serves imaginative seasonal food.

Elk

⓮ *39 mi north of Gualala on Hwy. 1.*

There's not much happening on the streets of this former timber town, but that's exactly why people love it. The setting is a beautiful, rocky coastline, and the entertainment is romance or quiet escape.

Where to Stay & Eat

$$$$ ✕⊡ **Harbor House.** Constructed in 1916, this redwood Craftsman-style house is as elegant as its location is rugged. Rooms in the main house are dressed with antiques; five of the six have fireplaces. The newer cottages are luxurious, each with a fireplace and deck. Room price includes breakfast and a four-course dinner (except on weeknights during January and February, when the rates drop drastically). The ocean-view restaurant ($$$$, reservations essential), which serves California cuisine on a prix fixe menu, is highly recommended; there's limited seating for nonguests. ⊠ *5600 S. Hwy. 1, 95432* ☎ *707/877–3203 or 800/ 720–7474* ⊕ *www.theharborhouseinn.com* ⤳ *6 rooms, 4 cottages* ⚲ *Restaurant* ⊟ *AE, MC, V* ⦿| *MAP.*

★ $$–$$$$ ✕⊞ **Elk Cove Inn.** Perched on a bluff above the surf that pounds on a virtually private beach, Elk Cove offers priceless views from most rooms. A stone-and-cedar-shingle Arts and Crafts–style building houses plush spa suites with cathedral ceilings. Spread among four cottages and a grand main house, the older accommodations are each unique and decorated in soothing and sensual palettes. All rooms have stereos and fireplaces; some have wood-burning stoves. The full bar is open daily. ⊠ *6300 S. Hwy. 1, 95432* ☎ *707/877–3321 or 800/275–2967* 🖷 *707/877–1808* ⊕ *www.elkcoveinn.com* ⤳ *7 rooms, 4 suites, 4 cottages* ⚲ *Refrigerators, hot tub, beach, spa, bar* ⊟ *AE, D, DC, MC, V* ⦿| *BP.*

Albion

⑮ *4 mi north of Elk on Hwy. 1.*

A hamlet nestled next to its namesake river, Albion has played host to myriad visitors—from the Pomo Indians to Sir Francis Drake. Over the years fires have taken most of the town's standing history, so Albion today is defined by its recent immigrants, particularly staunch environmentalists. The tiny town is less touristy than its neighbors.

Where to Stay & Eat

$$–$$$ ✕ **Ledford House.** There's nothing between this bluff-top wood-and-glass restaurant and the Pacific Ocean but a great view. Entrées include hearty bistro dishes—mainly stews and pastas—and equally large-portion examples of California cuisine—ahi, grilled meats, and the like. ⊠ *3000 N. Hwy. 1* ☎ *707/937–0282* ⊕ *www.ledfordhouse.com* ⊟ *AE, DC, MC, V* ⊘ *Closed Mon.–Tues. No lunch.*

$$$–$$$$ ✕⊞ **Albion River Inn.** Contemporary New England–style cottages at this inn overlook the dramatic bridge and seascape where the Albion River empties into the Pacific. All but two have decks facing the ocean. Six have spa tubs with ocean views; all have fireplaces. The rooms are filled with everything from antique furnishings to wide-back willow chairs. In the glassed-in dining room ($$$), which serves grilled dishes and fresh seafood, the food is as captivating as the views. ⊠ *3790 N. Hwy. 1, 95410* ☎ *707/937–1919, 800/479–7944 in CA* 🖷 *707/937–2604* ⊕ *www. albionriverinn.com* ⤳ *20 rooms* ⚲ *Restaurant, some in-room hot tubs, concierge; no smoking* ⊟ *AE, D, DC, MC, V* ⦿| *BP.*

Little River

⑯ *3 mi north of Albion on Hwy. 1.*

Van Damme State Park is best known for its beach and as one of the coast's best spots for abalone diving. Upland trails lead through lush riparian habitat and the bizarre Pygmy Forest, where acidic soil and poor drainage have produced mature cypress and pine trees that are no taller than a person. The visitor center has interesting displays on ocean life and Native American history. ⊠ *Hwy. 1* ☎ *707/937–5804 for park, 707/937– 4016 for visitor center* ⊕ *www.parks.ca.gov.*

Where to Stay & Eat

$$–$$$ ✕ **Little River Inn Restaurant.** There are fewer than a dozen entrées on the inn's menu, but they're varied: perhaps loin of lamb, local petrale sole

and salmon, or grilled polenta with vegetables. Main courses come with soup or salad. Less expensive appetizers, salads, and sandwiches are served in the ocean-view Ole's Whale Watch Bar. The adjoining inn is more like a laid-back resort, and has some relatively inexpensive rooms. ⊠ *7551 N. Hwy. 1* ☎ *707/937–5942* ▤ *AE, MC, V.*

$$–$$$$ ✕☷ **Heritage House.** Everywhere you go at this oceanside resort there is a stunning view. The cottages' decor ranges from frilly to tastefully spare, depending on the number of period antiques. The real draw is the amenities—private decks, fireplaces, and whirlpool tubs. The restaurant ($$$–$$$$) is more formal than most on the coast and has a superb wine list. Salmon, quail, sirloin, and elegant desserts are the standouts on the evening menu. The restaurant is closed from early December through mid-February. ⊠ *Hwy. 1, 95456* ☎ *707/937–5885 or 800/235–5885* ☷ *707/937–0318* ⊕ *www.heritagehouseinn.com* ⋑ *66 rooms* ♨ *Restaurant, some in-room hot tubs, refrigerators, lounge, massage, beach, concierge; no in-room phones* ▤ *AE, MC, V.*

★ **$$–$$$** ☷ **Glendeven Inn.** If Mendocino is the New England village of the West Coast, then Glendeven is the local country manor. The main house was built in 1867 and is surrounded by acres of gardens. Inside are five rooms, three with fireplaces. A converted barn holds an art gallery and a two-bedroom suite with a kitchen. The 1986 Stevenscroft building, whose four rooms have fireplaces, has a high gable roof and weathered barn-like siding. The carriage-house suite makes for a romantic retreat. ⊠ *8221 N. Hwy. 1, 95456* ☎ *707/937–0083 or 800/822–4536* ☷ *707/937–6108* ⊕ *www.glendeven.com* ⋑ *9 rooms, 2 suites* ♨ *Kitchenettes* ▤ *AE, MC, V* ⦿| *BP.*

Mendocino

★ ⑰ *2 mi north of Little River on Hwy. 1; 153 mi from San Francisco, north on U.S. 101, west on Hwy. 128, and north on Hwy. 1.*

Logging created the first boom in the windswept town of Mendocino, which flourished for most of the second half of the 19th century. As the timber industry declined during the early 20th century, many residents left, but the town's setting was too beautiful for it to remain neglected. Artists and craftspeople began flocking here in the 1950s, and in their wake came entrepreneurial types who opened restaurants, cafés, and inns. By the 1970s a full-scale revival was underway. A bit of the old town can be seen in such dives as Dick's Place, a bar near the Mendocino Hotel, but the rest of the small downtown area is devoted almost exclusively to contemporary restaurants and shops.

Mendocino may look familiar to fans of *Murder, She Wrote*; the town played the role of Cabot Cove, Maine, on the television show. The subterfuge worked because so many of the town's original settlers had come here from the Northeast and built houses in the New England style. The Blair House, at 45110 Little Lake Street, was the home of Jessica Fletcher (Angela Lansbury's character) in the series. Mendocino has also played a California town, most notably in the Elia Kazan film of John Steinbeck's novel *East of Eden*. The building on Main Street (at Kasten Street) that houses the astronomy-oriented Out of This World store was the Bay City Bank in the 1955 movie, which starred James Dean.

An 1861 structure holds the **Kelley House Museum,** whose artifacts include antique cameras, Victorian-era clothing, furniture, and historical photographs of Mendocino's logging days. ⊠ *45007 Albion St.* ☎ *707/937–5791* ▨ *$2* ⊙ *June–Aug., daily 1–4; Sept.–May, Fri.–Mon. 1–4.*

The **Mendocino Art Center** (⊠ 45200 Little Lake St. ☎ 707/937–5818 or 800/653–3328), which hosts exhibits and art classes and contains a gallery and a theater, is the nexus of Mendocino's flourishing art scene.

The tiny green-and-red **Temple of Kwan Tai** (⊠ Albion St. west of Kasten St. ☎ 707/937–5123) was built in 1852, making it the oldest Chinese temple on the North Coast. It's open only by appointment, but by peering in the window you can basically see everything there is to see.

The restored **Ford House,** built in 1854, serves as the visitor center for Mendocino Headlands State Park. The house has a scale model of Mendocino as it looked in 1890, when the town had 34 water towers and a 12-seat public outhouse. History walks leave from Ford House on Saturday afternoon at 1. The park itself consists of the cliffs that border the town. ⊠ *Main St. west of Lansing St.* ☎ *707/937–5397* 💲 *Free ($1 donation suggested)* ⊙ *Daily 11–4, with possible midweek closings in winter.*

Mendocino's ocean breezes might seem too chilly for grape growing, but summer days can be quite warm just over the hills in the **Anderson Valley,** where the cool nights permit a longer ripening period. Chardonnays and pinot noirs find the valley's climate particularly hospitable. Tasting here is a decidedly more laid-back affair than in the Napa and Sonoma valleys. Most tasting rooms are open from 11 to 5 daily and charge a nominal sampling fee (usually deducted if you purchase any wine).

Husch (⊠ 4400 Hwy. 128, Philo ☎ 707/895–3216 or 800/554–8724), one of the valley's oldest wineries, sells renowned chardonnays and a superb gewürztraminer. At the elegant tasting room at **Roederer Estate** (⊠ 4501 Hwy. 128, Philo ☎ 707/895–2288), you can taste (for $3) sparkling wines produced by the American affiliate of the famous French champagne maker. **Pacific Echo** (⊠ 8501 Hwy. 128, Philo ☎ 800/824–7754) was the first Anderson Valley winery to produce critically acclaimed sparkling wines. **Fetzer Vineyards** (⊠ Main St. between Lansing and Kasten Sts., Mendocino ☎ 707/937–6191 or 800/653–3328) has a tasting room next to the Mendocino Hotel & Garden Suites. To get to the Anderson Valley from Mendocino, take Highway 1 south to Highway 128 east. The valley begins about 10 miles in from the coast and continues all the way to U.S. 101.

Where to Stay & Eat

$$–$$$ ✕ **Cafe Beaujolais.** The Victorian cottage that houses this popular restaurant nestles in a garden of heirloom and exotic plantings. A commitment to the freshest possible organic, local, and hormone-free ingredients guides the chef here. Ever-evolving, the menu is cross-cultural, with free-range duck, line-caught fish, and Yucatecan-Thai crab cakes. The restaurant typically closes for a month or more in winter. ⊠ *961 Ukiah St.* ☎ *707/937–5614* ⊕ *www.cafebeaujolais.com* ▭ *D, MC, V.*

Fodor'sChoice
★

$–$$$ ✕ **955 Ukiah.** The interior of this smart restaurant is woodsy and the California cuisine creative. Specialties include fresh fish, duck cannelloni, peppercorn New York steak, and pastas topped with the house sauce. ⊠ *955 Ukiah St.* ☎ *707/937–1955* ⊕ *www.955restaurant.com* ▭ *MC, V* ⊙ *Closed Tues. July–Nov. and Mon.–Wed. Dec.–June. No lunch.*

$$$$ ✕▣ **Stanford Inn by the Sea.** This warm, family-run property feels like the Northern California version of an old-time summer resort. Several long buildings house guest rooms that range from cozy to chic, many with ocean views, fireplaces, and paintings by local artists. On the spacious grounds you'll find organic gardens, llamas, and a sandy river beach where you can rent a kayak or canoe and head 8 miles upstream. The spa, in-room massage, and daily yoga classes are complemented by The

Ravens vegetarian restaurant ($–$$$), which serves hearty breakfasts and inventive dinners. ⊠ *South of Mendocino, east on Comptche-Ukiah Rd. (off Hwy. 1), 95460* ☎ *707/937–5615 or 800/331–8884* 🖷 *707/937–0305* ⊕ *www.stanfordinn.com* 🖙 *23 rooms, 10 suites* ⚬ *Refrigerators, cable TV with movies, in-room VCRs, indoor pool, hot tub, sauna, bicycles, some pets allowed (fee); no smoking* ▭ *AE, D, DC, MC, V* ⁑ *BP.*

$$–$$$
Fodor'sChoice
★
✕⌨ **MacCallum House.** This inn makes the most of its 2 acres in the middle of town. Each room has its own character: the main house feels like the mansion of a wealthy friend, the cottages are bright and honeymooney, and the renovated barn and water tower house lavish, cedar-walled suites. The property is drenched in rose bushes, some planted by the original owner in the late 1800s. At the excellent restaurant ($$–$$$; reservations essential), recipes highlight local ingredients and are prepared daily from scratch (including the ice cream and mozzarella cheese). Lucky you, the lodging includes a sumptuous breakfast. The restaurant is closed mid-January through mid-February. ⊠ *45020 Albion St., 95460* ☎ *707/937–0289 or 800/609–0492* ⊕ *www.maccallumhouse. com* 🖙 *12 rooms, 7 cottages, 3 suites* ⚬ *Restaurant, in-room data ports, cable TV, bar* ▭ *AE, MC, V* ⁑ *BP.*

$–$$$
✕⌨ **Mendocino Hotel & Garden Suites.** From the street this hotel looks like something out of the Wild West, with a period facade and balcony that overhangs the raised sidewalk. Stained-glass lamps, polished wood, and Persian rugs lend the hotel a swank, 19th-century appeal. Most rooms have private baths. Deluxe garden rooms have fireplaces and TVs. The wood-paneled restaurant ($–$$$), fronted by a solarium, serves fine fish entrées and the best ollalieberry (common to the Northern California coast) deep-dish pie in California. ⊠ *45080 Main St., 95460* ☎ *707/ 937–0511 or 800/548–0513* 🖷 *707/937–0513* ⊕ *www.mendocinohotel. com* 🖙 *51 rooms, 37 with bath* ⚬ *Restaurant, room service, bar; no TV in some rooms* ▭ *AE, MC, V.*

★ **$$$–$$$$**
⌨ **Whitegate Inn.** With a white picket fence, latticework gazebo, and romantic garden, the Whitegate is a picture-book Victorian. High ceilings, floral fabrics, and pastel walls define the public spaces and the luxurious rooms, all of which have fireplaces. Best of all, you can watch the ocean breakers from the deck out back. ⊠ *499 Howard St., 95460* ☎ *707/ 937–4892 or 800/531–7282* 🖷 *707/937–1131* ⊕ *www.whitegateinn. com* 🖙 *6 rooms, 1 cottage* ⚬ *Some in-room hot tubs, some refrigerators, cable TV, some in-room VCRs, Internet; no kids under 10 or pets except in cottage, no smoking* ▭ *AE, D, DC, MC, V* ⁑ *BP.*

$$–$$$$
⌨ **Agate Cove Inn.** Facing the Mendocino Headlands across a rocky cove, this inn is ideally situated for winter whale watching. Adirondack chairs are set on a small deck for just that purpose; borrow the inn's binoculars for a closer look. Each blue-and-white cottage unit is individually decorated. There are four single and four duplex cottages; two more rooms are in the 1860s farmhouse, where country breakfasts are prepared on an antique woodstove in a kitchen with a full view of the Pacific. ⊠ *11201 N. Lansing St., 95460* ☎ *707/937–0551 or 800/527–3111* 🖷 *707/937–0550* ⊕ *www.agatecove.com* 🖙 *10 rooms* ⚬ *In-room VCRs, massage, concierge, shop; no room phones, no smoking* ▭ *AE, MC, V* ⁑ *BP.*

$$–$$$$
⌨ **Alegria.** A staircase from the back porch to Big River Beach makes this the only oceanfront lodging in Mendocino. Each room has something special and unique: perhaps beautiful bamboo floors and a woodstove or sunset views from a perfectly positioned window seat. Despite its central location, the property is more private than others in town; it feels like a quiet retreat. The hot tub, surrounded by jasmine vines, is a nighttime treat. ⊠ *44781 Main St., 95460* ☎ *707/937–5150, 800/780–*

7905 ⊕ *www.oceanfrontmagic.com* ⇆ *6 rooms, 1 suite* ⚘ *Some kitchenettes, some microwaves, refrigerators, in-room VCRs, hot tub, concierge* ▤ *AE, MC, V* ⦶ *BP.*

★ **$$–$$$$** ▦ **Brewery Gulch Inn.** This tasteful new inn is a modern twist on the elegance of Mendocino. Furnishings are dark wood and leather, beds are plush, and all rooms but one have jetted tubs with views. The luxury is in tune with the surrounding nature: large windows frame views of the 10-acre property's bird-filled trees, and winding paths lead through native-plant gardens. An organic farm that's on-site (but out of ear-shot) provides ingredients for the sumptuous breakfast menu. ⊠ *9401 Hwy. 1, 1 mile south of Mendocino, 95460* ☎ *707/937–4752 or 800/578–4454* 🖷 *707/937–1279* ⊕ *www.brewerygulchinn.com* ⇆ *10 rooms* ⚘ *In-room data ports, some in-room hot tubs, cable TV, massage, shop, concierge, meeting room; no smoking* ▤ *AE, MC, V.*

$$–$$$ ▦ **C. O. Packard House.** One of four landmark homes on Executive Row, this Carpenter Gothic Victorian is run by a husband-and-wife team of interior decorators. Four oddly shaped rooms are dazzlingly sophisticated, with custom wall finishes, jetted tubs, fireplaces, and a mix of French and English antiques. A garden cottage is large enough to accommodate four but is less elegant than the rooms in the main house. ⊠ *45170 Little Lake St., 95460* ☎ *707/937–2677 or 888/453–2677* 🖷 *707/937–1323* ⊕ *www.packardhouse.com* ⇆ *4 rooms, 1 suite* ⚘ *Cable TV, in-room VCRs, in-room hot tubs, massage, baby-sitting, concierge; no smoking* ▤ *MC, V* ⦶ *BP.*

$$–$$$ ▦ **Joshua Grindle Inn.** The original farmhouse of this B&B on a 2-acre hilltop has five guest rooms, a parlor, and a dining room. Two other buildings, the Watertower (an upper room has windows on all four sides) and the Cottage, hold five additional rooms. Furnishings throughout are simple but comfortable American antiques: Salem rockers, wing chairs, steamer-trunk tables, painted pine beds. ⊠ *44800 Little Lake Rd., 95460* ☎ *707/937–4143 or 800/474–6353* ⊕ *www.joshgrin.com* ⇆ *10 rooms* ⚘ *Some cable TVs with VCRs, some in-room hot tubs, massage, concierge; no in-room phones, no kids under 12, no smoking* ▤ *MC, V* ⦶ *BP.*

$–$$$ ▦ **Blackberry Inn.** Each single-story unit here has a false front, creating the image of a frontier town. There is a bank, a saloon, Belle's Place (of hospitality), and "offices" for doctors and sheriffs, as well as other themed accommodations. Rooms are cheery and spacious. Most have wood-burning stoves or fireplaces and at least partial ocean views. The inn is a short drive east of town down a quiet side street. ⊠ *44951 Larkin Rd., 95460* ☎ *707/937–5281 or 800/950–7806* ⊕ *www.mendocinomotel. com* ⇆ *17 rooms* ⚘ *In-room dataports, some kitchenettes, cable TV, some in-room hot tubs, some pets allowed; no smoking* ▤ *MC, V* ⦶ *CP.*

Nightlife & the Arts

Mendocino Theatre Company (⊠ Mendocino Art Center, 42500 Little Lake St. ☎ 707/937–4477) has been around for more than two decades. The community theater's repertoire ranges all over the contemporary map, including works by David Mamet, Neil Simon, and local playwrights.

Patterson's Pub (⊠ 10485 Lansing St. ☎ 707/937–4782), an Irish-style watering hole, is a friendly gathering place day or night, though it becomes boisterous as the evening wears on. Bands entertain on Friday night.

Sports & the Outdoors

Catch-a-Canoe and Bicycles Too (⊠ Stanford Inn by the Sea, Comptche-Ukiah Rd., off Hwy. 1, ☎ 707/937–0273) rents regular and outrigger canoes as well as mountain and suspension bicycles.

Shopping

Many artists exhibit their work in Mendocino, and the streets of this compact town are so easily walkable that you're sure to find a gallery with something that strikes your fancy. Start your gallery tour at the **Mendocino Art Center** (✉ 45200 Little Lake St. ☎ 707/937–5818 or 800/653–3328). **Old Gold** (✉ 6 Albion St. ☎ 707/937–5005) is a good place to look for locally crafted jewelry.

Fort Bragg

⑱ *10 mi north of Mendocino on Hwy. 1.*

Fort Bragg has changed more than any other coastal town in the past few years. The decline in what was the top industry, timber, is being offset in part by a boom in charter-boat excursions and other tourist pursuits. The city is also attracting many artists, some lured from Mendocino, where the cost of living is higher. This basically blue-collar town is the commercial center of Mendocino County.

The **Skunk Train,** a remnant of the region's logging days, dates from 1885 and travels a route—through redwood forests inaccessible to automobiles—from Fort Bragg 21 mi inland to the town of Northspur and back. A fume-spewing self-propelled train car that shuttled passengers along the railroad earned the nickname Skunk Train, and the entire line has been called that ever since. Excursions are now given on historic trains and replicas of the Skunk Train motorcar that smell less foul than the original. ✉ *Foot of Laurel St.* ☎ *707/964–6371 or 800/777–5865* ⊕ *www.skunktrain.com* ✉ *Round-trip $17–$35* ☉ *Departs Fort Bragg 10 AM and 2:15 PM.*

★ The **Mendocino Coast Botanical Gardens** offer something for nature lovers in every season. Even in winter, heather and Japanese tulips bloom. Along 2 mi of trails, with ocean views and observation points for whale-watching, is a splendid profusion of flowers. The rhododendrons are at their peak from April through June, and the dahlias are spectacular in August. ✉ *18220 N. Hwy. 1, 1 mi south of Fort Bragg* ☎ *707/964–4352* ⊕ *www.gardenbythesea.org* ✉ *$7.50* ☉ *Mar.–Oct., daily 9–5; Nov.–Feb., daily 9–4.*

★ **MacKerricher State Park** includes 10 mi of sandy beach and several square miles of dunes. Fishing (at two freshwater lakes, one stocked with trout), canoeing, hiking, jogging, bicycling, camping, and harbor-seal watching at Laguna Point are among the popular activities, many of which are accessible to travelers with disabilities. Whales can often be spotted from December to mid-April from the nearby headland. Rangers lead nature hikes throughout the year. ✉ *Hwy. 1, 3 mi north of Fort Bragg* ☎ *707/937–5804* ✉ *Free.*

Where to Stay & Eat

$$ ✕ **The Restaurant.** The name may be generic, but this place isn't. California cuisine is served in a dining room that doubles as an art gallery. Under the same ownership since 1973, The Restaurant is one of the few places in town serving Sunday brunch. ✉ *418 N. Main St.* ☎ *707/964–9800* ▭ *MC, V* ☉ *Closed Wed. No lunch.*

$–$$ ✕ **Sharon's by the Sea.** The views of Noyo Harbor are up close and scenic at this one-story restaurant at the end of the pier. The other reason to visit this unpretentious establishment is the excellent selection of seafood, all of which comes from local waters. Sauces, breads, and desserts made in-house complement these seafood dishes, as do a good selection of Mendocino County wines. ✉ *32096 N. Harbor Dr., at south* end of Fort Bragg ☎ 707/962–0680 ⊕ *www.sharonsbythesea.com* ⊟ *AE, MC, V.*

¢–$$ ✗ **Mendo Bistro.** On the second floor of the Company Store complex, downtown, the town's sole hip restaurant serves oodles of noodles, made fresh on the premises. You might find on the menu rotini with sun-dried tomatoes; shells stuffed with spinach, chard, and ricotta; and sweet-potato gnocchi with Gorgonzola sauce. ⊠ *301 N. Main St.* ☎ 707/964–4974 ⊟ *AE, D, DC, MC, V* ⊘ *No lunch.*

¢ ✗ **Headlands Coffee House.** The coffeehouse acts as a cultural center and local gathering place. Musicians perform most nights. ⊠ *120 E. Laurel St.* ☎ 707/964–1987 ⊟ *D, MC, V.*

$–$$ ⊡ **Weller House Inn.** Guest accommodations in this 1886 mansion are decorated with Victorian-style wallpaper and furnishings; the baths have hand-painted tiles. The third floor has a 900-square-foot ballroom (now the breakfast room) paneled in California redwood. Newer accommodations are in a water tower on the property—at 51 feet the tallest building in town—topped by a hot tub with spectacular ocean views. Guest rooms have jacks but no phones; request one if you need a lifeline. ⊠ *524 Stewart St., 95437* ☎ 707/964–4415 or 877/893–5537 ⊞ *707/964–4198* ⊕ *www.wellerhouse.com* ☜ *8 rooms* ⚬ *Some in-room hot tubs, refrigerators, microwaves; no room TVs, no smoking* ⊟ *AE, D, DC, MC, V* ⊺○⊢ *BP.*

¢–$$ ⊡ **Surf and Sand Lodge.** You have to go north of Fort Bragg to find lodgings with unimpeded ocean views, and they're just what you'll get at this souped-up motel. As its name implies, it's practically on the beach. Right out the door are pathways down to the rock-strewn shore. The six cheaper rooms don't have views, but all the bright and fresh accommodations come with enough amenities to make you feel you're staying somewhere grander than a motel. The fancier of the second-story rooms have hot tubs and fireplaces. ⊠ *1131 N. Main St., 95437* ☎ 707/ 964–9383 or 800/964–0184 ⊞ *707/964–0314* ⊕ *www.surfsandlodge. com* ☜ *30 rooms* ⚬ *Some in-room hot tubs, refrigerators, in-room VCRs, beach; no smoking* ⊟ *AE, D, MC, V.*

⚠ **MacKerricher State Park.** The campsites at MacKerricher are in woodsy spots a quarter mile or so from the ocean. There are no hook-ups. Make reservations for summer weekends as early as possible (reservations are taken April–mid-October), unless you want to try your luck getting one of the 25 sites that are available on a first-come, first-served basis each day. ⚬ *Flush toilets, drinking water, showers, fire pits, picnic tables* ☜ *142 sites* ⊠ *Hwy. 1 3 mi north of Fort Bragg* ☎ 800/444– 7275 for reservations ☑ $13.

Nightlife

Caspar Inn & Blues Cafe (⊠ 14957 Caspar Rd. ☎ 707/964–5565) presents blues, rock, and alternative rock from Thursday through Saturday. If you get a little tipsy, you can indeed stay at the inn, upstairs in one of the spartan, inexpensive rooms.

Sports & the Outdoors

Matlick's *Tally Ho II* (⊠ 11845 N. Main St. ☎ 707/964–2079) operates whale-watching trips from December through mid-April, as well as fishing excursions all year. **Ricochet Ridge Ranch** (⊠ 24201 N. Hwy. 1 ☎ 707/964–7669) guides groups on horseback to the Mendocino–Fort Bragg beaches.

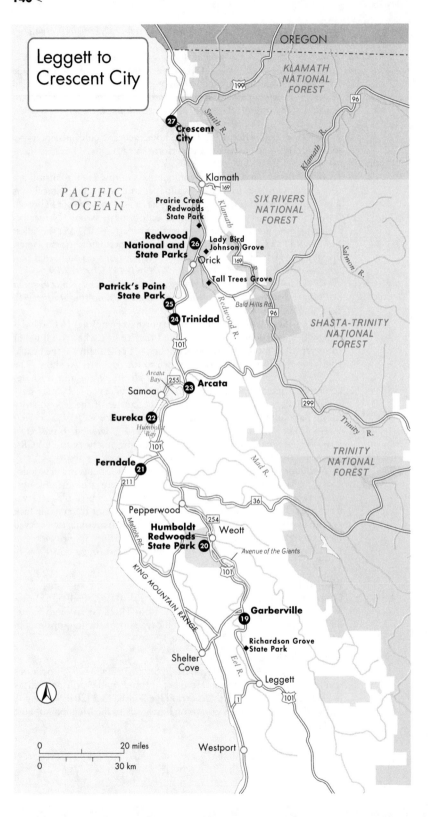

Leggett to
Crescent City

OREGON

KLAMATH
NATIONAL
FOREST

199

Smith R.

96

27 Crescent
City

Klamath
169

PACIFIC
OCEAN

Prairie Creek
Redwoods
State Park

SIX RIVERS
NATIONAL
FOREST

Klamath R.

Salmon R.

Redwood
National and
State Parks

26 Lady Bird
Johnson Grove

Orick

169

Tall Trees Grove

Patrick's Point
State Park

Bald Hills Rd.

96

SHASTA-TRINITY
NATIONAL
FOREST

25

24 Trinidad

Redwood R.

101

Arcata
Bay

255

23 Arcata

299

Samoa

Trinity R.

Eureka 22

Humboldt
Bay

101

TRINITY
NATIONAL
FOREST

Ferndale
21

211

Mad R.

Pepperwood

36

Mattole Rd.

254

Humboldt
Redwoods
State Park

Weott

20

Avenue of the Giants

101

KING MOUNTAIN RANGE

Garberville

19

Richardson Grove
State Park

Shelter
Cove

Eel R.

Leggett

1

101

20 miles

30 km

Westport

en route | North on Highway 1 from Fort Bragg past the mill town of Westport, the road cuts inland around the **King Range,** a stretch of mountain so rugged it was impossible to build the intended major highway through it. Highway 1 joins U.S. 101 at the town of Leggett. **Richardson Grove State Park,** north of Leggett along U.S. 101, marks your first encounter with the truly giant redwoods, but there are even more magnificent stands farther north, in Humboldt and Del Norte counties. Before heading into the wilderness, stop for an espresso or a beer at the **Lost Coast Inn** (⊠ 38921 Hwy. 1, Westport ☎ 707/964–5584), a B&B whose bar/coffeehouse has a chess set and friendly resident dog.

REDWOOD COUNTRY
FROM GARBERVILLE TO CRESCENT CITY

The majestic redwoods that grace California's coast become more plentiful as you head north. Their towering ancient presence defines the landscape.

Garberville

⑲ *70 mi from Fort Bragg, north and east on Hwy. 1 and north on U.S. 101; 197 mi north of San Francisco on U.S. 101.*

Although it's the largest town in the vicinity of Humboldt Redwoods State Park, Garberville hasn't changed much since timber was king. The town is a pleasant place to stop for lunch, pick up picnic provisions, or poke through arts-and-crafts stores. A few miles below Garberville is an elegant Tudor resort, the Benbow Inn. Even if you are not staying there, stop in for a drink or a meal and take a look at the architecture and gardens.

Where to Stay & Eat

¢ ✕ **Woodrose Cafe.** This unpretentious eatery serves basic breakfast items on the weekends and healthy lunches every day. Dishes include chicken, pasta, and vegetarian specials. ⊠ *911 Redwood Dr.* ☎ *707/923–3191* ⊟ *No credit cards* ⊘ *No dinner.*

★ $$–$$$$ ✕⛱ **Benbow Inn.** South of Garberville alongside the Eel River, this three-story Tudor-style manor resort is the equal of any in the region. The most luxurious of the antiques-filled rooms are on the terrace, with fine river views; some rooms have fireplaces. Guests have canoeing, tennis, golf, and pool privileges at an adjacent property. The wood-paneled restaurant ($$–$$$) serves American cuisine, with the focus on fresh salmon and trout. ⊠ *445 Lake Benbow Dr., 95542* ☎ *707/923–2124 or 800/ 355–3301* 🖶 *707/923–2897* ⊕ *www.benbowinn.com* ➥ *55 rooms, 1 cottage* ♿ *Restaurant, refrigerators, some in-room VCRs, golf privileges, lake, lobby lounge* ⊟ *AE, D, MC, V* ⊘ *Closed early Jan.–early Apr.*

Humboldt Redwoods State Park

☾ **⑳** *15 mi north of Garberville on U.S. 101.*

At the **Humboldt Redwoods State Park Visitor Center** you can pick up information about the redwoods, waterways, and recreational activities in the 53,000-acre park. One helpful brochure describes a self-guided auto tour of the park, with short and long hikes into redwood groves. ⊠ *Ave. of the Giants, 2 mi south of Weott* ☎ *707/946–2409 (park), 707/946–2263 (visitor center)* 🎫 *Free; $2 day-use fee for parking and facilities in Williams Grove and Women's Federation Grove* ⊘ *Park daily; visitor center Mar.–Oct., daily 9–5; Nov.–Feb., daily 10–4.*

The **Avenue of the Giants** (Highway 254) begins about 7 mi north of Garberville and winds north, more or less parallel to U.S. 101, toward Pepperwood. Some of the tallest trees on the planet tower over this stretch of two-lane blacktop. The road follows the south fork of the Eel River and cuts through part of Humboldt Redwoods State Park. Reached via a ½-mi trail off Avenue of the Giants is **Founders Grove** (✉ Hwy. 254, 4 mi north of Humboldt Redwoods State Park Visitor Center). One of the most impressive trees here—the 362-foot-long Dyerville Giant—fell to the ground in 1991; its root base points skyward 35 feet. **Rockefeller Forest** (✉ Mattole Rd., 6 mi north of Humboldt Redwoods State Park Visitor Center) is the largest remaining coast redwood forest. It contains 40 of the 100 tallest trees in the world.

Ferndale

㉑ *30 mi from Weott, north on U.S. 101 to Hwy. 211 west.*

The residents of the stately town of Ferndale maintain some of the most sumptuous Victorian homes in California, many of them built by 19th-century Scandinavian, Swiss, and Portuguese dairy farmers who were drawn to the area's mild climate. The queen of them all is the Gingerbread Mansion. A sweet, old-fashioned graveyard slopes down Ocean Avenue west of Main Street. Many shops carry a map with self-guided tours of some of the town's oldest and most interesting buildings.

The main building of the **Ferndale Museum** hosts changing exhibitions of Victoriana and has an old-style barbershop and a display of Wiyot Indian baskets. In the annex are a horse-drawn buggy, a re-created blacksmith's shop, and antique farming, fishing, and dairy equipment. ✉ *515 Shaw Ave.* ☎ *707/786–4466* ✍ *$1* ⊙ *June–Sept., Tues.–Sat. 11–4, Sun. 1–4; Oct.–Dec. and Feb.–May, Wed.–Sat. 11–4, Sun. 1–4.*

Where to Stay

$$–$$$ ⊞ **Gingerbread Mansion.** This photogenic Victorian B&B rivals San Francisco's "painted ladies" for dazzle. The mansion's carved friezes set off its gables, and turrets delight the eye. The comfortable parlors and spacious bedrooms are laid out in flowery Victorian splendor. Some rooms have views of the mansion's English garden, and one has side-by-side bathtubs. One spectacular suite is the Veneto, with hand-painted scenes of Venice on the walls and ceiling as well as marble floors. ✉ *400 Berding St., off Brown St., 95536* ☎ *707/786–4000 or 800/952–4136* ⊕ *www.gingerbread-mansion.com* ✍ *11 rooms, 4 suites* ☰ *AE, MC, V* ⦿| *BP.*

Sports & the Outdoors

Eel River Delta Tours (✉ 285 Morgan Slough Rd. ☎ 707/786–4187) conducts two-hour boat trips that emphasize the wildlife and history of the Eel River's estuary and salt marsh.

Shopping

Among the shops along Main Street, **Golden Gait Mercantile** (✉ 421 Main St. ☎ 707/786–4891) seems to be lost in a time warp, with Burma Shave products and old-fashioned long johns as well as penny candy.

Eureka

㉒ *10 mi north of Ferndale and 269 mi north of San Francisco on U.S. 101.*

Eureka, population 28,500, is the North Coast's largest city. It has gone through several cycles of boom and bust, first with mining and later with timber and fishing. Due in large part to the nearly 100 Victorian buildings here, tourism is becoming a healthy industry. And thanks to community efforts, the downtown area is now a vision into Eureka's past, with smart shops and a brand-new walking pier that looks onto the harbor and its colorful fishing boats. The splendid **Carson Mansion** (⊠ M and 2nd Sts.) was built in 1885 for timber baron William Carson. A private men's club now occupies the house. Don't miss the Victorian extravaganza popularly known as the **Pink Lady** (⊠ M and 2nd Sts.). For proof that contemporary architects have the skills to build lovely Victoriana, take a look at the **Carter House B&B** (⊠ 3rd and L Sts.), a stunning replica of a San Francisco building that burned in the 1906 earthquake.

At the **Chamber of Commerce** you can pick up maps with self-guided driving tours of Eureka's architecture and find out about organized tours. ⊠ *2112 Broadway* ☎ *707/442–3738 or 800/356–6381* ◷ *Weekdays 8:30–5, Sat. 10–4.*

The **Clarke Memorial Museum** contains extraordinary northwestern California Native American basketry and artifacts of Eureka's Victorian, logging, and maritime eras. ⊠ *240 E St.* ☎ *707/443–1947* ◲ *Donations accepted* ◷ *Feb.–Dec., Tues.–Sat. 11–4.*

The structure that gave **Fort Humboldt State Historic Park** its name once protected white settlers from Native Americans. Ulysses S. Grant was posted here in 1854. The old fort is no longer around, but on its grounds are a museum, ancient steam engines (operators rev them up on the third Saturday of the month), and a logger's cabin. The park is a good place for a picnic. ⊠ *3431 Fort Ave.* ☎ *707/445–6567 or 707/445–6547* ◲ *Free* ◷ *Daily 9–5.*

To explore the waters around Eureka, take a **Humboldt Bay Harbor Cruise.** You can observe some of the region's bird life while sailing past fishing boats and decaying timber mills during the 75-minute narrated cruise. ⊠ *Pier at C St.* ☎ *707/445–1910 or 707/444–9440* ◲ *Harbor cruise $9.50; cocktail cruise $6.50* ◷ *Harbor cruise departs May–Oct., Mon.–Sat. at 1, 2:30, and 4, Sun. 1 and 2:30. Cocktail cruise departs Tues.–Sat. at 5:30.*

Where to Stay & Eat

★ **$$-$$$$** ✕ **Restaurant 301.** Eureka's best restaurant is known for its outstanding wine list, which has so many vintages (including the owner's private label) that several rooms in the hotel upstairs have had to be converted into "cellars." The cuisine is no less exquisite. Ingredients are hand-selected from the farmers market and local cheesemakers and ranchers; the chef even has secret sources abroad for some key ingredients. Dishes are prepared with a delicate hand and a sensuous imagination. The thin, L-shaped dining room makes each table private, conducive to the romance the food inspires. Just passing through on the highway, you'd never know such elegance exists in Eureka. ⊠ *301 L St.* ☎ *707/444–8062* ⊟ *AE, D, DC, MC, V* ◷ *No lunch.*

★ **$** ✕ **Samoa Cookhouse.** The recommendation here is for rustic fun, of which there is plenty: this is a longtime loggers' hangout. The Samoa's cooks serve three substantial set meals family-style at long wooden tables. Meat dishes predominate. Save room (if possible) for the homemade apple pie or strawberry shortcake. ⊠ *Cookhouse Rd. (from U.S. 101 cross Samoa Bridge, turn left onto Samoa Rd., then left 1 block later onto Cookhouse Rd.)* ☎ *707/442–1659* ⊟ *AE, D, MC, V.*

¢-$$ ✕ **Cafe Waterfront.** This airy local landmark presents a solid basic menu of burgers and steaks, but the real standouts are the daily seafood specials—lingcod, shrimp, and other treats fresh from the harbor across the street. The building, listed on the National Register of Historic Places, was a saloon and brothel until the 1950s. Two rooms, named after former ladies of the house, are available as "rooms to let." ✉ *102 F St.* ☎ *707/443–9190* ⊟ *MC, V.*

¢ ✕ **Ramone's.** A casual bakery café, Ramone's serves light sandwiches from dawn to 6 PM. ✉ *209 E. St.* ☎ *707/442–6082* ⊟ *MC, V* ⊘ *No dinner.*

$$–$$$$ ⊡ **Carter House.** Mark Carter likes to say that his staff has been instructed to say "Yes." Whether it's breakfast-in-bed or an in-room massage, someone here will make sure you get what you want. Rooms—in two main buildings and several cottages—have varying floor plans and are individually decorated. The luscious honeymoon suite (nicknamed "The Loveshack") comes with a professional-grade kitchen, where you can have the restaurant's chef cook you a private dinner. Even the least expensive rooms cover all the bases of comfort, with thick comforters and classic, aristocratic design. ✉ *301 L St., 95501* ☎ *707/444–8062* ⊠ *707/444–8067* ⊕ *www.carterhouse.com* ⇥ *32 rooms, 15 suites* ⟠ *Restaurant, some in-room hot tubs, some kitchens, minibars, cable TV, massage, shop, concierge, meeting rooms; no smoking* ⊟ *AE, D, DC, MC, V* ⫲◯⫳ *BP.*

★ $–$$$ ⊡ **An Elegant Victorian Mansion.** This meticulously restored Eastlake mansion in a residential neighborhood east of the Old Town lives up to its name. Each room is completely decked out in period furnishings and wall coverings, down to the carved-wood beds, fringed lamp shades, and pull-chain commodes. The innkeepers may even greet you in vintage clothing and entertain you with silent movies on tape, croquet on the rose-encircled lawn, and guided tours of local Victoriana in their antique automobile. ✉ *1406 C St., 95501* ☎ *707/444–3144* ⊠ *707/442–3295* ⊕ *www.eureka-california.com* ⇥ *4 rooms* ⟠ *Sauna, bicycles, croquet, laundry service* ⊟ *MC, V* ⫲◯⫳ *BP.*

Nightlife

Lost Coast Brewery & Cafe (✉ 617 4th St. ☎ 707/445–4480), a bustling microbrewery, is the best place in town to relax with a pint of ale or porter. Soups, salads, and light meals are served for lunch and dinner (about $15).

Sports & the Outdoors

Hum-Boats (✉ 2 F St. ☎ 707/443–5157) provides sailing rides, sailboat rentals, guided kayak tours, and sea kayak rentals and lessons (year-round; by appointment only in winter). The company also runs a water-taxi service on Humboldt Bay.

Shopping

Eureka has several art galleries in the district running from C to I streets between 2nd and 3rd streets. Specialty shops in Eureka's Old Town include the original **Restoration Hardware** (✉417 2nd St. ☎707/443–3152), a good place to find stylish yet functional home and garden accessories and clever polishing and cleaning products. The **Irish Shop** (✉ 334 2nd St. ☎ 707/443–8343) carries imports from the Emerald Isle, mostly fine woolens.

Arcata

㉓ *9 mi north of Eureka on U.S. 101.*

The home of Humboldt State University is one of the few California burgs to retain a town square. A farmers' market takes place in the square on Saturday morning from May through November. For a self-guided tour of Arcata that includes some of its restored Victorian buildings, pick up a map from the **Chamber of Commerce** (✉ 1635 Heindon Rd. ☎ 707/822–3619 ⊕ www.arcatachamber.com), open daily from 9 to 5.

Where to Stay & Eat

$–$$ ✕ **Abruzzi.** Salads and hefty pasta dishes take up most of the menu at this upscale Italian restaurant in the lower level of Jacoby's Storehouse, off the town square. One specialty is *linguine pescara*, pasta with a spicy seafood-and-tomato sauce. ⊠ *H and 8th Sts.* ☎ *707/826–2345* ▭ *AE, D, MC, V* ⊙ *No lunch.*

¢ ✕ **Crosswinds.** This restaurant serves Continental cuisine in a sunny Victorian room, at prices that attract students from Humboldt State University. Hit it for an early breakfast and you'll have the place to yourself. ⊠ *10th and I Sts.* ☎ *707/826–2133* ▭ *MC, V* ⊙ *Closed Mon. No dinner.*

¢–$$ ▦ **Hotel Arcata.** Rooms are clean and modest, but flowered bedspreads and claw-foot bathtubs lend a bit of character to this historic landmark overlooking the town square. Tomo, the Japanese restaurant on the ground floor, serves sushi as well as cooked food. It is closed for lunch on weekends. ⊠ *708 9th St., 95521* ☎ *707/826–0217 or 800/344–1221* ▦ *707/826–1737* ⊕ *www.hotelarcata.com* ⇄ *32 rooms* ◬ *Restaurant, meeting room* ▭ *AE, D, DC, MC, V* ¶⊙ *CP.*

Shopping

Plaza Design (⊠ 808 G St. ☎ 707/822–7732), one of Arcata's impressive selection of book, housewares, clothing, fabric, and other shops, specializes in gifts, paper products, and innovative furnishings.

Trinidad

㉔ *14 mi north of Arcata on U.S. 101.*

Trinidad got its name from the Spanish mariners who entered the bay on Trinity Sunday, June 9, 1775. The town became a principal trading post for the mining camps along the Klamath and Trinity rivers. As mining, and then whaling, faded, so did the luster of this former boomtown. One family owns nearly all the commercial real estate in town, and it strives to keep Trinidad from becoming solely a tourist town. The result is that picturesque Trinidad Bay and the surrounding village have enough sights and activities to accommodate visitors but remain quiet, inexpensive, and genuinely charming.

Where to Stay & Eat

★ $$–$$$ ✕ **Larrupin' Cafe.** Considered by many locals one of the best places to eat on the North Coast, this restaurant has earned widespread fame for its mesquite-grilled ribs and fresh fish dishes, served in a bright yellow, two-story house on a quiet country road 2 mi north of Trinidad. ⊠ *1658 Patrick's Point Dr.* ☎ *707/677–0230* ◬ *Reservations essential* ▭ *No credit cards* ⊙ *Closed Tues.–Wed. in winter, Tues. in summer. No lunch.*

$–$$ ✕ **Seascape.** With its glassed-in main room and deck for outdoor dining, this casual spot takes full advantage of its location on Trinidad Bay. Dinners showcase local seafood, particularly Dungeness crab in winter, but are a bit pricey for the return: the food is of acceptable quality but dishes are not particularly imaginative. The lunches and huge breakfasts are best bets. ⊠ *At pier* ☎ *707/677–3762* ▭ *D, MC, V.*

¢ ✕ **Katy's Smokehouse.** This tiny smokehouse has been doing things the same way for 65 years, curing day-boat, line-caught fish in the original smokers. It's traditional but still imaginative, with smoked salmon cured with brown sugar alongside albacore jerky and smoked scallops. The shopkeepers are great talkers and have loads of information about fishing, from the local industry to tips on preparing what you buy. There's no seating or restaurant service, but if you buy bread and drinks in town, you can make a picnic with the fixings here and walk to waterside for lunch. ⊠ *740 Edwards St.* ☎ *707/677–0151* ⊕ *www.katyssmokehouse. com* ▭ *MC, V.*

$$$ 🏨 **Turtle Rocks Oceanfront Inn.** This comfortable inn has the best view in Trinidad, and the architects cleverly incorporated the stunning outdoors into their design. Each room's private, glassed-in deck overlooks the ocean and several sea stacks covered with sunning sea lions. The surrounding landscape has been left natural; tucked among the low bushes are sun decks for winter whale watching and summer catnaps. Patrick's Point State Park is a short walk away. ⊠ *3392 Patrick's Point Dr., 95570* ☎ *707/677–3707* ⊕ *www.turtlerocksinn.com* ↩ *6 rooms, 1 suite* ⊟ *AE, D, MC, V* ⦿❙ *BP.*

$$–$$$ 🏨 **Trinidad Bay Bed & Breakfast.** This Cape Cod–style shingle house overlooks the harbor and the coastline to the south. The innkeepers can provide a wealth of information about the nearby wilderness, beach, and top fishing spots. A crackling fire warms the living room in chilly weather; one room has its own fireplace. ⊠ *560 Edwards St., Box 849, 95570* ☎ *707/677–0840* 🖶 *707/677–9245* ⊕ *www.trinidadbaybnb. com* ↩ *4 rooms* ⚭ *Some microwaves, some refrigerators* ⊟ *MC, V* ⊙ *Closed Dec.–Feb.* ⦿❙ *BP.*

Patrick's Point State Park

★ ㉕ *5 mi north of Trinidad and 25 mi north of Eureka on U.S. 101.*

Patrick's Point is the ultimate California coastal park. On a forested plateau almost 200 feet above the surf, it has stunning views of the Pacific, great whale and sea-lion watching in season, picnic areas, bike paths, and hiking trails through old-growth forest. There are tidal pools at Agate Beach and a small museum with natural-history exhibits. Because the park is far from major tourist hubs, there are few visitors—most are local surfers—leaving the land sublimely quiet. ☎ *707/677–3570* ✉ *$2 per vehicle.*

Where to Stay

⚠ **Patrick's Point State Park Campground.** In a spruce and alder forest above the ocean (just a handful of sites have sea views), Patrick's Point has all the campground amenities except RV hook-ups. You should reserve in advance in summer. ⚭ *Flush toilets, drinking water, showers, bear boxes, fire pits* ↩ *124 sites* ⊠ *U.S. 101, 4150 Patrick's Point Dr.* ☎ *800/444–7275* ⊕ *www.reserveamerica.com* ⊙ *Year-round* ✉ *$12.*

Redwood National and State Parks

㉖ *22 mi north (Orick entrance) of Trinidad on U.S. 101.*

After 115 years of intensive logging, this 106,000-acre parcel of tall trees came under government protection in 1968, marking the California environmentalists' greatest victory over the timber industry. Redwood National and State Parks encompasses one national and three state parks (Prairie Creek Redwoods, Del Norte Coast Redwoods, and Jedediah Smith Redwoods) and is more than 40 mi long. There is no admission fee to the national park, but the state parks charge a $2 day-use fee that admits you to all three. ⊠ *Park Headquarters: 1111 2nd St., Crescent City* ☎ *707/464–6101 Ext. 5064.*

At the **Redwood Information Center** you can get brochures, advice, and a free permit to drive up the steep, 17-mi road (the last 6 mi are gravel) to reach the Tall Trees Grove. Whale-watchers will find the deck of the visitor center an excellent observation point, and birders will enjoy the nearby Freshwater Lagoon, a popular layover for migrating waterfowl. ⊠ *Off U.S. 101, Orick* ☎ *707/464–6101 Ext. 5265.*

At **Tall Trees Grove** a 3-mi round-trip hiking trail leads to the world's tallest redwood, as well as its third- and fifth-tallest ones.

Within **Lady Bird Johnson Grove,** off Bald Hills Road, is a short circular trail to resplendent redwoods. This section of the park was dedicated by and named for the former first lady. For additional views take Davison Road to Fern Canyon. This gravel road winds through 4 mi of second-growth redwoods, then hugs a bluff 100 feet above the pounding Pacific surf for another 4 mi.

To reach the entrance to **Prairie Creek Redwoods State Park** (☎ 707/464–6101 Ext. 5300), take the Prairie Parkway exit off the U.S. 101 bypass. Extra space has been paved alongside the parklands, providing fine vantage points from which to observe an imposing herd of Roosevelt elk grazing in the adjoining meadow. Prairie Creek's Revelation Trail is fully accessible to those with disabilities.

Where to Stay

¢ ▦ **Hostelling International–Redwood National Park.** This century-old inn is a stone's throw from the ocean; hiking begins just beyond its doors. Lodging is dormitory-style. Reserve well in advance for the hostel's one private room. ⊠ *14480 U.S. 101, at Wilson Creek Rd. (20 mi north of Orick), Klamath 95548* ☏ *707/482–8265* ⊕ *www.norcalhostels.org* ⊗ *Closed Dec.–Feb.* ⬩ *Kitchen, laundry facilities* ⊟ *MC, V.*

Crescent City

㉗ *40 mi north of Orick on U.S. 101.*

Del Norte County's largest town (population just under 5,000) is named for the shape of its harbor; during the 1800s this was an important steamship stop. At the bottom of B Street at **Popeye's Landing** you can rent a crab pot, buy some bait, and try your luck at crabbing. At low tide from April through September, you can walk from the pier across the ocean floor to the oldest lighthouse on the North Coast, **Battery Point Lighthouse** (☎ 707/464–3089). Tours ($2) of the 1856 structure are given from May through October, Wednesday through Sunday between 10 and 4, and by appointment the rest of the year.

Where to Stay & Eat

$–$$ ✕ **Harbor View Grotto.** This glassed-in dining hall overlooking the Pacific is known for its fresh fish entrées. The white, two-story building is marked only by a neon sign that reads RESTAURANT, but inside things are clean, friendly, and low-key. ⊠ *150 Starfish Way* ☎ *707/464–3815* ⊟ *D, MC, V.*

¢ ▦ **Curly Redwood Lodge.** A single redwood tree produced the 57,000 board feet of lumber used to build this lodge. The rooms make the most of that tree, with paneling, platform beds, and dressers built into the walls. ⊠ *701 U.S. 101 S, 95531* ☎ *707/464–2137* 🖶 *707/464–1655* ⊕ *www.curlyredwoodlodge.com* ⇜ *36 rooms* ⊟ *AE, DC, MC, V.*

en route | Travelers continuing north to the **Smith River** near the Oregon state line will find fine trout and salmon fishing as well as a profusion of flowers. Ninety percent of America's lily bulbs are grown in this area.

THE NORTH COAST A TO Z

To research prices, get advice from other travelers, and book travel arrangements, visit ⊕ www.fodors.com

AIRPORTS & TRANSFERS

Arcata/Eureka Airport receives United Express and Alaska Airlines flights from San Francisco. The airport is in McKinleyville, which is 16 mi north of Eureka. *See* Air Travel *in* Smart Travel Tips A to Z for airline phone numbers. A taxi costs about $40 and takes roughly 20 minutes. Door to Door Airport Shuttle costs $16 to Arcata and Trinidad, $19 to Eureka, and $45 to Ferndale for the first person, $3 for each additional person. Buses on Redwood Transit run to Arcata (33 min) and Eureka (51 min), both trips for $1.70. Note, however, that weekday buses operate only between 6 AM and 6 PM and Saturday buses are even more restricted. There is no Sunday bus service.

🛪 **Arcata/Eureka Airport** ⊠ 3561 Boeing Ave, McKinleyville ☎ 707/839-5401. **Door to Door Airport Shuttle** ☎ 707/442-9266 or 888/338-5497. Buses on **Redwood Transit** ☎ 707/443-0826.

BUS TRAVEL

Greyhound buses travel along U.S. 101 from San Francisco to Seattle, with regular stops in Eureka and Crescent City. Bus drivers will stop in other towns along the route if you specify your destination when you board. Humboldt Transit Authority connects Eureka, Arcata, Scotia, Fortuna, and Trinidad.

🚌 **Greyhound** ☎ 800/231-2222 ⊕ www.greyhound.com. **Humboldt Transit Authority** ☎ 707/443-0826 ⊕ www.hta.org.

CAR RENTAL

Hertz rents cars at the Arcata/Eureka Airport, but call the reservation desk in advance if your flight will arrive late in the evening—the staff sometimes goes home early. *See* Car Rental *in* Smart Travel Tips A to Z for national rental agency phone numbers.

CAR TRAVEL

Although there are excellent services along Highway 1 and U.S. 101, the main north–south coastal routes, gas stations and mechanics are few and far between on the smaller roads. If you're running low on fuel and see a gas station, stop for a refill. Highway 1 is often curvy and difficult all along the coast. Driving directly to Mendocino from San Francisco is quicker if, instead of driving up the coast on Highway 1, you take U.S. 101 north to Highway 128 northwest (from Cloverdale) to Highway 1 north. Once it gets into Humboldt County, U.S. 101 itself becomes as twisting as Highway 1 as it continues on to the northernmost corner of the state. For information on the condition of roads in northern California, call the Caltrans Highway Information Network's voice-activated system. At the prompt say the route number in which you are interested, and you'll hear a recorded message about current conditions.

🚗 **Road Conditions Caltrans Highway Information Network** ☎ 800/427-7623.

EMERGENCIES

In an emergency dial 911. In state and national parks park rangers serve as police officers and will help you in any emergency. Bigger towns along the coast have hospitals, but for major medical emergencies you will need to go to San Francisco.

🚑 Emergency Contacts **Central Hospital Health Direct** ⊠ 2200 Harrison Ave., Eureka, ☎ 707/445-3121. **Del Norte County Hospital** ⊠ 100 A St., Crescent City ☎ 707/

464-8511. **Eureka Police Department** ✉ 604 C St., Eureka ☎ 707/441-4060. **Mendocino Coast District Hospital** ✉ 700 River Dr., Fort Bragg ☎ 707/961-1234. **Mendocino County Sheriff** ✉ 951 Low Gap Rd., Ukiah ☎ 707/463-4411.

VISITOR INFORMATION

🛈 **Eureka/Humboldt County Convention and Visitors Bureau** ✉ 1034 2nd St., Eureka 95501 ☎ 707/443-5097 or 800/346-3482 ⊕ www.redwoodvisitor.org. **Fort Bragg-Mendocino Coast Chamber of Commerce** ⌂ 332 N. Main St., Fort Bragg 95437 ☎ 707/961-6300 or 800/726-2780 ⊕ www.mendocinocoast.com. **North Coast Visitors Bureau** ✉ The Cannery, 2801 Leavenworth St., 2nd floor, Fisherman's Wharf, San Francisco 94133 ☎ 415/394-5991. **Redwood Empire Association** ✉ Cannery, 2801 Leavenworth St., San Francisco 94133 ☎ 415/543-8334 ⊕ www.redwoodempire.com. **Sonoma County Tourism Program** ✉ 2300 County Center Dr., Room B260, Santa Rosa 95405 ☎ 707/565-5383 ⊕ www.sonomacounty.com. **West Marin Chamber of Commerce** ☎ 415/663-9232 ⊕ www.pointreyes.org.

THE PENINSULA & SOUTH BAY

SOUTH OF SAN FRANCISCO

4

FODOR'S CHOICE

Tech Museum of Innovation, *San Jose*

HIGHLY RECOMMENDED

RESTAURANTS   Cafe Gibraltar, *El Granada*

Emile's Restaurant, *San Jose*

Evvia, *Palo Alto*

Flea Street Café, *Palo Alto*

Sent Sovi, *Saratoga*

71 Saint Peter, *San Jose*

Three–Zero Cafe, *El Granada*

HOTELS   Garden Court Hotel, *Palo Alto*

The Hensley House, *San Jose*

Hotel De Anza, *San Jose*

SIGHTS   Cantor Center for Visual Arts, *museum in Palo Alto*

Filoli, *country estate in Woodside*

Rosicrucian Egyptian Museum, *San Jose*

Scenic Highway 9, *Saratoga*

Villa Montalvo, *mansion and art museum in Saratoga*

Updated by
Lisa M.
Hamilton

TWO PARALLEL WORLDS LIE SOUTH OF SAN FRANCISCO. The Inland Peninsula pulses with prosperity and draws innovative inspiration from Stanford University. Many visitors to the Bay Area associate the area with traffic congestion and suburban sprawl. Indeed, much of the region from San Francisco to Santa Clara County is clogged with office complexes and strip-mall shopping centers. But the Peninsula also has lovely hills and redwood forests. Former country estates built by the mining and transportation "bonanza kings" of the 19th century remain hidden away in dense forests and behind the vast stretches of tawny hills where hawks soar overhead. Seemingly even the "dot.com" bust cannot shake this area's resilient good fortune.

Farther south is the heart of Silicon Valley, the birthplace of the tiny electronic chips and circuits that support the information superhighway. Look beyond what seems to be an endless sprawl of office parks, intertwined highways, shopping centers, and high-rises, and you'll find that the South Bay contains old-fashioned neighborhoods and abundant green hills. There are diverse towns such as Santa Clara, with its 200-year-old mission; Saratoga, with its fine antiques stores and French restaurants; and San Jose—the third-largest city on the West Coast—with its burgeoning core, its many micro-neighborhoods, and a growing ribbon of urban green connecting the city from north to south.

The second world south of San Francisco lies over the Santa Cruz Mountains on the fog-shrouded San Mateo County coast, where rural towns perch between undeveloped hills and rugged coastline. Most of the hamlets that dot the coast are no more than a few blocks long, with just enough room for a couple of B&Bs, restaurants, and boutiques or galleries. As you wind your way from one to the other, past Christmas tree farms, pumpkin patches, and stunning beaches, you'll find that the pace of life is slower here than in the rest of the Bay Area.

Exploring the Peninsula & South Bay

You'll need a car to get around. The Inland Peninsula and South Bay is a tangle of freeways, especially in the area around San Jose, so avoid driving in rush hour. By contrast, the stretch of Highway 1 that leads south to the Monterey Bay area passes through a sparsely populated landscape punctuated by only a few small towns.

About the Restaurants

It used to be that for a an exceptional dining experience, Peninsula and South Bay food lovers would head to San Francisco. No longer. Today some of the country's greatest chefs have recognized the area's appeal, opening trendy bistros and eateries, especially in San Jose's revitalized downtown. Dining in the South Bay might be a notch more casual than in San Francisco—and a notch less expensive—but that doesn't mean you won't need reservations. Along the coast, however, restaurants are strictly casual, and unless otherwise noted, you can generally walk in without a wait for a table.

About the Hotels

Lodging in the Inland Peninsula and South Bay areas targets business travelers—most are chain motels and hotels, though a number of B&Bs have popped up. Plan ahead because during the week many Inland Peninsula and South Bay hotels are booked up to two weeks in advance. Conversely, many of the area's business- and convention-oriented hotels can be nearly empty on weekends, when rates plummet and package deals abound. You might consider smaller hotels in such outlying areas as Santa Clara and Stevens Creek Boulevard in San Jose. Along the coastal peninsula, accommodations tend to have some character and cater to weekend tourists and San Franciscans; distinctive inns and B&Bs are the norm. Because of the weekend demand on the coast you'd be wise to make reservations as far out as you can.

	WHAT IT COSTS				
	$$$$	$$$	$$	$	¢
RESTAURANTS	over $30	$23–$30	$16–$22	$10–$15	under $10
HOTELS	over $250	$176–$250	$121–$175	$90–$120	under $90

Restaurant prices are for a main course at dinner, excluding sales tax of 8¼% (depending on location). Hotel prices are for a standard double room in high season, excluding service charges and 10% tax.

Timing
The hills that separate the Santa Clara Valley from the coastal peninsula block summertime fog from blowing into the Inland Peninsula and South Bay, producing drastic variations in temperatures between the coast and inland from April through October. In July you can expect foggy weather and temperatures in the mid-60s along the coastline, while just inland the days are sunny, with temperatures in the mid-80s. The rainy season runs from about November through March, and temperatures are generally constant across the region; expect daytime highs in the 50s and 60s.

THE INLAND PENINSULA

Much of your first impression of the Inland Peninsula will depend on where and when you enter. Take the 30-mi stretch of U.S. 101 from San Francisco along the eastern side of the Peninsula, and you'll see office complex after shopping center after corporate tower—and you'll likely get caught in horrific morning and evening commuter traffic. On the west side, however, the less crowded I–280 takes you past soul-soothing hills, lakes, and reservoirs.

Woodside

▶ ❶ *31 mi south of San Francisco via I–280.*

West of Palo Alto, Woodside is a tiny, rustic town where weekend warriors stock up on espresso and picnic fare before charging off on their mountain bikes. Blink once, and you're past the town center. The main draw here is the wealth of surrounding lush parks and preserves.

★ One of the few great country houses in California that remains intact is **Filoli.** Built 1915–1917 for wealthy San Franciscan William B. Bourn II, it was designed by Willis Polk in a Georgian Revival style, with red-brick walls and a tile roof. The name is Bourn's acronym for "fight, love, live." As interesting as the house are the 16 acres of formal gardens, which encompass a sunken garden and a teahouse in the Italian Renaissance style. From June through September Filoli hosts a series of Sunday-afternoon jazz concerts. Bring a picnic or buy a box lunch; Filoli provides tables, sodas, wine, fruit, and popcorn. In December the mansion is festively decorated for a series of holiday events: brunches, afternoon teas, Christmas concerts, and more. ⊠ *Cañada Rd. near Edgewood Rd.* ☎ *650/364–2880* ⊕ *www.filoli.org* ☜ *$10* ☉ *Mid-Feb.–Oct., Tues.–Sat. 10–3* ☞ *Reservations essential for guided tours.*

Numbers in the text correspond to numbers in the margin and on the Peninsula and South Bay and Downtown San Jose maps.

If you have 1 day

Spend your morning in ▶ **Palo Alto ❷**, taking a look around town and a tour of **Stanford University.** In the afternoon head for ⊞ **San Jose ❺–⓰** and the **Tech Museum of Innovation ❾**, the **Rosicrucian Egyptian Museum ⓭**, and the **Winchester Mystery House ⓯**. Depending on your taste, have a raucous evening at **Big Lil's Barbary Coast Dinner Theater** or an evening of symphony, ballet, or theater at San Jose's **Center for Performing Arts.**

4

If you have 3 days

On your first day head south from San Francisco to ▶ **Woodside ❶**, where you can tour **Filoli** (except Mon. Dec.–Jan.). Drive south on I–280 to the Sand Hill Road exit and take that route to the central campus of **Stanford University.** Take an afternoon tour of the university and its **Iris and B. Gerald Cantor Center for Visual Arts,** then have dinner in ⊞ **Palo Alto ❷**. For an unusual evening outing visit the **Hewlett-Packard garage** before retiring to your hotel. On day two, stop in **Santa Clara ❸** to see **Mission Santa Clara de Asis,** or if you have kids in tow, you might want to treat them to a morning at **Paramount's Great America.** Devote your afternoon to ⊞ **San Jose ❺–⓰** and its attractions, then take a sunset drive to **Saratoga ❹**. Drive back up I–280 on your last day and exit onto Highway 92 to head west to the coast. Noodle around **Año Nuevo State Reserve ⓴**, **Pescadero State Beach,** ⊞ **Half Moon Bay ⓲**, and **Moss Beach ⓱**, then overnight in a Half Moon Bay B&B.

One Peninsula oddity unknown even to most residents is the **Pulgas Water Temple,** where exquisitely groomed grounds surround a Romanesque temple and a reflecting pool. The temple commemorates the massive underground pipeline project of the early 1930s that channeled water from Hetch Hetchy, near Yosemite, to the Crystal Springs Reservoir, on the Peninsula. Walk up the steps of the columned circular temple to feel the power of the water as it thunders under your feet. At press time the temple was scheduled to be closed for repairs until mid-2004, so make sure to call ahead. ⊠ *Cañada Rd. 1½ mi north of Edgewood Rd.* ☏ *650/872–5900* ☑ *Free* ☉ *Weekdays 9:30–4.*

Where to Stay & Eat

$$–$$$ ✕ **Bucks in Woodside.** Giant plastic alligators, Elvis paintings, a human-size Statue of Liberty reproduction, and framed computer chips on the walls make the aesthetic statement at this casual restaurant. The menu is a grab bag of crowd pleasers: soups, sandwiches, burgers, and salads. For breakfast there's a "U-do-it" omelet in addition to standard choices. ⊠ *3062 Woodside Rd.* ☏ *650/851–8010* ▭ *AE, D, MC, V.*

$–$$ ✕ **Woodside Bakery and Café.** Stop by the bakery section for a cup of hot cocoa and a fresh-baked pastry, or sit in the café for a glass of wine and a light meal. Everything is fresh and well presented. The menu tends toward light seasonal dishes such as fresh pastas and salads. But you'll also find more substantial entrées like oven-braised lamb shank and baked Dijon chicken. ⊠ *3052 Woodside Rd.* ☏ *650/851–0812* ▭ *AE, MC, V.*

Palo Alto

▶ ❷   *34 mi south of San Francisco via I–280 or U.S. 101; 3 mi south of Wood-side on I–280.*

Palo Alto's main attraction is the bucolic campus of Stanford University, 8,200 acres of grassy hills. Downtown Palo Alto is a hotbed of restaurants, shops, and attractions catering to high-income Peninsula residents as well as the university crowd. Wander up and down University Avenue and the surrounding side streets and you'll discover the historic Stanford Theatre, a 1920s-style movie palace—and a Barbie Hall of Fame.

Stanford University was former California governor Leland Stanford's horse-breeding farm, and the land is still known as The Farm. Founded in 1885 and opened in 1891, the university occupies a campus designed by Frederick Law Olmsted. Its unique California mission–Romanesque sandstone buildings, joined by arcades and topped by red-tile roofs, are mixed with newer buildings in variations on Olmstead's style. Lined with majestic palm trees, the main campus entrance, Palm Drive (an extension of University Avenue from Palo Alto) leads directly to the main quadrangle. The quadrangle, a group of 12 original classroom buildings, is the center of the university. There, the facade and interior walls of Memorial Church are covered with mosaics of biblical scenes. Students lounge or rush around the quadrangle and near the Clock Tower and White Plaza in a constant stream of bicycles and in-line skates. The 285-foot Hoover Tower is a landmark and a tourist attraction; an elevator ($2) leads to an observation deck that provides sweeping views. Free one-hour **walking tours** (⊠ Serra St., opposite Hoover Tower ☏ 650/723–2560 or 650/723–2053) of the Stanford campus leave daily at 11 and 3:15 from the visitor center in front of Memorial Hall. ⊠ *Galvez St. at Serra St.* ☏ *650/723–2300* ⊕ *www.stanford.edu.*

★   **Iris and B. Gerald Cantor Center for Visual Arts,** one of the most comprehensive and varied art collections in the Bay Area, spans the centuries as well as the globe, from pre-Columbian to modern. Included is the world's largest collection—180 pieces—of Rodin sculptures outside Paris, many of them displayed in the outdoor sculpture garden. Other highlights include a bronze Buddha from the Ming dynasty, wooden masks and carved figurines from 18th- and 19th-century Africa, paintings by Georgia O'Keeffe, and sculpture by Willem de Kooning and Bay Area artist Robert Arneson. The exceptional café has a menu—all organic—and clientele that's savvy but unpretentious. Choose to sit in the airy dining room or on the sunny terrace overlooking the Rodin garden. ⊠ *328 Lomita Dr. and Museum Way, off Palm Dr. at Stanford University* ☏ *650/723–4177* ⊕ *www.stanford.edu/dept/ccva* ⊠ *Free* ⊙ *Wed. and Fri.–Sun. 11–5, Thurs. 11–8. Rodin Sculpture Garden tours Sat. at 11, Sun. at 3.*

Tucked into a small, heavily wooded plot of land is the **Papua New Guinea Sculpture Garden.** The inconspicuous garden is filled with tall, ornately carved wooden poles, drums, and carved stones—all created on location in the 1990s by 10 artists from Papua New Guinea. A Stanford anthropology professor proposed the idea for the garden. Detailed plaques explain the concept and the works. ⊠ *Santa Teresa St. and Lomita Dr., at Stanford University* ⊠ *Free.*

Though it doesn't look like much, the **Hewlett-Packard garage** is a good place to get a sense of the humble origins of one of the world's largest technology companies. It all started in this one-car garage, where former Stanford freshman roommates William Hewlett and David Packard put their heads together back in the 1930s. The rest is history. Today

4

Beaches

The main draw of coastal San Mateo County is its beaches. From Montara to Pescadero the strands accessible from Highway 1 are surprisingly uncrowded. Fog and cool weather may keep many people out of the water for large portions of the year, but the unspoiled beauty and wildlife make these beaches a treasure of the Bay Area. Some standouts are San Gregorio and Pomponio for strolling and sunbathing; windy Waddell Creek for windsurfing and kite-surfing; and Fitzgerald Marine Preserve for tidepooling. With nearly three-quarters of the county (70%) in open space, there's enough beach that you can usually find a good one by simply pulling over wherever you see a patch of sand.

Historic Homesteads

The communities of the Peninsula and South Bay—once known not for computers but for their blossoming fruit orchards and vineyards—work hard to preserve their parklands and turn-of-the-20th-century homesteads. In Woodside, Filoli stands as one of the great California country houses that remain intact. The Winchester Mystery House, in San Jose, may be the best-known site, but look beyond the tales of ghosts to see the sprawling farmhouse it once was. You can also visit former vineyards and historic homes in the Santa Cruz Mountains, notably Villa Montalvo and the Mountain Winery in Saratoga.

---

the Hewlett-Packard garage is a California State Landmark, but it's also a private residence, so viewing is limited to sidewalk rubbernecking. ⊠ *Behind 367 Addison Ave.*

Two-hour tours of the **Stanford Linear Accelerator Center (SLAC)** reveal the workings of the 2-mi-long electron accelerator, which is used by Stanford University scientists for research into elementary particles. Call for times and reservations. ⊠ *Sand Hill Rd., 2 mi west of the central campus* ☎ *650/926–2204.*

> **off the beaten path**

PALO ALTO BAYLANDS NATURE PRESERVE – East of downtown Palo Alto is a wetlands area of creeks, sloughs, mudflats, and freshwater and saltwater marshland. The area supports abundant bird life (more than 150 species) and is an important stopover on the Pacific Flyway. You can walk the Bay Trail through the middle of the preserve and visit the Lucy Evans Nature Interpretive Center to learn about the wildlife of the Baylands. ⊠ *East end of Embarcadero Rd.* ☎ *650/329–2506* 🎟 *Free* ☉ *Tues.–Wed. 10–5, Thurs.–Fri. 2–5, weekends 1–5.*

SOUTH BAY
WEST OF SAN JOSE

To many the South Bay is synonymous with Silicon Valley, the center of high-tech research and the corporate headquarters of such giants as Apple, Sun Microsystems, Oracle, and Hewlett-Packard. But Silicon Valley is more a state of mind than a place—it is an attitude held by the legions of software engineers, programmers, and computerphiles who call the area home. And that home is increasingly visitor-friendly. Within the

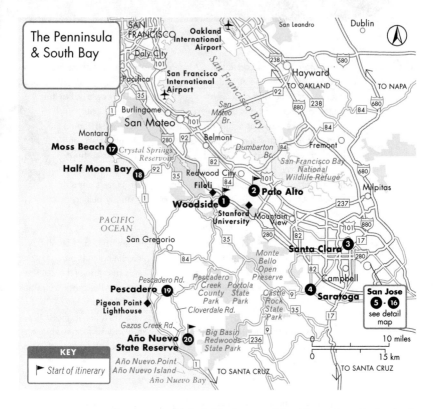

The Penninsula & South Bay

KEY

► Start of itinerary

sprawl are towns with individual personalities, history that stretches back to the Spanish, thriving arts scenes, and shops and restaurants to satisfy the most discerning wallet.

Santa Clara

3 *40 mi south of San Francisco and 6 mi south of Palo Alto on U.S. 101 101.*

Santa Clara's offerings include two major attractions at opposite ends of the sightseeing spectrum: Mission Santa Clara de Asis, founded in 1777, and Paramount's Great America, northern California's answer to Disneyland. Although many visitors head straight to the amusement park, Santa Clara has plenty of history and is worthy of a brief visit—despite the sprawling shopping malls and sterile business parks.

Santa Clara University, founded in 1851 by Jesuits, was California's first college. The campus's **de Saisset Art Gallery and Museum** shows a permanent collection that includes California mission artifacts and gold-rush-era pieces, California-themed artwork, and contemporary Bay Area art, especially prints. ⊠ *500 El Camino Real* ☎ *408/554–4528* ⊕ *www.scu.edu/desaisset* ☒ *Free* ☉ *Tues.–Sun. 11–4.*

In the center of Santa Clara University's campus is the **Mission Santa Clara de Asis,** the first of California's original missions to honor a female saint. In 1926 the mission chapel was destroyed by fire. Roof tiles of the current building, a replica of the original, were salvaged from earlier structures, which dated from the 1790s and 1820s. Early adobe walls and a spectacular rose garden with 4,500 roses—many varieties classified as antiques—remain as well. Part of the wooden Memorial Cross, from 1777, is set in front of the church. ⊠ *500 El Camino Real* ☎ *408/554–*

4023 ⊕ *www.scu.edu/visitors/mission* ⊠ *Free* ☉ *Daily 1–sundown for self-guided tours.*

☺ At the gigantic theme park **Paramount's Great America,** each section recalls a familiar part of North America: Hometown Square, Yukon Territory, Yankee Harbor, or County Fair. Popular attractions include the Drop Zone Stunt Tower, the tallest free-fall ride in North America; a *Top Gun* movie–theme roller coaster, whose cars travel along the outside of a 360-degree loop track; and Nickelodeon Splat City, 3 acres of obstacle courses apparently designed for kids who love to get wet and dirty. The park is served by Santa Clara County Transit and the Fremont BART station. ⊠ *Great America Pkwy. between U.S. 101 and Hwy. 237, 6 mi north of San Jose* ☎ *408/988–1776* ⊕ *www.pgathrills.com* ⊠ *$43.99, parking $6* ☉ *Apr.–May and Sept.–Oct., weekends; June–Aug., daily; opens 10 AM, closing times vary* ⊟ *AE, D, MC, V.*

At the **Intel Museum** you can learn how computer chips are made and follow the development of Intel Corporation's microprocessor, memory, and systems product lines. Guided tours are available by reservation. ⊠ *Robert Noyce Bldg., 2200 Mission College Blvd.* ☎ *408/765–0503* ⊕ *www.intel. com/intel/intelis/museum* ⊠ *Free* ☉ *Weekdays 9–6, Sat. 10–5.*

The **Carmelite Monastery** is a fine example of Spanish ecclesiastical architecture. Built in 1917, it's on the grounds of a mission-era ranch crossed by shady walkways and dotted with benches perfect for quiet contemplation. ⊠ *1000 Lincoln St.* ☎ *408/296–8412* ⊕ *http://members.aol. com/santaclaracarmel* ⊠ *Free* ☉ *Grounds open Mon.–Sat. 6:30–4:15, Sun. 8–5.*

In the Civic Center Park, a **statue of St. Clare,** patron saint of the city of Santa Clara, rises out of a fountain. The sculpture was cast in Italy in 1965 by Anne Van Kleeck, who used an ancient wax process. It was then shipped around Cape Horn and dedicated on this site in 1985. ⊠ *Civic Center Park, Lincoln St. at El Camino Real.*

Skylights cast natural light for viewing the exhibitions in the **Triton Museum of Art.** A permanent collection of 19th- and 20th-century sculpture by Bay Area artists is displayed in the garden, which you can see through a curved-glass wall at the rear of the building. Indoor galleries present excellent, eclectic shows of contemporary Native American work. ⊠ *1505 Warburton Ave.* ☎ *408/247–3754* ⊕ *www.tritonmuseum. org* ⊠ *$2 suggested donation* ☉ *Fri.–Tues. 11–5, Thurs. 11–9.*

Open only on Sunday afternoon, the tiny **Santa Clara Historic Museum** exhibits artifacts and photos that trace the history of the region. ⊠ *1509 Warburton Ave.* ☎ *408/248–2787* ⊠ *Free* ☉ *Sun. 1–4.*

Walk over to the grounds of City Hall to see noted San Francisco sculptor Benny Bufano's primitive *Universal Child,* facing the Santa Clara Historic Museum. The 85-foot statue depicts the children of the world standing as one. ⊠ *1500 Warburton Ave* ⊠ *Free.*

The **Harris-Lass Historic Museum** is built on Santa Clara's last farmstead. A restored house, summer kitchen, and barn convey a sense of life on the farm from the early 1900s through the 1930s. Guided tours take place every half hour until 3:30. ⊠ *1889 Market St.* ☎ *408/249–7905* ⊠ *$3* ☉ *Weekends noon–4.*

Where to Stay & Eat

$$–$$$ ✕ **Birk's.** Silicon Valley's businesspeople come to this sophisticated American grill to unwind. High-tech sensibilities will appreciate the modern, open kitchen and streamlined, multilevel dining area—yet the menu is traditional, strong on steaks and chops. An oyster bar adds a lighter element, as do the simply prepared but high-quality organic vegetable dishes such as garlic mashed potatoes and creamed spinach. ⊠ *3955 Freedom Cir., at U.S. 101 and Great America Pkwy.* ☎ *408/980–6400* ⊟ *AE, D, DC, MC, V* ☉ *No lunch weekends.*

$$ ✕ **Mio Vicino.** Mio's is a small, bare-bones, checkered-tablecloth Italian bistro in Old Santa Clara. The menu includes a long list of classic and contemporary pastas—and if you don't see it on the menu, just ask. The house specialties are shellfish pasta and chicken cannelloni. ⊠ *1290 Benton St.* ☎ *408/241–9414* ⊠ *384 E. Campbell Ave., Campbell* ☎ *408/ 378–0335* ⊟ *MC, V* ☉ *No lunch weekends.*

¢ ✕ **Chez Sovan.** This Cambodian jewel, with a pleasant setting and satisfying food, is a wonderful addition to the South Bay dining scene. The spring rolls are delectable, as are the noodle dishes, grilled meats, and flavorful curries. ⊠ *2425 S. Bascom Ave.* ☎ *408/371–7711* ⊟ *AE, MC, V.*

$$$ ▥ **Embassy Suites.** This upper-end chain hotel is ideal for Silicon Valley business travelers and families bound for Paramount's Great America. Every room is a two-room suite. Guests receive complimentary cooked-to-order breakfasts and evening beverages. ⊠ *2885 Lakeside Dr., 95054* ☎ *408/496–6400 or 800/362–2779* ⊟ *408/988–7529* ⊕ *www.embassy-suites.com* ⟿ *257 suites* ⟝ *Restaurant, room service, in-room data ports, refrigerators, cable TV with movies, pool, gym, hot tub, sauna, lounge, Internet, business services, meeting room, airport shuttle, free parking, no-smoking rooms* ⊟ *AE, D, DC, MC, V* ⍉⊙⍉ *BP.*

¢–$$ ▥ **Madison Street Inn.** At this Queen Anne Victorian, complimentary afternoon refreshments and a full breakfast are served on a brick garden patio with a bougainvillea-draped trellis. The inn has the distinct look of a private home, with a green-and-red-trim facade and individually styled rooms that range from homey to frilly. ⊠ *1390 Madison St., 95050* ☎ *408/249–5541 or 800/491–5541* ⊟ *408/249–6676* ⊕ *www. madisonstreetinn.com* ⟿ *6 rooms, 4 with bath* ⟝ *Some fans, in-room data ports, some microwaves, some refrigerators, cable TV, pool, hot tub, bicycles, laundry service, Internet, meeting room, some pets allowed; no a/c in some rooms, no TV in some rooms, no smoking* ⊟ *AE, D, DC, MC, V* ⍉⊙⍉ *BP.*

Nightlife and the Arts

ComedySportz (⊠ 3428 El Camino Real ☎ 408/985–5233) offers evenings of good-natured comedy appropriate for all ages. Book in advance or pay $7–$14 at the door.

Saratoga

❹ *12 mi southwest of Santa Clara on Hwy. 85.*

A 10-mi detour southwest from San Jose's urban core puts you in the heart of Saratoga, at the foot of the Santa Cruz Mountains. Once an artists' colony, the town is now home to many Silicon Valley CEOs, whose mansions dot the hillsides. Spend a slow-paced afternoon exploring Big Basin Way, the ⅓-mi main drag of the Village, as the downtown area is locally known. Here you'll find antiques stores, galleries, spas, and a handful of worthwhile restaurants.

★ Built in 1912 by former governor James Phelan, **Villa Montalvo** is a striking white mansion presiding over an expansive lawn. You can picnic and lounge on the lawn amidst sculptures or stroll through the art gallery, whose changing exhibits feature work by local artists and artists-in-residence. Additional draws are a gift shop and 175-acre park with several hiking trails, as well as a first-rate summer concert series and year-round literary events. ⊠ *15400 Montalvo Rd.* ☎ *408/961–5800*

⊕ *www.villamontalvo.org* ⊠ *Free* ⊙ *Park Oct.–Mar., daily 9–5; Apr.–Sept., daily 9–5; Gallery Wed.–Sun. 1–4.*

One of the most peaceful and meditative attractions in the area is the Zen-style **Hakone Gardens,** nestled on a steep hillside just south of downtown. Designed in 1918 by Aihara Naoharu, who had been an imperial gardener in Japan, the gardens have been carefully maintained, with koi (carp) ponds, sculptured shrubs, and a quiet grove of bamboo. Formal tea ceremonies, which cost $5 per person, are held from 1 to 4 on the first Thursday of the month; call for reservations. ⊠ *21000 Big Basin Way* ☏ *408/741–4994* ⊕ *www.hakone.com* ⊠ *Free; parking $5, free 1st Tues. of month* ⊙ *Weekdays 10–5, weekends 11–5.*

★ For a quick driving tour of the hills with their sweeping valley views, drive south out of Saratoga on Big Basin Way, which is **Scenic Highway 9.** The road leads into the Santa Cruz Mountains, all the way to the coast at the city of Santa Cruz. But you can take in some great views about 1½ mi out of town by taking a right on Pierce Road toward the **Mountain Winery** (☏ 408/741–2822). Built by Paul Masson in 1905 and now listed on the National Register of Historic Places, it is constructed of masonry and oak to resemble a French-country chateau. No longer serving its original purpose, Mountain Winery now hosts private events and a summer concert series, with bands playing against the backdrop of the ivy-covered winery building. Walking tours are available for free if you call in advance.

Where to Stay & Eat

★ $$$–$$$$ ✕ **Sent Sovi.** At this small, flower-draped restaurant, housed in a quaint cottage on Saratoga's quiet main street, chef and co-owner David Kinch offers a regularly changing menu of refined European fare. You might find potato-wrapped sea bass with wild mushrooms and red-wine broth, spice-glazed roast quail stuffed with gingerbread, or napoleon of lobster salad with toasted cumin crackers. Desserts are equally tantalizing. A five-course tasting menu lets you sample more widely from Kinch's remarkable repertoire. ⊠ *14583 Big Basin Way* ☏ *408/867–3110* ⌂ *Reservations essential* ⊟ *AE, MC, V* ⊙ *Closed Mon. No lunch.*

¢–$ ✕ **Willow Street Wood-Fired Pizza.** What began as a quaint "secret" pizzeria in the Willow Glen neighborhood just south of downtown has become one of the best and trendiest spots in the South Bay. Order an individual wood-fired pizza with classic cheese or try something less mundane, such as chicken Brie or artichoke and goat cheese. During lunch you can order from a quick and downsized version of the dinner menu. Reservations are accepted only for parties of eight or more, but smaller groups can call ahead to secure a spot on the waiting list. ⊠ *1072 Willow St.* ☏ *408/971–7080* ⌂ *Reservations not accepted* ⊟ *AE, MC, V.*

$$$–$$$$ ▦ **Inn at Saratoga.** Though this five-story, European-style inn is only 20 minutes from San Jose, its aura of calm makes it feel far from busy Silicon Valley. Rooms are decorated in soft earth tones and include secluded sitting alcoves overlooking a peaceful creek. A complimentary Continental breakfast is served in the morning; in the evening wine and hors d'oeuvres are set out in the cozy lobby. Modern business conveniences are available but discreetly hidden. ⊠ *20645 4th St., 95070* ☏ *408/867–5020 or 800/543–5020* 📠 *408/741–0981* ⊕ *www.innatsaratoga.com* 🛏 *42 rooms, 3 suites* ⌂ *In-room data ports, refrigerators, cable TV, in-room VCRs, exercise equipment, laundry service, Internet, business services, meeting room; no smoking* ⊟ *AE, DC, MC, V* �a� *CP.*

$$–$$$ ▦ **Saratoga Oaks Lodge.** This small and cozy place occupies a site that once housed the tollgate to a private road heading over the Santa Cruz Mountains. Several rooms have fireplaces and steam baths. Town is a

short stroll away, so the location is quiet but convenient. ⊠ *14626 Big Basin Way, 95070* ☎ *408/867–3307 or 888/867–3588* 🖷 *408/867–6765* ⊕ *www.saratogaoakslodge.com* ↪ *15 rooms, 5 suites* ♨ *In-room data ports, microwaves, refrigerators, cable TV; no smoking* ⊟ *AE, D, MC, V* ⏀⊙⏀ *CP.*

Nightlife and the Arts

Summer concerts at **Villa Montalvo** (⊠ 15400 Montalvo Rd. ☎ 408/961–5858) are performed on an intimate outdoor stage where seats give you a sweeping view of the valley—particularly spectacular at sunset. There's also a carriage house where concerts are performed throughout the rest of the year. Summer concerts at **The Mountain Winery** (⊠ 14831 Pierce Rd. ☎ 408/741–0763) are performed on a small stage outside the gorgeous, vine-covered winery building. Most of the acts are big-time, but openers are often local bands, which lends to the feeling of being at a local party rather than a concert.

Sports

Garrod Farms Stables (⊠ 22600 Mount Eden Rd. ☎ 408/867–9527) provides horse rentals and free weekend tastings of wines made on the premises.

Shopping

Stock up on dishes, linens, home accessories, and gifts at the **Butter Paddle** (⊠ 14510 Big Basin Way ☎ 408/867–1678), where all profits are donated to the local Eastfield Ming Quong Foundation for abused and troubled children.

SAN JOSE

San Jose has its own ballet, symphony, repertory theater, nationally recognized museums, downtown nightlife, and exclusive hotels. Downtown can be easily explored by foot, and Guadalupe River Park, a 3-mi belt of trees and gardens, connects downtown with the Children's Discovery Museum, to the south. The chain of parks and playgrounds extends all the way north to San Jose International Airport. A 21-mi light-rail system links downtown to the business district and to Paramount's Great America, to the north, and to various suburbs and malls to the south. You will still need a car to get to outlying communities and such sights as the Egyptian Museum and the Winchester Mystery House.

A walking tour of downtown San Jose is detailed in a brochure available from the convention and visitors bureau. The self-guided walk leads you past the 14 historic buildings described in the brochure. Vintage trolleys operate in downtown San Jose from 10:30 to 5:30 in summer and on some holidays throughout the year. Buy tickets for the trolleys at vending machines in any transit station.

Downtown San Jose and Vicinity

4 mi east of Santa Clara on Hwy. 82, 55 mi south of San Francisco on U.S. 101 or I–280.

a good tour

Much of downtown San Jose can be toured easily on foot. Start at the ► **Children's Discovery Museum** ❺ and be sure to wander around the outside of this outrageously purple building. Crossing through the surrounding park, take a stroll through the "herd" of larger-than-life animal sculptures facing San Carlos Street. The nearby steps lead down to Guadalupe Creek and a parallel walking path; a good detour leads north to the San Jose Arena and the **Guadalupe River Park** ❻, with a carousel and children's playground.

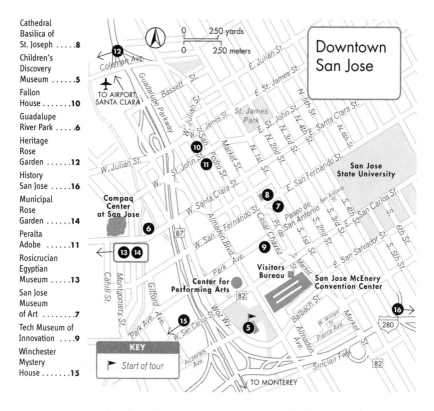

Back at the sculpture park, continue east on San Carlos Street into the heart of downtown San Jose. Immediately on the left is the Center for the Performing Arts, home to the city's ballet and symphony. San Jose's McEnery Convention Center and the visitor center are catercorner across the road. In front of the center an outdoor skating rink (open daily) is set up from mid-November to mid-January.

Continue down San Carlos Street and turn left on Market Street; ahead is Plaza de Cesar Chavez. On the square's northeast corner are the must-see **San Jose Museum of Art** ❼ and adjacent **Cathedral Basilica of St. Joseph** ❽. On the square's western edge at Park Avenue is the **Tech Museum of Innovation** ❾, with its children-friendly hands-on exhibits.

Follow Market Street north from the plaza and turn left on Santa Clara Street. For a glimpse of the historic Hotel De Anza, walk four blocks ahead to the corner of North Almaden Boulevard. Otherwise, walk one block, turn right on San Pedro Street, and continue two blocks—past the sidewalk cafés and restaurants—to St. John Street and turn left. The **Fallon House** ❿ will be on your right, the **Peralta Adobe** ⓫ on your left. At this point you can turn around and go east three blocks on St. John Street and board the light rail to return to your starting point.

Pick up your car and drive northwest from the center of town on Coleman Avenue. At Taylor Street take a right to reach **Heritage Rose Garden** ⓬. After you've strolled the grounds, head southwest on Taylor Street, which turns into Naglee Avenue at the Alameda, Naglee will take you to the **Rosicrucian Egyptian Museum** ⓭ and, across the street, the **Municipal Rose Garden** ⓮. When you're done there, continue southwest on Naglee until it turns into Forest Avenue, which intersects Winchester Boulevard. Turn left onto Winchester Boulevard to reach **Winchester Mys-**

tery House ⑮. Finally, take I–280 east to Highway 82 (Monterey Road) south and turn left on Phelan Avenue. At Kelley Park you can visit **History San Jose** ⑯. To return to downtown, backtrack to Monterey Road and turn right to drive north.

TIMING   The walking portion of this tour can easily be completed in about two hours. However, if you decide to spend time in the museums or at a café along San Pedro Street, give yourself at least four hours. The length of the driving tour depends on how long you spend at each sight. Plan on anywhere from three to six hours.

What to See

⑧ **Cathedral Basilica of St. Joseph.** This Renaissance-style cathedral is an embodiment of resurrection: it is the fifth church of St. Joseph built in San Jose (the fourth on this site), all its predecessors having perished in earthquakes and other natural disasters. The original adobe church began serving the residents of the pueblo of San Jose in 1803. The current and most long-standing incarnation, built in 1877, is a grand cathedral with extraordinary stained-glass windows and murals. ⊠ *90 S. Market St.* ☎ *408/283–8100* ⊕ *www.stjosephcathedral.org.*

⑤ **Children's Discovery Museum of San Jose.** You can't miss this angular purple building that seems to rise from the creek across from the convention center at the rear of Discovery Meadow Park. Installations on science, the humanities, and the arts are interactive: children can dress up in period costumes, create art from recycled materials, or play on a real fire truck. Outside, kids can crawl all over the oversize animal sculptures, nicknamed the Parade of Animals, while parents picnic on the lawn. ⊠ *180 Woz Way, at Auzerais St.* ☎ *408/298–5437* ⊕ *www.cdm.org* ⊠ *$7* ☉ *Tues.–Sat. 10–5, Sun. noon–5.*

⑩ **Fallon House.** San Jose's seventh mayor, Thomas Fallon, built this Victorian mansion in 1855. The house's period-decorated rooms can be viewed on a 90-minute tour that includes the Peralta Adobe and a screening of a video about the two houses. ⊠ *175 W. St. John St.* ☎ *408/993–8182* ⊕ *www.historysanjose.org* ⊠ *$6 (includes admission to Peralta Adobe)* ☉ *Guided tours weekends noon–5.*

⑥ **Guadalupe River Park.** This downtown park includes the Arena Green, next to the sports arena, with a carousel, children's playground, and artwork honoring five champion figure skaters from the area. The River Park path, which stretches for 3 mi, starts at the Children's Discovery Museum and runs north, ending at the Arena Green. ⊠ *345 W. Santa Clara St.* ☎ *408/277–5904* ⊕ *www.grpg.org* ⊠ *Free.*

⑫ **Heritage Rose Garden.** The newer of the city's two rose gardens has won national acclaim for its 5,000 rosebushes and trees. This quiet, 4-acre retreat has benches perfect for a break or a picnic and is alongside the still-developing Historic Orchard, which has fruit trees indigenous to the Santa Clara Valley. The garden is northwest of downtown, near the airport. ⊠ *Taylor and Spring Sts.* ☎ *408/298–7657* ⊠ *Free* ☉ *Daily dawn–dusk.*

⑯ **History San Jose.** Southeast of the city center, occupying 25 acres of Kelley Park, this outdoor "museum" highlights the history of San Jose and the Santa Clara Valley. You can see 28 historic and reconstructed buildings, hop a historic trolley, observe letterpress printing, and buy ice cream and candy at O'Brien's. On weekdays admission is free but the buildings are closed except for the galleries, Pacific Hotel, and ice cream and candy stores. ⊠ *1650 Senter Rd., at Phelan Ave.* ☎ *408/287–2290* ⊕ *www. historysanjose.org* ⊠ *$6* ☉ *Daily noon–5 call for weekend tour times.*

⓮ **Municipal Rose Garden.** Installed in 1931, the Municipal Rose Garden is one of several outstanding green spaces in the city's urban core—and certainly the best-smelling. West of downtown San Jose you'll find 5½ acres of roses with 4,000 shrubs and trees in 189 well-labeled beds, as well as marvelous walkways, fountains, and trellises. Some of the neighboring homes in the Rose Garden district date to the time of the city's founding. ☒ *Naglee and Dana Aves.* ☎ *408/277–4191* ⊕ *www.ci.san-jose.ca.us/cae/parks/rg* ☒ *Free* ⊙ *Daily 8 AM–sunset.*

⑪ **Peralta Adobe.** California pepper trees shade the last remaining structure (circa 1797) from the Pueblo de Guadalupe, the original settlement from which the modern city was born. The whitewashed, two-room home has been furnished to interpret life during the Spanish occupation and the Mexican rancho era. ☒ *184 W. St. John St.* ☎ *408/993–8182* ⊕ *www.historysanjose.org* ☒ *$6 (includes admission to Fallon House)* ⊙ *Guided tours weekends noon–5.*

★ ⑬ **Rosicrucian Egyptian Museum.** Owned by the Rosicrucian Order, the museum exhibits the West Coast's largest collection of Egyptian and Babylonian antiquities, including mummies, and an underground replica of a rock tomb. The museum's entrance is a reproduction of the Avenue of Ram Sphinxes from the Temple at Karnak in Egypt. The complex, 3 mi from downtown, is surrounded by a garden filled with palms, papyrus, and other plants recalling ancient Egypt. ☒ *1342 Naglee Ave., at Park Ave.* ☎ *408/947–3635* ⊕ *www.rosicrucian.org/park* ☒ *$9* ⊙ *Tues.–Fri. 10–5, weekends 11–6.*

❼ **San Jose Museum of Art.** Housed in a former post office building, this museum doesn't attempt to compete with its larger neighbor in San Francisco (SFMoFA) instead, it does its own thing. The permanent collection of paintings, sculpture, photography, and large-scale multimedia installations is solid, with an emphasis on cutting-edge California and Latino artists. The massive Dale Chihuly glass sculpture hanging above the lobby hints at the embrace of futuristic, high-tech pieces. ☒ *110 S. Market St.* ☎ *408/294–2787 or 408/271–6840* ⊕ *www.sjmusart.org* ☒ *Free* ⊙ *Tues.–Thurs. and weekends 11–5, Fri. 11–10.*

☾ ❾ **Tech Museum of Innovation.** Designed by renowned architect Ricardo Fodor'sChoice Legorreta of Mexico City, this museum of technology is high-tech and ★ hands-on. Exhibits allow you to create an action movie in a video editing booth, try to solve the story behind a crime scene using real forensic techniques, or talk with a roaming robot named Zaza. Another worthwhile attraction is the 299-seat Hackworth IMAX Dome Theater. ☒ *201 S. Market St., at Park Ave.* ☎ *408/294–8324* ⊕ *www.thetech. org* ☒ *Museum $9, IMAX $9, combination ticket $16* ⊙ *Tues.–Sun. 10–5; open some Mon., call for hrs.*

☾ ⓯ **Winchester Mystery House.** Convinced that spirits would harm her if construction ever stopped, firearms heiress and house owner Sarah Winchester constantly added to her house. For 38 years, beginning in 1884, she kept a revolving crew of carpenters at work creating a bizarre 160-room Victorian labyrinth with stairs going nowhere and doors that open into walls. Today, the brightly painted house (on the National Register of Historic Places) is a favorite family attraction, and though the grounds are no longer dark and overgrown, the place retains an air of mystery. Explore the house on the 65-minute estate tour and the 50-minute behind-the-scenes tour, or come on a Friday the 13th for an evening flashlight tour. Tours usually depart every 20–30 minutes. ☒ *525 S. Winchester Blvd., between Stevens Creek Blvd. and I–280* ☎ *408/247–2101* ⊕ *www.winchestermysteryhouse.com* ☒ *Estate tour $16.95, be-*

hind-the-scenes tour $13.95, combination ticket $23.95 ⊙ *Daily 9–5:30 (last admission at 5).*

Where to Stay & Eat

$$$–$$$$ ✕ **A. P. Stump's.** With its tin ceilings, dramatic lighting, and gold- and copper-tone walls, this restaurant's extravagant interior is well-matched to the food. Chef-partner Jim Stump offers creative dishes on his frequently changing menu, which may include sesame ahi with bok choy and soba noodle cake, molasses-glazed pork chop with huckleberry sauce, or one of his signature dishes like lobster corn pudding. If you plan to come during spring or summer, ask about the program of outdoor live-music performances. ⊠ *163 W. Santa Clara St.* ☎ *408/292–9928* ⊟ *AE, D, DC, MC, V* ⊙ *No lunch weekends.*

★ **$$$–$$$$** ✕ **Emile's Restaurant.** Swiss chef and owner Emile Mooser's menu is a blend of classical European and contemporary California influences. Specialties include house-cured gravlax, rack of lamb, fresh game, and Grand Marnier soufflé. Mooser is an expert at matching food and wine. He'll gladly make a selection from his restaurant's extensive list for you. The interior is distinguished by romantic lighting, stunning floral displays, and an unusual leaf sculpture on the ceiling. ⊠ *545 S. 2nd St.* ☎ *408/289–1960* ⊟ *AE, D, DC, MC, V* ⊙ *Closed Sun. and Mon. No lunch Tues.–Thurs. and Sat.*

$$–$$$$ ✕ **Blake's Steakhouse and Bar.** Blake's fully satisfies the carnivore while managing not to neglect even the staunchest non–beef eater. Uncluttered and tranquil for a steak house, the restaurant has intimate high-back booths, some with a view of bustling San Pedro Square. Order any cut of beef you fancy, as well as roasted fowl and charbroiled fish. ⊠ *17 N. San Pedro Sq.* ☎ *408/298–9221* ⊟ *AE, D, DC, MC, V.*

$$–$$$$ ✕ **Paolo's.** A longtime meeting ground for South Bay notables, Paolo's has a sponge-painted interior that is as contemporary as any in San Jose. Duck and delicate handmade pastas are among the appealing, up-to-the-moment dishes. At lunchtime the dining room is a sea of suits, with bankers and brokers entertaining clients. ⊠ *333 W. San Carlos St.* ☎ *408/294–2558* ⊟ *AE, D, DC, MC, V* ⊙ *Closed Sun. No lunch Sat.*

$$–$$$ ✕ **Menara Moroccan Restaurant.** The delicious cumin- and coriander-spiced food is only part of the reason to come here for a leisurely meal. Arched entryways, lazily spinning ceiling fans, and a tile fountain all lend to the faraway feel. Sit on jewel-tone cushions around low tables while feasting on lamb with honey, delicately spiced chicken kebabs, or hare with paprika. You can choose from five multicourse dinners—all include couscous, salad, dessert, and sweet mint tea. A nightly belly dancing performance completes the experience. ⊠ *41 E. Gish Rd.* ☎ *408/453–1983* ⊟ *AE, D, MC, V* ⊙ *No lunch.*

★ **$–$$** ✕ **71 Saint Peter.** The selection at this downtown restaurant is somewhat small, but each dish is prepared with care, from the seafood linguine (a mix of clams, shrimp, and scallops in a basil-tomato broth) to the roasted duck in a raspberry–black pepper demiglace. The ceramic-tile floors and wood-beam ceiling add rustic touches to the warm, elegant atmosphere. You can watch chef-owner Mark Tabak at work in the glass-wall kitchen. ⊠ *71 N. San Pedro St.* ☎ *408/971–8523* ⊟ *AE, D, DC, MC, V* ⊙ *Closed Sun. No lunch Sat.*

$–$$ ✕ **Bella Mia.** Locals love this restaurant for its elegant interior and good Italian food. There are plenty of fresh pastas to choose from, like salmon ravioli in tomato dill sauce and pasta carbonara, as well as flat-bread pizzas. You can also choose from a number of grilled entrées, like spit-roasted chicken and citrus-grilled pork chops. On some nights during spring and summer, jazz is performed on the patio. ⊠ *58 S. 1st St.* ☎ *408/280–1993* ⊟ *AE, D, DC, MC, V.*

¢–$ ✕ **Lou's Living Donut Museum.** If you want a real taste of San Jose, do like the locals and stop for a sweet breakfast or afternoon snack at Lou's, just two blocks from the Children's Discovery Museum. Lou's serves a variety of handmade doughnuts—from pumpkin to old-fashioned chocolate—and lets you watch the bakers in action. This family-run shop has been around since 1955; the owners are glad to talk to you about the history of the shop and of San Jose. ⊠ *387 Delmas Ave.* ☎ *408/295–5887* ▭ *No credit cards* ☉ *Closed Sun. No dinner.*

¢ ✕ **Señora Emma's.** This *taquería* serves up large and tasty portions of nachos, tacos, burritos, and quesadillas as well as full meals. You can help yourself to several kinds of salsas, limes, and jalapeños at the salsa bar and get a margarita at the full bar. The restaurant's interior may be nothing special to look at, but there's a great sidewalk patio that affords terrific people-watching opportunities. ⊠ *177 N. Santa Clara St.* ☎ *408/279–3662 or 408/261–8448* ▭ *AE, MC, V* ☉ *No dinner Mon.–Wed. No lunch Sun.*

¢ ✕ **White Lotus.** The Southeast Asian–influenced meatless dishes at this slightly worn restaurant are deliciously prepared using fresh ingredients. Choose from an extensive menu of vegetable and meat-substitute entreés, like soft, chewy, panfried rice noodles with tofu and crisp vegetables, curry "chicken," or spicy garlic eggplant. Start your meal with an order of crunchy imperial rolls or Thai sweet-and-sour soup. ⊠ *80 N. Market St.* ☎ *408/977–0540* ▭ *MC, V* ☉ *Closed Sun.*

★ $$$$ ▣ **Hotel De Anza.** This lushly appointed art deco hotel has hand-painted ceilings, a warm coral-and-green color scheme, and an enclosed terrace with towering palms and dramatic fountains. Business travelers appreciate the many amenities, including a full-service business center and personal voice-mail services. ⊠ *233 W. Santa Clara St., 95113* ☎ *408/286–1000 or 800/843–3700* 🖷 *408/286–0500* ⊕ *www.hoteldeanza.com* ⇢ *91 rooms, 9 suites ♿ Restaurant, in-room data ports, some in-room hot tubs, minibars, refrigerators, cable TV with movies, in-room VCRs, gym, bar, laundry service, business services, concierge, Internet, no-smoking rooms* ▭ *AE, D, DC, MC, V.*

$$$$ ▣ **Hyatt Sainte Claire.** The first American hotel to utilize an earthquake-protective roller system when it was built in 1926, the Sainte Claire has survived decades of quakes without a whimper. Its high ceilings, classic chandeliers, and courtyard lined in Spanish tiles, as well as the painted ceiling in the Palm Room parlor, are magnificent. Each room has something a little different about it, and many have a night-sky theme. ⊠ *302 S. Market St., 95113* ☎ *408/885–1234 or 800/233–1234* 🖷 *408/977–0403* ⊕ *www.hyatt.com* ⇢ *170 rooms, 17 suites ♿ Restaurant, café, in-room data ports, some in-room faxes, in-room safes, in-room hot tubs, minibars, cable TV with movies, pool, exercise equipment, bar, laundry service, concierge, Internet, business services, meeting rooms, no-smoking rooms* ▭ *AE, D, DC, MC, V.*

$$$–$$$$ ▣ **The Fairmont.** This downtown gem is as opulent as its sister property in San Francisco. Get lost in the lavish lobby sofas under dazzling chandeliers, or dip your feet in the fourth-floor pool, which is surrounded by exotic palms. Rooms have every imaginable comfort, from down pillows and custom-designed comforters to oversize bath towels changed twice a day. ⊠ *170 S. Market St., at Fairmont Pl., 95113* ☎ *408/998–1900 or 800/866–5577* 🖷 *408/287–1648* ⊕ *www.fairmont.com* ⇢ *541 rooms ♿ 3 restaurants, room service, in-room data ports, some in-room faxes, in-room safes, some in-room hot tubs, minibars, some refrigerators, cable TV with movies and video games, pool, health club, massage, steam room, lobby lounge, laundry service, concierge, Internet, business services, meeting rooms, no-smoking rooms, no-smoking floor* ▭ *AE, D, DC, MC, V.*

★ **$$–$$$$** 🏨 **The Hensley House.** This is the only B&B in downtown San Jose, with rooms in neighboring Victorian and craftsman-style houses. The antiques-decorated rooms have thoughtful touches like robes, feather mattresses, and down comforters and pillows. Breakfast frequently includes chorizo and eggs or quiche and homemade bread, and you can eat it in the tranquil breakfast room or on the patio. ✉ *456 N. 3rd St., 95112* ☎ *408/298–3537 or 800/498–3537* 🖷 *408/298–4676* ⊕ *www.hensleyhouse.com* ➯ *11 rooms, 4 suites* ⚲ *In-room data ports, some in-room hot tubs, some kitchens, minibars, refrigerators, cable TV, in-room VCRs, outdoor hot tub, laundry service, concierge, Internet, business services; no smoking* 🖃 *AE, D, DC, MC, V* 🍴 *BP.*

$$–$$$ 🏨 **Briar Rose Bed & Breakfast Inn.** This charming bed-and-breakfast in a restored 1875 Victorian farmhouse sits on nearly half an acre of gardens. There are plenty of special touches in the rooms, like antique furniture and feather mattresses, and a lovely front parlor with a marble fireplace. The complimentary breakfast often includes quiche, pancakes, waffles, and omelets. Groups of five or more can enjoy afternoon tea in the garden or back parlor with advance reservations. ✉ *897 E. Jackson St., 95112* ☎ *408/279–5999* 🖷 *408/279–4534* ⊕ *www.briarrose.com* ➯ *5 rooms, 1 cottage* ⚲ *In-room data ports, some refrigerators, cable TV, in-room VCRs; no smoking* 🖃 *AE, D, DC, MC, V* 🍴 *BP.*

$ 🏨 **Days Inn.** There's nothing fancy about these motel-style accommodations, but there's an Olympic-size pool on the premises and a coffeemaker in every room. The hotel is about 5 mi from downtown. ✉ *4170 Monterey Rd., 95111* ☎ *408/224–4122 or 800/329–7466* 🖷 *408/224–4177* ⊕ *www.daysinn.com* ➯ *34 rooms* ⚲ *Microwaves, refrigerators, pool, hot tub, no-smoking rooms* 🖃 *AE, D, DC, MC, V* 🍴 *CP.*

Nightlife and the Arts

NIGHTLIFE Try **Big Lil's Barbary Coast Dinner Theater** (✉ 157 W. San Fernando St. ☎ 408/295–7469) for an evening of turn-of-the-20th-century melodrama, vaudeville, and audience participation (lots of popcorn throwing) on Friday and Saturday evenings; there's also comedy and live music on Thursday. Just west of downtown, the **Garden City Lounge** (✉ 360 S. Saratoga Ave. ☎ 408/244–3333) has jazz nightly with no cover charge. **Agenda** (✉ 399 S. 1st St. ☎ 408/287–3991) is one of the most popular nightspots downtown, with a restaurant on the main floor, a bar upstairs, and a nightclub on the bottom floor. Pick up a pool cue at trendy **South First Billiards** (✉ 420 S. 1st St. ☎ 408/294–7800), amid the burgeoning cluster of small clubs in an area called SoFA—South of First Area—along 1st and 2nd streets south of San Carlos Avenue.

THE ARTS The **Center for Performing Arts** (✉ 255 Almaden Blvd. ☎ 408/277–3900) is the city's main performance venue. **American Musical Theatre of San Jose** (☎ 408/453–7108) presents four musicals per year. **San Jose Symphony** (☎ 408/288–2828) performs in the fall, winter, and spring. **Ballet San Jose Silicon Valley** (☎ 408/288–2800) performs from October through May. **San Jose Repertory Theatre** (✉ 101 Paseo de San Antonio ☎ 408/291–2255) occupies a contemporary four-story, 528-seat theater, dubbed the Blue Box because of its angular blue exterior. **City Lights Theater Co.** (☎ 408/295–4200) presents progressive and traditional programs in an intimate 99-seat theater.

Sports & the Outdoors

GOLF **San Jose Municipal Golf Course** (✉ 1560 Oakland Rd. ☎ 408/441–4653) is an 18-hole course. **Cinnabar Hills Golf Club** (✉ 23600 McKean Rd. ☎ 408/323–5200) is a 27-hole course.

SPECTATOR SPORTS The 17,483-seat **Compaq Center at San Jose** (✉ Santa Clara St. at Autumn St. ☎ 408/287–9200, 408/998–2277 for tickets), known locally as the Shark Tank (even just "the Tank"), is home to the National Hockey League's **San Jose Sharks.** The building looks like a giant hothouse, with its glass entrance, shining metal armor, and skylight ceiling. Inside, hockey alternates with other sporting events and concerts. **Spartan Stadium** (⊠ 7th St. between E. Alma Ave. and E. Humboldt St.) hosts the **San Jose Earthquakes** major league soccer team (formerly the San Jose Clash), as well as qualifying games for international competitions. The only venue of its type in Northern California, the **Hellyer Velodrome** (⊠ 985 Hellyer Ave. ☎ 408/226–9716) attracts national-class cyclists and Olympians in training to races from May through August.

Shopping

It opened in 1960 with only 20 sellers, but today the **San Jose Flea Market** (⊠ 1590 Berryessa Rd., between I–680 and U.S. 101 ☎ 408/453–1110) is part Mexican *mercado* (market), part carnival, and part garage sale. Some 2,700 vendors spread over 120 acres sell handicrafts, leather, jewelry, furniture, produce, and more. The flea market operates Wednesday–Sunday dawn–dusk; parking is $1 weekdays and $5 weekends. With more than 150 retail outlets and an ice rink, **Eastridge Mall** (⊠ Capitol Expressway and Tully Rd. ☎ 408/274–0360) is one of the area's largest commercial centers.

THE COASTAL PENINSULA

DOWN HIGHWAY 1 FROM MOSS BEACH TO AÑO NUEVO

The coastal towns between San Francisco and Santa Cruz were founded in the late 18th century, when Spanish explorer Gaspar de Portola arrived. After the Mexican government gained control, the land was used for agriculture by ranchers who provided food to San Francisco's Mission Dolores. Soon, lighthouses and ships were being built to facilitate the transport of goods to San Francisco. You can still visit the short, squat Point Montara Lighthouse, in Montara, Moss Beach. Drive all the way from San Francisco to Santa Cruz along scenic Highway 1, hugging the twists and turns of the coast, or venture 11 mi inland at Half Moon Bay, over hilly Highway 92 to San Mateo.

Moss Beach

🄌 *20 mi south of San Francisco on Hwy. 1.*

Moss Beach was a busy outpost during Prohibition, when regular shipments of liquid contraband from Canada were unloaded at the secluded beach and hauled off to San Francisco. The town itself by necessity kept under the radar, with only a local hotel and bar where impatient Bay Area politicians and gangsters would go for a drink. To this day it is all but invisible from the highway, and so the area remains a good hideaway for those allergic to crowds.

The biggest Moss Beach attraction is the **Fitzgerald Marine Reserve** (⊠ California and North Lake Sts., ☎ 650/728–3584), a 3-mi stretch of bluffs and tidepools. Since the reserve was protected in 1969, scientists have discovered 25 new aquatic species; depending on the tide, you'll find shells, anemones, or starfish.

Just off the coast at Moss Beach is **Mavericks:** when there's a big swell, it's one of the biggest surfing breaks in the world. Waves here have been reported at 60 feet high, and surfers get towed in by Jet Skis. The break is a mile offshore, so seeing it from the coast can be tough and requires a demanding hike. The intrepid can get photocopied directions at The Distillery restaurant, then drive 3 mi south for the trail out of **Pillar Point Harbor.** Even if you're not hunting for waves, the harbor is a nice place to wander, with its laid back restaurants and waters full of fishing boats and sea lions.

Built in 1928 after two horrible shipwrecks on the point, the **Point Montara Lighthouse** still has its original light keeper's quarters from the late 1800s. Gray whales pass this point during their migration from November through April, so bring your binoculars. Visiting hours coincide with morning and afternoon check-in and check-out times at the adjoining youth hostel ($17 dorm beds, $55 private room). ⊠ *16th St. at Hwy. 1, Montara* ☎ *650/728–7177* ⊘ *7:30–9:30 AM and 4:30–9:30 PM.*

Where to Stay & Eat

$$–$$$$ ✕ **The Distillery.** During Prohibition, this two-tier restaurant perched on a cliff was the first stop for the Canadian liquor unloaded on the beach below. History remains in the form of a ghost, the soul of a 1930s adulteress who is said to visit from time to time, dressed in blue. Upstairs is a candlelit restaurant with big views and a menu split between tenderloins and seafood. Things are more casual at the self-service lunch spot and bar downstairs, where the deck may get downright rowdy on sunny weekends. On chilly afternoons lovers cuddle under heavy woolen blankets on swinging benches as they and sip wine and watch the fog roll in. ⊠ *140 Beach Way* ☎ *650/728–5595* ⊕ *www.mossbeachdistillery. com* ▭ *D, DC, MC, V.*

★ **$$** ✕ **Cafe Gibraltar.** The cuisine at the best restaurant on the San Mateo coast is Mediterranean in the truest sense of the word: one meal can transport diners to Spain, Greece, Morocco, Turkey, or Italy. Chef/owner Jose Luiz Ugalde cooks each dish himself and is a master of creative sauces, particularly the sweet and spicy (most are reductions of fruits, such as apricots and currants). The flavors are unexpected—calamari baked with cinnamon, lavender crème brûlée—and the atmosphere is sensual, with peach walls lit by flickering candles and four booths draped with curtains and lined with pillows (no chairs). Located 2 mi south of Moss Beach on the east side of the highway, it's a bit hard to find, but well worth the hunt. At signs for Pillar Point Harbor, turn inland onto Capistrano, and then right onto Alhambra. ⊠ *425 Ave. Alhambra, at Palma Ave., El Granada* ☎ *650/560–9039* ⊕ *www.cafegibraltar.com* ▭ *AE, MC, V* ⊘ *Closed Mon.*

★ **¢** ✕ **Three–Zero Cafe.** This busy restaurant at the tiny Half Moon Bay Airport is a locals' favorite, especially for weekend breakfasts. The food is standard—burgers for lunch, eggs and pancakes for breakfast—but reliably good. Get a window table, and as you eat watch two-seater planes take off and land on the runway 20 feet away. ⊠ *Hwy. 1 2 mi south of Moss Beach El Granada* ☎ *650/573-3701* ▭ *MC, V* ⊘ *No dinner.*

$$$–$$$$ ▦ **Seal Cove Inn.** Travel writer Karen Brown has written guidebooks to inns all over the world, and this is what she has created at home. Her building is modern but charming and warm, with all windows looking onto flower gardens and toward cypress trees that border the marine reserve. Rooms have antique bed frames and writing desks, plush mattresses, and lounging chairs. Upstairs rooms have cathedral ceilings and balconies, and all have fireplaces. Full breakfast and evening wine and hors d'oeuvres are served in the parlor and dining room. ⊠ *221 Cypress Ave, 94038* ☎ *650/728–4114 or 800/995–9987* 🖷 *650/728–4116* ⊕ *www.sealcoveinn.com* ⇆ *10 rooms, 2 suites* ⚮ *In-room VCRs* ▯◎▮ *BP* ▭ *AE, D, MC, V.*

$–$$ ▦ **The Goose and Turrets.** Artifacts from the international travels of innkeepers Raymond and Emily Hoche-Mong fill the shelves of this inn

8 mi north of Half Moon Bay. A full home-cooked breakfast, afternoon goodies, and homemade chocolate truffles are sure to make anyone feel at home. Some rooms have fireplaces. ⊠ *835 George St., Montara 94037* ☎ *650/728–5451* 🖷 *650/728–0141* 📞 *5 rooms* ⌂ *Bocce, piano, no-smoking room* 🖃 *AE, D, DC, MC, V* ⊕ *goose.montara.com* 🍽 *BP.*

Half Moon Bay

⑱ *7 mi south of Moss Beach on Hwy. 1.*

The largest and most visited of the coastal communities, Half Moon Bay is nevertheless a small town with a population of fewer than 10,000. You'd never guess there was much of a town from the highway. Turn onto Main Street, though, and you'll find the town's heart: five blocks of small crafts shops, art galleries, and outdoor cafés, many housed in renovated 19th-century structures. Half Moon Bay comes to life on the third weekend in October, when 300,000 people gather for the **Half Moon Bay Art and Pumpkin Festival** (☎ 650/726–9652).

The 4-mi stretch of **Half Moon Bay State Beach** (⊠ Hwy. 1, west of Main St. ☎ 650/726–8819) is perfect for long walks, kite flying, and picnic lunches, though the 50°F water and dangerous currents discourage swimming.

Best western
726 - 9000

Where to Stay & Eat

$$–$$$ ✕ **Cetrella.** This is the coast at its most dressed up. The restaurant is all polished wood and pressed tablecloths, and hits every gourmet mark— adventurous wine list, sumptuous cheese course, and live jazz and salsa music Thursdays through Saturdays. The menu—which features local, organic ingredients—is largely Provençal, with some yummy Spanish surprises, such as a variety of *tapas* (small plates of different hors d'oeuvres. Seafood lovers, however, may want to slurp down some oysters or clams at the raw bar. ⊠ *845 Main St.* ☎ *650/726–4090* 🖃 *AE, MC, V.*

$$ ✕ **Pasta Moon.** The wood-burning oven tips you off to the thin-crust pizzas that are served in this small restaurant. The kitchen also turns out handmade pastas, a wonderful crisp-skinned roast chicken, grilled quail, and marinated flank steak. ⊠ *315 Main St.* ☎ *650/726–5125* 🖃 *AE, D, DC, MC, V.*

$$ ✕ **San Benito House.** Tucked inside a historic inn in the heart of Half Moon Bay, this ground-floor restaurant serves a limited dinner menu that changes weekly and often includes bouillabaisse, roasted quail, sea bass or other fresh fish, a vegetarian meal, and house-made ravioli or other pastas. By day the kitchen prepares memorable sandwiches with bread baked in the restaurant's oven and sells them, deli style, for a picnic by the sea. ⊠ *356 Main St.* ☎ *650/726–3425* 🖃 *AE, DC, MC, V* ⊙ *No dinner Mon.–Wed.*

¢–$ ✕ **Two Fools.** The kitchen tosses together big organic salads and packs contemporary burritos with a healthy mix of traditional Mexican and unexpected ingredients. A slice of old-fashioned American meat loaf topped with caramelized onions is sandwiched in a house-made bun at lunchtime. Dinnertime brings fresh fish, a daily risotto, roasted chicken, and a house-made nut loaf. ⊠ *408 Main St.* ☎ *650/712–1222* 🖃 *AE, D, MC, V* ⊙ *No dinner Mon.*

$$$–$$$$ 🛏 **Mill Rose Inn.** Pampering touches include fireplaces, brass beds stacked high with down comforters, coffee and cocoa, and baskets of fruit and candies in the guest rooms, as well as decanters of sherry and brandy in the parlor. The lush gardens are planted extensively with roses and climbing sweet peas. Room rates include a lavish champagne breakfast and afternoon snacks. ⊠ *615 Mill St., 94019* ☎ *650/726–8750 or 800/900–7673* 🖷 *650/726–3031* ⊕ *www.millroseinn.com* 📞 *4 rooms, 2 suites*

Refrigerators, some in-room hot tubs, cable TV, in-room VCRs, meeting room; no smoking ▭ *AE, D, DC, MC, V* 🍽 *BP.*

$$$–$$$$ **The Ritz-Carlton.** This golf and spa resort is everything the Ritz-Carlton name connotes. The massive but tastefully decorated building is secluded on the wild oceanfront and the ample staff waits hand and foot on guests. Attention to detail is considered right down to the silver service, china, and perfect linens. At the cocktail hour, view the ocean from the plush conservatory bar or tucked under a heavy blanket on a simple Adirondack chair on the lawn. ✉ *1 Miramontes Point Rd., 94019* ☎ *650/712–7000, 800/241–3333* 📠 *650/712–7070* 🌐 *www.ritzcarlton.com* *261 rooms, 22 suites* *Restaurant, room service, in-room data ports, in-room safes, 18-hole golf course, hot tub, sauna, spa, steam room, 6 tennis courts, bar, babysitting, laundry service, concierge, business services, meeting rooms, airport shuttle, no smoking rooms.* ▭ *AE, D, DC, MC,V.*

$$–$$$$ **Old Thyme Inn.** The owners of this 1898 Princess Anne Victorian have managed the rare feat of drenching their entire inn in flowers and floral motifs without sacrificing taste. The garden bursts with blossoms and herbs, which provide the stuff for multiple bouquets in guest rooms: each is named after an herb and decorated in its colors. The place is fresh and clean, and the innkeepers are perfectly attentive—appearing exactly (and only) when you want them. Antiques, a homemade breakfast, complimentary sherry, and afternoon snacks make this a lovely place to spend a relaxing weekend. ✉ *779 Main St., 94019* ☎ *650/726–1616 or 800/720–4277* 📠 *650/726–6394* 🌐 *www.oldthymeinn.com* *7 rooms* *In-room data ports, some in-room hot tubs, cable TV, in-room VCRs, concierge, no-smoking rooms* ▭ *AE, D, MC, V* 🍽 *BP.*

Sports

The **Bicyclery** (✉ 101 Main St. ☎ 650/726–6000) rents bikes and can provide information on organized rides up and down the coast. If you prefer to go it alone, try the 3-mi bike trail that leads from Kelly Avenue in Half Moon Bay to Mirada Road in Miramar.

en route

In addition to beautiful scenery and expansive state beaches, on your way from Half Moon Bay to Pescadero you will pass the town of San Gregorio and its idiosyncratic **San Gregorio General Store** (✉ Hwy. 84 at Stage Rd., 1 mi east of Hwy. 1 ☎ 650/726–0565). Part old-time saloon, part hardware store, part grocery, the place has been a fixture in town since the late 1800s. The current Spanish-style structure replaced the original wooden building when it burned down in 1930. Come to browse through the hodgepodge items—camp stoves, books, and boots, to name just a few—or to listen to Irish music and bluegrass on weekend afternoons.

Pescadero

19 *16 mi south of Half Moon Bay on Hwy. 1.*

As you walk down Stage Road, Pescadero's main street, it's hard to believe you're only 30 minutes from Silicon Valley. The few short blocks of the downtown area could almost serve as the backdrop for a Western movie, with Duarte's Tavern serving as the centerpiece. In fact, Pescadero was larger in the late 19th century than it is today. This is a good place to stop for a bite or to browse for antiques. The town's real attractions, though, are spectacular beaches and hiking.

If a quarantine is not in effect (watch for signs), from November through April you can look for mussels at **Pescadero State Beach** amid sandy expanses, tidal pools, and rocky outcroppings. Barbecue pits and picnic tables attract many families. Across U.S. 101, at the **Pescadero Marsh Natural Preserve,** hikers can spy on birds and other wildlife by following the trails that crisscross 600 acres of marshland. Early spring and fall are the best times to visit. ☎ 650/879–2170 ☜ *Free, parking $5* ☉ *Daily 8–sunset.*

If you prefer mountain trails to sand dunes, head for **Pescadero Creek County Park,** a 7,500-acre expanse of shady, old-growth redwood forests, grasslands, and mountain streams. The park is actually composed of three smaller ones: Heritage Grove Redwood Preserve, Sam McDonald Park, and San Mateo Memorial County Park. The Old Haul Road Trail, 6½ mi long, runs the length of the park. Campsites cost $15 per night. ☎ 650/ 879–0238 ☜ *$4 per vehicle.*

Where to Eat

$–$$ ✕ **Duarte's Tavern.** This 19th-century roadhouse serves simple American fare, with locally grown vegetables and fresh fish as standard items. If you really want a treat, order the abalone, for $45. Don't pass up the famed house artichoke soup or the old-fashioned berry pie à la mode. Breakfasts, of eggs, bacon, sausage, and hotcakes, are hearty here. ⊠ *202 Stage Rd.* ☎ *650/879–0464* ☰ *AE, MC, V.*

en route | About 6 mi south of Pescadero stands the 115-foot **Pigeon Point Lighthouse,** one of the tallest on the West Coast. Built in 1872, it has been used as a backdrop in numerous TV shows and commercials. The light from the 8,000-pound Fresnel lens can be seen 20 mi at sea. The former coast guard quarters now serves as a youth hostel. You can still visit the park, but the lighthouse itself is closed indefinitely for repairs. ⊠ *Pigeon Point Rd. and Hwy. 1* ☎ *650/879–2120* ☜ *$2* ☉ *Weekends 11–4, guided tours 10:30–3.*

Año Nuevo State Reserve

▶ ⑳ *12 mi south of Pescadero and 21 mi north of Santa Cruz on Hwy. 1.*

At the most southerly point of the San Mateo County Coast, Año Nuevo is the world's only approachable mainland rookery for elephant seals. If you know you'll be in the area between mid-December and March, make reservations early for a 2½-hour guided walking tour to view the huge (up to 3 tons), fat, furry elephant seals mating or birthing, depending on the time of year. Tours proceed rain or shine, so dress for anything. From April through November there's less excitement, but you can still watch the seals lounging on the beach. Pick up a free permit at the visitors center, which also has exhibits and a fascinating film. There are plenty of hiking trails in the area. ⊠ *Hwy. 1* ☎ *650/879–0227, 800/444–4445 for tour reservations* ☜ *$4, parking $5* ☉ *Tours leave every 15 mins 8:45–3.*

THE PENINSULA & SOUTH BAY A TO Z

To research prices, get advice from other travelers, and book travel arrangements, visit ⊕ *www.fodors.com.*

AIRPORTS & TRANSFERS

All the major airlines serve San Francisco International Airport, and most of them fly to San Jose International Airport. South & East Bay Airport Shuttle can transport you between the airport and Saratoga, Palo Alto, and other destinations. *See* Air Travel *in* Smart Travel Tips A to Z for airline phone numbers.

🛪 **San Francisco International Airport** ⊠ Off U.S. 101, 15 mi south of downtown, San Francisco ☎ 650/761-0800. **San Jose International Airport** ⊠ 1661 Airport Blvd., off

Hwy. 87, San Jose ☎ 408/277-4759 ⊕ www.sjc.org. **South & East Bay Airport Shuttle** ☎ 408/225-4444, 800/548-4664.

BUS TRAVEL

The Valley Transportation Authority (VTA) shuttle links downtown San Jose to the CalTrain station, across from the Arena, every 20 minutes during morning and evening commute hours. SamTrans buses travel to Moss Beach and Half Moon Bay from the Daly City BART station. Another bus connects Half Moon Bay with Pescadero. Each trip takes approximately one hour. Call for schedules, because departures are infrequent.
∄ SamTrans ☎ 800/660-4287. **VTA Shuttle** ☎ 408/321-2300 ⊕ www.vta.org.

CAR RENTAL

You can rent a car at the San Jose airport from any of the many major agencies. Specialty Rentals offers standard cars and luxury vehicles; it has an office in Palo Alto and will deliver a car to you anywhere on the Peninsula or at the airport. *See* Car Rental *in* Smart Travel Tips A to Z for national rental agency phone numbers.
∄ Local Agencies Specialty Rentals ☎ 650/856-9100, 800/400-8412.

CAR TRAVEL

By car the most pleasant route down the Inland Peninsula to Palo Alto, Woodside, Santa Clara, and San Jose is I–280, which passes along Crystal Springs Reservoir. U.S. 101, also known as the Bayshore Freeway, is more direct but also more congested. To avoid the often-heavy commuter traffic on U.S. 101, use I–280 during rush hours.

To reach Saratoga, take I–280 south to Highway 85 and follow Highway 85 south toward Gilroy. Exit on Saratoga–Sunnyvale Road, go south, and follow the signs to the Village—about 2½ mi. Signs will also direct you to Hakone Gardens, Villa Montalvo, and on concert nights, the Mountain Winery.

To get to Moss Beach or Half Moon Bay from San Francisco, take Highway 1, also known as the Coast Highway, south along the length of the San Mateo coast. When coastal traffic is heavy, especially on summer weekends, you can also reach Half Moon Bay via I–280, the Junipero Serra Freeway; follow it south as far as Highway 92, where you can turn west toward the coast. To get to Pescadero, drive south 16 mi on Highway 1 from Half Moon Bay. For Año Nuevo continue south on Highway 1 another 12 mi.

EMERGENCIES

In an emergency dial 911.
∄ Hospitals San Jose Medical Center ⊠ 675 E. Santa Clara St., San Jose ☎ 408/998-3212. **Stanford Hospital** ⊠ 300 Pasteur Dr., Palo Alto ☎ 650/723-4000.

TRAIN TRAVEL

CalTrain runs from 4th and Townsend streets in San Francisco to Palo Alto ($4.50 each way); from there take the free Marguerite shuttle bus to the Stanford campus and the Palo Alto area. Buses run about every 15 minutes 6 AM–7:45 PM and are timed to connect with trains and public transit buses.

CalTrain service continues south of Palo Alto to Santa Clara's Railroad and Franklin streets stop, near Santa Clara University ($5.25 one-way), and to San Jose's Rod Diridon station ($6 one-way). The trip to Santa Clara takes approximately 1¼ hours; to San Jose, it's about 1½ hours.

Valley Transportation Authority buses run efficiently throughout the Santa Clara Valley, although not as frequently as you might like. Operators can help you plan routes.

In San Jose, light-rail trains run 24 hours a day and serve most major attractions, shopping malls, historic sites, and downtown. Trains run every 10 minutes weekdays from 6 AM to 8 PM and vary during weekends and late-night hours from every 15 minutes to once an hour. Tickets are valid for two hours; they cost $1.40 one-way or $4 for a day pass. Buy tickets at vending machines in any transit station. For more information call or visit the Downtown Customer Service Center.

🚹 **CalTrain** ☎ 800/660-4287. **Downtown Customer Service Center** Light Rail ✉ 2 N. 1st St., San Jose ☎ 408/321-2300. **Marguerite Shuttle** ☎ 650/723-9362. **Valley Transportation Authority** ☎ 408/321-2300 or 800/894-9908.

VISITOR INFORMATION

🚹 **California State Parks Bay Area District Office** ✉ 250 Executive Park Blvd., Suite 4900, San Francisco 94134 ☎ 415/330-6300. **Half Moon Bay Chamber of Commerce** ✉ 520 Kelly Ave., Half Moon Bay 94019 ☎ 650/726-8380 ⊕ www.halfmoonbaychamber. org. **Palo Alto Chamber of Commerce** ✉ 325 Forest Ave., Palo Alto 94301 ☎ 650/324-3121. **San Jose Convention and Visitors Bureau** ✉ 125 S. Market St., 3rd floor, San Jose 95113 ☎ 800/726-5673, 408/295-2265, or 408/295-9600 ⊕ www.sanjose.org. **Santa Clara Chamber of Commerce and Convention and Visitors Bureau** ✉ 1850 Warburton Ave., Santa Clara 95052 ☎ 408/244-8244 ⊕ www.santaclarachamber.org. **Saratoga Chamber of Commerce** ✉ 14485 Big Basin Way, Saratoga 95070 ☎ 408/867-0753 ⊕ www.saratogachamber.org. **Woodside Town Hall** ✉ 2955 Woodside Rd., Woodside 94062 ☎ 650/851-6790.

MONTEREY BAY
FROM SANTA CRUZ TO CARMEL

5

FODOR'S CHOICE

Montrio Bistro, *Monterey*

Old Monterey Inn, *Monterey*

17-Mile Drive, *Pebble Beach*

Stonepine Estate Resort, *Carmel Valley*

HIGHLY RECOMMENDED

RESTAURANTS Bittersweet Bistro, *Aptos*

Casanova, *Carmel*

Fresh Cream, *Monterey*

Robert's Bistro, *Carmel*

Stokes Restaurant & Bar, *Monterey*

Theo's, *Soquel*

HOTELS Bernardus Lodge, *Carmel Valley*

Casa Palmero, *Pebble Beach*

Cobblestone Inn, *Carmel*

Green Gables Inn, *Pacific Grove*

Highlands Inn, *Carmel*

Historic Sand Rock Farm, *Aptos*

Lodge at Pebble Beach, *Pebble Beach*

Martine Inn, *Pacific Grove*

Monterey Plaza Hotel and Spa, *Monterey*

Quail Lodge, *Carmel Valley*

SIGHTS Carmel Mission, *Carmel*

Elkhorn Slough, *in the estuarine reserve, Watsonville*

Living History Day, *San Juan Bautista*

Monterey Bay Aquarium, *Monterey*

Point Lobos State Reserve, *Carmel*

Updated by
Daniel S.
Hindin

FAMED FOR ITS SCENIC BEAUTY, the Monterey Peninsula is also steeped in history. The town of Monterey was California's first capital, the Carmel Mission headquarters for California's mission system. John Steinbeck's novels immortalized the area in *Cannery Row,* and Robert Louis Stevenson strolled its streets, gathering inspiration for *Treasure Island.* The present is equally illustrious. Blessed with maritime bounty and cultural diversity, Monterey Bay is the setting for both high-tech marine habitats and luxurious resorts. Set along a 90-mi crescent of coastline like jewels in a tiara, the towns of Monterey Bay combine the somewhat funky, beachcomber aspects of California's culture with the state's more refined tendencies. Past and present merge gracefully here.

About 2,500 years ago, the Ohlone Indians recognized the region's potential and became its first settlers. Europeans followed in 1542, when the white-sand beaches, pine forests, and rugged coastline captivated explorer Juan Rodríguez Cabrillo, who claimed the Monterey Peninsula for Spain. Spanish missionaries, Mexican rulers, and land developers have come and gone throughout the centuries since then, yet the area's natural assets and historic sites remain remarkably untarnished.

In 1770 Monterey became the capital of the Spanish territory of Alta California. Commander Don Gaspar de Portola established the first of California's four Spanish presidios here, and Father Junípero Serra founded the second of 21 Franciscan missions (he later moved it to Carmel). Mexico revolted against Spain in 1810; a decade later, a treaty was signed and the now-independent nation claimed Alta California as its own. By the mid-1840s, Monterey had grown into a lively seaport that attracted Yankee sea traders, and land from California to Texas was coveted by the United States. On July 7, 1846, Commodore John Sloat raised the flag of the United States over the Custom House. For Anglos, being governed by the United States proved far more profitable than being aligned with Mexico. But for the Ohlone Indians, the transition to American rule was disastrous: state and federal laws passed in the late 1800s took away rights and property that had been granted them by Spain and Mexico.

California's constitution was framed in Monterey's Colton Hall, but the town was all but forgotten once gold was discovered at Sutter's Mill on the American River. After the gold rush the state capital moved to Sacramento, while in Monterey the whaling industry boomed until the early 1900s. Tourists began to arrive at the turn of the 20th century with the opening of the Del Monte Hotel, the most palatial resort the West Coast had ever seen. Writers and artists such as John Steinbeck, Henry Miller, Robinson Jeffers, and Ansel Adams also discovered Monterey Bay, adding their legacy to the region while capturing its magic on canvas, paper, and film. In the 1920s and 1930s Cannery Row's sardine industry took off, but by the late 1940s and early 1950s the fish had disappeared. The causes are still in dispute, though overfishing, water contamination, and a change in ocean currents were the likely culprits.

Today the Monterey Peninsula's diverse cultural and maritime heritage is evident in the town's 19th-century buildings and busy harbor. Cannery Row has been reborn as a tourist attraction, with shops, restaurants, hotels, and the Monterey Bay Aquarium. The bay itself is protected by the Monterey Bay National Marine Sanctuary, the nation's largest undersea canyon, bigger and deeper than the Grand Canyon. The preserve supports a rich brew of marine life, from fat barking sea lions to tiny plantlike anemones. Indeed, nature is still at its best around

Monterey Bay, as the view from almost anywhere along Highway 1 will tell you.

Exploring Monterey Bay

The individual charms of its towns complement Monterey Bay's natural beauty. Santa Cruz sits at the northern tip of the crescent formed by Monterey Bay; the Monterey Peninsula, including Monterey, Pacific Grove, and Carmel, occupies the southern end. In between, Highway 1 cruises along the coastline, passing windswept beaches piled high with sand dunes. Along the route are artichoke fields and the towns of Watsonville and Castroville.

About the Restaurants

Between San Francisco and Los Angeles, the finest dining is to be found around Monterey Bay (with the possible exception of Santa Barbara). The surrounding waters abound with fish, wild game roams the foothills, and the inland valleys are the vegetable basket of California; nearby Castroville dubs itself the "artichoke capital of the world." Except at beachside stands and inexpensive eateries, where anything goes, casual but neat resort wear is the norm. The few places where more formal attire is required are noted.

About the Hotels

Monterey-area accommodations range from no-frills motels to luxurious resorts. Many of the area's small inns and B&Bs pamper the traveler in grand style, serving not only full breakfasts but afternoon or early evening wine and hors d'oeuvres. Pacific Grove has quietly turned itself into the region's B&B capital; Carmel also has fine B&Bs. Truly lavish resorts, with everything from featherbeds to heated floors, cluster in exclusive Pebble Beach and pastoral Carmel Valley. Many of these accommodations are not suitable for children, so if you're traveling with kids, be sure to ask before you book. Likewise, because many hotels around Monterey Bay don't have air-conditioning (it is for the most part unneccessary), inquire in advance if you need a/c.

Around Monterey Bay high season runs April through October. Rates during winter, especially at the larger hotels, may drop by 50% or more, and B&Bs often offer midweek specials in the off-season. However, even the simplest of the area's lodgings are expensive, and most properties require a two-night stay on weekends.

WHAT IT COSTS				
$$$$	**$$$**	**$$**	**$**	**¢**
RESTAURANTS over $30	$23–$30	$16–$22	$10–$15	under $10
HOTELS over $250	$176–$250	$121–$175	$90–$120	under $90

Restaurant prices are for a main course at dinner, excluding sales tax of 7½–8¼% (depending on location). Hotel prices are for a standard double room in high season, excluding service charges and 10–10½% tax.

Timing

Summer is peak season, with crowds everywhere and generally mild weather. A sweater or windbreaker is nearly always necessary along the coast, where a cool breeze usually blows and fog is on the way in or out. Inland, temperatures in Salinas or Carmel Valley can be 15 or 20 degrees warmer than those in Carmel and Monterey. Off-season, from November through April, fewer people visit, and the mood is mellower. Rainfall is heaviest in January and February.

Although it is compact, the Monterey Peninsula is packed with diversions. If you have an interest in California history and historic preservation, the place to start is Monterey, with its adobe buildings along the downtown Path of History. Fans of Victorian architecture will want to search out the many fine examples in Pacific Grove. In Carmel you can shop 'til you drop, and when summer and weekend hordes overwhelm the town's clothing boutiques, art galleries, housewares outlets, and gift shops, you can slip off to enjoy the coast.

5

Numbers in the text correspond to numbers in the margin and on the Monterey Bay and Monterey maps.

If you have 3 days
Start in ► 🔢 **Monterey ❹–⓳**, with a tour of the the state historic park, **Cannery Row** and **Fisherman's Wharf ⓰**. Don't miss the **Monterey Bay Aquarium ⓳**. Catch the sunset from the bustling wharf or slip into the serene bar at the Monterey Plaza Hotel and Spa. On the following day, motor down **17-Mile Drive ㉑** in the morning, stopping at **Point Lobos State Reserve** to take in the views. Spend the afternoon in 🔢 **Carmel ㉒**, browsing the shops of **Ocean Avenue,** then stroll over to **Scenic Road** and take a break on **Carmel Beach** before dinner. On the morning of day three, visit **Carmel Mission** and **Tor House** if it's open. Head for **Carmel Valley ㉓** in the afternoon to do a little shopping or wine-tasting.

If you have 5 days
Kick off your trip with a morning in the state historic park of ► **San Juan Bautista ❷**, followed by an hour or two at the **National Steinbeck Center** in **Salinas ❸**. Wind down your afternoon with a stop at Ventana Vineyards, and check into a hotel in 🔢 **Monterey ❹–⓳**. The next morning, get up-close and personal with Monterey Bay marine life by boarding a whale-watching or other cruise vessel at **Fisherman's Wharf ⓰**. Spend the afternoon on the wharf, along **Cannery Row,** and at the **Monterey Bay Aquarium ⓳**. Start day three in **Monterey State Historic Park,** then explore the shoreline and Victorian houses of 🔢 **Pacific Grove ⓴**, where you'll overnight. Your fourth day is for meandering down **17-Mile Drive ㉑** and having lunch in **Pebble Beach.** Round out the day with an afternoon of golf or a hike in **Point Lobos State Reserve,** then have dinner in 🔢 **Carmel ㉒**. On day five explore Carmel and **Carmel Valley ㉓**.

SANTA CRUZ COUNTY

Less manicured than its upmarket Monterey Peninsula neighbors to the south, Santa Cruz is the big city on its stretch of the California coast. A haven for those opting out of the rat race and a bastion of 1960s-style counterculture values, Santa Cruz has been at the forefront of such quintessential "left coast" trends as organic food, medicinal marijuana, and environmentalism. Between Santa Cruz and the Monterey Peninsula, the quieter towns of Capitola, Soquel, and Aptos have their own quality restaurants, small inns, resorts, and antiques shops.

Santa Cruz

❶ *76 mi south of San Francisco and 21 mi south of Año Nuevo State Reserve on Hwy. 1.*

The surrounding mountains shelter the beach town of Santa Cruz from the coastal fog and from the smoggy skies of the San Francisco Bay area and Silicon Valley. The climate here is mild, and it is usually warmer and sunnier than elsewhere along the coast this far north. The heart of downtown Santa Cruz is along Pacific Avenue south of Water Street, where you'll find shops, restaurants, and other establishments in the outdoor **Pacific Garden Mall.**

Santa Cruz gets some of its youthful spirit from the nearby **University of California at Santa Cruz.** The school's harmonious redwood buildings are perched on the forested hills above the town, and the campus is tailor-made for the contemplative life, with a juxtaposition of sylvan settings and sweeping vistas over open meadows onto the bay. ⊠ *Bay and High Sts.* ☎ *831/459–0111* ⊕ *www.ucsc.edu.*

Santa Cruz has been a seaside resort since the mid-19th century. The Looff carousel and classic wooden Giant Dipper roller coaster at the ☉ **Santa Cruz Beach Boardwalk** date from the early 1900s. Elsewhere along the boardwalk, the Casino Fun Center has its share of video-game technology. But this is still primarily a place for good old-fashioned fun for toddlers, teens, and adults. Take a break from the rides with boardwalk favorites such as corn dogs or chowder fries. ⊠ *Along Beach St. west from San Lorenzo River* ☎ *831/423–5590 or 831/426–7433* ⊕ *www. beachboardwalk.com* ⊠ *$23.95 (day pass for unlimited rides)* ☉ *Memorial Day–Labor Day, daily; Labor Day–Memorial Day, weekends only, weather permitting (call for hrs).*

The **Santa Cruz Municipal Wharf** (☎ 831/420–6025 ⊕ www.santacruzwharf. com), just up the beach from the boardwalk, is lined with restaurants, shops, and seafood takeout windows. The barking of sea lions that lounge in heaps under the wharf's pilings enliven the area.

Drive southwest from the municipal wharf on West Cliff Drive about ¾ mi to the promontory at **Seal Rock,** where you can watch pinnipeds hang out, sunbathe, and occasionally frolic. The **Mark Abbott Memorial Lighthouse,** adjacent to the promontory, has a surfing museum with artifacts that include the remains of a board that a shark munched on. ⊠ *W. Cliff Dr.* ☎ *831/420–6289* ⊕ *www.santacruzmuseums.org* ⊠ *Free* ☉ *Memorial Day–Labor Day, Wed.–Mon. noon–4; Labor Day–Memorial Day, Thurs.–Mon. noon–4.*

☉ About 1¾ mi west of the lighthouse is secluded **Natural Bridges State Beach,** a stretch of soft sand with tidal pools and a natural rock bridge nearby. From October to early March a colony of monarch butterflies resides here. ⊠ *2531 W. Cliff Dr.* ☎ *831/423–4609* ⊕ *www.parks.ca.gov* ⊠ *Parking $3* ☉ *Park daily 8 AM–sunset. Visitor center Oct.–Feb., daily 10–4; Mar.–Sept., weekends 10–4.*

Where to Stay & Eat

★ **$$$–$$$$** ✗ **Theo's.** On a quiet side street in a residential neighborhood, Theo's serves mainly three- and five-course prix fixe dinners. Seasonal standouts include duck with garden vegetables and currants, as well as rack of lamb with ratatouille. Much of the produce comes from the ¾-acre organic garden behind the restaurant, where you can stroll between courses. Service is gracious and attentive, and the wine list is outstand-

Fine Dining

In California you can eat well, and around Monterey Bay you can eat very, very well. Monterey and Carmel fairly burst at the seams with exceptional restaurants, with Monterey's Montrio Bistro—a temple of California cuisine—leading the pack. In Monterey you can also find excellent Mediterranean (Stokes Restaurant & Bar) and French (Fresh Cream) cooking. For more great French food head to Carmel, where Casanova presents southern French and northern Italian cuisine, and Robert's Bistro offers classic French fare. Even in Santa Cruz, a town not famed for its restaurants, your palate can be more than pleased, at the Mediterranean-inspired Bittersweet Bistro and at Theo's, a specialist in seasonal American dishes.

Golf

Since the opening of the Del Monte Golf Course in 1897, golf has been an integral part of the Monterey Peninsula's social and recreational scene. Pebble Beach's championship courses host prestigious tournaments, and though the greens fees at these courses can run well over $200, elsewhere on the peninsula you'll find less expensive—but still challenging and scenic—options. Many hotels will help with golf reservations or have golf packages; inquire when you book your room.

Whale-Watching

On their annual migration between the Bering Sea and Baja California, thousands of gray whales pass not far off the Monterey coast. They are sometimes visible through binoculars from shore, but a whale-watching cruise is the best way to get a close look at these magnificent mammals. The migration south takes place from December through March. January is prime viewing time. The migration north occurs from March through June. In addition, some 2,000 blue whales and 600 humpbacks pass the coast and are easily spotted in late summer and early fall. Smaller numbers of minke whales, orcas, sperm whales, and fin whales have been sighted in mid-August. Even if no whales surface, bay cruises almost always encounter some unforgettable marine life, including sea otters, sea lions, and porpoises.

---

ing. ✉ *3101 N. Main St., Soquel* ☎ *831/462–3657* ⌔ *Reservations essential* ▤ *AE, MC, V* ⊘ *Closed Sun.–Mon. No lunch.*

★ **$$–$$$** ✕ **Bittersweet Bistro.** A large old tavern with cathedral ceilings houses the popular bistro of chef-owner Thomas Vinolus, who draws his culinary inspiration from the Mediterranean. The menu changes seasonally, but try one of the outstandingly fresh fish specials, a grilled vegetable platter, a seafood *puttanesca* (pasta with a distinctive sauce of garlic, tomatoes, anchovies, and olives), or grilled lamb tenderloins. Finish with any of the chocolate desserts. ✉ *787 Rio Del Mar Blvd., off Hwy. 1, Aptos* ☎ *831/662–9799* ▤ *AE, MC, V* ⊘ *No lunch.*

$$–$$$ ✕ **Oswald's.** Intimate and stylish, this tiny courtyard bistro serves sophisticated yet unpretentious European-inspired California cooking. The menu changes seasonally, but might include such items as perfectly prepared sherry-steamed mussels or sautéed veal livers. ✉ *1547-E Pacific Ave.* ☎ *831/423–7427* ⌔ *Reservations essential* ▤ *AE, D, DC, MC, V* ⊘ *Closed Mon. No lunch.*

$$–$$$ ✕ **Pearl Alley Bistro.** The menu changes monthly to focus on a particular country's cuisine at this bustling bistro, which encourages the sharing of entrées. Book a table in advance or sit at the marble-top bar and meet the bon vivants of Santa Cruz. ⊠ *110 Pearl Alley, off Walnut Ave.* ☎ *831/429–8070* ⌕ *Reservations essential* ▤ *AE, MC, V* ☉ *No lunch.*

$–$$$ ✕ **Shadowbrook.** Take the cable car or walk down the steep bank of fern-lined steps beside the running waterfall to this romantic favorite overlooking Soquel Creek. Dining room options include the rooftop Redwood Room, the wood-paneled Wine Cellar, and the airy, glass-enclosed Garden Room. Prime rib and grilled seafood are the stars of the simple menu. A cheaper menu of light entrées is available in the lounge. Champagne brunch is served on Sunday. ⊠ *1750 Wharf Rd., Capitola* ☎ *831/475–1571* ▤ *AE, D, DC, MC, V* ☉ *No lunch weekends.*

$$ ✕ **Gabriella Café.** This tiny, romantic café shows the work of local artists. The seasonal Italian menu highlights organic produce from farms in the area. Watch for such dishes as steamed mussels, braised lamb shank, and grilled Portobello mushrooms. ⊠ *910 Cedar St.* ☎ *831/457–1677* ▤ *AE, MC, V.*

$–$$ ✕ **O'mei.** Don't let its plain shopping-center location fool you; this unpretentious provincial Chinese restaurant serves outstanding seasonal dishes with fresh and dynamic flavors. ⊠ *2316 Mission St.* ☎ *831/425–8458* ⌕ *Reservations essential* ▤ *AE, MC, V* ☉ *No lunch weekends.*

¢–$ ✕ **Seabright Brewery.** Great burgers, seafood, and stellar house-made microbrews make this a favorite local hangout. Sit outside on the large patio or inside at one of the comfortable, spacious booths. ⊠ *519 Seabright Ave.* ☎ *831/426–2739* ▤ *AE, MC, V.*

¢ ✕ **Zachary's.** With its mostly young clientele, this noisy café defines the funky essence of Santa Cruz. It also dishes up great breakfasts: omelets, sourdough pancakes, artichoke frittatas, and "Mike's Mess"—eggs scrambled with bacon, mushrooms, and home fries, then topped with sour cream, melted cheese, and fresh tomatoes. ⊠ *819 Pacific Ave.* ☎ *831/427–0646* ⌕ *Reservations not accepted* ▤ *MC, V* ☉ *Closed Mon. No dinner.*

$$$$ ⌂ **Seascape Resort.** On a bluff overlooking Monterey Bay, Seascape is a place to unwind. The spacious suites sleep from two to six people; each has a kitchenette and fireplace, and most have an ocean-view patio with a barbecue grill. The resort is about 9 mi south of Santa Cruz. ⊠ *1 Seascape Resort Dr., Aptos 95003* ☎ *831/688–6800 or 800/929–7727* ⊟ *831/685–0615* ⊕ *www.seascaperesort.com* ⇗ *285 suites* ⌕ *Restaurant, room service, in-room data ports, some kitchens, some kitchenettes, cable TV with movies and video games, golf privileges, 3 pools, health club, 3 hot tubs, spa, beach, children's programs (ages 5–10), laundry service, Internet, business services, convention center, meeting room; no a/c, no smoking* ▤ *AE, D, DC, MC, V.*

$$$–$$$$ ⌂ **Inn at Depot Hill.** This inventively designed B&B in a former rail depot sees itself as a link to the era of luxury train travel. Each double room or suite, complete with fireplace and feather beds, is inspired by a different destination—Italy's Portofino, France's Côte d'Azur, Japan's Kyoto. One suite is decorated like a Pullman car for a railroad baron. Some accommodations have private patios with hot tubs. This is a great place for an adults-only weekend. ⊠ *250 Monterey Ave., Capitola 95010* ☎ *831/462–3376 or 800/572–2632* ⊟ *831/462–3697* ⊕ *www.innatdepothill.com* ⇗ *8 rooms, 4 suites* ⌕ *Fans, in-room data ports, cable TV, in-room VCRs, hot tub; no a/c, no smoking* ▤ *AE, D, MC, V* ⏀ *BP.*

$$$–$$$$ ⌂ **Pleasure Point Inn.** Tucked in a residential neighborhood at the east end of town, this modern Mediterranean-style B&B sits right across the street from the ocean and a popular surfing beach, where surfing lessons are available. The immaculate rooms are handsomely appointed with high-quality furnishings and perfectly outfitted with deluxe amenities, including wireless Internet access and dimmer switches; some rooms have

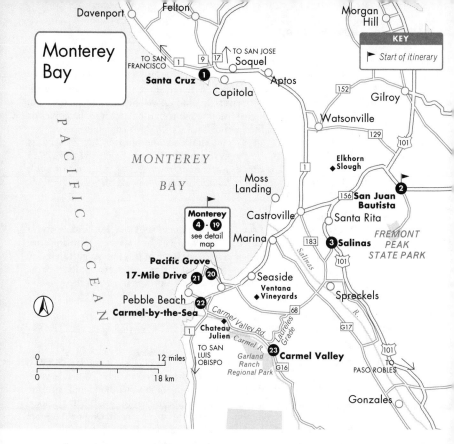

fireplaces. You have use of the large rooftop sun deck and hot tub overlooking the Pacific. Since this is a place for a romantic getaway, it's not a good place for kids. ⊠ *2–3665 E. Cliff Dr. 95062* ☎ *831/469–6161 or 877/557–2567* 🖷 *831/479–1347* ⊕ *www.pleasurepointinn.com* 🖙 *4 rooms* ⚇ *Fans, in-room data ports, in-room safes, some in-room hot tubs, minibars, refrigerators, cable TV, hot tub, beach; no a/c, no smoking* ▭ *MC, V* ◉ *CP.*

★ **$$$** 🏨 **Historic Sand Rock Farm.** On the site of a former winery, this century-old Arts and Crafts–inspired farmhouse, on 10 acres of traversable forest and meadow, has been lovingly restored and modernized. You are pampered with comfortable, spacious accommodations and a sumptuous breakfast. Most rooms have oversize Jacuzzi tubs; the others share a large outdoor hot tub. ⊠ *6901 Freedom Blvd., Aptos 95003* ☎ *831/ 688–8005* 🖷 *831/688–8025* ⊕ *www.sandrockfarm.com* 🖙 *5 rooms* ⚇ *Fans, in-room data ports, some in-room hot tubs, cable TV, in-room VCRs, outdoor hot tub, Internet; no a/c* ▭ *AE, MC, V* ◉ *BP.*

$$–$$$ 🏨 **Babbling Brook Inn.** Though smack in the middle of Santa Cruz, the lush gardens, running stream, and tall trees of this B&B make you feel as though you are in a secluded wood. All rooms have fireplaces (though a few are electric) and feather beds and most have private patios. Complimentary wine, cheese, and fresh-baked cookies are available in the afternoon. ⊠ *1025 Laurel St., 95060* ☎ *831/427–2456 or 800/866– 1131* 🖷 *831/427–2457* ⊕ *www.babblingbrookinn.com* 🖙 *13 rooms* ⚇ *In-room hot tubs, cable TV, in-room VCRs; no a/c, no smoking* ▭ *AE, D, DC, MC, V* ◉ *BP.*

$$–$$$ 🏨 **Ocean Pacific Lodge.** By staying a few blocks from the beach, you can save money at this modern, multi-story motel. ⊠ *120 Washington St., 95060* ☎ *831/457–1234 or 800/995–0289* 🖷 *831/457–0861* 🖙 *44* *rooms, 13 suites ☼ Refrigerators, cable TV, in-room VCRs, pool, gym, 2 hot tubs, some pets allowed ▤ AE, D, DC, MC, V ❍ CP.*

$$–$$$ ▦ **WestCoast Santa Cruz Hotel.** Within a short stroll of the boardwalk and wharf, this resort opens right onto Cowell Beach. Though the hotel is a monolithic concrete structure, all rooms have private balconies or patios overlooking the Pacific. If it's too cold to swim in the ocean, you can head for the heated swimming pool and hot tub. ✉ *175 W. Cliff Dr., 95060* ☎ *831/426–4330 or 800/426–0670* 🖷 *831/427–2025* ↻ *147 rooms, 16 suites ☼ Restaurant, room service, refrigerators, cable TV, pool, 2 hot tubs, bar, laundry service, no-smoking rooms ▤ AE, D, DC, MC, V.*

The Arts

Shakespeare Santa Cruz (✉ Performing Arts Complex, University of California at Santa Cruz ☎ 831/459–2121 ⊕ www.shakespearesantacruz. org) stages a six-week Shakespeare festival in July and August that also may include one modern work. Most performances are outdoors in the striking Redwood Glen. There is also a program around the holidays in December.

Sports & the Outdoors

BICYCLING   Rent a a bike at **Bike Shop Santa Cruz** (✉ 1325 Mission St. ☎ 831/454–0909).

BOATS &   **Chardonnay Sailing Charters** (☎ 831/423–1213) accommodates 49 pas-
CHARTERS   sengers for year-round cruises on Monterey Bay. The 70-ft *Chardonnay II* leaves from the yacht harbor in Santa Cruz. Food and wine are served on many of their cruises, and appearances by guest chefs and local astronomers are common. Reservations are essential. **Original Stagnaro Fishing Trips** (✉ center of Santa Cruz Municipal Wharf ☎ 831/427–2334) operates salmon-, albacore-, and rock cod–fishing expeditions; the fees ($45–$55) include bait. The company also runs whale-watching cruises ($30) December through April.

SURFING   **Manresa State Beach** (✉ Manresa Dr., La Selva Beach ☎ 831/761–1795), south of Santa Cruz, has premium surfing conditions, but the currents can be treacherous; campsites are available. The surf at **New Brighton State Beach** (✉ 1500 State Park Dr., Capitola ☎ 831/464–6330) is challenging; campsites are available. Surfers gather for spectacular waves and sunsets at **Pleasure Point** (✉ E. Cliff and Pleasure Point Drs.). **Steamer's Lane,** near the lighthouse on West Cliff Drive, has a decent break. The area plays host to several competitions in the summer.

Cowell's Beach 'n' Bikini Surf Shop (✉ 30 Front St. ☎ 831/427–2355) rents surfboards and wet suits and offers lessons.

en route   About halfway between Santa Cruz and Monterey, east of the tiny harbor town of Moss Landing, is one of only two federal research reserves in California, the **Elkhorn Slough at the National Estuarine** ★ **Research Reserve** (✉ 1700 Elkhorn Rd., Watsonville ☎ 831/728–2822 ⊕ www.elkhornslough.org). Its 1,400 acres of tidal flats and salt marshes form a complex environment that supports some 300 species of birds. A walk along the meandering waterways and wetlands can reveal hawks, white-tailed kites, owls, herons, and egrets. On weekends guided walks to the heron rookery are offered at 10 and 1. (☼ Wed.–Sun. 9–5 🎟 $2.50)

San Juan Bautista

▶ ❷ *32 mi southeast of Santa Cruz via Hwy. 1 south and Hwy. 152 east.*

Sleepy San Juan Bautista has been protected from development since 1933, when much of the town became a state park. This is about as close to early-19th-century California as you can get. Small antiques shops and art galleries line the side streets.

The centerpiece of **San Juan Bautista State Historic Park** is a wide green plaza ringed by historic buildings: a restored blacksmith shop, a stable, a pioneer cabin, and a jailhouse. The **Castro-Breen Adobe,** furnished with Spanish colonial antiques, presents a view of mid-19th-century domestic life in the village. Running along one side of the town square is **Mission San Juan Bautista** (✉ 408 S. 2nd St. ☎ 831/623–2127), founded by Father Fermin de Lasuen in 1797. Adjoining the long, low, colonnaded structure is the mission cemetery, where more than 4,300 Native Americans who converted to Christianity are buried in unmarked graves. (☉ Daily 9:30–5 ✎ $2).

After the mission era, San Juan Bautista became an important crossroads for stagecoach travel. The principal stop in town was the **Plaza Hotel,** a collection of adobe buildings with furnishings from the 1860s.
★ ☾ On **Living History Day,** which takes place on the first Saturday of each month, costumed volunteers engage in quilting bees, tortilla making, butter churning, and other frontier activities. ✉ *2nd and Franklin Sts., off Hwy. 156* ☎ *831/623–4881 or 831/623–4526* ⊕ *www.cal-parks. ca.gov* ✎ *$2* ☉ *Daily 10–4:30.*

Salinas

❸ *20 mi south of San Juan Bautista on U.S. 101.*

Salinas is the population center of a rich agricultural valley where fertile soil, an ideal climate, and a good water supply produce optimum growing conditions for crops such as lettuce, broccoli, tomatoes, strawberries, flowers, and wine grapes. This unpretentious town may lack the sophistication and scenic splendors of the coast, but it will interest literary and architectural buffs. Turn-of-the-20th-century buildings have been the focus of ongoing renovation, much of it centered on the original downtown area of South Main Street, with its handsome stone storefronts. The memory and literary legacy of Salinas native (and winner of Pulitzer and Nobel prizes) John Steinbeck are well honored here.

The **National Steinbeck Center** is a museum and archive dedicated to the life and works of John Steinbeck. Many exhibits are interactive, bringing to life Steinbeck worlds such as Cannery Row, Hooverville (from *The Grapes of Wrath*), and the Mexican Plaza (from *The Pearl*). The library and archives contain Steinbeck first editions, notebooks, photographs, and audiotapes. Access to the archives is by appointment only. The center has information about Salinas's annual Steinbeck Festival, in August, and about tours of area landmarks mentioned in his novels. ✉ *1 Main St.* ☎ *831/796–3833* ⊕ *www.steinbeck.org* ✎ *$10* ☉ *Daily 10–5.*

The **Jose Eusebio Boronda Adobe** contains furniture and artifacts depicting the California lifestyle of the 1840s. ✉ *333 Boronda Rd.* ☎ *831/ 757–8085* ✎ *Free (donation requested)* ☉ *Weekdays10–2; weekends by appt.*

Where to Eat

$–$$ ✕ **Spado's.** Spado's brings Monterey-style culinary sophistication to the valley. For lunch visit the antipasto bar for fresh salads and Mediterranean morsels; the *panini* (Italian-style sandwiches) are also excellent. For dinner try the pizza with chicken and sun-dried–tomato pesto, the angel-hair pasta and prawns, or the risotto of the day. ✉ 66 *W. Alisal St.* ☎ *831/424–4139* ⊟ *AE, D, DC, MC, V* ✆ *Closed Mon. No lunch weekends.*

$ ✕ **Steinbeck House.** John Steinbeck's birthplace, a Victorian frame house, has been converted into a lunch-only (11:30–2) eatery run by the volunteer Valley Guild. The restaurant displays some Steinbeck memorabilia. There's no à la carte service; the set menu includes soup or salad, vegetable, main dish, and non-alcoholic beverage. Dishes such as zucchini lasagna and spinach crepes are created using locally grown produce. ✉ *132 Central Ave.* ☎ *831/424–2735* ⊟ *MC, V* ✆ *Closed Sun. and 3 wks late Dec.–early Jan. No dinner.*

Sports & the Outdoors

The **California Rodeo** (☎ 831/775–3100 ⊕ www.carodeo.com), one of the oldest and most famous rodeos in the West, takes place in Salinas in mid-July.

MONTEREY

Early in the 20th century Carmel Martin, the first mayor of the city of Monterey, saw a bright future for his town: "Monterey Bay is the one place where people can live without being disturbed by manufacturing and big factories. I am certain that the day is coming when this will be the most desirable place in the whole state of California." It seems that Mayor Martin was not far off the mark.

Historic Monterey

▶ *42 mi south of Santa Cruz via Hwy. 1; 17 mi west of Salinas via Hwy. 68.*

a good tour

You can glimpse Monterey's early history in the well-preserved adobe buildings at **Monterey State Historic Park.** Far from being a hermetic period museum, the park facilities are an integral part of the day-to-day business life of the town—within some of the buildings are a store, a theater, and government offices. Some of the historic houses are graced with gardens that are worthy sights themselves. Free guided tours of Casa Soberanes, Larkin House, Cooper-Molera Adobe, and Stevenson House are given daily. Spend the first day of your Monterey visit exploring the historic park, starting at ▶ **Stanton Center** ❹, which also houses the **Maritime Museum of Monterey** ❺. Take the guided 90-minute tour of the park (call for times), after which you can tour some or all of the following historic adobes and their gardens. Start next door to the Maritime Museum at **Pacific House** ❻ and cross the plaza to the **Custom House** ❼. It's a short walk up Scott Street to **California's First Theatre** ❽, then one block down Pacific to **Casa Soberanes** ❾. Afterward, see the **Stevenson House** ❿, **Cooper-Molera Adobe** ⓫, **Larkin House** ⓬, and **Colton Hall** ⓭. Stop in at the **Monterey Museum of Art** ⓮, and finish the day at **La Mirada** ⓯.

Start day two on **Fisherman's Wharf** ⓰, then head for the **Presidio of Monterey Museum** ⓱. Spend the rest of the day on **Cannery Row**, which has undergone several transformations since it was immortalized in John Steinbeck's 1945 novel of the same name. The street that Steinbeck described was crowded with sardine canneries processing, at their peak, nearly 200,000 tons of the smelly silver fish a year. During the mid-1940s, how-

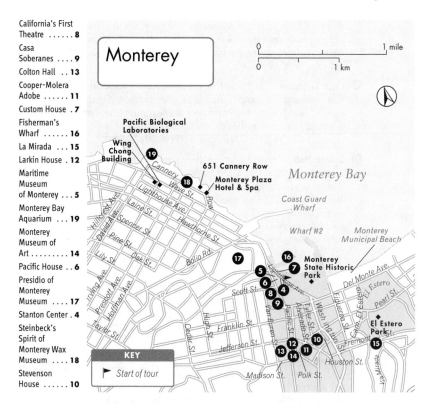

ever, the sardines disappeared from the bay, causing the canneries to close. Through the years the old tin-roof canneries have been converted into restaurants, art galleries, and malls with shops selling T-shirts, fudge, and plastic sea otters. Recent tourist development along the row has been more tasteful, however, and includes several stylish inns and hotels. The **Monterey Plaza Hotel and Spa,** on the site of a historic estate at 400 Cannery Row, is a great place to relax over a drink and watch for sea otters. Wisps of the neighborhood's colorful past appear at **651 Cannery Row,** whose tile Chinese dragon roof dates to 1929.

Poke around in **Steinbeck's Spirit of Monterey Wax Museum** ⑱ before heading for a weathered wooden building at 800 Cannery Row. This was the site of **Pacific Biological Laboratories,** where Edward F. Ricketts, the inspiration for Doc in *Cannery Row,* did much of his marine research. The **Wing Chong Building,** at 835 Cannery Row, is the former Wing Chong Market that Steinbeck called Lee Chong's Heavenly Flower Grocery in *Cannery Row.* Step back into the present at the spectacular **Monterey Bay Aquarium** ⑲ and commune with the marine life.

TIMING   Depending on how quickly you tour (it's easy to spend a couple of hours at both the maritime museum and the art museum), day one will be a long one, but all of the historic park sites are in a small area. Monterey Museum of Art and La Mirada are a short drive or taxi ride from the historic park. Day two will also be full; it's easy to linger for hours at Fisherman's Wharf and the aquarium.

What to See

❽ **California's First Theatre.** The theater was constructed in the 1840s as a saloon with adjoining apartments by Jack Swan, an English sailor who settled in Monterey. Soldiers from the New York Volunteers who were on assignment in Monterey put on plays in the building. Melo-dramas and other theatrical performances are still staged here. ✉ *Monterey State Historic Park, Scott and Pacific Sts.* ☎ *831/375–4916* 🎫 *Free* ⊙ *Call for hrs.*

⑨ Casa Soberanes. A classic low-ceilinged adobe structure built in 1842, this was once a Custom House guard's residence. Exhibits at the house survey life in Monterey from the era of Mexican rule to the present. There's a peaceful garden in back. ✉ *Monterey State Historic Park, 336 Pacific St.* ☎ *831/649–7118* 🎫 *Free* ⊙ *Daily 8–5.*

⑬ Colton Hall. A convention of delegates met in 1849 to draft the first state constitution at California's equivalent of Independence Hall. The stone building, which has served as a school, a courthouse, and the county hall, is a museum furnished as it was during the constitutional convention. The extensive grounds outside the hall surround the Old Monterey Jail. ✉ *Monterey State Historic Park, 500 block of Pacific St., between Madison and Jefferson Sts.* ☎ *831/646–5640* 🎫 *Free* ⊙ *Daily 10–noon and 1–4.*

⑪ Cooper-Molera Adobe. The restored 2-acre complex includes a house dating from the 1820s, a visitor center, a bookstore, and a large garden enclosed by a high adobe wall. The mostly Victorian-era antiques and memorabilia that fill the house provide a glimpse into the life of a prosperous pioneer family. ✉ *Monterey State Historic Park, Polk St. and Munras Ave.* ☎ *831/649–7118* 🎫 *Free* ⊙ *Call for hrs.*

⑦ Custom House. This adobe structure built by the Mexican government in 1827—now California's oldest standing public building—was the first stop for sea traders whose goods were subject to duties. At the beginning of the Mexican–American War, in 1846, Commodore John Sloat raised the American flag over the building and claimed California for the United States. The house's lower floor displays cargo from a 19th-century trading ship. ✉ *Monterey State Historic Park, 1 Custom House Plaza, across from Fisherman's Wharf* ☎ *831/649–2909* 🎫 *Free* ⊙ *Thurs.–Tues. 10–4.*

ᑕ ⑯ Fisherman's Wharf. The mournful barking of sea lions is the soundtrack for Monterey's waterfront. The whiskered marine mammals are best enjoyed while walking along this aging pier across from Custom House Plaza. Most of the commercial fishermen have moved to Wharf No. 2, a five-minute walk away, and Fisherman's Wharf is lined with souvenir shops, fish markets, seafood restaurants, and popcorn stands. It's a lively and entertaining place to bring children and is the departure point for fishing, diving, and whale-watching trips. ✉ *End of Calle Principal* ☎ *831/ 373–0600* ⊕ *www.montereywharf.com.*

⑮ La Mirada. Asian and European antiques fill this 19th-century adobe house. A newer 10,000-square-ft gallery space, designed by Charles Moore, houses Asian and California regional art. Outdoors are magnificent rose and rhododendron gardens. The entrance fee for La Mirada includes admission to the Monterey Museum of Art. ✉ *720 Via Mirada, at Fremont St.* ☎ *831/372–3689* 🎫 *$5* ⊙ *Wed.–Sat. 11–5, Sun. 1–4.*

> **need a break?** El Estero Park's **Dennis the Menace Playground** (✉ Pearl St. and Camino El Estero ☎ 831/646–3866) is an imaginative play area designed by the late Hank Ketcham, the well-known cartoonist. The equipment is on a grand scale and made for daredevils; there's a roller slide, a clanking suspension bridge, and a real Southern Pacific steam locomotive. You can rent a rowboat or a paddleboat to cruise about U-shaped Lake El Estero, populated with an assortment of ducks, mud hens, and geese. The park is closed Mondays except for holidays.

For a little down time, kick off your shoes at **Monterey Municipal Beach,** (⊠ North of Del Monte Ave., east of Wharf No. 2), where the shallow waters are usually warm and calm enough for wading.

⑫ Larkin House. A veranda encircles the second floor of this architecturally significant two-story adobe built in 1835, whose design bears witness to the Mexican and New England influences on the Monterey style. The rooms are furnished with period antiques, many of them brought from New Hampshire by the Larkin family. ⊠ *Monterey State Historic Park, 510 Calle Principal, between Jefferson and Pacific Sts.* ☎ *831/649–7118* 🖻 *Free* ☉ *Call for hrs.*

❺ Maritime Museum of Monterey. This collection of maritime artifacts belonged to Allen Knight, who was Carmel's mayor from 1950 to 1952. Among the exhibits of ship models, scrimshaw items, and nautical prints, the highlight is the enormous multifaceted Fresnel lens from the Point Sur Light Station. ⊠*Monterey State Historic Park, 5 Custom House Plaza* ☎ *831/375–2553* 🖻 *$5* 🖻 *Free* ☉ *Tues.–Sun. 11–5.*

★ ☺ ⑲ Monterey Bay Aquarium. The Outer Bay wing of this institution contains a million-gallon indoor ocean—observed through the largest window on Earth—that re-creates the sunlighted blue water where Monterey Bay meets the open sea. In this habitat soupfin sharks, barracuda, pelagic stingrays, ocean sunfish (which can weigh several hundred pounds), green sea turtles, and schools of fast-moving tuna swim together. The Outer Bay wing also houses a mesmerizing collection (the largest in the nation) of jellyfish. Expect long lines and sizable crowds at the aquarium on weekends, especially during the summer, but it's worth it. Don't miss the original wing's three-story Kelp Forest exhibit, the only one of its kind in the world, or the display of the sea creatures and vegetation found in Monterey Bay. Among other standouts are a petting pool where you can touch the velvet-like skin of the bat-rays a 55,000-gallon sea-otter tank; an enormous outdoor artificial tidal pool that supports anemones, crabs, sea stars, and other colorful creatures; and Splash Zone, a hands-on activity center geared to families with small children. ⊠ *886 Cannery Row* ☎ *831/648–4888, 800/756–3737 in CA for advance tickets* ⊕ *www.montereybayaquarium.org* 🖻 *$17.95* ☉ *Memorial Day–Labor Day, daily 9:30–6; Labor Day–Memorial Day, daily 10–6.*

⑭ Monterey Museum of Art. Here you can see the works of photographers Ansel Adams and Edward Weston and of other artists who have spent time on the Peninsula. Another focus is international folk art; the colorful collection ranges from Kentucky hearth brooms to Tibetan prayer wheels. The entrance fee for the Monterey Museum of Art includes admission to La Mirada. ⊠ *559 Pacific St., across from Colton Hall* ☎ *831/ 372-7591* ⊕ *www.montereyart.org* 🖻 *$5* ☉ *Wed.–Sat. 11–5, Sun. 1–4.*

❻ Pacific House. Once a hotel and saloon, this park visitor center and museum surveys life in early California with gold-rush relics and photographs of old Monterey. The upper floor displays Native American artifacts. ⊠ *Monterey State Historic Park, 10 Custom House Plaza* ☎ *831/649–7118* 🖻 *Free* ☉ *Tues.–Sun 10–4.*

⑰ Presidio of Monterey Museum. Learn about the cultural and military history of Monterey, from the 17th century to the present. Because of the important role of the military in Monterey in the 20th century, exhibits highlight the period between the two world wars. ⊠ *Corporal Ewing Rd., lower Presidio Park, Monterey Presidio* ☎ *831/646–3456* ⊕ *www.monterey.org/ museum/pom* 🖻 *Free* ☉ *Thurs.–Sat. 10–4, Sun. 1–4, Mon. 10–1.*

► ❹ **Stanton Center.** View a free 20-minute film about Monterey State Historic Park and gather maps and information. Then take the 90-minute walking tour along the 2-mi Path of History, marked by round gold tiles set into the sidewalk. The tour passes several landmark buildings and details the history and significance of the park's sites. You can do the walk on your own, or join a guided tour of the park. Admission to most sites along the walk is free, and most are open daily. ⊠ *Monterey State Historic Park, 5 Custom House Plaza* ☎ *831/649–7118* ⊕ *www.mbay. net/~mshp* ☒ *Free; park tours $5* ⊙ *Thurs.–Sat. 10–4, Sun. 1–4.*

⑱ **Steinbeck's Spirit of Monterey Wax Museum.** Characters from the novel *Cannery Row* are depicted in the displays here. An easy-to-digest, 25-minute summation of 400 years of Monterey history is narrated by an actor playing John Steinbeck. ⊠ *700 Cannery Row* ☎ *831/375–3770* ⊕ *www.wax-museum.com* ☒ *$4.95* ⊙ *Memorial Day–Labor Day, Sun.–Fri. 10:30–7, Sat. 10:30–8; Labor Day–Memorial Day, daily noon–8.*

⑩ **Stevenson House.** This house was named in honor of author Robert Louis Stevenson, who boarded here briefly in a tiny upstairs room. Items from his family's estate furnish Stevenson's room. Period-decorated chambers elsewhere in the house include a gallery of the author's memorabilia and a children's nursery stocked with Victorian toys and games. ⊠ *Monterey State Historic Park, 530 Houston St.* ☎ *831/649–7118* ☒ *Free* ⊙ *Weekends noon–2.*

off the beaten path

VENTANA VINEYARDS – A short drive from downtown Monterey leads to this winery known for its chardonnays and rieslings. Ventana's knowledgeable and hospitable owners, Doug and LuAnn Meador, invite you to bring a lunch to eat while tasting wines on the patio. ⊠ *2999 Monterey–Salinas Hwy. (Hwy. 68)* ☎ *831/372–7415* ⊕ *www.ventanavineyards.com* ⊙ *Daily 11–5.*

Where to Stay & Eat

★ **$$$–$$$$** ✕ **Fresh Cream.** The views of the bay are as superb as the imaginative French cuisine at this outstanding restaurant in Heritage Harbor. The menu, which changes weekly, might include rack of lamb Dijonnaise, roast boned duck in black-currant sauce, or blackened ahi tuna with pineapple rum-butter sauce. Service is formal, and though there is no requirement for dress, men will feel more comfortable in a jacket. ⊠ *99 Pacific St., Suite 100C* ☎ *831/375–9798* ⚲ *Reservations essential* ⊟ *AE, D, DC, MC, V* ⊙ *No lunch.*

$$$–$$$$ ✕ **Whaling Station Prime Steaks and Seafood.** A modern room with a lively crowd makes this restaurant above Cannery Row a festive yet comfortable place to enjoy prime beef and fresh seafood. ⊠ *763 Wave St.* ☎ *831/373–3778* ⚲ *Reservations essential* ⊟ *AE, D, DC, MC, V* ⊙ *No lunch.*

$$–$$$ ✕ **Domenico's.** Italian-style seafood, mesquite-grilled meats, and homemade pastas are the specialties at Domenico's. The nautical theme keeps the place comfortably casual; white drapery lends an air of elegance other wharf restaurants lack. ⊠ *50 Fisherman's Wharf* ☎ *831/372–3655* ⊟ *AE, D, DC, MC, V.*

$$–$$$ ✕ **Duck Club.** The elegant and romantic dining room of the Monterey Plaza Hotel and Spa is built over the waterfront on Cannery Row. The dinner menu highlights inventive dishes such as seared scallops with artichoke-potato mash, and air-dried, wood-roasted duck, and includes house-made pasta. Breakfast is served as well. ⊠ *400 Cannery Row* ☎ *831/646–1706* ⊟ *AE, D, DC, MC, V* ⊙ *Closed Mon. No lunch.*

$$–$$$ ✕ **Monterey's Fish House.** Casual yet stylish and away from the hubbub of the wharf, this always-packed seafood restaurant attracts locals and frequent visitors to the city. If the dining room is full, you can wait at the bar and savor deliciously plump oysters on the half shell. The bartenders and waitstaff will gladly advise you on the perfect wine to go with your poached, blackened, or oak-grilled seafood. ⊠ *2114 Del Monte Ave.* ☎ *831/373–4647* ⌥ *Reservations essential* ⊟ *AE, D, DC, MC, V* ⊘ *No lunch weekends.*

$$–$$$ ✕ **Montrio Bistro.** Style reigns at this trendy, eclectic downtown restau-
Fodor'sChoice rant, which was formerly Monterey's firehouse. Wrought-iron trellises,
★ metal sculpture, and rawhide complement the artful presentation of California cuisine, which includes prime beef and organic produce. Clean, strong flavors typify the cooking here. Grilled Portobello mushrooms with polenta and rotisserie chicken with garlic mashed potatoes are two of the menu highlights. ⊠ *414 Calle Principal* ☎ *831/648–8880* ⌥ *Reservations essential* ⊟ *AE, D, DC, MC, V* ⊘ *No lunch.*

$–$$$ ✕ **Mike's Seafood Restaurant.** A large, open brass fireplace and excellent water views make this a cozy and inviting spot for lunch or dinner on the wharf. Though standard seafood preparations are the focus, the chef also highlights some unusual Italian- and Japanese-inspired dishes. ⊠ *25 Fisherman's Wharf No. 1* ☎ *831/372–6153* ⌥ *Reservations essential* ⊟ *AE, D, DC, MC, V.*

★ **$–$$$** ✕ **Stokes Restaurant & Bar.** Chef Brandon Miller's restaurant, set inside an 1833 adobe, seamlessly balances innovative cooking and traditional design. Miller specializes in the cuisines of Provence, northern Italy, and Catalan Spain, turning out imaginative pasta, seafood, and vegetarian dishes that change seasonally. His creations have included slow-roasted duck breast on squash-chestnut risotto, rustic pasta tubes with fennel sausage and Manila clams, and a vegetable napoleon of crepes, and house-made ricotta with smoked tomato sauce. ⊠ *500 Hartnell St.* ☎ *831/ 373–1110* ⌥ *Reservations essential* ⊟ *AE, D, DC, MC, V* ⊘ *No lunch Sun.*

$–$$$ ✕ **Tarpy's Roadhouse.** Fun, dressed-down roadhouse lunch and dinner are served in this renovated farmhouse from the early 1900s. Out of the kitchen comes everything Mom used to make, only better. Eat indoors by a fireplace or outdoors in the courtyard. ⊠ *2999 Monterey–Salinas Hwy. (Hwy. 68), at Canyon Del Rey Rd.* ☎ *831/647–1444* ⌥ *Reservations essential* ⊟ *AE, D, MC, V.*

$–$$ ✕ **Cafe Fina.** Mesquite-grilled fish dishes and linguine in clam sauce with baby shrimp and tomatoes are among the highlights at this understated Italian restaurant on the wharf. The wine list is extensive. ⊠ *47 Fisherman's Wharf* ☎ *831/372–5200* ⊟ *AE, MC, V.*

$–$$ ✕ **Paradiso Trattoria and Oyster Bar.** Follow the aroma of marinating olives, roasted garlic, and platters of focaccia to this bright Cannery Row establishment. Mediterranean specialties and pizzas from a wood-burning oven are the main luncheon fare. Seafood is a good choice for dinner, served in a dining room overlooking a lighted beachfront. ⊠ *654 Cannery Row* ☎ *831/375–4155* ⊟ *AE, D, DC, MC, V.*

¢–$$ ✕ **Thai Bistro.** In a former residence on one of Monterey's main drags, this airy and bright mom-and-pop restaurant serves excellent, authentic Thai cuisine from family recipes. Though technically just over the city line in Pacific Grove, it is within walking distance of Cannery Row and the Monterey Aquarium. ⊠ *159 Central Ave., Pacific Grove* ☎ *831/ 372–8700* ⊟ *AE, D, MC, V.*

¢ ✕ **Old Monterey Cafe.** Breakfast here, which is served until closing time (2:30 PM), might include fresh-baked muffins and eggs Benedict. Soups, salads, and sandwiches appear on the lunch menu. This is also a good place to relax with a cappuccino after touring Monterey's historic adobes. ⊠ *489 Alvarado St.* ☎ *831/646–1021* ⌥ *Reservations not accepted* ⊟ *D, MC, V* ⊘ *No dinner.*

$$$–$$$$ ⊞ **Embassy Suites.** As you drive into Monterey from the north on Highway 1, you can't miss this high-rise property, which towers over the town of Seaside. Two blocks from the beach, it has views of Laguna Grande Lake and Monterey Bay. All accommodations here are smallish two-room suites. Complimentary cocktails are available each evening. ⊠ *1441 Canyon Del Rey, Seaside 93955* ☎ *831/393–1115* 🖷 *831/393–1113* ⊕ *www.embassymonterey.com* 🛏 *225 suites* ☖ *Restaurant, in-room data ports, kitchenettes, cable TV with movies and video games, indoor pool, gym, hot tub, sauna, bar, video game room, business services, meeting rooms, no-smoking rooms* ⊟ *AE, D, DC, MC, V* ⦿ *BP.*

$$$–$$$$ ⊞ **Hotel Pacific.** All the rooms at this modern adobe-style hotel are junior suites, handsomely appointed with featherbeds, hardwood floors, fireplaces, and balconies or patios. The rates include afternoon tea and cheese. ⊠ *300 Pacific St., 93940* ☎ *831/373–5700 or 800/554–5542* 🖷 *831/373–6921* ⊕ *www.hotelpacific.com* 🛏 *105 rooms* ☖ *Fans, in-room data ports, refrigerators, cable TV, in-room VCRs, 2 hot tubs, meeting rooms; no a/c, no smoking* ⊟ *AE, D, DC, MC, V* ⦿ *CP.*

$$$–$$$$ ⊞ **Hyatt Regency Monterey.** Although its rooms and overall vibe are less glamorous than those at some other resorts in the region, the facilities here are very good. ⊠ *1 Old Golf Course Rd., 93940* ☎ *831/372–1234, 800/824–2196 in CA* 🖷 *831/372–4277* ⊕ *www.montereyhyatt.com* 🛏 *575 rooms* ☖ *Restaurant, café, fans, some refrigerators, cable TV with movies, 18-hole golf course, 5 tennis courts, 2 pools, gym, 2 hot tubs, massage, bicycles, bar, recreation room, laundry service, concierge, Internet, business services, meeting room, some pets allowed (fee), no-smoking rooms; no a/c* ⊟ *AE, D, DC, MC, V.*

$$$–$$$$
Fodor'sChoice
★ ⊞ **Old Monterey Inn.** One of just two residential-area B&Bs in Monterey, the three-story Tudor-style country manor, completed in 1929, is replete with hand-carved window frames, balustrades, and Gothic archways. Loving restoration by proprietors Gene and Ann Swett included a rose garden, which is surrounded by giant holly trees, gnarled oaks, and majestic redwoods. The inn is legendary for its 20 bathroom amenities, featherbeds with down comforters, sumptuous breakfast, and solicitous service. Because of the expensive and fragile furnishings, this is not a suitable place to bring children of any age. ⊠ *500 Martin St., 93940* ☎ *831/375–8284 or 800/350–2344* 🖷 *831/375–6730* ⊕ *www. oldmontereyinn.com* 🛏 *7 rooms, 2 suites, 1 cottage* ☖ *In-room data ports, cable TV, in-room VCRs, concierge; no a/c, no smoking* ⊟ *MC, V* ⦿ *BP.*

$$$–$$$$ ⊞ **Spindrift Inn.** This boutique hotel on Cannery Row, under the same management as the Hotel Pacific and the Monterey Bay Inn, has beach access and a rooftop garden that overlooks the water. Spacious rooms with sitting areas, hardwood floors, fireplaces, and down comforters are among the indoor pleasures. This is a place for adults; families would not be comfortable here. ⊠ *652 Cannery Row, 93940* ☎ *831/646–8900 or 800/841–1879* 🖷 *831/646–5342* ⊕ *www.spindriftinn.com* 🛏 *42 rooms* ☖ *In-room data ports, refrigerators, cable TV, in-room VCRs, concierge; no a/c, no smoking* ⊟ *AE, D, DC, MC, V* ⦿ *CP.*

★ **$$–$$$$** ⊞ **Monterey Plaza Hotel and Spa.** This full-service hotel commands a waterfront location on Cannery Row, where frolicking sea otters can be observed from the wide outdoor patio and many room balconies. The architecture and design blend early California and Mediterranean styles and retain elements of the old cannery design. The property is meticulously maintained and offers accommodations from simple to luxurious. You have use of a state-of-the-art full-service spa facility. ⊠ *400 Cannery Row, 93940* ☎ *831/646–1700, 800/631–1339, 800/334–3999 in CA* 🖷 *831/646–0285* ⊕ *www.montereyplazahotel.com* 🛏 *285 rooms, 3 suites* ☖ *2 restaurants, room service, fans, in-room data ports,* *minibars, cable TV with movies, health club, spa, laundry service, con-cierge, Internet, business services, meeting rooms; no a/c, no smoking* ⊟ *AE, D, DC, MC, V.*

$$–$$$ ☷ **The Beach Resort.** The rooms here may be nondescript, but this Best Western hotel has a great waterfront location about 2 mi north of town, which affords views of the bay and the city skyline. The grounds are pleasantly landscaped, and there's a large pool with a sunbathing area. ⊠ *2600 Sand Dunes Dr., 93940* ☎ *831/394–3321 or 800/242–8627* 🖷 *831/393–1912* ⊕ *www.montereybeachresort.com* ⇨ *196 rooms* ⌖ *Restaurant, some fans, in-room data ports, refrigerators, cable TV with movies, pool, exercise equipment, hot tub, lounge, business ser-vices, some pets allowed (fee); no smoking* ⊟ *AE, D, DC, MC, V.*

$$–$$$ ☷ **Monterey Hotel.** Standard rooms in this restored Victorian are small but contain well-chosen reproduction antique furniture. The master suites have fireplaces and oval bathtubs. Afternoon tea and cake and bedtime milk and cookies are included. ⊠ *406 Alvarado St., 93940* ☎ *831/375–3184 or 800/727–0960* 🖷 *831/373–2899* ⊕ *www. montereyhotel.com* ⇨ *39 rooms, 6 suites* ⌖ *Fans, in-room data ports, some refrigerators, cable TV; no a/c, no smoking* ⊟ *AE, D, DC, MC, V* ❙◎❙ *CP.*

$–$$$ ☷ **Fireside Lodge.** Proximity to downtown and Fisherman's Wharf is key at this motel. Room furnishings are basic and clean, and some rooms have gas fireplaces. ⊠ *1131 10th St., 93940* ☎ *831/373–4172 or 800/ 722–2624 in CA* 🖷 *831/655–5640* ⊕ *www.montereyfireside.com* ⇨ *20 rooms, 1 suite* ⌖ *In-room data ports, cable TV, some refrigerators, some kitchenettes, some microwaves, some pets allowed (fee), hot tub; no a/c, no smoking* ⊟ *AE, D, DC, MC, V* ❙◎❙ *CP.*

$–$$ ☷ **Cypress Tree Inn.** Because of the 2 mi drive from town, large, spotless rooms are available for less money than those of comparable competi-tors located closer to the wharf and downtown. ⊠ *2227 N. Fremont St., 93940* ☎ *831/372–7586 or 800/446–8303* 🖷 *831/372–2940* ⊕ *www.cypresstreeinn.com* ⇨ *55 rooms* ⌖ *In-room data ports, some kitchenettes, refrigerators, microwaves, some in-room hot tubs, sauna, hot tub, laundry facilities; no a/c, no smoking* ⊟ *AE, D, DC, MC, V.*

☾ **$–$$** ☷ **Monterey Bay Lodge.** Its location on the edge of Monterey's El Estero Park and its superior amenities give this motel an edge over those along the busy Munras Avenue motel row. Indoor plants and a secluded court-yard with a heated pool are other pluses at this friendly facility. ⊠ *55 Camino Aguajito, 93940* ☎ *831/372–8057 or 800/558–1900* 🖷 *831/ 655–2933* ⊕ *www.montereybaylodge.com* ⇨ *45 rooms* ⌖ *Restau-rant, in-room data ports, cable TV, in-room VCRs, pool, hot tub, some pets allowed (fee), no-smoking rooms* ⊟ *AE, D, DC, MC, V.*

¢–$ ☷ **Quality Inn Monterey.** This attractive motel has a friendly, country-inn feeling. Rooms are light and airy, and some have fireplaces. ⊠ *1058 Munras Ave., 93940* ☎ *831/372–3381* 🖷 *831/372–4687* ⊕ *www. qualityinnmonterey.com* ⇨ *55 rooms* ⌖ *In-room data ports, mi-crowaves, refrigerators, cable TV, in-room VCRs, indoor pool, hot tub; no smoking* ⊟ *AE, D, DC, MC, V* ❙◎❙ *CP.*

Nightlife & the Arts

NIGHTLIFE **Bluefin** (⊠ 685 Cannery Row ☎ 831/375–7000) offers live music, danc-ing, and 19 pool tables. **Planet Gemini** (⊠ 625 Cannery Row ☎ 831/373–1449) presents comedy shows on weekends and dancing to a DJ or live music. **Sly McFlys** (⊠ 700-A Cannery Row ☎ 831/649–8050) has live jazz and blues every night.

THE ARTS **Dixieland Monterey** (☎ 831/443–5260 or 888/349–6879 ⊕ www. dixieland-monterey.com), held on the first full weekend of March, pre-sents trad-jazz bands in cabarets, restaurants, and hotel lounges on the

Monterey waterfront. The **Monterey Bay Blues Festival** (☎ 831/394–2652 ⊕ www.montereyblues.com) draws blues fans to the Monterey Fairgrounds over a June weekend. The **Monterey Jazz Festival** (☎ 831/373–3366 ⊕ www.montereyjazzfestival.org), the world's oldest, attracts jazz and blues greats from around the world to the Monterey Fairgrounds on the third full weekend of September.

The **Barbary Coast Theater** (✉ 324 Hoffman ☎ 831/655–4992) performs comedy melodramas near Cannery Row. **Monterey Bay Theatrefest** (☎ 831/622–0700) presents free outdoor performances at Custom House Plaza on weekend afternoons and evenings from late June to mid-July. The **Wharf Theater** (✉ Fisherman's Wharf ☎ 831/649–2332) focuses on American musicals past and present.

Sports & the Outdoors

Throughout most of the year, the Monterey Bay area is a paradise for those who love the outdoors. Residents are on the whole an active bunch. Tennis, golf, surfing, fishing, biking, hiking, scuba diving and kayaking are popular activities. Golf and tennis are less popular in the rainy winter months—a time when the waves grow larger and adventurous surfers flock to the water.

BICYCLING For bicycle rentals, visit **Bay Bikes** (✉ 640 Wave St. ☎ 831/646–9090). **Adventures by the Sea Inc.** (✉ 299 Cannery Row ☎ 831/372–1807) rents tandem and standard bicycles.

FISHING **Monterey Fishing** (✉ 96 Fisherman's Wharf ☎ 831/372–2203 or 800/200–2203) has one of the largest boats in the area and can accommodate up to 100 people for half- or full-day fishing trips. **Randy's Fishing Trips** (✉ 66 Fisherman's Wharf ☎ 831/372–7440 or 800/251–7440) has been operating under the same skippers since 1958. **Sam's Fishing Fleet** (✉ 84 Fisherman's Wharf ☎ 831/372–0577 or 800/427–2675) has been fishing the Monterey Bay since 1914.

GOLF The greens fee at the 18-hole **Del Monte Golf Course** (✉ 1300 Sylvan Rd. ☎ 831/373–2700) is $95, plus $20 per person for an optional cart. The $22 twilight special (plus cart rental) begins two hours before sunset.

KAYAKING **Monterey Bay Kayaks** (✉ 693 Del Monte Ave. ☎ 831/373–5357, 800/649–5357 in CA ⊕ www.montereybaykayaks.com) rents equipment and conducts classes and natural-history tours. Their **Moss Landing** store (✉ 2390 Hwy. 1, Moss Landing ☎ 800/649–5357), about 20 mi north of Monterey, offers the same services and is a good departure point for exploration of the Elk Horn Slough.

ROLLER-SKATING & IN-LINE SKATING **Del Monte Gardens** (✉ 2020 Del Monte Ave. ☎ 831/375–3202) is an old-fashioned rink for roller-skating and in-line skating. **Monterey Skate Park** (✉ next to Lake El Estero behind Sollecito Ballpark ☎ 831/646–3866) is an unsupervised park open daily from 9 AM to dusk.

SCUBA DIVING Even during summer, Monterey Bay waters never warm to the temperatures of their southern California counterparts. But throw on a wetsuit and one of the world's most diverse marine ecosystems is yours to explore. The Monterey Bay National Marine Sanctuary, home to mammals, seabirds, fishes, invertebrates, and plants, encompasses a 276-mi shoreline and 5,322 square mi of ocean. The staff at **Aquarius Dive Shops** (✉ 2040 Del Monte Ave. ☎ 831/375–1933 ✉ 32 Cannery Row ☎ 831/375–6605) gives diving lessons and tours and rents equipment. The **scuba-diving conditions information line** (☎ 831/657–1020) is updated regularly.

WALKING From Custom House Plaza, you can walk along the coast in either direction on the 29-mi long **Monterey Bay Coastal Trail** (☎ 831/372–3196 ⊕ www.mprpd.org/parks/coastaltrail.html) for spectacular views of the sea. It runs all the way from north of Monterey to Pacific Grove, with sections continuing around Pebble Beach.

WHALE-
WATCHING

Monterey Whale Watching (⊠ 96 Fisherman's Wharf ☎ 831/372–2203 or 800/200–2203) offers trips throughout the migration season in boats large enough to carry 100 people. **Randy's Fishing Trips** (⊠ 66 Fisherman's Wharf ☎ 831/372–7440 or 800/251–7440) has been operating under the same two skippers since 1958. **Sam's Fishing Fleet** (⊠ 84 Fisherman's Wharf ☎ 831/372–0577 or 800/427–2675) offers whale watching in season.

Shopping

Antiques and reproductions of merchandise popular in Monterey in the 1850s are available at the **Boston Store** (⊠ Monterey State Historic Park, 1 Custom House Plaza, across from Fisherman's Wharf ☎831/649–3364). You can sometimes find little treasures at the **Cannery Row Antique Mall** (⊠ 471 Wave St. ☎ 831/655–0264), which houses a number of local vendors under one roof. **The Cooper Store** (⊠ Polk St. and Munras Ave., in the Cooper-Molera Adobe ☎ 831/649–7111) is an 1800s-themed shop that is dedicated to the preservation of antiquities in the Monterey State Historic Park. **Old Monterey Book Co.** (⊠ 136 Bonifacio Pl., off Alvarado St. ☎ 831/372–3111) specializes in antiquarian books and prints. Historical Society–operated, **The Pickett Fence** (⊠ Monterey State Historic Park, 1 Custom House Plaza, across from Fisherman's Wharf ☎831/649–3364) sells high-end garden accessories and furnishings.

MONTEREY PENINSULA

If you want to see small towns and spectacular vistas, be sure to visit the stretch of coast between Monterey and Big Sur. Each of the communities here is different from the next, and you'll see everything from thatch-roofed cottages to palatial estates, rolling hills to craggy cliffs.

Pacific Grove

20 *2 mi northwest of Monterey via Lighthouse Avenue.*

If not for the dramatic strip of coastline in its backyard, Pacific Grove could easily pass for a typical small town in the heartland. The town, which began as a summer retreat for church groups more than a century ago, recalls its prim and proper Victorian heritage in its host of tiny board-and-batten cottages and stately mansions.

Even before the church groups flocked here, Pacific Grove had been receiving thousands of annual pilgrims in the form of bright orange-and-black monarch butterflies. Known as Butterfly Town USA, Pacific Grove is the winter home of monarchs that migrate south from Canada and the Pacific Northwest to take residence in pine and eucalyptus groves from October through March. The sight of a mass of butterflies hanging from the branches like a long, fluttering veil is unforgettable.

A prime way to enjoy Pacific Grove is to walk or bicycle along its 3 mi of city-owned shoreline, a cliff-top area following Ocean View Boulevard that is landscaped with native plants and has benches on which to sit and gaze at the sea. You can spot many types of birds here, including colonies of web-footed cormorants drawn to the massive rocks rising out of the surf.

Among the Victorians of note is the **Pryor House** (⊠ 429 Ocean View Blvd.), a massive, shingled, private residence with a leaded- and beveled-glass doorway. **Green Gables** (⊠ 5th St. and Ocean View Blvd. ☎ 831/

375–2095), a romantic Swiss Gothic–style mansion with steeply peaked gables and stained-glass windows, is a B&B.

🕓 The view of the coast is gorgeous from **Lovers Point Park** (☎ 831/648-5730), on Ocean View Boulevard midway along the waterfront. The park's sheltered beach has a children's pool and picnic area. Glass-bottom boat rides, which provide views of the plant and sea life below, are offered in summer.

🕓 At the 1855-vintage **Point Pinos Lighthouse,** the oldest continuously operating lighthouse on the West Coast, you can learn about the lighting and foghorn operations and wander through a small museum containing U.S. Coast Guard memorabilia. ⊠ *Lighthouse Ave. off Asilomar Blvd.* ☎ *831/648–5716* ⊕ *www.pgmuseum.org* 🎫 *Free* 🕓 *Thurs.–Mon. 1–4.*

Monarchs sometimes vary their nesting sites from year to year, but the **Monarch Grove Sanctuary** (⊠ 1073 Lighthouse Ave., at Ridge Rd. ⊕ www.pgmuseum.org) is a fairly reliable spot for viewing the butterflies. If you are in Pacific Grove when the monarch butterflies aren't, you can view

🕓 the well-crafted butterfly tree exhibit at the **Pacific Grove Museum of Natural History.** The museum also displays 400 mounted birds and has a touch gallery for children. ⊠ *165 Forest Ave.* ☎ *831/648–3116* ⊕ *www.pgmuseum.org* 🎫 *Free* 🕓 *Tues.–Sun. 10–5.*

Asilomar State Beach (☎ 831/372–4076), a beautiful coastal area, is on Sunset Drive between Point Pinos and the Del Monte Forest in Pacific Grove. The 100 acres of dunes, tidal pools, and pocket-size beaches form one of the region's richest areas for marine life.

Where to Stay & Eat

$$–$$$ ✕ **Old Bath House.** A romantic, nostalgic air permeates this converted bathhouse overlooking the water at Lovers Point. The classic regional menu makes the most of local produce and seafood (such as Monterey Bay prawns) and specializes in game meats. The restaurant has a less expensive menu for late-afternoon diners. ⊠ *620 Ocean View Blvd.* ☎ *831/375–5195* 🍽 *AE, D, DC, MC, V* 🕓 *No lunch.*

$–$$$ ✕ **Fandango.** With its stone walls and country furniture, Fandango has the earthy feel of a southern European farmhouse. Complementing the appointments are the robust flavors of cuisine from the Mediterranean, including paella, cannelloni, and couscous. ⊠ *223 17th St.* ☎ *831/372–3456* 🍽 *AE, D, DC, MC, V.*

$–$$$ ✕ **Taste Café and Bistro.** A favorite of locals, Taste serves hearty European-inspired California cuisine in a casual, airy room with high ceilings and an open kitchen. Meats are excellent here, particularly the marinated lamb fillets and the filet mignon. ⊠ *1199 Forest Ave.* ☎ *831/655–0324* 🍴 *Reservations essential* 🍽 *AE, MC, V* 🕓 *Closed Mon.*

$$ ✕ **Fifi's Café.** Despite its location at the edge of a strip mall a few blocks from downtown, this French bistro is intimate, cozy, and popular with locals, many of whom come for the $19 three-course prix fixe dinner. Try the roast duck with huckleberry sauce. The extensive wine list is reasonably priced, and there are a number of fine choices by the glass. ⊠ *1188 Forest Ave.* ☎ *831/372–5325* 🍴 *Reservations essential* 🍽 *AE, D, DC, MC, V* 🕓 *No lunch Wed.*

$$ ✕ **Joe Rombi's.** Pastas, fish, and veal are the specialties at this modern trattoria, which is the best in town for Italian food. The mood is convivial and welcoming. Try the sautéed veal with red-wine reduction, mozzarella, and herbs. ⊠ *208 17th St.* ☎ *831/373–2416* 🍽 *AE, MC, V* 🕓 *Closed Mon.–Tues.*

$–$$ ✕ **Passion Fish.** South American artwork and artifacts decorate the room, but both Latin and Asian flavors permeate many of the adventurous dishes. Fresh fish is paired with creative sauces; try the crispy squid with spicy orange-cilantro vinaigrette. Wines are an exceptional value

here. ✉ *701 Lighthouse Ave.* ☎ *831/655–3311* ▤ *AE, D, MC, V*
⊘ *Closed Tues. No lunch.*

$ ✕ **Fishwife.** Fresh fish with a Latin accent makes this a favorite of lo-
cals for lunch or a casual dinner. ✉ *1996½ Sunset Dr., at Asilomar Blvd.*
☎ *831/375–7107* ▤ *AE, D, MC, V.*

¢–$ ✕ **Peppers Mexicali Cafe.** This cheerful white-walled restaurant serves fresh
seafood and traditional dishes from Mexico and Latin America. The red
and green salsas are excellent. ✉ *170 Forest Ave.* ☎ *831/373–6892* ▤ *AE,
D, DC, MC, V* ⊘ *Closed Tues. No lunch Sun.*

¢–$ ✕ **Toasties Cafe.** Three-egg omelets, burritos, pancakes, waffles, French toast,
and other breakfast items are served at this crowded café until 3 PM. Lunch
selections include burgers and other sandwiches. Toasties also serves dinner—fish-and-chips, seafood pasta—but it's best to stick to daytime meals.
✉ *702 Lighthouse Ave.* ☎ *831/373–7543* ▤ *AE, D, MC, V.*

★ $$$–$$$$ ▥ **Martine Inn.** In a pink-stucco Mediterranean-style villa overlooking
the water, the glassed-in parlor and several guest rooms have stunning
ocean views. The many antiques include a mahogany suite exhibited at
the 1893 Chicago World's Fair, movie costume designer Edith Head's
bedroom suite, and an 1860 Chippendale Revival four-poster bed. Lav-
ish breakfasts—and elaborate dinners of up to 12 courses—are served
on lace-clad tables set with china, crystal, and silver. Because of the fragility
of the antiques, the inn is not suitable for children. ✉ *255 Ocean View
Blvd., 93950* ☎ *831/373–3388 or 800/852–5588* ▤ *831/373–3896*
⊕ *www.martineinn.com* ⟿ *25 rooms, 1 suite* ⌕ *Some fans, in-room
data ports, refrigerators, hot tub, Internet, meeting rooms, game room,
no-smoking rooms; no room TVs, no a/c* ▤ *AE, D, MC, V* ⦿ *BP.*

$$–$$$$ ▥ **Centrella Inn.** A handsome century-old Victorian mansion two blocks
from Lovers Point Beach, the Centrella Inn fills its guest rooms and cot-
tages with wicker and brass furnishings and claw-foot bathtubs. A side-
board in the large parlor is laden with cookies and hors d'oeuvres in
the afternoon. Because sound can easily travel in a Victorian building,
families are asked to stay in the cottages. ✉ *612 Central Ave., 93950*
☎ *831/372–3372 or 800/233–3372* ▤ *831/372–2036* ⊕ *www.
centrellainn.com* ⟿ *17 rooms, 4 suites, 5 cottages* ⌕ *In-room data ports,
some minibars, some refrigerators, some cable TV, concierge; no a/c, no
smoking* ▤ *AE, D, MC, V* ⦿ *BP.*

★ $$–$$$ ▥ **Green Gables Inn.** Stained-glass windows framing an ornate fireplace
and other interior details compete with the spectacular ocean views at
this Queen Anne–style mansion built by a businessman for his mistress
in 1888. Rooms in a carriage house perched on a hill out back are larger,
have more modern amenities, and afford more privacy, but rooms in
the main house have more charm. ✉ *301 Ocean View Blvd., 93950*
☎ *831/375–2095 or 800/722–1774* ▤ *831/375–5437* ⊕ *www.foursisters.
com* ⟿ *10 rooms, 6 with bath; 1 suite* ⌕ *Some fans, some in-room data
ports, some in-room hot tubs, some cable TV, some in-room VCRs, bicycles; no a/c, no smoking* ▤ *AE, MC, V* ⦿ *BP.*

$–$$$ ▥ **The Inn at 213 Seventeen Mile Drive.** Set in a residential area just past
town, this carefully restored 1920s craftsman-style home and cottage
has spacious, well-appointed rooms. The affable innkeepers offer com-
plimentary wine and hors d'oeuvres in the evening and tea and snacks
throughout the day. Redwood, cypress, and eucalyptus trees tower over
the garden and outdoor hot tub. ✉ *213 17-Mile Dr., 93950* ☎ *831/
642–9514 or 800/526–5666* ▤ *831/642–9546* ⊕ *www.innat17.com*
⟿ *14 rooms* ⌕ *Some fans, in-room data ports, cable TV, hot tub; no
a/c, no smoking* ▤ *AE, MC, V* ⦿ *BP.*

$–$$ ▥ **Asilomar Conference Center.** A summer-camp congeniality prevails at
this assortment of 28 rustic but comfortable lodges in the middle of a
woodsy 105-acre oceanfront state park. Activities include volleyball, bi-

cycle rentals, and ranger-led walking tours. Rooms are available to the general public when they're not booked for conferences. ⊠ *800 Asilomar Blvd. 93950* 🕿 *831/372–8016* 🖷 *831/372–7227* ⊕ *www.visitasilomar.com* 🖙 *313 rooms* ⟁ *Dining room, some refrigerators, pool, business services, meeting rooms; no room phones, no room TVs, no a/c, no smoking* 🖃 *AE, MC, V* ⊧◎⊧ *BP.*

$–$$ 🎛 **Gosby House Inn.** Though in the town center, this turreted yellow Queen Anne Victorian has an informal country air. The two most private rooms are in the rear carriage house; they have fireplaces, balconies, and whirlpool tubs. Buffet breakfast is served in the parlor or garden. ⊠ *643 Lighthouse Ave., 93950* 🕿 *831/375–1287 or 800/527–8828* 🖷 *831/655–9621* ⊕ *www.foursisters.com* 🖙 *22 rooms, 20 with bath* ⟁ *In-room data ports, some in-room hot tubs, some refrigerators, some cable TV, some in-room VCRs; no TV in some rooms, no a/c, no smoking* 🖃 *AE, DC, MC, V* ⊧◎⊧ *BP.*

¢–$$$ 🎛 **The Wilkie's Inn.** Great service and a friendly staff make for a pleasant stay here. One block from 17-Mile Drive, this clean, well-kept motel lies on a quiet, tree-lined street and boasts ocean views. ⊠ *1038 Lighthouse Ave. 93950* 🕿 *831/372–5960 or 866/372-5960* 🖷 *831/655–1681* ⊕ *www.wilkiesinn.com* 🖙 *24 rooms* ⟁ *Kitchenettes, refrigerators, microwaves, cable TV, in-room VCRs; no a/c, no smoking* 🖃 *AE, D, MC, V* ⊧◎⊧ *CP.*

¢–$$ 🎛 **Lighthouse Lodge and Suites.** Near the tip of the peninsula, this complex straddles Lighthouse Avenue—the lodge is on one side, the all-suites facility on the other. With daily afternoon barbecues, it's a woodsy alternative to downtown Pacific Grove's B&B scene. Suites have fireplaces and whirlpool tubs. Standard rooms are simple, but they're decent in size and much less expensive. ⊠ *1150 and 1249 Lighthouse Ave., 93950* 🕿 *831/655–2111 or 800/858–1249* 🖷 *831/655–4922* ⊕ *www.lhls.com* 🖙 *64 rooms, 31 suites* ⟁ *Fans, in-room data ports, some kitchenettes, microwaves, refrigerators, cable TV with movies, pool, hot tub, some pets allowed (fee), meeting rooms; no a/c, no smoking* 🖃 *AE, D, DC, MC, V* ⊧◎⊧ *BP.*

Sports & the Outdoors

GOLF The greens fee at the 18-hole **Pacific Grove Municipal Golf Links** (⊠ 77 Asilomar Blvd. 🕿 831/648–5777) runs between $32 and $38 (you can play 9 holes for between $18 and $20), with an 18-hole twilight rate of $20. Optional carts cost $28. The course has spectacular ocean views on its back nine. Tee times may be reserved up to seven days in advance.

TENNIS The **Pacific Grove Municipal Courts** (⊠ 515 Junipero St. 🕿 831/648–5729) are available for public play for a small hourly fee.

Shopping

American Tin Cannery Outlet Center (⊠ 125 Ocean View Blvd. 🕿 831/372–3071) carries designer clothing, jewelry, accessories, and home decorating items at discounts between 25% and 65%. **Wooden Nickel** (⊠ Central and Fountain Aves. 🕿 831/646–8050) sells accent pieces for the home.

17-Mile Drive

㉑ *Off Sunset Dr. in Pacific Grove or off North San Antonio Rd. in Carmel.*

Fodor'sChoice
★

Primordial nature resides in quiet harmony with palatial late-20th-century estates along 17-Mile Drive, which winds through an 8,400-acre microcosm of the Monterey coastal landscape. Dotting the drive are rare Monterey cypresses, trees so gnarled and twisted that Robert Louis Stevenson described them as "ghosts fleeing before the wind." Some sightseers balk at the $8-per-car fee collected at the gates—this is the only private toll road west of the Mississippi—but most find the drive well worth the price. An alternative is to grab a bike: cyclists tour for free, as do those with confirmed lunch or dinner reservations at one of the hotels.

You can take in views of the impeccable greens at **Pebble Beach Golf Links** (⌧ 17-Mile Dr. near the Lodge at Pebble Beach ☎ 800/654–9300 ⊕ www.pebblebeach.com) over a drink or lunch at the Lodge at Pebble Beach. The ocean plays a major role in the 18th hole of the famed golf course. Each winter the course is the main site of the AT&T Pebble Beach Pro-Am (formerly the Bing Crosby Pro-Am), where show business celebrities and golf pros team up for one of the nation's most glamorous tournaments.

Many of the stately homes along 17-Mile Drive reflect the classic Monterey or Spanish mission style typical of the region. A standout is the **Crocker Marble Palace,** about a mile south of the Lone Cypress; it's a private waterfront estate inspired by a Byzantine castle. This mansion is easily identifiable by its dozens of marble arches.

Bird Rock, the largest of several islands at the southern end of the Monterey Country Club's golf course, teems with harbor seals, sea lions, cormorants, and pelicans. Sea creatures and birds also make use of **Seal Rock,** the largest of a group of islands south of Bird Rock. The most-photographed tree along 17-Mile Drive is the weather-sculpted **Lone Cypress,** which grows out of a precipitous outcropping above the waves about 2 mi south of Seal Rock. You can stop for a view of the Lone Cypress at a parking area, but you can't walk out to the tree.

Where to Stay & Eat

$$$$ ✕⊡ **Inn at Spanish Bay.** This resort sprawls across a breathtaking stretch of shoreline. Under the same management as the Lodge at Pebble Beach—where you have privileges—the inn has a slightly more casual feel, though its 600-square-ft rooms are no less luxurious. Peppoli's restaurant ($–$$$), which serves Tuscan cuisine, overlooks the coast and the golf links. Try Roy's Restaurant ($–$$$) for more casual and innovative Euro–Asian fare. ⌧ *2700 17-Mile Dr., Pebble Beach 93953* ☎ *831/647–7500 or 800/654–9300* ⊟*831/644–7960* ⊕*www.pebblebeach.com* ⌁ *252 rooms, 17 suites* ♢ *3 restaurants, room service, in-room data ports, minibars, refrigerators, cable TV with movies and video games, in-room VCRs, 18-hole golf course, 8 tennis courts, pro shop, pool, aerobics, health club, sauna, steam room, beach, bicycles, hiking, bar, lobby lounge, laundry service, concierge, Internet, business services, meeting rooms; no smoking* ⊟ *AE, D, DC, MC, V.*

★ $$$$ ✕⊡ **Lodge at Pebble Beach.** Luxurious rooms with fireplaces and wonderful views set the tone at this resort that was built in 1919. The golf course, tennis club, and equestrian center are highly regarded; you also have privileges at the Inn at Spanish Bay. Overlooking the 18th green, Club XIX restaurant ($$$$; jackets recommended) is an intimate, clublike dining room serving expertly prepared French cuisine. ⌧ *1700 17-Mile Dr., Pebble Beach 93953* ☎ *831/624–3811 or 800/654–9300* ⊟*831/644–7960* ⊕*www.pebblebeach.com* ⌁*142 rooms, 19 suites* ♢*No a/c, 3 restaurants, coffee shop, in-room data ports, some in-room hot tubs, minibars, refrigerators, cable TV with movies and video games, in-room VCRs, 18-hole golf course, 12 tennis courts, pro shop, pool, gym, health club, sauna, spa, beach, bicycles, horseback riding, 2 bars, lobby lounge, laundry service, concierge, Internet, business services, meeting rooms, some pets allowed; no a/c, no smoking* ⊟ *AE, D, DC, MC, V.*

★ $$$$ ⊡ **Casa Palmero.** This exclusive spa resort captures the essence of a Mediterranean villa. Rooms are decorated with sumptuous fabrics and fine art, each has a wood-burning fireplace and heated floor, and some have a private outdoor patio with an in-ground Jacuzzi. Complimentary cocktail service is offered each evening in the main hall and library. The spa is state-of-the-art, and you have use of all facilities at the Lodge at Pebble Beach and the Inn at Spanish Bay. ⊠ *1518 Cypress Dr., Pebble Beach, 93953* ☏ *831/622–6650 or 800/654–9300* ⎙ *831/622–6655* ⊕ *www.pebblebeach.com* ⟳ *21 rooms, 3 suites* ⟳ *Room service, in-room data ports, some in-room hot tubs, minibars, refrigerators, cable TV with movies and video games, in-room VCRs, golf privileges, pool, health club, spa, bicycles, billiards, lounge, library, laundry service, concierge, meeting rooms; no a/c, no smoking* ⊟ *AE, D, DC, MC, V.*

Sports & the Outdoors

GOLF The **Links at Spanish Bay** (⊠ 17-Mile Dr., north end ☏ 831/624–3811, 831/624–6611, or 800/654–9300), which hugs a choice stretch of shoreline, is designed in the rugged manner of a traditional Scottish course, with sand dunes and coastal marshes interspersed among the greens. The greens fee is $210, plus $25 for cart rental (cart included for resort guests); nonguests can reserve tee times two months in advance.

Pebble Beach Golf Links (⊠ 17-Mile Dr. near the Lodge at Pebble Beach ☏ 831/624–3811, 831/624–6611, or 800/654–9300) attracts golfers from around the world, despite a greens fee of $350, plus $25 for an optional cart (complimentary cart for guests of the Pebble Beach and Spanish Bay resorts). Nonguests can reserve a tee time only one day in advance on a space-available basis (up to a year for groups); resort guests can reserve up to 18 months in advance.

Peter Hay (⊠ 17-Mile Dr. ☏ 831/625–8518 or 831/624–6611), a 9-hole, par-3 course, charges $20 per person, no reservations necessary. **Poppy Hills** (⊠ 3200 Lopez Rd., at 17-Mile Dr. ☏ 831/625–2035), a splendid 18-hole course designed in 1986 by Robert Trent Jones Jr., has a greens fee of $125–$150; an optional cart costs $30. Individuals may reserve up to one month in advance, groups up to a year.

Spyglass Hill (⊠ Stevenson Dr. and Spyglass Hill Rd. ☏ 831/624–3811, 831/624–6611, or 800/654–9300) is among the most challenging Pebble Beach courses. With the first five holes bordering on the Pacific and the rest of the 18 reaching deep into the Del Monte Forest, the views offer some consolation. The greens fee is $250; an optional cart costs $25 (the cart is complimentary for resort guests). Reservations are essential and may be made up to one month in advance (18 months for guests).

HORSEBACK The **Pebble Beach Equestrian Center** (⊠ Portola Rd. and Alva La. ☏ 831/
RIDING 624–2756) offers guided trail rides along the beach and through 26 mi of bridle trails in the Del Monte Forest.

Carmel-by-the-Sea

㉒ *4 mi south of Monterey on Hwy. 1.*

Although the community has grown quickly through the years and its population quadruples with tourists on weekends and in summer, Carmel-by-the-Sea, known simply as Carmel, retains its identity as a quaint village. Self-consciously charming, the town is populated by many former celebrities, major and minor, and it has a lot of quirky ordinances. For instance, women wearing high heels do not have the right to pursue legal action if they trip and fall on the cobblestone streets; drivers who hit a tree and leave the scene are charged with hit-and-run; live music is banned in local watering holes; and ice cream parlors are not allowed to sell cones—only cups—because children might drop them, leaving unsightly puddles on the pretty streets. Buildings still have no street numbers—and consequently no mail delivery (if you really want to see the locals, go to the post office). Artists started this community, and their legacy is evident in the numerous galleries. Wander the side streets off Ocean Avenue, poking into hidden courtyards and stopping at cafés to recharge on tea and crumpets.

Downtown Carmel's chief lure is shopping, especially along its main street, **Ocean Avenue,** between Junipero Avenue and Camino Real; the architecture here is a mishmash of ersatz Tudor, Mediterranean, and other styles. **Carmel Plaza** (⊠ Ocean and Junipero Aves. ☎ 831/624–0137), in the east end of the village proper, holds more than 50 shops and restaurants.

★ Long before it became a shopping and browsing destination, Carmel was an important religious center during the establishment of Spanish California. That heritage is preserved in the Mission San Carlos Borroméo del Rio Carmelo, more commonly known as the **Carmel Mission.** Founded in 1771, it served as headquarters for the mission system in California under Father Junípero Serra. Adjoining the stone church is a tranquil garden planted with California poppies. Museum rooms at the mission include an early kitchen, Serra's spartan sleeping quarters, and the first college library in California. ⊠ *3080 Rio Rd. (at Lasuen Dr.)* ☎ *831/624–3600* ⊕ *www.carmelmission.org* ☜ *$4* ⊙ *Sept.–May, Mon.–Sat. 9:30–4:30, Sun. 10:30–4:30; June–Aug., Mon.–Sat. 9:30–7:30, Sun. 10:30–7:30.*

Scattered throughout the pines in Carmel are the houses and cottages that were built for the writers, artists, and photographers who discovered the area decades ago. Among the most impressive dwellings is **Tor House,** a stone cottage built in 1919 by poet Robinson Jeffers on a craggy knoll overlooking the sea. Portraits, books, and unusual art objects fill the low-ceiling rooms. The highlight of the small estate is Hawk Tower, a detached edifice set with stones from the Carmel coastline as well as one from the Great Wall of China. The docents who lead tours (six persons maximum) are well informed about the poet's work and life. ⊠ *26304 Ocean View Ave.* ☎ *831/624–1813 or 831/624–1840* ⊕ *www.torhouse.org* ☜ *$7* ☞ *No children under 12* ⊙ *Tours on the hour Fri.–Sat. 10–3; reservations recommended.*

Carmel's greatest beauty is its rugged coastline, with pine and cypress forests and countless inlets. **Carmel Beach** (⊠ End of Ocean Ave.), an easy walk from downtown shops, has sparkling white sands and magnificent sunsets. **Carmel River State Beach** stretches for 106 acres along Carmel Bay. On sunny days the waters appear nearly as turquoise as those of the Caribbean. The sugar-white beach is adjacent to a bird sanctuary, where you might spot pelicans, kingfishers, hawks, and sandpipers. ⊠ *Off Scenic Rd., south of Carmel Beach* ☎ *831/624–4909 or 831/ 649–2836* ⊕ *www.cal-parks.ca.gov* ☜ *Free* ⊙ *Daily 9 AM–sunset.*

★ **Point Lobos State Reserve,** a 350-acre headland harboring a wealth of marine life, lies a few miles south of Carmel. The best way to explore the reserve is to walk along one of its many trails. The Cypress Grove Trail leads through a forest of Monterey cypress (one of only two natural groves remaining) clinging to the rocks above an emerald-green cove. Sea Lion Point Trail is a good place to view sea lions. From those and other trails you may also spot otters, harbor seals, and (during winter and spring) migrating whales. An additional 750 acres of the reserve is an undersea marine park open to qualified scuba divers. Arrive early (or in late afternoon) to avoid crowds; the parking lots fill up. No pets are allowed. ⊠ *Hwy. 1* ☎ *831/624–4909, 831/624–8413 for scuba-diving reservations* ⊕ *www.pointlobos.org* ☜ *$6 per vehicle* ⊙ *Apr.–Oct., daily 9–7; Nov.–Mar., daily 9–5.*

★ **$$$–$$$$** ✕ **Casanova.** Southern French and northern Italian cuisine come together at Casanova, one of the most romantic restaurants in Carmel. A heated outdoor garden and more than 1,800 domestic and imported vintages from the hand-dug wine cellar enhance the dining experience. The seasonal menu includes such delights as grilled veal chop with sautéed morel mushrooms. All entrées come with an antipasto plate and choice of appetizers. Private dining and a special menu are offered at Van Gogh's Table, a very special table imported from France's Auberge Ravoux. ⊠ *5th Ave. between San Carlos and Mission Sts.* ☎ *831/625–0501* ⟨ *Reservations essential* ⊟ *AE, MC, V.*

$$$ ✕ **Anton and Michel.** Expect superb European cuisine at this elegant restaurant in Carmel's shopping district. The tender lamb dishes are fantastic, and well complemented by the wines. The ultimate treats, however, are the flaming desserts. You can dine in the outdoor courtyard in summer. ⊠ *Mission St. and 7th Ave.* ☎ *831/624–2406* ⟨ *Reservations essential* ⊟ *AE, D, DC, MC, V.*

$$$ ✕ **La Bohème.** The chefs at campy La Bohème prepare one entrée each night, accompanied by soup and salad. You may find yourself bumping elbows with your neighbor in the faux-European-village courtyard, but the predominantly French cuisine is very good, and the mood is convivial. ⊠ *Dolores St. and 7th Ave.* ☎ *831/624–7500* ⟨ *Reservations not accepted* ⊟ *MC, V* ✆ *Closed Jan. No lunch.*

$$–$$$$ ✕ **French Poodle.** Specialties on the traditional French menu at this intimate restaurant include the duck breast in port and the abalone. The floating island—a meringue-and-custard combo—is a delicious dessert. The staff takes a vacation in the second and third weeks of January. ⊠ *Junipero and 5th Aves.* ☎ *831/624–8643* ⟨ *Reservations essential* ⊟ *AE, DC, MC, V* ✆ *Closed Sun. No lunch.*

$$–$$$$ ✕ **Kurt's Carmel Chop House.** USDA-prime steaks and chops are cooked over almond and oak woods at this stylish steak house, which serves up an abundance of seafood and inventive appetizers. ⊠ *5th Ave. and San Carlos St.* ☎ *831/625–1199* ⟨ *Reservations essential* ⊟ *AE, MC, V* ✆ *No lunch.*

★ **$$–$$$$** ✕ **Robert's Bistro.** Chef-owner Robert Kincaid is a master culinarian, and the menu at his French bistro stresses seasonal ingredients. Dried sage and lavender hanging from exposed ceiling beams, painted floors, and ocher-washed walls will make you feel as if you've stepped into an old farmhouse in Provence. Cassoulet made with white beans, duck confit, rabbit sausage, and garlic prawns are always on the stove. Leave room for dessert, particularly the soufflé with lemon and orange zest or the chocolate bag with chocolate shake, a masterful invention. ⊠ *Crossroads Center, 217 Crossroads Blvd.* ☎ *831/624–9626* ⟨ *Reservations essential* ⊟ *AE, D, DC, MC, V* ✆ *Closed Mon. No lunch.*

$$–$$$ ✕ **Flying Fish.** Simple in appearance yet bold with its flavors, this Japanese–California seafood restaurant has quickly established itself as one of Carmel's most inventive eateries. Among the best entrées is the almond-crusted sea bass served with Chinese cabbage and rock shrimp stir-fry. ⊠ *Mission St. between Ocean and 7th Aves.* ☎ *831/625–1962* ⊟ *AE, D, MC, V* ✆ *Closed Tues. No lunch.*

$$–$$$ ✕ **The Forge in the Forest.** This former blacksmith's shop houses a lively bar and restaurant suited to all ages and tastes. The menu has excellent prime steaks, sandwiches, and pizzas. You can sit under the trees outside by a fireplace on cool evenings. ⊠ *5th Ave. and Junipero Ave.* ☎ *831/ 624–2233* ⊟ *AE, MC, V.*

$$–$$$ ✕ **Grasing's Coastal Cuisine.** Chef Kurt Grasing's contemporary adaptations of European provincial and American cooking include a roast rack of lamb marinated in pomegranate juice, and medallions of pork with shiitake mushrooms, bacon, peas, and polenta. A casually elegant room, gracious service, and an extensive wine list make this one of Carmel's top restaurants. ☒ *6th Ave. and Mission St.* ☎ *831/624–6562* ⌕ *Reservations essential* ▭ *AE, D, DC, MC, V.*

$$–$$$ ✕ **Loutas/L'Escargot.** Great care and attention go into every plate at this cozy, romantic, unpretentious, and understated classic French restaurant. Menu highlights include a caramelized onion and goat cheese tart, bouillabaisse, and beef Wellington. Or choose the $27 prix-fixe dinner. Service is warm and attentive. ☒ *Mission St. between 4th and 5th Aves.* ☎ *831/620–1942* ⌕ *Reservations essential* ▭ *AE, DC, MC, V* ☺ *Closed Tues. No lunch.*

$–$$$ ✕ **Bahama Billy's.** The energy is electric at always-bustling Bahama Billy's. An excellent and diverse menu of Caribbean food combined with the colorful and lively action in the dining room make this a prime spot for fun and good eating in Carmel. Because it's outside the area covered by the town's strict zoning laws, there is often live music in the bar. ☒ *2690 The Barnyard, Barnyard Shopping Center Hwy. 1 and Carmel Valley Rd.* ☎ *831/626–0430* ⌕ *Reservations essential* ▭ *AE, D, MC, V.*

$–$$$ ✕ **Lugano Swiss Bistro.** Fondue is the centerpiece here. The house specialty is a version made with Gruyère, Emmentaler, and Appenzeller. Rosemary chicken, plum-basted duck, and fennel pork loin rotate on the rotisserie. Ask for a table in the back room, which contains a hand-painted street scene of Lugano. ☒ *The Barnyard, Barnyard Shopping Center Hwy. 1 and Carmel Valley Rd.* ☎ *831/626–3779* ▭ *AE, DC, MC, V* ☺ *Closed Mon.*

$–$$$ ✕ **Rio Grill.** The best bets in this lively Santa Fe–style roadhouse are the meat and seafood cooked over an oak-wood grill. The fire-roasted artichoke and the Monterey Bay squid are exceptional starters. ☒ *Crossroads Center, 101 Crossroads Blvd., Hwy. 1 and Rio Rd.* ☎ *831/625–5436* ⌕ *Reservations essential* ▭ *AE, D, DC, MC, V.*

$–$$ ✕ **Caffé Napoli.** Redolent of garlic and olive oil, this small, atmospheric Italian restaurant is a favorite of locals, who come for the crisp-crusted pizzas, house-made pastas, and fresh seafood. Specialties include grilled artichokes, fresh salmon and grilled vegetable risotto, and fisherman's pasta. There's a good Italian wine list. ☒ *Ocean Ave. and Lincoln St.* ☎ *831/625–4033* ⌕ *Reservations essential* ▭ *MC, V.*

¢–$$ ✕ **Jack London's.** Most anyone who's awake after dinner in Carmel can be found at Jack London's. This publike spot is the only Carmel restaurant to serve food until 12:30 AM, and it's where the locals eat and drink. The menu includes everything from snacks to steaks. ☒ *Su Vecino Court, on Dolores St. between 5th and 6th Aves.* ☎ *831/624–2336* ▭ *AE, D, DC, MC, V.*

¢–$ ✕ **The Cottage Restaurant.** The best breakfast in Carmel is served here. This local favorite offers six different preparations of eggs Benedict, sweet and savory crepes, and sandwiches and homemade soups at lunch. Good dinners are served on weekends, but the best meals here are served in the daytime. ☒ *Lincoln St. between Ocean and 7th Aves.* ☎ *831/625–6260* ▭ *MC, V* ☺ *No dinner Sun.–Wed.*

★ $$$$ ✕▣ **Highlands Inn.** High on a hill overlooking the Pacific, this place has superb views. Accommodations are in spa suites (each with its own Jacuzzi) and condominium-style units, a number with full kitchens, fireplaces, and decks overlooking the ocean. The excellent prix-fixe menus at the inn's Pacific's Edge restaurant ($$$$; jackets recommended) blend French technique and California cooking; the sommelier pairs the perfect wines. ☒ *120 Highlands Dr., 93921* ☎ *831/624–3801, 800/682–4811, 831/622–5445 for restaurant* 🖷 *831/626–1574* ⊕ *highlandsinn. hyatt.com* ⬱ *105 suites, 37 rooms* ♿ *2 restaurants, room service, in-room data ports, in-room safes, some in-room hot tubs, some kitchenettes,* *refrigerators, cable TV with movies, some in-room VCRs, pool, gym, 3 hot tubs, bicycles, 2 lounges, piano, baby-sitting, laundry service, concierge, Internet, business services, meeting rooms, some pets allowed (fee), no-smoking rooms; no a/c ☰ AE, D, DC, MC, V.*

$$$$ 🏨 **Carriage House Inn.** This small inn with a wood-shingle exterior has spacious rooms with beam ceilings, fireplaces, down comforters, and, in most, whirlpool baths. Afternoon wine and hors d'oeuvres are included. ⊠ *Junipero Ave. between 7th and 8th Aves., 93921* 🕾 *831/625–2585 or 800/422–4732* 🖷 *831/624–0974* ⊕ *www.innsbythesea.com* 🛏 *11 rooms, 2 suites* ♨ *In-room safes, some in-room hot tubs, minibars, refrigerators, cable TV, in-room VCRs; no a/c* ☰ *AE, D, MC, V* *CP.*

$$$$ 🏨 **Tickle Pink Inn.** Atop a towering cliff, this inn has views of the Big Sur coastline, which you can contemplate from your private balcony. Fall asleep to the sound of surf crashing below and wake up to Continental breakfast and the morning paper in bed. If you prefer the company of fellow travelers, breakfast is also served buffet style in the lounge, as are complimentary wine and cheese in the afternoon. Many rooms have wood-burning fireplaces, and there are six luxurious spa suites. ⊠ *155 Highlands Dr., 93923* 🕾 *831/624–1244 or 800/635–4774* 🖷 *831/626– 9516* ⊕ *www.ticklepink.com* 🛏 *24 rooms, 11 suites* ♨ *Fans, in-room data ports, some in-room hot tubs, refrigerators, cable TV with in-room VCRs, outdoor hot tub, concierge; no a/c, no smoking* ☰ *AE, DC, MC, V* *CP.*

★ $$$–$$$$ 🏨 **Cobblestone Inn.** Stones from the Carmel River completely cover the lower level of the inn; the work of local artisans is featured throughout. Guest rooms have stone fireplaces too, as well as thick quilts on the beds. Country antiques in the sitting-room area and afternoon wine and hors d'oeuvres contribute to the homey feel at this English-style inn. ⊠ *Junipero Ave. between 7th and 8th Aves. 93921* 🕾 *831/625–5222 or 800/833–8836* 🖷 *831/625–0478* ⊕ *www.foursisters.com* 🛏 *22 rooms, 2 suites* ♨ *In-room data ports, refrigerators, cable TV, bicycles no a/c, no smoking* ☰ *AE, DC, MC, V* *BP.*

$$–$$$$ 🏨 **Briarwood Inn.** This ivy-covered B&B offers comfortable accommodations within steps of Carmel's shops and galleries. Most rooms have fireplaces and some have flower-lined verandas. A Continental breakfast is available in your room or in the common area. ⊠ *San Carlos St. between 4th and 5th Aves., Box 5245, 93921* 🕾 *831/626–9056 or 800/999–8788* 🖷 *831/626–8900* ⊕ *www.briarwood-inn-carmel.com* 🛏 *12 rooms* ♨ *Fans, refrigerators, cable TV, in-room VCRs; no a/c, no smoking* ☰ *AE, MC, V* *CP.*

$$–$$$$ 🏨 **La Playa Hotel.** Norwegian artist Christopher Jorgensen built the original structure in 1902 for his bride, a member of the Ghirardelli chocolate clan. The property has since undergone many additions and now resembles a Mediterranean estate. Though some rooms are small and could use a few modern amenities, the history and location more than compensate. You can also opt for a cottage; most have full kitchens and wood-burning fireplaces, and all have a patio or a terrace. ⊠ *Camino Real at 8th Ave., 93921* 🕾 *831/624–6476 or 800/582–8900* 🖷 *831/ 624–7966* ⊕ *www.laplayahotel.com* 🛏 *75 rooms, 5 cottages* ♨ *Restaurant, refrigerators, cable TV, pool, bar, laundry service, business services, meeting rooms, massage; no a/c, no smoking* ☰ *AE, DC, MC, V.*

$$–$$$ 🏨 **Pine Inn.** A favorite with generations of Carmel visitors, the Pine Inn has red-and-black Victorian style, complete with grandfather clock, padded fabric wall panels, antique tapestries, and marble-top furnishings. Only four blocks from the beach, the complex includes a brick courtyard of specialty shops and a modern Italian restaurant. ⊠ *Ocean Ave. and Lincoln St., 93921* 🕾 *831/624–3851 or 800/228–3851* 🖷 *831/624– 3030* ⊕ *www.pine-inn.com* 🛏 *43 rooms, 6 suites* ♨ *Restaurant, fans,*

some in-room data ports, some refrigerators, cable TV, laundry service, meeting room; no smoking ═ AE, D, DC, MC, V.

$$–$$$$ 🏨 **Mission Ranch.** Sheep graze in the ocean-side pasture near the 19th-century farmhouse at Mission Ranch. The six rooms in the main house are set around a Victorian parlor; other options include a cottage, a hayloft, and converted barn rooms. Handmade quilts and carved wooden beds complement the country location. ✉ *26270 Dolores St., 93923* ☎ *831/ 624–6436 or 800/538–8221* 🖷 *831/626–4163* 🖙 *31 rooms* ♻ *Restaurant, fans, in-room data ports, some in-room hot tubs, some refrigerators, cable TV, 6 tennis courts, pro shop, gym, piano bar; no a/c, no smoking ═ AE, MC, V* ⦿ *CP.*

$$–$$$ 🏨 **Cypress Inn.** When Doris Day became part-owner of this inn in 1988, she added her own touches, such as posters from her many movies and photo albums of her favorite canines (pets are welcome in most rooms here). In nice weather you can enjoy your Continental breakfast in a garden surrounded by bougainvillea. ✉ *Lincoln St. and 7th Ave., Box Y, 93921* ☎ *831/624–3871 or 800/443–7443* 🖷 *831/624–8216* ⊕ *www. cypress-inn.com* 🖙 *33 rooms, 1 suite* ♻ *Fans, in-room data ports, some in-room hot tubs, cable TV, bar, laundry service, concierge, some pets allowed (fee); no a/c in some rooms, no smoking ═ AE, MC, V* ⦿ *CP.*

$$–$$$ 🏨 **Tally Ho Inn.** Boasting an English garden courtyard, this is one of the few small hotels in Carmel's center with good views of the ocean. Penthouse units have fireplaces. ✉ *Monte Verde St. and 6th Ave., 93921* ☎ *831/ 624–2232 or 877/482–5594* 🖷 *831/624–2661* ⊕ *www.tallyho-inn.com* 🖙 *12 rooms, 2 suites* ♻ *Some fans, some in-room data ports, cable TV, laundry service; no a/c, no smoking ═ AE, D, DC, MC, V* ⦿ *CP.*

$–$$$ 🏨 **Best Western Carmel Mission Inn.** This motel on the edge of Carmel Valley has a lushly landscaped pool and hot tub area and is close to the Barnyard and Crossroads shopping centers. Rooms vary in size; request a large one. ✉ *3665 Rio Rd., at Hwy. 1, 93923* ☎ *831/624–1841 or 800/348– 9090* 🖷 *831/624–8684* ⊕ *www.bestwestern.com* 🖙 *163 rooms, 2 suites* ♻ *Restaurant, room service, in-room data ports, refrigerators, cable TV, pool, exercise equipment, 2 hot tubs, bar, business services, some pets allowed (fee), no-smoking rooms ═ AE, D, DC, MC, V.*

$–$$$ 🏨 **Carmel River Inn.** Besides attracting those looking for a relative bargain in pricey Carmel, this mid-20th-century inn appeals to travelers who enjoy a bit of distance from the madding crowd. Yet the area's beaches are only 1½ mi away. The blue-and-white motel at the front of the property contains units with cable TV, small refrigerators, and coffeemakers. Cabins out back sleep up to six; some have fireplaces and kitchens. ✉ *Hwy. 1 at Carmel River Bridge, 93922* ☎ *831/624–1575 or 800/882– 8142* 🖷 *831/624–0290* ⊕ *www.carmelriverinn.com* 🖙 *19 rooms, 24 cabins* ♻ *Some microwaves, refrigerators, cable TV, pool, Internet, some pets allowed (fee), no-smoking rooms; no a/c ═ MC, V.*

$–$$ 🏨 **Lobos Lodge.** The white-stucco motel units here are set amid cypress, oaks, and pines on the edge of the business district. All accommodations have fireplaces, and some have private patios. ✉ *Monte Verde St. and Ocean Ave., 93921* ☎ *831/624–3874* 🖷 *831/624–0135* ⊕ *www. loboslodge.com* 🖙 *28 rooms, 2 suites* ♻ *Fans, in-room data ports, refrigerators, cable TV, no-smoking rooms, no a/c ═ AE, MC, V* ⦿ *CP.*

$–$$ 🏨 **Sea View Inn.** In a residential area a few hundred feet from the beach, this restored 1905 home has a double parlor with two fireplaces, Oriental rugs, canopy beds, and a spacious front porch. Afternoon tea and evening wine and cheese are offered daily. Because of the fragile furnishings and quiet atmosphere, families with kids would be more comfortable elsewhere. ✉ *Camino Real between 11th and 12th Aves., 93921* ☎ *831/ 624–8778* 🖷 *831/625–5901* ⊕ *www.seaviewinncarmel.com* 🖙 *8 rooms,*

6 with private bath ♿ *No room phones, no room TVs, no a/c, no smoking* ⊟ *AE, MC, V* ⊠ *CP.*

The Arts

Carmel Bach Festival (☎ 831/624–2046 ⊕ www.bachfestival.org) has presented the works of Johann Sebastian Bach and his contemporaries in concerts and recitals since 1935. The festival runs for three weeks, starting mid-July. **Monterey County Symphony** (☎ 831/624–8511 ⊕ www.montereysymphony.org) performs classical concerts from October through May at the Sunset Community Cultural Center.

The **Pacific Repertory Theater** (☎ 831/622–0700 ⊕ www.pacrep.org) puts on the Carmel Shakespeare Festival from August through October and performs contemporary dramas and comedies from February through July. **Sunset Community Cultural Center** (⊠ San Carlos St. between 8th and 10th Aves. ☎ 831/624–3996), which presents concerts, lectures, and headline performers, is the Monterey Bay area's top venue for the performing arts.

Shopping

ART GALLERIES **Carmel Art Association** (⊠ Dolores St. between 5th and 6th Aves. ☎ 831/624–6176 ⊕ www.carmelart.org) exhibits the paintings, sculpture, and prints of local artists. **Galerie Pleine Aire** (⊠ Dolores St. between 5th and 6th Aves. ☎ 831/625–5686) showcases oil paintings by a group of seven local artists. **Highlands Sculpture Gallery** (⊠ Dolores St. between 5th and 6th Aves. ☎ 831/624–0535) is devoted to contemporary indoor and outdoor sculpture, primarily works in stone, bronze, wood, metal, and glass. **Masterpiece Gallery** (⊠ Dolores St. and 6th Ave. ☎ 831/624–2163) shows early California impressionist art. **Photography West Gallery** (⊠ Ocean Ave. and Dolores St. ☎ 831/625–1587) exhibits photography by Ansel Adams and other 20th-century artists.

SPECIALTY SHOPS **Madrigal** (⊠ Carmel Plaza and Mission St. ☎ 831/624–3477) carries sportswear, sweaters, and accessories for women. **Mischievous Rabbit** (⊠ Lincoln Ave. between 7th and Ocean Aves. ☎ 831/624–6854) sells toys, nursery accessories, books, music boxes, china, and children's clothing, with a specialty in Beatrix Potter items. **Pat Areias Sterling** (⊠ Ocean Ave. between Lincoln Ave. and Delores St. ☎ 831/626–8668) puts a respectfully modern spin on the Mexican tradition of silversmithing with its line of sterling silver belt buckles, jewelry, and accessories. **Shop in the Garden** (⊠ Lincoln Ave. between Ocean and 7th Aves. ☎ 831/624–6047) is an indoor-outdoor sculpture garden where you can buy fountains or garden accoutrements. You'll hear the tinkle of its wind chimes before you see the courtyard establishment.

Carmel Valley

❷❸ *10 mi east of Carmel-by-the-Sea, Hwy. 1 to Carmel Valley Rd.*

Carmel Valley Road, which heads inland from Highway 1 south of Carmel, is the main thoroughfare through the town of Carmel Valley, a secluded enclave of horse ranchers and other well-heeled residents who prefer the area's sunny climate to the fog and wind on the coast. Tiny Carmel Valley Village, about 13 mi southeast of Carmel via Carmel Valley Road, has several crafts shops and art galleries.

Garland Ranch Regional Park (⊠ Carmel Valley Rd., 9 mi east of Carmel ☎ 831/659–4488 ⊕ www.mprpd.org/parks/garland.html) has hiking trails and picnic tables. The beautiful **Château Julien** winery, recognized internationally for its chardonnays and merlots, gives tours on weekdays at 10:30 and 2:30 and weekends at 12:30 and 2:30, all by appointment.

The tasting room is open daily. ⊠ *8940 Carmel Valley Rd.* ☎ *831/624–2600* ⊕ *www.chateaujulien.com* ⊗ *Weekdays 8–5, weekends 11–5.*

Where to Stay & Eat

$–$$ ✕**Café Rustica.** Italian-inspired country cooking is the focus at this lively roadhouse. Specialties include roasted meats, pastas, and pizzas from the wood-fired oven. Because of the tile floors, it can get quite noisy inside; opt for a table outside for a quieter meal. ⊠ *10 Delfino Pl.* ☎ *831/659–4444* ⚖ *Reservations essential* ⊟ *MC, V* ⊗ *Closed Wed.*

¢ ✕**Wagon Wheel Coffee Shop.** Grab a seat at the counter or wait for a table at this local hangout decorated with wood-beam ceilings, hanging wagon wheels, cowboy hats, and lassos. Then chow down on substantial breakfasts of *huevos rancheros* (Mexican-style fried eggs on corn tortillas, covered in a mild chilie sauce), Italian sausage and eggs, or trout and eggs; this is also the place to stoke up on biscuits and gravy. For lunch choose among a dozen types of burgers and other sandwiches. ⊠ *Valley Hill Center, Carmel Valley Rd. next to Quail Lodge* ☎ *831/624–8878* ⊟ *No credit cards* ⊗ *No dinner.*

★ $$$$ ✕🏠**Bernardus Lodge.** A first-rate spa and outstanding cuisine are the focus at this luxury resort, where services are geared to oenophiles and gourmands. Spacious guest rooms have vaulted ceilings, featherbeds, fireplaces, patios, and double-size bathtubs. Marinus, the intimate, formal dining room ($$$$; jacket recommended), emphasizes modern French technique. Chef Cal Stamenov is one of the area's few master culinarians; he changes the menu daily to reflect availability of local game and produce. ⊠ *415 Carmel Valley Rd., 93924* ☎ *831/659–3131 or 888/648–9463* 🖷 *831/659–3529* ⊕ *www.bernardus.com* ⤶ *57 rooms* ⚙ *2 restaurants, room service, in-room data ports, minibars, refrigerators, cable TV with movies, some in-room VCRs, tennis court, pool, gym, hair salon, hot tub, sauna, spa, steam room, croquet, hiking, lawn bowling, bar, lobby lounge, laundry service, concierge, Internet, meeting room; no smoking* ⊟ *AE, D, DC, MC, V.*

★ $$$$ ✕🏠 **Quail Lodge.** At this resort on the grounds of a private country club you have access to an 850-acre wildlife preserve frequented by deer and migratory fowl. Modern rooms with European styling are clustered in several low-rise buildings. Each room has a private deck or patio overlooking the golf course, gardens, or lake. The Covey at Quail Lodge ($$–$$$$; jacket recommended) serves Continental cuisine in a romantic lakeside dining room. Standouts include rack of lamb, mustard-crusted salmon, and mousseline of sole. ⊠ *8205 Valley Greens Dr., 93923* ☎ *831/624–1581 or 800/538–9516* 🖷 *831/624–3726* ⊕ *www.quaillodge. com* ⤶ *83 rooms, 14 suites* ⚙ *2 restaurants, room service, some fans, in-room data ports, some in-room faxes, some in-room safes, some in-room hot tubs, minibars, refrigerators, cable TV with movies and video games, 18-hole golf course, putting green, 4 tennis courts, pro shop, 2 pools, gym, hot tub, sauna, spa, steam room, bicycles, croquet, hiking, 2 bars, baby-sitting, laundry service, concierge, Internet, business services, meeting rooms, some pets allowed (fee), no-smoking rooms no a/c in some rooms* ⊟ *AE, DC, MC, V.*

$$$$ 🏠 **Carmel Valley Ranch Resort.** This all-suites Wyndham resort, well off Carmel Valley Road on a 400-acre estate overlooking the valley, is typical of contemporary California architecture. Standard amenities include wood-burning fireplaces and watercolors by local artists. Rooms have cathedral ceilings, fully stocked wet bars, and large decks. If you're staying here, the greens fee at the resort's 18-hole golf course is $150, including cart; special golf packages can reduce this rate considerably. ⊠ *1 Old Ranch Rd., 93923* ☎ *831/625–9500 or 800/422–7635* 🖷 *831/624–2858* ⊕ *www.wyndham.com* ⤶ *144 suites* ⚙ *2 restaurants, in-room* data ports, in-room safes, some in-room hot tubs, minibars, some microwaves, refrigerators, cable TV with movies and video games, some in-room VCRs, 18-hole golf course, 13 tennis courts, 2 pools, 2 hot tubs, 2 saunas, steam room, 2 bars, laundry service, concierge, Internet, business services, meeting rooms; no smoking ⊟ AE, D, DC, MC, V.

$$$$
Fodor'sChoice
★
  Stonepine Estate Resort. Set on 330 pastoral acres, the former estate of the Crocker banking family has been converted to an ultradeluxe inn. The oak-paneled, antiques-laden main château holds eight elegantly furnished rooms and suites and a dining room for guests, though with advance reservations it is possible for others to dine here. The property's romantic cottages include one that is straight out of *Hansel and Gretel*. Fresh flowers, afternoon tea, and evening champagne are daily delights. An equestrian center offers riding lessons. This is a quiet property, best suited to couples traveling without children. ⊠ *150 E. Carmel Valley Rd., 93924* ☎ *831/659–2245* 🖶 *831/659–5160* ⊕ *www.stonepinecalifornia. com* ⤶ *8 rooms, 4 suites, 3 cottages* ⌕ *Dining room, room service, fans, in-room data ports, some in-room safes, some in-room hot tubs, minibars, cable TV, in-room VCRs, 5-hole golf course, 2 tennis courts, 2 pools, gym, massage, mountain bikes, archery, hiking, horseback riding, library, piano, recreation room, laundry service, concierge, Internet; no a/c, no smoking* ⊟ *AE, MC, V* ⦿⧈ *BP.*

$$–$$$
  Carmel Valley Lodge. This small inn has rooms surrounding a garden patio and separate one- and two-bedroom cottages with fireplaces and full kitchens. ⊠ *8 Ford Rd., at Carmel Valley Rd. 93924* ☎ *831/659– 2261 or 800/641–4646* 🖶 *831/659–4558* ⊕ *www.valleylodge.com* ⤶ *19 rooms, 4 suites, 8 cottages* ⌕ *Kitchenettes, refrigerators, cable TV, in-room VCRs, pool, exercise equipment, hot tub, sauna, horseshoes, Ping-Pong, Internet, some pets allowed (fee), no-smoking rooms* ⊟ *AE, MC, V* ⦿⧈ *CP.*

The Arts

The **Magic Circle Center** (⊠ 8 El Caminito ☎ 831/659–1108) presents three comedies, two dramas, and a music series annually in an intimate 60-seat theater.

Sports & the Outdoors

Golf Club at Quail Lodge (⊠ 8000 Valley Greens Dr. ☎ 831/624–2770) incorporates several lakes into its course. Depending on the season and day of the week, greens fees range from $115 to $140 for guests and $125 to $175 for nonguests, including cart rental. **Rancho Cañada Golf Club** (⊠ 4860 Carmel Valley Rd., 1 mi east of Hwy. 1 ☎ 831/624–0111) is a public course with 36 holes, some of them overlooking the Carmel River. Fees range from $35 to $80, plus $34 for cart rental, depending on course and tee time.

Shopping

You'll find high-end linens as well as stunning, one-of-a-kind provincial French antiques, such as 18th-century stone mantelpieces, at **Jan de Luz** (⊠ 4 E. Carmel Valley Rd. ☎ 831/659–7966).

MONTEREY BAY A TO Z

To research prices, get advice from other travelers, and book travel arrangements, visit ⊕ *www.fodors.com.*

AIRPORTS & TRANSFERS

Monterey Peninsula Airport is 3 mi east of downtown Monterey (take Olmstead Road off Highway 68). It is served by American, American Eagle, America West, United, and United Express. *See* Air Travel *in* Smart

Travel Tips A to Z for airline phone numbers. Taxi service is available for about $9–$10, and Monterey–Salinas Transit has buses to and from the airport Monday through Saturday.

🏢**Monterey Peninsula Airport** ⊠200 Fred Kane Dr., Monterey 🕾831/648-7000 ⊕www. montereyairport.com. **Carmel Taxi** 🕾 831/624-3885. **Monterey Airport Taxi** 🕾 831/ 626-3385. **Monterey-Salinas Transit** 🕾 831/899-2555. **Yellow Checker Cabs** 🕾 831/ 646-1234.

BUS TRAVEL

Greyhound serves Santa Cruz and Monterey from San Francisco three or four times daily. The trips take about 3 or 4½ hours, respectively. Monterey-Salinas Transit provides frequent service between the peninsula's towns and many major sightseeing spots and shopping areas. The base fare is $1.75, with an additional $1.75 for each zone you travel into. A day pass costs $3.50–$7, depending on how many zones you'll be traveling through. Monterey-Salinas Transit also runs the WAVE shuttle, which links major attractions on the Monterey waterfront. The free shuttle operates Memorial Day through Labor Day, daily from 9 to 6:30.

🏢 **Greyhound** 🕾 800/231-2222 ⊕ www.greyhound.com. **Monterey-Salinas Transit** 🕾 831/424-7695 ⊕ www.mst.org.

CAR RENTAL

Most of the major agencies have locations in downtown Santa Cruz and at the Monterey Airport. *See* Car Rental *in* Smart Travel Tips A to Z for national car-rental agency phone numbers.

CAR TRAVEL

Parking is especially difficult in Carmel and in the heavily touristed areas of Monterey.

Two-lane Highway 1 runs north–south along the coast, linking the towns of Santa Cruz, Monterey, and Carmel. Highway 68 runs east from Pacific Grove toward Salinas at U.S. 101. North of Salinas, the freeway (U.S. 101) links up with Highway 156 to San Juan Bautista. The drive south from San Francisco to Monterey can be made comfortably in three hours or less. The most scenic way is to follow Highway 1 down the coast past flower, pumpkin, and artichoke fields and the seaside communities of Pacifica, Half Moon Bay, and Santa Cruz. Unless you drive on sunny weekends when locals are heading for the beach, the two-lane coast highway may take no longer than the freeway.

A sometimes faster route is I–280 south from San Francisco to Highway 17, north of San Jose. Highway 17 crosses the redwood-filled Santa Cruz Mountains between San Jose and Santa Cruz, where it intersects with Highway 1. The traffic can crawl to a standstill, however, heading into Santa Cruz. Another option is to follow U.S. 101 south through San Jose to Prunedale and then take Highway 156 west to Highway 1 south into Monterey.

EMERGENCIES

In the event of an emergency, dial 911. Monterey Bay Dental Society provides dentist referrals and Monterey County Medical Society can refer you to a doctor. The Surf 'n' Sand pharmacy in Carmel is open on weekdays from 9 to 6, Saturday from 9 to 1. There is a 24-hour Walgreen's pharmacy in Seaside, about 4 mi northeast of Monterey via Highway 1.

🏢 Hospitals **Community Hospital of Monterey Peninsula** ⊠ 23625 Holman Hwy., Monterey 🕾 831/624-5311. **Dominican Hospital** ⊠ 1555 Soquel Dr., Santa Cruz 🕾 831/462-7700.

🏢 Pharmacies **Surf 'n' Sand** ⊠ 6th and Junipero Aves., Carmel 🕾 831/624-1543. **Walgreen's** ⊠ 1055 Fremont Blvd., Seaside 🕾 831/393-9231.

🛈 Referrals **Monterey Bay Dental Society** ☎ 831/658-0168. **Monterey County Medical Society** ☎ 831/655-1019.

LODGING

Bed and Breakfast Innkeepers of Santa Cruz County is an association of innkeepers that can help you find a B&B. Monterey County Conventions and Visitors Bureau Visitor Services operates a lodging referral line and publishes an informational brochure with discount coupons that are good at restaurants, attractions, and shops. Monterey Peninsula Reservations will assist you in booking lodgings.

🛈 **Bed and Breakfast Innkeepers of Santa Cruz County** ☎ 831/688-0444 ⊕ www. santacruzbnb.com. **Monterey County Conventions and Visitors Bureau Visitor Services** ☎ 800/555-9283 ⊕ www.gomonterey.org. **Monterey Peninsula Reservations** ☎ 888/655-3424 ⊕ www.monterey-reservations.com.

TOURS

California Parlor Car Tours operates motor-coach tours from San Francisco that include one or two days in the Monterey Peninsula.

🛈 **California Parlor Car Tours** ☎ 415/474-7500 or 800/227-4250 ⊕ www. calpartours.com.

TRAIN TRAVEL

Amtrak's *Coast Starlight,* which runs between Los Angeles, Oakland, and Seattle, stops in Salinas. Connecting Amtrak Thruway buses serve Monterey and Carmel.

🛈 **Amtrak** ✉ 11 Station Pl., Salinas ☎ 800/872-7245 ⊕ www.amtrakcalifornia.com.

VISITOR INFORMATION

🛈 **Monterey County Vintners and Growers Association** ☎ 831/375-9400 ⊕ www. montereywines.org. **Monterey County Convention & Visitors Bureau** ☎ *800/555-9283* ⊕ *www.gomonterey.org.* **Monterey Peninsula Visitors and Convention Bureau** ✉ 380 Alvarado St., Monterey 93942 ☎ 831/649-1770 ⊕ www.monterey.com. **Salinas Valley Chamber of Commerce** ✉ 119 E. Alisal St., Salinas 93901 ☎ 831/424-7611 ⊕ www. salinaschamber.com. **Santa Cruz County Conference and Visitors Council** ✉ 1211 Ocean St., Santa Cruz 95060 ☎ 831/425-1234 or 800/833-3494 ⊕ www.scccvc.org. **Santa Cruz Mountain Winegrowers' Association** ✉ 7605-A Old Dominion Ct., Aptos 95003 ☎ 831/479-9463 ⊕ www.scmwa.com.

THE CENTRAL VALLEY

HIGHWAY 99 FROM FRESNO TO LODI

6

HIGHLY RECOMMENDED

RESTAURANTS   DeAngelo's, *Merced*

HOTELS   Wine & Roses Hotel and Restaurant, *Lodi*

SIGHTS   Forestiere Underground Gardens, *Fresno*
Haggin Museum, *Stockton*
Jessie's Grove, *winery in Lodi*
Knights Ferry Recreation Area, *Oakdale*
McHenry Mansion, *Modesto*
Woodward Park, *Fresno*

Updated by
Alison Lucian

AMONG THE WORLD'S MOST FERTILE working land, the Central Valley is California's heartland and the country's breadbasket. Lush fields and orchards crisscrossed by miles of back roads define the landscape of this sunbaked region, and a wealth of rivers, lakes, and waterways provide relief from the flat farmland that carpets much of the valley. The agriculturally rich area hosts a tremendous diversity of wildlife. Nearly every telephone post is crowned by a hawk or kestrel hunting the land below. Humans, in turn, have created a profusion of vineyards, dairy farms, orchards, and pastures that stretch to the horizon. In the towns, museums and historical societies display artifacts of the valley's eccentric past, and museums, concert halls and restored theaters host a vibrant contemporary cultural life. From the back roads to the main streets, the people are not only friendly but proud to help outsiders see the beauty of the Central Valley.

If the well-populated Central Valley appears at first glance to be a traveler's void, it's because most folks never leave the highway. Many choose to drive boring I–5 instead of Highway 99, which is framed by farms, vineyards, and dairies. The valley's history of being passed over dates back hundreds of years. Until the mid-19th century, the area was a desert. Gold discoveries, starting in the 1850s, sparked the birth of some towns; the arrival of the railroad in following decades spurred the development of others. But it was the coming of water, courtesy of private dams and, in the 1930s, the Central Valley Project, that transformed this land into the country's most vital agricultural region.

As soon as irrigation gave potential to the valley's open acres, the area became a magnet for farmers, ranchers, developers, World War II refugees, and immigrants from places as diverse as Portugal, China, Armenia, and Laos. Today refugees from the state's big cities come in search of cheaper real estate, safer neighborhoods, and more space. With development has come some unsightly sprawl, air pollution, and pressure on crucial water supplies. Nevertheless, the valley still retains many of its traditional charms. The region's cultural diversity and agricultural roots have woven a textured social fabric that has been chronicled by some of the country's finest writers, including Fresno native William Saroyan, Stockton native Maxine Hong Kingston, and *Grapes of Wrath* author John Steinbeck.

Just as these authors found inspiration in a place you cannot view while speeding down the highway, you must invest time and footwork to appreciate the Central Valley. The rewards can be surprising, relaxing, thrilling. . . even poetic.

Exploring the Central Valley

The upper Central Valley cuts through San Joaquin, Stanislaus, Merced, Madera, and Fresno counties. It is bounded on the east by the mighty Sierra Nevada and on the west by the smaller coastal ranges. I–5 runs south–north through the valley, as does Highway 99.

About the Restaurants

Fast-food places and chain restaurants dominate valley highways, but away from the main drag, independent and family-owned eateries will awaken your taste buds. Many cutting-edge bistros and fine restaurants take advantage of the local produce and locally raised meats that are the cornerstone of California cuisine. Even simple restaurants produce hearty, tasty fare that often reflects the valley's ethnic mix. Some of the nation's best Mexican restaurants call the valley home. Chinese, Italian, Armenian, and Basque restaurants also are abundant; many serve

Numbers in the text correspond to numbers in the margin and on the Central Valley and Fresno Area maps.

6

If you have
1 day

Touring the **Fresno** area is a good strategy if you only have a day to spend in the valley. ▶ **Roeding Park** ❶ has a striking tropical rain forest within **Chaffee Zoological Gardens**; the park's **Playland** and **Storyland** are great stops if you are traveling with children. Don't miss the **Forestiere Underground Gardens** ❼, on Shaw Avenue. In springtime take the self-guided **Blossom Trail** driving tour through orchards, vineyards, and fields. Along the trail in Reedley is the **Mennonite Quilt Center.** Depending on your mood and the weather, you can spend part of the afternoon at **Wild Water Adventures** or visit the **Fresno Metropolitan Museum** ❷, whose highlights include an exhibit about author William Saroyan.

If you have
3 days

Start your trip through the Central Valley in ▶ ▣ **Fresno** ❶–❽ and spend the day there, as in the one-day itinerary above. In the evening take in a show at Roger Rocka's or the Tower Theatre, both in Fresno's Tower District. On day two drive up Highway 99 and stop off at the Castle Air Museum, north of **Merced** ❾ in Atwater. **Modesto** ❿ is a good place to stop for lunch. In the afternoon, take a rafting trip on the Stanislaus River near **Oakdale** ⓫. Reserve your last day for more refined pursuits, spending an hour or two at the Haggin Museum in **Stockton** ⓬, and making an afternoon tour of the wineries around **Lodi** ⓭. Lodi is a pleasant place to overnight.

---

massive, many-course meals. While dress at most valley eateries is casual, diners at some of the finer establishments won't feel out of place in jacket and tie or cocktail dress. Such attire, however, is not required.

About the Hotels
The Central Valley has many chain motels and hotels, but independently owned hotels and bed-and-breakfasts also can be found. There's a large selection of upscale lodgings as well as ones that are simply utilitarian while clean and comfortable. The Victorian-style B&Bs in the area are a good bet because they offer a taste of local life.

WHAT IT COSTS				
$$$$	**$$$**	**$$**	**$**	**¢**
RESTAURANTS over $30	$23–$30	$16–$22	$10–$15	under $10
HOTELS over $250	$176–$250	$121–$175	$90–$120	under $90

Restaurant prices are for a main course at dinner, excluding sales tax of 7–10% (depending on location). Hotel prices are for a standard double room in high season, excluding service charges and 8–13% tax.

Timing
Spring, when wildflowers are in bloom and the scent of fruit blossoms is in the air, and fall, when the air is brisk and leaves turn red and gold, are the best times to visit. Many of the valley's biggest festivals take place during these seasons. (If you're an allergy-sufferer, though, beware of spring, when stone-fruit trees blossom.) Summer, when temperatures often top 100°F, can be oppressive. June-August, though, are great months to visit

area water parks and lakes or to take in the museums, where air-conditioning provides a reprieve from the heat. Many attractions close in winter, which can get cold and dreary. Thick, ground-hugging fog, called tule fog by locals, is a common driving hazard November–February.

MID-CENTRAL VALLEY
FRESNO & MERCED

The Mid-Central Valley, which includes Fresno, Madera, and Merced counties, is perhaps the richest agricultural zone in America. Cotton, grapes, and tomatoes are among the major crops; poultry and milk are other important products. The area is a crossroads of sorts. Highway 152 travels over the mountains from Monterey Bay to I–5 and Highway 99, the valley's major north–south arteries. Along Highway 99 lie Fresno and Merced, from which you can travel easily to the southern Sierra or the Gold Country. From Fresno, Highway 41 runs north 65 mi to Yosemite National Park. From Merced, Highway 140 runs 65 mi northeast to the park, along the way crossing Highway 49, the main line of the Mother Lode.

Fresno

▶ *153 mi southeast of San Jose via U.S. 101 and Rtes. 152 and 99; 150 mi east of Monterey via Hwy. 1, U.S. 101, and Hwys. 152 and 99.*

Sprawling Fresno, with more than 450,000 people, has about 75 ethnic communities, including Armenian, Laotian, and Indian. The city has a burgeoning arts scene, several public parks, and an abundance of low-priced restaurants serving tasty food. The Tower District, with its chic restaurants, coffeehouses, and boutiques, is the trendy spot. The city's most famous native, Pulitzer Prize–winning playwright and novelist William Saroyan (*The Time of Your Life, The Human Comedy*), was born here in 1908.

☾ ▶ ❶ Tree-shaded **Roeding Park** is a place of respite on hot summer days; it has picnic areas, playgrounds, tennis courts, horseshoe pits, and a zoo. The most striking exhibit at **Chaffee Zoological Gardens** (☎ 559/498–2671 ⊕ www.chaffeezoo.org) is the tropical rain forest, where you'll encounter exotic birds along the paths and bridges. Elsewhere you'll find tigers, grizzly bears, sea lions, tule elk, camels, elephants, and hooting siamangs. Also here are a high-tech reptile house and a petting zoo. Open year-round, the zoo charges $6 admission. A miniature train, little race cars, and other rides for kids are among the amusements that operate February–November at **Playland** (☎ 559/486–2124). Children can explore attractions with fairy-tale themes and attend puppet shows at **Storyland** (☎ 559/264–2235), which is open February–November. Admission to Storyland is $3.75. ⊠ *Olive and Belmont Aves.* ☎ *559/498–1551* ▭ *Parking $1 Feb.–Oct.* ☉ *Daily 6 AM–11 PM.*

☾ ❷ The **Fresno Metropolitan Museum** mounts art, history, and hands-on science exhibits, many of them quite innovative. The William Saroyan History Gallery presents a riveting introduction in words and pictures to the author's life and times. ⊠ *1515 Van Ness Ave.* ☎ *559/441–1444* ⊕ *www.fresnomet.org* ▭ *$7, $1 Thursday nights only* ☉ *Tues.–Sun. 11–5 and Thurs. 5–8.*

❸ The **Legion of Valor Museum** is a real find for military history buffs of all ages. It has German bayonets and daggers, a Japanese Namby pistol, a Gatling gun, and an extensive collection of Japanese, German, and

6

Taste of the Valley
The Central Valley is a great destination for anyone who likes produce fresh from the fields. As billboards announce, fruit and nut orchards as well as cheese factories offer educational tours that include tastings. Better yet, there are farmers' markets in virtually every town, and roadside stands in between. Good places to find produce stands are Herndon Avenue in Fresno and Clovis and Highway 12 in Lodi. Prime season for farmers' markets is May through October, though many larger ones are open year-round, including those held every Saturday in Fresno, Merced, and Stockton. Especially in fall check with chambers of commerce for festivals celebrating everything from asparagus to raisins.

Sports & the Outdoors
Several cities and towns serve as convenient starting points for white-water rafting trips on the Stanislaus, Merced, and Kings rivers. Fishing in the rivers and lakes is another favored activity; the lakes are also prime spots for boating and swimming. Stockton is a popular rental area for houseboating on the Sacramento River delta. The San Francisco Giants' Triple-A team, the Fresno Grizzlies, plays in a stadium opened in 2002 in Fresno. Wildlife refuges are world-class sites for watching birds, especially migrating waterfowl.

American uniforms. The staff is extremely enthusiastic. ☒ *2425 Fresno St.* ☎ *559/498–0510* ☒ *Free* ☙ *Mon.–Sat. 10–3.*

❹ Inside a restored 1889 Victorian, the **Meux Home Museum** displays furnishings typical of early Fresno. Guided tours proceed from the front parlor to the backyard carriage house. ☒ *Tulare and R Sts.* ☎ *559/233–8007* ⊕ *www.meux.mus.ca.us* ☒ *$5* ☙ *Fri.–Sun. noon–3:30.*

❺ The **Fresno Art Museum** exhibits American, Mexican, and French art; highlights of the permanent collection include pre-Columbian works and graphic art from the postimpressionist period. The 152-seat Bonner Auditorium hosts lectures, films, and concerts. ☒ *Radio Park, 2233 N. 1st St.* ☎ *559/441–4221* ⊕ *www.fresnoartmuseum.com* ☒ *$4; free Tues.* ☙ *Tues.–Fri. 10–5, weekends noon–5.*

★ ❻ **Woodward Park,** 300 acres of jogging trails, picnic areas, and playgrounds in the northern reaches of the city, is especially pretty in the spring, when plum and cherry trees, magnolias, and camellias bloom. Outdoor concerts take place in summer. The **Shinzen Friendship Garden** has a teahouse, a koi pond, arched bridges, a waterfall, and Japanese art. ☒ *Audubon Dr. and Friant Rd.* ☎ *559/498–1551* ☒ *$2 per car Feb.–Oct.; additional $1 for Shinzen Garden* ☙ *Apr.–Oct., daily 7 AM–10 PM; Nov.–Mar., daily 7–7.*

★ ☾ ❼ Sicilian immigrant Baldasare Forestiere spent four decades (1906–46) carving out the **Forestiere Underground Gardens,** a subterranean realm of rooms, tunnels, grottoes, alcoves, and arched passageways that extends for more than 10 acres beneath busy, mall-pocked Shaw Avenue. Only a fraction of Forestiere's prodigious output is on view, but you can tour his underground living quarters, including bedrooms (one with a fireplace), the kitchen, living room, and bath, as well as a fish pond and an aquarium. Skylights allow exotic full-grown fruit trees, including one

Fresno Area

that bears seven kinds of citrus as a result of grafting, to flourish more than 20 feet below ground. You have to make reservations for the tour. ✉ *5021 W. Shaw Ave., 2 blocks east of Hwy. 99* ☎ *559/271–0734* 💲*$8* ⊘ *Tours: weekends noon and 2. Call for other tour times.*

⑧ The drive along palm-lined Kearney Boulevard is one of the best reasons to visit the **Kearney Mansion Museum,** which stands in shaded 225-acre **Kearney Park,** 7 mi west of town. The century-old home of M. Theo Kearney, Fresno's onetime "raisin king," is accessible only by taking a guided 45-minute tour. ✉ *7160 W. Kearney Blvd.* ☎ *559/441–0862* 💲*$4 (park entrance $3, waived for museum visitors)* ⊘ *Park hours: 7 AM–10 PM; museum tours Fri.–Sun. at 1, 2, and 3.*

> **off the beaten path**

BLOSSOM TRAIL – This 62-mi self-guided driving tour takes in Fresno-area orchards, citrus groves, and vineyards during spring blossom season. Pick up a route map at the **Fresno Convention & Visitors Bureau** (✉ 848 M St., 3rd floor ☎ 559/233–0836 or 800/ 788–0836). The route passes through small towns and past rivers, lakes, and canals. The most colorful and aromatic time to go is from late February to mid-March, when almond, plum, apple, orange, lemon, apricot, and peach blossoms shower the landscape with shades of white, pink, and red. Directional and crop identification signs mark the trail. Allow at least 2–3 hours for the tour.

Along the Blossom Trail, roughly halfway between Fresno and Visalia, the colorful handiwork of local quilters is on display at the **Mennonite Quilt Center** (✉ 1012 G St. [take Manning Ave. exit off Hwy. 99 and head east 12 mi], Reedley ☎ 559/638–3560). The center is open weekdays 9:30–4:30 and Saturday 10–4, but try to visit on Monday (except holidays) between 8 and noon, when two dozen quilters stitch, patch, and chat over coffee. Prime viewing time—with the largest number of quilts—is in February and March, before the center's early-April auction. Ask a docent to take you to the locked upstairs room, where most of the quilts hang; she'll explain the fine points of patterns such as the Log Cabin Romance, the Dahlia, and the Snowball-Star. Admission is free.

Where to Stay & Eat

$$-$$$ ✕ **Echo.** This Tower District restaurant has a well-appointed dining room and a chic sensibility. Its tantalizing menu draws largely on food grown locally, much of it organic, with exquisite results. Worth mentioning are the grilled quail marinated in Dijon, garlic, and herbs; organic beef with red wine and yellowfoot mushrooms; and Meyer lemon pudding cake. The food is tasty, but portions are small. ⊠ *609 E. Olive Ave.* ☎ *559/442–3246* ▤ *AE, D, MC, V* ⊗ *Closed Sun.–Mon.*

$-$$ ✕ **La Rocca's Ristorante Italiano.** The sauces that top these pasta and meat dishes will make your taste buds sing. The rich tomato sauce, which comes with or without meat, has a nice zing. The marsala sauce—served on either chicken or veal—is rich yet not overpowering. Typical red-sauce dishes, such as spaghetti, rigatoni, and lasagna, are offered here, but you'll also be happily surprised with offerings such as the bowtie pasta with cream, peas, bacon, tomato sauce, and olive oil. Pizzas also are served. Reservations recommended on weekend evenings. ⊠ *6735 N. 1st St.* ☎ *559/431–1278* ▤ *AE, D, MC, V* ⊗ *No lunch weekends.*

$-$$ ✕ **Tahoe Joe's.** While this restaurant is known for its steaks, other selections include the slow-roasted prime rib, center-cut pork chops, and chicken breast served with a whiskey peppercorn sauce. But if it's a steak you want, all cuts, including sirloin, rib eye, strip, and filet mignon, will satisfy. The baked potato that accompanies almost every dish is loaded tableside with your choice of butter, sour cream, chives, and bacon bits. Tahoe Joe's has two Fresno locations. ⊠ *7006 N. Cedar Ave.* ☎ *559/ 299–9740* ⚐ *Reservations not accepted* ▤ *AE, D, MC, V* ⊗ *No lunch* ⊠ *2700 W. Shaw Ave.* ☎ *559/277–8028* ⚐ *Reservations not accepted* ▤ *AE, D, MC, V* ⊗ *No lunch.*

¢-$ ✕ **El Rosal.** Authentic Mexican food served in a friendly atmosphere draws locals to this eatery. Try the Modesto Meat Combo, which includes *carne asada* (thin strips of marinated and grilled beef), pork chop, and grilled chicken breast. Other good choices include beef, chicken, or shrimp fajitas, and the jumbo burritos stuffed with rice, beans, and a meat of your choice. Carnitas (tender bits of pork served with condiments and hot tortillas) and menudo (tripe stew) are served Friday and Saturday. ⊠ *5730 N. 1st St.* ☎ *559/437–9614* ▤ *AE, D, MC, V* ⊗ *Closed Sun.*

¢ ✕ **Irene's.** Downtown workers pack this Tower District restaurant at lunchtime. Handmade, half-pound burgers are the most popular, and most filling, items on the menu. Other popular dishes include the smoked ham and melted Swiss cheese sandwich served on a hard roll, and fresh salads. For breakfast, homemade granola, huge buttermilk pancakes, and the Denver omelet (with ham, onions, and green peppers) will fill up even those with the most hearty appetites. ⊠ *747 E. Olive Ave.* ☎ *559/ 237–9919* ▤ *AE, D, MC, V.*

$$ ▦ **Piccadilly Inn Shaw.** This two-story property has 7½ attractively landscaped acres and a big swimming pool. The sizable rooms have king- and queen-size beds, full-size robes, ironing boards, and coffeemakers; some rooms have fireplaces. ⊠ *2305 W. Shaw Ave., 93711* ☎ *559/226– 3850* 🖷 *559/226–2448* ⊕ *www.piccadilly-inn.com/shaw.html* ⇥ *188 rooms, 6 suites* ⚴ *Some microwaves, some refrigerators, cable TV,* *pool, gym, hot tub, laundry facilities, laundry service, business services, meeting rooms, no-smoking rooms* 🖴 *AE, D, DC, MC, V.*

¢ 📺 **La Quinta Inn.** Rooms are ample at this basic three-story motel near downtown. Most rooms have large desks that prove helpful for business travelers. ✉ *2926 Tulare St., 93721* ☎ *559/442–1110* 🖨 *559/237–0415* 💬 *130 rooms* ⚭ *Some microwaves, some refrigerators, cable TV, pool, no-smoking rooms* 🖴 *AE, D, MC, V* ❍ *CP.*

Nightlife & the Arts

The **Fresno Philharmonic Orchestra** (☎ 559/261–0600) performs classical concerts (sometimes pops) on weekends, usually at the **William Saroyan Theatre** (✉ 700 M St.), from September through June. **Roger Rocka's Music Hall** (✉ 1226 N. Wishon Ave. ☎ 559/266–9494 or 800/371–4747), a dinner theater in the Tower District, stages six Broadway-style musicals a year. The **Tower Theatre for the Performing Arts** (✉ 815 E. Olive Ave. ☎ 559/485–9050) has given its name to the trendy Tower District of theaters, clubs, restaurants, and cafés. The restored 1930s art deco movie house presents theater, ballet, concerts, and other cultural events year-round.

Sports & the Outdoors

Kings River Expeditions (✉ 211 N. Van Ness Ave. ☎ 559/233–4881 or 800/846–3674) arranges white-water rafting trips on the Kings River. **Wild Water Adventures** (✉ 11413 E. Shaw Ave., Clovis ☎ 559/299–9453 or 800/564–9453 ⊕ www.wildwater.net 💬 $22, $16 after 4 PM), a 52-acre water theme park about 10 mi east of Fresno, is open from late May to early September.

Shopping

Old Town Clovis (✉ Upper Clovis Ave., Clovis) is an area of restored brick buildings with numerous antiques shops and art galleries (along with restaurants and saloons). Be warned, though: not much here is open on Sunday. Head east on Fresno's Herndon Avenue about 10 mi, and then turn right onto Clovis Ave.

Merced

❾ *50 mi north of Fresno on Hwy. 99.*

Thanks to a branch of the University of California set to open in 2004 and an aggressive community redevelopment plan, the downtown of county seat Merced is coming back to life. The transformation is not yet complete, but there are promising signs: a brewpub, several boutiques, the restoration of numerous historic buildings, and foot traffic won back from outlying strip malls.

Even if you don't go inside, be sure to swing by the **Merced County Courthouse Museum.** The three-story former courthouse, built in 1875, is a striking example of Victorian Italianate style. The upper two floors are a museum of early Merced history. Highlights include ornate restored courtrooms and an 1870 Chinese temple with carved redwood altars. ✉ *21st and N Sts.* ☎ *209/723–2401* 💬 *Free* ☉ *Wed.–Sun. 1–4.*

The **Merced Multicultural Arts Center** displays paintings, sculpture, and photography. Threads, a festival that celebrates the area's ethnic diversity, is held here on a mid-October weekend. ✉ *645 W. Main St.* ☎ *209/388–1090* 💬 *Free* ☉ *Weekdays 9–5, Sat. 10–2.*

> off the
> beaten
> path

MILLERTON LAKE STATE RECREATION AREA – This lake at the top of Friant Dam is a great place for boating, fishing, and camping and is a popular summer swimming spot. The lake and its surrounding hills are wintering grounds for bald eagles, and if you are patient, you can almost surely spot them here between December and February. ⊠ *5290 Millerton Rd., 20 mi northeast of Fresno via Hwy. 41 and Hwy. 145, Friant* ☎ *559/822–2332* ⊠ *$3 per car* ☉ *Oct.–Mar. sunrise–sunset; Apr.–Sept. 6 AM–10 PM.*

Where to Stay & Eat

★ $$ ✕ **DeAngelo's.** Not only the best restaurant in Merced, it's one of the best in the Central Valley. Chef Vincent DeAngelo, a graduate of the Culinary Institute of America, brings his considerable skill to everything from basic ravioli to Portobello mushrooms stuffed with sausage, peppers, and cheese. The delicious crusty bread comes from the Golden Sheath bakery, in Watsonville. ⊠ *350 W. Main St.,* ☎ *209/383–3020* ⊟ *AE, D, MC, V* ☉ *No lunch weekends.*

$–$$ ✕ **The Branding Iron.** Beef is what this restaurant is all about. The juicy cut of prime rib paired with potato and Parmesan-cheese bread will satisfy diners with even the most ravenous appetites. This restaurant is a favorite among farmers and ranchers looking for a place to refuel as they travel through cattle country. California cattle brands decorate the walls, and when the weather is nice, cooling breezes refresh diners on the outdoor patio. ⊠ *640 W. 16th St.* ☎ *209/722–1822* ⊟ *AE, MC, V.*

¢ ✕ **Main Street Café.** This bright downtown café dishes up soups, pizza, salads, sandwiches, and pastries. Sandwiches (try the chicken breast with pesto mayonnaise on French bread) are served with tasty side salads. Espresso and cappuccino are available. ⊠ *460 W. Main St.* ☎ *209/725–1702* ⊟ *AE, MC, V* ☉ *Closed Sun. No dinner.*

$–$$ ▥ **Hooper House Bear Creek Inn.** This 1931 neocolonial home regally stands at the corner of M Street. The 1½ acres of tightly clipped grounds host fruit trees and grapevines, while the house offers a sunroom, well-chosen antiques, and big, soft beds. Breakfast is hearty and imaginative, featuring locally grown foods such as fried sweet potatoes and black walnuts. ⊠ *575 W. N. Bear Creek Dr., at M St., 95348* ☎ *209/723–3991* 🖶 *209/723–7123* ⊕ *www.hooperhouse.com* ⇝ *2 rooms, 1 suite, 1 cottage* ♿ *In-room data ports, no-smoking rooms* ⊟ *AE, MC, V* �ⓄⒾ *BP.*

Sports & the Outdoors

At **Lake Yosemite Regional Park** (⊠ N. Lake Rd. off Yosemite Ave., 5 mi northeast of Merced ☎ 209/385–7426 ⊠ $4 per car Memorial Day–Labor Day), you can boat, swim, windsurf, water-ski, and fish on a 387-acre reservoir. Boat rentals and picnic areas are available.

en route

Heading north on Highway 99 from Merced, stop at the outdoor **Castle Air Museum,** adjacent to the former Castle Air Force Base (now Castle Aviation, an industrial park). You can stroll among fighter planes and other historic military aircraft. The 44 restored vintage war birds include the B-25 Mitchell medium-range bomber (best known for the Jimmy Doolittle raid on Tokyo following the attack on Pearl Harbor) and the speedy SR-71 Blackbird, used for reconnaissance over Vietnam and Libya. ⊠ *Santa Fe Ave. and Buhach Rd. (6 mi north of Merced, take the Buhach Rd. exit off Hwy. 99 in Atwater and follow signs), Atwater* ☎ *209/723–2178* ⊠ *$7* ☉ *May–Sept., daily 9–5; Oct.–Apr., daily 10–4.*

NORTH CENTRAL VALLEY
FROM MODESTO TO LODI

The northern section of the valley occupies Stanislaus and San Joaquin counties, encompassing the flat, abundantly fertile terrain south of

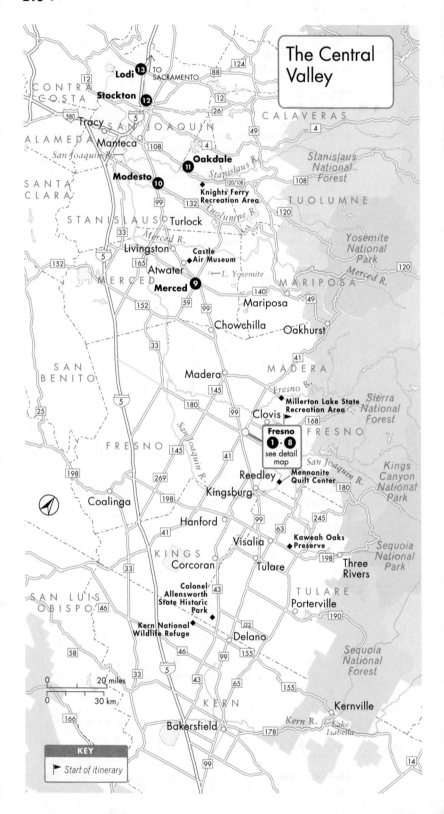

Modesto north to the edges of the Sacramento River delta and the fringes of the Gold Country. If you're heading to Yosemite National Park from northern California, chances are you'll pass through (or very near) at least one of these gateway cities.

Modesto

❿ *38 mi north of Merced on Hwy. 99.*

Modesto, a gateway to Yosemite and the southern reaches of the Gold Country, was founded in 1870 to serve the Central Pacific Railroad. The frontier town was originally to be named Ralston, after a railroad baron, but as the story goes, he modestly declined—thus the name Modesto. The Stanislaus County seat, a tree-lined city of 180,000, is perhaps best known as the site of the annual Modesto Invitational Track Meet and Relays and birthplace of film producer-director George Lucas, creator of *Star Wars* and *American Graffiti.*

The **Modesto Arch** (⊠ 9th and I Sts.) bears the city's motto: WATER, WEALTH, CONTENTMENT, HEALTH. The prosperity that water brought to Modesto has attracted people from all over the world. The city holds a well-attended **International Festival** (☎ 209/521–3852) in early October that celebrates the cultures, crafts, and cuisines of many nationalities. You can witness the everyday abundance of the Modesto area at the **Blue Diamond Growers Store** (⊠ 4800 Sisk Rd. ☎ 209/545–3222), which offers free samples, shows a film about almond-growing, and sells nuts in many flavors.

★ A rancher and banker built the 1883 **McHenry Mansion,** the city's sole surviving original Victorian home. The Italianate-style mansion has been decorated to reflect Modesto life in the late 19th century. Oaks, elms, magnolias, redwoods, and palms shade the grounds. ⊠ *15th and I Sts.* ☎ *209/577–5341* ⊕ *www.mchenrymuseum.org* ⌖ *Free* ☺ *Dec.–mid-Nov., Sun.–Thurs. 1–4, Fri. noon–3.*

The **McHenry Museum of Arts** is a jumbled repository of early Modesto and Stanislaus County memorabilia, including re-creations of an old-time doctor's office, a blacksmith's shop, and a general store stocked with period goods such as hair crimpers and corsets. ⊠ *14th and I Sts.* ☎ *209/577–5366* ⌖ *Free* ☺ *Tues.–Sun. noon–4.*

Where to Stay & Eat

$$–$$$ ✕ **Hazel's Elegant Dining.** Hazel's is *the* special-occasion restaurant in Modesto. The seven-course dinners include Continental entrées served with appetizer, soup, salad, pasta, and dessert. Members of the Gallo family, which owns much vineyard land in the Central Valley, eat here often, perhaps because the wine cellar's offerings are so comprehensive. ⊠ *431 12th St.* ☎ *209/578–3463* ⊟ *AE, D, DC, MC, V* ☺ *Closed Sun.–Mon. No lunch Sat.*

$–$$ ✕ **Tresetti's World Café.** An intimate setting with white tablecloths and contemporary art draws diners to this eatery—part wine shop, part restaurant—with a seasonally changing menu. For a small fee, the staff will uncork any wine you select from the shop. The Creole buttermilk fried chicken is outstanding, as are the Cajun-style crab cakes. ⊠ *927 11th St.* ☎ *209/572–2990* ⊟ *AE, D, DC, MC, V* ☺ *Closed Sun.*

¢–$ ✕ **India Palate.** A statue of the Hindu god Shiva greets diners when they enter this popular eatery; dark leather elephants watch over those already seated. Although Indian food traditionally is very spicy, the chef here will make any dish to your specifications—from ultramild to ultrahot. House favorites are tandoori chicken cooked in a rich sauce, and samosas: crispy puffs of dough filled with potatoes or ground lamb and peas. Indian tea and coffee and mango *lassi* (a combination of yogurt, ice, and mango) are among the specialty drinks offered. ⊠ *915 Yosemite Blvd.* ☎ *209/523-0324* ⊟ *AE, D, MC, V.*

¢–$ ✕ **St. Stan's.** Modesto's renowned microbrewery makes St. Stan's beers. The 14 on tap include the delicious Whistle Stop pale ale and Red Sky ale. The restaurant is casual and serves up good corned beef sandwiches loaded with sauerkraut as well as a tasty beer-sausage nibbler. ⊠ *821 L St.* ☎ *209/524–2337* ⊟ *AE, D, MC, V.*

$ ▦ **Doubletree Hotel.** Modesto's largest lodging towers 15 stories over downtown. Each room has a coffeemaker, iron, and desk. The convention center is adjacent, and a good brewpub, St. Stan's, is across the street. ⊠ *1150 9th St., 95354* ☎ *209/526–6000* ⊟ *209/526-6096* ⊕ *www.doubletree. com* ⌑ *258 rooms* ⌂ *Café, room service, pool, gym, hot tub, sauna, nightclub, laundry service, meeting rooms, airport shuttle, no-smoking rooms* ⊟ *AE, D, DC, MC, V.*

¢ ▦ **Best Western Town House Lodge.** The downtown location is the primary draw for this hotel. The county's historical library is across the street, and the McHenry Mansion and the McHenry Museum are nearby. All rooms come equipped with a coffeemaker and a hair dryer. ⊠ *909 16th St., 95354* ☎ *209/524-7261 or 800/780–7234* ⊟ *209/579-9546* ⊕ *www.bestwestern.com* ⌑ *56 rooms* ⌂ *Refrigerators, pool, hot tub, free parking, no-smoking rooms* ⊟ *AE, D, DC, MC, V* ⏏ *CP.*

┌─────────┐
│ **en route** │ The top attraction in Manteca, the largest town between Modesto and Stockton, is **Manteca Waterslides.** Kids will head to the wild Thunder Falls, which has three three-story slides. ⊠ *874 E. Woodward Ave.,* ☾ *between I–5 and Hwy. 99* ☎ *209/249-2520 or 877/625–9663* ⊕ *www.oakwoodlake.com* ⌑ *$23* ☉ *Daily Memorial Day–Labor Day, weekends in May and Sept.; hours vary by day.*

Oakdale

⑪ *15 mi northeast of Modesto on Hwy. 108.*

Oakdale is a bit off the beaten path from Modesto. You can sample the wares at **Oakdale Cheese & Specialties** (⊠ 10040 Hwy. 120 ☎ 209/848–3139), which has tastings (try the aged Gouda) and cheese-making tours. There's a picnic area and a petting zoo.

If you're in Oakdale—home of a Hershey's chocolate factory—the third weekend in May, check out the **Oakdale Chocolate Festival** (☎ 209/847–2244), which attracts 50,000–60,000 people each year. The event's main attraction is Chocolate Avenue, where vendors proffer cakes, cookies, ice cream, fudge, and cheesecake.

★ ☾ The featured attraction at the **Knights Ferry Recreation Area** is the 355-foot-long Knights Ferry covered bridge. The beautiful and haunting structure, built in 1863, crosses the Stanislaus River near the ruins of an old gristmill. The park has picnic and barbecue areas along the riverbanks, as well as three campgrounds accessible only by boat, bicycle, or by foot. You can hike, fish, canoe, and raft on 4 mi of rapids. ⊠ *Corps of Engineers Park, 17968 Covered Bridge Rd., Knights Ferry, 12 mi east of Oakdale via Hwy. 108* ☎ *209/881-3517* ⌑ *Free* ☉ *Daily dawn–dusk.*

Sports & the Outdoors

Rafting on the Stanislaus River is a popular activity near Oakdale. **River Journey** (⊠ 14842 Orange Blossom Rd. ☎ 209/847–4671 or 800/292–2938 ⊕ www.riverjourney.com) will take you out for a few hours of fun. To satisfy your white-water or flat-water cravings, contact **Sunshine River Adventures** (☎ 209/848–4800 or 800/829–7238).

Stockton

⑫ *29 mi north of Modesto on Hwy. 99.*

California's first inland port—connected since 1933 to San Francisco via a 60-mi-long deepwater channel—is wedged between I–5 and Highway 99, on the eastern end of the Sacramento River delta. Stockton, founded during the gold rush as a way station for miners traveling from San Francisco to the Mother Lode and now a city of 254,000, is where many of the valley's agricultural products begin their journey to other parts of the world. If you're here in late April, don't miss the **Stockton Asparagus Festival** (☎ 800/350–1987), in Oak Grove Park. The highlight of the festival is the food; organizers try to prove that almost any dish can be made with asparagus. A car show, kids' activity area, and musical entertainment also are part of the event.

★ The **Haggin Museum,** in pretty Victory Park, has one of the Central Valley's finest art collections. Highlights include landscapes by Albert Bierstadt and Thomas Moran, a still life by Paul Gauguin, a Native American gallery, and an Egyptian mummy. ⊠ *1201 N. Pershing Ave.* ☎ *209/940–6300* 🎫 *$5* 🕐 *Tues.–Sun. 1:30–5.*

Where to Stay & Eat

$$$–$$$$ ✕ **Le Bistro.** The dishes at one of the valley's most upscale restaurants are fairly standard Continental fare—rack of lamb, fillet of sole, sautéed prawns, soufflé Grand Marnier—and you can count on high-quality ingredients and presentation with a flourish. ⊠ *Marina Center Mall, 3121 W. Benjamin Holt Dr. (off I–5, behind Lyon's)* ☎ *209/951–0885* 🍽 *AE, D, DC, MC, V* 🕐 *No lunch weekends.*

¢–$ ✕ **On Lock Sam.** Operating since 1898, this Stockton landmark is in a modern pagoda-style building with framed Chinese prints on the walls, a garden outside one window, and a sparkling bar area. One touch of old-time Chinatown remains: a few booths have curtains that can be drawn for complete privacy. The Cantonese food is among the valley's best Chinese offerings. ⊠ *333 S. Sutter St.* ☎ *209/466–4561* 🍽 *AE, D, MC, V.*

¢ 🏨 **Best Western Stockton Inn.** Four miles from downtown, this large motel has a convenient location off Highway 99. The central courtyard with a pool and lounge chairs is a big plus on hot days. Most rooms are spacious. ⊠ *4219 Waterloo Rd., 95215* ☎ *209/931–3131 or 877/293–8697* 🖨 *209/931–0423* ⊕ *www.bestwesterncalifornia.com* 🛏 *141 rooms* 🍴 *Restaurant, pool, wading pool, hot tub, bar, laundry service, meeting room, no-smoking rooms* 🍽 *AE, D, DC, MC, V.*

¢ 🏨 **La Quinta Inn.** Close to downtown and near many upscale restaurants, this is a good choice for business and pleasure travelers alike. The spacious and quiet rooms have large desks and televisions with access to first-run movies. ⊠ *2710 W. March La., 95219* ☎ *209/952–7800* 🖨 *209/472–0732* ⊕ *www.laquinta.com* 🛏 *151 rooms* 🍴 *In-room data ports, pool, laundry service, meeting rooms, no-smoking rooms* 🍽 *AE, D, DC, MC, V.*

Sports & the Outdoors

Several companies rent houseboats (of various sizes, usually for three, four, or seven days) on the Sacramento River delta waterways near Stockton. Houseboats, patio boats, and ski boats can be rented through the **Delta Houseboat Rental Hotline** (⊠ 6333 Pacific Ave., Suite 152 ☎ 209/477–1840). **Herman & Helen's Marina** (⊠ Venice Island Ferry ☎ 209/951–4634) has houseboats with hot tubs and fireplaces. **Paradise Point Marina** (⊠ 8095 Rio Blanco Rd. ☎ 209/952–1000) offers a variety of rentals, including patio boats and personal watercraft.

Lodi

🔞 *13 mi north of Stockton and 34 mi south of Sacramento on Hwy. 99.*

Founded on agriculture, Lodi was once the watermelon capital of the country, and today it is surrounded by fields of asparagus, pumpkins, beans, safflowers, sunflowers, kiwis, melons, squashes, peaches, and cherries. It also has become a wine grape capital of sorts, producing zinfandel, merlot, cabernet sauvignon, chardonnay, and sauvignon blanc grapes. For years California wineries have built their reputations on the juice of grapes grown around Lodi. Now the area that includes Lodi, Lockeford, and Woodbridge is a wine destination boasting about 40 wineries, many offering tours and tastings. Lodi still retains an old rural charm. You can stroll downtown or visit a wildlife refuge, all the while benefiting from a Sacramento River delta breeze that keeps this microclimate cooler in summer than anyplace else in the area. With a short, mild winter and a long, rain-free summer, Lodi is ideal for outdoor recreation.

🖑 The 65-acre **Micke Grove Park and Zoo,** an oak-shaded county park off I–5, includes a Japanese garden, picnic areas, a golf course, and an agricultural museum with a collection of 94 tractors. Geckos and frogs, black-and-white ruffed lemurs, and hissing cockroaches found only on the African island of Madagascar inhabit "An Island Lost in Time," an exhibit at the **Micke Grove Zoo** (☎ 209/953–8840 ⊕ www.mgzoo.com ⊙ Daily 10–5). California sea lions bask on rocks much as they do off the coast of San Francisco in the "Islands Close to Home" exhibit, another highlight of this compact facility. Most rides and other diversions at Micke Grove's **Funderwoods** (☎ 209/369–5437 ⊙ Daily 8–dusk), a family-oriented amusement park, are geared to children. ⊠ *11793 N. Micke Grove Rd.* ☎ *209/331–7400* 🖾 *Zoo admission $2; parking $2 weekdays, $4 weekends and holidays.*

Stop by the **Lodi Wine & Visitor Center** (⊠ 2545 W. Turner Rd. ☎ 209/ 365–0621) to see exhibits on Lodi's viticultural history. Here you can pick up a map of area wineries, as well as buy wine. One of the stand-
★ out wineries in the area is **Jessie's Grove** (⊠ 1973 W. Turner Rd. ☎ 209/ 368–0880 ⊕ www.jgwinery.com), a wooded horse ranch and vineyard that has been in the same family since 1863. In addition to producing outstanding old-vine zinfandels, it presents blues concerts on the second Saturday of the month April–October. At the **Woodbridge by Robert Mondavi** winery (⊠ 5950 E. Woodbridge Rd., Acampo ☎ 209/365–2839 ⊕ www.woodbridgewines.com), you can take a free 30-minute tour of the vineyard and aging room. At its homey facility, kid-friendly **Phillips Farms** (⊠ 4580 W. Hwy. 12 ☎ 209/368–7384) offers tastings from its affordable Michael-David Vineyard. You can also cut flowers from the garden, pet the animals, eat breakfast and lunch at the café, and buy Phillips' produce. **Vino Piazza** (⊠ 12470 Locke Rd., Lockeford ☎ 209/ 727–9770) is a sort of wine co-op housed in the old Lockeford Winery building, where 13 vineyards operate tasting rooms. At the expense of not seeing the vineyards themselves, this is a good way to sample the area's many wines in a short time.

Where to Stay & Eat

$–$$ ✕ **Rosewood Bar & Grill.** In downtown Lodi, Rosewood offers fine dining without formal dress. Operated by the folks at Wine & Roses Hotel and Restaurant, this low-key spot serves American fare with a twist, such as meatloaf wrapped in bacon and grilled pork chops with barbecue sauce. There's a large bar with its own menu, plus live jazz nightly. ⊠ *28 S. School St.* ☎ *209/369–0470* ⊕ *rosewoodbarandgrill.com* 🗏 *MC, V* ⊙ *Closed Sun.–Mon. No lunch.*

¢–$ ✕ **Habanero Hots.** If your mouth can handle the heat promised by the restaurant's name, try the tamales. If you want to take it easy on your taste buds, stick with the rest of the menu. ⊠ *1024 E. Victor Rd.* ☎ *209/369–3791* ▭ *AE, D, MC, V.*

¢ ✕ **Angelo's.** Authentic Mexican dishes such as chile verde, steak ranchero and all-meat chimichangas draw locals to this downtown eatery. The service is friendly and quick, and the atmosphere is casual. ⊠ *28 N. School St.* ☎ *209/366–2728* ▭ *AE, DC, MC, V.*

★ $$–$$$ ✕▥ **Wine & Roses Hotel and Restaurant.** Set on 7 acres amid a tapestry of informal gardens, this hotel cultivates a sense of refinement typically associated with Napa or Carmel. Rooms are decorated in rich earth tones, and linens are imported from Italy. Some rooms have fireplaces; all have coffeemakers, irons, and hair dryers. Some of the bathrooms even have TVs. The restaurant is *the* place to eat in Lodi. Lunch and dinner served in the light and airy dining room feature fresh local produce. The Sunday buffet champagne brunch includes ham, prime rib, and made-to-order crepes and omelets. ⊠ *2505 W. Turner Rd., 95242* ☎ *209/334–6988* 🖷 *209/334–6570* ⊕ *www.winerose.com* ⇗ *36 rooms, 4 suites* ⌂ *Restaurant, room service, in-room data ports, refrigerators, cable TV, bar, laundry service, no-smoking rooms* ▭ *AE, D, DC, MC, V.*

$ ▥ **The Inn at Locke House.** Built in 1865, this B&B was a pioneer family's home and is on the National Register of Historic Places. Rooms are filled with antique furnishings, and all have fireplaces. The centerpiece of the Watertower Room is a queen canopy bed; the room also has a deck and a private sitting room. In the oak-paneled parlor, you'll find books, games, historical artifacts, and an old pump organ. Refreshments are served when you arrive. ⊠ *19960 N. Elliott Rd., Lockeford 95237* ☎ *209/727–5715* 🖷 *209/727–0873* ⊕ *www.theinnatlockehouse.com* ⇗ *4 rooms, 1 suite* ⌂ *Library, no-smoking rooms; no room TVs* ▭ *AE, D, DC, MC, V* ¶◎¶ *BP.*

¢ ▥ **Lodi Comfort Inn.** This downtown motel has quiet rooms with contemporary furnishings and blow dryers in the bathrooms. It's easily accessible from Highway 99. Donuts, waffles, bagels, juice, and coffee make up the complimentary breakfast. ⊠ *118 N. Cherokee La.* ☎ *209/367–4848* 🖷 *209/367–4898* ⇗ *55 rooms* ⌂ *Refrigerators, microwaves, cable TV, pool, hot tub, laundry facilities, laundry service* ▭ *AE, D, MC, V* ¶◎¶ *CP.*

Sports & the Outdoors

Even locals need respite from the heat of Central Valley summers, and **Lodi Lake Park** (⊠ Turner Rd. at Holly Dr. ☎ 209/333–6742) is where they find it. The banks, shaded by grand old elms and oaks, are much cooler than other spots in town. Swimming, bird-watching, and picnicking are possibilities, as is renting a kayak, canoe, or pedal boat ($2–$4 per half hour, Tuesday–Sunday, Memorial Day–Labor Day only).

THE CENTRAL VALLEY A TO Z

To research prices, get advice from other travelers, and book travel arrangements, visit ⊕ *www.fodors.com.*

AIRPORTS & TRANSFERS

Fresno Yosemite International Airport is serviced by America West, Alaska, Allegiant, American and American Eagle, Continental, Delta, Hawaiian, Horizon, Northwest, Skywest, United and United Express. United Express flies from San Francisco to Modesto City Airport. *See* Air Travel *in* Smart Travel Tips A to Z for airline phone numbers.

◪ **Fresno Yosemite International Airport** ⊠ 4995 E. Clinton Way, Fresno ☎ 559/498–4700. **Modesto City Airport** ⊠ 617 Airport Way, Modesto ☎ 209/577–5318.

BUS TRAVEL
Greyhound provides service between major valley cities. Orange Belt Stages provides bus service, including Amtrak connections, to many valley locations, including Fresno, Madera, Merced, and Stockton.

🔁 **Greyhound** 📞 800/231-2222 🌐 www.greyhound.com. **Orange Belt Stages** 📞 888/299-7433 🌐 www.orangebelt.com.

CAR RENTAL
Avis, Budget, Dollar, Hertz, and National rent cars at Fresno Yosemite International Airport. Avis, Enterprise, and Hertz rent cars at Modesto City Airport. *See* Car Rental *in* Smart Travel Tips A to Z for national rental-agency phone numbers.

CAR TRAVEL
To reach the Central Valley from San Francisco, take I–80 east to I–580 and then I–580 east to I–5, which leads south into the valley (several roads from I–5 head east to Highway 99); or continue east on I–580 to I–205, which leads to I–5 north to Stockton or (via Highway 120) east to Highway 99 at Manteca.

Highway 99 is the main route between the valley's major cities and towns. Interstate 5 runs roughly parallel to it to the west but misses the major population centers; its main use is for quick access from San Francisco or Los Angeles. Major roads that connect I–5 with Highway 99 are Highways 152 (to Chowchilla, via Los Banos), 140 (to Merced), 132 (to Modesto), and 120 (to Manteca). For road conditions, call the California Department of Transportation hot line.

🔁 **California Department of Transportation** 📞 916/445-1534 or 800/427-7623.

EMERGENCIES
In an emergency dial 911.

🔁 Hospitals **St. Joseph's Medical Center** ✉ 1800 North California St., Stockton 📞 209/943-2000. **University Medical Center** ✉ 445 S. Cedar Ave., Fresno 📞 559/459-4000.

TOURS
Central Valley Tours provides general and customized tours of the Fresno area and the valley.

🔁 **Central Valley Tours** ✉ 1869 E. Everglade Ave., Fresno 93720 📞 559/323-5552.

TRAIN TRAVEL
Amtrak's daily *San Joaquin* travels between Bakersfield, San Jose, and Oakland, stopping in Fresno, Merced, Riverbank (near Modesto), and Stockton.

🔁 **Amtrak** 📞 800/872-7245 🌐 www.amtrakcalifornia.com.

VISITOR INFORMATION
🔁 **Fresno City & County Convention and Visitors Bureau** ✉ 848 M St., Fresno 93721 📞 559/233-0836 or 800/788-0836. **Lodi Conference and Visitors Bureau** ✉ 2545 W. Turner Dr., Lodi 95242 📞 209/365-1195 or 800/798-1810. **Merced Conference and Visitors Bureau** ✉ 710 W. 16th St., Merced 95340 📞 209/384-7092 or 800/446-5353. **Modesto Convention and Visitors Bureau** ✉ 1150 9th St., Suite C, Modesto 95353 📞 800/266-4282. **Stockton/San Joaquin Convention and Visitors Bureau** ✉ 46 W. Fremont St., Stockton 95202 📞 209/943-1987 or 800/350-1987.

YOSEMITE & THE SOUTHERN SIERRA

WITH MAMMOTH LAKES

7

FODOR'S CHOICE

Ahwahnee Hotel & Dining Room, *Yosemite Village*
Bodie Ghost Town, *Bodie State Historic Park*
Château du Sureau, *inn in Oakhurst*
Erna's Elderberry House, *restaurant in Oakhurst*
Glacier Point, *scenic overlook near Yosemite Village*
Tamarack Lodge Resort, *Mammoth Lakes*

HIGHLY RECOMMENDED

RESTAURANTS The Restaurant at Convict Lake, *Mammoth Lakes*
Restaurant 1881, *Bridgeport*

HOTELS Tenaya Lodge, *Fish Camp*

SIGHTS Bridalveil Fall, *Yosemite Village*
El Capitan, *Yosemite Village*
Half Dome, *Yosemite Village*
Mono Lake, *Lee Vining*
Yosemite Falls, *Yosemite Village*

Revised by
John A.
Vlahides

VAST, SOARING GRANITE PEAKS AND GIANT SEQUOIAS are among the mind-boggling natural wonders of the southern Sierra. Yosemite, California's most famous national park, is renowned for its staggering U-shape valleys carved by glaciers during the Ice Age. Outside the park, pristine lakes, stunning ski resorts, and small towns complete the picture of the southern Sierra. Without a doubt, the southern Sierra should be on your "don't miss" California vacation list. Unfortunately, it's on everyone else's as well, so lodging reservations are essential when you visit this spectacular region. If possible, visit in winter or early spring, when you can take it all in without tripping over throngs of tourists.

Exploring the Southern Sierra

For the full Sierra experience, explore the national forests as well as Yosemite. Stop at any of the ranger stations near the forests' borders and pick up information on lesser-known sights and attractions. Spend a few nights in the small towns outside the park. If, however, you're tight on time and want to focus on the attractions that make the region famous, then stay in the park itself instead of the "gateway cities" in the foothills or the Central Valley; you won't want to lose time shuttling back and forth.

Yosemite Valley is the primary destination for many visitors. Because the valley is only 7 mi long and averages less than 1 mi wide, you can visit its attractions in whatever order you choose and return to your favorites at different times of the day.

About the Restaurants

Towns in the Sierra Nevada are small, but they usually have at least one diner or restaurant. In Yosemite, snack bars, coffee shops, and cafeterias are not expensive. The three fanciest lodgings within the national park are prime dining spots, with hefty price tags to match. With few exceptions, which are noted, dress is casual at the restaurants listed in this chapter.

When you're traveling in the area, you can expect to spend a lot of time in the car, so pick up snacks and drinks to keep with you, and keep the gas tank full—especially in winter, when roads sometimes close due to inclement weather. Stopping at a grocery store and filling the ice chest before you set out will also allow you to explore Yosemite without having to search for food. With picnic supplies on hand you can enjoy a meal under giant trees; just be certain to clean up after yourself and leave no food or trash behind. It's not just polite; human food is bad for wildlife and can cause health and behavioral problems. Leave no trace!

About the Hotels

Towns are few and far between in the southern Sierra. Whenever possible, book lodging reservations in advance—especially in summer—or plan to camp out. If you don't, you may find yourself driving long distances to find a place to sleep.

Most accommodations inside Yosemite National Park can best be described as "no frills"—many have no electricity or indoor plumbing. Other than the Ahwahnee and Wawona hotels in Yosemite, lodgings tend to be basic motels or rustic cabins. Except during the off-peak season, from November through March, rates in Yosemite are pricey, given the general quality of the lodging.

Numbers in the text correspond to numbers in the margin and on the Yosemite National Park and Southern Sierra maps.

If you have 3 days

If your time is limited, choose ▸ 🏞 **Yosemite National Park** to explore. Enter the park via the Big Oak Flat entrance on Highway 120, and head east on Big Oak Flat Road. Once you reach the valley floor, traffic is diverted onto a one-way loop road. Continue east, following the signs to **Yosemite Village** ⑤ and the **Valley Visitor Center.** Loop back west for a short hike near **Yosemite Falls** ⑦, the highest waterfall in North America. Continue west for a valley view of the famous **El Capitan** ⑫ monolith. This area is a good place for a picnic. Backtrack onto Southside Drive, stopping at misty **Bridalveil Fall** ⑧; then follow Highway 41/Wawona Road south 14 mi to the Chinquapin junction and make a left turn onto Glacier Point Road. From **Glacier Point** ⑭ (road closed in winter) you'll get a phenomenal bird's-eye view of the entire valley, including **Half Dome** ⑬, **Vernal Fall** ⑩, and **Nevada Fall** ⑪. If you want to avoid the busloads of tourists at Glacier Point, stop at **Sentinel Dome** ⑮ instead. After a moderately strenuous 1-mi hike you get a view similar to that from Glacier Point. Head back to the valley for an early evening beverage at the **Ahwahnee Hotel**'s bar (try out the patio in good weather), and view the lobby's paintings of Native American leaders.

On day two, head south again on Highway 41/Wawona Road and visit the **Mariposa Grove of Big Trees** ⑰ at the southern end of the park. Afterward, head north to the **Wawona Hotel** (closed weekdays much of the winter), where you can have lunch or a relaxing drink on the veranda or in the charming lobby bar. (If the restaurant is closed, there's a general store in town to pick up basic provisions; alternatively, carry a picnic basket in the car.) Afterward tour the **Pioneer Yosemite History Center.** Head back to Yosemite Valley on Wawona Road, and stop at the mouth of the tunnel on Highway 41, just before you drop into the valley, for one of the park's most famous and spectacular views. On the third day, have breakfast near the Valley Visitor Center before hiking to **Vernal Fall** or **Nevada Fall.** If you are up for a strenuous hike, you can climb to the top of **Yosemite Falls.**

If you have 5 days

Follow the three-day itinerary above, and plan your last two days depending on the season. If it's not winter, on day four pack a picnic and drive 55 mi east on Tioga Road to **Tuolumne Meadows,** the largest subalpine meadow in the Sierra. Follow the road over 9,900-foot Tioga Pass to **Lee Vining** ⑲, where you'll turn north on U.S. 395 to reach **Bodie Ghost Town** ⑳ and historic 🏞 **Bridgeport** ㉑. On day five, drive south on U.S. 395 to see **Mono Lake, Mammoth Mountain,** and **Devils Postpile National Monument. Mammoth Lakes** ⑱ is a good place to overnight. In winter, when Tioga Road is closed, it's a long and circuitous route to the east face of the Sierra, so you'll want to stay in Yosemite for the last two days of your trip. Check out the many winter sports options, such as **Badger Pass Ski Area** and the ice-skating rink at **Curry Village,** or take a snowshoeing, cross-country skiing, telemarking, or skate-skiing class at **Yosemite Mountaineering School.**

7

	WHAT IT COSTS				
	$$$$	**$$$**	**$$**	**$**	**¢**
RESTAURANTS	over $30	$23–$30	$16–$22	$10–$15	under $10
HOTELS	over $250	$176–$250	$121–$175	$90–$120	under $90

Restaurant prices are for a main course at dinner, excluding sales tax of 7¼%. Hotel prices are for a standard double room in high season, excluding service charges and 9–10% tax.

Timing

Summer brings crowds to the Sierra Nevada. Because much of the range is covered by deep snow in winter, trails in the backcountry and in wilderness areas aren't accessible until late spring. As you rise in elevation, you'll see "spring" wildflowers blooming late in summer.

Summer is also the most crowded season. During extremely busy periods—when snow closes high-country roads in late spring or on crowded summer weekends—Yosemite Valley may be closed to all vehicles unless their drivers have overnight reservations. Avoid these restrictions by visiting from mid-April through Memorial Day and from Labor Day to mid-October, when the park is less busy and the weather is usually hospitable.

The falls at Yosemite are at their most spectacular in May and June. By the end of summer some will have dried up. They begin flowing again in late fall with the first storms, and during winter they may be hung with ice, a dramatic sight. Snow on the floor of Yosemite Valley is never deep, so you can often camp there even in winter (January highs are in the mid-40s, lows in the mid-20s). Tioga Road is usually closed from late October through May; unless you ski or snowshoe in, you can't get to Tuolumne Meadows then. The road to Glacier Point beyond the turnoff for Badger Pass is not cleared in winter, but it is groomed for cross-country skiing.

SOUTH OF YOSEMITE
FROM BASS LAKE TO EL PORTAL

Several gateway towns to the south and west of Yosemite National Park, most within an hour's drive of Yosemite Valley, have food, lodging, and other services. Highway 140 heads east from the Central Valley to El Portal. Highway 41 heads north from Fresno to Oakhurst and Fish Camp; Bass Lake is off Highway 41.

Bass Lake

1 *Approx. 50 mi north of Fresno; take Hwy. 41 to Bass Valley Rd.*

For the most part surrounded by the Sierra National Forest, Bass Lake is a warm-water lake whose waters can reach 80° in summer. Created by a dam on a tributary of the San Joaquin River, the lake is owned by Pacific Gas and Electric Company, and is used to generate electricity as well as for recreation.

Where to Eat

¢–$$$ ✕ **Ducey's on the Lake/Ducey's Bar & Grill.** With elaborate chandeliers sculpted from deer antlers, the lodge-style restaurant at Ducey's (part of the larger Pines Resort complex) attracts boaters, locals, and tourists with its lake views and standard lamb, beef, seafood, and pasta dishes. For cheap eats, head upstairs to Ducey's Bar & Grill for burgers, sal-

Camping

Camping in the Sierra Nevada means awakening to the sights of nearby meadows and streams and the unforgettable landscape of giant granite. Camping here also means gazing up at an awe-inspiring collection of constellations and spying a shooting star in the night sky. Campgrounds from remote, tents-only areas to sprawling full-service facilities close to the main attractions operate in Yosemite National Park. Of the numerous campgrounds in the park, Tuolumne Meadows campground may be the prettiest of the easily accessible spots, so it's also among the most popular. Spectacular camping abounds outside the national park, as well, at sites such as Lake Mary Campground in the Mammoth Lakes area.

Hiking & Walking

Hiking is the primary outdoor activity in the Sierra Nevada. Whether you walk the paved loops that pass by major attractions or head off the beaten path into the backcountry, a hike through groves and meadows or alongside streams and waterfalls will allow you to see, smell, and feel nature up close. Some of the most popular trails are described briefly in this chapter; stop by the visitor centers for maps and advice from park rangers. No matter which trail you decide to take, always carry lots of water.

Winter Sports

Famous for its massive snowfalls, the Sierra Nevada has something for every winter sports fan. At Yosemite Mountaineering School you can learn how to snowshoe, cross-country ski, telemark ski, and skate-ski, and at Yosemite's Badger Pass Ski Area you can schuss down the slopes alpine-style. But Mammoth Mountain Ski Area is the star of the southern Sierra winter sports scene. One of the biggest ski resorts in the western United States, Mammoth offers terrain to suit every taste and ability level, plus ample facilities for snowboarders.

---

ads, tacos, and sandwiches. ⊠ *54432 Rd. 432,* ☎ *559/642–3121* ▭ *AE, D, DC, MC, V.*

Sports & the Outdoors

Bass Lake Water Sports & Marina (⊠ Bass Lake Reservoir ☎ 559/642–3565), open from April through October, rents ski boats, houseboats, and fishing boats.

Oakhurst

❷ *40 mi north of Fresno (23 mi south of Yosemite National Park's South Entrance) on Hwy. 41.*

Motels and restaurants line both sides of Highway 41 as it cuts through the town of Oakhurst. You can stock up on provisions at the grocery and general stores.

Where to Stay & Eat

$$$$ ✕ **Erna's Elderberry House.** The restaurant, operated by Vienna-born
Fodor'sChoice Erna Kubin, owner of Château du Sureau, is an expression of her pas-
★ sion for beauty, charm, and impeccable service. Red walls and dark beams accent the dining room's high ceilings, and arched windows reflect the glow of candles. A seasonal six-course prix fixe dinner is elegantly paced and accompanied by superb wines. When the waitstaff places all the plates on the table in perfect synchronicity, you'll know this will be

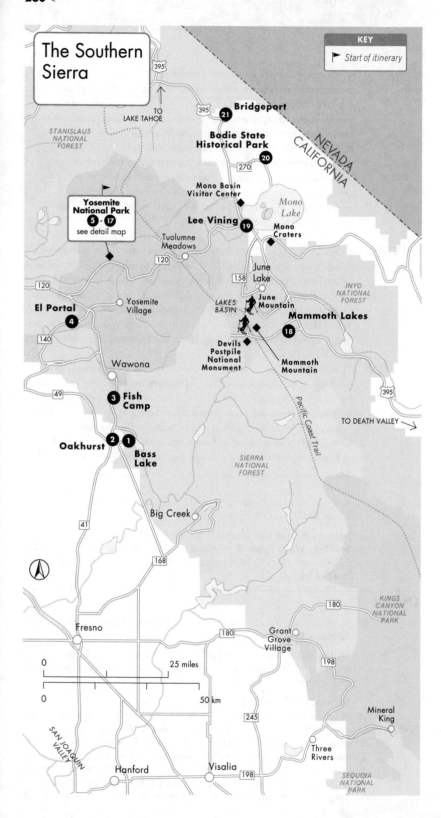

The Southern Sierra

395

TO LAKE TAHOE

STANISLAUS
NATIONAL
FOREST

395

Bridgeport
21

Bodie State
Historical Park
20
270

Mono Basin
Visitor Center

Mono
Lake

Lee Vining
19

Mono
Craters

Yosemite
National Park
5 - 17
see detail map

Tuolumne
Meadows

120

June
Lake

158

LAKES
BASIN

June
Mountain

INYO
NATIONAL
FOREST

120

Yosemite
Village

El Portal
4

Mammoth Lakes
18

140

Devils
Postpile
National
Monument

Mammoth
Mountain

Wawona

49

3 Fish
Camp

395

TO DEATH VALLEY →

Oakhurst
2 1

Bass
Lake

Pacific Coast Trail

SIERRA
NATIONAL
FOREST

Big Creek

41

168

Fresno

180

KINGS
CANYON
NATIONAL
PARK

180

Grant
Grove
Village

198

0   25 miles

0   50 km

245

Mineral
King

SAN JOAQUIN VALLEY

Hanford

Visalia

198

Three
Rivers

SEQUOIA
NATIONAL
PARK

a meal to remember. ⊠ *48688 Victoria La.* ☎ *559/683–6800* ☰ *AE, MC, V* ⚒ *Reservations essential* ⊘ *Closed 1st 3 wks in Jan. No lunch except Sun. (brunch).*

$$$$ 🏨 **Château du Sureau.** This romantic inn, adjacent to Erna's Elderberry
Fodor's Choice House, is out of a children's book. From the moment you drive through
★ the wrought-iron gates and up to the fairy-tale castle, you will be pampered. You'll fall asleep in the glow of a crackling fire amid goose-down pillows and a fluffy comforter. In the morning, after a hearty European breakfast in the dining room, relax in the piano room, which has an exquisite ceiling mural. ⊠ *48688 Victoria La., Box 577, 93644* ☎ *559/ 683–6860* 🖷 *559/683–0800* ⊕ *www.elderberryhouse.com* ⇆ *10 rooms, 1 villa* ⚒ *Restaurant, dining room, in-room data ports, pool, boccie ball; TV by request only, no smoking* ☰ *AE, MC, V* ⧖❘ *BP.*

$$–$$$ 🏨 **The Homestead Cottages.** Serenity is the order of the day at this secluded getaway in Ahwahnee, 6 mi west of Oakhurst. On 160 acres that once held a Miwok village, these cottages have fireplaces, living rooms, fully equipped kitchens, and queen-size beds. The cottages, built by hand by the owners, are stocked with soft green robes, oversize towels, and a good supply of paperback books. ⊠ *41110 Rd. 600, 2½ mi off Hwy. 49, Ahwahnee 93601* ☎ *559/683–0495 or 800/483–0495* 🖷 *559/683–8165* ⊕ *www.homesteadcottages.com* ⇆ *4 cottages, 1 loft* ⚒ *Kitchenettes, microwaves, cable TV; no room phones, no smoking* ☰ *AE, D, MC, V.*

$–$$ 🏨 **Shilo Inn.** Rooms at this upscale multi-story motel are spacious and sunny and offer amenities such as in-room coffeemakers, irons, and hair dryers. ⊠ *40644 Hwy. 41, 93644* ☎ *559/683–3555 or 800/222–2244* 🖷 *559/683–3386* ⊕ *www.shiloinns.com* ⇆ *80 rooms, 1 suite* ⚒ *Microwaves, refrigerators, cable TV with movies, pool, gym, hot tub, sauna, steam room, laundry facilities, no-smoking rooms* ☰ *AE, D, DC, MC, V* ⧖❘ *CP.*

Fish Camp

❸ *57 mi north of Fresno (4 mi south of Yosemite National Park's south entrance) on Hwy. 41.*

In the small town of Fish Camp there is a post office and a general store.
Ⓒ The **Yosemite Mountain Sugar Pine Railroad** has a narrow-gauge steam engine that chugs through the forest. It follows 4 mi of the route the Madera Sugar Pine Lumber Company cut through the forest in 1899 in order to harvest timber. Saturday evening's Moonlight Special dinner excursion (reservations essential) includes music by the Sugar Pine Trio. ⊠ *56001 Hwy. 41* ☎ *559/683–7273* 🎟 *$13; Moonlight Special $36* ⊘ *Mar.–Oct., daily.*

Where to Stay & Eat

$$$–$$$$ ✕🏨 **Tenaya Lodge.** One of the region's largest hotels, the Tenaya Lodge
★ Ⓒ is ideal for people who enjoy wilderness treks by day but prefer luxury at night. A Southwestern motif prevails in the ample regular rooms. The deluxe rooms have minibars and other extras, and the suites have balconies. The cozy Sierra Restaurant ($$–$$$$) serves Continental cuisine; the fare at the lodge's casual Jackalopes Bar and Grill ($–$$) includes burgers, salads, and sandwiches. ⊠ *1122 Hwy. 41, Box 159, 93623* ☎ *559/683–6555 or 888/514–2167* 🖷 *559/683–0249* ⊕ *www. tenayalodge.com* ⇆ *244 rooms, 6 suites* ⚒ *2 restaurants, snack bar, room service, in-room data ports, some minibars, cable TV with movies and video games, indoor pool, health club, hot tub, mountain bikes, hiking, cross-country skiing, bar, recreation room, baby-sitting, children's programs (ages 5–12), playground, laundry service, concierge, business services, meeting room; no smoking* ☰ *AE, D, DC, MC, V.*

$$ ✕⚏ **Narrow Gauge Inn.** This motel-style property is comfortably furnished with old-fashioned accents and railroad memorabilia. The inn's restaurant ($–$$$, open Apr.–Oct.), which serves standard American fare, is festooned with moose, bison, and other wildlife trophies. ⊠ *48571 Hwy. 41, 93623* ☎ *559/683–7720 or 888/644–9050* 📠 *559/683–2139* ⊕ *www.narrowgaugeinn.com* 🛏 *25 rooms, 1 suite* � *Restaurant, in-room data ports, cable TV, some in-room VCRs, pool, hot tub, bar, some pets allowed (fee); no a/c in some rooms, no smoking* ⊟ *D, MC, V.*

El Portal

❹ *14 mi west of Yosemite Valley on Hwy. 140.*

The market in town is a good place to pick up provisions before you get to Yosemite. There is also a post office and a gas station.

Where to Stay

⟳ **$$** ⚏ **Yosemite View Lodge.** Many rooms with balconies overlook the boulder-strewn Merced River and majestic pines. Also in view is a picnic patio with hot tubs and heated pools. The pleasant facility is on the public bus route to Yosemite National Park and near fishing and river rafting. Many rooms have spa baths, fireplaces, and kitchenettes. ⊠ *11136 Hwy. 140, 95318* ☎ *209/379–2681* 📠 *209/379–2704* ⊕ *www.yosemite-motels.com* 🛏 *276 rooms* � *Restaurant, pizzeria, some kitchenettes, cable TV, indoor pool, pool, 5 hot tubs, bar, laundry facilities, meeting room, some pets allowed (fee), no-smoking rooms* ⊟ *AE, MC, V.*

$–$$ ⚏ **Cedar Lodge.** The lobby of this rustic lodge in the pines is filled with teddy bears. Rooms range from suites with kitchenettes to family units to romantic accommodations with whirlpool tubs for two. ⊠ *9966 Hwy. 140, 95318* ☎ *209/379–2612* 📠 *209/379–2712* ⊕ *www.yosemite-motels.com* 🛏 *188 rooms, 22 suites, 2 apartments, 1 house* � *Restaurant, some kitchenettes, cable TV, 2 pools, hot tub, no-smoking rooms* ⊟ *AE, MC, V.*

YOSEMITE NATIONAL PARK

▶ Yosemite, with 1,169 square mi of parkland, is 93% undeveloped wilderness, most of it accessible only on foot or horseback. The western boundary dips as low as 2,000 feet in the chaparral-covered foothills; the eastern boundary rises to 13,000 feet at points along the Sierra crest.

Yosemite is so large you can think of it as five different parks. Yosemite Valley, famous for waterfalls and cliffs, and Wawona, where the giant sequoias stand, are open all year. Hetch Hetchy, home of less-used backcountry trails, closes after the first big snow and reopens in May or June. The subalpine high country, Tuolumne Meadows, is open for summer hiking and camping; in winter it's accessible only by cross-country skis or snowshoes. Badger Pass Ski Area is open in winter only. The fee to visit Yosemite National Park (good for seven days) is $20 per car, $10 per person if you don't arrive in a car. (Fees must be paid in cash or traveler's checks only.)

From early May to late September and during some holiday periods, actor Lee Stetson portrays naturalist John Muir, bringing to life Muir's wit, wisdom, and storytelling skill. You can also join park rangers on free 60- to 90-minute nature walks focusing on geology, wildlife, waterfalls, forest ecology, and other topics. Locations and times for both are listed in the *Yosemite Guide,* the newspaper that you receive on entering the park.

Yosemite Valley

214 mi east of San Francisco, I–80 to I–580 to I–205 to Hwy. 120; 330 mi northeast of Los Angeles, I–5 to Hwy. 99 to Hwy. 41.

Yosemite Valley has been so extravagantly praised (John Muir described it as "a revelation in landscape affairs that enriches one's life forever") and so beautifully photographed (by Ansel Adams, who said, "I knew my destiny when I first experienced Yosemite") that you may wonder if the reality can possibly measure up. For almost everyone it does. It's a true reminder of what "breathtaking" really means. The Miwok people, the last of several Native American tribes who inhabited the Yosemite area, named the valley "Ahwahnee," which is thought to mean "the place of the gaping mouth." Members of the tribe, who were forced out of the area by gold miners in 1851, called themselves the Ahwahneechee. The roads at the eastern fringes of the valley are closed to private cars, but a free shuttle bus runs frequently from the village (between 7 AM and 10 PM May–September, between 9 AM and 10 PM the rest of the year). Be aware that bears are a huge problem in Yosemite; be sure to speak with a ranger about taking proper precautions while in the park.

❺ The center of activity in Yosemite Valley is **Yosemite Village,** which contains restaurants, stores, a post office, the Ahwahnee Hotel, Yosemite Lodge, and a clinic. You can get your bearings, pick up maps, and obtain information from park rangers at the village's **Valley Visitor Center.** At the **Wilderness Center** you can find out everything you need to know about backcountry activities like hiking and camping. A 1-mi paved loop from the visitor center, called **A Changing Yosemite,** traces the park's natural evolution and includes a couple of interesting stops. The **Yosemite Museum** has an Indian cultural exhibit, with displays about the Miwok and Paiute people who lived in the region; there's a re-created Ahwahneechee village behind it. The **Ansel Adams Gallery** shows works of the master photographer and sells prints and camera equipment. ✉ *Off Northside Dr.* ☎ *209/372–0200 for park information, 209/372-0299 for visitor center, 209/372–4413 for gallery* ☉ *Visitor center fall–spring, daily 9–5; summer, daily 9–6.*

Yosemite Concession Services Corporation (☎ 209/372–1240 ⊕ www. yosemitepark.com) operates daily guided bus tours of the Yosemite Valley floor year-round, plus seasonal tours of Glacier Point and the Mariposa Grove of Big Trees. The company's Grand Tour ($55), offered between Memorial Day and October 29, weather permitting, covers the park's highlights.

❻ As you venture through the valley amid Yosemite's natural wonders, stop at **Happy Isles Nature Center,** about half a mile east of Curry Village, to see ecology exhibits and find books for children. ☉ *May–Oct., daily 9–5.*

★ ❼ Yosemite Valley is famed for its waterfalls, and the mightiest of them all is **Yosemite Falls,** the highest waterfall in North America and the fifth highest in the world. The upper fall (1,430 feet), the middle cascades (675 feet), and the lower fall (320 feet) combine for a total drop of 2,425 feet. When viewed from the valley, the three sections appear as a single waterfall. A ¼-mi trail leads from the parking lot to the base of the falls. The Upper Yosemite Fall Trail, a strenuous 3½-mi climb rising 2,700 feet, takes you above the top of the falls. It starts at Camp 4, formerly known as Sunnyside Campground.

★ ❽ **Bridalveil Fall,** a filmy fall of 620 feet that is often diverted as much as 20 feet one way or the other by the breeze, is the first view of Yosemite Valley for those who arrive via Wawona Road. Native Americans called

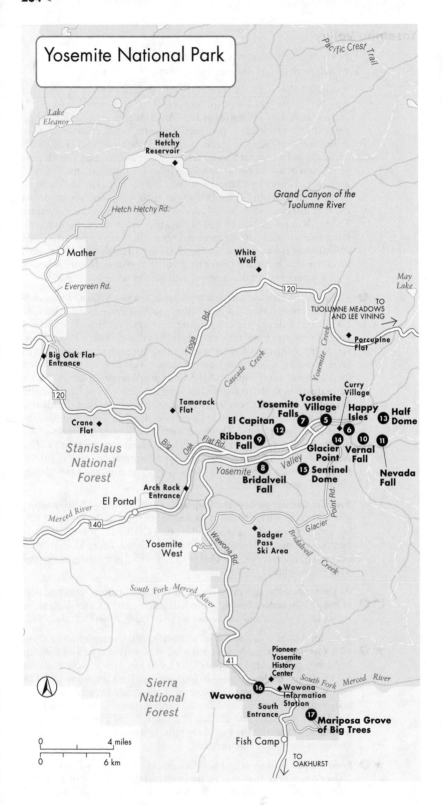

Yosemite National Park

Lake Eleanor

Hetch Hetchy Reservoir

Hetch Hetchy Rd.

Grand Canyon of the Tuolumne River

Mather

Evergreen Rd.

White Wolf

120

May Lake

TO TUOLUMNE MEADOWS AND LEE VINING

Big Oak Flat Entrance

Tioga Rd.

Cascade Creek

Porcupine Flat

120

Tamarack Flat

Crane Flat

Stanislaus National Forest

Big Oak Flat Rd.

Yosemite Creek

Curry Village

Yosemite Falls

Yosemite Village

Happy Isles

Half Dome

El Capitan

12

7

5

13

Ribbon Fall

9

14

6

10

11

Glacier Point

Vernal Fall

Yosemite Valley

8

15

Sentinel Dome

Nevada Fall

Bridalveil Fall

Arch Rock Entrance

El Portal

Merced River

140

Glacier Point Rd.

Yosemite West

Badger Pass Ski Area

Bridalveil Creek

Wawona Rd.

South Fork Merced River

Pioneer Yosemite History Center

41

South Fork Merced River

Sierra National Forest

Wawona

16

Wawona Information Station

South Entrance

17

Mariposa Grove of Big Trees

Fish Camp

TO OAKHURST

0 ——— 4 miles

0 ——— 6 km

the fall Pohono (spirit of the puffing wind). A ¼-mi trail leads from the parking lot off Wawona Road to the base of the fall.

❾ At 1,612 feet **Ribbon Fall** is the highest single fall in North America. It is also the first waterfall in the valley to dry up; the rainwater and melted snow that create the slender fall evaporate quickly at this height.

❿ Fern-covered black rocks frame **Vernal Fall** (317 feet), and rainbows play in the spray at its base. The hike on a paved trail from the Happy Isles Nature Center to the bridge at the base of Vernal Fall is only moderately strenuous and less than 1 mi long. It's another steep (and often wet) ¾ mi up the Mist Trail—which is open only from late spring to early fall—to the top of Vernal Fall. Allow two–four hours for the 3-mi round-trip hike.

⓫ **Nevada Fall** (594 feet) is the first major fall as the Merced River plunges out of the high country toward the eastern end of Yosemite Valley. A strenuous 2-mi section of the Mist Trail leads from Vernal Fall to the top of Nevada Fall. Allow 6–8 hours for the full 7-mi round-trip hike.

Yosemite Valley's waterfalls tumble past magnificent geological scenery.
★ ⓬ **El Capitan,** rising 3,593 feet above the valley, is the largest exposed granite monolith in the world, almost twice the height of the Rock of Gibraltar.

★ ⓭ Astounding **Half Dome** rises 4,733 feet from the valley floor to a height 8,842 feet above sea level. The west side of the dome is fractured vertically and cut away to form a 2,000-foot cliff. The highly strenuous **John Muir Trail** (which incorporates the Mist Trail) leads from Yosemite Valley to the top of Half Dome. Allow 10–12 hours round-trip for the 16¾-mi round-trip hike; start early in the morning and beware of afternoon thunderstorms. If you plan to take this hike, inquire about preparations at one of the ranger stations.

⓮ **Glacier Point** yields what may be the most spectacular vistas of the valley and the High Sierra that you can get without hiking, especially at
Fodor'sChoice ley and the High Sierra that you can get without hiking, especially at
★ sunset. Glacier Point Road splits off from Wawona Road (Highway 41) about 23 mi southwest of the valley; then it's a 16-mi drive, with fine views, into higher country. From the parking area walk a few hundred yards, and you'll be able to see Nevada, Vernal, and Yosemite Falls as well as Half Dome and other peaks. You can hike to the valley floor (3,214 feet below) via the Panorama or Four-Mile Trails. To avoid a grueling round-trip, catch a ride to Glacier Point on one of the three daily hikers' buses (☎ 209/372–1240 for reservations ✉ $15 one-way, $29.50 round-trip), which run from late spring through October. In winter, Glacier Point Road is closed beyond the turnoff for the Badger Pass Ski Area, making Glacier Point inaccessible.

⓯ The view from **Sentinel Dome** is similar to that from Glacier Point, except you can't see the valley floor. A 1.1-mi path begins at a parking lot on Glacier Point Road a few miles below Glacier Point. The trail is long and steep enough to keep the crowds and tour buses away, but not overly rugged.

off the beaten path

HETCH HETCHY RESERVOIR AND TUOLUMNE MEADOWS – Hetch Hetchy Reservoir, which supplies water and hydroelectric power to San Francisco, is about 40 mi from Yosemite Valley via Big Oak Flat Road to Highway 120 to Evergreen Road to Hetch Hetchy Road. Some say John Muir died of heartbreak when this valley was dammed and flooded beneath 300 feet of water in 1913. Tioga Road (Highway 120) stays open until the first big snow of the year, usually about mid-October. This spectacularly scenic route is the only road to Tuolumne Meadows, which sits at 8,575 feet in altitude—it's about 55 mi from Yosemite Valley. The largest subalpine meadow in the Sierra and the trailhead for many backpack trips into the High Sierra, the area contains campgrounds, a gas station, a store (with limited and expensive provisions), stables, a lodge, and a visitor center open from late June until Labor Day from 9 to 5.

Where to Stay & Eat

$$-$$$ ✕ **Mountain Room Restaurant.** The food becomes secondary when you see Yosemite Falls through this dining room's wall of windows. Almost every table has a view of the falls. Sesame-seared ahi tuna, grilled rainbow trout, steak, pasta, and several children's dishes are on the menu. ⊠ *Yosemite Lodge, off Northside Dr.* ☎ *209/372–1281* ☐ *AE, D, DC, MC, V* ☉ *Closed weekdays Thanksgiving–Easter except for holiday periods. No lunch.*

$$$$ ✕⌂ **Ahwahnee Hotel & Dining Room.** This grand 1920s-era mountain lodge,
Fodor'sChoice designated a National Historical Landmark, is constructed of rocks
★ and sugar-pine logs. In the Ahwahnee's comfortable rooms you'll enjoy some of the amenities found in a luxury hotel, including turn-down service and guest bathrobes. The Ahwahnee Dining Room ($$$–$$$$), with its 34-foot-tall trestle-beam ceiling, full-length windows, and wrought-iron chandeliers, is by far the most impressive eating establishment in the park. Specialties include sautéed salmon, roast duckling, and prime rib. Jackets are required, and reservations are essential. ⊠ *Ahwahnee Rd. north of Northside Dr., 95389* ⌂ *Yosemite Reservations, 5410 E. Home Ave., Fresno, 93727* ☎ *559/252–4848 for lodging reservations, 209/372–1489 for restaurant,* ⊕ *www.yosemitepark.com* ⤴ *99 rooms, 4 suites, 24 cottages* ↻ *Restaurant, in-room data ports, refrigerators, tennis court, pool, lounge, concierge, no-smoking rooms; no a/c in some rooms* ☐ *AE, D, DC, MC, V.*

$–$$ ✕⌂ **Yosemite Lodge.** This lodge near Yosemite Falls, which dates from 1915, once housed the U.S. army cavalry. Today it looks like a discrete 1950s motel-resort complex, with several satellite buildings painted brown and white to blend in with the landscape. Rooms have two double beds, and the larger rooms also have dressing areas and balconies. Of the lodge's eating places, the Mountain Room Restaurant ($$–$$$) is the most formal. The cafeteria-style Food Court (¢–$) serves three meals a day and offers salads, soups, sandwiches, pastas, and roasted meats. ⊠ *Off Northside Dr., 95389* ⌂ *Yosemite Reservations, 5410 E. Home Ave., Fresno, 93727* ☎ *559/252–4848 for lodging reservations, 209/372–1274 for front desk* ⊟ *559/456–0542* ⊕ *www.yosemitepark.com* ⤴ *239 rooms* ↻ *Restaurant, cafeteria, fans, in-room data ports, pool, bicycles, bar, no-smoking rooms; no a/c* ☐ *AE, D, DC, MC, V.*

¢–$ ⌂ **Curry Village.** Opened in 1899 as a place where travelers could enjoy the beauty of Yosemite for a modest price, Curry Village has plain accommodations: standard motel rooms, cabins, and tent cabins, which have rough wood frames and canvas walls and roofs. The latter are a step up from camping, with linens, blankets, and maid service provided. Most of the cabins share shower and toilet facilities. ⊠ *South side of Southside Dr., 95389* ⌂ *Yosemite Reservations, 5410 E. Home Ave., Fresno, 93727* ☎ *559/252–4848 for lodging reservations, 209/372–8333 for front desk* ⊟ *559/456–0542* ⊕ *www.yosemitepark.com* ⤴ *19 rooms; 182 cabins, 102 with bath; 427 tent cabins* ↻ *Cafeteria, pizzeria, pool, bicycles, ice-skating, no-smoking rooms; no a/c, no room phones, no room TVs* ☐ *AE, D, DC, MC, V.*

¢ ⌂ **Housekeeping Camp.** These rustic three-sided concrete units with canvas roofs, set on a beach along the Merced River, are difficult to come by; reserving a year in advance is advised. They are not the prettiest sites in the valley, but they're good for travelers with RVs or those without a tent who want to camp. You can cook here on gas stoves rented from the front desk, or you can use the fire pits. Toilets and showers are in a central building, and there is a camp store for provisions. ☖ *Picnic area, beach, laundry facilities; no a/c, no room phones, no room TVs* ☜ *226 units* ✉ *North side of Southside Dr. near Curry Village, 95389* ☎ *Yosemite Reservations, 5410 E. Home Ave., Fresno, 93727* ☎ *209/ 372–8338, 559/252–4848 for reservations* 🖷 *559/456–0542* ⊕ *www. yosemitepark.com* ☰ *AE, D, DC, MC, V* ⊘ *Closed early Oct.–late Apr.*

△ **Camp 4.** Formerly known as Sunnyside Walk-In, this is the only valley campground available on a first-come, first-served basis, and the only one west of Yosemite Lodge. It is a favorite for rock climbers and solo campers, so it fills quickly and is typically sold out by 9 AM every day from spring through fall. ☖ *Flush toilets, drinking water, showers, bear boxes, fire grates, picnic tables, public telephone, ranger station* ☜ *35 sites* ✉ *At base of Yosemite Falls Trail, near Yosemite Lodge* ☎ *209/ 372–0265* 🖷 *209/372–0371* ☒ *$5* ☖ *Reservations not accepted* ☰ *No credit cards* ⊘ *Year-round.*

△ **Crane Flat.** Also on the western boundary, south of Hodgdon Meadow, this camp is just 17 mi from the valley but far from its bustle. A small grove of sequoias is nearby. ☖ *Flush toilets, drinking water, bear boxes, fire pits, picnic tables, general store, ranger station* ☜ *166 sites (tent or RV)* ✉ *From Big Oak Flat entrance on Hwy. 120, drive 10 mi east to campground entrance on right* ☎ *209/372–0265 or 800/436–7275* 🖷 *209/372–0371* ⊕ *reservations.nps.gov* ☒ *$18* ☖ *Reservations essential* ☰ *AE, D, MC, V* ⊘ *June–Oct.*

△ **Tuolumne Meadows.** The campground is in a wooded area at 8,600 feet, just south of a subalpine meadow, and it affords easy access to high peaks with spectacular views. Campers here can use the hot showers at the Tuolumne Meadows Lodge (only at certain strictly regulated times). Half the sites are first-come, first-served, but arrive very early if you hope to get one. Because of the beautiful scenery, this is one of the most sought-after campgrounds in Yosemite. ☖ *Flush toilets, dump station, drinking water, bear boxes, fire grates, picnic tables, public telephone, general store, ranger station* ☜ *314 sites (tent or RV)* ✉ *Hwy. 120, 46 mi east of Big Oak Flat entrance station,* ☎ *209/372–4025 or 800/436–7275* 🖷 *209/372–0371* ⊕ *reservations.nps.gov* ☒ *$18* ☖ *Reservations essential* ☰ *AE, D, MC, V* ⊘ *June–Sept.*

△ **Upper Pines.** This is the valley's largest campground and is closest to the trailheads. Expect large crowds in the summer—and little privacy. ☖ *Flush toilets, dump station, drinking water, showers, bear boxes, fire grates, picnic tables, public telephone, ranger station, swimming (river)* ☜ *238 sites (tent or RV)* ✉ *At east end of valley,* ☎ *800/436–7275* ⊕ *reservations.nps.gov* ☒ *$18* ☖ *Reservations essential* ☰ *AE, D, MC, V* ⊘ *Year-round.*

Sports & the Outdoors

BICYCLING For those who wish to explore the 8 mi of bike paths in eastern Yosemite Valley, **Yosemite Lodge** (☎ 209/372–1208) rents bicycles all year. Bikes are $5.50 an hour or $21 per day. You can ride on 196 mi of paved park roads in Yosemite; rental bikes are available at **Curry Village** (☎ 209/ 372–8319) from April through October. Baby jogger strollers and bikes with child trailers are also available.

HIKING Yosemite's 840 mi of hiking trails range from short strolls to rugged multiday treks. The park's visitor centers have trail maps and information. Rangers will recommend easy trails to get you acclimated to the altitude. The staff at the **Wilderness Center** in Yosemite Village provides free wilderness permits for overnight backpackers which are required for overnight camping (reservations are available for $5 and are highly recommended for popular trailheads from May through September and on weekends). They also provide maps and advice to hikers heading into the backcountry. ⊠ *Yosemite Village near Ansel Adams Gallery* 🖃 *Yosemite Wilderness Reservations, Box 545, Yosemite 95389* ☎ *209/372–0740* ⊕ *www.nps.gov/yose.*

HORSEBACK
RIDING

Tuolumne Meadows Stables (☎ 209/372–8427) has day trips costing from $40 to $80 and High Sierra four- to six-day camping treks on mules beginning at $617. **Wawona Stables** (☎ 209/375–6502) has several rides, starting at $40. You can tour the backcountry on two-hour, four-hour, and all-day rides at **Yosemite Valley Stables** (☎ 209/372–8348).

ROCK CLIMBING

Yosemite Mountaineering School (☎ 209/372–8344) conducts rock-climbing, backpacking, snowshoeing, cross-country skiing, telemarking, and skate-skiing classes. It also has guided hiking trips or can design a customized hike for you.

WINTER SPORTS

Badger Pass Ski Area, off Yosemite's Glacier Point Road, has nine downhill runs, 90 mi of groomed cross-country trails, and two excellent ski schools. Free shuttle buses from Yosemite Valley to Badger Pass operate in ski season. The gentle slopes of Badger Pass make **Yosemite Ski School** (☎ 209/372–8430) an ideal spot for children and beginners to learn downhill skiing or snowboarding. The highlight of Yosemite's cross-country skiing center is a 21-mi loop from Badger Pass to Glacier Point. You can rent cross-country skis for $17 per day at the **Cross-Country Ski School** (☎ 209/372–8444). They also rent snowshoes ($15 per day), telemarking equipment ($21.50), and skate-skis ($19.50). ⊠ *Badger Pass Rd. off Glacier Point Rd., approx. 18 mi from Yosemite Valley* ☎ *209/372–8430* 🖃 *Lift tickets, $31; downhill equipment rental, $22.50; snowboard rental, $32.50* ☉ *Dec.–early Apr., weather permitting.* The outdoor **ice-skating rink** at Curry Village in Yosemite Valley is open from Thanksgiving Day through April. Admission is $9.75, including skate rental. ⊠ *South side of Southside Dr.* ☎ *209/372–8341.*

Wawona

16 *25 mi south of Yosemite Valley (16 mi north of Fish Camp) on Hwy. 41.*

The historic buildings in **Pioneer Yosemite History Center** were moved to Wawona from their original sites in the park. From Wednesday through Sunday in summer, costumed docents re-create life in 19th-century Yosemite in a blacksmith's shop, a Wells Fargo office, a jail, and other structures. Near the center are a post office, a general store, an information center (Memorial Day–Labor Day), and a gas station. Ask about ranger-led walks and horse-drawn stage rides. ⊠ *Hwy. 41 near south entrance gate, Wawona,* ☎ *209/375–9531 or 209/379–2646* 🖃 *Free* ☉ *Daily year-round; building interiors accessible mid-June–Labor Day, Wed. 2–5, Thurs.–Sun. 10–1 and 2–5.*

17 **Mariposa Grove of Big Trees,** Yosemite's largest grove of giant sequoias, can be visited on foot—trails all lead uphill—or, during the summer, on one-hour tram rides (reservations essential). The Grizzly Giant, the oldest tree here, is estimated to be 2,700 years old. In summer, a free shuttle connects Wawona to the Mariposa Grove of Big Trees between 9 and 4:30. The last return shuttle from the grove departs at 5. If the road to the grove is closed (which happens when Yosemite is crowded), park in Wawona and take the free shuttle; passengers are picked up near the gas station. The access road to the grove may also be closed by snow for extended periods from November to mid-May. You can still usually walk, snowshoe, or ski in. ⊠ *Off Hwy. 41, 2 mi north of south entrance gate* ☎ *209/375–1621 or 209/375–6551* 🎫 *Free; tram tour $11* ⏱ *Tram May–Oct., daily 9–4; shuttle Memorial Day–Labor Day, daily 9–5.*

Where to Stay & Eat

$–$$ ✕🖼 **Wawona Hotel and Dining Room.** This 1879 National Historic Landmark sits at the southern end of Yosemite National Park, near the Mariposa Grove of Big Trees. It's an old-fashioned New England–style estate of whitewashed buildings with wraparound verandas. The hotel has small but pleasant rooms decorated with period pieces. Dine in the romantic, candlelit dining room ($$–$$$, reservations essential), which dates from the late 1800s. The smoky corn trout soup hits the spot on cold winter nights. ⊠ *Hwy. 41, 95389* 🏛 *Yosemite Reservations, 5410 E. Home Ave., Fresno, 93727* ☎ *559/252–4848 for lodging reservations, 209/375–6556 for front desk, 209/375–1425 for dining reservations* 🖨 *559/456–0542* ⊕ *www.yosemitepark.com* 🛏 *104 rooms, 52 with bath* ⚙ *Restaurant, 9-hole golf course, putting green, tennis court, pool, horseback riding, bar; no room phones, no room TVs, no smoking* 🗇 *AE, D, DC, MC, V* ⏱ *Closed weekdays Nov.–Easter except holidays.*

⚠ **Wawona.** Near the Mariposa Grove, just downstream from a good fishing spot, this campground has larger, less closely packed sites than campgrounds in the valley. The downside is that it's an hour's drive to the valley's major attractions. ⚙ *Flush toilets, drinking water, bear boxes, fire grates, picnic tables, ranger station, swimming (river)* 🛏 *93 sites (tent or RV)* ⊠ *Hwy. 41, 1 mi north of village of Wawona* ☎ *800/ 436–7275 or 209/372–0265* 🖨 *209/372–0371* ⊕ *reservations.nps.gov* 🎫 *$18* ⚙ *Reservations essential* 🗇 *AE, D, MC, V* ⏱ *Year-round.*

MAMMOTH AREA

A jewel in the vast eastern Sierra Nevada, the Mammoth Lakes area provides California's finest skiing and snowboarding south of Lake Tahoe. Skiers hit the slopes at 11,053-foot-high Mammoth Mountain as late as June or even July. As soon as the snows melt, Mammoth transforms itself into a warm-weather playground—fishing, mountain biking, golfing, hiking, and horseback riding are among the activities available. Nine deep-blue lakes are spread through the Mammoth Lakes Basin, and another 100 lakes dot the surrounding countryside. Crater-pocked Mammoth Mountain hasn't had a major eruption for 50,000 years, but the region is alive with hot springs, mud pots, fumaroles, and steam vents.

Mammoth Lakes

🔵 *30 mi south of eastern edge of Yosemite National Park on U.S. 395.*

Much of the architecture in the hub town of Mammoth Lakes (elevation 7,800 feet) is in the faux-alpine category. You'll find basic services here, plus plenty of dining and lodging, the latter of which is often in condominium units. Highway 203 heads west from U.S. 395, becoming Main Street as it passes through the town of Mammoth Lakes, and later Minaret Road (which makes a right turn) as it continues west to the Mammoth Mountain ski area and Devils Postpile National Monument.

The lakes of the **Mammoth Lakes Basin,** reached by Lake Mary Road off Highway 203 southwest of town, are popular for fishing and boating in summer. First comes Twin Lakes, at the far end of which is Twin Falls, where water cascades 300 feet over a shelf of volcanic rock. Also popular are Lake Mary, the largest lake in the basin, Lake Mamie, and Lake George. Horseshoe Lake is the only lake in which you can swim.

The glacial-carved sawtooth spires of the Minarets, the remains of an ancient lava flow, are best viewed from the **Minaret Vista,** off Highway 203 west of Mammoth Lakes.

☺ Even if you don't ski, you'll want to see **Mammoth Mountain,** the aptly named landmass that gives Mammoth Lakes its name. Gondolas serve skiers in winter and mountain bikers and sightseers in summer. The high-speed, eight-passenger *Panorama Gondola* whisks you from the chalet to the summit, where you can read interpretive panels about the area's volcanic history. The boarding area is at the main lodge. ⊠ *Off Hwy. 203, Mammoth Lakes* ☎ *760/934–2571 Ext. 3850 (gondola station) or Ext. 2400 (information)* ⊠ *$16* ☉ *July 4–Oct., daily 9–4:30; Nov.–July 3, daily 8:30–4.*

The overwhelming popularity of Mammoth Mountain has generated a real estate boom, and the once sleepy town with no center point has seen big changes in the first years of the 21st century. A huge new complex called the **Village at Mammoth,** a cluster of four-story wood-and-stone multi-use buildings slated for completion in summer of 2004, seeks to become the town's tourist center, with shops, restaurants, and luxury accommodations. The **Village Gondola** (⊠ Minaret Rd. at Forest Trail ☎ 760/934–1982 or 800/626–6684) runs from the Village complex to Canyon Lodge, giving you access to the entire mountain while reliev-ing you of the hassle of fighting for a parking space at the base area.

☺ An easy 10-minute walk from the ranger station at **Devils Postpile Na-tional Monument** takes you to a geologic formation of smooth, vertical basalt columns sculpted by volcanic and glacial forces. A short but steep trail winds to the top of the 60-foot-high rocky cliff, where you'll find a bird's-eye view of the columns. A 2-mi hike past the Postpile leads to the monument's second scenic wonder, **Rainbow Falls,** where a branch of the San Joaquin River plunges more than 100 feet over a lava ledge. When the water hits the pool below, sunlight turns the resulting mist into a spray of color. Walk down a bit from the top of the falls for the best view.

During summer, Devils Postpile National Monument is accessible only via a shuttle bus that begins operation as soon as the road is cleared of snow—usually in June, but sometimes as late as July. The shuttle de-parts from Mammoth Mountain Inn approximately every 20 minutes from 7 AM to 7 PM. The shuttle stops running after Labor Day, but you can drive to the falls until the snows come again, usually around the be-ginning of November. Scenic picnic spots dot the bank of the San Joaquin River. ⊠ *Hwy. 203, 13 mi west of Mammoth Lakes* ☎ *760/ 934–2289, 760/924–5502 for shuttle bus information* ⊠ *$7* ☉ *Late June–late Oct., daily, weather permitting.*

off the beaten path

HOT CREEK GEOLOGIC SITE/HOT CREEK FISH HATCHERY – Forged by an ancient volcanic eruption, the Hot Creek Geologic Site is a landscape of boiling hot springs, fumaroles, and occasional geysers about 10 mi southeast of the town of Mammoth Lakes. You can soak (at your own risk) in hot springs or walk along boardwalks through the canyon to view the steaming volcanic features. Fly-fishing for trout is popular upstream from the springs. En route to the geologic site is the Hot Creek Fish Hatchery, the breeding ponds for most of the fish (3–5 million annually) with which the state stocks eastern Sierra lakes and rivers. ⊠ *Hot Creek Hatchery Rd. east of U.S. 395* ☎ *760/924–5500 for geologic site, 760/934–2664 for hatchery* ⊠ *Free* ☉ *Site daily sunrise–sunset; hatchery June–Oct., daily 8–4, depending on snowfall.*

Where to Stay & Eat

$$-$$$ ✕ **Nevados.** You can't go wrong at Nevados, the top choice of many locals. You'll find contemporary California cuisine that draws from European and Asian cooking. The menu presents imaginative preparations of seafood, duck, veal, beef, and game. Everything is made in-house, and there's an excellent three-course prix-fixe menu. The atmosphere is convivial and welcoming, and the bar is always bustling. ⊠ *Main St. and Minaret Rd.* ☎ *760/934–4466* ⌂ *Reservations essential* ▭ *AE, D, DC, MC, V* ⊘ *No lunch.*

★ **$-$$$** ✕ **The Restaurant at Convict Lake.** Tucked in a grove of aspens, ten minutes south of town, is one of the best restaurants in the eastern Sierra. In the rustic dining room you can sit beside the fire, under the knotty-pine cathedral ceiling, and sup on such dishes as sautéed venison medallions, pan-seared local trout, and beef Wellington. This is a haven for wine aficionados, with an extensive selection of reasonably priced European and California varietals. The service is as good as the food. ⊠ *2 mi off U.S. 395, 4 mi south of Mammoth Lakes* ☎ *760/934–3803* ⌂ *Reservations essential* ⊘ *No lunch Labor Day–July 4th* ▭ *AE, D, MC, V.*

$$ ✕ **Ocean Harvest.** This is the place to go for fresh fish. All the seafood is broiled over mesquite-wood charcoal, unless you request it be blackened Cajun style or served Jamaican Jerk style. Considering the nearest ocean is 200 mi away, prices are very reasonable; soup or salad comes with all dinners. ⊠ *248 Old Mammoth Rd.* ☎ *760/934–8539* ▭ *AE, D, DC, MC, V* ⊘ *No lunch.*

$-$$ ✕ **Berger's.** Don't even think about coming to this bustling pine-panel restaurant unless you're hungry. Berger's is known, appropriately enough, for burgers and generously sized sandwiches. Everything comes in mountainous portions. For dinner try the beef ribs or the buffalo steak. ⊠ *Minaret Rd. near Canyon Blvd.* ☎ *760/934–6622* ▭ *MC, V* ⊘ *Closed 2 wks May and 4–6 wks Oct.–Nov.*

$-$$ ✕ **The Mogul.** This longtime steakhouse serves excellent prime rib, charbroiled shrimp, grilled beef, and fresh fish. There are no surprises here, just hearty, straightforward American food. Dinners come with soup or salad, and you won't leave hungry. There's also a kids' menu. ⊠ *Mammoth Tavern Rd. off Old Mammoth Rd.* ☎ *760/934–3039* ▭ *AE, D, MC, V* ⊘ *No lunch.*

¢-$ ✕ **Giovanni's Pizza.** Children love this casual restaurant. It serves standard Italian dinners, but stick to the delicious pizza. Don't come here for quiet conversation—it's a high-decibel joint. ⊠ *Minaret Village Mall, Old Mammoth Rd. and Meridian St.* ☎ *760/934–7563* ▭ *AE, MC, V* ⊘ *No lunch Sun.*

¢ ✕ **Blondie's Kitchen and Waffle Shop.** This comic strip–theme diner serves the best waffles in town and delicious traditional breakfasts every morning, starting at 6 AM. ⊠ *Main and Lupin Sts.* ☎ *760/934–4048* ▭ *AE, D, DC, MC, V* ⊘ *No dinner.*

¢ ✕ **Schat's Bakery & Café Vermeer.** Part restaurant, part bakery, this family-run business serves everything from huge, perfectly cooked omelets to monster pancakes and terrific French toast. The pastries and breads are fresh and delicious. You can also get great sandwiches to go. ⊠ *3305 Main St.* ☎ *760/934–6055 or 760/934–4203* ▭ *MC, V* ⊘ *No dinner.*

$–$$$$ ✕⊡ **Tamarack Lodge Resort.** Tucked away on the edge of the John Muir
Fodor'sChoice Wilderness Area, this original 1924 log lodge has the most rustic and
★ charming of all accommodations in the Mammoth Lakes area. Rooms
in the main lodge can be fairly spartan in their furnishings, and some
share a bathroom. If you prefer more privacy, you can opt for one of
the cabins, which range from simple to luxurious and come in a vari-
ety of sizes. The main building is surrounded by quiet woods, and cross-
country ski trails loop past the cabins. In warm months, fishing, canoeing,
hiking, and mountain biking are close by. The cozy cabins are modern,
neat, and clean, with knotty-pine kitchens and private baths; some have
fireplaces or wood-burning stoves. The romantic Lakefront Restaurant
($$–$$$; reservations essential; no lunch) serves outstanding contem-
porary French-inspired cuisine, with an emphasis on game. ⬡ *Box 69,*
93546 ✦ *Lake Mary Rd. off Hwy. 203* ☎ *760/934–2442 or 800/626–*
6684 🖷 *760/934–2281* ⊕ *www.tamaracklodge.com* ⇨ *11 rooms, 25*
cabins ⚫ *Restaurant, fans, some kitchenettes, cross-country skiing, ski*
shop; no a/c, no room TVs, no smoking ▭ *AE, MC, V.*

$$$–$$$$ ⊡ **Juniper Springs Lodge.** If you're planning to ski and must have slope-
side luxury, this is one of the top choices in the area. Accommodations
are in a four-story stone-and-timber building directly adjacent to one
of the ski lifts. All rooms are condominium-style units, with full kitchens
and ski-in, ski-out access to the mountain. Amenities include stone fire-
places, balconies, and stereos with CD players. The heated outdoor pool—
surrounded by a heated deck—is open year-round. ✉ *4000 Meridian*
Blvd., Box 2129, 93546 ☎ *800/626–6684 for lodging reservations, 760/*
924–1102 for front desk 🖷 *760/924–8152* ⊕ *www.mammothmountain.*
com ⇨ *10 studios, 99 1-bedrooms, 92 2-bedrooms, 5 3-bedrooms*
⚫ *Restaurant, café, room service, fans, in-room data ports, kitchens,*
microwaves, refrigerators, cable TV, in-room VCRs, 18-hole golf course,
pool, exercise equipment, 2 hot tubs, mountain bikes, downhill skiing,
ski shop, ski storage, bar, laundry service, concierge, meeting rooms; no
a/c, no smoking ▭ *AE, MC, V.*

$$–$$$$ ⊡ **Mammoth Mountain Inn.** If you want to be within walking distance of
the main lodge of Mammoth Mountain, this is the place to stay. Check
your skis with the concierge, pick them up in the morning, and head directly to the lifts. The accommodations, which vary in size, include standard hotel rooms and condo units; the latter have kitchenettes, and many
have lofts. The inn has licensed on-site child care. ✉ *Minaret Rd., Box*
353 (4 mi west of Mammoth Lakes), 93546 ☎ *760/934–2581 or 800/*
626–6684 🖷 *760/934–0701* ⊕ *www.mammothmountain.com* ⇨ *124*
rooms, 91 condos ⚫ *2 restaurants, fans, some in-room data ports,*
some kitchenettes, some microwaves, some refrigerators, cable TV, hot
tub, bar, video game room, baby-sitting, playground, meeting room, no-
smoking rooms; no a/c ▭ *AE, MC, V.*

$$–$$$$ ⊡ **Snowcreek Resort.** In a valley surrounded by mountain peaks, this 355-
acre condominium community on the outskirts of Mammoth Lakes con-
tains one- to four-bedroom units. All have kitchens, living and dining
rooms, and fireplaces; some have washers and dryers. You will have free
use of the well-supplied athletic club. ✉ *Old Mammoth Rd., Box 1647,*
93546 ☎ *760/934–3333 or 800/544–6007* 🖷 *760/934–1619* ⊕ *www.*
snowcreekresort.com ⇨ *195 condos* ⚫ *In-room data ports, kitchens,*
microwaves, refrigerators, cable TV, 9-hole golf course, 9 tennis courts,
2 pools, health club, hot tub, sauna, racquetball, meeting room; no a/c,
no smoking ▭ *AE, D, MC, V.*

$–$$$ ⊡ **Convict Lake Resort.** This resort stands beside a lake named for an
1871 gunfight between local vigilantes and an escaped posse of six pris-
oners. The cabins range from rustic to luxurious and come with everything you need, including a fully equipped kitchen (with coffeemaker

and premium coffee). Large luxury homes ($$$$) can sleep up to 35 people. ⊠ *2 mi off U.S. 395, 35 mi north of Bishop* ☎ *760/934–3800 or 800/992–2260* ⊕ *www.convictlakeresort.com* ⬢ *29 cabins* ⛆ *Restaurant, kitchens, some microwaves, lake, boating, fishing, bicycles, horseback riding, shop, Internet, some pets allowed (fee); no a/c, no room phones* ⊟ *AE, D, MC, V.*

¢–$$$ ⊡ **Alpenhof Lodge.** You can walk to restaurants and shops from this Swiss-style, family-owned motel. Accommodations are simple, rates reasonable, and the service good. Some rooms have fireplaces. In winter, the rates jump because of the motel's proximity to the new Village Gondola. ⊠ *6080 Minaret Rd., Box 1157, 93546* ☎ *760/934–6330 or 800/828–0371* ⊟ *760/934–7614* ⊕ *www.alpenhof-lodge.com* ⬢ *54 rooms, 3 cabins* ⛆ *Restaurant, some kitchens, some microwaves, some refrigerators, cable TV, pool, hot tub, bar, recreation room, laundry facilities; no a/c, no smoking* ⊟ *AE, D, MC, V.*

¢–$$ ⊡ **Sierra Lodge.** This modern motel on Main Street has spacious rooms. A covered parking garage with ski lockers is helpful in winter. Free shuttles take skiers to Mammoth Mountain. ⊠ *3540 Main St.,* ☎ *760/ 934–8881, 800/356–5711* ⊟ *760/934–7231* ⊕ *www.sierralodge.com* ⬢ *35 rooms* ⛆ *Fans, in-room data ports, kitchenettes, microwaves, refrigerators, cable TV, hot tub, ski storage, Internet, some pets allowed (fee); no a/c, no smoking* ⊟ *AE, D, MC, V* ⊓⊙⊏ *CP.*

¢–$ ⊡ **Swiss Chalet.** One of the most reasonably priced motels in town, the Swiss Chalet has great views of the mountains. Among the amenities are a fish-cleaning area and a freezer to keep your summer catch fresh. In winter, the shuttle to Mammoth Mountain stops out front. ⊠ *3776 Viewpoint Rd., Box 16, 93546* ☎ *760/934–2403 or 800/937–9477* ⊟ *760/934–2403* ⊕ *www.mammoth-swisschalet.com* ⬢ *20 rooms* ⛆ *Kitchenettes, some microwaves, refrigerators, cable TV, hot tub, sauna, some pets allowed (fee); no a/c, no smoking* ⊟ *AE, D, MC, V.*

⚠ **Convict Lake Campground.** This campground, near the Convict Lake Resort, is run by the U.S. Forest Service. Sites are available on a first-come, first-served basis and are extremely popular. ⛆ *Flush toilets, dump station, drinking water, showers, fire pits, general store, lake* ⬢ *88 campsites* ⊠ *2 mi off U.S. 395, 35 mi north of Bishop* ☎ *760/ 924–5500* ⊕ *www.fs.fed.us/r5/inyo* ⬚ *$15* ⊟ *No credit cards* ⊙ *May–Oct.*

⚠ **Lake Mary Campground.** You can catch trout in Lake Mary, the biggest lake in the region. The campground is set on its shores at 8,900 feet, and there are few sites as beautiful. Accordingly, it is extremely popular. If it's full, try the adjacent Coldwater campground. There is a general store nearby. ⛆ *Flush toilets, drinking water, fire grates, picnic tables* ⬢ *48 sites (tent or RV)* ⊠ *Hwy. 203 west to Lake Mary Loop Dr. (turn left and go ¼ mi)* ☎ *760/924–5500* ⊟ *760/924–5537* ⬚ *$14* ⊟ *No credit cards* ⊙ *June–Sept.*

Nightlife & the Arts

The summertime **Mammoth Lakes Jazz Jubilee** (☎ 760/934–2478 or 800/ 367–6572 ⊕ www.mammothjazz.org) is hosted by the local Temple of Folly Jazz Band and takes place in 10 venues, most with dance floors. For one long weekend every summer, Mammoth Lakes hosts **Bluesapalooza** (☎760/934–0606 or 800/367–6572 ⊕www.mammothconcert. com), a blues and beer festival—with emphasis on the beer tasting. Concerts occur throughout the year on Mammoth Mountain; call **Mammoth Mountain Music** (☎ 760/934–0606 ⊕ www.mammothconcert.com) for listings.

You can dance six nights a week to a DJ (and sometimes a band) at **La Sierra's** (⊠ Main St. near Minaret Rd. ☎ 760/934–8083), which has

Mammoth's largest dance floor. On Tuesday and Saturday evenings, you can sing karaoke at **Shogun** (⊠ 452 Old Mammoth Rd. ☎ 760/934–3970), Mammoth's only Japanese restaurant. The bar at **Whiskey Creek** (⊠ Main St. and Minaret Rd. ☎ 760/934–2555) hosts musicians on weekends year-round and on most nights in winter.

Sports & the Outdoors

For information on winter conditions around Mammoth, call the **Snow Report** (☎ 760/934–7669 or 888/766–9778). The **U.S. Forest Service ranger station** (☎ 760/924–5500) can provide information year-round.

BICYCLING **Mammoth Mountain Bike Park** (☎ 760/934–0706), at the ski area, opens when the snow melts, usually by July, with 70-plus mi of single-track trails—from mellow to superchallenging. Chairlifts and shuttles provide trail access, and rentals are available.

DOGSLEDDING **Mammoth Dog Teams** (☎ 760/934–6270) operates rides through the forest on sleds pulled by teams of 10 dogs. Options range from 25-minute rides to overnight excursions. In summer, you can tour the kennels and learn about the dogs.

FISHING Crowley Lake is the top trout-fishing spot in the area; Convict Lake, June Lake, and the lakes of the Mammoth Basin are other prime spots. One of the best trout rivers is the San Joaquin, near Devils Postpile. Hot Creek, a designated Wild Trout Stream, is renowned for fly-fishing (catch and release only). The fishing season runs from the last Saturday in April until the end of October. **Kittredge Sports** (⊠ Main St. and Forest Trail ☎ 760/934–7566) rents rods and reels and conducts guided trips.

GOLF Because it's nestled right up against the forest, you might see deer and bears on the fairways at the 18-hole **Sierra Star Golf Course** (⊠ 2001 Sierra Star Pkwy., 93546 ☎ 760/924–2200).

HIKING Trails wind around the Lakes Basin and through pristine alpine scenery. Stop at the **U.S. Forest Service ranger station** (⊠ On right-hand side of Hwy. 203, just before town of Mammoth Lakes ☎ 760/924–5500) for a Mammoth area trail map and permits for backpacking in wilderness areas.

HORSEBACK RIDING Stables around Mammoth are typically open from June through September. There are several outfitters. Call or write **Mammoth Lakes Pack Outfit** (🖃 Box 61, 93546 ✛ Along Lake Mary Rd. ☎ 760/934–2434) to find out about their horseback trips. **McGee Creek Pack Station** (🖃 Box 162, Rte. 1, 93546 ☎ 760/935–4324 or 800/854–7407) can set you up with horses and gear.

HOT-AIR BALLOONING The balloons of **Mammoth Balloon Adventures** (☎ 760/937–8787) glide over the countryside in the morning from spring until fall, weather permitting.

SKIING & SNOWBOARDING **June Mountain Ski Area.** This low-key resort 20 mi north of Mammoth Mountain is a favorite of snowboarders, who have a half-pipe all to themselves, and there are three freestyle terrain areas for both skiers and boarders. Seven lifts service the area, which has a 2,664-foot vertical drop; the skiing ranges from beginner to expert. There's rarely a line for the lifts, and the area is better protected than Mammoth from wind and storms. (If it starts to storm, you can use your Mammoth ticket at June.) A rental and repair shop, a ski school, and a sport shop are all on the premises. ⊠ *Off June Lake Loop (Hwy. 158) north of Mammoth Lakes, 🖃 Box 146, June Lake 93529 ☎ 760/648–7733 or 888/586–3686 ☜ Lift ticket $47 ☞ 35 trails on 500 acres, rated 35% beginner, 45% intermediate, 20% expert. Longest run 2½ mi, base 7,510′, summit, 10,174′. Lifts: 7.*

Mammoth Mountain Ski Area. One of the West's largest and best ski resorts, Mammoth has 28 lifts (nine high-speed) and more than 3,500 acres of skiable terrain, from beginning to expert. The base elevation is 7,953 feet and the summit an ear-popping 11,053 feet, making for a 3,100-foot vertical drop. You'll find a 6½-mi-wide swath of groomed boulevards and canyons, as well as tree skiing and a dozen vast bowls, one of them a staggering 13,000 feet wide. Snowboarders are welcome on all slopes; there are three outstanding freestyle terrain parks, with jumps, rails, table tops, and superpipes to rip. Mammoth's season begins in November and often lingers until June or beyond. Lessons and rental equipment are available, and there's a children's ski and snowboard school. Mammoth Mountain runs five free **shuttle bus** (☎ 760/934–0687 or 760/934–2571) routes around town which will take you to and from the ski area. Buses run from 7:30 to 5:30 daily in snow season, with limited evening service until midnight. ⊠ *Minaret Rd. west of Mammoth Lakes, Box 24, 93546* ☎ *760/934–2571 or 800/626–6684* ☜ *Lift ticket $60* ☞ *150 trails on 3,500 acres, rated 30% beginner, 40% intermediate, 30% expert. Longest run 3 mi, base 7,953', summit 11,053'. Lifts: 28.*

Trails at **Tamarack Cross Country Ski Center** (⊠ Lake Mary Rd. off Hwy. 203 ☎ 760/934–5293), adjacent to Tamarack Lodge, meander around several lakes. Rentals are available.

Mammoth Sporting Goods (⊠ 1 Sierra Center Mall, Old Mammoth Rd. ☎ 760/934–3239) tunes and rents skis, and sells equipment, clothing, and accessories.

SNOWMOBILING **Mammoth Snowmobile Adventures** (☎ 760/934–9645 or 800/626–6684), at the Main Lodge at the Mammoth Mountain Ski Area, conducts guided tours along wooded trails.

EAST OF YOSEMITE
FROM LEE VINING TO BRIDGEPORT

The area to the north and east of Yosemite National Park includes some ruggedly handsome terrain, most notably around Mono Lake. Bodie State Historic Park is north of the lake. The area is best visited by car: Distances are great and public transportation in the region is limited. US 395 is the main north–south road on the eastern side of the Sierra Nevada.

Lee Vining

⑲ *20 mi east of Tuolumne Meadows, Hwy. 120 to U.S. 395; 30 mi north of Mammoth Lakes on U.S. 395.*

Lee Vining is mostly known as an eastern gateway to Yosemite National Park and the location of Mono Lake. Pick up supplies or stop for lunch here before or after a drive through the high country.

★ Eerie tufa towers—calcium carbonate formations that often resemble castle turrets—rise from impressive **Mono Lake.** Since the 1940s the city of Los Angeles has diverted water from streams that feed the lake, lowering its water level and exposing the tufa. Court victories by environmentalists in the 1990s forced a reduction of the diversions, and the lake has since risen about 9 feet. From April through August, millions of migratory birds nest in and around Mono Lake. The best place to view the tufa is at the south end of the lake along the mile-long **South Tufa Trail.** To reach it, drive 5 mi south from Lee Vining on U.S. 395, then 5 mi east on Highway 120. There is a $3 fee. You can swim (or float) in the salty water at Navy Beach near the South Tufa Trail or take a kayak or canoe trip for close-up views of the tufa (check with rangers for boating restrictions during bird-nesting season). The **Scenic Area Visitor Center** (⊠ U.S. 395 ☎ 760/647–3044) is open daily from 9–4:30 (daily from May through October; 3–4 days a week from November through April–call for exact hours.) Rangers and naturalists lead walking tours of the tufa daily in summer and on weekends (sometimes on cross-country skis) in winter.

Where to Stay & Eat

¢–$ ✕ **Nicely's.** Plants and pictures of local attractions decorate this eatery that has been around since 1965. Try the blueberry pancakes and home-made sausages at breakfast. For lunch or dinner try the chicken-fried steak or the fiesta salad. There's also a kids' menu. ⊠ *U.S. 395 and 4th St.* ☎ *760/647–6477* ▤ *MC, V* ☉ *Closed Wed. in winter.*

$ ▦ **Tioga Lodge.** Just 2½ mi north of Yosemite's eastern gateway, this 19th-century building has been by turns a store, a saloon, a tollbooth, and a boarding house. Now restored and expanded, it's a popular lodge that's close to ski areas and fishing spots. Ask about their summer boat tours of Mono Lake. ⊠ *U.S. 395, Box 580, 93541* ☎ *760/647–6423 or 888/647–6423* ᵬ *760/647–6074* ⊕ *www.tiogalodge.com* ⇱ *13 rooms* ⚴ *Restaurant; no a/c, no room phones, no room TVs, no smoking* ▤ *AE, D, MC, V* ☉ *Closed Nov.–Mar.*

en route   Heading south from Lee Vining, U.S. 395 intersects the **June Lake Loop** (⊠ Hwy. 158 W). This wonderfully scenic 17-mi drive follows an old glacial canyon past Grant, June, Gull, and other lakes before reconnecting with Route 395 on its way to Mammoth Lakes. The loop is especially colorful in fall.

Bodie State Historic Park

㉓ *23 mi northeast of Lee Vining, U.S. 395 to Hwy. 270 (last 3 mi are unpaved). Snow may close Hwy. 270 in winter and early spring, but park stays open.*

Old shacks and shops, abandoned mine shafts, a Methodist church, the mining village of Rattlesnake Gulch, and the remains of a small Chinatown are among the sights at fascinating **Bodie Ghost Town.** The town, at an elevation of 8,200 feet, boomed from about 1878 to 1881 as gold prospectors, having worked the best of the western Sierra mines, headed to the high desert on the eastern slopes. Bodie was a mean place—the booze flowed freely, shootings were commonplace, and licentiousness reigned. The big strikes were made during the boom years, and though some mining continued into the 1930s, the town had long since begun its decline. By the late 1940s all its residents had departed. A state park was established in 1962, with a mandate to preserve the town in a state of "arrested decay," but not to restore it. Evidence of Bodie's wild past survives at an excellent museum, and you can tour an old stamp mill (where ore was stamped into fine powder to extract gold and silver) and a ridge that contains many mine sites. No food, drink, or lodging is available in Bodie, and the nearest picnic area is a half mile away. Winter access depends on snowfall. Roads aren't plowed, so if you want to visit when there's snow on the ground, you'll have to hike or ski as much as 13 mi from the highway to reach the park. ⊠ *Museum: Main and Green Sts.* ☎ *760/647–6445* ☙ *Park $2; museum free* ☉ *Park: Memorial Day–Labor Day, daily 8–7; Labor Day–Memorial Day, daily 8–4. Museum: Memorial Day–Labor Day, daily 9–6; Sept.–May, hrs vary.*

Bridgeport

㉑ *25 mi north of Lee Vining (55 mi north of Mammoth Lakes) on U.S. 395.*

Historic Bridgeport lies within striking distance of a myriad of alpine lakes and streams and both forks of the Walker River, making it a prime spot for fishing. It is also the gateway to Bodie Ghost Town.

Where to Stay & Eat

$–$$$ ✕ **Bridgeport Inn.** Tables spread with white linen grace the dining room of this clapboard Victorian inn, built in 1877. The prime rib and fresh seafood are complemented by homemade soups, pastas, and a large wine list. Victorian-appointed guest rooms are available upstairs. ✉ *205 Main St.* ☎ *760/932–7380* ⊘ *Closed Dec.–Feb.* ▤ *MC, V.*

★ $–$$$ ✕ **Restaurant 1881.** Everything is made in-house at one of the eastern Sierra's only haute-cuisine restaurants. Specialties include marinated chateaubriand with a black-truffle butter and cabernet glaze, rack of lamb with a pistachio crust, and fillet of local Alpers trout with a chive-leek sauce. ✉ *362 Main St.* ☎ *760/932–1918* ⌲ *Reservations essential* ▤ *AE, D, MC, V* ⊘ *Closed Jan.–mid-Feb; Nov. 15–Apr. 15 Mon.–Wed. No lunch.*

$–$$ ⌂ **Cain House.** This old home has been refurbished as a B&B in elegant country style. Afternoon wine-and-cheese service is offered daily, and all beds have down comforters. ✉ *340 Main St., 93517* ☎ *760/932–7040 or 800/433–2246* ▤ *760/932–7419* ⊕ *www.cainhouse.com* ⥃ *7 rooms* ⌂ *Some refrigerators, cable TV, tennis court; no smoking* ▤ *AE, D, MC, V* ⊘ *Closed Nov.–Mar.* ⦿⊙⦿ *BP.*

$–$$ ⌂ **Walker River Lodge.** Right in the center of Bridgeport, this hotel has a charming antiques shop in its lobby. Many rooms overlook the East Walker River. ✉ *100 Main St., 93517* ☎ *760/932–7021 or 800/688–3351* ▤ *760/932–7914* ⊕ *www.walkerriverlodge.com* ⥃ *36 rooms* ⌂ *Some microwaves, refrigerators, cable TV, some in-room VCRs, pool, spa, fishing, some pets allowed, no-smoking rooms* ▤ *AE, D, MC, V.*

¢–$ ⌂ **Silver Maple Inn.** Next to the Mono County Courthouse (1880), this inn is in central Bridgeport, on attractive wooded grounds with views of the nearby Sierra. Built in the 1940s, the motel provides fish cleaning and freezing facilities and barbecue pits in which to cook your catch. ✉ *310 Main St., 93517* ☎ *760/932–7383 or 800/433–2246* ▤ *760/932–7419* ⊕ *www.silvermapleinn.com* ⥃ *20 rooms* ⌂ *Fans, refrigerators, cable TV, some pets allowed, no-smoking rooms; no a/c* ▤ *AE, D, MC, V* ⊘ *Closed Nov.–Mar.*

YOSEMITE & THE SOUTHERN SIERRA A TO Z

To research prices, get advice from other travelers, and book travel arrangements, visit ⊕ www.fodors.com

AIRPORTS & TRANSFERS

Fresno Yosemite International Airport (FYI) is the nearest airport to Yosemite National Park. Alaska, Allegiance, American, America West, Continental, Delta, Hawaiian, Horizon, Northwest, United Express, and several regional carriers fly here. *See* Air Travel *in* Smart Travel Tips A to Z for airline phone numbers.

🛈 **Fresno Yosemite International Airport** ✉ 5175 E. Clinton Ave., Fresno ☎ 559/498-4095 ⊕ www.flyfresno.org.

BUS TRAVEL

Greyhound serves Fresno, Merced, and Visalia from many California cities. VIA Adventures runs three daily buses from Merced to Yosemite

Valley; buses also depart daily from Mariposa. The 2½-hour ride from Merced costs $20 round-trip, which includes admission to the park.

🟦 **Greyhound** ☎ 800/231-2222 ⊕ www.greyhound.com. **VIA Adventures** ☎ 209/384-1315 or 800/369-7275 ⊕ www.via-adventures.com.

CAMPING

In Yosemite National Park you can camp only in designated areas, but in the national forests you can pitch a tent anywhere you want, so long as there are no signs specifically prohibiting camping in that area. Always know and obey fire regulations; you can find out what they are in a specific area by checking with Forest Service rangers, either by telephone or at any of the ranger stations just inside park boundaries.

Most of Yosemite's 14 campgrounds are in Yosemite Valley and along the Tioga Road. Glacier Point and Wawona have one each. Several campgrounds operate on a first-come, first-served basis year-round (some 400 of the park's sites remain open year-round), while some take reservations in high season; during summer reservations are strongly recommended. It's sometimes possible to get a campsite on arrival by stopping at the campground reservations office in Yosemite Valley, but this is a risky strategy. Yosemite Campground Reservations handles all bookings for the reservable campgrounds within the park. During the last two weeks of each month, beginning on the 15th, you can reserve a site up to five months in advance. Yosemite Concession Services Corporation handles reservations for the tent-cabin and other sites at Curry Village and for the camping shelters at Housekeeping Camp.

RVs and trailers are permitted in most national park campgrounds, though space is scarce at some. The length limit is 40 feet for RVs and 35 feet for trailers, but the park service recommends that trailers be no longer than 22 feet. Disposal stations are available in most of the main camping areas.

The Sierra Nevada is home to thousands of bears, and if you plan on camping, you should take all necessary precautions to keep yourself—and the bears—safe. Bears that acquire a taste for human food can become very aggressive and destructive and often must eventually be destroyed by rangers. Yosemite's campgrounds and some campgrounds outside the park provide food-storage boxes that can keep bears from pilfering your edibles (portable canisters for backpackers can be rented in most park stores). It is imperative that you move all food, coolers, and items with a scent (including toiletries, toothpaste, and air fresheners) from your car (including the trunk) to the storage box at your campsite. If you don't, a bear may break into your car by literally peeling off the door or ripping open the trunk, or it may ransack your tent. The familiar tactic of hanging your food from high tree limbs is not an effective deterrent, as bears can easily scale trees. In the southern Sierra, bear canisters are the only effective and proven method for preventing bears from getting human food. Whether hiking or camping, it's important to respect the landscape and wildlife around you. For detailed information about responsible outdoor recreation, visit the web site of the Leave No Trace Center for Outdoor Ethics.

🟦 **Inyo National Forest** ☎ 760/873-2400 🖷 760/873-2458 ⊕ www.r5.fs.fed.us/inyo. **Leave No Trace Center for Outdoor Ethics** ⊕ www.lnt.org. **Lodgepole/Dorst campgrounds** ☎ 301/722-1257 or 800/365-2267. **Sequoia National Forest** ☎ 559/784-1500 🖷 559/781-4744 ⊕ www.r5.fs.fed.us/sequoia. **Wilderness Permit Office** ☎ 559/565-3766 ⊕ www.nps.gov/seki. **Yosemite Campground Reservations** ☎ 301/722-1257 or 800/436-7275 ⊕ reservations.nps.gov. **Yosemite Concession Services Corporation** ☎ 559/252-4848 ⊕ www.yosemitepark.com.

CAR RENTAL

The car-rental outlets closest to the southern Sierra are at Fresno Yosemite International Airport, where the national chains have outlets. *See* Car Rental *in* Smart Travel Tips A to Z for national rental agency phone numbers.

CAR TRAVEL

From San Francisco, I–80 and I–580 are the fastest routes toward the Central Sierra Nevada; avoid driving these routes during weekday rush hours. Through the Central Valley, I–5 and Highway 99 are the fastest north–south routes, but the latter is narrower and has heavy farm-truck traffic. To get to Yosemite, plan on driving 4–5 hours. Enter the park either on Highway 140, which is the best route in inclement weather, or on Highway 120, which is the fastest route when the roads are clear. To get to Mammoth Lakes in summer and early fall (or whenever snows aren't blocking Tioga Road), you can travel via Highway 120 (to U.S. 395 south) through the Yosemite high country; the quickest route in winter is I–80 to U.S. 50 to Highway 207 (Kingsbury Grade) to U.S. 395 south; either route takes 6–7 hours.

Keep your tank full, especially in winter. Distances between gas stations can be long, and there is no fuel available in Yosemite Valley. If you're traveling from October through April, rain on the coast can mean heavy snow in the mountains. Carry tire chains, and know how to put them on (on I–80 and U.S. 50 you can pay a chain installer $20 to do it for you, but on other routes you'll have to do it yourself). Always check road conditions before you leave. Traffic in Yosemite in summer can be heavy, and there are sometimes travel restrictions.

🚩 **Northern California Road Conditions** ☎ 800/427-7623. **Yosemite Area Road and Weather Conditions** ☎ 209/372-0200.

EMERGENCIES

In an emergency dial 911.

🚩 **Emergency Services Mammoth Hospital** ✉ 85 Sierra Park Rd., Mammoth Lakes ☎ 760-934-3311 ⊕ www.mammothhospital.com. **Yosemite Medical Clinic** ✉ Ahwahnee Rd. north of Northside Dr. ☎ 209/372-4637.

LODGING

Most lodgings in the southern Sierra are simple and basic. A number of agencies can help you find a room.

🚩 **Reservation Services Mammoth Lakes Visitors Bureau Lodging Referral** ☎ 760/934-2712 or 888/466-2666 ⊕ www.visitmammoth.com. **Mammoth Reservations** ☎ 760/934-5571 or 800/223-3032 ⊕ www.mammothreservations.com. **Three Rivers Reservation Center** ☎ 559/561-0410. **Yosemite Concession Services Corporation** ☎ 559/252-4848 ⊕ www.yosemitepark.com.

TOURS

California Parlor Car Tours, in San Francisco, serves Yosemite. Lodging and some meals are included with the rail fare. VIA Adventures runs bus tours from Merced to Yosemite Valley, some of them in conjunction with Amtrak. For $63 you get transportation, lunch, park admission, and a two-hour tour.

🚩 **California Parlor Car Tours** ☎ 415/474-7500 or 800/227-4250 ⊕ www.calpartours.com. **VIA Adventures** ✉ 300 Grogan Ave., Merced ☎ 209/384-1315 or 800/369-7275 ⊕ www.via-adventures.com.

VISITOR INFORMATION

🚩 **Bridgeport Chamber of Commerce** 🗂 Box 541, Bridgeport 93517 ☎ 760/932-7500 ⊕ www.ca-biz.com/bridgeportchamber. **Lee Vining Chamber of Commerce** 🗂 Box 29, Lee Vining 93541 ☎ 760/647-6595 ⊕ www.monolake.org/chamber. **Mammoth Lakes Visitors Bureau** ✉ Along Hwy. 203 [Main St.], near Sawmill Cutoff Rd.,

Box 48, Mammoth Lakes 93546 ☎ 760/934-2712 or 888/466-2666 ⊕ www.visitmammoth. com. **Mono Lake** ⌖ Box 49, Lee Vining 93541 ☎ 760/647-3044 ⊕ www.monolake.org. **National Park Service** ✉ Three Rivers 93271 ☎ 559/565-3341 or 559/565-3134 ⊕ www. nps.gov/seki. **Yosemite Concession Services Corporation** ☎ 209/372-1000 ⊕ www. yosemitepark.com. **Yosemite National Park** ⌖ Information Office, Box 577, Yosemite National Park, 95389 ☎ 209/372-0200 or 209/372-0264 ⊕ www.nps.gov/yose. **Yosemite Sierra Visitors Bureau** ✉ 40637 Hwy. 41, Box 1998, Oakhurst 93644 ☎ 559/683-4636 ⊕ www.yosemite-sierra.org.

THE GOLD COUNTRY
WITH SACRAMENTO

8

FODOR'S CHOICE

California State Railroad Museum, *Sacramento*

Columbia State Historic Park, *Columbia*

HIGHLY RECOMMENDED

RESTAURANTS   Biba, *Sacramento*

Latitudes, *Auburn*

The Waterboy, *Sacramento*

Zachary Jacques, *Placerville*

HOTELS   Amber House Bed & Breakfast Inn, *Sacramento*

Dunbar House 1880, *Murphys*

The Foxes Bed & Breakfast, *Sutter Creek*

Hyatt Regency at Capitol Park, *Sacramento*

Imperial Hotel, *Amador City*

Red Castle Historic Lodgings, *Nevada City*

SIGHTS   California State Capitol, *Sacramento*

Empire Mine State Historic Park, *Grass Valley*

Hangtown's Gold Bug Mine, *Placerville*

Marshall Gold Discovery State Historic Park, *Coloma*

Sutter Creek, *town south of Amador City*

Sutter's Fort, *living-history museum in Sacramento*

Updated by
Reed Parsell

A NEW ERA DAWNED FOR CALIFORNIA when James Marshall turned up a gold nugget in the tailrace of a sawmill he was constructing along the American River. Before January 24, 1848, Mexico and the United States were still wrestling for ownership of what would become the Golden State. With Marshall's discovery the United States tightened its grip on the region, and prospectors from all over the world came to seek their fortunes in the Mother Lode.

As gold fever seized the nation, California's population of 15,000 swelled to 265,000 within three years. The mostly young, mostly male adventurers who arrived in search of gold—the '49ers—became part of a culture that discarded many of the conventions of the eastern states. It was also a violent time. Yankee prospectors chased Mexican miners off their claims, and California's leaders initiated a plan to exterminate the local Native American population. Bounties were paid and private militias hired to wipe out the Native Americans or sell them into slavery. California was now to be dominated by the Anglo.

The boom brought on by the gold rush lasted scarcely 20 years, but it changed California forever. It produced 546 mining towns, of which fewer than 250 remain. The hills of the Gold Country were alive, not only with prospecting and mining but also with business, the arts, gambling, and a fair share of crime. Opera houses went up alongside brothels, and the California State Capitol, in Sacramento, was built with the gold dug out of the hills. A lot of important history was made in Sacramento, the center of commerce during this period. Pony Express riders ended their nearly 2,000-mile journeys in the city in the 1860s. The transcontinental railroad, completed in 1869, was conceived here.

By the 1960s the scars that mining had inflicted on the landscape had largely healed. To promote tourism, locals began restoring vintage structures, historians developed museums, and the state established parks and recreation areas to preserve the memory of this extraordinary episode in American history.

One of California's least expensive—and least sophisticated—destinations, the gold-mining region of the Sierra Nevada foothills is not without its pleasures, natural and cultural. Today you can come to Nevada City, Auburn, Coloma, Sutter Creek, and Columbia not only to relive the past but also to explore art galleries and to stay at inns full of character. Spring brings wildflowers, and in fall the hills are colored by bright red berries and changing leaves. Because it offers a mix of indoor and outdoor activities, the Gold Country is a great place to take the kids.

Exploring the Gold Country

Visiting Old Sacramento's museums is a good way to steep yourself in history, but the Gold Country's heart lies along Highway 49, which winds the 325-mi north–south length of the historic mining area. The highway, often a twisting, hilly two-lane road, begs for a convertible with the top down.

About the Restaurants
American, Italian, and Mexican fare are common in the Gold Country, but chefs also prepare ambitious Continental, French, and California cuisine. Grass Valley's pasties (meat pies), introduced by 19th-century gold miners from the Welsh city of Cornwall, are one of the region's more unusual treats.

Numbers in the text correspond to numbers in the margin and on the Sacramento and Gold Country maps.

8

If you have 1 day

Drive northeast from Sacramento on I–80 to **Auburn** ㉚ ▶ for a tour of the Placer County Courthouse and its museum. Travel south on Highway 49 to the Marshall Gold Discovery State Historic Park, at **Coloma** ㉙. Head back to Sacramento for a drink at the bar on the *Delta King* and an evening stroll and dinner along the waterfront in **Old Sacramento** ❶–⓮. The historical attractions will be closed, but you'll still get a feel for life here during the last half of the 19th century.

If you have 5 days

Start your trip in ▦ **Sacramento** ❶–⓰ ▶, where you can visit the **California State Railroad Museum** ❶ and **Sutter's Fort** ⓯, and take a riverboat cruise. On the second day, drive to **Placerville** ⓳ to see Hangtown's Gold Bug Mine and continue to ▦ **Sutter Creek** ㉑. Day three starts with a visit to the Amador County Museum, in **Jackson** ㉒, after which you can head south on Highway 49 and northeast on Highway 4 for lunch in **Murphys** ㉔. Return to Highway 49 and continue south to Columbia State Historic Park, in ▦ **Columbia** ㉕. You can relive the 1800s by dining and spending the night at the City Hotel. If you've been itching to pan for gold, do that in the morning of day four. Drive back north on Highway 49 to **Coloma** ㉙ and Marshall Gold Discovery State Historic Park, and head to ▦ **Auburn** ㉚ to spend the night. On your last day, stop at Empire Mine State Historic Park in **Grass Valley** ㉛ and pay a visit to **Nevada City** ㉜.

About the Hotels

Full-service hotels, budget motels, small inns, and even a fine hostel can all be found in Sacramento. The main accommodations in the larger towns along Highway 49—among them Placerville, Nevada City, Auburn, and Mariposa—are chain motels and inns. Many Gold Country B&Bs occupy former mansions, miners' cabins, and other historic buildings.

WHAT IT COSTS				
$$$$	**$$$**	**$$**	**$**	**¢**
RESTAURANTS over $30	$23–$30	$16–$22	$10–$15	under $10
HOTELS over $250	$176–$250	$121–$175	$90–$120	under $90

Restaurant prices are for a main course at dinner, excluding sales tax of 7¾% (depending on location). Hotel prices are for a standard double room in high season, excluding service charges and 7¼% tax.

Timing

The Gold Country is most pleasant in the spring, when the wildflowers are in bloom, and in the fall. Summers are beautiful but hot: temperatures of 100°F are common. Sacramento winters tend to be cold and foggy. Throughout the year Gold Country towns stage community and ethnic celebrations. In December many towns deck themselves out for Christmas. Sacramento hosts the annual Jazz Jubilee over Memorial Day weekend and the California State Fair in August and early September. East of the town of Sutter Creek, flowers bloom on Daffodil Hill in March.

SACRAMENTO & VICINITY

The gateway to the Gold Country, the seat of state government, and an agricultural hub, the city of Sacramento plays many important contemporary roles. Nearly 2 million people live in the metropolitan area. The continuing influx of newcomers seeking opportunity, sunshine, and lower housing costs than in coastal California has made it one of the nation's fastest-growing regions. The central "midtown" area contains most of the city's culture and much of its charm, though pedestrians-only K Street Mall is not quite as clean and vibrant as city planners would have hoped when the downtown-revitalization project was conceived. Ten miles west is the college town of Davis, which, like nearby Woodland, is beginning to feel more suburban than agricultural because many Sacramento workers are settling there.

Sacramento contains more than 2,000 acres of natural and developed parkland. Grand old evergreens, deciduous and fruit-bearing trees (some streets are littered with oranges in springtime), and even giant palms give it a shady, lush quality. Genteel Victorian edifices sit side-by-side with art deco and postmodern skyscrapers.

Old Sacramento & Downtown

▶ *87 mi northeast of San Francisco, I–80 to Hwy. 99 or I–5 north.*

Wooden sidewalks and horse-drawn carriages on cobblestone streets lend a 19th-century feel to Old Sacramento, a 28-acre district along the Sacramento River waterfront. The museums at the north end hold artifacts of state and national significance. Historic buildings house shops and restaurants. River cruises and train rides bring gold-rush history to life. Call the **Old Sacramento Events Hotline** (☎ 916/558–3912) for information about living-history re-creations and merchant hours. An entertaining audio tour of Old Sacramento can be found at kiosks placed throughout the historic district, which, when fed with special tokens or 50¢ in quarters, activate the voice of "Mark Twain" telling tales of the gold-rush days. A water taxi run by **River Otter Taxi Co.** (☎ 916/446–7704) serves the Old Sacramento waterfront during spring and summer, stopping at points near restaurants and other sights. **Channel Star Excursions** (✉ 110 L St. ☎ 916/552–2933 or 800/433–0263) operates the *Spirit of Sacramento,* a riverboat that takes passengers on happy-hour, dinner, lunch, and champagne-brunch cruises in addition to one-hour narrated tours.

A Good Tour

Old Sacramento, the capitol and park surrounding it, and Sutter's Fort lie on an east–west axis that begins in the west at the Sacramento River. The walk from Old Sacramento to the state's capitol is easy, passing through the Downtown Plaza shopping mall and down K Street. This area becomes quite festive during the Thursday evening outdoor market. A DASH (Downtown Area Shuttle) bus and the No. 30 city bus both link Old Sacramento, the K Street Mall, the convention center, downtown, midtown, and Sutter's Fort in a loop that travels eastward on J Street and westward on L Street. The fare is 50¢ within this area, and buses run every 15 minutes weekdays, every 20 minutes Saturday, and every 30 minutes Sunday.

Park your car in the municipal garage under I–5 at 2nd Street (enter on I Street between 2nd and 3rd streets), and head to the superb **California State Railroad Museum** ❶ ▶; then browse the hardware and house-

8

Historic Hotels and Inns

The Gold Country abounds in well-preserved examples of gold rush–era architecture, so why not experience the history up-close by staying at an inn or hotel that dates back to those colorful years? Plenty of old mansions have been converted to inns and B&Bs, and several hotels have been in operation since the gold rush. The very Victorian Imperial Hotel in Amador City opened in 1879, while the stone Murphys Historic Hotel & Lodge in Murphys has served guests such as Mark Twain and Black Bart since 1855. Columbia has the 1856 City Hotel and the 1857 Fallon Hotel, the latter of which was restored by the state of California. In Jamestown, the National Hotel offers an authentic 1859 experience.

Shopping

Shoppers visit the Gold Country in search of antiques, collectibles, fine art, quilts, toys, tools, decorative items, and furnishings. Handmade quilts and crafts can be found in Sutter Creek, Jackson, and Amador City. Auburn and Nevada City support many gift boutiques. Sacramento's commuter communities, such as Elk Grove, Folsom, and Roseville, are exploding with subdivisions and with them inevitably come the standard suburban assortment of chain stores and strip malls.

Theater

For weary miners in search of diversion, theater was a popular form of entertainment in the Gold Country. It still is, and you can take in a show at several venues dating from the era. The Woodland Opera House, opened in 1885, mounts musical theater productions September through July. Nevada City's Nevada Theatre, built in 1865, is the home of the Foothill Theater Company. In Columbia State Historic Park, the Historic Fallon House Theater presents plays, comedies, and musicals. A reconstruction of the original 1849 building, Sacramento's canvas and ship's-timber Eagle Theater is the scene of everything from puppet shows to juggling acts.

---

hold items at the **Huntington, Hopkins & Co. ❷** store. Next door are the hands-on exhibits of the **Discovery Museum ❸**.

To learn more about Sacramento's role in rail history, walk a few paces south to the **Central Pacific Passenger Depot ❹**. The **Central Pacific Freight Depot,** next to the passenger depot, houses a public market (closed Monday), where merchants sell food and gifts. Across Front Street is a replica of the 19th-century **Eagle Theater ❺**. The foot of K Street (at Front Street) is a great spot for viewing the Sacramento River wharf and the restored stern-wheeler the *Delta King.*

At the corner of 2nd and J streets is the **B. F. Hastings Building ❻**. The **Old Sacramento Visitor Information Center ❼** is on 2nd Street in the same block as the **California Military Museum ❽**. A must-see a few blocks south of Old Sacramento is the **Crocker Art Museum ❾**, the oldest art museum in the American West. From here walk south on Front Street to the **Towe Auto Museum ❿**. If you'd rather skip the automotive museum, walk up 3rd Street to the Capitol Mall, which leads to the **capitol ⓫**. If you're still going strong, explore the **Golden State Museum ⓬**, at O and 10th streets, one block south of the capitol, and the **Leland Stanford Mansion ⓭**, a block

west of that. Or walk north to H Street and then east to the **Governor's Mansion** ⑭. Otherwise, walk back to your car via J Street.

A bit more than a mile to the east, accessible via the DASH or No. 30 city bus, is **Sutter's Fort** ⑮. It was Sacramento's earliest Euro-American settlement; evocative exhibits bring that era back to life. North of the fort is the **State Indian Museum** ⑯.

TIMING This tour makes for a leisurely day. Most of the attractions are open daily, except for the Military Museum, the Crocker Art Museum, the Golden State Museum, and the Eagle Theater, which are closed on Monday. The latter is closed on weekends as well.

What to See

⑥ **B. F. Hastings Building.** A reconstruction of the first chambers of the California Supreme Court occupies the second floor of this 1853 building. On the first floor there's a Wells Fargo History Museum and an ATM. ⊠ *1000 2nd St.* ☎ *916/440–4263* ⊗ *Daily 10–5.*

⑧ **California Military Museum.** A storefront entrance leads to three floors containing more than 30,000 artifacts—uniforms, weapons, photographs, documents, medals, and flags of all kinds—that trace Californians' roles in the military throughout U.S. history. Among the exhibits are one documenting the role of women in the U.S. armed forces, and another that relates the military history of African-Americans. ⊠ *1119 2nd St.* ☎ *916/442–2883* ⊠ *$3* ⊗ *Tues.–Thur. 11–3, Fri.–Sun. 10–5.*

☺ ▶ ① **California State Railroad Museum.** Near what was once the terminus of
Fodor'sChoice the transcontinental and Sacramento Valley railroads (the actual terminus
★ was at Front and K streets), this 100,000-square-foot museum has 21 locomotives and railroad cars on display and 46 exhibits. You can walk

through a post-office car and peer into cubbyholes and canvas mailbags, enter a sleeping car that simulates the swaying on the roadbed and the flashing lights of a passing town at night, or glimpse the inside of the first-class dining car. Allow at least two hours to enjoy the museum. ☒ *125 I St.* ☎ *916/445–6645* ⊕ *www.csrmf.org* ☒ *$4* ☉ *Daily 10–5.*

★ ⑪ **Capitol.** The Golden State's capitol was built in 1869. The lacy plaster-work of the 120-foot-high rotunda has the complexity and colors of a Fabergé egg. Underneath the gilded dome are marble floors, glittering chandeliers, monumental staircases, replicas of 19th-century state offices, and legislative chambers decorated in the style of the 1890s. Guides conduct tours of the building and the 40-acre Capitol Park, which contains a rose garden, an impressive display of camellias (Sacramento's city flower), and the California Vietnam Veterans Memorial. ☒ *Capitol Mall and 10th St.* ☎ *916/324–0333* ☒ *Free* ☉ *Daily 9–5; tours hourly 9–4.*

☾ ④ **Central Pacific Passenger Depot.** At this reconstructed 1876 station there's rolling stock to admire, a typical waiting room, and a small restaurant. A steam-powered train departs hourly (April through September) from the freight depot, south of the passenger depot, making a 40-minute loop along the Sacramento riverfront. ☒ *930 Front St.* ☎ *916/445–6645* ☒ *$3 (free with same-day ticket from California State Railroad Museum); train ride $5 additional* ☉ *Depot daily 10–5. Train Apr.–Sept., every weekend; Oct.–Dec., 1st weekend of the month.*

⑨ **Crocker Art Museum.** The oldest art museum in the American West has a collection of art from Europe, Asia, and California, including *Sunday Morning in the Mines* (1872), a large canvas by Charles Christian Nahl depicting aspects of the original mining industry, and the magnificent *The Great Canyon of the Sierra, Yosemite* (1871), by Thomas Hill. The museum's lobby and ballroom retain the original 19th-century woodwork, plaster moldings, and English tiles. ☒ *216 O St.* ☎ *916/264–5423* ⊕ *www.crockerartmuseum.org* ☒ *$6* ☉ *Tues.–Wed. and Fri.–Sun. 10–5, Thurs. 10–9.*

☾ ③ **Discovery Museum.** The building that holds this child-oriented museum is a replica of the 1854 city hall and waterworks. Interactive history, science, and technology exhibits examine the evolution of everyday life in the Sacramento area. You can sift for gold, examine a Native American thatch hut, or experience the goings-on in the former print shop of the *Sacramento Bee* newspaper. The Gold Gallery displays nuggets and veins. ☒ *101 I St.* ☎ *916/264–7057* ☒ *$5* ☉ *June–Aug., daily 10–5; Sept.–May, Tues.–Sun. 10–5.*

⑤ **Eagle Theater.** When the Eagle opened in 1849, audiences paid between $3 and $5 in gold dust or coin to sit on rough boards and watch professional actors. This replica was constructed with the tentlike canvas and ship's-timber walls of the original structure, though now there's insulation, and the bench seats are cushioned. The theater hosts programs that range from a 13-minute slide show called *City of the Plains* to puppet shows and juggling acts. ☒ *925 Front St.* ☎ *916/323–6343* ☒ *Fees vary depending on program* ☉ *Tues.–Fri. 10–4.*

☾ ⑫ **Golden State Museum.** Drawing from the vast collections of the California State Archives, this state-of-the-art museum vividly portrays the story of California's land, people, and politics. Exhibits utilize modern technology, but there are also scores of archival drawers that you can pull out to see the real artifacts of history and culture—from the California State Constitution to surfing magazines. Board a 1949 cross-country bus to view a video on immigration, visit a Chinese herb shop maintained by a holographic proprietor, or stand on a gubernatorial balcony overlooking a sea of cameras and banners. Admission includes the use of an innovative personal audio guide—choose an adult or children's program and the level of detail you desire for each exhibit. There's also a café where you can take a break from the fun. ⊠ *1020 O St., at 10th St.* ☎ *916/653–7524* ⊕ *www.goldenstatemuseum.org* ⊠ *$5* ☉ *Tues.–Sat. 10–5, Sun. noon–5.*

⑭ **Governor's Mansion.** This 15-room house was built in 1877 and used by the state's chief executives from the early 1900s until 1967, when Ronald Reagan vacated it in favor of a newly built home in the more upscale suburbs. Many of the Italianate mansion's interior decorations were ordered from the Huntington, Hopkins & Co. hardware store, one of whose partners, Albert Gallatin, was the original occupant. Each of the seven marble fireplaces has a petticoat mirror that ladies strolled past to see if their slips were showing. The mansion is said to have been one of the first homes in California with an indoor bathroom. ⊠ *1526 H St.* ☎ *916/323–3047* ⊠ *$1* ☉ *Daily 10–4; tours hourly.*

② **Huntington, Hopkins & Co. Store.** This museum is a replica of the 1855 hardware store opened by Collis Huntington and Mark Hopkins, two of the Big Four businessmen who established the Central Pacific Railroad. Picks, shovels, gold pans, and other paraphernalia used by miners during the gold rush are on display, along with household hardware and appliances from the 1880s. Some items, such as blue enamelware, wooden toys, and oil lamps, are for sale. ⊠ *113 I St.* ☎ *916/323–7234* ☉ *Daily 10–5.*

⑬ **Leland Stanford Mansion.** The home of Leland Stanford, a railroad baron, California governor, and U.S. senator, was built in 1856, with additions in 1862 and the early 1870s. The once-grand edifice is undergoing major renovations. Some floors of the mansion—which will operate as a museum and a site for state government functions—will be featured in tours that may not be launched until 2004 or 2005. It is interesting in the meantime to view the transformation of the exterior. ⊠ *802 N St.* ☎ *916/324–0575.*

⑦ **Old Sacramento Visitor Information Center.** Obtain brochures about nearby attractions, check local restaurant menus, and get advice from the helpful staff here. ⊠ *1101 2nd St., at K St.* ☎ *916/442–7644* ⊕ *www. oldsacramento.com* ☉ *Daily 10–5.*

☾ ⑯ **State Indian Museum.** Among the interesting displays at this well-organized museum is one devoted to Ishi, the last Yahi Indian to emerge from the mountains, in 1911. Ishi provided scientists with insight into the traditions and culture of this group of Native Americans. Arts-and-crafts exhibits, a demonstration village, and an evocative 10-minute video bring to life the multifaceted past and present of California's native peoples. ⊠ *2618 K St.* ☎ *916/324–0971* ⊕ *www.parks.ca.gov* ⊠ *$2* ☉ *Daily 10–5.*

★ ☾ ⑮ **Sutter's Fort.** Sacramento's earliest Euro-American settlement was founded by German-born Swiss immigrant John Augustus Sutter in 1839. Audio speakers at each stop along a self-guided tour give information about exhibits, including a blacksmith's shop, a bakery, a prison, living quarters, and livestock areas. Costumed docents sometimes reenact fort life, demonstrating crafts, food preparation, and firearms maintenance. ⊠ *2701 L St.* ☎ *916/445–4422* ⊕ *www.parks.ca.gov* ⊠ *$2* ☉ *Daily 10–5.*

☾ ⑩ **Towe Auto Museum.** With more than 150 vintage automobiles on display, and exhibits ranging from the Hall of Technology to Dreams of Speed and Dreams of Cool, this museum explores automotive history and car culture. Docents provide information about specific models, including a 1931 Chrysler, a 1960 Lotus, and a luxurious and sleek 1927 Hispano-Suiza. A 1920s roadside café and garage exhibit re-creates the early days of motoring. The gift shop sells vintage-car magazines, model kits, and other car-related items. ⊠ *2200 Front St., 1 block off Broadway* ☎ *916/442–6802* ⊕ *www.toweautomuseum.org* ⊠ *$6* ☉ *Daily 10–6.*

Where to Stay & Eat

$$–$$$$ ✕ **The Firehouse.** The menu includes such rich and well-presented meals as seared foie gras and pan-roasted elk with a blueberry-and-chestnut chutney in such formal surroundings that a gentlemen in a tuxedo would not feel out of place. Consistently rated by local publications as among the city's top 10 restaurants, the Firehouse features a full bar and courtyard seating. In Old Sacramento, visitors who can afford to treat themselves to a fine and leisurely meal can do no better. ⊠ *1112 2nd St.* ☎ *916/442–4772* ▤ *AE, MC, V* ☉ *Closed Sun. No lunch Sat.*

★ **$$–$$$** ✕ **Biba.** Owner Biba Caggiano is an authority on Italian cuisine, author of several cookbooks, and the star of a national TV show on cooking. The capitol crowd flocks here for homemade ravioli, osso buco, grilled pork loin, and veal and rabbit specials. Reservations are a must on Fridays and Saturdays; a pianist adds to the upscale ambience nightly. ⊠ *2801 Capitol Ave.* ☎ *916/455–2422* ▤ *AE, DC, MC, V* ☉ *Closed Sun. No lunch Sat.*

$$ ✕ **Frank Fat's.** A longtime favorite of lawmakers and lobbyists, Frank Fat's is renowned more as a watering hole than as a restaurant. The menu of so-so Chinese food emphasizes Cantonese cuisine, but there are items from other regions as well. Signature dishes include brandy-fried chicken, honey-glazed walnut prawns, plus a couple of American items: New York steak and banana cream pie. ⊠ *806 L St.* ☎ *916/442–7092* ▤ *AE, MC, V* ☉ *No lunch weekends.*

$$ ✕ **Rio City Café.** Eclectic lunch and dinner menus and huge floor-to-ceiling windows with views of an Old Sacramento wharf are the dual attractions of this bright restaurant. Rio City serves both light and hearty fare: calamari salad, New York steak with wild-mushroom demiglace, mesquite-grilled salmon on garlic mashed potatoes, and duck breast with ginger-apple marmalade over couscous. ⊠ *1110 Front St.* ☎ *916/442–8226* ▤ *AE, D, DC, MC, V.*

★ **$–$$** ✕ **The Waterboy.** Rural French cooking and California cuisine are the culinary treasures at this increasingly popular midtown restaurant. Patrons always seem to be in a good mood, enjoying each other and dishes as chicken potpie, veal sweetbreads, and beet salad. The Waterboy is where the top local restaurateurs go when they want a good meal. ⊠ *2000 Capitol Ave.* ☎ *916/498–9891* ▤ *AE, D, DC, MC, V* ☉ *Closed Mon. No lunch weekends.*

$ ✕ **Paragary's Bar and Oven.** Pastas and brick-oven pizzas are the specialties of this casual spot. You won't go hungry here—portions are enormous. A waterfall flows near the back patio, which holds hundreds of plants. ⊠ *1401 28th St.* ☎ *916/457–5737* ▤ *AE, D, DC, MC, V* ☉ *No lunch weekends.*

¢–$$ ✕ **Centro.** The motorcycle with a skeleton rider in the front window denotes the vibrant wackiness that spices up this popular midtown Mexican eatery. Bright yellow booths and salsa music add to the ambience, but the tasty food—well outside the taco-burrito realm—is the real attraction. Dishes include citrus-marinated rotisserie chicken with plantains and pork slow-roasted in banana leaves. The bar carries more than 60 Mexican tequilas, but it's easy to lose count after the first two. ⊠ *2730 J St.* ☎ *916/442–2552* ▤ *AE, DC, MC, V* ☉ *No lunch weekends.*

¢–$$ ✕ **Tapa the World.** As defined at this midtown bar and restaurant, tapas are bite-size portions of meats, seafood, chicken, and veggies shared at the table. One of Sacramento's liveliest night spots (it's open till midnight), Tapa presents Flamenco and Spanish classical music performers nightly. ✉ *2125 J St.* ☎ *916/442–4353* ▤ *AE, D, DC, MC, V.*

¢ ✕ **Ernesto's Mexican Food.** This is one of the midtown area's most popular dinner restaurants, with customers waiting up to an hour on Friday and Saturday evenings. Fresh ingredients are stressed in the wide selection of entrées, and the margaritas are especially refreshing. A lively bar helps kill time before tables become available. Request an outdoor table if you're more interested in conversation than too-loud, canned Mexican music. ✉ *16th and S Sts.* ☎ *916/441–5850* ▤ *AE, D, DC, MC, V.*

$$$ ✕▥ **The Sterling Hotel.** This gleaming white Victorian mansion just three blocks from the capitol has been transformed into a small luxury hotel. Rose-hue guest rooms have handsome furniture, including four-poster or canopy beds. The bathrooms are tiled in Italian marble and have Jacuzzi tubs. Cookies or pastries baked on the premises are delivered to guests' rooms each evening. Restaurant Chanterelle ($$) serves contemporary Continental cuisine in its candlelit dining room and pleasant patio area. ✉ *1300 H St., 95814* ☎ *916/448–1300 or 800/365–7660* 🖷 *916/448–8066* ⊕ *www.sterlinghotel.com* ⇙ *17 rooms, 2 suites* ⌂ *Restaurant, room service, in-room data ports, cable TV, bar, dry cleaning, business services, meeting room, parking (fee), no-smoking rooms* ▤ *AE, D, DC, MC, V.*

★ $$–$$$$ ▥ **Amber House Bed & Breakfast Inn.** This B&B near the capitol encompasses four separate homes. The original house, the Poet's Refuge, is a craftsman-style home with five bedrooms named for famous writers. The 1913 Mediterranean-style Artist's Retreat has a French Impressionist motif. The third, an 1897 Dutch Colonial–revival home named Musician's Manor, has gardens where weddings occasionally take place. Novelist Haven was added in early 2003. Baths are tiled in Italian marble; some have skylights and two-person spa tubs. The Emily Dickenson Room's double-sided fireplace warms both the bathroom and bedroom. ✉ *1315 22nd St., 95816* ☎ *916/444–8085 or 800/755–6526* 🖷 *916/552–6529* ⊕ *www.amberhouse.com* ⇙ *20 rooms* ⌂ *In-room data ports, cable TV, in-room VCRs, some in-room hot tubs, concierge, no-smoking rooms* ▤ *AE, D, DC, MC, V* ⏐⊙⏐ *BP.*

★ $$$ ▥ **Hyatt Regency at Capitol Park.** With a marble-and-glass lobby and luxurious rooms, this hotel across from the capitol and adjacent to the convention center is arguably Sacramento's finest. The multi-tiered, glass-dominated hotel has a striking Mediterranean design. The best rooms have Capitol Park views. The service and attention to detail are outstanding. ✉ *1209 L St., 95814* ☎ *916/443–1234* 🖷 *916/321–3799* ⊕ *www.hyatt.com* ⇙ *500 rooms, 24 suites* ⌂ *2 restaurants, pool, gym, hot tub, bar, dry cleaning, laundry service, concierge, business services, meeting room, car rental, parking (fee)* ▤ *AE, D, DC, MC, V.*

$$–$$$ ▥ **Delta King.** This grand old riverboat, now permanently moored on Old Sacramento's waterfront, once transported passengers between Sacramento and San Francisco. Among many notable design elements are its main staircase, mahogany paneling, and brass fittings. The best of the 43 staterooms are on the river side toward the back of the boat. The boat's theater gains more critical acclaim every year, though patrons sometimes must tune out the creaking floorboards above. ✉ *1000 Front St., 95814* ☎ *916/444–5464 or 800/825–5464* 🖷 *916/447–5959* ⊕ *www.deltaking.com* ⇙ *44 rooms* ⌂ *Restaurant, lounge, theater, meeting room, parking (fee)* ▤ *AE, D, DC, MC, V* ⏐⊙⏐ *CP.*

$–$$ ▥ **Holiday Inn Capitol Plaza.** Despite its decided lack of charm, this highrise hotel has modern rooms and the best location for visiting Old

Sacramento and the Downtown Plaza. It's also within walking distance of the capitol. Rooms are typical of others in the Holiday Inn chain—geared toward comfort and practicality, not opulence or distinctive decor. Here it's all about location, and there may be none better in downtown Sacramento. ⊠ *300 J St., 95814* ☎ *916/446–0100* 🖶 *916/446–7371* ⊕ *www.holiday-inn.com* ➪ *362 rooms, 4 suites* ⚲ *Restaurant, minibars, cable TV, pool, gym, bar, shop, concierge floor, convention center, no-smoking rooms* ☰ *AE, DC, MC, V.*

$ 🏨 **Best Western Sutter House.** Many of the pleasant, modern rooms in this downtown hotel open onto a courtyard surrounding a pool. The stylish restaurant, Grape's, serves contemporary cuisine. A complimentary full breakfast is offered, which along with covered parking make Sutter House a bargain among downtown's pricey options. ⊠ *1100 H St., 95814* ☎ *916/441–1314, 800/830–1314* 🖶 *916/441–5961* ⊕ *www.thesutterhouse. com* ➪ *97 rooms, 1 suite* ⚲ *Restaurant, pool, lounge, laundry service, free parking, no-smoking floor* ☰ *AE, D, DC, MC, V* ⦿ *CP.*

$ 🏨 **Radisson Hotel Sacramento.** Mediterranean-style two-story buildings cluster around a large artificial lake on an 18-acre landscaped site. Rooms are enlivened with art deco appointments and furnishings; many have a patio or balcony. More resort-like than other Sacramento-area hotels, the Radisson presents summer jazz concerts in a lakeside amphitheater and holds barbecues on warm evenings. ⊠ *500 Leisure La., 95815* ☎ *916/922–2020 or 800/333–3333* 🖶 *916/649–9463* ⊕ *www. radisson.com/sacramentoca* ➪ *307 rooms, 22 suites* ⚲ *2 restaurants, room service, pool, lake, gym, outdoor hot tub, boating, bicycles, bar, convention center* ☰ *AE, D, DC, MC, V.*

¢ 🏨 **Sacramento International Hostel.** This 1885 Victorian mansion has a grand mahogany staircase, a stained-glass atrium, frescoed ceilings, and carved and tiled fireplaces. Dormitory rooms and bedrooms suitable for singles, couples, and families are available, as is a communal kitchen. In 2002, the building was moved across the street and spruced up considerably. Its access to downtown remains superb. ⊠ *925 H St., 95814* ☎ *916/443–1691 or 800/909–4776 Ext. 40* 🖶 *916/443–4763* ⊕ *www. norcalhostels.org* ➪ *70 beds* ⚲ *Kitchen* ☰ *MC, V.*

Nightlife & the Arts

Downtown Events Line (☎ 916/442–2500) has recorded information about seasonal events in the downtown area.

NIGHTLIFE The **Blue Cue** (⊠ 1004 28th St. ☎ 916/442–7208), upstairs from Centro restaurant, is an eclectic billiard lounge known for its large selection of single-malt scotches. The **Fox and Goose** (⊠ 1001 R St. ☎ 916/443–8825) is a casual pub with live music (including open-mike Monday). Traditional pub food (fish-and-chips, Cornish pasties) is served on weekday evenings from 5:30 to 9:30. **Harlow's** (⊠ 2708 J St. ☎ 916/441–4693) draws a young crowd to its art deco bar-nightclub for live music after 9. **Streets of London Pub** (⊠ 1804 J St. ☎ 916/498–1388) is popular among Anglophiles and stays open until 2 AM every night except Sunday, when it closes an hour earlier.

THE ARTS **Sacramento Community Center Theater** (⊠ 13th and L Sts. ☎ 916/264–5181) hosts concerts, opera, and ballet. The **Sacramento Light Opera Association** (⊠ 1419 H St. ☎ 916/557–1999) presents Broadway shows at the Sacramento Community Center Theater and in the huge Music Circus tent during summer. If you want the really *big* picture, the **Esquire Theater** (⊠ 13th Street on the K Street Mall ☎ 916/446–2333), screens IMAX movies. For art films, visit the funky **Tower Theater** (⊠ 2508 Land Park Drive ☎ 916/442–4700), a few minutes southeast of downtown.

Sports & the Outdoors

The basement-level **California Family Health & Fitness** (⊠ 428 J St., at 5th St. ☎ 916/442–9090) has a workout area, weight machines, and sauna. The fee for nonmembers is $10. **Jedediah Smith Memorial Bicycle Trail** runs for 23 mi from Old Sacramento to Beals Point in Folsom, mostly along the American River. The recently formidable **Sacramento Kings** of the National Basketball Association play at the **Arco Arena** (⊠ 1 Sports Pkwy. ☎916/928–6900), though tickets are difficult to obtain. The minor-league **Sacramento River Cats** baseball team is a major hit, playing before mostly sold-out crowds its first three seasons at West Sacramento's **Raley Field** (⊠ 400 Ballpark Dr. ☎ 916/371–4487).

Shopping

Top local artists and craftspeople exhibit their works at **Artists' Collaborative Gallery** (⊠ 1007 2nd St. ☎ 916/444–3764). The **Elder Craftsman** (⊠ 130 J St. ☎ 916/264–7762) specializes in items made by local senior citizens. **Gallery of the American West** (⊠ 121 K St. ☎ 916/446–6662) has a large selection of Native American arts and crafts. **Downtown Plaza,** comprising the K Street Mall along with many neighboring shops and restaurants, has shopping and entertainment. There's a Thursday-night market in the summer and an outdoor ice-skating rink in winter.

Woodland

⑰ *20 mi northwest of Sacramento on I–5.*

Woodland's downtown lies frozen in a quaint and genteel past. In its heyday it was one of the wealthiest cities in California, established in 1861 by gold seekers and entrepreneurs. Once the boom was over, attention turned to the rich surrounding land, and the area became an agricultural gold mine. The legacy of the old land barons lives on in the Victorian homes that line Woodland's wide streets. Many of the houses have been restored and are surrounded by lavish gardens.

More than 300 touring companies, including John Philip Sousa's marching band, and Frank Kirk, the Acrobatic Tramp, appeared at **The Woodland Opera House,** built in 1885 (and rebuilt after it burned in 1892). Now restored, the building hosts concerts and, September through July, a season of musical theater. Free weekly guided tours reveal old-fashioned stage technology. ⊠ *Main and 2nd Sts.* ☎ *530/666–9617* ⊕ *www.wohtheatre. org* ☉ *Mon. and Tues. 10–2, weekends 2–4; tours Tues. noon–4.*

The 10-room Classic Revival home of settler William Byas Gibson was purchased by volunteers and restored as the **Yolo Country Historical Museum.** You can see collections of furnishings and artifacts from the 1850s to 1930s. Old trees and an impressive lawn cover the 2-acre site off Highway 113. ⊠ *512 Gibson Rd.,* ☎ *530/666–1045* 🖭 *$2* ☉ *Mon.–Tues. 10–4, weekends noon–4.*

Ancient trucks and farm machinery seem to rumble to life within this ⟳ shedlike **Heidrick Ag History Center,** where you can see the world's largest collection of antique agricultural equipment. Also here are interactive exhibits, a food court, gift shop, and kids' play area. ⊠ *1962 Hays La.,* ☎ *530/666–9700* 🖶 *530/666–9712* ⊕ *www.aghistory.org* 🖭 *$6* ☉ *Weekdays 10–5, Sat. 10–6, Sun. 10–4.*

Where to Stay & Eat

$–$$$ ✕ **Morrison's Upstairs.** A Victorian building registered as a State Historic Landmark houses this restaurant. Downstairs is a bar, deli, and patio. The

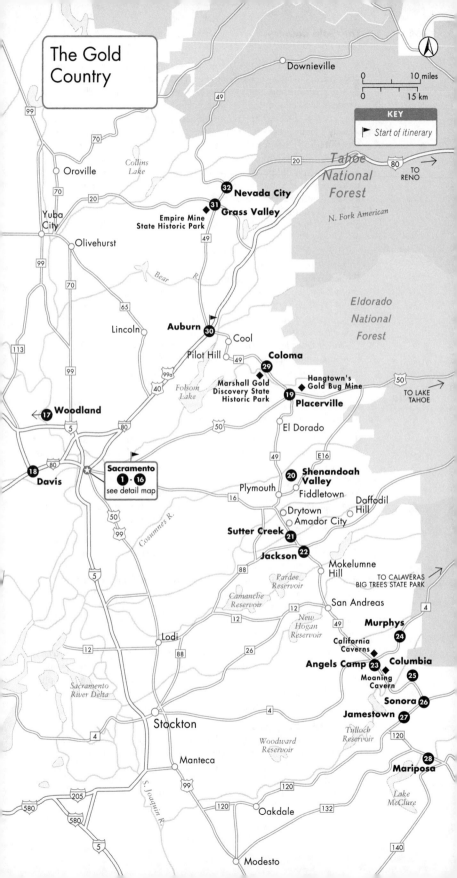

The Gold Country

0 ——————— 10 miles
0 ——————— 15 km

Downieville

99

70

Oroville

70

20

Yuba City

Olivehurst

99

70

65

Lincoln

113

99

40

17 **Woodland**

5

18 **Davis**

80

Collins Lake

Bear R.

49

32 Nevada City

31 Grass Valley

Empire Mine State Historic Park

Tahoe National Forest

20

80

TO RENO

N. Fork American

Eldorado National Forest

99a

Auburn 30

Cool

Pilot Hill

49

Coloma

29

Marshall Gold Discovery State Historic Park

Hangtown's Gold Bug Mine

50

TO LAKE TAHOE

Folsom Lake

19

Placerville

El Dorado

Sacramento
1 · 16
see detail map

50

49

E16

20 Shenandoah Valley

Fiddletown

Daffodil Hill

Plymouth

16

Drytown

Amador City

Sutter Creek

21

Jackson 22

88

Mokelumne Hill

TO CALAVERAS BIG TREES STATE PARK

Pardee Reservoir

Camanche Reservoir

San Andreas

4

5

50

99

Cosumnes R.

5

Lodi

12

88

12

New Hogan Reservoir

49

Murphys

24

California Caverns

Columbia

Angels Camp 23

25

Moaning Cavern

Sonora 26

Jamestown

27

120

Sacramento River Delta

Stockton

4

Woodward Reservoir

Tulloch Reservoir

28

Mariposa

Lake McClure

4

Manteca

205

580

580

5

99

120

120

132

Oakdale

140

Modesto

top floor, once the attic, is full of nooks and alcoves where you can have your meal. It's furnished throughout with polished wood tables that suit the style of the house. The menu lists burgers and sandwiches, scampi, Chinese chicken salad, pasta, and prime rib, and includes vegetarian selections. ⊠ *428½ 1st St.,* ☎ *530/666–6176* ⊟ *AE, D, DC, MC, V.*

¢–$$ ✕ **Ludy's Main Street BBQ.** Here's a big, casual restaurant next door to the Opera House that looks like something out of the *Beverly Hillbillies.* You can tuck into huge portions of ribs, beef, chicken, or fish-and-chips, or have a half-pound burger slathered in red sauce. On the patio water misters cool you in summer and heaters keep you toasty in winter. There is a kids' menu. ⊠ *667 Main St.* ☎ *530/666–4400* ⊟ *AE, MC, V.*

$ 🏨 **Best Western Shadow Inn.** Palm trees wave over the landscaped pool area at this two-story hotel. Some rooms have wet bars and kitchenettes. ⊠ *584 N. East St.* ☎ *530/666–1251* 🖷 *530/662–2804* ⊕ *www.bestwestern.com* ➽ *120 rooms* ⬤ *Cable TV, pool, hot tub, laundry facilities, business services* ⊟ *AE, D, DC, MC, V* ⦿ *CP.*

¢ 🏨 **Cinderella Motel Woodland.** Rooms here are clean and basic, which makes this a good middle-range choice in a town without many lodging options. ⊠ *99 W. Main St.* ☎ *530/662–1091* 🖷 *530/662–2804* ➽ *30 rooms* ⬤ *Refrigerators, cable TV, in-room VCRs (and movies), pool, hot tub, some pets allowed (fee); no smoking* ⊟ *AE, D, DC, MC, V.*

¢ 🏨 **Valley Oaks Inn.** Rooms in this two-story motel have basic furnishings and amenities. ⊠ *600 N. East St.* ☎ *530/666–5511* ➽ *62 rooms* ⬤ *Refrigerators, cable TV, pool* ⊟ *AE, D, DC, MC, V.*

Davis

⓲ *10 mi west of Sacramento; take I–80 to I–5.*

Though it began as and still is a rich agricultural area, Davis doesn't feel like a cow town. It's home to the University of California at Davis, whose students hang at the cafés and bookstores in the central business district, making the city feel a little more cosmopolitan. The city is known for its energy conservation programs and projects, including a solar village. The university is a leader in viticulture education, and has one of the West Coast's top veterinary programs.

The center of action in town is the **Davis Campus of the University of California,** which ranks among the top 25 research universities in the United States. You can take tours of the campus, which depart from Buehler Alumni and Visitors Center. The **Mondavi Center for the Performing Arts,** a strikingly modern glass structure off I–80, opened in 2002 with much fanfare and a jam-packed schedule of cultural events. ⊠ *1 Shields Ave.* ☎ *530/752–8111* ⊕ *www.ucdavis.edu* ⊙ *Tours weekends at 11:30 and 1:30, weekdays by appointment.*

The work by northern California craftspeople displayed at the **Artery,** an artists' cooperative, includes decorative and functional ceramics, glass, wood, jewelry, fiber arts, painting, sculpture, drawing, and photography. ⊠ *207 G St.* ☎ *530/758–8330* ⊕ *www.arteryart.com* ⊙ *Mon.–Thurs. and Sat. 10–6, Fri. 10–9, Sun. noon–5.*

Where to Stay & Eat

$$ ✕ **Soga's.** Watercolors by local artists hang on the walls of this elegant restaurant. The California-style menu features various presentations of salmon fillet, swordfish, and veal and also offers vegetable plates. You can eat on the long, covered patio in good weather. ⊠ *217 E St.* ☎ *530/757–1733* ⬧ *Reservations essential* ⊙ *No lunch weekends.* ⊟ *AE, D, MC, V.*

$ ✕ **Café California.** The locals who gather at this downtown Davis eatery favor such dishes as a salad of prawns and baby greens with avocado-tarragon vinaigrette, Cajun-style prime rib with chili onion rings, and roast chicken with garlic mashed potatoes. The contemporary dining room set with white linens. ✉ *808 2nd St., 95616* ☎ *530/757–2766* 🖷 *530/758–5236* 🖃 *AE, MC, V.*

¢–$$ 🏨 **Aggie Inn.** This hotel, less than a block from the campus, is named for the University of California at Davis "Aggies," the school's team name. Rooms are clean and basic; convenience is what this place is about. ✉ *245 First St., 95616* ☎ *530/756–0352* 🖷 *530/753–5738* ⊕ *www.stayanight. com* ⚘ *Some in-room hot tubs, some kitchenettes, outdoor hot tub, sauna, laundry service* ↩ *25 rooms, 9 suites* 🖃 *AE, D, DC, MC, V.*

$ 🏨 **Best Western University Lodge.** This three-story hotel is a good place to stop if you have business at the university, which is one block away. ✉ *123 B St.* ☎ *530/756–7890* 🖷 *530/756–0245* ⊕ *www.bestwestern.com* ↩ *53 rooms* ⚘ *Some kitchenettes, microwaves, refrigerators, cable TV, exercise equipment, spa, some pets allowed* 🖃 *AE, D, DC, MC, V.*

$ 🏨 **Hallmark Inn.** Two buildings make up this inn, which is five blocks from the University of California campus and is next door to a restaurant. ✉ *110 F St.* ☎ *800/753–0035* ⊕ *www.hallmarkinn.com* ↩ *135 rooms* ⚘ *Restaurant, some refrigerators, pool, free parking* 🖃 *AE, D, DC, MC, V.*

THE GOLD COUNTRY—SOUTH
HIGHWAY 49 FROM PLACERVILLE TO MARIPOSA

South of its junction with U.S. 50, Highway 49 traces in asphalt the famed Mother Lode. The sleepy former gold-rush towns strung along the road have for the most part been restored and made presentable to visitors with an interest in one of the most frenzied episodes of American history.

Placerville

⑲ *44 mi east of Sacramento via U.S. 50.*

It's hard to imagine now, but in 1849 about 4,000 miners staked out every gully and hillside in Placerville, turning the town into a rip-roaring camp of log cabins, tents, and clapboard houses. The area was then known as Hangtown, a graphic allusion to the nature of frontier justice. It took on the name Placerville in 1854 and became an important supply center for the miners. Mark Hopkins, Philip Armour, and John Studebaker were among the industrialists who got their starts here.

★ ♵ **Hangtown's Gold Bug Mine,** owned by the City of Placerville, centers around a fully lighted mine shaft open for self-guided touring. A shaded stream runs through the park, and there are picnic facilities. ✉ *1 mi off U.S. 50, north on Bedford Ave.* ☎ *530/642–5207* ⊕ *www.goldbugpark.org* 🎫 *$3* ⊙ *Tours mid-Apr.–Oct., daily 10–4; Nov.–mid-Apr., weekends 10–4. Gift shop Mar.–Nov., daily 10–4.*

off the beaten path | **APPLE HILL –** Roadside stands sell fresh produce from more than 50 family farms in this area. During the fall harvest season (from September through December) members of the Apple Hill Growers Association open their orchards and vineyards for apple and berry picking, picnicking, and wine and cider tasting. Many sell baked items and picnic food. ✉ *About 5 mi east of Hwy. 49; take Camino exit from U.S. 50* ☎ *530/644–7692.*

Where to Stay & Eat

★ $$-$$$ ✕ **Zachary Jacques.** It's not easy to locate, so call for directions, because finding this country-French restaurant is worth the effort. Appetizers on the seasonal menu might include escargots or mushrooms prepared in several ways, roasted garlic with olive oil served on toast, or spicy lamb sausage. Standard entrées include roast rack of lamb, beef stew, and scallops and prawns in lime butter. The attached wine bar opens at 4:30 in the afternoon. ⊠ *1821 Pleasant Valley Rd. (3 mi east of Diamond Springs)* ☎ *530/626–8045* ⊟ *AE, MC, V* ⊗ *Closed Mon.–Tues. No lunch.*

$$ ✕ **Café Luna.** Tucked into the back of the Creekside Place shopping complex is a small restaurant with about 30 seats inside, plus outdoor tables overlooking a creek. The menu, which changes weekly, encompasses many cuisines, including Indian, Russian, and Thai. ⊠ *451 Main St.* ☎ *530/642–8669* ⊟ *AE, D, MC, V* ⊗ *Closed Sun. No dinner Mon.–Tues.*

$-$$ ✕ **Lil' Mama D. Carlo's Italian Kitchen.** This comfortable Italian restaurant with a pleasant staff serves large portions of homemade pasta and chicken; the vegetarian dishes are heavy on the garlic. A wine bar features local varieties. ⊠ *482 Main St.* ☎ *530/626–1612* ⊟ *AE, MC, V* ⊗ *Closed Mon.–Tues. No lunch.*

$$ ▦ **Shadowridge Ranch and Lodge.** In the wooded hills outside Placerville, you'll find a beautifully restored rustic lodge complex. The immaculate hand-hewn log-and-stone cottages, most with wood-burning stoves, are filled with interesting artifacts of ranch and lodge life—including some dramatic stuffed specimens—and modern amenities. Each unit has its own patio. In the afternoon complimentary local wines and a huge appetizer platter are offered. ⊠ *3700 Fort Jim Rd., 95667* ☎ *530/295–1000 or 800/644–3498* 📠 *530/626–5613* ⊕ *www.shadowridgeranch.com* ⤶ *4 suites* ⚬ *Minibars, refrigerators, hiking, no-smoking rooms* ⊟ *AE, MC, V* ⊗ *Closed Jan.–Mar.* ⦿ *BP.*

$-$$ ▦ **The Seasons Bed & Breakfast.** A 10-minute walk from downtown, one of Placerville's oldest homes has been transformed into a lovely and relaxing oasis. The main house, two cottages, and the gardens are filled with paintings and sculptures. Privacy is treasured here. A suite with a sitting room and stained-glass windows occupies the main house's top floor. One cottage has a little white picket fence around its own mini-garden; the other has a two-person shower. ⊠ *2934 Bedford Ave., 95667* ☎ *530/626–4420* ⊕ *www.theseasons.net* ⤶ *3 rooms, 1 suite* ⚬ *No-smoking rooms* ⊟ *MC, V* ⦿ *BP.*

$ ▦ **Best Western Placerville Inn.** This motel's serviceable rooms are decorated in the chain's trademark pastels. The pool comes in handy during hot summer months. ⊠ *6850 Greenleaf Dr., near Missouri Flats exit of U.S. 50, 95667* ☎ *530/622–9100 or 800/854–9100* 📠 *530/622–9376* ⊕ *www.bestwestern.com* ⤶ *105 rooms* ⚬ *Cable TV, pool, free parking* ⊟ *AE, D, DC, MC, V.*

Shenandoah Valley

⓴ *20 mi south of Placerville on Shenandoah Rd., east of Hwy. 49.*

The most concentrated Gold Country wine-touring area lies in the hills of the Shenandoah Valley, east of Plymouth. Robust zinfandel is the primary grape grown here, but vineyards also produce cabernet sauvignon, sauvignon blanc, and other varietals. Most wineries are open on weekend afternoons; several have shaded picnic areas, gift shops, and galleries or museums; all have tasting rooms.

Sobon Estate (⊠ 14430 Shenandoah Rd. ☎ 209/245–6554) operates the Shenandoah Valley Museum, illustrating pioneer life and wine making in the valley. It's open daily from 9:30 to 5. **Charles Spinetta Winery** (✉ 12557 Steiner Rd. ☎ 209/245–3384 ⊕ www.charlesspinettawinery. com), where you can see a wildlife art gallery in addition to tasting the wine, is open daily between 9 and 4. The gallery at **Shenandoah Vineyards** (✉ 12300 Steiner Rd. ☎ 209/245–4455), open daily from 10 to 5, displays contemporary art.

Where to Stay

$$ 🏨 **Amador Harvest Inn.** This B&B adjacent to Deaver Vineyards occupies a bucolic lakeside spot in the Shenandoah Valley. A contemporary Cape Cod–style structure has homey guest rooms with private baths. Public areas include a living room with fireplace and a music room with a view of the lake. ✉ *12455 Steiner Rd., 95669* ☎ *209/245–5512 or 800/217–2304* 🖷 *209/245–5250* ⊕ *www.amadorharvestinn.com* ⛱ *4 rooms* ▤ *AE, MC, V* ⦿⚬ *BP.*

Amador City

6 mi south of Plymouth on Hwy. 49.

The history of tiny Amador City mirrors the boom-bust-boom cycle of many Gold Country towns. With an output of $42 million in gold, its Keystone Mine was one of the most productive in the Mother Lode. After all the gold was extracted, the miners cleared out, and the area suffered. Amador City now derives its wealth from tourists, who come to browse through its antiques and specialty shops, many of them on or off Highway 49.

Where to Stay & Eat

★ **$** ✕🏨 **Imperial Hotel.** The whimsically decorated mock-Victorian rooms at this 1879 hotel give a modern twist to the excesses of the era. Antique furnishings include iron and brass beds, gingerbread flourishes, and, in one room, art deco appointments. The two front rooms, which can be noisy, have balconies. The hotel's fine dinner-only restaurant ($–$$; closed Monday), whose menu changes quarterly, serves meals in a bright dining room and on the patio. The cuisine ranges from vegetarian to country hearty to contemporary eclectic. There is a two-night minimum stay on weekends. ✉ *Hwy. 49, 95601* ☎ *209/267–9172 or 800/242–5594* 🖷 *209/267–9249* ⊕ *www.imperialamador.com* ⛱ *6 rooms* ⚠ *Restaurant, bar* ▤ *AE, D, DC, MC, V* ⦿⚬ *BP.*

Sutter Creek

★ **㉑** *2 mi south of Amador City on Hwy. 49.*

Sutter Creek is a charming conglomeration of balconied buildings, Victorian homes, and neo–New England structures. The stores along Highway 49 (called Main Street in the town proper) are worth visiting for works by the many local artists and craftspeople. Seek out the **J. Monteverde General Store** (✉ 3 Randolph St. ☉ weekends 10–3; closed Jan.), a typical turn-of-the-20th-century emporium with vintage goods on display (but not for sale), an elaborate antique scale, and a chair-encircled potbellied stove in the corner. You can also stop by the **Sutter Creek Visitor Center** (✉ 11A Randolph St. ☎ 209/267–1344 or 800/400–0305 ☉ weekends 10–3) for more information.

off the beaten path

DAFFODIL HILL – Each spring a 4-acre hillside east of Sutter Creek erupts in a riot of yellow and gold as 300,000 daffodils burst into bloom. The garden is the work of members of the McLaughlin family, which has owned this site since 1887. Daffodil plantings began in the 1930s. The display usually takes place between mid-March and mid-

April. ⊠ *From Main St. (Hwy. 49) in Sutter Creek take Shake Ridge Rd. east 13 mi* ☎ *209/223–0350* ⊕ *www.amadorcountychamber.com* 🎫 *Free* ⊘ *Mid-Mar.–mid-Apr., daily 9–5.*

Where to Stay & Eat

$$–$$$ ✗ **Zinfandel's.** Black-bean chili in an edible bread tureen and smoked mussels and bay shrimp with roasted garlic cloves are among the appetizers at this casual restaurant. On the adventurous menu are such entrées as rack of lamb marinated in red wine, garlic, and rosemary on garlic smashed potatoes with mushroom port sauce. There's also a cozy wine-and-espresso bar with a fireplace, open Friday and Saturday nights only. ⊠ *51 Hanford St.* ☎ *209/267–5008* ⊟ *AE, D, MC, V* ⊘ *Closed Mon.–Wed. No lunch.*

¢–$ ✗ **Chatterbox Café.** This classic 1940s luncheonette has only five tables and 14 counter stools. Read a vintage newspaper or examine the jazz instruments and Disney memorabilia on the shelves while you wait for your chicken-fried steak, burger, homemade pie, or hot-fudge sundae. The menu is as big as the Chatterbox is small. Beer and wine are available. ⊠ *39 Main St.* ☎ *209/267–5935* ⊟ *AE, D, MC, V* ⊘ *No dinner Wed.–Mon.*

¢ ✗ **Back Roads Coffee House.** Airy and spacious, Back Roads is roughly in the middle of a frenzied four-block stretch of Highway 49 where traffic crawls and sidewalks bulge. Muffins, pastries, and coffee seem to be the biggest draws here, though hot, simple breakfasts are available. The lunch menu includes soups and salads. All the tables have a small stack of Trivial Pursuit cards, which should amuse baby boomers. ⊠ *74 Main St.* ☎ *209/267–0440* ⊟ *D, MC, V* ⊘ *No dinner.*

★ $$–$$$ ⬚ **The Foxes Bed & Breakfast.** The rooms in this 1857 white-clapboard house are handsome, with high ceilings, antique beds, and armoires. All have queen-size beds; five have wood-burning fireplaces. Breakfast is cooked to order and delivered on a silver service to your room or to the gazebo in the garden. Innkeepers Min and Pete Fox have pampered guests here since 1980, and they are full of local lore. ⊠ *77 Main St., 95685* ☎ *209/267–5882 or 800/987–3344* ⊟ *209/267–0712* ⊕ *www.foxesinn. com* ⇨ *5 rooms, 2 suites* ⚬ *Some cable TVs, some in-room VCRs, no-smoking rooms* ⊟ *D, MC, V* ⦿ *BP.*

$$–$$$ ⬚ **Grey Gables Inn.** Charming yet modern, this inn brings a touch of the English countryside to the Gold Country. The rooms, named after British literary figures, have gas-log fireplaces. Afternoon tea and evening refreshments are served in the parlor; birds flit about the wisteria in the terraced garden. ⊠ *161 Hanford St., 95685* ☎ *209/267–1039 or 800/ 473–9422* ⊟ *209/267–0998* ⊕ *www.greygables.com* ⇨ *8 rooms* ⊟ *MC, V* ⦿ *BP.*

$–$$ ⬚ **Eureka Street Inn.** Original redwood paneling, wainscoting, beams, and cabinets as well as lead- and stained-glass windows lend the Eureka Street Inn—formerly the Picture Rock Inn—a certain coziness. The craftsman-style bungalow was built in 1914 as a family home. Most rooms have gas-log fireplaces. ⊠ *55 Eureka St., 95685* ☎ *209/ 267–5500 or 800/399–2389* ⊕ *www.eurekastreetinn.com* ⇨ *4 rooms* ⊟ *AE, D, MC, V* ⦿ *BP.*

¢ ⬚ **Aparicio's Hotel.** If you're touring the Gold Country on a budget, this hotel is a good choice. The rooms contain coffee-makers and two queen-size beds, and three rooms are wheelchair accessible. ⊠ *271 Hanford St., 95685* ☎ *209/267–9177* ⊟ *209/267–5303* ⇨ *52 rooms* ⚬ *Cable TV* ⊟ *D, MC, V.*

Jackson

㉒ *8 mi south of Sutter Creek on Hwy. 49.*

Jackson wasn't the Gold Country's rowdiest town, but the party lasted longer here than most anywhere else: "Girls' dormitories" (brothels) and nickel slot machines flourished until the mid-1950s. Jackson also had the world's deepest and richest gold mines, the Kennedy and the Argonaut, which together produced $70 million in gold. These were deep-rock mines with tunnels extending as much as a mile underground. Most of the miners who worked the lode were of Serbian or Italian origin, and they gave the town a European character that persists to this day. Jackson has pioneer cemeteries whose headstones tell the stories of local Serbian and Italian families. The terraced cemetery on the grounds of the handsome **St. Sava Serbian Orthodox Church** (⊠ 724 N. Main St.) is the most impressive of the town's burial grounds.

The heart of Jackson's historic section is the **National Hotel** (⊠ 2 Water St.), which operates an old-time saloon in the lobby. The hotel is especially active on weekends, when people come from miles around to participate in Saturday-night sing-alongs.

The **Amador County Museum,** built in the late 1850s as a private home, provides a colorful take on gold-rush life. Displays include a kitchen with a woodstove, the Amador County bicentennial quilt, and a classroom. A time line recounts the county's checkered past. The museum conducts hourly tours of large-scale working models of the nearby Kennedy Mine. ⊠ *225 Church St.* ☎ *209/223–6386* 🖾 *Museum free; building with mine $1* ⊗ *Wed.–Sun. 10–4.*

Where to Stay & Eat

$$–$$$ ✕ **Upstairs Restaurant.** Chef Layne McCollum takes a creative approach to contemporary American cuisine with a menu that changes weekly. The baked-Brie and roast-garlic appetizer and the soups are specialties. Local wines are reasonably priced. Downstairs from the 12-table restaurant there's a street-side bistro and wine bar. ⊠ *164 Main St.* ☎ *209/ 223–3342* ⊟ *AE, D, MC, V* ⊗ *Closed Mon.–Tues.*

¢ ✕ **Rosebud's Classic Café.** Art deco accents and music from the 1930s and 1940s set the mood at this homey café. Among the classic American dishes served are hot roast beef, turkey, and meat loaf with mashed potatoes smothered in gravy. Charbroiled burgers, freshly baked pies, and espresso coffees round out the lunch menu. Omelets, hotcakes, and many other items are served for breakfast. ⊠ *26 Main St.* ☎ *209/223– 1035* ⊟ *MC, V* ⊗ *No dinner.*

$–$$$ 🏨 **Court Street Inn.** This Victorian has tin ceilings and a redwood staircase. The cozy first-floor Burgundy Court Room has a fireplace; the Champagne Court Room has a large whirlpool bathtub and a Wedgwood stove. The Indian House, a two-bedroom cottage, has a large bathroom, a 61-inch TV with VCR, and a stereo. A third building, Vintage Court, is decorated in wine colors and contains two guest rooms that share a parlor and deck. ⊠ *215 Court St., 95642* ☎ *209/223–0416 or 800/200–0416* 🖷 *209/223–5429* ⊕ *www.courtstreetinn.com* ☚ *5 rooms, 2 suites* ⟁ *Some in-room VCRs, outdoor hot tub* ⊟ *AE, D, MC, V* ⊖⊗ *BP.*

¢ 🏨 **Best Western Amador Inn.** Convenience and price are the main attractions of this two-story motel right on the highway. Many rooms have gas fireplaces. Guests who want in-room refrigerators and microwaves pay $5 extra. ⊠ *200 S. Hwy. 49, 95642* ☎ *209/223–0211 or 800/543–5221* 🖷 *209/223–4836* ⊕ *www.bestwestern.com* ☚ *118 rooms* ⟁ *Restaurant, pool, laundry service* ⊟ *AE, D, DC, MC, V.*

Angels Camp

23 *20 mi south of Jackson on Hwy. 49.*

Angels Camp is famed chiefly for its May jumping-frog contest, based on Mark Twain's "The Jumping Frog of Calaveras County." The writer reputedly heard the story of the jumping frog from Ross Coon, proprietor of Angels Hotel, which has been in operation since 1856.

Angels Camp Museum has gold-rush relics—photos, rocks, petrified wood, old blacksmith and mining equipment, and a horse-drawn hearse. The carriage house out back holds 31 carriages and an impressive display of mineral specimens. ⊠ *753 S. Main St.* ☎ *209/736–2963* ✉ *$2* ⊙ *Jan.–Feb., weekends 10–3; Mar.–Dec., daily 10–3.*

> **off the beaten path**

CALIFORNIA CAVERNS AND MOANING CAVERN – A ½-mi subterranean trail at the California Caverns winds through large chambers and past underground streams and lakes. There aren't many steps to climb, but it's a strenuous walk, with some narrow passageways and steep spots. The caverns, at a constant 53°F, contain crystalline formations not found elsewhere; the 80-minute guided tour explains local history and geology. A 235-step spiral staircase leads into the vast Moaning Cavern. More adventurous sorts can rappel into the chamber—ropes and instruction are provided. Otherwise, the only way inside is via the 45-minute tour, during which you'll see giant (and still growing) stalactites and stalagmites and an archaeological site that holds some of the oldest human remains yet found in America (an unlucky person has fallen into the cavern about once every 130 years for the last 13,000 years). ⊠ *California Caverns: 9 mi east of San Andreas on Mountain Ranch Rd., then about 3 mi on Cave City Rd. (follow signs)* ☎ *209/736–2708* ✉ *$10* ⊙ *Usually May–Dec., but call ahead* ⊠ *Moaning Cavern: Parrots Ferry Rd., 2 mi south of town of Vallecito, off Hwy. 4 east of Angels Camp* ☎ *209/736–2708* ⊕ *www.caverntours.com* ✉ *$10* ⊙ *May–Oct., daily 9–6; Nov.–Apr., weekdays 10–5, weekends 9–5.*

Murphys

24 *10 mi east of Angels Camp on Hwy. 4.*

Murphys is a well-preserved town of white picket fences, Victorian houses, and interesting shops. Horatio Alger and Ulysses S. Grant are among the guests who have signed the register at **Murphys Historic Hotel and Lodge.** The men were among the 19th-century visitors to the giant sequoia groves in nearby Calaveras Big Trees State Park.

The **Kautz Ironstone Winery and Caverns** is worth a visit even if you don't drink wine. Tours take you into underground tunnels cooled by a waterfall from a natural spring; they include a performance on a massive automated pipe organ. The winery schedules concerts during spring and summer in its huge outdoor amphitheater, plus art shows and other events on weekends. On display is a 44-pound specimen of crystalline gold. A deli offers lunch items. ⊠ *1894 Six Mile Rd.* ☎ *209/728–1251* ⊙ *Daily 11–5.*

> **off the beaten path**

CALAVERAS BIG TREES STATE PARK – This state park protects hundreds of the largest and rarest living things on the planet— magnificent giant sequoia redwood trees. Some are nearly 3,000 years old, 90 feet around at the base, and 250 feet tall. The park's self-guided walks range from a 200-yard trail to 1-mi and 5-mi (closed in winter) loops through the groves. There are campgrounds and picnic areas; swimming, wading, fishing, and sunbathing on the Stanislaus River are popular in summer. ⊠ *Off Hwy. 4, 15 mi northeast of Murphys (4 mi northeast of Arnold)* ☎ *209/795–2334* ⌑ *$4 per vehicle (day use); campsites $16* ☉ *Park daily sunrise–sunset (day use). Visitor center May–Oct., daily 10–4; Nov.–Apr., weekends 11–3.*

Where to Stay & Eat

$–$$ ✕ **Grounds.** Light Italian entrées, grilled vegetables, chicken, seafood, and steak are the specialties at this bistro and coffee shop. Sandwiches, salads, and homemade soups are served for lunch. The crowd is friendly and the service attentive. ⊠ *402 Main St.* ☎ *209/728–8663* ▤ *MC, V* ☉ *Closed Tues. No dinner Mon.*

★ **$$$** ▦ **Dunbar House 1880.** The oversize rooms in this elaborate Italianate-style home have brass beds, down comforters, gas-burning stoves, and claw-foot tubs. Broad wraparound verandas encourage lounging, as do the colorful gardens and large elm trees. The Cedar Room's sunporch has a two-person whirlpool tub; in the Sequoia Room you can gaze at the garden while soaking in a bubble bath. In the afternoon you are treated to trays of appetizers and wine in your room. ⊠ *271 Jones St., 95247* ☎ *209/728–2897 or 800/692–6006* 🖶 *209/728–1451* ⊕ *www.dunbarhouse.com* ↪ *3 rooms, 2 suites* ♿ *Refrigerators, in-room VCRs* ▤ *AE, MC, V* ❙◐❙ *BP.*

¢–$ ✕▦ **Murphys Historic Hotel & Lodge.** This 1855 stone hotel, whose register has seen the signatures of Mark Twain and the bandit Black Bart, figured in Bret Harte's short story "A Night at Wingdam." Accommodations are in the hotel and a modern motel-style addition. The older rooms are furnished with antiques, many of them large and hand-carved. The hotel has a convivial old-time saloon, which can be noisy into the wee hours. ⊠ *457 Main St., 95247* ☎ *209/728–3444 or 800/532–7684* 🖶 *209/728–1590* ⊕ *www.murphyshotel.com* ↪ *29 rooms, 20 with bath* ♿ *Restaurant, bar, meeting room* ▤ *AE, D, DC, MC, V.*

Columbia

㉕ *14 mi south of Angels Camp, Hwy. 49 to Parrots Ferry Rd.*

Columbia is the gateway for Columbia State Historic Park, which is one of the Gold Country's most visited sites.

☾ **Columbia State Historic Park,** known as the Gem of the Southern Mines,
Fodor'sChoice comes as close to a gold-rush town in its heyday as any site in the Gold
★ Country. You can ride a stagecoach, pan for gold, and watch a blacksmith working at an anvil. Street musicians perform in summer. Restored or reconstructed buildings include a Wells Fargo Express office, a Masonic temple, stores, saloons, two hotels, a firehouse, churches, a school, and a newspaper office. All are staffed to simulate a working 1850s town. The park also includes the **Historic Fallon House Theater,** where a full schedule of entertainment is presented. ☎ *209/532–0150* ⊕ *www.parks.ca.gov* ⌑ *Free* ☉ *Daily 9–5.*

Where to Stay & Eat

$ ✕▦ **City Hotel.** The rooms in this restored 1856 hostelry are furnished with period antiques. Two have balconies overlooking Main Street, and six rooms open onto a second-floor parlor. All the accommodations have private half-baths, with showers nearby; robes and slippers are provided. The restaurant ($$; closed Monday), one of the Gold Country's best, serves French-accented California cuisine complemented by a large selection of the state's respected wines. The What Cheer Saloon is right out of a western movie. Combined lodging, dinner, and theater packages are available. ⊠ *22768 Main St., 95310* ☎ *209/532–1479 or 800/ 532–1479* 🖷 *209/532–7027* ⊕ *www.cityhotel.com* 🛏 *10 rooms* ⌂ *Restaurant, bar* ▤ *AE, D, MC, V* ⦿❘ *CP.*

¢–$ 🏨 **Fallon Hotel.** The state of California restored this 1857 hotel. All rooms have antiques and a private half-bath; there are separate men's and women's showers. If you occupy one of the five balcony rooms, you can sit outside with your morning coffee and watch the town wake up. ⊠ *11175 Washington St., 95310* ☎ *209/532–1470* 🖷 *209/532–7027* ⊕ *www.cityhotel.com* 🛏 *14 rooms* ▤ *AE, D, MC, V* ⦿❘ *CP.*

Nightlife & the Arts

Sierra Repertory Theater Company (☎ 209/532–4644) presents a full season of plays, comedies, and musicals at the Historic Fallon House Theater and another venue in East Sonora.

Sonora

㉖ *4 mi south of Columbia, Parrots Ferry Rd. to Hwy. 49.*

Miners from Mexico founded Sonora and made it the biggest town in the Mother Lode. Following a period of racial and ethnic strife, the Mexican settlers moved on. Yankees built the commercial city that is visible today. Sonora's historic downtown section sits atop the Big Bonanza Mine, one of the richest in the state. Another mine, on the site of nearby Sonora High School, yielded 990 pounds of gold in a single week in 1879. Reminders of the gold rush are everywhere in Sonora, in prim Victorian houses, typical Sierra-stone storefronts, and awning-shaded sidewalks. Reality intrudes beyond the town's historic heart, with strip malls, shopping centers, and modern motels. If the countryside surrounding Sonora seems familiar, that's because it has been the backdrop for many movies over the years. Scenes from *High Noon, For Whom the Bell Tolls, The Virginian, Back to the Future III,* and *Unforgiven* were filmed here.

The **Tuolumne County Museum and History Center** occupies a building that served as a jail until 1951. Restored to an earlier period, it houses a jail museum, vintage firearms and paraphernalia, a case with gold nuggets, a cute exhibit on soapbox derby racing in hilly Sonora, and the libraries of a historical society and a genealogical society. ⊠ *158 W. Bradford St.* ☎ *209/532–1317* 🖾 *Free* ⊙ *Sun.–Fri. 10–4, Sat. 10–3:30.*

Where to Stay & Eat

¢–$ ✕ **Banny's Cafe.** Its pleasant environment and hearty yet refined dishes make Banny's a quiet alternative to Sonora's noisier eateries. Try the grilled salmon fillet with scallion rice and ginger-wasabi-soy aioli. ⊠ *83 S. Stewart St.* ☎ *209/533–4709* ▤ *D, MC, V.*

¢ ✕ **Garcia's Taqueria.** This casual, inexpensive eatery serves Mexican and southwestern fare with an emphasis on seafood. Murals of Yosemite and other California landscapes adorn the walls. The spicy roasted-garlic soup is popular. ⊠ *145 S. Washington St.* ☎ *209/588–1915* ▤ *No credit cards* ⊙ *Closed Sun.*

$ 🏨 **Barretta Gardens Bed and Breakfast Inn.** This inn is perfect for a romantic getaway or a special business meeting. Its elegant Victorian rooms vary in size, but all are furnished with period pieces. The three antiques-filled parlors carry on the Victorian theme. A French bakery on the property provides the fresh pastries at breakfast. ⊠ *700 S. Barretta St., 95370* ☎ *209/532–6039* 🖨 *209/532–8257* ⊕ *www. barrettagardens.com* ↗ *5 rooms* ⚏ *Hot tub* ▤ *AE, MC, V* ⟨◯⟩ *CP.*

¢ ⌗ **Best Western Sonora Oaks Motor Hotel.** The standard motel–issue rooms at this East Sonora establishment are clean and roomy; the larger ones have outdoor sitting areas. Suites have fireplaces, whirlpool tubs, and tranquil hillside views. Because the motel is right off Highway 108, the front rooms can be noisy. ⊠ *19551 Hess Ave., 95370* ☎ *209/533– 4400 or 800/532–1944* 🖨 *209/532–1964* ⊕ *www.bestwestern.com* ↗ *96 rooms, 4 suites* ⚏ *Restaurant, pool, outdoor hot tub, lounge, meeting room* ▤ *AE, D, DC, MC, V.*

Jamestown

㉗ *4 mi south of Sonora on Hwy. 49.*

Compact Jamestown supplies a touristy, superficial view of gold-rush-era life. Shops in brightly colored buildings along Main Street sell antiques and gift items.

The California State Railroad Museum operates **Railtown 1897** at what were the headquarters and general shops of the Sierra Railway from 1897 to 1955. The railroad has appeared in more than 200 movies and television productions, including *Petticoat Junction, The Virginian, High Noon,* and *Unforgiven.* You can view the roundhouse, an air-operated 60-ft turntable, shop rooms, and old locomotives and coaches. Six-mile, 40-minute steam train rides through the countryside operate on weekends during part of the year. ⊠ *5th Ave. and Reservoir Rd., off Hwy. 49* ☎ *209/984–3953* ⊕ *www.csrmf.org* 🎫 *Roundhouse tour $2; train ride $6* ☉ *Daily 9:30–4:30. Train rides Apr.–Oct., weekends 11–3; Nov., Sat. 11–3.*

Where to Stay & Eat

$–$$ ✕⌗ **National Hotel.** The National has been in business since 1859, and the furnishings—brass beds, patchwork quilts, and lace curtains—are authentic but not overly embellished. Some rooms have no phone. The saloon, which still has its original redwood bar, is a great place to linger. The popular restaurant ($–$$) serves big lunches: hamburgers and fries, salads, and Italian entrées. More upscale Continental cuisine is prepared for dinner (reservations essential). ⊠ *18183 Main St., 95327* ☎ *209/984–3446, 800/894–3446 in CA* 🖨 *209/984–5620* ⊕ *www. national-hotel.com* ↗ *9 rooms* ⚏ *Restaurant, bar* ▤ *AE, D, DC, MC, V* ⟨◯⟩ *CP.*

Mariposa

㉘ *50 mi south of Jamestown on Hwy. 49.*

Mariposa marks the southern end of the Mother Lode. Much of the land in this area was part of a 44,000-acre land grant Colonel John C. Fremont acquired from Mexico before gold was discovered and California became a state.

At the **California State Mining and Mineral Museum** a glittering 13-pound chunk of crystallized gold makes it clear what the rush was about. Displays include a replica of a typical tunnel dug by hard-rock miners, a miniature stamp mill, and a panning and sluicing exhibit. ⊠ *Mariposa County Fairgrounds, Hwy. 49* ☎ *209/742–7625* 🎫 *$2* ☉ *May–Sept., daily 10–6; Oct.–Apr., Wed.–Mon. 10–4.*

Where to Stay & Eat

$–$$$ ✕ **Charles Street Dinner House.** Ed Uebner moved here from Chicago to become the owner-chef in 1980, and Charles Street is firmly established as the classiest dinner joint in town—plus, it's centrally located. The extensive menu, which won't appeal to vegetarians, includes beef, chicken, pork, lamb, duck and lobster. ⊠ *Hwy. 140 at 7th St.* ☎ *209/966–2366* ▭ *D, MC, V* ⊘ *Closed Mon.–Tues. No lunch.*

¢–$ ✕ **Castillo's Mexican Food.** Tasty tacos, enchiladas, *chiles rellenos* (stuffed, batter-fried, mild chili peppers) and burrito combinations plus chimichangas, fajitas, steak, and seafood are served in a casual storefront. ⊠ *4995 5th St.* ☎ *209/742–4413* ▭ *MC, V.*

$–$$ ⊡ **Little Valley Inn.** Pine paneling, historical photos, and old mining tools recall Mariposa's heritage at this modern B&B with six bungalows. A suite that sleeps five people includes a full kitchen. All rooms have private entrances, baths, and decks. The large grounds include a creek where you can pan for gold. The enthusiastic innkeepers will also take you to their off-site claim for prospecting. ⊠ *3483 Brooks Rd., off Hwy. 49, 95338* ☎ *209/742–6204 or 800/889–5444* ◰ *209/742–5099* ⊕ *www. littlevalley.com* ⟿ *Private cabin, 4 rooms, 2 suites* ⚬ *Refrigerators, in-room VCRs, horseshoes* ▭ *AE, MC, V* ⦿⧉ *BP.*

¢ ⊡ **The Mariposa Lodge.** Thoroughly modern and somewhat without character, the Mariposa nevertheless is a solid option for those who want to stay warm and within 30 miles of Yosemite National Park without spending a fortune. ⊠ *5052 Hwy. 140, 95338* ☎ *209/966–3607 or 800/ 341–8000* ◰ *209/742–7038* ⟿ *45 rooms* ⚬ *Pool, outdoor hot tub, no-smoking rooms* ▭ *AE, MC, V.*

THE GOLD COUNTRY—NORTH
HIGHWAY 49 FROM COLOMA TO NEVADA CITY

Highway 49 north of Placerville links the towns of Coloma, Auburn, Grass Valley, and Nevada City. Most are gentrified versions of once-rowdy mining camps, vestiges of which remain in roadside museums, old mining structures, and restored homes now serving as inns.

Coloma

㉙ *8 mi north of U.S. 50 on Hwy. 49.*

The California gold rush started in Coloma. "My eye was caught with the glimpse of something shining in the bottom of the ditch," James Marshall recalled. Marshall himself never found any more "color," as gold came to be called.

★ Most of Coloma lies within **Marshall Gold Discovery State Historic Park.** Though crowded with tourists in summer, Coloma hardly resembles the mob scene it was in 1849, when 2,000 prospectors staked out claims along the streambed. The town's population grew to 4,000, supporting seven hotels, three banks, and many stores and businesses. But when reserves of the precious metal dwindled, prospectors left as quickly as they had come. A working replica of an 1840s mill lies near the spot where James Marshall first saw gold. A trail leads to a monument marking Marshall's discovery. The museum is not as interesting as the outdoor exhibits. ⊠ *Hwy. 49* ☎ *530/622–3470* ⊕ *www.parks. ca.gov* ⧉ *$4 per vehicle (day use)* ⊘ *Park daily 8 AM–sunset. Museum Memorial Day–Labor Day, daily 10–5; Labor Day–Memorial Day, daily 10–4:30.*

Where to Stay

$$ ⊞ **Coloma Country Inn.** Five of the rooms at this B&B on 5 acres in the state historic park are inside a restored 1852 Victorian. Two suites, one with a kitchenette, are in the carriage house. Appointments include antique double and queen-size beds, handmade quilts, stenciled friezes, and fresh flowers. The owners can direct you to tour operators offering rafting trips on the American River. ⊠ *345 High St., 95613* ☎ *530/622–6919* 🖶 *530/622–1795* ⊕ *www.colomacountryinn.com* 🖙 *5 rooms, 3 with bath; 2 suites* ⚲ *Kitchenette* 🖃 *No credit cards* ⟨◯⟩ *BP.*

Auburn

▶ **30** *18 mi north of Coloma on Hwy. 49, 34 mi northeast of Sacramento on I–80.*

Auburn is the Gold Country town most accessible to travelers on I–80. An important transportation center during the gold rush, Auburn has a small Old Town district with narrow climbing streets, cobblestone lanes, wooden sidewalks, and many original buildings. Fresh produce, flowers, baked goods, and gifts are for sale at the farmers' market, held Saturday morning year-round.

A $1 **trolley** (☎ 530/887–2111 or 800/427–6463) operated by the Placer County Visitor Information Center loops through downtown and Old Town, with stops at some hotels and inns.

Auburn's standout structure is the **Placer County Courthouse.** The classic gold-dome building houses the Placer County Museum, which documents the area's history—Native American, railroad, agricultural, and mining—from the early 1700s to 1900. ⊠ *101 Maple St.* ☎ *530/889–6500* 🖾 *Free* ⊙ *Tues.–Sun. 10–4.*

The **Bernhard Museum Complex,** whose centerpiece is the former Traveler's Rest Hotel, was built in 1851. A residence and adjacent winery buildings reflect family life in the late Victorian era. The carriage house contains period conveyances. ⊠ *291 Auburn-Folsom Rd.* ☎ *530/889–6500* 🖾 *Free* ⊙ *Tues.–Fri. 10:30–3, weekends noon–4.*

The **Gold Country Museum** surveys life in the mines. Exhibits include a walk-through mine tunnel, a gold-panning stream, and a replica saloon. ⊠ *1273 High St., off Auburn-Folsom Rd.* ☎ *530/889–6500* 🖾 *Free* ⊙ *Tues.–Fri. 10–3:30, weekends 11–4.*

Where to Stay & Eat

★ **$$–$$$$** ✕ **Latitudes.** Delicious multicultural cuisine is served up in an 1870 Victorian. The menu (with monthly specials from diverse geographical regions) includes seafood, chicken, beef, and turkey entrées prepared with the appropriate Mexican spices, curries, cheeses, or teriyaki sauce. Vegetarians and vegans have several inventive choices, too. Sunday brunch is deservedly popular. ⊠ *130 Maple St.* ☎ *530/885–9535* 🖃 *AE, D, MC, V* ⊙ *Closed Mon.–Tues.*

$$–$$$ ✕ **Le Bilig French Café.** Simple and elegant cuisine is the goal of the chefs at this country-French café on the outskirts of Auburn. Escargots, coq au vin, and quiche are standard offerings; specials might include salmon in parchment paper. ⊠ *11750 Atwood Rd., off Hwy. 49 near the Bel Air Mall* ☎ *530/888–1491* 🖃 *MC, V* ⊙ *Closed Mon.–Tues. No lunch.*

¢ ✕ **Awful Annie's.** Big patio umbrellas (and outdoor heaters when necessary) allow patrons to take in the view of the Old Town from this popular spot for breakfast—one specialty is a chili omelet—or lunch. ⊠ *160 Sacramento St.* ☎ *530/888–9857* 🖃 *AE, MC, V* ⊙ *No dinner.*

$–$$ ⊞ **Powers Mansion Inn.** This inn hints at the lavish lifestyle enjoyed by the gold-rush gentry. Two light-filled parlors have gleaming oak floors, Asian antiques, and ornate Victorian chairs and settees. A second-floor maze of narrow corridors leads to the guest rooms, which have brass and pencil-post beds. The honeymoon suite has a fireplace and heart-shape hot tub. ✉ *164 Cleveland Ave., 95603* ☎ *530/885–1166* ▣ *530/ 885–1386* ⊕ *www.vfr.net/~powerinn* ⇨ *10 rooms, 3 suites* ▤ *AE, MC, V* ⊚| *BP.*

$ ⊞ **Holiday Inn.** On a hill above the freeway across from Old Auburn, this hotel has an imposing columned entrance but a welcoming lobby. Rooms are chain-standard but attractively furnished. All have work areas and coffeemakers. Those nearest the parking lot can be noisy. ✉ *120 Grass Valley Hwy., 95603* ☎ *530/887–8787 or 800/814–8787* ▣ *530/ 887–9824* ⊕ *www.6c.com* ⇨ *96 rooms, 6 suites* ⌂ *Restaurant, room service, in-room data ports, pool, gym, spa, bar, business services, convention center* ▤ *AE, D, DC, MC, V.*

¢ ⊞ **Comfort Inn.** The contemporary-style rooms at this well-maintained property are softened with teal and pastel colors. Though just a short distance from the freeway, the hotel is fairly quiet. The expanded Continental breakfast includes many choices of baked goods, cereals, fruits, and juices. ✉ *1875 Auburn Ravine Rd. (Forest Hill exit north from I–80), 95603* ☎ *530/885–1800 or 800/626–1900* ▣ *530/888–6424* ⇨ *77 rooms, 2 suites* ⌂ *Pool, gym, spa, laundry facilities, meeting room, no-smoking floor* ▤ *AE, D, DC, MC, V* ⊚| *CP.*

Grass Valley

③ *23 mi north of Auburn on Hwy. 49.*

More than half of California's total gold production was extracted from mines around Grass Valley. Unlike in neighboring Nevada City, urban sprawl surrounds Grass Valley's historic downtown. The Empire Mine and the North Star Power House are among the Gold Country's most fascinating attractions.

In the center of town, on the site of the original, stands a reproduction of the **Lola Montez House,** home of the notorious dancer. Montez, who arrived in Grass Valley in the early 1850s, was no great talent—her popularity among miners derived from her suggestive "spider dance"—but her loves, who reportedly included composer Franz Liszt, were legendary. According to one account, she arrived in California after having been "permanently retired from her job as Bavarian king Ludwig's mistress," literary muse, and political adviser. She seems to have pushed too hard for democracy, which contributed to his overthrow and her banishment as a witch—or so the story goes. The memory of licentious Lola lingers in Grass Valley, as does her bathtub (on the front porch of the house). The Grass Valley/Nevada County Chamber of Commerce is headquartered here. ✉ *248 Mill St.* ☎ *530/273–4667 or 800/655–4667.*

The landmark **Holbrooke Hotel,** built in 1851, hosted Lola Montez and Mark Twain as well as Ulysses S. Grant and a stream of other U.S. presidents. Its restaurant-saloon is one of the oldest operating west of the Mississippi. ✉ *212 W. Main St.* ☎ *530/273–1353 or 800/933–7077.*

★ The hard-rock gold mine at **Empire Mine State Historic Park** was one of California's richest. An estimated 5.8 million ounces were extracted from its 367 mi of underground passages between 1850 and 1956. On the 50-minute tours you can walk into a mine shaft, peer into the mine's deeper recesses, and view the owner's "cottage," which has exquisite woodwork. The visitor center has mining exhibits, and a picnic area is nearby.

⊠ *10791 E. Empire St. (exit south from Hwy. 49)* ☎ *530/273–8522* ⊕ *www.parks.ca.gov* ⊠ *$1* ⊘ *May–Aug., daily 9–6; Sept.–Apr., daily 10–5; tours May–Aug., daily on the hr 11–4; Sept.–Apr., weekends at 1 (cottage only) and 2 (mine yard only), weather permitting.*

Ⓒ Housed in the former North Star powerhouse, the **North Star Mining Museum** displays a 32-ft-high enclosed Pelton waterwheel said to be the largest ever built. It was used to power mining operations and was a forerunner of the modern turbines that generate hydroelectricity. Hands-on displays are geared to children. There's a picnic area nearby. ⊠ *Empire and McCourtney Sts. (Empire St. exit north from Hwy. 49)* ☎ *530/273–4255* ⊠ *Donation requested* ⊘ *May–mid-Oct., daily 10–5.*

Where to Stay & Eat

¢ ✕ **Cousin Jack Pasties.** Meat- and vegetable-stuffed pasties in effect are a taste of the region's history, having come across the Atlantic with Cornish miners and their families in the mid-19th century. The flaky crusts practically melt in your mouth. A simple food stand that sometimes closes early on dreary winter days, Jack's is nonetheless a local landmark and dear to its loyal clientele. ⊠ *Auburn and Main Sts.* ☎ *530/272–9230* ⊟ *No credit cards.*

¢ ⌸ **Holiday Lodge.** This modest hotel is close to many of the town's main attractions and its staff can help arrange gold-panning excursions and historical tours of the gold country. ⊠ *1221 E. Main St., 95945* ☎ *530/273–4406 or 800/742–7125* ⤳ *35 rooms* ⌂ *Pool, sauna* ⊟ *AE, MC, V* ⏀ *CP.*

Nevada City

❸❷ *4 mi north of Grass Valley on Hwy. 49; 62 mi north of Sacramento via I–80 to Hwy. 49.*

Nevada City, once known as the Queen City of the Northern Mines, is the most appealing of the northern Mother Lode towns. The iron-shutter brick buildings that line the narrow downtown streets contain antiques shops, galleries, bookstores, boutiques, B&Bs, restaurants, and a winery. Horse-drawn carriage tours add to the romance, as do gas streetlamps. At one point in the 1850s Nevada City had a population of nearly 10,000, enough to support much cultural activity.

With its gingerbread-trim bell tower, **Firehouse No. 1** is one of the Gold Country's most photographed buildings. A museum, it houses gold-rush artifacts and a Chinese joss house (temple). Also on display are relics of the ill-fated Donner Party, a group of 19th-century travelers who, trapped in the Sierra Nevada by winter snows, were forced to cannibalize their dead in order to survive. ⊠ *214 Main St.* ☎ *530/265–5468* ⊠ *Donation requested* ⊘ *Apr.–Nov., daily 11–4; Dec.–Mar., Thurs.–Sun. 11:30–4.*

The redbrick **Nevada Theatre**, constructed in 1865, is California's oldest theater building in continuous use. Mark Twain, Emma Nevada, and many other notable persons appeared on its stage. Housed in the theater, the **Foothill Theater Company** (☎ *530/265–8587 or 888/730–8587*) hosts theatrical and musical events. Old films are screened here too. ⊠ *401 Broad St.* ☎ *530/265–6161, 530/274–3456 for film show times.*

The **Miners Foundry**, erected in 1856, produced machines for gold mining and logging. The Pelton Water Wheel, a source of power for the mines (the wheel also jump-started the hydroelectric power industry), was invented here. A cavernous building, the foundry hosts plays, concerts, an antiques show, weddings, receptions, and other events. ⊠ *325 Spring St.* ☎ *530/265–5040.*

You can watch wine being created while you sip at the **Nevada City Winery,** where the tasting room overlooks the production area. ⊠ *Miners Foundry Garage, 321 Spring St.* ☎ *530/265–9463 or 800/203–9463* ⊕ *www.ncwinery.com* ✉ *Free* ⊙ *Tastings daily noon–5.*

THE GOLD COUNTRY A TO Z

To research prices, get advice from other travelers, and book travel arrangements, visit ⊕ *www.fodors.com*

AIRPORTS & TRANSFERS

Sacramento International Airport is served by Alaska, America West, American, Delta, Frontier, Horizon Air, Northwest, Southwest, TWA, United Airlines, and US Airways. *See* Air Travel *in* Smart Travel Tips A to Z for airline phone numbers. A private taxi from the airport to downtown Sacramento is about $20. The cost of the Super Shuttle from the airport to downtown Sacramento is $11. Call in advance to arrange transportation from your hotel to the airport.

🛫 **Sacramento International Airport** ⊠ 6900 Airport Blvd., 12 mi northwest of downtown off I-5, Sacramento ☎ 916/874-0700 ⊕ www.sacairports.org. **Super Shuttle** ☎ 800/258-3826.

BUS TRAVEL

Getting to and from SIA can be accomplished via taxi, the Super Shuttle, or by Yolo County Public Bus 42, which operates a circular service around SIA, downtown Sacramento, West Sacramento, Davis, and Woodland. Other Gold Country destinations are best reached by private car.

Greyhound serves Sacramento, Davis, Auburn, and Placerville. It's a two-hour trip from San Francisco's Transbay Terminal, at 1st and Mission streets, to the Sacramento station, at 7th and L streets.

Sacramento Regional Transit buses and light-rail vehicles transport passengers in Sacramento. Most buses run from 6 AM to 10 PM, most trains from 5 AM to midnight. A DASH (Downtown Area Shuttle) bus and the No. 30 city bus both link Old Sacramento, midtown, and Sutter's Fort in a loop that travels eastward on J Street and westward on L Street. The fare is 50¢ within this area.

🚌 **Greyhound** ☎ 800/231-2222 ⊕ www.greyhound.com. **Sacramento Regional Transit** ☎ 916/321-2877 ⊕ www.sacrt.com. **Yolo County Bus** 530/666-2837 ☎ 530/666-2837 ⊕ www.yolobus.com.

CAR RENTAL

You can rent a car from any of the major national chains at Sacramento International Airport. *See* Car Rental *in* Smart Travel Tips A to Z for national rental agency phone numbers.

CAR TRAVEL

Traveling by car is the most convenient way to see the Gold Country. From Sacramento three highways fan out toward the east, all intersecting with Highway 49: I–80 heads 30 mi northeast to Auburn; U.S. 50 goes east 40 mi to Placerville; and Highway 16 angles southeast 45 mi to Plymouth. Highway 49 is an excellent two-lane road that winds and climbs through the foothills and valleys, linking the principal Gold Country towns.

Sacramento lies at the junction of I–5 and I–80, about 90 mi northeast of San Francisco. The 406-mi drive north on I–5 from Los Angeles takes 7–8 hours. I–80 continues northeast through the Gold Country toward Reno, about 136 mi (three hours or so) from Sacramento.

EMERGENCIES

In an emergency dial 911. Each of the following medical facilities has an emergency room open 24 hours a day.

⚑ Hospitals Mercy Hospital of Sacramento ✉ 4001 J St., Sacramento ☎ 916/453-4424. **Sutter General Hospital** ✉ 2801 L St., Sacramento ☎ 916/733-8900. **Sutter Memorial Hospital** ✉ 52nd and F Sts., Sacramento ☎ 916/733-1000.

LODGING

A number of organizations can supply information about Gold Country B&Bs and other accommodations.

⚑ Amador County Innkeepers Association ☎ 209/267-1710 or 800/726-4667. **Gold Country Inns of Tuolumne County** ☎ 209/533-1845. **Historic Bed & Breakfast Inns of Grass Valley & Nevada City** ☎ 530/477-6634 or 800/250-5808.

TOURS

Gold Prospecting Adventures, LLC, based in Jamestown, arranges gold-panning trips. Gray Line/Frontier Tours operates city tours for groups of 40 or more.

⚑ Gold Prospecting Adventures, LLC ☎ 209/984-4653 or 800/596-0009 ⊕ www.goldprospecting.com. **Frontier Tours** ☎ 916/564-8687 or 800/356-9838.

TRAIN TRAVEL

Several trains operated by Amtrak stop in Sacramento and Davis. Trains making the 2½-hour trip from Jack London Square, in Oakland, stop in Emeryville (across the bay from San Francisco), Richmond, Martinez, and Davis before reaching Sacramento; some stop in Berkeley and Suisun-Fairfield as well.

⚑ Amtrak ☎ 800/872-7245 ⊕ www.amtrakcalifornia.com.

VISITOR INFORMATION

⚑ Amador County Chamber of Commerce ✉ 125 Peek St., Jackson 95642 ☎ 209/223-0350 ⊕ www.amadorcountychamber.com. **Davis Chamber of Commerce** ✉ 130 G St., Davis 95616 ☎ 530/756-5160 ⊕ www.davischamber.com. **El Dorado County Chamber of Commerce** ✉ 542 Main St., Placerville 95667 ☎ 530/621-5885 or 800/457-6279 ⊕ www.eldoradocounty.org. **Grass Valley/Nevada County Chamber of Commerce** ✉ 248 Mill St., Grass Valley 95945 ☎ 530/273-4667 or 800/655-4667 ⊕ www.ncgold.com/chamber. **Mariposa County Visitors Bureau** ✉ 5158 Hwy. 140, Mariposa 95338 ☎ 209/966-7081 or 800/208-2434 ⊕ mariposa.yosemite.net/visitor. **Nevada City Chamber of Commerce** ✉ 132 Main St., Nevada City ☎ 530/265-2692. **Sacramento Convention and Visitors Bureau** ✉ 1303 J St., Suite 600, Sacramento 95814 ☎ 916/264-7777 ⊕ www.sacramentocvb.org. **San Joaquin Convention & Visitors Bureau** ✉ 46 W. Freemont St., Stockton 95202 ☎ 209/943-1987 or 800/350-1987 ⊕ www.ssjcvb.org. **Tuolumne County Visitors Bureau** ✉ 542 Stockton St., Sonora 95370 ☎ 209/533-4420 or 800/446-1333 ⊕ www.thegreatunfenced.com. **Woodland Chamber of Commerce** ✉ 307 1st St., Woodland 95695 ☎ 530/662-7327 or 888/843-2636 ⊕ www.woodlandchamber.org.

LAKE TAHOE
WITH RENO, NEVADA

FODOR'S CHOICE

Black Bear Inn B&B, *South Lake Tahoe*

Emerald Bay State Park, *South Shore*

Heavenly Gondola, *South Lake Tahoe*

PlumpJack, *restaurant in Olympic Valley*

PlumpJack Squaw Valley Inn, *Olympic Valley*

Wild Goose, *restaurant in Tahoe Vista*

HIGHLY RECOMMENDED

SIGHTS   Cave Rock, *north of Zephyr Cove*

Gatekeeper's Cabin Museum, *Tahoe City*

Sand Harbor Beach, *Lake Tahoe–Nevada State Park*

Sugar Pine Point State Park, *South of Tahoma*

OUTDOORS   Alpine Meadows Ski Area, *Tahoe City*

Squaw Valley USA, *Olympic Valley*

Many other great hotels and restaurants enliven Lake Tahoe. For other favorites, look for the black stars as you read this chapter.

John A.
Vlahides

THE LARGEST ALPINE LAKE IN NORTH AMERICA, Lake Tahoe is famous for its clarity, deep blue water, and surrounding snowcapped peaks. Straddling the state line between California and Nevada, the lake lies 6,225 feet above sea level in the Sierra Nevada. The border gives this popular resort region a split personality. About half its visitors are intent on low-key sightseeing, hiking, fishing, camping, and boating. The rest head directly for the Nevada side, where bargain dining, big-name entertainment, and the lure of a jackpot draw them into the glittering casinos.

The first white explorer to gaze upon this spectacular region was Captain John C. Fremont, in 1844, guided by the famous scout Kit Carson. Not long afterward, silver was discovered in Nevada's Comstock Lode, at Virginia City. As the mines grew larger and deeper, the Tahoe Basin's forests were leveled to provide lumber for subterranean support. By the early 1900s wealthy Californians were building lakeside estates here, some of which still stand. Improved roads brought the less affluent in the 1920s and 1930s, when modest bungalows began to appear. The first casinos opened in the 1940s. Ski resorts inspired another development boom in the 1950s and 1960s, turning the lake into a year-round destination.

Though Lake Tahoe possesses abundant natural beauty and accessible wilderness, nearby towns are highly developed, and roads around the lake are often congested with traffic. Those who prefer solitude can escape to the many state parks, national forests, and protected tracts of wilderness that ring the 22-mi-long, 12-mi-wide lake. At a vantage point overlooking Emerald Bay, on a trail in the national forests that ring the basin, or on a sunset cruise on the lake itself, you can forget the hordes and the commercial development. You can even pretend that you're Mark Twain, who found "not 15 other human beings throughout its wide circumference" when he visited the lake in 1861 and wrote that "the eye never tired of gazing, night or day, calm or storm."

Exploring Lake Tahoe

The typical way to explore the Lake Tahoe area is to drive the 72-mi road that follows the shore through wooded flatlands and past beaches, climbing to vistas on the rugged southwest side of the lake and passing through busy commercial developments and casinos on its northeastern and southeastern edges. Undeveloped Lake Tahoe–Nevada State Park occupies more than half of the Nevada side of Lake Tahoe, stretching along the shore from just north of Zephyr Cove to just south of the upscale community of Incline Village. The California side, particularly South Lake Tahoe, is more developed, though much wilderness remains.

About the Restaurants

On weekends and in high season expect a long wait in the more popular restaurants. Always try to reserve a table in advance. During slower periods some places may close temporarily or limit their hours, so call to make sure your choice is open. Casinos use their restaurants to attract gaming customers. Marquees often tout "$5.99 prime rib dinners" or "$1.99 breakfast specials." Some of these meal deals, usually found in the coffee shops and buffets, may not be top quality, but at those prices, it's hard to complain. The finer restaurants in casinos, however, generally deliver good food and service, and a bit of atmosphere. Unless otherwise noted, even the most expensive area restaurants welcome customers in casual clothes—not surprising in this year-round vacation spot—but don't expect to be served in most places if you're barefoot, shirtless, or wearing a skimpy bathing suit.

About the Hotels

Quiet inns on the water, motels near the casino area, rooms at the casinos themselves, lodges close to ski runs, and condos everywhere else are among your Tahoe lodging options. During summer and ski season the lake is crowded; reserve space as far in advance as possible. Spring and fall give you a little more leeway and lower—sometimes significantly lower—rates.

WHAT IT COSTS					
	$$$$	**$$$**	**$$**	**$**	**¢**
RESTAURANTS	over $30	$23–$30	$16–$22	$10–$15	under $10
HOTELS	over $250	$176–$250	$121–$175	$90–$120	under $90

Restaurant prices are for a main course at dinner, excluding sales tax of 7%–7¼% (depending on location). Hotel prices are for a standard double room in high season, excluding service charges and 9%–12% tax.

Timing

Most Lake Tahoe accommodations, restaurants, and even a handful of parks are open year-round, but most visitor centers, mansions, state parks, and beaches are closed from November through May. During those months, multitudes of skiers and winter-sports enthusiasts are attracted to Tahoe's downhill resorts and cross-country centers, North America's largest concentration of skiing facilities. Ski resorts try to open by Thanksgiving, if only with machine-made snow, and can operate through May or later. During the ski season Tahoe's population swells on the weekends. If you're able to come midweek, you'll have the resorts and neighboring towns almost to yourself. Bear in mind, though, that Tahoe is a popular wedding and honeymoon destination: on Valentine's Day the chapels become veritable assembly lines.

Unless you want to ski, you'll find that Tahoe is most fun during the summer, when it's cooler here than in the scorched Sierra Nevada foothills, and the clean mountain air is bracingly crisp. But on some summer weekends it seems that absolutely every tourist at the lake—100,000 at peak periods—is in a car on the main road that circles the 72-mi shoreline. Weekdays are busy as well. The crowds and congestion increase as the day wears on, so the best strategy for avoiding the crush is to do as much as you can early in the day. The parking lots of the Lake Tahoe Visitor Center, Vikingsholm, and Gatekeeper's Log Cabin Museum can be jammed at any time, and the lake's beaches can be packed. Even in the warmest months the water of Lake Tahoe is brisk—except for in small, shallow, and sheltered coves, its temperature averages 39°F. September and October, when the throngs have dispersed but the weather is still pleasant, are among the most satisfying—and cheapest—months to visit Lake Tahoe.

Numbers in the text correspond to numbers on the Lake Tahoe map.

CALIFORNIA SIDE

California and Nevada share Lake Tahoe. With the exception of Stateline, Nevada, the California side is the more developed, both with commercial enterprises—restaurants, motels, lodges, resorts, residential subdivisions—and public-access facilities, such as historic sites, parks, campgrounds, marinas, and beaches.

It takes only one day to "see" Lake Tahoe—to drive around the lake, stretch your legs at a few overlooks, take a nature walk, and wander among the casinos at Stateline. But if you have more time, you can laze on a beach and swim, venture onto the lake or into the mountains, and sample Tahoe's finer restaurants. If you have five days, you may become so attached to Tahoe that you begin visiting real-estate agents.

9

**If you have
3 days**

On your first day stop in 🖼 **South Lake Tahoe** ❶ ⌐ and pick up provisions for a picnic lunch. Start in **Pope-Baldwin Recreation Area** ❷ and check out Tallac Historic Site. Head west on Highway 89, stopping at the **Lake Tahoe Visitor Center** and the **Emerald Bay State Park** ❸ lookout. Have lunch at the lookout, or hike down to Vikingsholm, a Viking castle replica. In the late afternoon explore the trails and mansions at **Sugar Pine Point State Park** ❺; then backtrack on Highway 89 and U.S. 50 for dinner in 🖼 **Stateline** ⓮ or in South Lake Tahoe. On day two cruise on the *Tahoe Queen* out of South Lake Tahoe or the MS *Dixie II* out of **Zephyr Cove** ⓭ then ride the **Heavenly Gondola** at Heavenly Ski Resort in South Lake Tahoe. Pack a picnic and have lunch high above the lake and (except in snow season) take a walk on one of Heavenly's nature trails. You can try your luck at the Stateline casinos before dinner. Start your third day by heading north on U.S. 50, stopping at **Cave Rock** and (after turning north on Highway 28) at **Sand Harbor Beach.** If there's no snow on the ground, tour the **Thunderbird Lodge** (reservations essential) for a glimpse of life at an old-Tahoe estate. If *Bonanza* looms large in your memory, drop by **Ponderosa Ranch,** just south of **Incline Village** ⑪, or else continue on to **Crystal Bay** ❿ to hike the Stateline Lookout Trail. If you have time, drive to **Tahoe City** ❼ to see Gatekeeper's Log Cabin Museum, or make the 45-minute drive down to 🖼 **Reno** ⑫ for dinner and some nightlife.

**If you have
5 days**

Spend your first morning at **Pope-Baldwin Recreation Area** ❷ ⌐. After a picnic lunch head to **Lake Tahoe Visitor Center** and the **Emerald Bay State Park** ❸ lookout. Hike to Vikingsholm or move on to **Sugar Pine Point State Park** ❺. Have dinner in 🖼 **South Lake Tahoe** ❶. On your second day cruise on the *Tahoe Queen* or MS *Dixie II,* then pack a picnic and ride the **Heavenly Gondola** and possibly take a hike. Spend the late afternoon or early evening sampling the worldly pleasures of the 🖼 **Stateline** ⓮ casinos. On day three visit **Cave Rock,** the **Thunderbird Lodge** (reservations essential), and the **Ponderosa Ranch,** just south of **Incline Village** ⑪, and hike the Stateline Lookout Trail, above **Crystal Bay** ❿. Have lunch in Crystal Bay and spend the afternoon at nearby **Kings Beach State Recreation Area.** That evening, drive down to 🖼 **Reno** ⑫ for dinner and entertainment. On your fourth day hang out at **Sand Harbor Beach.** If the high-mountain desert appeals, spend day five in the Great Basin, touring **Carson City and Virginia City,** and the vast expanse of the eastern Sierra. Alternatively, head to **D. L. Bliss State Park** ❹ for a hike, then drive to **Tahoe City** ❼ for lunch and a tour of the Gatekeeper's Log Cabin Museum; afterward, visit **Olympic Valley** ❽ and ride the cable car to High Camp at Squaw Valley for a sunset cocktail.

South Lake Tahoe

▶ ❶ *50 mi south of Reno on U.S. 395 and U.S. 50, 198 mi northeast of San Francisco on I–80 and U.S. 50.*

South Lake Tahoe's raison d'être is tourism. The evidence is all there: the casinos at Stateline; the ski slopes at Heavenly Valley; the beaches, docks, bike trails, and campgrounds of the south shore; and the backcountry of Eldorado National Forest and Desolation Wilderness. Motels, lodges, and restaurants line U.S. 50 heading into town. But if you go northwest on Highway 89, which follows the lakefront, commercial development gives way to national forests and state parks.

Fodor'sChoice
★

Whether you ski or not, you'll appreciate the impressive view of Lake Tahoe from the **Heavenly Gondola,** which has 138 eight-passenger cars that travel from the middle of town 2½ mi up the mountain in 11 minutes. When the weather's fine, you can take one of three hikes around the mountaintop. During ski season, you can also ride the **Heavenly Tram** and have lunch at Monument Peak Restaurant, which serves both cafeteria-style food and fancier fare from a dining room that affords stunning lake views. ⊠ *Gondola leaves from downtown South Lake Tahoe; tram leaves from the California base area, at the end of Ski Run Blvd., off U.S. 50 in South Lake Tahoe* ☎ *775/586–7000 or 800/243–2836* ⊕ *www.skiheavenly.com* ☒ *$20* ⊘ *Gondola: winter, daily 9–4, summer, daily 9–9. Tram: winter only, daily 9–4.*

The 500-passenger ***Tahoe Queen*** (⊠ Ski Run Marina, off U.S. 50 ☎ 530/ 541–3364 or 800/238–2463), a glass-bottom paddle-wheeler, makes 2¼-hour sightseeing cruises year-round and three-hour dinner-dance cruises from April through October. Fares range from $22 to $49. In winter the boat becomes the only waterborne ski shuttle in the world: $79 covers hotel transfers, breakfast, transportation across the lake to Squaw Valley, and dinner; $119 includes a ski lift ticket.

Where to Stay & Eat

★ $$–$$$ ✕ **Café Fiore.** Café Fiore may be the most romantic spot in town. There are only seven candlelit tables at this northern Italian restaurant, where the menu lists a wide variety of pastas and meat dishes, as well as several daily fish specials. Sautéed veal dishes are the house specialty. Leave room for the homemade white-chocolate ice cream. ⊠ *1169 Ski Run Blvd.* ☎ *530/541–2908* ⌕ *Reservations essential* ☰ *AE, MC, V* ⊘ *No lunch.*

★ $$–$$$ ✕ **Evan's.** It's unusual in a resort town to find inventive, sophisticated food of the caliber served at Evan's. The contemporary California menu includes specialties like seared foie gras with curried ice cream and roast pineapple, and venison with balsamic-roasted cherries. The 40-seat dining room is intimate, with tables a little close together, but the service and food are excellent. ⊠ *536 Emerald Bay Rd.* ☎ *530/542–1990* ⌕ *Reservations essential* ☰ *MC, V* ⊘ *No lunch.*

$–$$$ ✕ **Fresh Ketch.** Fish is the specialty at this dockside restaurant, where you can look out at the yachts in the Tahoe Keys marina. The upstairs dining room serves full dinners, with a variety of fresh seafood and meats. Downstairs in the lively fireside seafood bar, the menu is lighter and more eclectic, with a good selection of reasonably priced hot and cold appetizers, salads, and sandwiches. ⊠ *2433 Venice Dr.* ☎ *530/541–5683* ⌕ *Reservations essential upstairs; reservations not accepted downstairs* ☰*. AE, D, DC, MC, V* ⊘ *No lunch upstairs.*

¢–$$ ✕ **Freshies.** When you've had your fill of junk food, come here for delicious, healthful meals. Specialties include seafood and vegetarian dishes, but there are always good grilled meats available, like Hawaiian spare ribs and free-range New York steaks. Though it's in a mini-

Camping

Campgrounds abound in the Tahoe area, operated by the California and Nevada state park departments, the U.S. Forest Service, city utility districts, and private operators. Sites range from primitive and rustic to upscale and luxurious. Make reservations far ahead for summer, when sites are in high demand.

Gambling

Six casinos are clustered on a strip of U.S. 50 in Stateline, and five casinos operate on the north shore. And, of course, in Reno there are more than a dozen major and a dozen minor casinos. Open 24 hours a day, 365 days a year, these gambling halls have table games, race and sports books, and thousands of slot and video poker machines. There is no charge to enter, and there is no dress code; as long as you're wearing money, you'll be welcome.

Great Golf

The Tahoe area is nearly as popular with golfers as it is with skiers. Over a dozen superb courses dot the mountains around the lake, with magnificent views, thick pines, fresh cool air, and lush fairways and greens. Encountering wildlife is not uncommon if you have to search for your ball out-of-bounds.

Hiking

There are five national forests in the Tahoe Basin and a half-dozen state parks. The main areas for hiking include the Tahoe Rim Trail, a 165-mi path along the ridgelines that now completely rings the lake; Desolation Wilderness, a vast 63,473-acre preserve of granite peaks, glacial valleys, subalpine forests, the Rubicon River, and more than 50 lakes; and the trail systems in D. L. Bliss, Emerald Bay, Sugar Pine Point, and Lake Tahoe–Nevada state parks and near Lake Tahoe Visitor Center. The Pacific Crest Trail, a high-mountain foot trail connecting Mexico to Canada, runs along the Sierra Crest just west of the lake. To the south of Lake Tahoe sits the Mokelumne Wilderness, a whopping 100,848-acre preserve, one of several undeveloped tracts that extend toward Yosemite, which is accessible via the Tahoe-Yosemite Trail, a 186-mi trek.

Skiing & Snowboarding

The mountains around Lake Tahoe are bombarded by blizzards throughout most winters and sometimes in the fall and spring; 10- to 12-foot bases are not uncommon. The Sierra often boasts the deepest snowpack on the continent, but because of the relatively mild temperatures over the Pacific, falling snow can be very heavy and wet—it's nicknamed "Sierra Cement" for a reason. The upside is that you can sometimes ski and board as late as July, you probably won't get frostbite, and you'll likely get a tan. The profusion of downhill resorts guarantees an ample selection of terrains, conditions, and challenges, including backcountry access at several resorts, most notably at Alpine Meadows, Sugar Bowl, and Sierra-at-Tahoe. Snowboarding is permitted at all Tahoe ski areas.

The Lake Tahoe area is also a great destination for Nordic skiers. You can even cross-country ski on fresh snow right on the lakeshore beaches. "Skinny" (i.e. cross-country) skiing at the resorts can be costly, but you get the benefits of machine grooming and trail preparation. If it's bargain Nordic you're after, take advantage of thousands of acres of public forest and parkland trails.

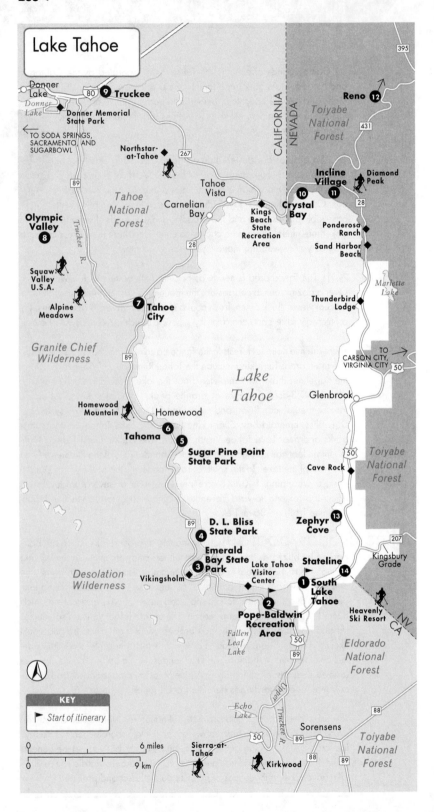

Lake Tahoe

Donner Lake
Donner Lake
Donner Memorial State Park
9 **Truckee**

TO SODA SPRINGS, SACRAMENTO, AND SUGARBOWL

Northstar-at-Tahoe

Tahoe Vista

Carnelian Bay

Kings Beach State Recreation Area

CALIFORNIA / NEVADA

Reno **12**

Toiyabe National Forest

Incline Village **11**   Diamond Peak

Crystal Bay **10**

Ponderosa Ranch

Sand Harbor Beach

Tahoe National Forest

Olympic Valley 8

Squaw Valley U.S.A.

Alpine Meadows

Marlette Lake

Thunderbird Lodge

7 **Tahoe City**

Granite Chief Wilderness

Lake Tahoe

TO CARSON CITY, VIRGINIA CITY

Glenbrook

Homewood Mountain   Homewood

Tahoma **6**
5 **Sugar Pine Point State Park**

Cave Rock

Toiyabe National Forest

D. L. Bliss State Park **4**

Zephyr Cove **13**

Emerald Bay State Park **3**
Vikingsholm

Lake Tahoe Visitor Center

Stateline

1 **South Lake Tahoe** **14**

Kingsbury Grade

Desolation Wilderness

2
Pope-Baldwin Recreation Area

Fallen Leaf Lake

Heavenly Ski Resort

NV / CA

Eldorado National Forest

Echo Lake

Sorensens

Toiyabe National Forest

KEY
Start of itinerary

0 — 6 miles
0 — 9 km

Sierra-at-Tahoe

Kirkwood

mall and you may have to wait for a table, it's worth it. ✉ *3300 Lake Tahoe Blvd.* ☎ *530/542–3630* ⌔ *Reservations not accepted* ▭ *MC, V.*

¢–$$ ✕ **Scusa!** The kitchen here turns out big plates of linguine with clam sauce, veal Marsala, and chicken piccata. There's nothing fancy or esoteric about the menu, just straightforward Italian–American food for everyday eating. Try the exceptionally good bread pudding for dessert. ✉ *1142 Ski Run Blvd.* ☎ *530/542–0100* ▭ *AE, MC, V* ☉ *No lunch.*

¢–$ ✕ **The Cantina.** The Cantina serves generous portions of traditional Mexican-American dishes, like burritos, enchiladas and tamales, as well as more stylized Southwestern cooking, like sautéed salmon breaded with blue corn, and crab cakes in jalapeño cream sauce. The bar makes great margaritas and serves 30 different kinds of beer. ✉ *765 Emerald Bay Rd.* ☎ *530/544–1233* ⌔ *Reservations not accepted* ▭ *MC, V.*

¢–$ ✕ **Dixon's Brew Pub.** This lively, stripped-down roadhouse near the outskirts of town serves everything from soups, sandwiches, and salads to barbecued chicken, pot pies, pastas, and coq au vin. The bar serves 15 beers on tap and packs 'em in on the weekends, when there's live music. ✉ *675 Emerald Bay Rd.* ☎ *530/542–3389* ⌔ *Reservations not accepted* ▭ *AE, MC, V.*

¢ ✕ **Red Hut Café.** A vintage-1959 Tahoe diner, all chrome and red plastic, the Red Hut is a tiny place with a dozen counter stools and a dozen booths. It's a traditional breakfast spot for those in the know. Come here for the huge omelets; the banana, pecan, and coconut waffles; and other tasty vittles. ✉ *2749 U.S. 50* ☎ *530/541–9024* ⌔ *Reservations not accepted* ▭ *No credit cards* ☉ *No dinner.*

$$$–$$$$ 🛏 **Black Bear Inn Bed and Breakfast.** South Lake Tahoe's best and most Fodor'sChoice luxurious inn feels like one of the great old lodges of the Adirondacks, ★ its living room complete with rough-hewn timber beams, plank floors, knotty-pine cathedral ceilings, hand-knotted Persian rugs, and even an elk's head over the giant river-rock fireplace. Built in the 1990s with meticulous attention to detail, the five inn rooms and three cabins feature 19th-century American antiques, fine art, and fireplaces; cabins also have kitchenettes. Never intrusive, the affable innkeepers provide a sumptuous breakfast in the morning and wine and cheese in the afternoon. ✉ *1202 Ski Run Blvd., 96150* ☎ *530/544–4451 or 877/232–7466* ⊕ *www.tahoeblackbear.com* ⚲ *5 rooms, 3 cabins* ⌂ *Dining room, in-room data ports, some kitchenettes, cable TV with movies, in-room VCRs, outdoor hot tub, some in-room hot tubs, ski storage, lounge; no kids under 16, no smoking* ▭ *MC, V* ⍟�‖ *BP.*

$$$–$$$$ 🛏 **Marriott's Grand Residence and Timber Lodge.** At the base of Heavenly Gondola, right in the center of town, are these two giant, modern condominium properties operated by Marriott. Though both are extremely comfortable, Timber Lodge feels more like a family vacation resort; Grand Residence is geared toward luxury travelers. Units vary in size from studios to three bedrooms, and some have amenities like stereos, fireplaces, daily maid service, and full kitchens. Ask about vacation packages. ✉ *1001 Park Ave., 96150* ☎ *530/542–8400 or 800/627–7468* 🖶 *530/524–8410* ⊕ *www.marriott.com* ⚲ *431 condos* ⌂ *In-room data ports, some in-room hot tubs, cable TV, some kitchens, outdoor pool, gym, 2 indoor hot tubs, ice skating, ski shop, ski storage, laundry facilities, laundry service, concierge; no smoking* ▭ *AE, D, DC, MC, V.*

$$$ 🛏 **Tahoe Seasons Resort.** It's a 150-yard walk to California Lodge of Heavenly Ski Resort from this all-suites hotel, where every room has a two-person sunken hot tub. Most units have gas fireplaces, and some can sleep up to six people. The lobby is decorated in retro-contemporary early-'80s style, but the rooms are very comfortable, and the service is great. ✉ *3901 Saddle Rd., 96157* ☎ *530/541–6700 or 800/540–4874* 🖶 *530/541–0653* ⊕ *www.tahoeseasons.com* ⚲ *183 suites* ⌂ *Restau-*

rant, room service, in-room hot tubs, minibars, kitchenettes, microwaves, refrigerators, cable TV, in-room VCRs, 2 tennis courts, outdoor pool, outdoor hot tub, volleyball, downhill skiing, billiards, ski shop, ski storage, lounge, video game room, concierge, meeting rooms; no smoking ☰ *AE, DC, MC, V.*

★ $$–$$$$ ▦ **Embassy Suites.** All rooms are suites at this large, full-service hotel, just over the state line in California, where there's no casino disturbing the quiet of the nine-story atrium lobby. Accommodations are extra-spacious and perfect for families, since there's a pull-out sofa in the living room of every suite. Rates include a full breakfast and evening cocktails. ☒ *4130 Lake Tahoe Blvd., 96150* ☎ *530/544–5400 or 800/362–2779* ▤ *530/544–4900* ⊕ *www.embassysuites.com* ➮ *400 suites* ⌂ *Restaurant, in-room data ports, microwaves, refrigerators, cable TV with movies and video games, indoor pool, exercise equipment, indoor hot tub, sauna, ski storage, bar, lounge, laundry facilities, meeting rooms, parking (fee)* ☰ *AE, D, DC, MC, V* ⦿ *BP.*

$–$$$$ ▦ **Lakeland Village Beach and Mountain Resort.** This 19-acre lakefront condominium complex has one- to five-bedroom semi-detached town houses, and studios and suites in the lodge building. Each unit is individually owned and decorated, so there's no uniformity to the furnishings, but all are spacious and come with fireplaces and fully equipped kitchens. Some have decks overlooking the lake, but others face the highway; ask when you book. This is a great place for families and couples traveling together: the largest unit sleeps 10. ☒ *3535 Lake Tahoe Blvd., 96150* ☎ *530/544–1685 or 800/822–5969* ▤ *530/544–0193* ⊕ *www. lakeland-village.com* ➮ *210 units* ⌂ *Room service, in-room data ports, kitchens, cable TV, in-room VCRs, outdoor pool, outdoor hot tub, indoor hot tub, sauna, gym, beach, boating, fishing, 2 tennis courts, ski shop, ski storage, dry cleaning, laundry facilities, meeting rooms, some pets allowed* ☰ *AE, D, MC, V.*

$–$$$ ▦ **Forest Inn Suites.** The location is excellent—5½ acres bordering a forest, a half block from the casinos, and adjacent to a supermarket, cinema, and shops. Rooms are among the largest at the lake, and there are six classes of suites. Ski rentals are available, and the Heavenly Gondola flies right over the roof. ☒ *1 Lake Pkwy., 96150* ☎ *530/541–6655 or 800/822–5950* ▤ *530/544–3135* ⊕ *www.forestinn.com* ➮ *17 rooms, 101 suites* ⌂ *Restaurant, in-room data ports, in-room safes, kitchenettes, cable TV, 5 putting greens, 2 pools, health club, 2 outdoor hot tubs, sauna, steam room, Ping-Pong, bicycles, volleyball, ski shop, bar, video game room, laundry facilities, meeting rooms, some pets allowed* ☰ *AE, D, DC, MC, V.*

$–$$$ ▦ **Inn by the Lake.** Across the road from a beach, this luxury motel has spacious rooms and suites furnished in contemporary style. All have balconies; some have lake views, wet bars, and kitchens. In the afternoon the staff sets out cookies and cider. ☒ *3300 Lake Tahoe Blvd., 96150* ☎ *530/542–0330 or 800/877–1466* ▤ *530/541–6596* ⊕ *www. innbythelake.com* ➮ *87 rooms, 13 suites* ⌂ *Room service, in-room data ports, some in-room hot tubs, some kitchenettes, some minibars, cable TV with movies and video games, outdoor pool, bicycles, sauna, ski storage, dry cleaning, laundry facilities, meeting rooms* ☰ *AE, D, DC, MC, V* ⦿ *CP.*

★ $–$$$ ▦ **Sorensen's Resort.** Escape civilization by staying in Eldorado National Forest, 20 minutes south of town. In a log cabin at this woodsy 165-acre resort you can lie on a hammock and listen to the wind in the aspens or sit in a rocker on your own front porch. All but three of the housekeeping cabins have a kitchen and wood-burning stove or fireplace. There are also three modern homes that sleep six. ☒ *14255 Hwy. 88, Hope Valley 96120* ☎ *530/694–2203 or 800/423–9949* ⊕ *www.*

sorensensresort.com ➰ *28 cabins with bath, 2 rooms with shared bath, 4 houses △ Restaurant, some fans, some kitchens, some kitchenettes, pond, sauna, fishing, bicycles, croquet, hiking, cross-country skiing, ski shop, ski storage, tobogganing, library, baby-sitting, children's programs (ages 3–18), playground, some pets allowed; no a/c, no room phones, no room TVs, no smoking.*

$–$$ 🏨 **Camp Richardson.** A 1920s lodge, a few dozen cabins, and a small inn comprise this resort, nestled beneath giant pine trees on 80 acres of land bordering the southwest shore of Lake Tahoe. The rustic log-cabin–style lodge has simple, attractive accommodations. The cabins (one-week minimum in summer) have lots of space and come with a fireplace or wood stove and a kitchenette; some can sleep eight. The Beachside Inn has more modern amenities and sits right on the lake, but its rooms feel like those in a run-of-the-mill motel. Far from the glitter of the casinos, this is a terrific place for families. ✉ *1900 Jameson Beach, 96150* ☎ *530/ 542–6550 or 800/544–1801* 🖷 *530/541–1802* ⊕ *www.camprichardson. com* ➰ *28 lodge rooms, 47 cabins, 7 inn rooms, 300 campsites △ Restaurant, some microwaves, some refrigerators, beach, boating, fishing, marina, waterskiing, bicycles, cross-country skiing, sleigh rides, shop; no phone in some rooms, no TV in some rooms, no smoking* ⊟ *AE, D, MC, V.*

★ **¢–$$** 🏨 **Best Western Station House Inn.** It's a short walk to the beach, the Heavenly Gondola, or the casinos from this modern, well-kept, two-story motel off the main drag, near the state line. The beds are comfortable, and the entire property is immaculate. ✉ *901 Park Ave., 96150* ☎ *530/542–1101 or 800/822–5953* 🖷 *530/542–1714* ⊕ *www.stationhouseinn.com* ➰ *100 rooms, 2 suites △ Restaurant, cable TV, pool, outdoor hot tub, bar, ski storage, dry cleaning, Internet* ⊟ *AE, D, DC, MC, V* ⟩◌⟨ *BP.*

¢–$$ 🏨 **Travelodge.** There are three branches of this motel chain in South Lake Tahoe. All are convenient to casinos, shopping, and recreation and have no-smoking rooms. ✉ *3489 U.S. 50, at Bijou Center, 96150* ☎ *530/ 544–5266 or 800/578–7878* 🖷 *530/544–6985* ⊕ *www.travelodge.com* ➰ *59 rooms △ Restaurant, cable TV, pool* ⊟ *AE, D, DC, MC, V* ✉ *4011 U.S. 50, 96150* ☎ *530/544–6000 or 800/578–7878* 🖷 *530/ 544–6869* ➰ *50 rooms △ Cable TV, pool* ⊟ *AE, D, DC, MC, V* ✉ *4003 U.S. 50, 96150* ☎ *530/541–5000 or 800/578–7878* 🖷 *530/ 544–6910* ➰ *66 rooms △ Cable TV, pool* ⊟ *AE, D, DC, MC, V.*

¢–$ 🏨 **Best Tahoe West Inn.** The Tahoe West is three blocks from the beach and casinos. There's nothing fancy about the place, but rooms are neatly furnished and have queen-size beds. The inn offers every possible kind of discount; ask and ye might receive. ✉ *4107 Pine Blvd., 96150* ☎ *530/544–6455 or 800/522–1021* 🖷 *530/544–0508* ⊕ *www.besttahoe. com* ➰ *60 rooms △ Some kitchenettes, cable TV with movies, pool, hot tub, sauna* ⊟ *AE, D, DC, MC, V.*

¢–$ 🏨 **Ridgewood Inn.** Great for get-up-and-go travelers, this single-story mom-and-pop motel has simple accommodations. On the outskirts of town, it makes a good jumping-off point for skiing or exploring the mountains. Every room has a gas fireplace. ✉ *1341 Emerald Bay Rd. (U.S. 50), 96150* ☎ *530/541–8589* 🖷 *530/542–4638* ⊕ *www.ridgewoodinn. com* ➰ *11 rooms, 1 suite △ Refrigerators, some kitchenettes, cable TV, outdoor hot tub* ⊟ *AE, D, MC, V.*

Sports & the Outdoors

CROSS-COUNTRY SKIING **Kirkwood Ski Resort** (☎ 209/258–7248) has 58 mi of superb groomed-track skiing, with skating lanes, instruction, and rentals. At Sorensen's Resort, **Hope Valley Cross Country** (☎ 530/694–2266) provides instruction and equipment rentals to prepare you for striding and telemarking. The outfit has 36 mi of trails, 6 of which are groomed, through Eldorado National Forest.

DOWNHILL SKIING

Straddling two states, vast **Heavenly Ski Resort**—composed of nine peaks, two valleys, and four base-lodge areas, and boasting the largest snow-making equipment in the western United States—has something for every skier. Beginners can choose wide, well-groomed trails—accessed via the Heavenly Tram or the gondola from downtown South Lake Tahoe—or short and gentle runs in the Enchanted Forest area. The Sky Express high-speed quad chair whisks intermediate and advanced skiers to the summit for wide cruisers or steep tree skiing. Mott and Killebrew canyons draw expert skiers to the Nevada side for the steep chutes and thick-timber slopes. For snowboarders there's Airport Park, near the Olympic lift. The ski school, like everything else at Heavenly, is large, and offers everything from learn-to-ski packages to canyon-adventure tours. Skiing lessons are available for children age four and up; there's day care for infants older than six weeks. ⊠ *Ski Run Blvd. off Hwy. 89/U.S. 50, Stateline NV* ☎ *775/586–7000, 800/243–2836, 530/541–7544 snow phone* ☞ *84 trails on 4,800 acres, rated 20% beginner, 45% intermediate, 35% expert. Longest run 5½ mi, base 6,540', summit 10,067'. Lifts: 29, including 1 aerial tram, 1 gondola, 1 high-speed 6-passenger lift, and 5 high-speed quads.*

Thirty-six miles south of Lake Tahoe, **Kirkwood Ski Resort** is a destination resort with 135 condominiums, shops and restaurants, and a spa. But with 500 annual inches of snowfall, Kirkwood really draws the crowds with outstanding skiing. The rocky chutes off the very top are rated expert-only, but intermediate and beginner skiers enjoy vast bowls, where they can ski through trees or on wide, open trails. There are three freestyle terrain parks with varying degrees of difficulty; one is so technically challenging that it requires a separate ticket. Nonskiers can snowshoe, snowmobile, or go on a dog-sled ride. There's also an ice-skating rink. The children's ski school has programs for ages 4–12, and there's day care for children two to six years old. ⊠ *Hwy. 88, 14 mi west of Hwy. 89* ☎ *209/258–6000, 209/258–7000 for lodging information, 209/258–3000 snow phone* ☞ *72 trails on 2,300 acres, rated 15% beginner, 50% intermediate, 20% advanced, 15% expert. Longest run 2½ mi, base 7,800', summit 9,800'. Lifts: 14.*

Often overlooked by skiers and boarders rushing to Heavenly or Kirkwood, **Sierra-at-Tahoe** has meticulously groomed intermediate slopes, some of the best tree skiing in California, and guided backcountry access. There are also two terrain parks, including a superpipe with 17-ft walls. For nonskiers there's a snow-tubing hill. Sierra has both challenging terrain and a low-key atmosphere that's great for families. ⊠ *12 mi from South Lake Tahoe off of U.S. 50, near Echo Summit* ☎ *530/659–7453* ☞ *46 trails on 2,000 acres, rated 25% beginner, 50% intermediate, 25% advanced. Longest run 2½ mi, base 6,640', summit 8,852'. Lifts: 11, including 3 high-speed quads*

FISHING

Tahoe Sports Fishing is one of the largest and oldest fishing-charter services on the lake. Trips include all necessary gear and bait, and the crew cleans and packages your catch. ⊠ *Ski Run Marina, South Lake Tahoe* ☎ *530/541–5448, 800/696–7797 in CA.*

GOLF

The 18-hole, par-71 **Lake Tahoe Golf Course** (⊠ U.S 50, between Lake Tahoe Airport and Meyers ☎ 530/577–0788) has a driving range. Greens fees start at $45 a cart (mandatory from Friday through Sunday) costs $20.

HIKING

The south shore is a great jumping-off point for day treks into nearby Eldorado National Forest and Desolation Wilderness. Hike a couple of miles on the **Pacific Crest Trail** (⊠ Echo Summit, about 12 mi southwest from South Lake Tahoe off U.S. 50 ☎ 916/349–2109 or 888/728–7245 ⊕ www.pcta.org). The Pacific Crest Trail leads into **Desolation Wilderness** (✉ El Dorado National Forest Information Center ☎ 530/644–6048), where you can pick up trails to gorgeous backcountry lakes and mountain peaks (bring a map). Memorial Day through Labor Day, the easiest way to access Desolation Wilderness is via boat taxi ($14 round-trip) across Echo Lake from **Echo Chalet** (✉ Echo Lakes Rd., off U.S. 50 near Echo Summit ☎ 530/659–7207 ⊕ www.echochalet.com).

KAYAKING **Kayak Tahoe** has long been teaching people to kayak on Lake Tahoe and the Truckee River. Lessons and excursions (Emerald Bay, Cave Rock, Zephyr Cove) are offered from June through September. You can also rent a kayak and paddle solo. ✉ *Timber Cove Marina at Tahoe Paradise* ☎ *530/544–2011.*

SCUBA DIVING **Sun Sports** (✉ 3564 Lake Tahoe Blvd. ☎ 530/541–6000) is a full-service PADI dive center with rentals and instruction.

Pope-Baldwin Recreation Area

▶ **②** *5 mi west of South Lake Tahoe on Hwy. 89.*

George S. Pope, who made his money in shipping and lumber, hosted the business and cultural elite of 1920s America at his home, the **Pope House.** The magnificently restored 1894 mansion and two other estates—those of entrepreneur "Lucky" Baldwin (which houses a museum of Baldwin memorabilia and Washoe Indian artifacts) and Walter Heller (the Valhalla, used for community events)—form the heart of the Pope-Baldwin Recreation Area's **Tallac Historic Site.** The lakeside site, a pleasant place to take a stroll or have a picnic, hosts summertime cultural activities including a Renaissance festival. Docents conduct tours of the Pope House in summer. ☎ *530/541–5227* ⊕ *www.tahoeheritage. org* ✆ *Free; Pope House tour $2* ۞ *Tallac Historic Site grounds daily dawn–sunset; house and museum hrs vary.*

The U.S. Forest Service operates the **Lake Tahoe Visitor Center,** on Taylor Creek. You can visit the site of a Washoe Indian settlement; walk self-guided trails through meadow, marsh, and forest; and inspect the Stream Profile Chamber, an underground underwater display with windows that afford views right into Taylor Creek (in the fall you may see spawning kokanee salmon digging their nests). In summer U.S. Forest Service naturalists organize discovery walks and nighttime campfires with singing and marshmallow roasts. ✉ *Hwy. 89* ☎ *530/573–2674 (in season only)* ⊕ *www.r5.fs.fed.us/ltbmu* ۞ *June–Sept., daily 8–5:30; Oct., weekends 8–5:30.*

Emerald Bay State Park

③ *4 mi west of Pope-Baldwin Recreation Area on Hwy. 89.*

Fodor'sChoice
★

Emerald Bay, a 3-mi-long and 1-mi-wide fjord-like inlet on Lake Tahoe's shore, was carved by a massive glacier millions of years ago. Famed for its jewel-like shape and colors, it surrounds Fannette, Tahoe's only island. Highway 89 curves high above the lake through Emerald Bay State Park; from the Emerald Bay lookout, the centerpiece of the park, you can survey the whole scene.

A steep 1-mi-long trail from the lookout leads down to **Vikingsholm,** a 38-room estate completed in 1929. The original owner, Lora Knight, had this precise replica of a 1,200-year-old Viking castle built out of materials native to the area. She furnished it with Scandinavian antiques and hired artisans to build period reproductions. The sod roof sprouts wildflowers each spring. There are picnic tables nearby and a gray-sand beach for strolling. The hike back up is hard (especially if you're not yet acclimated to the elevation), but there are benches and stone culverts to rest on. At the 150-ft peak of Fannette Island are the remnants of a stone structure known as the Tea House, built in 1928 so that guests of Lora Knight could have a place to enjoy afternoon refreshments after a motorboat ride. The island is off-limits from February through June to protect nesting Canada geese. The rest of the year it's open for day use. ☎ 530/541–3030 (summer only) or 530/525–7277 ✉ $3 ⊙ Mid-June–Sept. 30, 10–4.

Sports & the Outdoors

HIKING   Leave your car in the parking lot for Eagle Falls picnic area (near Vikingsholm; arrive early for a good spot), and head to **Eagle Falls,** a short but fairly steep walk up-canyon; you'll have a brilliant panorama of Emerald Bay from this spot, near the boundary of Desolation Wilderness. If you want a full-day's hike and you're in good shape, continue 5 mi, past Eagle Lake, to Upper and Middle Velma Lakes (bring a map).

SWIMMING   Hike past Eagle Falls (about 1 mi from the parking lot) to **Eagle Lake,** where you can shed your clothes and dive into cold water.

D. L. Bliss State Park

❹ *3 mi north of Emerald Bay State Park on Hwy. 89.*

D. L. Bliss State Park takes its name from Duane LeRoy Bliss, a 19th-century lumber magnate. At one time Bliss owned nearly 75% of Tahoe's lakefront, along with local steamboats, railroads, and banks. The Bliss family donated these 1,200 acres to the state in the 1930s. The park now shares 6 mi of shoreline with Emerald Bay State Park. At the north end of Bliss is Rubicon Point, which overlooks one of the lake's deepest spots. Short trails lead to an old lighthouse and Balancing Rock, which weighs 250,000 pounds and balances on a fist of granite. A 4¼-mi trail leads to Vikingsholm and affords stunning lake views. Two white-sand beaches front some of Tahoe's warmest water. ☎ 530/525–7277 ✉ $2 per vehicle (day use) ⊙ Memorial Day–Sept., daily sunrise–sunset.

Camping

⚠ **D. L. Bliss State Park Campground.** In one of California's most beautiful spots, quiet, wooded hills make for blissful family camping near the lake. Reservations are accepted up to seven months in advance. ⚲ *Grills, flush toilets, drinking water, showers, bear boxes, fire pits, picnic tables, public telephone, swimming; no hook-ups* ⇆ *168 sites* ✉ *Off Hwy. 89, 17 mi south of Tahoe City on lake side* ☎ *800/444–7275* ⊕ *www.reserveamerica.com* ✉ *$14–$16* ⊙ *June–Sept.*

Sugar Pine Point State Park

★ ❺ *8 mi north of D. L. Bliss State Park on Hwy. 89.*

The main attraction at Sugar Pine Point State Park is Ehrman Mansion, a 1903 stone-and-shingle summer home furnished in period style. In its day it was the height of modernity, with a refrigerator, an elevator, and an electric stove. Also in the park are a trapper's log cabin from the mid-19th century, a nature preserve with wildlife exhibits, a lighthouse, the start of the 10-mi-long biking trail to Tahoe City, and an extensive system of hiking and cross-country skiing trails. ☎ 530/525–7232 year-round, 530/525–7982 in season ✉ $2 per vehicle (day use) ⊙ Mansion open July–Labor Day, daily 11–4.

Camping

⚠ **General Creek Campground.** This homey campground on the mountain side of Highway 89 is beautiful and one of the few public ones to remain open in winter, when it is popular with cross-country skiers. There are no hookups here, and the showers operate from Memorial Day to Labor Day only. ⚘ *Grills, flush toilets, drinking water, showers, bear boxes, fire pits, public telephone, swimming* ⇨ *175 sites* ✉ *Hwy. 89, 1 mi south of Tahoma* ☎ *800/444–7275* ⊕ *www.reserveamerica.com* ⊟ *$14–$18* ⊙ *Year-round.*

Tahoma

❻ *1 mi north of Sugar Pine Point State Park on Hwy. 89; 23 mi south of Truckee on Hwy. 89.*

The quiet west shore offers a glimpse back in time to "Old Tahoe." Tahoma exemplifies life on the lake in its early days, with rustic, lakeside vacation cottages that are far from the blinking lights of the South Shore's casinos. In 1960 Tahoma hosted the Olympic nordic skiing competitions. Today there's little to do here except stroll by the lake and listen to the wind in the trees.

Where to Stay

$–$$$ 🏠 **Tahoma Meadows B&B Cottages.** Rooms in these freestanding vacation cabins are individually decorated, and some have clawfoot tubs and fireplaces. Some of the cabins are a bit small, so if you want to lounge in your room, ask for a big one. Tariffs for cabins without kitchens include a delicious family-style breakfast. ✉ *6821 W. Lake Blvd., Box 810, 96142* ☎ *530/525–1553 or 866/525–1553* ⊕ *www.tahomameadows.com* ⇨ *15 cabins* ⚘ *Restaurant, some kitchens, cable TV, outdoor hot tub, some pets allowed (fee); no room phones, no smoking* ⊟ *AE, D, MC, V.*

Sports & the Outdoors

You'll feel as though you're going to ski into the lake when you schuss down the face of **Homewood Mountain Resort**—and you could if you really wanted to, since the mountain rises right off the shoreline. This is the favorite area of locals on a fresh-snow day, since you can find lots of untracked powder. It's also the most protected and least windy Tahoe ski area during a storm. There aren't any high-speed lifts, but there are rarely any lines and the ticket prices are some of the cheapest around. It may look small as you drive by, but most of the resort is not visible from the road. ✉ *Hwy. 89* ☎ *530/525–2992* ⊕ *www.skihomewood. com* ⚡ *56 trails on 1,260 acres, rated 15% beginner, 50% intermediate, and 35% advanced. Base 6,240′, summit 7,880′. Lifts: 4 chair lifts, 4 surface lifts.*

Tahoe City

❼ *10 mi north of Sugar Pine Point State Park on Hwy. 89, 14 mi south of Truckee on Hwy. 89.*

Tahoe City's many stores and restaurants lie within a compact area, all within walking distance of the Outlet Gates, where water is spilled into the Truckee River to control the surface level of the lake. Giant trout are commonly seen in the river from Fanny Bridge, so-called for the views of the backsides of sightseers leaning over the railing. Here, Highway 89 turns north from the lake and leads to Squaw Valley, Donner Lake, and Truckee, and Highway 28 continues northeast around the lake toward Kings Beach and Nevada.

★ The **Gatekeeper's Cabin Museum,** in Tahoe City, preserves a little-known part of the region's history. Between 1910 and 1968 the gatekeeper who lived on this site was responsible for monitoring the level of the lake, using a hand-turned winch system to keep the water at the correct level. That winch system is still used today. ⊠ *130 W. Lake Blvd.* ☎ *530/583–1762* 🖅 *Free* ☉ *Mid-June–Labor Day, daily 11–5; May–mid-June and Labor Day–late Sept., Wed.–Sun. 11–5.*

The **Watson Cabin Living Museum,** a 1909 log cabin built by Robert M. Watson and his son and filled with century-old furnishings, is in the middle of Tahoe City. Costumed docents act out the daily life of a typical pioneer family. ⊠ *560 N. Lake Blvd.* ☎ *530/583–8717 or 530/583–1762* 🖅 *Free* ☉ *Memorial Day–June 30, weekends noon–4; July–Labor Day, daily noon–4.*

Where to Stay & Eat

$$–$$$$ ✕ **Christy Hill.** Sit near the fireplace in the sparsely decorated, whitewashed dining room. While you take in great views of the lake, you can dine on sophisticated yet unpretentious seasonal California cuisine, including fresh seafood, beef, Australian lamb loin, and pasta. The service is professional, desserts are delicious (try the pecan ice cream or fruit cobbler), and the wine list includes several inexpensive vintages. ⊠ *Lakehouse Mall, 115 Grove St.* ☎ *530/583–8551* ⚲ *Reservations essential* ☰ *AE, MC, V* ☉ *Closed Mon. Labor Day–Thanksgiving and Apr.–May. No lunch.*

$$–$$$ ✕ **Jake's on the Lake.** Overlooking the water, large, handsome rooms of oak and glass are the backdrop for steaks and an extensive selection of seafood. The lounge gets crowded with bar-hopping boaters, who pull up to the big pier outside. ⊠ *Boatworks Mall, 780 N. Lake Blvd.* ☎ *530/583–0188* ☰ *AE, MC, V* ☉ *No lunch weekdays.*

★ **$$–$$$** ✕ **Wolfdale's.** Wolfdale's brought contemporary California cuisine to Lake Tahoe in 1984. The weekly menu draws from Asian and European cooking and includes imaginative entrées like sea bass tempura, Asian braised duck leg and breast, and coconut crepe stuffed with stir-fried vegetables. Tables in the comfortable dining room are well-spaced. ⊠ *640 N. Lake Blvd.* ☎ *530/583–5700* ⚲ *Reservations essential* ☰ *MC, V* ☉ *No lunch.*

★ **$–$$$** ✕ **Fiamma.** Everything from soup stock to gelato is made from scratch at this modern northern Italian trattoria. Settle into one of the comfy, romantic booths, where hot focaccia hits the table as soon as you arrive, or sit at the always-bustling wine bar with wine aficionados and hip, young singles. The menu includes roasted and grilled meats, homemade pastas, and pizzas from the wood-fired oven. ⊠ *521 N. Lake Blvd.* ☎ *530/581–1416* ⚲ *Reservations essential* ☰ *AE, MC, V* ☉ *No lunch.*

¢–$ ✕ **Hacienda del Lago.** If you need a margarita fix and you're craving Mexican, you can fill up on nachos in the bar during happy hour (4–6), or sit at a table by the window for burritos, enchiladas, or fajitas and a great lake view. You won't leave hungry. ⊠ *760 N. Lake Blvd., upstairs in the Boatworks Mall* ☎ *530/583–0358* ⚲ *Reservations not accepted* ☰ *MC, V* ☉ *No lunch.*

¢ ✕ **Fire Sign Café.** There's often a wait at the west shore's best spot for breakfast and lunch, but it's worth it. The pastries are made from scratch, the salmon is smoked in-house, and there's real maple syrup for the many flavors of pancakes and waffles. The eggs Benedict are delicious here. ✉ *1785 W. Lake Blvd.* ☎ *530/583–0871* 🖃 *AE, MC, V* ◯ *No dinner.*

★ **$–$$$** ✕🖼 **Sunnyside Restaurant and Lodge.** The views are superb at this pretty little lodge, right on the lake, just 3 mi south of Tahoe City. All but four rooms have balconies and locally crafted furnishings; some have river-rock fireplaces and wet bars, and some have pull-out sofas. The lodge is great for couples, but it's a little too low-key for families. The restaurant ($$–$$$) serves standard preparations of seafood, steaks, and pasta. The dockside bar gets packed with boaters and partiers. ✉ *1850 W. Lake Blvd., Box 5969, 96145* ☎ *530/583–7200 or 800/822–2754* 🖷 *530/583–2551* ⊕ *www.sunnysidetahoe.com* ⌨ *18 rooms, 5 suites* ⟐ *Restaurant, room service, fans, in-room data ports, cable TV, in-room VCRs, bar, beach; no a/c, no smoking* 🖃 *AE, MC, V* ⏀ *CP.*

$$$–$$$$ 🖼 **Chinquapin Resort.** A deluxe development on 95 acres of forested land and a mile of lakefront lies 3 mi northeast of Tahoe City. Within are one- to four-bedroom town houses and condos with great views of the lake and the mountains. Each unit has a fireplace, a fully equipped kitchen, and a washer and dryer. A one-week minimum stay is required in summer and late December; two- and three-night minimums apply the rest of the year. ✉ *3600 N. Lake Blvd., 96145* ☎ *530/583–6991 or 800/732–6721* 🖷 *530/583–0937* ⊕ *www.chinquapin.com* ⌨ *172 town houses and condos* ⟐ *Kitchens, cable TV, 7 tennis courts, pool, sauna, 2 beaches, hiking, horseshoes* 🖃 *AE, D, MC, V.*

$$–$$$$ 🖼 **The Cottage Inn.** Avoid the crowds by staying just south of town in one of these tidy, circa-1938 log cottages under the towering pines on the west shore of the lake. Cute as a button, with knotty-pine paneling and a gas-flame stone fireplace, each unit typifies old-Tahoe style while embracing you with up-to-date comfort. There's also a private beach. ✉ *1690 W. Lake Blvd.* ⌂ *(Box 66, 96145)* ☎ *530/581–4073 or 800/581–4073* 🖷 *530/581–0226* ⊕ *www.thecottageinn.com* ⌨ *17 rooms, 10 suites* ⟐ *Some in-room hot tubs, in-room VCRs, lake, sauna, beach; no kids under 12, no smoking* 🖃 *MC, V* ⏀ *BP.*

$$–$$$$ 🖼 **Mayfield House.** This cozy B&B, constructed of wood and stone, is a classic example of 1930s Tahoe architecture. Rooms are decorated with alpine country furnishings, some of them antiques. There are down comforters, fresh flowers, and books in the rooms, each of which has a queen- or king-size bed. There's a large living room with a fireplace, and a full breakfast every morning in the dining room. ✉ *236 Grove St.* ⌂ *(Box 8529, 96145)* ☎*530/583–1001 or 888/518–8898* ⊕*www.mayfieldhouse. com* ⌨ *4 rooms, 1 suite, 1 cabin* ⟐ *Dining room, some in-room hot tubs, some in-room VCRs; no TV in some rooms, no smoking* 🖃 *AE, MC, V* ⏀ *BP.*

$–$$ 🖼 **Tahoe City Travelodge.** As motels go, this one is excellent. Rooms are well-maintained and larger than average, and have either double or king-size beds, big bathrooms with massage showers and hair dryers, and coffeemakers. There's also a great lake-view deck with a hot tub and a sauna. ✉ *455 N. Lake Blvd., Box 84, 96145* ☎ *530/583–3766 or 800/578–7878* 🖷*530/583–8045* ⊕*www.travelodge.com* ⌨*47 rooms* ⟐ *In-room data ports, microwaves, refrigerators, cable TV, some in-room VCRs, hot tub, sauna* 🖃 *AE, D, DC, MC, V.*

Nightlife

Bands play several nights a week at **Sierra Vista** (✉ 700 N. Lake Blvd. ☎ 530/583–0233), where you can also have lunch or dinner.

Sports & the Outdoors

MOUNTAIN BIKING   **Cyclepaths Mountain Bike Adventures** (✉ 1785 W. Lake Blvd., Tahoe City ☎ 530/581–1171 or 800/780–2453) is a combination full-service bike shop and bike-adventure outfitter. It offers instruction in mountain biking, guided tours (from half-day to weeklong excursions), tips for self-guided bike touring, bike repairs, and books and maps on the area.

GOLF Golfers use pull carts or caddies at the 9-hole **Tahoe City Golf Course** (⊠ Hwy. 28, Tahoe City ☎ 530/583–1516), which opened in 1917. Though rates vary by season, the maximum greens fees are $30 for 9 holes, $50 for 18; a power cart costs $16 to $24.

RIVER RAFTING In summer, you can take a self-guided raft trip down a 5-mi stretch of the Truckee River with **Truckee River Rafting** (☎ 530/583–7238 or 888/584–7238). They will shuttle you back to your car at the end of your two- to four-hour trip.

SKIING
★ The locals' favorite place to ski, **Alpine Meadows Ski Area** is also the unofficial telemarking hub of the Sierra. With 495 inches of snow annually, Alpine has some of Tahoe's most reliable conditions; this is usually one of the first areas to open in November and one of the last to close in May or June. Alpine isn't the place for arrogant show-offs; instead, you'll find down-to-earth alpine fetishists. The two peaks here are well suited to intermediate skiers, but for experts there's also an open boundary to the backcountry. Snowboarders and hot-dog skiers will find a terrain park with a half-pipe, superpipe, rails, and tabletops, as well as a boardercross course. Alpine is a great place to learn to ski, and the Tahoe Adaptive Ski School here teaches and coaches those with physical and mental disabilities. There's also an area for overnight RV parking. ⊠ 6 *mi northwest of Tahoe City off Hwy. 89, 13 mi south of I–80 🗇 (Box 5279, 96145)* ☎ *530/583–4232 or 800/441–4423, 530/581–8374 snow phone ☞ 100 trails on 2,000 acres, rated 25% easier, 40% more difficult, 35% most difficult. Longest run 2½ mi, base 6,835', summit 8,637'. Lifts: 12, including 1 high-speed 6-passenger lift and 1 high-speed quad.*

If you plan to ski or board the backcountry, you'll find everything from crampons to transceivers at **The Backcountry** (⊠ 690 N. Lake Blvd. ☎ 530/581–5861). You can rent skis, boards, and snowshoes at **Tahoe Dave's Skis and Boards** (⊠ 620 N. Lake Blvd. ☎ 530/583–0400), which has the area's best selection of downhill rental equipment.

Olympic Valley

❽ *7 mi north of Tahoe City via Hwy. 89 to Squaw Valley Rd., 8½ mi south of Truckee via Hwy. 89 to Squaw Valley Rd.*

Olympic Valley got its name in 1960, when Squaw Valley USA, the ski resort here, hosted the winter Olympics. Snow sports remain the primary activity, but once summer comes, you can hike into the adjacent Granite Chief Wilderness, ride horseback through alpine meadows, or lie by a swimming pool in one of the Sierra's prettiest valleys.

Ride the Squaw Valley Cable Car up to **High Camp,** which at 8,200 feet commands superb views of Lake Tahoe and the surrounding mountains. In summer, you can go for a hike, sit by the pool at the High Camp Bath and Tennis Club, or have a cocktail and watch the sunset. In winter, you can ski, ice skate, or snow tube. There's also a restaurant, a lounge, and a small Olympic museum. ⊠ *The Village at Squaw Valley* ☎ *530/583–6985 (cable car), 530/581–7278 (restaurant reservations)* ⊕ *www.squaw.com* ☑ *$15 for cable car; inquire about special prices that include swimming or skating* ☉ *Open daily; call for hrs.*

Where to Stay & Eat

$$$ ✕ **Graham's of Squaw Valley.** Sit by a floor-to-ceiling river-rock hearth under a knotty-pine peaked ceiling in the intimate dining room in the Christy

Inn Lodge. The mostly southern European menu changes often, but expect dishes like cassoulet seafood paella, pheasant ragout with pasta, or a simple grilled rib eye with sautéed onions. You can also stop in at the bar for wine and appetizers by the fire. ⊠ *1650 Squaw Valley Rd.* ☎ *530/ 581–0454* ▭ *MC, V* ⚴ *Reservations essential* ⊘ *Closed Mon. No lunch.*

$$–$$$ ✕ **Balboa Café** The top choice for lunch at Squaw is also a cushy, romantic spot for dinner. Aside from having the best burger in the valley, Balboa serves a varied menu of contemporary California cuisine, including steak frites and Cobb salad at lunch, and ahi tuna tartare, Muscovy duck breast, and grilled lamb chops at dinner. ⊠ *The Village at Squaw Valley, 1995 Squaw Valley Rd.* ☎ *530/583-5850* ⚴ *Reservations essential* ▭ *AE, MC, V.*

$$–$$$ ✕ **PlumpJack.** In the luxurious, beautifully lighted dining room, there
Fodor'sChoice   is little adornment on the walls to distract you from the exquisite con-
★   temporary haute cuisine. Expect seafood, game, and meats, most garnished with reductions of natural juices that maximize the food's flavors. If you have dietary restrictions, the chef will make something special—and delicious—for you. The wine list is exceptional for its variety and surprisingly low prices. ⊠ *1920 Squaw Valley Rd.* ☎ *530/583–1576 or 800/323–7666* ⚴ *Reservations essential* ▭ *AE, MC, V.*

$ ✕ **Fireside Pizza Company.** All the pizzas at this modern Italian restaurant in the Village at Squaw Valley come with a three-cheese blend of fontina, provolone, and mozzarella. There are also respectable pasta dishes and salads. ⊠*The Village at Squaw Valley, 1985 Squaw Valley Rd.* ☎*530/ 584–6150* ▭ *AE, D, MC, V.*

$$$$ ✕▦ **Resort at Squaw Creek.** This vast, 650-acre resort-within-a-resort offers all the amenities and services you could possibly want. The glass-and-concrete buildings are more typical of Scottsdale than the Sierra, but the resort's extensive facilities make it great for large groups and families with kids. Some units have fireplaces and full kitchens, and all have original art, custom furnishings, and good views. Glissandi ($$$$) serves excellent contemporary California cuisine in a dramatic glass-walled room. In winter the resort operates its own chair lift to the mountain. ⊠ *400 Squaw Creek Rd., 96146* ☎ *530/583–6300 or 800/327–3353* 🖷 *530/581–5407* ⊕ *www.squawcreek.com* ⇨ *203 rooms, 200 suites* ⚴ *3 restaurants, coffee shop, some kitchens, minibars, cable TV with movies and video games, 18-hole golf course, 2 tennis courts, 3 outdoor pools, health club, hair salon, 4 hot tubs, sauna, spa, cross-country skiing, downhill skiing, ice skating, ski shop, ski storage, sleigh rides, sports bar, shops, children's programs (ages 4–12), dry cleaning, laundry service, concierge, Internet, business services, meeting rooms, free parking* ▭ *AE, D, DC, MC, V.*

$$$$ ▦ **The Village at Squaw Valley USA.** Right at the base of the slopes sits a cluster of four-story stone-and-timber buildings, the latest additions to Squaw Valley's luxury lodging scene. Each one-, two-, or three-bedroom condominium comes complete with gas fireplace, daily maid service, and heated slate-tiled bathroom floor. The individually owned units are uniformly decorated with granite counters, wood cabinets, and comfortable furnishings. On the ground floor of each of the four-story buildings are shops, restaurants, and bars. ⊠ *1985 Squaw Valley Rd., 96146* ☎. *530/584-6205 or 888/805-5022* 🖷 *530/584-6290* ⊕ *www. thevillageatsquaw.com* ⇨ *290 suites* ⚴ *In-room data ports, kitchens, cable TV with movies, in-room VCRs, exercise equipment, 2 outdoor hot tubs, billiards, downhill skiing, shops, laundry facilities, video game room, concierge, free parking; no smoking.* ▭ *AE, D, DC, MC, V.*

$$$–$$$$ ▦ **PlumpJack Squaw Valley Inn.** If style and luxury are a must, Plump-
Fodor'sChoice   Jack should be your first choice. Located right next to the The Village
★   at Squaw Valley, the inn building originally housed visiting dignitaries

during the 1960 Olympics. Every room comes equipped with down comforters, luxurious linens, and hooded terrycloth robes to wear on your way to the outdoor hot tubs. The bar is a happening après-ski destination, and the restaurant (*above*) is superb. PlumpJack may not have an on-site spa or fitness center, but the service—personable and attentive—can't be beat. Not all of the rooms have bathtubs, so if it matters, request one when you book. ⊠ *1920 Squaw Valley Rd., 96146* ☎ *530/583–1576 or 800/323–7666* ⚏ *530/583–1734* ⊕ *www.plumpjack.com* ↴ *56 rooms, 5 suites* △ *Restaurant, some in-room hot tubs, minibars, cable TV, in-room VCRs, 2 outdoor hot tubs, massage, cross-country skiing, downhill skiing, ski storage, bar, shop, dry cleaning, laundry service, concierge, meeting rooms, free parking* ▭ *AE, MC, V* � *BP.*

$$–$$$$ ▦ **Squaw Valley Lodge.** You can ski right to the doors of this all-suites condo complex, which offers many of the amenities of a full-service hotel. The units are individually owned and styled, so there's no uniformity to the décor, but all of them come with down comforters, daily maid service, oversize soaking tubs, and well-stocked kitchens or kitchenettes. There's also an excellent fitness center with plenty of sports-conditioning equipment. ⊠ *201 Squaw Peak Rd., 96146* ☎ *530/583–5500 or 800/922–9970* ⚏ *530/583–0326* ⊕ *www.squawvalleylodge.com* ↴ *142 units* △ *Some kitchens, some kitchenettes, cable TV, outdoor pool, 3 outdoor hot tubs, 4 indoor hot tubs, sauna, steam room, downhill skiing, laundry facilities, concierge, Internet, meeting rooms, free parking* ▭ *AE, DC, MC, V.*

Sports & the Outdoors

CROSS-COUNTRY SKIING
Cross-country skiers will enjoy looping through the valley's giant alpine meadow. **The Resort at Squaw Creek** (☎ 530/583–6300) rents cross-country equipment and provides trail maps.

DOWNHILL SKIING
★
Known for some of the toughest skiing in the Tahoe area, **Squaw Valley USA** was the centerpiece of the 1960 Olympics. Although the immense resort has changed significantly since then, the skiing is still world-class, with steep chutes and cornices on six peaks. Expert skiers often head directly to the untamed terrain of the infamous KT-22 face, which has bumps, cliffs, and gulp-and-go chutes. For beginners, there are plenty of wide, groomed trails near the High Camp lift and around the more challenging Snow King Peak. Snowboarders and hot-dog skiers can shred the two fantastic terrain parks, which include a giant superpipe. Lift prices include night skiing until 9 PM, and tickets for skiers under 12 are only $5. ⊠ *Hwy. 89, 5 mi northwest of Tahoe City* ⌂ *(Box 2007, Olympic Valley 96146)* ☎ *530/583–6985, 800/545–4350 for reservations, 530/583–6955 for snow phone* ☞ *100 trails on 4,300 acres, rated 25% beginner, 45% intermediate, 30% advanced. Longest run 3 mi, base 6,200′, summit 9,050′. Lifts: 31, including a funitel, a cable car, 7 high-speed chairs, and 18 fixed-grip chairs, which together can move up to 49,000 skiers an hour.*

If you don't want to pay resort prices, you can rent and tune downhill skis and snowboards at **Tahoe Dave's Skis and Boards** (⊠ Squaw Valley Rd. at Hwy. 89 ☎ 530/583–5665).

GOLF
The **Resort at Squaw Creek Golf Course** (⊠ 400 Squaw Creek Rd. ☎ 530/583–6300), an 18-hole championship course, was designed by Robert Trent Jones Jr. The $90 to $120 greens fee includes the use of a cart.

HIKING
The Granite Chief Wilderness and the high peaks surrounding Olympic Valley are accessible by foot, but save yourself a 2,000-foot elevation gain by riding the Squaw Valley Cable Car to **High Camp** (☎ 530/583–6985), where you can begin a trek to Shirley Lake, then head back down-

canyon to the valley for a beautiful 4-mi, half-day hike. In late summer, there are full-moon night hikes from High Camp.

HORSEBACK
RIDING

You can rent a horse or a pony from **Squaw Valley Stables** (⊠ 1525 Squaw Valley Rd. ☎ 530/583–7433), which offers instruction as well as group and private rides.

ROCK CLIMBING

Before you rappel down a granite monolith, you can hone your skills at the **Headwall Climbing Wall** (⊠ The Village at Squaw Valley ☎ 530/583–7673) at the base of the cable car.

At the **Adventure Center at High Camp** (☎ 530/583–6985), at the top of the cable car, there's an extensive ropes course, including a 50-foot tower and a giant swing.

SWIMMING

There are dramatic views from the pool deck at the **High Camp Bath and Tennis Club** (☎ 530/581–7255), where you can swim laps or soak in the 25-person hot tub. The **Resort at Squaw Creek** (⊠ 400 Squaw Creek Rd. ☎ 530/583–6300) has a giant swimming pool and a miniature water park; nonguests pay $20 for day use.

TENNIS

You'll find two tennis courts at the **Resort at Squaw Creek** (⊠ 400 Squaw Creek Rd. ☎ 530/583–6300). **High Camp Bath and Tennis Club** (☎ 530/583–6985) has six courts. Call for reservations and information on lessons and clinics.

Truckee

❾ *13 mi northwest of Kings Beach on Hwy. 267, 14 mi north of Tahoe City on Hwy. 89.*

Old West facades line the main street of Truckee, a favorite stopover for people traveling from the San Francisco Bay area to the north shore of Lake Tahoe. Around 1863, the town was officially established, and by 1868, it had gone from a stagecoach station to a major stopover for trains bound for the Pacific via the new transcontinental railroad. Freight and passenger trains still stop every day at the depot right in the middle of town. There are many galleries and boutiques, but you will also find low-key diners, discount skiwear, and an old-fashioned five-and-dime store. Stop by the **information booth** (⊠ Railroad St. at Commercial Rd.) in the Amtrak depot for a walking-tour map of historic Truckee.

Donner Memorial State Park and Emigrant Trail Museum commemorates the Donner Party, a group of 89 westward-bound pioneers who were trapped in the Sierra in the winter of 1846–47 in snow 22 feet deep. Only 47 survived, some by resorting to cannibalism and others by eating animal hides. The Emigrant Museum's hourly slide show details the Donner Party's plight. Other displays and dioramas relate the history of other settlers and of railroad development through the Sierra. In the park, you can picnic, hike, and go boating, fishing, water-skiing in summer; winter brings cross-country skiing and snowshoeing on groomed trails. ⊠ *Donner Pass Rd., off I–80, 2 mi west of Truckee* ☎ *530/582–7892* ☑ *Museum $2* ☉ *Museum daily 9–4.*

The **Old Truckee Jail Museum** occupies a former lock-up that first opened its doors in 1875. Until 1964 it was the longest-operating jail in the state. You can tour the cells and see exhibits by the town's historical society and displays of Native American artifacts. ⊠ *10142 Jibboom St.* ☎ *530/582–0893* ⊕ *http://truckeehistory.tripod.com* ☑ *Free* ☉ *May–Labor Day, weekends 11–4.*

Draped along the Sierra Nevada Crest above Lake Tahoe, the **Tahoe National Forest** offers abundant outdoor recreation. There's picnicking and camping in summer, and in winter, you can snowshoe, ski, and sled over some of the deepest snowpack in the West. The **Big Bend Visitor Center** occupies a state historic landmark within the forest, 10 mi west of Donner Summit. This area has been on major cross-country routes for centuries, ever since Native Americans passed through trading acorns and salt for pelts, obsidian, and other materials. Between 1844 and 1860, more than 200,000 emigrants traveled to California along the Emigrant Trail, which passed nearby; you can see rut marks left by wagon wheels scraping the famously hard granite. Later the nation's first transcontinental railroad ran through here (and still does), as did U.S. 40 (the old National Road), and its successor, I–80. Exhibits in the visitor center explore the area's transportation history. There are also occasional exhibits focusing on natural history. Take the Rainbow–Big Bend exit off I–80. ⊠ *49685 Hampshire Rocks Road (Old Hwy. 40), Soda Springs* ☎*530/426–3609 or 530/587–3558* ⊕*www.fs.fed.us/r5/tahoe/index.html* ☎ *Free* ⊗ *Thurs.–Mon. 8:30–5.*

Where to Stay & Eat

$$–$$$ ✕ **Cottonwood.** High above Truckee, on the site of the first chairlift in North America, sits the Cottonwood restaurant. The bar is decked out with old wooden skis, sleds, skates, and photos of the town's early days. In the dining area, California cuisine is served on white linen beneath an open-truss ceiling. The ambitious menu offers everything from grilled New York strip steak to free-range rabbit stew to red-curry and coconut-milk vegetable stir fry. This is a favorite of many locals, and there's something for everyone here there's even live music on weekends. ⊠ *Old Brockway Rd., just off Hwy. 267, ¼ mi south of downtown* ☎ *530/587–5711* ⌂ *Reservations essential* ▤ *AE, DC, MC, V* ⊗ *No lunch.*

$$ ✕ **Dragonfly.** The eclectic pan-Asian menu draws primarily from Japanese and Thai cooking at this bright, contemporary, second-floor restaurant in old-town Truckee. The noodle bowls at lunch are a bargain, and there are lots of choices for vegetarians. DId ⊠ *10118 Donner Pass Rd.* ☎*530/587–0557* ⌂ *Reservations essential* ▤*D, MC, V* ⊗ *Closed Tues.*

★ $$ ✕ **Moody's.** In a town known for burgers and Mexican grub, Moody's stands out as a culinary oasis. Half of the offerings on the contemporary northern California menu change daily and often include organically grown ingredients. Look for the ahi tuna "four ways," seared foie gras with Port wine sauce, braised short ribs, and roasted or stewed free-range chicken. In summer you can dine outside on a large brick patio surrounded by potted flowers, or sit in the warm and inviting dining room with its pumpkin-colored walls, burgundy velvet banquettes, and art deco fixtures. The restaurant serves a limited afternoon menu, and on weekends there's live jazz in the always-busy bar. ⊠ *1007 Bridge St.* ☎ *530/587–8831* ▤ *AE, D, DC, MC, V* ⌂ *Reservations essential.*

$–$$ ✕ **O.B.'s Pub and Restaurant.** You'll find mountainous portions of meat and potatoes at this long-standing bar and grill, where Old West memorabilia hangs from the rafters and pictures of Truckee's early days adorn the walls. At lunch, there are sandwiches and hot entrées, and at dinner there's slow-roasted Harris Ranch prime rib. ⊠ *10046 Donner Pass Rd.* ☎ *530/587–4164* ▤ *D, MC, V.*

$–$$ ✕ **Pianeta.** Flavors are bold at this northern Italian trattoria, right on the main drag of old-town Truckee. You'll find a variety of pastas, including homemade ravioli and lasagna Bolognese, as well as entrées like double-cut marinated lamb chopss with mint pesto and jumbo-shrimp scampi. If you don't want a full meal, sit in the bar and order from the extensive list of appetizers. The exposed stone walls may make you feel as if you're eating inside a Tuscan farmhouse. ⊠ *10069 Donner Pass Rd.* ☎ *530/587–4694* ☰ *AE, MC, V.* ⌣ *Reservations essential.* ◔ *No lunch.*

¢–$ ✕ **Village Pizzeria.** North Lake Tahoe's best pizza comes either with a thin crust or in a deep dish. For something different, try the stuffed pizza, a two-crust pie topped with marinara sauce. There are also Italian-American dishes on the menu. This is a great place for families, but expect a wait on weekends. ⊠ *11329 Deerfield Dr., in the Crossroads Shopping Center, just south of I–80 on Hwy. 89* ☎ *530/587-7171* ☰ *No credit cards.*

¢ ✕ **Squeeze In.** Eat breakfast with the locals and choose from 57 different omelets. At lunch there are homemade soups and sandwiches. ⊠ *10060 Donner Pass Rd.* ☎ *530/587–9814* ☰ *No credit cards.* ◔ *No dinner.*

$$–$$$$ ✕▣ **Northstar-at-Tahoe Resort.** The center of action at the Truckee area's most complete destination resort is the Village Mall, a concentration of restaurants, shops, recreation facilities, and accommodations. The many sports activities—from golf and tennis to skiing and snowmobiling—make the resort especially popular with families. Lodgings range from hotel rooms to condos to private houses. Some of the units have ski-in, ski-out access. Guests receive free lift tickets and on-site shuttle transportation, and have complimentary access to the Swim and Racquet Club's swimming pools, outdoor hot tubs, fitness center, and teen center. Summer rates are lower than winter rates. ⊠ *Hwy. 267, 6 mi southeast of Truckee* ☐ *(Box 129, Truckee 96160)* ☎ *530/562–1010 or 800/466–6784* ☐ *530/562-2215* ⊕ *www.northstarattahoe.com* ⇨ *270 units* ⑁ *3 restaurants, some kitchenettes, some microwaves, cable TV, in-room VCRs, 18-hole golf course, 12 tennis courts, bicycles, horseback riding, downhill skiing, ski storage, ski shop, dog-sled rides, snowmobiling, recreation room, video game room, shops, baby-sitting, children's programs (ages 2–6), laundry facilities, meeting rooms; no smoking* ☰ *AE, D, MC, V.*

$–$$ ▣ **Richardson House.** This beautifully maintained 1881 Victorian is filled with period furnishings. You'll find fresh flowers and a featherbed in every room. After a day of sightseeing, you can sit in the comfortable parlor and munch on freshly baked cookies. ⊠ *10154 High St., Box 2011, 96160* ☎ *530/587–5388 or 888/229–0365* ⊕ *www. richardsonhouse.com* ⇨ *8 rooms, 6 w/bath* ⑁ *Dining room; no a/c, no room TVs, no room phones, no smoking, no kids under 12* ☰ *AE, D, MC, V* ☉ *BP.*

¢–$$ ▣ **Truckee Hotel.** Constructed in 1873, this four-story hotel is one of the town's oldest buildings. Antiques fill the Victorian-style rooms; several have private bathrooms with claw-foot tubs. All rooms are clean and comfortable, if a bit small. ⊠ *10007 Bridge St., 96161* ☎ *916/587–4444 or 800/659–6921* ☐ *916/587–1599* ⊕ *www.truckeehotel.com* ⇨ *37 rooms, 29 with shared bath.* ⑁ *Restaurant, bar; no a/c, no TV in some rooms, no smoking* ☰ *AE, MC, V.*

Sports & the Outdoors

GOLF **Northstar** (☎ 530/562–1010) has open links–style play and tight, tree-lined fairways, including water hazards; fees range from $40 to $110, including cart. The **Coyote Moon Golf Course** (☎ 530/587–0886) is both challenging and beautiful, with no houses to spoil the view; fees range from $75 to $145, including cart.

HORSEBACK **Northstar Stables** offers guided 45-minute, half-day, and full-day (for ex-
RIDING perienced riders only) rides. Instruction is provided, ponies are available for tots, and you can even board your own horse here. ⊠ *Hwy. 267 at Northstar Dr.* ☎ *530/562-2480.*

MOUNTAIN In summer you can rent a bike and ride the lifts up the mountain at **North-
BIKING star at Tahoe** (☎ 530/562–1010) for 100 mi of challenging terrain.

SKIING   Six alpine ski resorts blanket the mountains around Truckee. The two largest local areas are described here, but take note that the four smaller resorts give you access to the Sierra's fabled slopes for a lot less cash. Though you'll sacrifice vertical rise and high-speed lifts, you can ski or board and still have money left over for room and board. Check out **Boreal** (⊠ Boreal/Castle Peak exit off I–80 ☎ 530/426–3666 ⊕ www.borealski.com), **Donner Ski Ranch** (⊠ 19320 Donner Pass Rd., Norden ☎ 530/426–3635), **Soda Springs** (⊠ Soda Springs exit off I–80, Soda Springs ☎ 530/426–1010), and **Tahoe Donner** (⊠ 11603 Slalom Way ☎ 530/587–9444 ⊕ www.tahoedonner.com).

Northstar-at-Tahoe may be the best all-around family ski resort at Tahoe. With two tree-lined, northeast-facing, wind-protected bowls, it's the ideal place to ski in a storm. The meticulous grooming and long cruisers make it an intermediate skier's paradise. Boarders are especially welcome, with an awesome terrain park, including a 400-foot-long superpipe, a half pipe, rails and boxes, and lots of kickers. Experts can ski the steeps and bumps off Lookout Mountain, where there's never a line for the high-speed quad. Northstar-at-Tahoe has 28 mi of groomed trails, including double-set tracks and skating lanes. The school has programs for skiers ages four and up, and day care is available for toilet-trained tots. ⊠ *Hwy. 267, 6 mi southeast of Truckee* ☎ *530/562–1010, 530/562–1330 for snow phone* 🖨 *530/562–2215* ☞ *72 trails on 2,420 acres, rated 25% beginner, 50% intermediate, 25% advanced. Longest run 2.9 mi, base 6,400′, summit 8,600′. Lifts: 17, including a gondola and 5 high-speed quads.*

For the ultimate in groomed conditions, head to the nation's largest cross-country ski resort, **Royal Gorge**, which has 197 mi of 18-foot-wide track for all abilities, 88 trails on 9,172 acres, two ski schools, and 10 warming huts. Four cafés, two hotels, and a hot tub and sauna are among the facilities. ⊠ *Follow signs from Soda Springs–Norden exit off I–80* 🖃 *(Box 1100, Soda Springs 95728)* ☎ *530/426–3871.*

Opened in 1939 by Walt Disney, **Sugar Bowl** is the oldest—and one of the best—resorts at Tahoe. Atop Donner Summit, it receives an incredible 500 inches of snowfall annually. Four peaks are connected by 1,500 acres of skiable terrain, with everything from gentle groomed corduroy to wide-open bowls to vertical rocky chutes and outstanding tree-skiing. Snowboarders can hit two terrain parks and an 18½-foot superpipe. Because it's more compact than some of the area's megaresorts, there's a certain gentility here that distinguishes Sugar Bowl from its competitors, making this a great place for families and a low-pressure, low-key place to learn to ski. There's limited lodging at the base area. ⊠ *Donner Pass Rd., 3 mi east of I–80 off the Soda Springs/ Norden exit, 10 mi west of Truckee* ☎ *530/426–9000 (information and lodging reservations), 530/426–1111 (snowphone), 866/843–2695 (lodging referral)* ⊕ *www.sugarbowl.com* ☞ *84 trails on 1,500 acres, rated 17% beginner, 45% intermediate, 38% advanced. Longest run 3 mi, base 6883′, summit 8383′ Lifts: 12, including 4 high-speed quads.*

You can save money by renting skis and boards at **Tahoe Dave's** (⊠ 10200 Donner Pass Rd. ☎ 530/582–0900), which has the area's best selection. They also repair and tune equipment.

Carnelian Bay to Kings Beach

5–10 mi northeast of Tahoe City on Hwy. 28.

The small lakeside commercial districts of Carnelian Bay and Tahoe Vista service the thousand or so locals who live in the area year-round and the thousands more who have summer residences or launch their boats here. Kings Beach, the last town heading east on Highway 28 before the Nevada border, is to Crystal Bay what South Lake Tahoe is to Stateline: a bustling California village full of motels and rental condos, restaurants and shops, used by the hordes of hopefuls who pass through on their way to the casinos.

The 28-acre **Kings Beach State Recreation Area,** one of the largest such areas on the lake, is open year-round. The 700-foot-long beach becomes crowded with people swimming, sunbathing, jet-skiing, riding in paddleboats, spiking volleyballs, and tossing Frisbees. There's a good playground and picnic area here. ⊠ *N. Lake Blvd., Kings Beach* ☎ *530/ 546–7248* ⊑ *Free.*

Where to Eat

$$–$$$$
FodorsChoice
★ ✕ **Wild Goose.** The food is as sublime as the view at Wild Goose. Buttery-soft leather banquettes, polished mahogany tables, impeccable lighting, and the smartly dressed clientele might make you feel like you're in L.A. But look out the window at the stunning lake views (come early to see the sun set), and you'll remember where you are. Dine on exquisite contemporary French–California cuisine, like poached crab and artichoke hearts, roasted lobster and chanterelles, or a deliciously simple sirloin steak and french fries. Sliding glass doors line the chic, casually elegant, 100-seat dining room, opening up to a lakeside deck beneath towering pines. Desserts are impeccable, and the wine list superb. There's also a happening bar scene. You'll pay high resort prices, but you won't soon forget what you ate. ⊠ *7320 N. Lake Blvd., Tahoe Vista* ☎ *530/ 546–3640* ⌖ *Reservations essential* ⊟ *AE, D, MC, V* ⊘ *Closed Mon. No lunch Oct.–May.*

$$–$$$ ✕ **Gar Woods Grill and Pier.** Here you can take in terrific views through the dining room's plate glass windows and from the heated outdoor deck. There are salads and sandwiches at lunch, and steaks and grilled fish at dinner, but the best meal here is Sunday brunch. At all hours in season, the bar gets packed with boaters who pull up to the restaurant's pier. ⊠*5000 N. Lake Blvd., Carnelian Bay* ☎ *530/546–3366* ⊟ *AE, MC, V.*

★ **$$–$$$** ✕ **Le Petit Pier.** The lake views are superb at this contemporary French restaurant, which sits on stilts above the shoreline. Specialties include rack of lamb and New Zealand venison. The wine list and food are as good as the views. ⊠ *7238 N. Lake Blvd., Tahoe Vista* ☎ *530/546–7508* ⌖ *Reservations essential* ⊟ *AE, MC, V* ⊘ *Closed Tues. No lunch.*

$–$$ ✕ **Lanza's.** Lanza's serves good old-fashioned Italian-American food on red-and-white checked tablecloths in a knotty-pine–paneled dining room. There's lasagna, manicotti, veal piccata, and eggplant Parmesan, but you can also order your own pasta-and-sauce combination. Leave room for the homemade spumoni. ⊠ *7739 N. Lake Blvd., next to Safeway, Kings Beach* ☎ *530/546–2434* ⌖ *Reservations not accepted* ⊟ *MC, V* ⊘ *No lunch.*

¢–$ ✕ **The Naughty Dawg Baja Grill.** After a day at the beach, throw back a Dos Equis and eat a delicious fish taco at this raucous Cal-Mex bar. There's a separate dining room appropriate for families. ⊠ *8791 N. Lake Blvd., Kings Beach* ☎ *530/546–7297* ⊟ *AE, D, MC, V* ⊘ *Sometimes closed for weekday lunch in slow seasons; call to confirm.*

¢ ✕ **Log Cabin Caffe.** Almost always hopping, this Kings Beach eatery specializes in hearty breakfast and lunch entrées—five kinds of eggs Benedict, Mexican and smoked salmon scrambles, omelets, pancakes, and waffles. They also serve sandwiches and freshly baked pastries. Get here early on weekends for the popular brunch. ⊠ *8692 N. Lake Blvd., Kings Beach* ☎ *530/546–7109* ⊟ *MC, V* ⊘ *No dinner.*

¢ ✕ **Sancho's.** It's little more than a hole in the wall, but Sancho's serves delicious Mexican food, including ceviches, tacos, burritos, and several daily specials. ⊠ *7019 N. Lake Blvd., Tahoe Vista* ☎ *530/546–7744* ⊟ *MC, V.*

$$$–$$$$ 🏨 **Shore House.** Every room has a gas fireplace and featherbed at this lakefront B&B in Tahoe Vista. The comfortable guest rooms all have private entrances and extra touches like bathrobes and rubber duckies in the bathtubs; many have great views of the water. There's also a private beach. ⊠ *7170 N. Lake Blvd., Tahoe Vista 96148* ☎ *530/546–7270 or 800/207–5160* ⊕ *www.shorehouselaketahoe.com* 🛏 *8 rooms, 1 cottage* ⟡ *Refrigerators, outdoor hot tub, beach; no a/c, no in-room TVs, no in-room telephones, no smoking* ⊟ *D, MC, V* ⦿ *BP.*

¢–$$$ 🏨 **Rustic Cottages.** Detached clapboard cottages sit in a semicircle across the road from Lake Tahoe. In fairly good shape, they offer an inexpensive alternative to a motel (though the cheaper units are small). All have patios, and some have fireplaces and kitchens. ⊠ *7449 N. Lake Blvd.* ⌖ *(Box 18, Tahoe Vista 96148)* ☎ *530/546–3523 or 888/778–7842* 🖷 *530/546–0146* ⊕ *www.rusticcottages.com* 🛏 *20 cottages* ⟡ *Some kitchenettes, cable TV, in-room VCRs, microwaves, refrigerators, some pets allowed (fee); no a/c, no room phones, no smoking* ⊟ *AE, D, MC, V* ⦿ *CP.*

Sports & the Outdoors

SNOWMOBILING   **Snowmobiling Unlimited** (⊠ Hwy. 267, 3 mi north of Hwy. 28, Kings Beach ☎ 530/583–7192) conducts 1½-, 2-, and 3-hour guided cross-country tours, mostly along the trails in nearby Tahoe National Forest. They provide open-face helmets and mittens, but bring your own goggles or sunglasses.

WINDSURFING   Learn to skitter across the icy blue waters of the lake with one of Tahoe's kindest instructors at **Windsurf North Tahoe** (⊠ 7276 N. Lake Blvd., Tahoe Vista ☎ 530/546–5857 or 800/294–6378).

NEVADA SIDE

You don't need a highway sign to know when you've crossed from California into Nevada: the flashing lights and elaborate marquees of casinos announce legal gambling in garish hues.

Crystal Bay

❿ *1 mi east of Kings Beach on Hwy. 28; 30 mi north of South Lake Tahoe via U.S. 50 to Hwy. 28.*

Right at the Nevada border, Crystal Bay has a cluster of casinos. The **Cal-Neva Lodge** (⊠ 2 Stateline Rd. ☎ 775/832–4000) is bisected by the state line. Opened in 1927, this joint has weathered many scandals, the largest involving former owner Frank Sinatra (he lost his gaming license in the 1960s for alleged mob connections). The **Tahoe Biltmore** (⊠ Hwy. 28 at Stateline Rd. ☎ 775/831–0660) serves its popular $1.99 breakfast special 24 hours a day. **Jim Kelley's Nugget** (⊠ Hwy. 28 at Stateline Rd. ☎ 775/831–0455) serves 101 kinds of beers.

Where to Stay & Eat

★ **$$–$$$** ✕ **Soule Domain.** Some of Lake Tahoe's most creative and delicious dinners are served in this 1927 pine-log cabin. Chef-owner Charles Edward Soule IV's specialties include curried cashew chicken, smoked rabbit ravioli, rock shrimp with sea scallops, and a vegan sauté. ⊠ *Cove St., ½ block up Stateline Rd. from Hwy. 28, across from the Tahoe Biltmore* ☎ *530/546–7529* ⟡ *Reservations essential* ⊟ *AE, DC, MC, V* ⦿ *No lunch.*

$$–$$$$ 🏨 **Cal-Neva Lodge.** All the rooms in this hotel-casino have views of Lake Tahoe and the mountains. The hotel also rents seven two-bedroom chalets and 12 cabins with living rooms. There is an arcade for children, and cabaret entertainment for grown-ups. Though some of the public areas look a bit shabby, the rooms are generally well maintained. ⊠ *2 Stateline Rd., Box 368, 89402 ☎ 775/832–4000 or 800/225–6382 🖷 775/831–9007 ⊕ www.calnevaresort.com ⤳ 220 rooms, 20 suites, 19 cabins ⚬ Restaurant, coffee shop, room service, cable TV with movies, in-room VCRs, tennis court, pool, indoor hot tub, gym, spa, sauna, massage, bar, casino, dry cleaning, concierge, video game room, airport shuttle, some pets allowed. ☰ AE, D, DC, MC, V.*

Incline Village

⓫ *3 mi east of Crystal Bay on Hwy. 28.*

Incline Village, Nevada's only privately owned town, dates to the early 1960s, when an Oklahoma developer bought 10,000 acres north of Lake Tahoe. His idea was to sketch out a plan for a town without a central commercial district, hoping to prevent congestion and to preserve the area's natural beauty. One-acre lakeshore lots originally fetched $12,000 to $15,000; today you couldn't buy even the land for less than several million. Check out **Lakeshore Drive,** along which you'll see some of the most expensive real estate in Nevada. Incline Village's **recreation center** (⊠ 980 Incline Way ☎ 775/832–1300) has an eight-lane swimming pool and a fitness area, basketball court, game room, and snack bar.

off the beaten path | **MOUNT ROSE –** If you want to ski some of the highest slopes in the Lake Tahoe region, take Highway 431 north out of Incline Village to Mt. Rose. Reno is another 30 mi farther. On the way is Tahoe Meadows, the most popular area near North Lake for noncommercial sledding, tubing, snowshoeing, cross-country skiing, and snowmobiling. ☎ 775/849–0704.

☾ The 1960s television western *Bonanza* inspired the **Ponderosa Ranch** theme park. Attractions include the Cartwrights' ranch house, a Western town complete with museums, shops, snack bars, gunfight and stunt show, roping demonstrations, petting zoo, and a big saloon. There's a self-guided nature trail, free pony rides for children, and if you're here from 8 to 9:30, a breakfast hayride. ⊠ *Hwy. 28, 2 mi south of Incline Village ☎ 775/ 831–0691 ⤳ $9.50, breakfast $2 extra ☉ Mid-Apr.–Oct., daily 9:30–5.*

George Whittell, a San Francisco socialite who once owned 50,000 acres of property along the lake, built the **Thunderbird Lodge** in 1936. You can tour the mansion and the grounds by reservation only, and though it's pricey, it offers a rare glimpse back to a time when only the very wealthy had homes at Tahoe. ⊠ *5000 Hwy. 28 ☎ 775/832–8750 or 800/468–2463 ⤳ $27 ☉ May–Oct., Wed. and Thurs. 9–3.*

The *Sierra Cloud* (☎ 775/831–1111), a large trimaran, cruises the north shore area morning and afternoon, from May through October, from the Hyatt Regency Hotel in Incline Village. The fare is $40.

Where to Stay & Eat

$$–$$$ ✕ **Frederick's.** Sit at one of the 15 copper-covered tables at this intimate bistro, which serves a mishmash of European and Asian cooking. Try the braised lamb shank, Parmesan gnocchi, or the deliciously fresh sushi rolls. Ask for a table by the fire. ⊠ *907 Tahoe Blvd. ☎ 775/832–3007 ⚬ Reservations essential ☰ AE, MC, V ☉ Closed Tues. No lunch.*

$–$$ ✕ **Azzara's.** An Italian family restaurant with a light, inviting dining room, Azzara's serves a dozen pasta dishes and many pizzas, as well as chicken, lamb, veal, shrimp, and beef. Dinners include soup or salad, a vegetable, and olive-oil garlic bread. ✉ *Incline Center Mall, 930 Tahoe Blvd.* ☎ *775/831–0346* ▭ *MC, V* ⊙ *Closed Mon.*

¢ ✕ **T's Rotisserie.** There's nothing fancy about T's, which looks like a snack bar, but the mesquite-grilled chicken and tri-tip steaks are delicious. ✉ *901 Tahoe Blvd.* ☎ *775/831–2832* ▭ *No credit cards.*

$$$–$$$$ ✕▣ **Hyatt Lake Tahoe Resort Hotel/Casino.** Though the casino-hotel tower looks more like a transplant from the south shore, all the rooms, suites, and cottages in this luxurious hotel on the lake are top-notch. The praiseworthy Lone Eagle Grille ($$–$$$$) serves steaks and seafood in one of the north shore's most handsome lake-view dining rooms. ✉ *Lakeshore and Country Club Drs., 89450* ☎ *775/831–1111 or 888/ 899–5019* 🖷 *775/831–7508* ⊕ *www.hyatt-tahoe.com* ➷ *432 rooms, 28 suites* ⚴ *4 restaurants, coffee shop, room service, cable TV with movies, pool, health club, 2 saunas, spa, beach, bicycles, lobby lounge, casino, children's programs (ages 18 months–16 years), laundry service* ▭ *AE, D, DC, MC, V.*

Sports & the Outdoors

GOLF **Incline Championship** (✉ 955 Fairway Blvd. ☎ 775/325–8801) is an 18-hole, par-72 course with a driving range. The greens fee is $125. **Incline Mountain** (✉ 690 Wilson Way ☎ 775/325–8801) is an easy 18-holer; par is 58. The greens fee starts at $50; optional power carts at both courses cost $15.

SKIING A fun family mood prevails at **Diamond Peak,** which has many special programs and affordable rates. Snowmaking covers 75% of the mountain, and runs are groomed nightly. The ride up the 1-mi Crystal chair rewards you with some of the best views of the lake from any ski area. Diamond Peak is less crowded than some of the larger areas and provides free shuttles to nearby lodging. A first-timer's package, which includes rentals, a lesson, and a lift ticket, is $48. A parent-and-child ski package is $54 each additional child's lift ticket is $13. There are a half-pipe and superpipe for snowboarders. **Diamond Peak Cross-Country** (✉ off Hwy. 431 ☎ 775/832–1177) has 22 mi of groomed track with skating lanes. The trail system rises from 7,400 feet to 9,100 feet, with endless wilderness to explore. ✉ *1210 Ski Way, off Hwy. 28 to Country Club Dr.* ☎ *775/832–1177 or 800/468–2463* ⛷ *29 trails on 655 acres, rated 18% beginner, 46% intermediate, 36% advanced. Longest run 2½ mi, base 6,700', summit 8,540'. Lifts: 6, including 2 high-speed quads.*

Reno

⓬ *45 mi northeast of Crystal Bay on I–80.*

Established in 1859 as a trading station at a bridge over the Truckee River, Reno grew along with the silver mines of nearby Virginia City (starting in 1860), the railroad (railroad officials named the town in 1868), and gambling (legalized in 1931). Once the gaming and divorce capital of the United States, the city built itself a monument: The famous Reno Arch, a sign over the upper end of Virginia Street, proclaims it THE BIGGEST LITTLE CITY IN THE WORLD. Reno is still a gambling town, with most of the casinos crowded into five square blocks downtown. Besides the casino-hotels, Reno has a number of cultural and family-friendly attractions. Temperatures year-round in this high-mountain-desert climate are warmer than at Tahoe, though it rarely gets as hot here as in Sacramento and the Central Valley, making strolling around town a pleasure. In recent years, a few excellent restaurants have shown up outside the hotels, but aside from a few notable exceptions, lodging continues to be nothing special.

Circus Circus (⊠ 500 N. Sierra St. ☎ 775/329–0711 or 800/648–5010 ⊕ www.circusreno.com), marked by a neon clown sucking a lollipop, is the best stop for families with children. Complete with clowns, games, fun-house mirrors, and circus acts, the midway on the mezzanine above the casino floor is open from 10 AM to midnight. **Eldorado** (⊠ 345 N. Virginia St. ☎ 775/786–5700 or 800/648–5966 ⊕ www.eldoradoreno. com) is action packed, with tons of slots, good bar-top video poker, and great coffee-shop and food-court fare. **Harrah's** (⊠ 219 N. Center St. ☎ 775/ 786–3232 or 800/648–3773 ⊕ www.harrahs.com) occupies two city blocks, with a sprawling casino and an outdoor promenade; it also has a 29-story Hampton Inn annex. Minimums are low, and service is friendly. **Silver Legacy** (⊠ 407 N. Virginia St. ☎ 775/329–4777 or 800/ 687–8733 ⊕ www.silverlegacyresort.com) has a Victorian-themed casino with a 120-foot-tall mining rig that mints silver-dollar tokens. The **Club Cal- Neva** (⊠ 140 N. Virginia St. ☎ 775/323–1046 or 877/777–7303 ⊕ www.clubcalneva.com) is known for its race-and-sports book.

The **Downtown River Walk** (⊠ S. Virginia St. and the Truckee River ☎ 775/ 348–8858) often hosts special events featuring street performers, musicians, dancers, food, art exhibits, and games. On the University of Nevada campus, the sleekly designed **Fleischmann Planetarium** (⊠ 1600 N. Virginia St. ☎ 775/784–4811 ⊕ www.planetarium.unr.nevada.edu ✉ free) has films and astronomy shows. The **Nevada Museum of Art** (⊠ 160 W. Liberty St. ☎ 775/329–3333 ⊕ www.nevadaart.org ✉ $7.50), the state's largest art museum, has changing exhibits in a dramatic modern building. More than 220 antique and classic automobiles, including an Elvis Presley Cadillac, are on display at the **National Automobile Museum** (⊠ Mill and Lake Sts. ☎ 775/333–9300 ⊕ www.automuseum.org ✉ $8). **Victorian Square** (⊠ Victorian Ave. between Rock Blvd. and Pyramid Way), in downtown Sparks—Reno's sister city to the east—is fringed by restored turn-of-the-20th-century houses and Victorian-dressed casinos and storefronts; its bandstand is the focal point of the many festivals held here.

off the beaten path

CARSON CITY AND VIRGINIA CITY – Nevada's capital, Carson City, is a 30-minute drive from Stateline. At Spooner Junction, about 10 mi north of Stateline, head east on U.S. 50 for 10 mi. When you reach U.S. 395, go 1 mi north to Carson City. Most of its historic buildings and other attractions, including the Nevada State Museum and the Nevada Railroad Museum, are along U.S. 395, the main street through town. About a 30-minute drive up Highway 342 northeast of Carson City is the fabled mining town of Virginia City, one of the largest and most authentic historical mining towns in the West. It's chock full of mansions, museums, saloons, and, of course, dozens of shops selling everything from amethysts to yucca. For information on the area contact the **CARSON CITY CHAMBER OF COMMERCE** (⊠ 1900 S. Carson St., Carson City 87901 ☎ 775/882–1565 ⊕ www.carsoncitychamber.com) –

Where to Stay & Eat

★ **$$–$$$** ✕ **Fourth St. Bistro.** You'll find deliciously simple, perfectly prepared, contemporary cooking that bursts with flavor at this charming bistro, where the chef-owner uses organic produce and meats whenever possible. The casual white-tablecloth dining room, with its sponge-painted walls, is comfortable and inviting. ⊠ 3065 W. 4th St. ☎ 775/323–3200 ⌖ Reservations essential ☉ Closed Mon.–Tues. No lunch.

$$–$$$ ✗ **Galena Forest.** Surrounded by forest, this white-tablecloth roadhouse on the outskirts of town serves big portions of eclectic contemporary food in a casually elegant dining room. Ask for a table by the window, and look for foraging deer in the illuminated hills outside. ⊠ *17025 Mt. Rose Hwy.* ☎ *775/849–2100* ✍ *Reservations essential* ☰ *AE, D, MC, V.*

★ **$$–$$$** ✗ **LuLou's.** Modern art adorns the exposed brick walls of the small dining room at Reno's most innovative restaurant. Drawing influences from Europe and Asia, the chef has imported contemporary urban cooking to the Great Basin. The menu changes often, and you can expect to see anything from foie gras and duck confit to pot stickers and chicken curry. ⊠ *1470 South Virginia St.* ☎ *775/329–9979* ✍ *Reservations essential* ⊘ *Closed Sun.–Mon. No lunch.*

$–$$$ ✗ **Washoe.** When you're hungry for a good steak and you've had enough of the casinos, head out the old main highway to the Washoe and feast on mountainous portions of certified Angus beef. The wine list is great. ⊠ *4201 E. 4th St.* ☎ *775/786–1323* ✍ *Reservations essential* ☰ *AE, D, MC, V.*

$–$$ ✗ **Beaujolais Bistro.** Modern adaptations of classic French dishes are served in a comfortable, airy dining room with exposed brick walls and parquet floor. Everything here is French—the waiters, the wine, and even the music—but service is warm and friendly. On the menu, expect beef Bourguignon, roast duck, seafood sausage, and steak frites. ⊠ *130 West St.* ☎ *775/323–2227* ✍ *Reservations essential* ☰ *AE, D, MC, V.*

$ ✗ **Louis' Basque Corner.** Basque shepherds once populated northern Nevada; sample their heritage at this family-style restaurant, which specializes in oxtail, lamb, and tongue. ⊠ *301 E. 4th St.* ☎ *775/323–7203* ☰ *AE, DC, MC, V.*

¢–$$ ✗ **Café de Thai.** It's worth the ten-minute drive from downtown to reach this simple but very good Thai restaurant, where the soups, salads, stir-fries, and curries are expertly prepared by a professionally trained Thai national. ⊠ *7499 Longley La.* ☎ *775/829–8424* ☰ *MC, V.*

¢–$ ✗ **Bertha Miranda's Mexican Restaurant.** Begun as a hole-in-the-wall, this has grown into a highly successful establishment. The food is made by Bertha's family, and the salsa is the best in town. ⊠ *336 Mill St.* ☎ *775/786–9697* ☰ *MC, V.*

¢–$ ✗ **John A's Oyster Bar.** Entirely nautical in theme, John A's restaurant and bar serves the best steamers, pan roasts, cioppino, chowder, shrimp Louie, and cocktails this side of San Francisco's Fisherman's Wharf. ⊠ *1100 Nugget Ave., Sparks* ☎ *775/356–3300* ☰ *AE, D, DC, MC, V.*

¢–$$$ ✗▭ **Harrah's.** This is one of the nicer hotels in downtown Reno. Large guest rooms decorated in blues and mauves overlook downtown and the entire mountain-ringed valley. The dark and romantic dining room at Harrah's Steak House ($$$–$$$$) serves excellent prime steaks and seafood. ⊠ *219 N. Center St., 89501* ☎ *775/786–3232 or 800/648–3773* ⊕ *www.harrahs.com* ⇗ *565 rooms* ♨ *6 restaurants, room service, in-room safes, some in-room hot tubs, some refrigerators, cable TV with movies and games, pool, health club, video game room, dry cleaning* ☰ *AE, D, DC, MC, V.*

¢–$$$ ✗▭ **Peppermill.** Three miles from downtown, the Peppermill has Reno's most colorful casino. Rooms vary in size, but all are comfortable. The White Orchid restaurant ($$$$) is the fanciest and some say best restaurant in northern Nevada; the changing menu features seasonal contemporary cuisine, and there's an excellent wine list. ⊠ *2707 S. Virginia St., 89502* ☎ *775/826–2121 or 800/648–6992* ⊟ *775/826–5205* ⊕ *www.peppermillcasinos.com* ⇗ *1,070 rooms, 185 suites* ♨ *7 restaurants, room service, minibars, in-room data ports, cable TV with movies, pool, health club, hair salon, spa, video game room, concierge, meeting rooms* ☰ *AE, D, DC, MC, V.*

★ $–$$$ ✕⌂ **Siena Hotel Spa Casino.** Reno's most luxurious hotel also has beautiful rooms and deliciously comfortable beds, which are made up with Egyptian cotton sheets and down comforters. At check-in, you won't have to navigate past miles of slot machines to find the front desk, since the casino is in a self-contained room off the elegant lobby. Lexie's ($$$–$$$$) serves organic steaks and fresh seafood in a sleek and elegant modern dining room overlooking the river. There's also a full-service spa. ⊠ *1 S. Lake St., 89501* ☎ *775/337–6260 or 877/743–6233* 🖷 *775/321–5870* ⊕ *www.sienareno.com* ⇨ *193 rooms, 21 suites* △ *Restaurant, coffee shop, room service, minibars, refrigerators, in-room data ports, cable TV, pool, health club, spa, lounge, wine bar, casino, dry cleaning, laundry service, concierge, Internet, business center, meeting rooms, airport shuttle* ⊟ *AE, D, DC, MC, V.*

¢–$$ ✕⌂ **Eldorado.** Smack dab in the middle of glittering downtown sits the Eldorado, an all-suites tower whose rooms overlook the mountains or the lights of the city. La Strada ($$–$$$) serves great northern Italian cooking in a romantic room; the Roxy ($$$) serves roasted meats in an over-the-top, faux-European courtyard. Both restaurants have excellent wine lists. ⊠ *345 N. Virginia St., 89501* ☎ *775/786–5700 or 800/648–5966* 🖷 *702/322–7124* ⊕ *www.eldoradoreno.com* ⇨ *836 rooms* △ *8 restaurants, room service, in-room data ports, some in-room hot tubs, cable TV with movies, pool, hot tub, casino, video game room, meeting rooms* ⊟ *AE, D, DC, MC, V.*

¢–$$$ ⌂ **Reno Hilton.** This 27-story hotel near the airport is Nevada's largest hotel north of Las Vegas. In fact, almost everything here is the area's largest: the buffet, race and sports books, showroom, convention facilities, bowling alley, arcade, wedding chapel, driving range, and RV park. ⊠ *2500 E. 2nd St., 89595* ☎ *775/789–2000 or 800/648–5080* 🖷 *775/789–2418* ⊕ *www.renohilton.com* △ *6 restaurants, cable TV with movies, pool, health club, video game room, meeting rooms* ⊟ *AE, D, DC, MC, V.*

¢–$$$ ⌂ **Silver Legacy.** This two-tower mega-resort centers on a 120-foot-tall mining machine that coins dollar tokens. Skywalks connect it to Circus Circus and the Eldorado. The Victorian-theme rooms are comfortable and well kept. ⊠ *407 N. Virginia St., 89501* ☎ *775/329–4777 or 800/687–8733* ⊕ *www.silverlegacy.com* ⇨ *1,700 rooms* △ *5 restaurants, cable TV with movies, pool, health club, shops, casino, meeting rooms* ⊟ *AE, D, DC, MC, V.*

$–$$ ⌂ **Plumas House.** Escape the madding crowds and blinking lights by staying at this quiet and charming B&B in a residential area south of downtown. The owners, who have backgrounds in the antiques and decorating industries, have attended to every detail in the individually styled rooms. ⊠ *1000 Plumas St., 89509* ☎ *775/786-1164* ⊕ *www.plumashouse. com* ⇨ *3 rooms, 1 cottage* △ *Some kitchenettes, some pets allowed; no TV in some rooms, no smoking* ⊟ *MC, V* ⧖ *BP.*

⧖ ¢–$ ⌂ **Circus Circus.** This smaller version of the giant Las Vegas hotel has the same family-oriented theme, including circus midway games. The rooms, though small and garish, are good values. ⊠ *500 N. Sierra St., 89503* ☎ *775/329–0711 or 800/648–5010* 🖷 *775/329–0599* ⊕ *www. circusreno.com* ⇨ *1,625 rooms* △ *3 restaurants, cable TV, meeting rooms* ⊟ *AE, DC, MC, V.*

Lake Tahoe–Nevada State Park

Hwy. 28, between Incline Village and Zephyr Cove.

Protecting much of the lake's eastern shore from development, Lake Tahoe–Nevada State Park comprises several units. Beaches and trails provide access to a wilder side of the lake, whether you are into cross-country skiing, hiking, or just relaxing at a picnic.

★ ☾ **Sand Harbor Beach** is sometimes filled to capacity by 11 AM on summer weekends. Stroll the boardwalk and read the information signs to get a good lesson in the local ecology. A **pop-music festival** (☎ 775/832–1606 or 800/468–2463) is held at the beach in July, and the **Lake Tahoe Shakespeare Festival** (☎ 775/832–1616 or 800/747–4697) is held outdoors, with the lake as a backdrop, from mid-July through August. ⊠ *Hwy. 28, 4 mi south of Incline Village* ☎ *775/831–0494.*

★ **Cave Rock,** 25 yards of solid stone at the southern end of Lake Tahoe–Nevada State Park, is the throat of an extinct volcano. Tahoe Tessie, the lake's version of the Loch Ness monster, is reputed to live in a cavern below the impressive outcropping. For the Washoe Indians, this area is a sacred burial site. Cave Rock towers over a parking lot, a lakefront picnic ground, and a boat launch. ⊠ *U.S. 50, 13 mi south of Sand Harbor Beach* ☎ *775/831–0494.*

Sports & the Outdoors

CROSS-COUNTRY SKIING   You'll find superbly groomed tracks and fabulous views of Lake Tahoe at **Spooner Lake Cross-Country** (⊠ Spooner Summit, Hwy. 28, ½ mi north of U.S. 50, Glenbrook ☎ 775/887–8844 ski phone or 775/749–5349 reservations ⊕ www.spoonerlake.com), which has more than 50 mi of trails on more than 9,000 acres. They also rent two charming, secluded cabins for overnight treks.

MOUNTAIN BIKING   You can rent bikes and get helpful tips from **Flume Trail Bikes** (⊠ Spooner Summit, Hwy. 28, ½ mi north of U.S. 50 ☎ 775/887–8844 ⊕ www.theflumetrail.com), which also operates a bike shuttle to popular trailheads. Ask about their secluded rental cabins for overnight rides.

Zephyr Cove

⑬ *U.S. 50, 22 mi south of Incline Village.*

The largest settlement between Incline Village and Stateline is Zephyr Cove, a tiny resort. It has a beach, marina, campground, picnic area, coffee shop in a historic log lodge, rustic cabins, and nearby riding stables. The 550-passenger **MS Dixie II** (☎ 775/588–3508), a stern-wheeler, sails year-round from Zephyr Cove Marina to Emerald Bay on lunch and dinner cruises. Fares range from $25 to $51. The **Woodwind** (☎ 775/588–3000), a glass-bottom trimaran, sails on regular and champagne cruises from April through October from Zephyr Cove Resort. Fares range from $26 to $32. In winter Zephyr Cove Resort rents out snowmobiles and snowshoes.

> off the beaten path

KINGSBURY GRADE – This road, also known as Highway 207, is one of three roads that access Tahoe from the east. Originally a toll road used by wagon trains to get over the crest of the Sierra, it has sweeping views of the Carson Valley. Off Highway 206, which intersects Highway 207, is Genoa, the oldest settlement in Nevada. Along Main Street are a museum in Nevada's oldest courthouse, a small state park, and the state's longest-standing saloon.

Where to Stay

¢ ✕ **Coyote Grill.** Coyote Grill serves delicious fish tacos, made with fresh halibut or ahi tuna, sautéed cabbage, and chipotle aioli. There are also sandwiches, burgers, and a full bar. ⊠ *Safeway Shopping Center, 212 Elks Point Dr.* ☎ *775/586–1822* ⌣ *Reservations not accepted* ▭ *AE, MC, V.*

⚠ **Zephyr Cove Resort.** This sprawling campground on the mountain side of U.S. 50 is one of the largest on the lake and remains open all winter. It's mostly for RVers but has drive-in and walk-in tent sites. Across the highway are 28 lakefront cabins, a marina with boat rentals, and horse-back-riding and snowmobiling facilities. Be careful crossing the road! ⚐ *Restaurant, grills, snack bar, playground, laundry facilities, flush toilets, full hook-ups, partial hook-ups, dump station, drinking water, showers, fire pits, picnic tables, general store, swimming* ⚓ *175 sites* ✉ *U.S. 50, 5 mi north of Stateline* ☎ *775-589-4981* ✉ *$25–$46* ☉ *Year-round.*

Stateline

⑭ *5 mi south of Zephyr Cove on U.S. 50.*

Stateline is a great border town in the Nevada tradition. Its four high-rise casinos are as vertical and contained as the commercial district of South Lake Tahoe, on the California side, is horizontal and sprawling. And Stateline is as relentlessly indoors-oriented as the rest of the lake is focused on the outdoors. This strip is where you'll find the most concentrated action at Lake Tahoe: restaurants (including typical casino buffets), showrooms with famous headliners and razzle-dazzle revues, tower-hotel rooms and suites, and 24-hour casinos.

Where to Stay & Eat

★ **$$–$$$** ✕ **Mirabelle.** The French-Alsatian–born chef-owner prepares everything on the menu himself, from puff pastry to chocolate cake to homemade bread. Specialties include an Alsatian onion tart, escargots, and rack of lamb. Leave room for the dessert soufflés. On Mondays from April through June, the chef holds cooking classes that culminate with a grand repast in the casual, airy dining room; call for details. ✉ *290 Kingsbury Grade* ☎ *775/586–1007* ✉ *AE, MC, V* ☉ *Closed Mon. No lunch.*

★ **$$–$$$$** ✕⌂ **Harvey's Resort Hotel/Casino.** Harvey's, which started as a cabin in 1944, is now the largest resort in Tahoe. Rooms have custom furnishings, oversize marble baths, and minibars. Use of the health club, spa, and pool is free to guests—a rarity for this area. Llewelyn's ($$$–$$$$), atop the hotel, has drop-dead views and excellent Continental food in an elegant dining room. ✉ *U.S. 50 at Stateline Ave., 89449* ☎ *775/588–2411 or 800/648–3361* 🖶 *775/782–4889* ⊕ *www.harrahs.com/our casinos/hlt* ⚓ *705 rooms, 38 suites* ⚐ *8 restaurants, minibars, cable TV with movies, pool, health club, hair salon, hot tub, spa, casino, meeting rooms* ✉ *AE, D, DC, MC, V.*

$$–$$$$ ✕⌂ **Harrah's Tahoe Hotel/Casino.** Luxurious guest rooms here have two full bathrooms, each with a television and telephone. All rooms have views of the lake and the mountains. Top-name entertainment is presented in the South Shore Room. Among the restaurants, the romantic 16th-floor Summit is a standout; the buffet is also on the 16th floor. A tunnel runs under U.S. 50 to Harvey's, which Harrah's now owns. ✉ *U.S. 50 at Stateline Ave., 89449* ☎ *775/588–6611 or 800/427–7247* 🖶 *775/588–6607* ⊕ *www.harrahstahoe.com* ⚓ *470 rooms, 62 suites* ⚐ *7 restaurants, room service, in-room data ports, cable TV with movies, indoor pool, health club, hair salon, hot tub, casino, laundry service, meeting rooms, kennel* ✉ *AE, D, DC, MC, V.*

$$–$$$ ⌂ **Horizon Casino Resort.** Many rooms at this hotel-casino have lake views. The casino has a beaux-arts look, brightened by pale molded wood and mirrors. The Grande Lake Theatre, Golden Cabaret, and Aspen Lounge present shows, as well as up-and-coming and name entertainers. Le Grande Buffet has a nightly prime-rib special. ✉ *U.S. 50 at Lake Pkwy., 89449* ☎ *775/588–6211 or 800/322–7723* 🖶 *775/588–1344* ⊕ *www.*

horizoncasino.com ➪ 516 rooms, 23 suites ⚭ 3 restaurants, in-room data ports, cable TV with movies, pool, gym, 3 hot tubs, casino, meeting rooms ☰ AE, D, DC, MC, V.

$–$$$ 🏨 **Caesars Tahoe.** Most of the luxury-kitsch rooms and suites at Caesars have oversize tubs, king-size beds, two telephones, and a view of Lake Tahoe or the encircling mountains (some overlook the parking lot). Famous entertainers perform in the 1,600-seat Circus Maximus. Planet Hollywood is also here. *⊠ 55 U.S. 50 ⓓ (Box 5800, 89449) ☎ 775/588–3515 or 800/648–3353 🖷 775/586–2068 ⊕ www.caesars.com ➪ 328 rooms, 112 suites ⚭ 5 restaurants, coffee shop, in-room data ports, cable TV with movies, 4 tennis courts, indoor pool, health club, hot tub, sauna, spa, showroom, meeting rooms ☰ AE, D, DC, MC, V.*

¢–$ 🏨 **Lakeside Inn and Casino.** With the smallest of the Stateline casinos, the Lakeside has good promotional room rates and simple, attractive accommodations in two-story motel-style buildings away from the casino. *⊠ U.S. 50 at Kingsbury Grade, Box 5640, 89449 ☎ 775/588–7777 or 800/624–7980 🖷 775/588–4092 ⊕ www.lakesideinn.com ➪ 115 rooms, 9 suites ⚭ Restaurant, in-room data ports, pool, casino ☰ AE, D, DC, MC, V.*

Nightlife

The top entertainment venues, featuring everything from comedy to magic acts to floor shows to Broadway musicals, include the **Circus Maximus** (☎ 775/588–3515), at Caesars Tahoe; the **Emerald Theater** (☎ 775/588–2411), at Harvey's; the **South Shore Room** (☎ 775/588–6611), at Harrah's; and Horizon's **Grand Lake Theatre** (☎ 775/588–6211).

Sports & the Outdoors

Edgewood Tahoe (⊠ U.S. 50 and Lake Pkwy., behind Horizon Casino ☎ 775/588–3566), right on the lake, is an 18-hole, par-72 course with a driving range. The $200 greens fee includes a cart (though you can walk if you wish).

LAKE TAHOE A TO Z

To research prices, get advice from other travelers, and book travel arrangements, visit ⊕ www.fodors.com

AIR TRAVEL

Reno–Tahoe International Airport, in Reno, 35 mi northeast of the closest point on the lake, is served by Alaska, American, America West, Continental, Delta, Northwest, Skywest, Southwest, and United airlines. (*See* Air Travel *in* Smart Travel Tips A to Z for airline phone numbers.) 🛈 **Reno–Tahoe International Airport** ⊠ U.S. 395, exit 65B, Reno, NV ☎ 775/328–6400 ⊕ www.renoairport.com.

BUS TRAVEL

Greyhound stops in Sacramento, Truckee, South Lake Tahoe, and Reno, Nevada. South Tahoe Area Ground Express runs along U.S. 50 and through the neighborhoods of South Lake Tahoe daily from 6 AM to 12:15 AM. Tahoe Area Regional Transit (TART) operates buses along Lake Tahoe's northern and western shores between Tahoma (from Meeks Bay in summer) and Incline Village daily from 6:30 to 6:30. Free shuttle buses run among the casinos, major ski resorts, and motels of South Lake Tahoe. Tahoe Casino Express runs 14 daily buses between Reno–Tahoe Airport and hotels in Stateline.

🛈 **Greyhound** ☎ 800/231-2222. **South Tahoe Area Ground Express** (STAGE) ☎ 530/542-6077. **Tahoe Area Rapid Transit** (TART) ☎ 530/550-1212 or 800/736-6365. **Tahoe Casino Express** ☎ 775/785-2424 or 800/446-6128.

CAR RENTAL

The major car-rental agencies—Hertz, Avis, Budget, National, Thrifty, Enterprise, and Dollar—all have counters at Reno–Tahoe International Airport. Enterprise has an outlet at the South Lake Tahoe Airport; Avis has one at Harrah's Stateline; and Dollar has counters at the Reno Hilton, Circus Circus, and Caesars Tahoe. *See* Car Rental *in* Smart Travel Tips A to Z for national rental agency phone numbers.

CAR TRAVEL

Lake Tahoe is 198 mi northeast of San Francisco, a drive of less than four hours in good weather. Avoid the heavy traffic leaving the San Francisco area for Tahoe on Friday afternoon and returning on Sunday afternoon. The major route is I–80, which cuts through the Sierra Nevada about 14 mi north of the lake. From there Highway 89 and Highway 267 reach the west and north shores, respectively. U.S. 50 is the more direct route to the south shore, taking about 2½ hours from Sacramento. From Reno you can get to the north shore by heading west on Highway 431 for 35 mi. For the south shore, head south on U.S. 395 through Carson City, and then turn west on U.S. 50 (50 mi total).

The scenic 72-mi highway around the lake is marked Highway 89 on the southwest and west shores, Highway 28 on the north and northeast shores, and U.S. 50 on the east and southeast. Sections of Highway 89 sometimes close during winter, making it impossible to complete the circular drive. Interstate 80, U.S. 50, and U.S. 395 are all-weather highways, but there may be delays as snow is cleared during major storms. Carry tire chains from October through May, or rent a four-wheel-drive vehicle (rental agencies do not offer tire chains for rent).

🚗 **California Highway Patrol** ☎ 530/587-3510. **Cal-Trans Highway Information Line** ☎ 800/427-7023. **Nevada Department of Transportation Road Information** ☎ 877/687-6237. **Nevada Highway Patrol** ☎ 775/687-5300.

EMERGENCIES

In an emergency dial 911.

🏥 Hospitals **Barton Memorial Hospital** ✉ 2170 South Ave., South Lake Tahoe ☎ 530/541-3420. **St. Mary's Regional Medical Center** ✉ 235 W. 6th St., Reno ☎ 775/770-3188 **Tahoe Forest Hospital** ✉ 10121 Pine Ave., Truckee ☎ 530/587-6011.

LODGING

The Lake Tahoe Visitors Authority provides information on south-shore lodging. North Lake Tahoe Resort Association can give you information about accommodations on the north shore. Contact the Reno-Sparks Convention and Visitors Authority for lodging reservations in the Reno metropolitan area.

🏨 **Lake Tahoe Visitors Authority** ☎ 800/288-2463 ⊕ www.virtualtahoe.com. **North Lake Tahoe Resort Association** ☎ 800/824-6348 ⊕ www.tahoefun.org. **Reno-Sparks Convention and Visitors Authority** ☎ 775/827-7647 or 888/448-7366 ⊕ www.renolaketahoe.com.

SPORTS & THE OUTDOORS

If you are planning to spend any time outdoors around Lake Tahoe, whether hiking, climbing, or camping, be aware that weather conditions can change quickly in the Sierra: to avoid a life-threatening case of hypothermia, always bring a pocket-sized, fold-up rain poncho (available in all sporting goods stores) to keep you dry. Wear long pants and a hat. Carry plenty of water. Because you'll likely be walking on granite, wear sturdy, closed-toe hiking boots, with soles that grip rock. If you're going into the backcountry, bring a signaling device (such as a mirror), energy bars, emergency whistle, compass, map, and water purifier. When heading out alone, tell someone where you're going and when you're coming back.

If you plan to ski, be aware of resort elevations. In the event of a winter storm, determine the snow level before you choose the resort you'll ski. Often the level can be as high as 7,000 ft, which means rain at some resorts but snow at others. For storm information, check the National Weather Service's Web page. To save money on lift tickets, look for packages offered by lodges and resorts. It's usually cheaper to ski midweek, and some resorts offer family discounts. Free shuttle-bus service is available between most ski resorts and nearby lodgings.

If you plan to camp in the backcountry, you'll likely need a wilderness permit, which you can pick up at the Lake Tahoe Visitor Center or at a ranger station at the entrance to any of the national forests. For reservations at campgrounds in California state parks, contact Park.net.
🏢 **Lake Tahoe Visitor Center.** ⊠ Hwy. 89 ☎ 530/573-2674 (in season only) ⊕ www. r5.fs.fed.us/ltbmu. **National Weather Service** ⊕ www.wrh.noaa.gov/reno. **Park.net** ☎ 800/444-7275 ⊕ www.reserveamerica.com

TOURS

Outfits in South Lake Tahoe and Zephyr Cove operate guided boat tours (*see* South Lake Tahoe *and* Zephyr Cove *for more information*). Gray Line/Frontier Tours runs daily tours to South Lake Tahoe, Carson City, and Virginia City. Lake Tahoe Balloons conducts excursions year-round over the lake or over the Carson Valley for $129 per person for half-hour flights and $195 for hour-long flights (champagne brunch included). Soar Minden offers glider rides and instruction over the lake and the Great Basin. Flights cost $95 to $210 and depart from Minden-Tahoe Airport, a municipal facility in Minden, Nevada.
🏢 **Gray Line/Frontier Tours** ☎ 775/331-8687 or 800/831-2877. **Lake Tahoe Balloons** ☎ 530/544-1221 or 800/872-9294. **Soar Minden** ☎ 775/782-7627 or 800/345-7627.

TRAIN TRAVEL

Amtrak's cross-country rail service makes stops in Reno. The *California Zephyr* stops in the heart of downtown Reno once daily eastbound (Salt Lake, Denver, and Chicago) and once daily westbound (Truckee, Sacramento, and Oakland), blocking traffic for 5 to 10 minutes. Amtrak also operates several buses daily between Reno and Sacramento to connect with the *Coast Starlight,* which runs south to southern California and north to Oregon and Washington.
🏢 **Amtrak** ☎ 775/329-8638 or 800/872-7245 ⊕ www.amtrakcalifornia.com.

VISITOR INFORMATION

🏢 **California State Department of Parks and Recreation** ⊠ Box 942896, Sacramento 94296 ☎ 916/653-6995 or 800/777-0369 🖨 916/654-6374 ⊕ www.cal-parks.ca.gov. **Lake Tahoe Visitors Authority** ⊠1156 Ski Run Blvd., South Lake Tahoe, CA 96150 ☎ 530/ 544-5050 or 800/288-2463 ⊕ www.virtualtahoe.com. **North Lake Tahoe Resort Association** 📇 Box 5578, Tahoe City, CA 96145) ☎ 530/583-3494 or 800/824-6348 🖨 530/581-4081 ⊕ www.tahoefun.org. **Reno-Sparks Convention and Visitors Authority** ⊠ 4590 S. Virginia St., Reno 89502 ☎ 775/827-7600 or 800/367-7366 ⊕ www. renolaketahoe.com. **U.S. Forest Service** ☎ 530/587-2158 backcountry recording ⊕ www.fs.fed.us/r5.

THE FAR NORTH

WITH LAKE SHASTA, MOUNT SHASTA & LASSEN VOLCANIC NATIONAL PARK

FODOR'S CHOICE

Lassen Volcanic National Park, *Mineral*

HIGHLY RECOMMENDED

RESTAURANTS   Benassi's, *Chester*

Grand Cafe, *Susanville*

St. Francis Champion Steakhouse, *Susanville*

Trinity Café, *Mount Shasta*

HOTELS   Bidwell House, *Chester*

Feather Bed, *Quincy*

Mount Shasta Resort, *Mount Shasta*

The Red Lion, *Redding*

SIGHTS   Bidwell Mansion State Historic Park, *Chico*

Bidwell Park, *Chico*

Castle Crags State Park, *Dunsmuir*

Lake Shasta Area, *north of Redding*

McArthur–Burney Falls Memorial State Park, *Burney*

Sierra Nevada Brewing Company, *Chico*

Turtle Bay Exploration Park, *Redding*

Weaverville Joss House, *temple in Weaverville*

Updated by
Christine
Vovakes

THE WONDROUS LANDSCAPE of California's northeastern corner, relatively unmarred by development, congestion, and traffic, is the product of volcanic activity. At the southern end of the Cascade Range, Lassen Volcanic National Park is the best place to witness the far north's fascinating geology. Beyond the sulfur vents and bubbling mud pots, the park owes much of its beauty to 10,457-foot Mt. Lassen and 50 wilderness lakes. But the enduring image of the region has to be Mt. Shasta: at 14,162 feet its snow-capped peak is visible for miles, beckoning outdoor adventurers of all kinds. There are many versions of Shasta to enjoy—the mountain, the lake, the river, the town, the dam, and the forest—all named after the Native Americans known as the Shatasla, or Sastise, who once inhabited the region.

Its soaring mountain peaks, wild rivers teaming with trout, and almost unlimited recreational possibilities make the far north the perfect destination for sports lovers. You won't find many hot nightspots and cultural enclaves, but you will find some of the best hiking and fishing in the state. The region offers a glimpse of old California—natural, rugged, and inspiring.

Exploring the Far North

The far north encompasses all of four vast counties—Tehama, Shasta, Siskiyou, and Trinity—as well as parts of Butte, Modoc, and Plumas Counties. The area stretches from the valleys east of the Coast Range to the Nevada border and from the almond and olive orchards north of Sacramento to the Oregon border. A car is essential for touring the area unless you arrive by public transportation and plan to stay put in one town or resort.

About the Restaurants

Redding, the urban center of the far north, has the greatest selection of restaurants. In the smaller towns, cafés and simple eateries are the rule, though trendy, innovative restaurants have been opening. Dress is always informal.

About the Hotels

Aside from the large chain hotels and motels in the Redding area, most accommodations in the far north blend rusticity, simplicity, and coziness. That's just fine with most of the folks who visit, as they spend much of their time outdoors. Wilderness resorts close in fall and reopen after the snow season ends in May.

The far north—especially the mountainous backcountry—is gaining popularity as a tourist destination. For summer holiday weekends make lodging reservations well in advance. The Web site of the California Association of Bed & Breakfast Inns (☎ www.cabbi.com) lists numerous B&Bs in the far north region.

WHAT IT COSTS				
$$$$	**$$$**	**$$**	**$**	**¢**
RESTAURANTS over $30	$23–$30	$16–$22	$10–$15	under $10
HOTELS over $250	$176–$250	$121–$175	$90–$120	under $90

Restaurant prices are for a main course at dinner, excluding sales tax of 7¾% (depending on location). Hotel prices are for a standard double room in high season, excluding service charges and 7¼% tax.

Timing

The far north attracts more tourists during the summer than at any other time of year. Residents of the Sacramento Valley, which is usually dry

Numbers in the text correspond to numbers in the margin and on the Far North map.

If you have 3 days

From I–5 north of Redding, head northeast on Highways 299 and 89 to ▶ **McArthur–Burney Falls Memorial State Park** ❽. To appreciate the falls, take a short stroll to the overlook or hike down for a closer view. Continue north on Highway 89. Long before you arrive in the town of ▦ **Mount Shasta** ❼, you will spy the conical peak for which it is named. The central Mount Shasta exit east leads out of town along **Everitt Memorial Highway.** Take this scenic drive, which climbs to almost 8,000 feet. The views of the mountain and the valley below are extraordinary. Stay overnight in town. On the second day head south on I–5 toward **Lake Shasta** ❺, visible on both sides of the highway. Have a look at **Lake Shasta Caverns** and the **Shasta Dam** before heading west on Highway 299 to spend the night in ▦ **Weaverville** ❹ or south on I–5 to overnight in ▦ **Redding** ❸. The next day visit **Shasta State Historic Park** and **Weaverville Joss House,** on Highway 299.

10

If you have 5 or 6 days

Get a glimpse of the far north's heritage in ▶ **Red Bluff** ❷ before heading north on I–5 to the town of ▦ **Mount Shasta** ❼. On day two, drop by the Forest Service ranger station to check on trail conditions on the mountain and to pick up maps. Pack a picnic lunch before taking **Everitt Memorial Highway** up the mountain. After exploring it, head south on I–5 and spend the night in ▦ **Dunsmuir** ❻ at the **Railroad Car Resort,** where all the accommodations are old cabooses. On your third day take an early morning hike in nearby **Castle Crags State Park.** Continue south on I–5 to **Lake Shasta** ❺ and tour **Shasta Dam Visitor's Center.** Spend the night camping in the area or in ▦ **Redding** ❸. On your fourth morning head west on Highway 299, stopping at **Shasta State Historic Park** on your way to ▦ **Weaverville** ❹. Spend the night there or back in Redding. If you will be leaving the area on your fifth day but have a little time, zip north and visit **Lake Shasta Caverns.** If you're spending the night in Redding and it's between late May and early October, spend the next day and a half exploring **Lassen Volcanic National Park** ⓫. Highway 44 heads east from Redding into the park.

and scorching during the dog days of summer, tend to flee to the milder climes of the mountains to the north and east. The valley around Redding is mild in winter, while snow falls at higher elevations. In winter Mt. Shasta is a great place for downhill and cross-country skiing—and even ice fishing at the area's many high-elevation lakes. Snow closes the roads to some of the region's most awesome sights, including much of Lassen Volcanic National Park, from October until late May. During the off-season many restaurants and museums here have limited hours, sometimes closing for extended periods.

FROM CHICO TO MOUNT SHASTA
ALONG I–5

The far north is bisected, south to north, by I–5. Along this route you will find historic towns, museums, and state parks. Halfway to the Oregon border is Lake Shasta, a favorite recreation destination, and farther north stands the spectacular snowy peak of Mt. Shasta.

Chico

❶ *180 mi from San Francisco, east on I–80, north on I–505 to I–5, and east on Hwy. 32; 86 mi north of Sacramento on Hwy. 99.*

Chico sits just west of Paradise in the Sacramento Valley and offers a welcome break from the monotony of Highway I–5. The Chico campus of California State University heavily influences the town's character. With scores of local artisans and acres of almond orchards in the mix, Chico (which is Spanish for "small") successfully blends academics, the arts, and agriculture. It has many art galleries, but Chico's true claim to fame is the popular Sierra Nevada Brewery, which keeps locals and beer drinkers across the country happy with its distinctive microbrews.

★ The sprawling 3,670-acre **Bidwell Park** (⊠ River Rd. south of Sacramento St. ☎ 530/895–4972), a community green space that straddles Big Chico Creek, is where scenes from *Gone With the Wind* and the 1938 version of *Robin Hood,* starring Errol Flynn, were filmed. It provides the region with a recreational oasis of playgrounds; a golf course; swimming areas; and paved biking, hiking, and in-line skating trails. The third-largest city-run park in the country starts as a slender strip downtown and expands eastward toward the Sierra foothills.

★ In **Bidwell Mansion State Historic Park** you can take a one-hour tour of approximately 20 of the mansion's rooms. Built between 1865 and 1868 by General John Bidwell, the founder of Chico, the 26-room home was designed by Henry W. Cleaveland, a San Francisco architect. Bidwell and his wife welcomed many distinguished guests to the distinctive pink Italianate mansion, including President Rutherford B. Hayes, naturalist John Muir, suffragist Susan B. Anthony, and General William T. Sherman. ⊠ 525 The Esplanade ☎ 530/895–6144 ☜ $2 ☉ Wed.–Sun. noon–5, last tour at 4.

★ The renowned **Sierra Nevada Brewing Company,** one of the pioneers of the microbrewery movement, still has a hands-on approach to beer making that makes touring its sparkling brewery a pleasure. You can enjoy a hearty lunch or dinner in the brewpub, which serves standard pub fare and interesting entrées. There is also a gift shop. The brewery is closed Monday. ⊠ 1075 E. 20th St. ☎ 530/345–2739 ☟ 530/893–9358 ⊕ www.sierranevada.com ☜ Free ☉ Tours Tues.–Fri. at 2:30, Sat. noon–3 on the ½ hr.

Where to Stay & Eat

$–$$$ ✕ **Red Tavern.** With its warm, butter-yellow walls and mellow lighting, this is one of Chico's most refined restaurants. The menu, often inspired by fresh local produce, changes frequently. If you're lucky, it might include lamb chops with a lemon–pine nut crust or stuffed Atlantic salmon with Swiss chard, bacon, and sage butter. Choose from the California wine list or full bar. ⊠ 1250 The Esplanade ☎ 530/894–3463 ☰ AE, MC, V ☉ No lunch.

$ ✕ **Kramore Inn.** Crepes—from ham and avocado to crab cannelloni—are the inn's specialty, along with Hungarian mushroom soup. The menu also includes salads, stir-fries, Asian dishes, and pastas. Brunch is available on Sunday from 9 to 2. ⊠ 1903 Park Ave. ☎ 530/343–3701 ☰ AE, D, MC, V.

¢ ✕ **Madison Bear Garden.** This downtown favorite two blocks south of the Chico State campus is a great spot for checking out the vibrant col-

10

Camping In the vast expanses of the far north, pristine campgrounds make overnighting in the great outdoors a singular pleasure. There are hundreds of campgrounds here: some small and remote with few facilities; others with nearly all the conveniences of home; and still others somewhere in between.

Fishing Cascading rivers, lakes of many shapes and sizes, and bountiful streams draw sportfishers to the Far North. The Trinity River below the Lewiston Dam offers excellent fly-fishing. The large trout of Eagle Lake are renowned far and wide as especially feisty quarry. Lake Shasta holds 21 varieties of fish, including rainbow trout and salmon.

Hiking With so much wilderness, it's no wonder the far north has some of California's finest—and least crowded—hiking areas. In the shadow of Mt. Shasta, Castle Crags State Park has 28 mi of hiking trails, including rewarding routes at lower altitudes. Plumas National Forest, a protected area of 1.2 million acres, is laced with trails. Hikers in Lassen Volcanic National Park can access bizarre landscapes.

lege scene while enjoying a delicious burger and a vast selection of brews. ⊠ 316 W. 2nd St. ☎ 530/891-1639 ▭ MC, V.

¢–$ ▣ **Johnson's Country Inn.** Nestled in an almond orchard five minutes from downtown, this Victorian-style farmhouse with a wraparound veranda is a welcome change from motel row. It is full of antique furnishings and modern conveniences. ⊠ 3935 Morehead Ave., 95928 ☎☎ 530/345–7829 ⊕ www.now2000.com/johnsonsinn ⇆ 4 rooms ▭ AE, MC, V ⏹ BP.

Shopping
Made in Chico (⊠ 232 Main St. ☎ 530/894–7009) carries Woof and Poof products and locally made goods, including handwoven scarves, pottery, salad dressings, mustards, olives, and almonds. Beautiful custommade etched, stained, and beveled glass is created at **Needham Studios** (⊠ 237 Broadway ☎ 530/345–4718). Shop and watch demonstrations of glass blowing at the **Satava Art Glass Studio** (⊠ 819 Wall St. ☎ 530/345–7985).

Red Bluff

▶ ❷ *41 mi north of Chico on Hwy 99.*

Historic Red Bluff is a gateway to Lassen Volcanic National Park. Established in the mid-19th century as a shipping center and named for the color of its soil, the town is filled with dozens of restored Victorians, resulting in a downtown that resembles a stage set for a Western movie. It's a great home base for outdoor adventures in the area.

The **Kelly-Griggs House Museum,** a beautifully restored 1880s home, holds an impressive collection of antique furniture, housewares, and clothing arranged as though a refined Victorian-era family were still in residence. A Venetian glass punch bowl sits on the dining room table. In the upstairs parlor costumed mannequins seem eerily frozen in time. *Persephone,* the painting over the fireplace, is by Sarah Brown, daughter of abolitionist John Brown, whose family settled in Red Bluff. ⊠ 311 Washington St. ☎ 530/527–1129 ▧ Donation suggested ☉ Thurs.–Sun. 1–3.

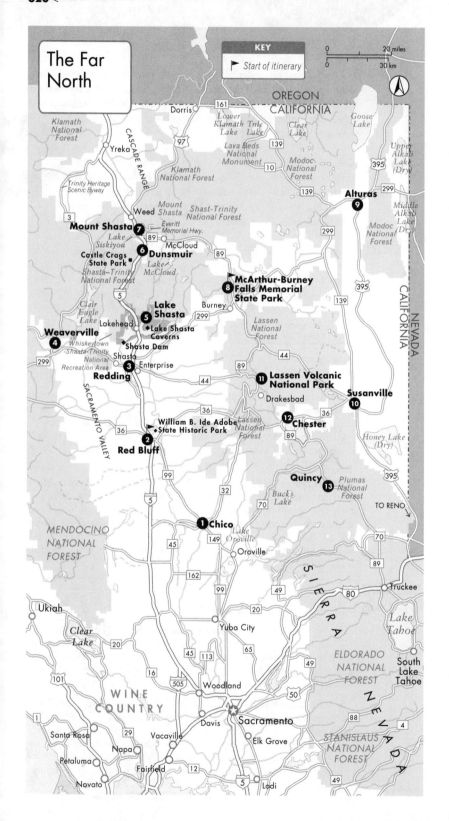

The Far
North

KEY
▶ Start of itinerary

0   20 miles
0   30 km

OREGON
CALIFORNIA

Klamath
National
Forest

Dorris

161

97

Lower
Klamath
Lake

Tule
Lake

Clear
Lake

Goose
Lake

Yreka

139

Lava Beds
National
Monument

10

Modoc
National
Forest

Upper
Alkali
Lake
(Dry)

Trinity Heritage
Scenic Byway

3

Weed

Klamath
National Forest

Mount
Shasta

Shast-Trinity
National Forest

139

Alturas
9

299

Middle
Alkali
Lake
(Dry)

395

Mount Shasta 7

89

Everitt
Memorial Hwy.

McCloud

89

299

Modoc
National
Forest

Dunsmuir 6

Castle Crags
State Park

Shasta-Trinity
National Forest

Lake
Siskiyou

Lake
McCloud

McArthur-Burney
Falls Memorial
State Park 8

395

5

Burney

139

Clair
Eagle
Lake

Lake
Shasta 5

Lakehead

Lake Shasta
Caverns

299

Lassen
National
Forest

Weaverville
4

Whiskeytown
-Shasta-Trinity
National
Recreation Area

Shasta Dam

Shasta

299

Enterprise

Redding 3

44

44

89

Lassen Volcanic
National Park 11

Susanville
10

Drakesbad

36

36

SACRAMENTO VALLEY

36

William B. Ide Adobe
State Historic Park

Lassen
National
Forest

Chester 12

89

Honey Lake
(Dry)

2

Red Bluff

99

395

32

Quincy 13

Plumas
National
Forest

TO RENO

Buck's
Lake

70

MENDOCINO
NATIONAL
FOREST

45

1 Chico

149

Lake
Oroville

70

89

Oroville

162

99

49

80

Truckee

20

Ukiah

Clear
Lake

20

Yuba City

65

SIERRA

Lake
Tahoe

101

45

113

49

ELDORADO
NATIONAL
FOREST

South
Lake
Tahoe

16

505

Woodland

50

1

WINE
COUNTRY

NEVADA

Santa Rosa

29

Vacaville

Davis

Sacramento

88

4

Napa

Elk Grove

STANISLAUS
NATIONAL
FOREST

Petaluma

Novato

Fairfield

12

5

Lodi

49

CASCADE RANGE

William B. Ide Adobe State Historic Park is named for the first and only president of the short-lived California Republic of 1846. The Bear Flag Party proclaimed California a sovereign nation, no longer under the dominion of Mexico, and the republic existed for 25 days before it was occupied by the United States. The flag concocted for the republic has survived, with only minor refinements, as California's state flag. The park's main attraction is an adobe home built in the 1850s and outfitted with period furnishings. There's also a carriage shed, a blacksmith shop, and a small visitor center. Home tours are available on request. ⊠ *21659 Adobe Rd.* ☎ *530/529–8599* ⊕ *www.ideadobe.tehama.k12. ca.us* ⊑ *$4 per vehicle* ☉ *Park and picnic facilities daily 8 AM–sunset.*

Where to Stay & Eat

¢–$$ ✕ **Crystal Steak & Seafood Co.** This place is one of the most popular steak houses in California, and no wonder—the meat is tender, flavorful, and cooked to perfection. ⊠ *343 S. Main St.* ☎ *530/527–0880* ⊟ *AE, D, MC, V* ☉ *Closed Mon. No lunch.*

¢–$ ✕ **Snack Box.** Unabashedly corny pictures and knickknacks decorate the renovated Victorian cottage that holds the family-owned Snack Box. But the hearty soups, omelets, burgers, and sandwiches are what keep folks coming back for more. ⊠ *257 Main St., 1 block from Kelly-Griggs House Museum* ☎ *530/529–0227* ⊟ *AE, MC, V* ☉ *No dinner.*

¢ ✕ **Countryside Deli.** If you've got a hankering for home cooking, this deli serves up delectable lunch and dinner platters heaped with traditional favorites like country-fried steak and meat loaf with mashed potatoes and gravy. With its old-fashioned soda fountain, lined with a row of red-topped swivel seats, the restaurant's atmosphere is as authentic as its hot fudge sundaes and banana splits. ⊠ *1007 Main St.* ☎ *530/529–3869* ⊟ *MC, V* ☉ *Closed weekends.*

¢–$$ ▥ **The Jeter Victorian Inn.** This two-story 1881 Victorian home is elegantly decorated with antiques and period furnishings. Two of the four rooms have private baths, including a Jacuzzi in the Imperial Room. A separate cottage is available. On nice days, breakfast is served in the garden pavilion. ⊠ *1107 Jefferson St., 96080* ☎ *530/527–7574* ⊕ *www. jetervictorianinn.com* ➥ *4 rooms, 2 with bath; 1 cottage* ⚘ *No phone in some rooms, no TV in some rooms, no smoking* ⊟ *MC, V* ▯◻ *BP.*

¢ ▥ **Lamplighter Lodge.** Despite its somewhat romantic name, this is a motel on the town's main street, not a lodge with wood cabins. There's not much to rave about: simple rooms are equipped with minifridges and microwaves, but the pool area is a great place to relax on sweltering summer days. ⊠ *210 S. Main St., 96080* ☎ *530/527–1150* ➥ *50 rooms, 2 suites* ⚘ *Microwaves, refrigerators, pool* ⊟ *AE, D, MC, V* ▯◻ *CP.*

Redding

❸ *32 mi north of Red Bluff on I–5.*

As the largest city in the far north, Redding is an ideal headquarters for exploring the surrounding countryside. Curving along the Sacramento River, **Turtle Bay Exploration Park** has a museum, Paul Bunyan's Forest Camp, and an arboretum with walking trails. Interactive exhibits focus on natural resources, waterways, and Northern California's Indian heritage. In the outdoor play area, Old West history and culture come to life with gold panning, a working miniature dam that children can operate, and logging displays. During summer, you can wander through the Butterfly House and watch monarchs emerge from their cocoons. Children 4–16 pay about half the adult admission, and there's no charge for kids under 3. ⊠ *800 Auditorium Dr.* ☎ *530/243–8850* ⊕ *www. turtlebay.org* ⊑ *$11* ☉ *Closed Mon. Sept.–May.*

Where to Stay & Eat

$–$$$ ✕ **Hatch Cover.** This establishment's dark-wood paneling and views of the adjacent Sacramento River create the illusion of dining aboard a ship, especially on the outside deck with its views of Mt. Shasta. The menu emphasizes seafood, but you can also get steaks, chicken, pasta, and combination plates. The appetizer menu is extensive. ✉ *202 Hemsted Dr. (from Cypress Ave. exit off I–5, turn left, then right on Hemsted Dr.)* ☎ *530/223–5606* ⊟ *AE, D, MC, V* ☺ *No lunch weekends.*

$–$$$ ✕ **Jack's Grill.** Famous for its 16-ounce steaks, this popular bar and steak house also serves prawns and chicken. A town favorite, the place is usually jam-packed and noisy. ✉*1743 California St.* ☎*530/241–9705* ⊟*AE, D, MC, V* ☺ *Closed Sun. No lunch.*

¢ ✕ **Klassique Kafe.** Two sisters run this small restaurant that caters to locals looking for simple but hearty breakfast and lunch fare served in a bustling room where the owners know the regulars on a first-name basis. ✉ *2427 Athens Ave.* ☎ *530/244–4939* ⊟ *AE, D, MC, V* ☺ *Closed Sat.*

★ ¢–$$ ✕▥ **The Red Lion.** Landscaped grounds surrounding a large patio entice guests to relax and enjoy the outdoor food service available here. Rooms are spacious and comfortable. There are irons, ironing boards, and hair dryers in the rooms, and video games in the public areas. The hotel's restaurant, Waters Seafood Grill is a popular place for locals. ✉ *1830 Hilltop Dr. (Hwy. 44/299 exit east from I–5), 96002* ☎ *530/221–8700* ▤ *530/221–0324* ⊕ *www.redlion.com* ⟿ *192 rooms, 2 suites* ♿ *Restaurant, coffee shop, room service, pool, wading pool, gym, hot tub, bar* ⊟ *AE, D, DC, MC, V.*

$$$–$$$$ ▥ **Brigadoon Castle Bed & Breakfast.** Fifteen winding miles from I–5 is an 86-acre estate crowned with an Elizabethan-style castle. Marble baths, antiques, and luxurious fabrics make the Brigadoon an elegant retreat. A separate 1,250-square-foot cottage is available. In the game room are a fireplace, a satellite TV, and a wall of videos. Evening snacks are included. ✉ *9036 Zogg Mine Rd., Igo 96047* ☎ *530/396–2785 or 888/343–2836* ▤ *530/396–2784* ⊕ *www.brigadooncastle.com* ⟿ *4 rooms* ♿ *Hot tub; no room phones, no room TVs* ⊟ *AE, MC, V* ⍾ *BP.*

¢ ▥ **Howard Johnson Express.** Here's a budget option off I–5's Cypress exit. There's complimentary coffee and breakfast, and no charge for local phone calls. ✉ *2731 Bechelli La.* ☎ *530/223–1935 or 800/354–5222* ▤ *530/ 223–1176* ⊕ *www.hojo.com* ⟿ *75 rooms, 2 suites* ♿ *Cable TV with movies, pool, no-smoking rooms* ⊟ *AE, D, MC, V* ⍾ *CP.*

Sports & the Outdoors

The **Fly Shop** (✉ 4140 Churn Creek Rd. ☎ 530/222–3555) sells fishing licenses and has information about guides, conditions, and fishing packages.

en route | Six miles west of Redding on Highway 299, **Shasta State Historic Park** (☎ 530/243–8194 ⌑ $2) stands where Shasta City thrived in the mid- to late 1800s. Its 19 acres of half-ruined brick buildings and overgrown graveyards, accessed via trails, are a reminder of the glory days of the California gold rush. The former county courthouse building, jail, and gallows have been restored to their 1860s appearance. The Courthouse Museum (Wed.–Sun. 10–5) houses a visitor center, information desk, art gallery, and interactive exhibits, including a storytelling "ghost" locked in the jail. The Litsch General Store, in operation from 1850 to 1950, is now a museum, with displays of many items that were sold here.

Weaverville

4 *46 mi west of Redding on Hwy. 299 (called Main St. in town).*

Weaverville is an enjoyable amalgam of gold-rush history and tourist kitsch. Named after John Weaver, who was one of three men who in 1850 built the first cabin here, the town has an impressive downtown historic district. Weaverville is a popular headquarters for family vacations and biking, hiking, fishing, and gold-panning excursions.

★ Weaverville's real attraction is the **Weaverville Joss House,** a Taoist temple built in 1874 and called Won Lim Miao (The Temple of the Forest Beneath the Clouds) by Chinese miners. The oldest continuously used Chinese temple in California, it attracts worshipers from around the world. With its golden altar, carved wooden canopies, and intriguing artifacts, the Joss House is a piece of California history that can best be appreciated on a guided 40-minute tour. The original temple building and many of its furnishings—some of which came from China—were lost to fire in 1873, but members of the local Chinese community soon rebuilt it. ✉ *Oregon and Main Sts.* ☎ *530/623–5284* ✉ *Museum free; guided tour $2* ☼ *Wed.–Sun. 10–5.*

Trinity County Courthouse (✉ Court and Main Sts.), built in 1856 as a store, office building, and hotel, was converted to county use in 1865. The Apollo Saloon, in the basement, became the county jail. It is the oldest courthouse still in use in California.

Trinity County Historical Park houses the **Jake Jackson Memorial Museum,** which has a blacksmith shop, a stamp mill (where ore is crushed) from the 1890s that is still in use, and the original jail cells of the Trinity County Courthouse. ✉ *508 Main St.* ☎ *530/623–5211* ☼ *May–Oct., daily noon–4; Nov.–Apr., Tues. and Sat. noon–4.*

> **off the beaten path**
>
> **TRINITY HERITAGE SCENIC BYWAY –** This road, shown on many maps as Highway 3, runs north from Weaverville for 120 mi up to its intersection with I–5, south of Yreka. The Trinity Alps and Lewiston Lake, formed by the Trinity Dam, are visible all along this beautiful, forest-lined road, which is often closed during the winter months. As it climbs from 2,000 to 6,500 feet, the route for the most part follows a path established by early miners and settlers.

Where to Stay & Eat

$–$$ ✕ **La Grange Café.** In two brick buildings dating from the 1850s (they're among the oldest edifices in town), this eatery always has buffalo, venison, pasta, fresh fish, and chicken on its menu, and farmers' market vegetables when available. There's a full premium bar, and the wine list boasts 135 vintages. ✉ *226 Main St.* ☎ *530/623–5325* ▭ *AE, D, MC, V* ☼ *No lunch Sun.*

¢ ✕ **La Casita.** Here you'll find the traditional selection—all the quesadillas (including one with roasted chili peppers), tostadas, enchiladas, tacos, and tamales you could want, many of them available in a vegetarian version. Open from late morning through early evening, this casual spot is great for a mid-afternoon snack. ✉ *254 Main St.* ☎ *530/ 623–5797* ▭ *No credit cards.*

¢ ▥ **Red Hill Motel.** Built in the 1940s, this is a favorite with perennial visitors; it's the best choice among Weaverville motels. The cozy cabin with full kitchen is popular with families; two others have kitchenettes, and the rest have minifridges and microwaves. ✉ *Red Hill Rd. 96093* ☎ *530/623–4331* ⊕ *www.redhillresorts.com* ⚲ *4 rooms, 10 cabins*

⚙ *Some kitchens, some microwaves, some refrigerators, cable TV*
🍴 *AE, D, MC, V.*

Sports & the Outdoors
Below the Lewiston Dam, east of Weaverville on Highway 299, is the
Fly Stretch of the Trinity River, a world-class fly-fishing area. The **Pine
Cove Boat Ramp,** on Lewiston Lake, provides quality fishing access for
those with disabilities—decks here are built over prime trout-fishing waters. Contact the **Weaverville Ranger Station** (☎ 530/623–2121) for maps
and information about hiking trails in the Trinity Alps Wilderness.

Shopping
Hays Bookstore (✉ 106 Main St. ☎ 530/623–2516) is a general bookstore that includes books on the natural history, attractions, and sights
of the far north.

Lake Shasta Area
★ ❺ *12 mi north of Redding on I–5.*

Twenty-one varieties of fish inhabit **Lake Shasta,** including rainbow
trout and salmon. The lake region also has the largest nesting population of bald eagles in California. You can rent fishing boats, ski boats,
sailboats, canoes, paddleboats, jet skis, and windsurfing boards at one
of the many marinas and resorts along the 370-mi shoreline.

Stalagmites, stalactites, flowstone deposits, and crystals entice people
of all ages to the **Lake Shasta Caverns.** To see this impressive spectacle,
you must take the two-hour tour, which includes a catamaran ride
across the McCloud arm of Lake Shasta and a bus ride up Grey Rock
Mountain to the cavern entrance. The caverns are 58°F year-round, making them a cool retreat on a hot summer day. The high point is the awe-
inspiring Cathedral Room. During peak summer months (June–Aug.),
tours depart every half hour; in April, May, and Sept. it's every hour. A
gift shop is open from 8 to 4:30. ✉ *Shasta Caverns Rd. exit from I–5*
☎ *530/238–2341 or 800/795–2283* ⊕ *www.lakeshastacaverns.com*
💳 *$18* ◷ *Daily 9–4 June–Aug. with departures every half hour; Daily
9–3 Apr., May, and Sept. with departures every hour; daily 10–2
Oct.–Mar. with departures every 2 hours.*

Shasta Dam is the second-largest concrete dam in the United States (Grand
Coulee in Washington is bigger). At dusk the sight of Mt. Shasta gleam-
ing above the not-quite-dark water of its namesake lake is magical. The
worthwhile visitor center has computerized photographic tours of the
dam construction, video presentations, fact sheets, and historic displays.
You can walk across the top of the dam or take a tour behind the scenes.
✉ *16349 Shasta Dam Blvd.* ☎ *530/275–4463* ⊕ *www.usbr.gov/mp/
ncao* ◷ *Pedestrian access daily 6AM–10PM; visitor center weekdays
8:30–4:30, weekends 8:30–5; tours daily at 9, 11, 1, and 3* 💳 *Free.*

Where to Stay & Eat
$$–$$$ ✕ **Tail o' the Whale.** With a name like this, it's no surprise that this restau-
rant has a nautical theme. Diners enjoy a panoramic view of Lake
Shasta as they indulge in spicy Cajun pepper shrimp, charbroiled salmon,
seafood fettuccine in a garlic cream sauce, and steak with scampi.
✉ *10300 Bridge Bay Rd., Bridge Bay exit from I–5* ☎ *530/275–3021*
🍴 *D, MC, V.*

⚠ **Antlers Campground.** On a level bluff above the Sacramento River Arm
of Lake Shasta, this campground sits in oak and pine forest. Open year-
round, the campground is adjacent to Antlers Boat Ramp, and a nearby
marina resort has watercraft rentals, on-water fueling, and a small store.

Some campsites are near the lakeshore, but direct access to the water is difficult. Reservations are taken mid-May through early September only. △ *Flush toilets, pit toilets, drinking water, fire pits, picnic tables* 🖘 *59 sites, no hook-ups* ✉*Antlers Rd., 1 mi east of I-5* ☎*530/275-8113* 🖷*530/275-8344* ⊕ *www.reserveusa.com* 🖾 *$16–$26* 🖃 *AE, D, MC, V.*

Sports & the Outdoors

FISHING **The Fishin' Hole** (✉ 3844 Shasta Dam Blvd., Shasta Lake City ☎ 530/275–4123) is a bait-and-tackle shop just a couple of miles from the lake. It sells fishing licenses and provides information about conditions.

HOUSEBOATING Houseboats here come in all sizes except small. As a rule, rentals are outfitted with cooking utensils, dishes, and most of the equipment you'll need—you just supply the food and the linens. When you rent a house-boat, you will receive a short course in how to maneuver your launch before you set out. You can fish, swim, sunbathe on the flat roof, or sit on the deck and watch the world go by. The shoreline of Lake Shasta is beautifully ragged, with countless inlets; it's not hard to find privacy. Expect to spend a minimum of $300 a day for a craft that sleeps six. A three-day, two-night minimum is customary. Prices are often lower during the off-season (Sept.–May). The **Shasta Cascade Wonderland Association** (✉ 1699 Hwy. 273, Anderson 96007 ☎ 530/365–7500 or 800/474–2782 ⊕ www.shastacascade.com) provides names of rental companies and prices for Lake Shasta houseboating. **Bridge Bay Resort** (✉ 10300 Bridge Bay Rd., Redding ☎ 800/752–9669) rents houseboats, jet skis, fishing boats, and patio boats.

Dunsmuir

❻ *10 mi south of Mt. Shasta on I–5.*

Castle Crags State Park surrounds the town of Dunsmuir, which was named for a 19th-century Scottish coal baron who offered to build a fountain if the town was renamed in his honor. The town's other major attraction is the Railroad Park Resort, where you can spend the night in restored railcars.

★ Named for its 6,000-ft glacier-polished crags, which tower over the Sacramento River, **Castle Crags State Park** offers fishing in Castle Creek, hiking in the backcountry, and a view of Mt. Shasta. The crags draw climbers and hikers from around the world. The 4,350-acre park has 28 mi of hiking trails, including a 2¾-mi access trail to **Castle Crags Wilderness,** part of the **Shasta-Trinity National Forest.** There are excellent trails at lower altitudes, along with picnic areas, rest rooms, showers, and campsites. ✉ *¼ mi off I–5, 6 mi south of Dunsmuir* ☎ *530/235–2684* 🖾 *$4 per vehicle (day use).*

Where to Stay

𝒞 ¢-$ 🖭 **Railroad Park Resort.** The antique cabooses here were collected over more than three decades and have been converted into cozy motel rooms in honor of Dunsmuir's railroad legacy. The resort has a vaguely *Orient Express*–style dining room and a lounge fashioned from vintage railcars. The landscaped grounds contain a huge steam engine and a restored water tower. There's also an RV park and campground. ✉ *100 Railroad Park Rd., 96025* ☎ *530/235–4440 or 800/974–7245* 🖷 *530/235–4470* ⊕ *www.rrpark.com* 🖘 *23 cabooses, 4 cabins* △ *Restaurant, cable TV with movies, some kitchenettes, refrigerators, pool, hot tub, some pets allowed (fee)* 🖃 *AE, D, MC, V.*

△ **Castle Crags State Park Campground.** Craggy peaks tower above this campground surrounded by tall evergreens. It's a great base for hiking and rock climbing. The site can accommodate RVs up to 27 feet long.

Six environmental sites—with pit toilets, and no parking or running water—in relatively undisturbed areas are for tents only. ⑂ *Flush toilets, pit toilets, showers, picnic tables.* ⚑ *76 sites, no hook-ups* ⊠ *15 mi south of Mt. Shasta (Castella exit off I–5)* ☎ *530/235–2684* ⊕ *www. parks.ca.gov* ⚐ *$14* ⚲ *Reservations essential late May–early Sept.* ▭ *D, MC, V* ☉ *Year-round.*

Mt. Shasta

❼ *34 mi north of Lake Shasta on I–5.*

The crown jewel of the 2.5-million-acre Shasta-Trinity National Forest, Mt. Shasta is popular with day hikers, especially in spring, when the fragrant Shasta lily and other flowers adorn the rocky slopes. The paved road reaches only as far as the timberline of this 16-million-year-old dormant volcano, and the final 6,000 feet are a tough climb of rubble, ice, and snow (the summit is perpetually ice-packed). Only a hardy few are qualified to make the trek to the top.

The town of Mount Shasta has real character and some fine restaurants. Lovers of the outdoors and backcountry skiers abound, and they are more than willing to offer advice on the most beautiful spots in the region, which include out-of-the-way swimming holes, dozens of high mountain lakes, and a challenging 18-hole golf course with 360 degrees of spectacular views.

Where to Stay & Eat

$$–$$$ ✕ **Michael's Restaurant.** Wood paneling, candlelight, and wildlife prints by local artists create an unpretentious backdrop for favorites like prime rib and filet mignon, and Italian specialties such as stuffed calamari, scallopini, and linguine pesto. ⊠ *313 N. Mt. Shasta Blvd.* ☎ *530/926–5288* ▭ *AE, D, MC, V* ☉ *Closed Sun.–Mon.*

$–$$ ✕ **Lily's.** This restaurant in a white-clapboard home, framed by a picket fence and arched trellis, serves everything from steaks and pastas to Mexican and vegetarian dishes. The tasty salads include the Jalisco—marinated rib-eye steak slices with greens, tomatoes, and Asiago cheese. The *huevos rancheros* (sunny-side-up eggs on tortillas in a mildly spicy sauce) or the scrambled eggs with salsa are delicious choices for brunch. ⊠ *1013 S. Mt. Shasta Blvd.* ☎ *530/926–3372* ▭ *AE, D, MC, V.*

★ $–$$ ✕ **Trinity Café.** Once a small home, this cozy restaurant has a bistro feel and a dinner menu that the owner-chef calls California Seasonal. The nightly special might be fresh sea bass, wild King Salmon, roasted duck breast with seared foie gras, or a pasta specialty such as potato gnocchi. Desserts also depend on seasonal ingredients; try the poppy-seed strawberry shortcake or orange cake with sugared cherries during spring and summer months. ⊠ *622 N. Mt. Shasta Blvd.* ☎ *530/926–6200* ▭ *MC, V* ☉ *No lunch.*

¢ ✕ **Has Beans.** This coffee shop is a favorite gathering spot for locals. Flyers posted inside offer loads of insider information on life in Mount Shasta. The coffee beans are roasted on-site. Enjoy the pastries, made daily. ⊠ *1011 S. Mt. Shasta Blvd.* ☎ *530/926–3602* ▭ *No credit cards.*

★ $–$$$ ✕▥ **Mount Shasta Resort.** Private chalets are nestled among tall pine trees along the shore of Lake Siskiyou, all with gas-log fireplaces and hot tubs, some with complete kitchens. The resort's Highland House Restaurant, above the clubhouse of a spectacular 18-hole golf course, has uninterrupted views of Mt. Shasta. Large steaks and herb-crusted calamari are menu highlights. Take the Central Mount Shasta exit west from I–5, then go south on Old Stage Road. ⊠ *1000 Siskiyou Lake Blvd., 96067* ☎ *530/926–3030 or 800/958–3363* ⊟ *530/926–0333* ⊕ *www.*

mountshastaresort.com ↝ *65 units* �còs *Restaurant, some kitchenettes, some microwaves, some refrigerators, 18-hole golf course, spa, sports bar, meeting room.* ⊟ *AE, D, DC, MC, V.*

$–$$ ⊞ **Best Western Tree House Motor Inn.** The clean, standard rooms at this motel less than a mile from downtown Mount Shasta are decorated with natural-wood furnishings. Some of the nicer ones have vaulted ceilings and mountain views. ⊠ *111 Morgan Way, at I–5 and Lake St., 96067* ☎ *530/926–3101 or 800/545–7164* ⊟ *530/926–3542* ⊕ *www.bestwestern.com* ↝ *98 rooms, 5 suites* �còs *Restaurant, refrigerators, indoor pool, hot tub* ⊟ *AE, D, DC, MC, V* ⅨⅪ *BP.*

⚠ **Lake Siskiyou Camp Resort.** On the west side of Lake Siskiyou, the sites on this 250-acre resort sit beneath tall pine trees that filter the light. Group sites, evening movies, and power boat and kayak rentals make it a great spot for families; there are also a marina, a free boat-launch ramp, and a fishing dock. ⅗ *Flush toilets, full hook-ups, showers, general store, swimming (lake)* ↝ *200 tent sites, 150 RV sites* ⊠ *4239 W. A. Barr Rd., 3 mi southwest of city of Mount Shasta* ☎ *530/926–2618 or 888/926–2618* ⊕ *www.lakesis.com* ✉ *$18–25* ⅗ *Reservations essential* ⊟ *D, MC, V* ⊘ *Apr.–Oct.*

Sports & the Outdoors

GOLF   At 6,100 yards, the **Mount Shasta Resort** golf course isn't long, but it's beautiful and challenging, with narrow, tree-lined fairways and several lakes and other waterways. Greens fees range from $35 to $50, depending on the day of the week and the season; carts rent for another $10, and clubs can be rented. ⊠ *1000 Siskiyou Lake Blvd.* ☎ *530/926–3052* ⊕ *www.mountshastaresort.com/golfing.htm.*

HIKING   The **Forest Service Ranger Station** (☎ 530/926–4511 or 530/926–9613) keeps tabs on trail conditions and offers avalanche reports.

MOUNTAIN **Fifth Season Mountaineering Shop** (⊠ 300 N. Mt. Shasta Blvd. ☎ 530/
CLIMBING 926–3606 or 530/926–5555) rents skiing and climbing equipment and operates a recorded 24-hour climber-skier report. **Shasta Mountain Guides** (☎ 530/926–3117) leads hiking, climbing, and ski-touring groups to the summit of Mt. Shasta.

SKIING   On the southeast flank of Mt. Shasta, **Mt. Shasta Board & Ski Park** has
ℭ three lifts on 425 skiable acres. It's a great place for novices because three-quarters of the trails are for beginning or intermediate skiers. The area's vertical drop is 1,390 feet, with a top elevation of 6,600 feet. The longest of the 31 trails is 1¾ mi. A package for beginners, available through the ski school, includes a lift ticket, ski rental, and a lesson. The school also runs ski and snowboard programs for children. Within the base lodge are food and beverage facilities, a ski shop, and a ski/snowboard rental shop. The park's Cross-Country Ski and Snowshoe Center, with 30 km (18 mi) of trails, is on the same road. ⊠ *Hwy. 89 exit east from I–5, south of Mt. Shasta* ☎ *530/926–8686 or 800/754–7427* ⊘ *Sun.–Tues. 9–4; Wed.–Sat. 9–10* ⊕ *www.skipark.com.*

THE BACKCOUNTRY

INCLUDING LASSEN VOLCANIC NATIONAL PARK

East of I–5, the far north's main corridor, dozens of scenic two-lane roads crisscross the wilderness, leading to dramatic mountain peaks and fascinating natural wonders. Small towns settled in the second half of the 19th century seem frozen in time, except that they are well equipped with tourist amenities.

McArthur–Burney Falls Memorial State Park

★ ☾ ☞ ❽ *Hwy. 89, 52 mi southeast of Mt. Shasta and 41 mi north of Lassen Volcanic National Park.*

Just inside the park's southern boundary, Burney Creek wells up from the ground and divides into two cascades that fall over a 129-foot cliff and into a pool below. Countless ribbonlike falls stream from hidden moss-covered crevices—an ethereal backdrop to the main cascades. Each day 100 million gallons of water rush over these falls. Resident bald eagles are frequently seen soaring overhead. A self-guided nature trail descends to the foot of the falls, which Theodore Roosevelt—according to legend—called "the eighth wonder of the world." You can swim at Lake Britton, lounge on the beach, or rent motorboats, paddleboats, and canoes. A campground, picnic sites, and other facilities are available. The camp store is open from early May to the end of October. ⊠ *24898 Hwy. 89, Burney 96013* ☎ *530/335-2777* 🖙 *$5 per vehicle for day use.*

Where to Stay

🛏 **McArthur–Burney Falls Memorial State Park.** Campsites here sit within evergreen forests near Burney Falls, several springs, a half dozen hiking trails, and Lake Britton. Boating and fishing are popular pursuits. Some sites can accommodate 35-foot RVs. ♿ *Flush toilets, dump station, showers, picnic tables, general store, swimming (lake)* 🗲 *98 RV sites, no hook-ups, 24 tent sites* ⊠ *McArthur–Burney Falls Memorial State Park, Hwy. 89* ☎ *530/335-2777* ⊕ *www.parks.ca.gov* 🖙 *$14* 🖎 *Reservations essential from Memorial Day to Labor Day* ⊟ *D, MC, V* ☉ *Year-round.*

Alturas

❾ *86 mi northeast of McArthur–Burney Falls Memorial State Park on Hwy. 299.*

Alturas is the county seat and largest town in Modoc County, in the remote upper reaches of northeastern California. The Dorris family arrived in the area in 1874, built Dorris Bridge over the Pit River, and later opened a small wayside stop for travelers. Today the Alturas area is a land of few people but much rugged natural beauty. Travelers come to see eagles and an abundance of other wildlife, geologic history in the Modoc National Forest, and active geothermal areas.

Modoc County Museum exhibits—which include Native American artifacts, firearms, and a steam engine—explore the development of the area from the 15th century through World War II. ⊠ *600 S. Main St.* ☎ *530/ 233-6328* 🖙 *Donations accepted* ☉ *May–Oct., Tues.–Sat. 10–4.*

Modoc National Forest encompasses 1.6 million acres and protects 300 species of wildlife. In spring and fall look for migratory waterfowl, as the Pacific Flyway passes above the forest. Hiking trails lead to Petroglyph Point, one of the largest panels of rock art in the United States. ⊠ *800 W. 12th St.* ☎ *530/233-5811* 🖷 *530/233-8709* ⊕ *www.r5.fs. fed.us/modoc.*

Canada geese, mallards, teal, wigeon, and pintail can be found everywhere in summer and fall within 6,280-acre **Modoc National Wildlife Refuge,** established to protect migratory waterfowl. In summer, white pelicans, cormorants, and snowy egrets arrive. The refuge is open for hiking, birding, and photography, but one area is set aside for hunters. Regulations and seasons vary. ☎ *530/233-3572* 🖙 *Free* ☉ *Daily dawn–dusk.*

<table>
<tr><td>

off the
beaten
path

</td><td>

LAVA BEDS NATIONAL MONUMENT – Volcanic activity created the rugged landscape of this intriguing monument. It is distinguished by cinder cones, lava flows, spatter cones, pit craters, and more than 400 underground lava tube caves. During the Modoc War (1872–73), Modoc Indians under the leadership of Captain Jack took refuge in a natural lava fortress now known as Captain Jack's Stronghold. They managed to hold off for five months U.S. army forces that outnumbered them 20 to 1. When exploring, wear hard-sole boots, and pick up necessary equipment (they lend lights and sell hard hats for $3.25 each) at the Indian Well Visitor Center, at the park's south end. Guided walks and cave tours, which take place during summer, depart from the visitor center. Campfire programs are offered nightly in summer. Bird-watching is popular in the spring and fall. ⊠ *Forest Service Rte. 10, 72 mi northwest of Alturas (Hwy. 299 west from Alturas to Hwy. 139, northwest to Forest Service Rte. 97, to Forest Service Rte. 10)* ☎ *530/667–2282* ⊕ *www.nps.gov/labe* ⊡ *$5 per vehicle; $3 per person on foot, bicycle, or motorcycle* ☉ *Visitor center Memorial Day–Labor Day, daily 8–6; Labor Day–Memorial Day, daily 8–5.*

</td></tr>
</table>

Where to Stay & Eat

$$ ✕ **Brass Rail.** This restaurant offers hearty meals in a comfortable space. Try the Basque lamb, the rib-eye steak, or the shrimp and scallops. There is a full bar and lounge. ⊠ *395 Lakeview Hwy.* ☎ *530/233–2906* ▭ *MC, V* ☉ *Closed Mon.*

¢–$ ✕ **Black Bear Diner.** This is one of a chain of diners, with the big black bear standing in front, that have been sprouting up throughout the far north. The menu is basic, offering everything from spaghetti to barbecued pork ribs and prime rib. Serving sizes are generous. Breakfast is served any time of day. ⊠ *449 N. Main St.* ☎ *530/233–3332* ▭ *AE, D, DC, MC, V.*

¢ ▥ **Best Western Trailside Inn.** This is the only lodging in town with a swimming pool. It's near local outdoor recreational areas: 2 mi north of Rachael Dorris Park, 3 mi south of Devils Garden, and 5 mi north of Modoc Wildlife Reserve. It's also five blocks south of the Modoc County Museum. You have access to a fax machine and a coffee machine. ⊠ *343 N. Main St., 96101* ☎ *530/233–4111* 🖷 *530/233–3180* ⇱ *38 rooms* ⚐ *Some kitchenettes, some microwaves, cable TV, pool, Internet, some pets allowed* ▭ *AE, DC, MC, V.*

¢ ▥ **Hacienda.** In the heart of farm country, this motel is marked with a large 19th-century wagon wheel out front. A gas station, fast-food restaurants, and a supermarket are all within five blocks. ⊠ *201 E. 12th St., 96101* ☎ *530/233–3459* ⇱ *20 rooms* ⚐ *Some kitchenettes, some microwaves, refrigerators, cable TV, some pets allowed, no-smoking rooms* ▭ *AE, D, DC, MC, V.*

△ **Medicine Lake Campground.** One of several small campgrounds on the shores of Medicine Lake, this spot lies at 6,700 feet above sea level, near the western border of Modoc National Forest. Sites can accommodate vehicles up to 22 feet. The lake, 14 mi south of Lava Beds National Monument, is a popular vacation spot for Northern California residents and tourists alike. Fishing, boating, and waterskiing are among the available recreational activities. ⚐ *Pit toilets, drinking water, fire pits, picnic tables, swimming (lake)* ⇱ *22 sites, no hook-ups* ⊠ *Off Forest Service Rd. 44N38 (Hwy. 139 to Forest Service Rte. 97 west to Forest Service Rd. 44N38, follow signs)* ☎ *530/667–2246* ⊕ *www.r5.fs.fed.us/modoc* ⊡ *$7* ⚐ *Reservations not accepted* ▭ *No credit cards.* ☉ *July–Oct.*

Susanville

⑩ *104 mi south of Alturas via U.S. 395, 65 mi east of Lassen Volcanic National Park via Hwy. 36.*

Susanville wears its history on its walls, telling the tale of its rich history through murals painted on buildings in the historic uptown area. Established as a trading post in 1854, Susanville is the second-oldest town in the western Great Basin. Take the self-guided tour that winds around the original buildings, and stop for lunch or dinner at one of several restaurants now housed within them. Plenty of outdoor recreation awaits just outside town at such sites as the Bizz Johnson Trail and Eagle Lake.

Bizz Johnson Trail follows a defunct line of the Southern Pacific Railroad for 25 mi. Known to locals as the Bizz, the trail is open for hikers, walkers, mountain bikers, and horseback riders. It follows the Susan River through a scenic landscape of canyons, bridges, and forests abundant with wildlife. ⊠ *Trailhead: 601 Richmond Rd.* ☎ *530/257–0456* ⊕ *www.ca.blm.gov/eaglelake/bizztrail.html* ☞ *Free.*

Anglers travel great distances to fish the waters of **Eagle Lake.** California's second-largest natural lake is surrounded by high desert to the north and alpine forests to the south. The Eagle Lake trout is prized for its size and fighting ability. The lake is also popular for picnicking, hiking, boating, waterskiing, and windsurfing. Wildlife watchers can see ospreys, pelicans, western grebes, and many other waterfowl on the lake. On land, you'll see mule deer, small mammals, and even pronghorn antelope. ⊠ *20 mi north of Susanville on Eagle Lake Rd.* ☎ *530/257–0456 for Eagle Lake Recreation Area, 530/825–3454 for Eagle Lake Marina* ⊕ *www. reserveusa.com.*

Where to Stay & Eat

★ **$$–$$$** ✕ **St. Francis Champion Steakhouse.** On the ground floor of the historic St. Francis Hotel, this steak house is decorated in an Old West theme and is all about meat. Those who succeed in finishing the "grand champion" 64-ounce steak dinner get their meal on the house; otherwise, it'll cost you $54.95. ⊠ *830 Main St.* ☎ *530/257–4820* ▤ *AE, MC, V* ⊙ *Closed Sun.–Mon.*

¢–$ ✕ **Josefina's.** Popular with the locals, Josefina's makes its own salsas and tamales. The interior's Aztec accents are a perfect accompaniment to the menu's traditional Mexican fare of *chile rellenos* (mild, batter-fried chile peppers stuffed with cheese or a cheese-meat mixture), enchiladas, tacos, and fajitas. ⊠ *1960 Main St.* ☎ *530/257–9262* ▤ *MC, V.*

★ **¢** ✕ **Grand Cafe.** Step back in time at this downtown coffee shop, which has been owned and operated by the same family since the 1920s. You can sit at the old-fashioned fountain counter or in a booth with its own nickel jukebox. The swiveling fountain seats have hat clips on the back, and wooden refrigerators are still in use. The chili is homemade, and so are the fruit cobblers. ⊠ *730 Main St.* ☎ *530/257–4713* ▤ *No credit cards* ⊙ *Closed Sun. No dinner.*

¢–$ 🏨 **Best Western Trailside Inn.** This large, modern, business-friendly motel is in the heart of Susanville but only a quick drive from the area's recreational sites. Some rooms have wet bars. Enjoy home-style cooking next door at the Black Bear Diner. ⊠ *2785 Main St., 96130* ☎ *530/257–4123* 🖷 *530/257–2665* ⊕ *www.bestwesterncalifornia.com* ⇆ *85 rooms* ⌂ *In-room data ports, some refrigerators, cable TV, pool, meeting room, no-smoking rooms* ▤ *AE, D, MC, V* ⧖ *CP.*

¢ 🏨 **High Country Inn.** Spacious rooms open onto indoor corridors in this two-story, colonial-style motel on the east edge of town. The hotel provides complimentary Continental breakfast; more extensive dining is available next door at Country Chicken, a local outlet of the chain. All rooms have hair dryers and coffeepots; business suites have in-room data ports. ⊠ *3015 Riverside Dr., 96130* ☎ *530/257–3450* 🖷 *530/257–2460* ➡ *66 rooms* ⚴ *Some in-room data ports, microwaves, refrigerators, cable TV with movies, pool, outdoor hot tub; no smoking* ⊟ *AE, D, DC, MC, V* ⦿ *CP.*

¢ 🖾 **St. Francis Hotel.** Susanville's oldest continuously operated guest house was built of brick in 1914. The rooms, furnished with wooden antiques, are simple and clean. ⊠ *830 Main St., 96130* ☎ *530/257–4820* ➡ *28 rooms* ⚴ *Cable TV* ⊟ *AE, D, MC, V.*

⚶ **Eagle Campground.** One of 11 campgrounds surrounding Eagle Lake, this site nestled amid pine trees has a boat ramp. ⚴ *Flush toilets, dump station, drinking water, showers, picnic tables* ➡ *35 tent/RV sites, no hook-ups, 14 tent-only sites* ⊠ *County Rd. A-1, 14 mi north of Hwy. 36* ☎ *530/825–3212* ⊕ *www.reserveusa.com* 🖾 *$14* ⚴ *Reservations essential* ⊟ *AE, D, MC, V* ⊗ *Late May–mid-Oct.*

Lassen Volcanic National Park

⓫ *45 mi east of Redding on Hwy. 44, 48 mi east of Red Bluff on Hwy. 36.*

FodorśChoice
★
Lassen Volcanic National Park provides a look at three sides of one of the world's largest plug-dome volcanoes. Much of the park is inaccessible from late October to late May because of heavy snow. The Lassen Park Road (the continuation of Highway 89 within the park) is closed to cars in winter but open to intrepid cross-country skiers and snowshoers, conditions permitting. In summer, food service and gifts are available at the Lassen Chalet, near the southwest entrance, and at the Manzanita Lake Camper Store, near the north entrance. Maps and road guides are available at the Loomis Museum, park headquarters, southwest information station, park entrance, and ranger stations. The park newspaper, *Peak Experiences,* available at the visitor contact stations, details these and other facilities. *Park Headquarters* ⊠ *38050 Hwy. 36E, Mineral 96063* ☎ *530/595–4444* ⊕ *www.nps.gov/lavo* 🖾 *$10 per vehicle, $5 on foot or bicycle* ⊗ *Park headquarters weekdays 8–4:30.*

In 1914 the 10,457-foot Lassen Peak came to life, the first of 300 eruptions to occur over the next seven years. Molten rock overflowed the crater, and the mountain emitted clouds of smoke and hailstorms of rocks and volcanic cinders. Proof of the volcanic landscape's volatility becomes evident shortly after you enter the park at the **Sulphur Works Thermal Area.** Boardwalks take you over bubbling mud and boiling springs and through sulfur-emitting steam vents. ⊠ *Lassen Park Rd., south end of park.*

The **Lassen Peak Hike** winds 2½ mi to the mountaintop. It's a tough climb—2,000 feet uphill on a steady, steep grade—but the reward is a spectacular view. At the peak you can see into the rim and view the entire park (and much of the Far North on a clear day). Bring sunscreen and water. ⊠ *Off Lassen Park Rd., 7 mi north of southwest entrance.*

Along **Bumpass Hell Trail,** a scenic 3-mi round-trip hike to the park's most interesting thermal-spring area, you can view boiling springs, steam vents, and mud pots up close. You'll take a gradual climb of 500 feet to the highest point before you descend 250 feet toward the hissing steam of Bumpass Hell. Near the thermal areas, stay on trails and boardwalks; what appears to be firm ground may be only a thin crust over scalding mud. ⊠ *Off Lassen Park Rd., 6 mi north of southwest entrance.*

Hot Rock, a 400-ton boulder, tumbled down from the summit during the volcano's active period and was still hot to the touch when locals dis-

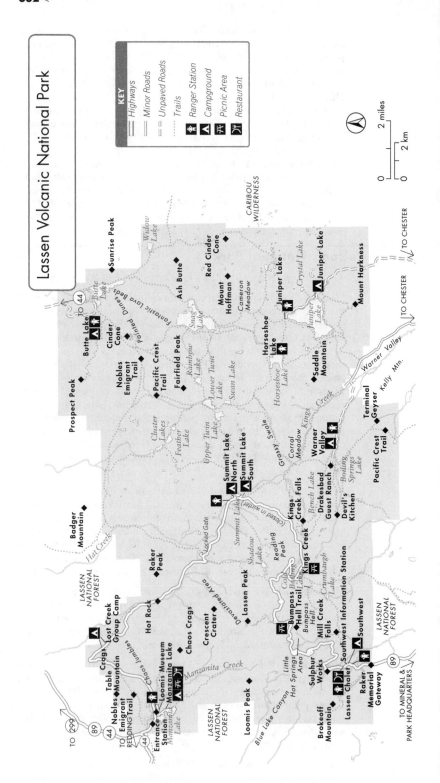

Lassen Volcanic National Park

KEY

Highways
Minor Roads
Unpaved Roads
Trails
Ranger Station
Campground
Picnic Area
Restaurant

0   2 miles
0   2 km

CARIBOU
WILDERNESS

TO CHESTER

TO CHESTER

Warner Valley

TO MINERAL &
PARK HEADQUARTERS

LASSEN
NATIONAL
FOREST

LASSEN
NATIONAL
FOREST

LASSEN
NATIONAL
FOREST

TO 299
TO 89
44

TO
REDDING Trail

Sunrise Peak

Widow
Lake

Ash Butte

Red Cinder
Cone

Mount
Hoffman

Crystal Lake

Juniper Lake

Juniper Lake

Mount Harkness

Butte Lake

Cinder
Cone

Fantastic Lava Beds

Painted Dunes

Snag
Lake

Cameron
Meadow

Butte
Lake

Prospect Peak

Nobles
Emigrant
Trail

Pacific Crest
Trail

Fairfield Peak

Rainbow
Lake

Lower Twin
Lake

Swan Lake

Horseshoe
Lake

Saddle
Mountain

Horseshoe
Lake

Terminal
Geyser

Badger
Mountain

Cluster
Lakes

Feather
Lake

Upper Twin
Lake

Summit Lake
North

Summit Lake
South

Grassy Swale

Corral
Meadow

Kings Creek

Warner
Valley

Boiling
Springs
Lake

Pacific Crest
Trail

Kelly Mtn.

Hat Creek

Raker
Peak

Locked Gate

Summit Lake (closed in winter)

Shadow
Lake

Reading
Peak

Kings
Creek Falls

Bench Lake

Drakesbad
Guest Ranch

Devil's
Kitchen

Lost Creek
Group Camp

Chaos Jumbles

Hot Rock

Chaos Crags

Crescent
Crater

Lassen Peak

Cold
Boiling
Lake

Bumpass
Hell Trail

Kings Creek

Crumbaugh
Lake

Bumpass
Hell

Mill Creek
Falls

Southwest Information Station

Nobles
Emigrant Trail

Table
Mountain

Loomis Museum
Manzanita Lake

Manzanita Creek

Manzanita
Lake

Entrance
Station

Loomis Peak

LASSEN
NATIONAL
FOREST

Blue Lake Canyon

Little
Hot Springs
Canyon

Sulphur
Works

Southwest

Lassen Chalet

Raker
Memorial
Gateway

Brokeoff
Mountain

Devastated Area

covered it nearly two days later. Although cool now, it's still an impressive sight. ⊠ *Lassen Park Rd., north end of park.*

Chaos Jumbles was created 300 years ago when an avalanche from the Chaos Crags lava domes spread hundreds of thousands of rocks, many of them 2–3 feet in diameter, over a couple of square miles. ⊠ *Lassen Park Rd., north end of park.*

Where to Stay & Eat

$$$$ ✕⌗ **Drakesbad Guest Ranch.** Situated at an elevation of 5,700 ft, this guest ranch is near Lassen Volcanic National Park's southern border, but it can't be reached from within the park. It's accessible only by a dirt road leading out of the town of Chester. The property is more than 100 years old, and guest rooms don't have electricity, but are lighted by kerosene lamps; propane furnaces provide the heat. Although rustic, the rooms—which occupy the lodge as well as bungalows and cabins—are comfortable. Each has either a half or full bath. Meals, casual during the day and rather elegant in the evening, are included in the room rate. The waiting list for room reservations can be up to two years long; non-guests who want to eat here should call several days in advance. ⊠ *Chester–Warner Valley Rd., north from Hwy. 36 ℗ (booking office: 2150 N. Main St., Suite 5, Red Bluff 96080)* ☎ *530/529–1512* 🖷 *530/529–4511* ⊕ *www.drakesbad.com* ↪ *19 rooms* ⚭ *Dining room, pool, fishing, badminton, horseback riding, horseshoes, Ping-Pong, volleyball; no a/c, no room phones, no room TVs* ▭ *D, MC, V* ⊗ *Closed early Oct.–early June.* ¶⦿¶ *FAP.*

¢–$ ✕⌗ **Lassen Mineral Lodge.** Reserve rooms at this motel-style property, at 5,000 feet, as far ahead as possible. You can rent cross-country skis, snowshoes, and snowboards at the lodge's ski shop. There's also a general store. ⊠ *Hwy. 36 E, Mineral 96063* ☎ *530/595–4422* ⊕ *www.minerallodge.com* ↪ *20 rooms* ⚭ *Restaurant, bar* ▭ *AE, D, MC, V.*

⚠ **Manzanita Lake Campground.** The largest of Lassen Volcanic National Park's eight campgrounds is near the northern entrance. It can accommodate vehicles up to 35 feet. A trail near the campground leads to Crags Lake. Summer reservations for group campgrounds can be made up to seven months in advance. From the end of September until snow closes the campground there is no running water. ⚭ *Flush toilets, dump station, drinking water, showers, fire pits, picnic tables* ↪ *149 tent/RV sites, no hook-ups, 31 tent sites* ⊠ *Off Lassen Park Rd., 2 mi east of junction of Hwys. 44 and 89* ☎ *530/595–4444* ⊕ *www.nps.gov/lavo/pphtml/camping.html* 🖾 *$16* ▭ *D, MC, V* ⊗ *Late June–late Oct., depending on snowfall.*

Chester

⑫ *36 mi west of Susanville on Hwy. 36.*

Chester's population swells from 2,500 to nearly 5,000 in the summer months as the small town at the edge of Lake Almanor comes alive with tourist activity. Perched along the Lassen Scenic Byway, the town serves as a gateway to Lassen Volcanic National Park.

Lake Almanor's 52 mi of shoreline lie in the shadow of Mt. Lassen. It's a popular draw for camping, swimming, boating, waterskiing, and fishing. At an elevation of 4,500 feet, the lake warms to above 70°F for about eight weeks in summer. Information is available at the Almanor Ranger District headquarters. ⊠ *900 W. Hwy. 36* ☎ *530/258–2141* ⊗ *Open mid-May–mid-October.*

Lassen Scenic Byway is a 172-mi drive through the forested terrain, volcanic peaks, geothermal springs, and lava fields of Lassen National Forest and Lassen National Park. Along the way you'll pass through five rural communities where refreshments and basic services are available. Information is available at Almanor Ranger District headquarters. ⊠ *900 W. Hwy. 36* ☎ *530/258–2141* ⊇ *$10 per vehicle within Lassen National Park* ⊙ *Partially inaccessible in winter; call for road conditions.*

Where to Stay & Eat

$$–$$$ ✕ **Peninsula Station Bar and Grill.** The big meals of steak, prime rib, and seafood are popular with hungry outdoor recreationists. Next door to the Almanor Country Club, the restaurant draws customers with its patio seating and full bar. ⊠ *401 Peninsula Dr., on Lake Almanor Peninsula* ☎ *530/596–3538* ⊙ *Closed Mon. No lunch.* ⊟ *AE, DC, MC, V.*

★ **$–$$** ✕ **Benassi's.** Small and nondescript from the outside but homey inside, this restaurant on the north end of town specializes in northern Italian food. Everything served is homemade, including sauces, ravioli, and tortellini. Other selections include fish, chicken, and beef dishes along with vegetables cooked tender-crisp. ⊠ *159 Main St.* ☎ *530/258–2600* ⊙ *Closed Mon. Oct.–Apr. No dinner Sun.* ⊟ *MC, V.*

¢–$$ ✕ **Cynthia's.** Bordering a brook near the center of town, Cynthia's serves California home-style cuisine with a French touch. Specialties include light meat dishes, pastas, and salads, all made with fresh seasonal ingredients. The bakery is known for rustic pizzas and artisan breads. The bar offers wines and microbrews. Hours change frequently, so call to check. ⊠ *278 Main St.* ☎ *530/258–1966* ⊙ *Closed Sun.–Mon. No dinner Tues.–Thurs. Labor Day–Memorial Day* ⊟ *MC, V.*

¢–$ ✕ **Kopper Kettle Cafe.** Locals return again and again to this tidy restaurant that serves savory home-cooked lunch and dinner, and breakfast whenever you've got a hankering for eggs with biscuits and gravy or other morning fare. Half-orders, a junior–senior menu, and beer and wine are available. The patio is open during summer months. ⊠ *243 Main St.* ☎ *530/258–2698* ⊟ *AE, D, MC, V.* ⊙ *No dinner Nov.–Mar.*

★ **¢–$$** 🏨 **Bidwell House.** With Mt. Lassen as a backdrop, this two-story, 1901 ranch house sits on 2 acres of cottonwood-studded lawns and gardens with a view of Lake Almanor. Chairs and swings make the front porch inviting, and there are plenty of puzzles and games in the sunroom. Some rooms offer wood-burning stoves, claw-foot or Jacuzzi tubs, hardwood floors, and antiques. A separate cottage, which sleeps six, has a kitchen. The inn's specialties—omelets and blueberry-walnut pancakes—are the stars of the daily full breakfast. ⊠ *1 Main St., 96020* ☎ *530/258–3338* ⊕ *www.bidwellhouse.com* ⮎ *14 rooms, 2 with shared bath* ⚭ *Cable TV; no a/c, no room phones, no smoking* ⊟ *MC, V* ⦿ *BP.*

¢ 🏨 **Chester Manor Motel.** This remodeled 1950s-era one-story motel is within easy walking distance of restaurants and offers picnic tables among the pine groves on its 2½-acre lot. Six of the 18 rooms are two-bedroom suites; all rooms have hair dryers. ⊠ *306 Main St., 96020* ☎ *530/258–2441 or 888/571–4885* ⊞ *530/258–3523* ⮎ *12 rooms, 6 suites* ⚭ *Microwaves, refrigerators, cable TV with movies, Internet; no a/c, no smoking* ⊟ *AE, MC, V.*

Quincy

⓭ *67 mi southwest of Susanville via Hwys. 36 and 89.*

A center for mining and logging in the 1850s, Quincy is nestled against the western slope of the Sierra Nevada. The county seat and largest community in Plumas County, the town is rich in historic buildings that have been the focus of preservation and restoration efforts. The four-story courthouse on Main Street, one of several stops on a self-guided tour, was built in 1921 with marble posts and staircases. The arts are thriving in Quincy, too. Catch one of the plays or bluegrass groups on stage at the Town Hall Theatre.

Considered the centerpiece of recreation in central Plumas County, **Bucks Lake Recreation Area** is 17 mi southwest of Quincy at the 5,200-foot level. During warm months the lake's 17-mile shoreline, two marinas, and eight campgrounds attract anglers and water-sports enthusiasts. Trails through the tall pines beckon hikers and horseback riders. In winter, much of the area remains open for snowmobiling and cross-country skiing. ✉ *Bucks Lake Rd.* ☎ *530/283–5465 or 800/326–2247* ⊕ *www.plumas.ca.us.*

Plumas County is known for its wide-open spaces, and the 1.2-million-acre **Plumas National Forest** is a large part of that. High alpine lakes and crystal-clear streams sparkle in this forest, which attracts outdoor enthusiasts year-round. Hundreds of campsites are maintained in the forest, and picnic areas and hiking trails abound. You can explore Gold Country (Chapter 8) history or ride the rapids in canoes, rafts, and inner tubes. There's access to the forest at numerous sites along Highways 70 and 89. ✉ *159 Lawrence St.* ☎ *530/283–2050* 🖷 *530/283–4156* ⊕ *www.r5.fs.fed.us/plumas* ☉ *U.S. Forest Service office weekdays 8–4:30.*

The cultural, home arts, and industrial history displays at the **Plumas County Museum** contain artifacts dating to the 1850s. Highlights include collections of Maidu Indian basketry, pioneer weapons, and rooms depicting life in the early days of Plumas County. There are a blacksmith shop and gold-mining cabin, equipment from the early days of logging, a restored buggy, and railroad and mining exhibits. ✉ *500 Jackson St.* ☎ *530/283–6320* 🖷 *530/283–6080* 🖃 *$1* ☉ *Weekdays 8–5, year-round; weekends 10–4, May–Oct.*

Where to Stay & Eat

$–$$ ✗ **Moon's.** This restored 1930 building houses a dinner-only restaurant that serves such delights as honey-almond chicken, prime rib (on weekends), ravioli, and Tuscan pasta. The pastas and breads are homemade, and the pizza is wonderful. Top off the meal with a slice of chocolate Kahlua pie. A verdant garden patio adds to Moon's allure. ✉ *497 Lawrence St.* ☎ *530/283–0765* ▤ *AE, D, MC, V* ☉ *Closed Mon.*

$–$$ ✗ **Sweet Lorraine's Good Food Good Feelings.** You can choose to eat upstairs by candlelight or in the more casual downstairs bar and dining area. Sweet Lorraine's serves hearty fare such as Cajun meat loaf with roasted-garlic mashed potatoes, as well as lighter items; it also has a great assortment of microbrews and wine. ✉ *384 Main St.* ☎ *530/283–5300* 🍴 *Reservations essential* ▤ *MC, V* ☉ *Closed Sun.*

★ **$–$$** 🖽 **Feather Bed.** Stay here and you'll enjoy the quaint romanticism of an 1893 Queen Anne Victorian plus the convenience of proximity to the sites in Quincy's town center. Furnishings are antiques, and the views of the Sierra Nevada spectacular. The five rooms in the main house have claw-foot tubs. Two private guest cottages have fireplaces and outside decks. Classical music plays softly in the morning, and breakfast begins with smoothies made with homegrown blackberries or raspberries. Fresh fruit or baked fruit crunch and home-baked bread or muffins accompany a hot entrée. ✉ *542 Jackson St., 95971* ☎ *530/283–0102 or 800/696–8624* ⊕ *www.featherbed-inn.com* ⇆ *5 rooms, 2 cottages* ᐤ *Cable TV, bicycles, airport shuttle; no a/c in some rooms* ▤ *AE, D, DC, MC, V* 🍴🛏 *BP.*

¢ 🖽 **Ranchito.** Rough-hewn beams both decorate and support the front exterior of this rustic Spanish-style motel 1½ mi east of downtown. A brook runs through the mostly wooded 2½-acre grounds. ✉ *2020 E. Main St., 95971* ☎ *530/283–2265* 🖷 *530/283–2316* ⇆ *30 rooms*

⚸ *Picnic area, some kitchenettes, cable TV, no-smoking rooms; no a/c in some rooms* ⊟ *AE, D, MC, V.*

⚠ **Haskins Valley Campground.** At an elevation of 5,200 feet, this campground lies on the south shore of Bucks Lake and has a boat ramp. ⚸ *Pit toilets, dump station, drinking water* ⇨ *65 sites, no hook-ups* ⊠ *Bucks Lake Rd., 16½ mi off Hwy. 70* ☏ *530/283–2050* ⊕ *http://plumas-county.org/camping/buckslake.htm* ⚏ *$15* ⚐ *Reservations not accepted* ⊟ *No credit cards* ⊘ *Mid-May–mid-Oct.*

THE FAR NORTH A TO Z

To research prices, get advice from other travelers, and book travel arrangements, visit ⊕ www.fodors.com

AIRPORTS & TRANSFERS

Chico Municipal Airport and Redding Municipal Airport are served by United Express. Horizon Air also uses the airport in Redding. *See* Air Travel *in* Smart Travel Tips A to Z for airline phone numbers. There is no shuttle service from either airport, but taxis can be ordered. The approximate cost from the airport to downtown Redding is $20–25, and it's $12–15 from the Chico airport to downtown.

🛈 **Chico Municipal Airport** ⊠ 150 Airpark Blvd., off Cohasset Rd. ☏ 530-879-3910. **Redding Municipal Airport** ⊠ Airport Rd. ☏ 530/224-4320. **Taxi Service, Chico** ☏ 530/893-4444 or 530/342-2929. **Taxi Service, Redding** ☏ 530/246-0577 or 530/222-1234

BUS TRAVEL

Greyhound buses travel I–5, serving Chico, Red Bluff, Redding, Dunsmuir, and Mount Shasta. Butte County Transit serves Chico, Oroville, and elsewhere. Chico Area Transit System, which is affiliated with Butte County Transit, provides bus service within Chico. The vehicles of the Redding Area Bus Authority operate daily except Sunday within Redding. STAGE buses serve Siskiyou County, on weekdays only, from Yreka to Dunsmuir, stopping in Mount Shasta and other towns, and provide service in Scott Valley, Happy Camp, and the Klamath River area. Lassen Rural Bus serves the Susanville, northeast Lake Almanor, and south Lassen County areas, running weekdays except holidays. Lassen Rural Bus connects with Plumas County Transit, which serves the Quincy area, and with Modoc County Sage Stage, which serves the Alturas area.

🛈 **Butte County Transit/Chico Area Transit System** ☏ 530/342-0221 ⊕ www.bcag. org/transit.htm. **Greyhound** ☏ 800/229-9424 ⊕ www.greyhound.com. **Lassen Rural Bus** ☏ 530/252-7433. **Modoc County Sage Stage** ☏ 530/233-3883. **Plumas County Transit** ☏ 530/283-2538 ⊕ www.aworkforce.org/ptransit. **Redding Area Bus Authority** ☏ 530/241-2877 ⊕ www.ci.redding.ca.us. **STAGE** ☏ 530/842-8295 ⊕ www. co.siskiyou.ca.us.

CAMPING

Some campgrounds in California's Far North get booked as much as a year in advance for the Fourth of July, although that's not the norm. Still, it's a good idea to make summer reservations two–three months in advance. You can reserve a site at many of the region's campgrounds through ReserveAmerica and ReserveUSA.

🛈 Campground Reservations **ReserveAmerica** ☏877/444-6777 ⊕www.reserveamerica. com. **ReserveUSA** ☏ 800/444-7275 ⊕ www.reserveusa.com.

CAR RENTAL

Avis and Hertz serve Redding Municipal Airport. Budget and Hertz serve Chico Municipal Airport. Enterprise has branches in Chico, Red Bluff, and Redding. *See* Car Rental *in* Smart Travel Tips A to Z for national rental agency phone numbers.

CAR TRAVEL

An automobile is virtually essential for touring the far north unless you arrive by bus, plane, or train and plan to stay put in one town or resort. I–5, an excellent four-lane divided highway, runs up the center of California through Red Bluff and Redding and continues north to Oregon. The other main roads in the area are good two-lane highways that are, with few exceptions, open year-round. Chico is east of I–5 on Highway 32. Lassen Volcanic National Park can be reached by Highway 36 from Red Bluff or (except in winter) Highway 44 from Redding. Highway 299 connects Redding and Alturas. Highway 139 leads from Susanville to Lava Beds National Monument. Highway 89 will take you from Mount Shasta to Quincy. Highway 36 links Chester and Susanville. If you are traveling through the far north in winter, always carry snow chains in your vehicle. For information on the condition of roads in Northern California, call the Caltrans Highway Information Network's voice-activated system. At the prompt say the route number in which you are interested, and you'll hear a recorded message about current conditions.

⚡ Caltrans Highway Information Network ☎ 800/427-7623.

EMERGENCIES

In an emergency dial 911.

⚡ Hospitals Enloe Medical Center ⊠ 1531 Esplanade, Chico ☎ 530/891-7300. **Lassen Community Hospital** ⊠ 560 Hospital La., Susanville ☎ 530/257-5325. **Mercy Medical Center** ⊠ 2175 Rosaline Ave., Redding ☎ 530/225-6000.

TRAIN TRAVEL

Amtrak has stations in Chico, Redding, and Dunsmuir and operates buses that connect to Greyhound service through Redding, Red Bluff, and Chico.

⚡ Amtrak ⊠ W. 5th and Orange Sts., Chico ⊠ 1620 Yuba St., Redding ⊠ 5750 Sacramento Ave., Dunsmuir ☎ 800/872-7245 ⊕ www.amtrakcalifornia.com.

VISITOR INFORMATION

⚡ Alturas Chamber of Commerce ⊠ 522 S. Main St., Alturas 96101 ☎ 530/233-4434 ⊕ www.alturaschamber.org. **Chester–Lake Almanor Chamber of Commerce** ⊠ 529 Main St., Chester 96020 ☎ 530/258-2426 or 800/350-4838 ⊕ www.chester-lakealmanor. com. **Chico Chamber of Commerce** ⊠ 300 Salem St., 95928 ☎ 530/891-5556 or 800/ 852-8570 ⊕ www.chicochamber.com. **Lassen County Chamber of Commerce** ⊠ 84 N. Lassen St., Susanville 96130 ☎ 530/257-4323 ⊕ lassencountychamber.org. **Plumas County Visitors Bureau** ⊠ Hwy. 70, ½ mi west of downtown, Quincy 95971 ☎ 530/283-6345 or 800/326-2247 ⊕ www.plumas.ca.us. **Quincy Chamber of Commerce** ⊠ 464 Main St., Quincy 95971 ☎ 530/283-0188 ⊕ www.psln.com/qchamber. **Red Bluff–Tehama County Chamber of Commerce** ⊠ 100 Main St., Red Bluff 96080 ☎ 530/527-6220 or 800/655-6225 ⊟ 530/527-2908 ⊕ www.redbluffchamberofcommerce.com. **Shasta Cascade Wonderland Association** ⊠ 1699 Hwy. 273, Anderson 96007 ☎ 530/365-7500 or 800/474-2782, ⊕ www.shastacascade.org. **Siskiyou County Visitors Bureau** ⊠ 508 Chestnut St., Mt. Shasta 96067 ☎ 530/926-3850 or 877/847-8777 ⊟ 530/926-3680 ⊕ www. visitsiskiyou.org.

INDEX

NOTES

NOTES

NOTES

NOTES

NOTES

NOTES

NOTES

NOTES

Huntington → 2 beds
city − $425

NOTES

FODOR'S KEY TO THE GUIDES

America's guidebook leader publishes guides for every kind of traveler. Check out our many series and find your perfect match.

FODOR'S GOLD GUIDES

America's favorite travel-guide series offers the most detailed insider reviews of hotels, restaurants, and attractions in all price ranges, plus great background information, smart tips, and useful maps.

COMPASS AMERICAN GUIDES

Stunning guides from top local writers and photographers, with gorgeous photos, literary excerpts, and colorful anecdotes. A must-have for culture mavens, history buffs, and new residents.

FODOR'S CITYPACKS

Concise city coverage in a guide plus a foldout map. The right choice for urban travelers who want everything under one cover.

FODOR'S EXPLORING GUIDES

Hundreds of color photos bring your destination to life. Lively stories lend insight into the culture, history, and people.

FODOR'S TRAVEL HISTORIC AMERICA

For travelers who want to experience history firsthand, this series gives in-depth coverage of historic sights, plus nearby restaurants and hotels. Themes include the Thirteen Colonies, the Old West, and the Lewis and Clark Trail.

FODOR'S POCKET GUIDES

For travelers who need only the essentials. The best of Fodor's in pocket-size packages for just $9.95.

FODOR'S FLASHMAPS

Every resident's map guide, with dozens of easy-to-follow maps of public transit, restaurants, shopping, museums, and more.

FODOR'S CITYGUIDES

Sourcebooks for living in the city: thousands of in-the-know listings for restaurants, shops, sports, nightlife, and other city resources.

FODOR'S AROUND THE CITY WITH KIDS

Up to 68 great ideas for family days, recommended by resident parents. Perfect for exploring in your own backyard or on the road.

FODOR'S HOW TO GUIDES

Get tips from the pros on planning the perfect trip. Learn how to pack, fly hassle-free, plan a honeymoon or cruise, stay healthy on the road, and travel with your baby.

FODOR'S LANGUAGES FOR TRAVELERS

Practice the local language before you hit the road. Available in phrase books, cassette sets, and CD sets.

KAREN BROWN'S GUIDES

Engaging guides—many with easy-to-follow inn-to-inn itineraries—to the most charming inns and B&Bs in the U.S.A. and Europe.

BAEDEKER'S GUIDES

Comprehensive guides, trusted since 1829, packed with A–Z reviews and star ratings.

OTHER GREAT TITLES FROM FODOR'S

Baseball Vacations, The Complete Guide to the National Parks, Family Vacations, Golf Digest's Places to Play, Great American Drives of the East, Great American Drives of the West, Great American Vacations, Healthy Escapes, National Parks of the West, Skiing USA.